THE AGE OF DESCARTES

DESCARTES ET SON TEMPS

VOLUME 9

*Centro Dipartimentale di Studi su Descartes
e il Seicento 'Ettore Lojacono' Università del Salento*

Series Editor
Giulia Belgioioso (Università del Salento)

Editorial Board
Igor Agostini (Università del Salento)
Roger Ariew (Tampa University, Florida)
Jean-Robert Armogathe (EPHE, Paris)
Carlo Borghero (Università di Roma, La Sapienza)
Vincent Carraud (Sorbonne Université)
Alan Gabbey (Barnard College)
Daniel Garber (Princeton University)
Tullio Gregory + (Accademia dei Lincei)
Jean-Luc Marion (Académie française)

Descartes and Medicine

Problems, Responses and Survival of a Cartesian Discipline

edited by
FABRIZIO BALDASSARRI

BREPOLS

An earlier version of some of the essays contained in this volume was presented at the VivaMente Conference organized by Fabrizio Baldassarri and funded by the Centre for the Study of Medicine and the Body in the Renaissance (CSMBR) under ref. CSMBR_VIV003.2020

CENTRE FOR THE STUDY OF
MEDICINE AND THE BODY
IN THE RENAISSANCE

VIVAMENTE
The Garden of Ideas

© 2023, Brepols Publishers n. v., Turnhout, Belgium.

All rights reserved. No part of this publication may be reproduced, stored in a retrieval system, or transmitted, in any form or by any means, electronic, mechanical, photocopying, recording, or otherwise without the prior permission of the publisher.

D/2023/0095/28
ISBN 978-2-503-59461-3
eISBN 978-2-503-59462-0
DOI 10.1484/M.DESCARTES-EB.5.123382

ISSN 2736-7010
eISSN 2566-0276

Printed in the EU on acid-free paper.

Acknowledgments

This volume is the result of several meetings and seminars in Padua, Venice, Lecce, Utrecht, Leiden, Bologna, Bloomington, and a conference, organized online on November 18, 19 and 20, 2020, with the technical support of CSMBR and Vivamente, and sponsored by the Institutio Santoriana, University of Exeter, UEFISCDI, Università degli Studi di Padova, and Studio Firmano. I must thank the president, vice-president, director, and vice-directors of the CSMBR, namely, Vivian Nutton, Jonathan Barry, Fabrizio Bigotti, Fabio Zampieri and Fabiola Zurlini, for their help at different stages, as well as Tomaso Maria Pedrotti dell'Acqua and Mark Ferretti for their technical help. On all these very well-attended seminars, the rich presentations and productive discussions led all of us to the belief that Descartes's study of medicine, and its reception, would be a major feature of his natural philosophy, although not an easy one to deal with in its entirety. Obscurities appear now and then in Descartes's medical enterprise, although this latter represents a prominent discipline of his entire philosophical project. During the pandemic nothing has been easy: neither the organization of online events, nor the planning of a volume. When I developed the aim to collect a re-elaboration of a few papers discussed in seminars and meetings, I also asked a few colleagues to add their own contribution to enlarge the picture of Cartesian medicine. As a result, I hope that the reader may appreciate the importance of (and the problems and difficulties related to) medicine in the age (and the philosophy) of Descartes, and the strives for survival that Cartesian medicine deployed throughout the seventeenth century. This is the main topic of the present volume, now published in Giulia Belgioioso's series with Brepols. And I hope that further investigations may develop on this topic to enrich the studies in early modern philosophy, sciences, and medicine.

I thank Giulia Belgioioso and Igor Agostini for having guided me through the difficulties of editing the volume, and Theo Verbeek, who has been a safe haven for the study of Descartes and Cartesianism throughout the years. I also thank Marco Sgarbi and Domenico Bertoloni Meli, who have supported me through the Marie Skłodowska-Curie fellowship scheme.

Bloomington (IN), September 2022

Table of Contents

Acknowledgments — 5

List of illustrations — 11

List of contributors — 13

Descartes's Abbreviations — 19

Introduction — 21
Lights & Shadows in Descartes's Medicine
Fabrizio BALDASSARRI

Part I
Descartes's Medical Philosophy
Sources and Texts, Dissections and Reflections

Descartes's Cartesian Medicine — 43
Past, Present, and Future
Gideon MANNING

Epigenesis and Generative Power in Descartes' Late Scholastic Sources — 59
Simone GUIDI

Ambroise Paré and René Descartes on Sensation in Amputated Limbs — 81
Jil MULLER

Anatomical Debates on Hearts and Brains and Philosophical Issues from Descartes' Writing of *L'Homme* to its Posthumous Publications — 99
Annie BITBOL-HESPÉRIÈS

The Medical Context of Descartes's *Dioptrique* — 121
Tawrin BAKER

A Medicine in the Shadows — 141
The Bio-Medical Manuscripts and a *Compendium* Descartes Never Published
Fabrizio BALDASSARRI

Fermentation as 'Heat-Rarefaction' and Animal Spirits in Descartes' Medical Philosophy   161
Carmen SCHMECHEL

What Descartes's Embryology Tells Us about his Dualism   185
Lynda GAUDEMARD

From the Animal Instinct to the Mind's Acknowledgement of the (In)*Commoda* in Descartes   203
Clément RAYMOND

Madness and Dream in Descartes's *First Meditation*   215
Jan FORSMAN

Malattie e metafisica   229
La prova patologica
Franco A. MESCHINI

Part 2
Reception And Opposition
Cartesian Medicine and Cartesianism

Mercurius Cosmopolita alias Andreas of Habernfeld   263
The Hermetic Response to Descartes
Erik-Jan BOS

The Rules of Anatomy: On the Empiricisms of Descartes and Harvey   285
Benjamin GOLDBERG

The Lost *Dictata* of Henricus Regius   315
Andrea STRAZZONI

A British Response to *The Passions of the Soul*   345
Daniel SAMUEL

Jacques Rohault on Medicine   361
Mihnea DOBRE

On Cartesian Embryology   377
A Debate on Monsters at the Bourdelot Academy
Elena RAPETTI

The Cartesian Physiology of Johann Jakob Waldschmidt   393
Nabeel HAMID

Cartesianism between Northern Europe, Germany, and the Medici Court   411
Charting a New Map
Stefano GULIZIA

"Se fusse meno cartesiano lo stimarei molto"   437
Anti-Cartesian Motifs in Italian Medicine
Maria CONFORTI

Embodied Difference and the Cartesian Soul   451
Pierre-Sylvain Régis and the Pineal Gland Problem
Aaron SPINK

Beyond Mechanical Life   467
Biological Processes in the Seventeenth Century
Laurynas ADOMAITIS

List of illustrations

Gideon MANNING, *Descartes's Cartesian Medicine*

Figure 1. René Descartes, *Principia philosophiae*, Amsterdam, Elsevier, 1644, p. 220. RB 336030, the Huntington Library, San Marino, California.   52

Figure 2. "Frontispiece" of a manuscript English language translation of Louis de la Forge, *Traité de l'esprit de l'homme*, MS/76, The Royal Society, London.   57

Jil MULLER, *Ambroise Paré and René Descartes*

Figure 1. Nerves of the arm, photo taken at the exposition 'Bodies', hosted at the *Coque* in Luxembourg, from 8-11 October 2020.   85

Figure 2. 'Pinces à bec de corbin', in Ambroise Paré, *Œuvres complètes d'Ambroise Paré*, edition from 1585, ed. by J.-F. Malgaigne, Paris, Baillière, 2 vols, 1840-1841, vol. 2, Book 10, ch. 22, p. 224. Source: www.gallica.fr/BNF.   88

Figure 3. 'Artifical devices', in Ambroise Paré, *Œuvres d'Ambroise Paré*, edition from 1585, ed. by J.-F. Malgaigne, Paris, Baillière, 2 vols, 1840-1841, vol. 2, Book 17, ch. 22, p. 617. Source: www.gallica.fr/BNF.   89

Figure 4. 'Artificial hand' in Ambroise Paré, *Œuvres d'Ambroise Paré*, edition from 1585, ed. by J.-F. Malgaigne, Paris, Baillière, 2 vols, 1840-1841, vol. 2, Book 17, ch. 22, p. 616. Source: www.gallica.fr/BNF.   93

Annie BITBOL-HESPÉRIÈS, *Anatomical Debates on Hearts and Brains*

Figure 1. Brain in CASPAR BAUHIN, *Theatrum anatomicum* (ed. 1621), text followed by and bound with *Vivae imagines partium corporis humani ex Theatro Anatomico*, [Frankfurt and Rheinland]: J. T. de Bry publisher, 1620, Lib. II, p. 107. Published with the kind permission from the BIUS, Paris.   110

Figure 2. Heart in CASPAR BAUHIN, *Theatrum anatomicum* (ed.1621), text followed by and bound with *Vivae imagines partium corporis humani ex Theatro Anatomico*, [Frankfurt and Rheinland]: J. T. de Bry

LIST OF ILLUSTRATIONS

	publisher, 1620, Lib. III, p. 143. Published with the kind permission from the BIUS, Paris.	111
Figure 3.	Heart in DESCARTES, *De Homine*, ed. F. Schuyl, Leyden, 1662 [2nd ed. 1664], p. 8 (the image is already present on p. 6). Published with the kind permission from the BIUS, Paris.	114
Figure 4.	Heart with the valves in DESCARTES, *De Homine*, ed. F. Schuyl, Leyden, 1662 [& 2nd ed. 1664], folio between p. 8 and p. 9. [This folio is missing in many editions.] Published with the kind permission from the BIUS, Paris.	115
Figure 5.	Heart in DESCARTES, *L'Homme*, ed. C. Clerselier, Paris, 1664, p. 9. [This is the only representation of the heart in this edition, and this image is also reproduced on p. 10.] Published with the kind permission from the BIUS, Paris.	118

Tawrin BAKER, *The Medical Context of Descartes's* Dioptrique

Figure 1.	Descartes's anatomical eye. DESCARTES, *Dioptrique*, 26. Courtesy Bibliothèque nationale de France.	125
Figure 2.	A mechanical prosthesis described by the barber-surgeon AMBROISE PARÉ, *Les oeuvres d'Ambroise Paré 5e edition*, Paris, Gabriel Buon, 1598, p. 902. Courtesy Bibliothèque nationale de France.	136

Stefano GULIZIA, *Cartesianism between Northern Europe, Germany, and the Medici Court*

Figure 1.	Copy of Cosimo Brunetti's letter to Leopoldo de' Medici of September 9, 1660, with the illustration of a telescopic instrument used by Hevelius; Florence, Biblioteca Nazionale Centrale, MS Gal. 276, c. 61r.	422
Figure 2.	Front page of CORNELIS VAN HOGELANDE, *Cogitationes quibus Dei existentia [...] explicantur*, Amsterdam, Elzevir, 1646; copy marked as Phil 1632 at the Staats- und Stadtbibliothek in Augsburg.	429

List of contributors

Laurynas ADOMAITIS has defended his doctoral thesis cum laude at the Scuola Normale Superiore and carried out research visits at the École Normale Supérieure in Paris, the University of Münster and at the University of Montreal, studying Leibniz and early modern science. He is currently a researcher at the Atomic Energy Commission (CEA) in Paris. His main areas of research are data ethics, AI ethics, and the ethical issues of extended reality.

Fabrizio BALDASSARRI is a Marie Skłodovska-Curie postdoc at Ca' Foscari University of Venice and Indiana University Bloomington, with a project on plants in early modern philosophy. He co-edited several special issues and volumes such as *Vegetative Powers* (2021), and has widely published on Descartes's naturalistic studies and philosophy in journals such as the *BJHS*, *ESM*, *Physis*, *Historia philosophica* and the *Rivista di storia della filosofia*. In 2021, he has published a monograph entitled, *Il metodo al tavolo anatomico. Descartes e la medicina* (Rome, 2021).

Tawrin BAKER is currently Visiting Assistant Professor in the History and Philosophy of Science at the University of Notre Dame. In 2014 he received his PhD in the History and Philosophy of Science and Medicine from Indiana University, Bloomington. He was a 2016-2017 Dibner Research Fellow in the History of Science at the Huntington Library in San Marino, California, and has also been a Mellon Postdoctoral Fellow in the History and Philosophy of Science at the University of Pittsburgh and a Visual Studies Postdoctoral Fellow at the University of Pennsylvania. He works on the intersection of anatomy and medicine, natural philosophy, and mathematics in the early modern period, focusing especially on vision and physical color theory, and more recently on images, diagrams, and visual cultures of science and medicine, in the sixteenth and early seventeenth centuries.

Annie BITBOL-HESPÉRIÈS published *Le principe de vie chez Descartes* in 1990 (Paris, Vrin) and edited René Descartes' *Le Monde, L'Homme* in 1996 (Paris, Le Seuil). She has worked on *Monsters from the Renaissance to the Age of Reason* for a virtual exhibition on the website of the main medical library in France : Bibliothèque interuniversitaire de santé (BIUS, Médecine, 2004). She is presently editing Descartes' medical texts to be published in René Descartes, *Œuvres complètes* edited by the late Jean-Marie Beyssade and Denis Kambouchner (Paris, Gallimard-Tel, vol. II). Her critical edition of Descartes' biography by Adrien Baillet (*La vie de Monsieur Descartes*, 2 vols, Paris, 1691) will be published by Encre marine (Les Belles Lettres).

LIST OF CONTRIBUTORS

Erik-Jan BOS (Erasmus University Rotterdam) is a specialist of the life and works of René Descartes and also interested in the history of Dutch Cartesianism. He is one of the editors-in-chief of the new critical edition of Descartes' correspondence with complete English translation (Oxford University Press).

Maria CONFORTI is professor at La Sapienza University of Rome, where she teaches History of medicine and directs the museum of medical history. She has widely published on the history of medicine in the early modern period, especially focusing on the Italian context, but also on the communication of medicine from the seventeenth to the twentieth century. She has edited several volumes and special issues; in 2014, she co-edited with Marco Beretta a volume entitled *Fakes!? Hoaxes, Counterfeits and Deception in Early Modern Science*, just to name one. She has been editor in chief of *Nuncius: Journal of the Material and Visual History of Science* between 2017 and 2020, and is a member of the editorial board of several journals and institutions of history of medicine and history of science.

Mihnea DOBRE teaches and does research at the University of Bucharest. He has a PhD in philosophy (Radboud University Nijmegen and University of Bucharest), and his research focus is in the history of philosophy and science; in particular on the relations between philosophy, science, and religion in the early modern period. He is also interested in new scholarly approaches (Digital Humanities) and different ways of communication and dissemination of research results (Open Science). He has published two monographs, *Cosmologia carteziană* [*Cartesian Cosmology*; in Romanian, 2021] and *Descartes and Early French Cartesianism: between metaphysics and physics* (Zeta Books, 2017), and co-edited the volume on *Cartesian Empiricisms* (Springer, 2013).

Jan FORSMAN is a recent PhD in Philosophy from Tampere University, Finland. His doctoral thesis concentrated on Descartes's skepticism in the *Meditations*. He is currently working on postdoc resarch at the University of Iowa on the skeptical influence of early modern women philosophers. In his spare time, he enjoys writing, playing basketball and taking care of animals.

Lynda GAUDEMARD is lecturer at the Department of philosophy of the University of Aix-Marseille, where she received her Ph.D in 2012. In addition to her research, she works for the French Ministry of Justice. She held several positions at the University of Geneva and the University of Lausanne. She published extensively on Descartes's philosophy of mind, metaphysics and embryology, as well as on bioethics, children's rights and legal epistemology. Her publications include the monograph *Rethinking Descartes's Substance Dualism* (Springer, 2021). Recently, she was also invited by the *Annals of the University of Bucharest* to be a guest editor of a special issue dedicated to emotions and cognition in early modern philosophy. In 2021, she received a Harvard certificate in child protection. She is currently working on ethics of children's rights.

Benjamin GOLDBERG is a historian and philosopher of science at the University of South Florida. His work concentrates on the intersection between medicine and philosophy in the early modern Europe, as well on larger philosophical issues concerning the nature of experience and evidence, underdetermination, and the philosophy of experiment. He is currently working on the pedagogical aspects of William Harvey's lecture notes for the Lumleian Lectures. You can find him at http://metabenny.com.

Stefano GULIZIA is an intellectual historian specializing in the early modern period, with a focus on scholarly networks, print culture, and other themes. Trained as a classicist and philologist, he taught extensively in the U.S. (after his PhD from Indiana University) and held fellowships in California, Oxford, Chicago, Montreal, Berlin, Wolfenbüttel, Bucharest and Warsaw. He has joined the University of Milan as a member of TACITROOTS, and he is the editor-in-chief of the *Scientiae Studies* series at Amsterdam UP.

Simone GUIDI is a Researcher in the Institute for the European Intellectual Lexicon and History of Ideas (CNR-ILIESI) at the National Research Council of Italy. He teaches at the Roma Tre University in Italy. His work focuses on the history of early modern philosophy, with particular attention to Descartes and early modern Scholasticism. He authored and edited several monographs, articles, book chapters, and collective volumes, among which are *L'angelo e la macchina. Sulla genesi della* res cogitans *cartesiana* (2018), *Francisco Suárez. Metaphysics, Politics and Ethics* (2020, with Mário Santiago de Carvalho and Manuel Lazáro Pulido), and *Pedro da Fonseca. Humanism and Metaphysics* (2022, with Mário Santiago de Carvalho). He is the scientific coordinator of the Conimbricenses.org project (directed by Mário Santiago de Carvalho).

Nabeel HAMID is Assistant Professor of Philosophy at Concordia University (Montreal). He works on the history of German philosophy, in particular on early modern German scholasticism and the reception of Cartesianism in German universities. He has published articles in venues such as *Oxford Studies in Early Modern Philosophy*, *Journal of Modern Philosophy*, *History of Universities*, and *British Journal for the History of Philosophy*.

Gideon MANNING is Associate Professor of History of Medicine and Humanities at the Cedars-Sinai Medical Center in Los Angeles, California, where he directs the Program in the History of Medicine. He is also Research Associate Professor at Claremont Graduate University. The author of numerous articles and book chapters, as well as the editor or co-editor of four books, his most recent publications include "Women, Medicine, and the Life Sciences," "Circulation and the New Physiology" and, with Anna Marie Roos, the edited volume *Collected Wisdom of the Early Modern Scholar*. He continues his research on René Descartes and his long reception, but is also trying to productively bring together the history of medicine, science and philosophy to address questions about illustrations and visualization in science, the early modern fate of Galenism, the history of surgery, philosophies of the good death, and translational science and evidence-based medicine.

Franco A. MESCHINI is an Associate Professor at the University of Salento, Lecce (Department of Humanities). He has been scholar of Tullio Gregory (Roma, La Sapienza). His interests focus on the philosophical and scientific thought of seventeenth century scholars, especially dealing with the medical writings of René Descartes. On Descartes, he has published: *Neurofisiologia cartesiana* (1998); *Materiali per una storia della medicina cartesiana* (2013); *La dottrina della digestione secondo Descartes* (2015), of which he is now retracing and defining the concept of disease, *Descartes su vita, morte e malattia. In margine alla questione del rapporto di anima e corpo* (2019).

Jil MULLER, after a PhD thesis on Montaigne, Descartes and the original sin, has turned her research focus on French Women Philosophers and Scientists in the early modern period, such as Marie de Gournay, Sophie Germain and Emilie du Châtelet. She has mainly focused on their moral theories and their understanding of man in society, as well as with the status or role of man in the creation of God. Recently, she published a book by Classiques Garnier: *Soigner l'humain — Péchés et remèdes chez Montaigne et Descartes*, in May 2022.

Elena RAPETTI is Assistant Professor at the Catholic University of Milan, where she teaches History of Philosophy. Her research is carried out in two main directions: the philosophical, scientific, and theological debates of post-Cartesian philosophy and the reception of Origen's thought in the seventeenth century. She has published on the reception of Descartes and Spinoza, mostly focusing on the figure of the anti-Cartesian thinker Pierre-Daniel Huet and his milieu.

Clément RAYMOND is a former student of the Ecole Normale Supérieure d'Ulm, holder of the agrégation in philosophy. He is currently a PhD student in philosophy at the Université Jean Moulin Lyon 3 and member of the "Institut d'Histoire des Représentations et des Idées dans les Modernités" (IHRIM). His research interests include Descartes, Cartesianism(s) and the women's quarrel.

Daniel SAMUEL is a PhD candidate at the Warburg Institute, University of London. His thesis examines how developments in natural philosophy and medicine influenced the formation of new theories of emotion in seventeenth-century England. He studied medicine at the University of Cambridge and Imperial College London and worked as medical doctor before commencing his doctoral studies.

Carmen SCHMECHEL is a historian of science and medicine. She currently holds a German Research Foundation-sponsored postdoctoral fellowship at the Institute for Philosophy of the Freie Universität Berlin, exploring theories about ferments and fermentation in premodern European medicine and chemistry. Her broader interests extend to other theories of transformation of matter, such as distillation, sublimation, or metabolism, including the metaphorical usages of these terms and their *longue-durée* philosophical backgrounds. Most recently she has authored "Descartes on Fermentation in Digestion: Iatromechanism, Analogy and Teleology," in *The British Journal for the History of Science*, 2022, 101-116.

Aaron SPINK is currently a lecturer in philosophy at Dartmouth College. He works primarily on methodological issues related to the early adoption of Cartesian philosophy in the seventeenth century. He is also co-editor and translator for an upcoming collection of selected philosophical works from Blaise, Jacqueline, and Gilberte Pascal.

Andrea STRAZZONI, Ph.D. (Erasmus University Rotterdam, 2015), is Marie-Curie fellow at the Ca' Foscari University of Venice. He has published monographs and articles on the history of early modern philosophy and science, and editions of primary sources.

Descartes's Abbreviations

Alquié	François Alquié, *Œuvres philosophiques de René Descartes*, 3 vols, Paris, Garnier, 1963-1973.
AT	*René Descartes. Œuvres*, édités par Charles Adam et Paul Tennry, 13 vols, Paris, Léopold Cerf, 1897-1913. Nouvelle présentation par J. Beaude, P. Constable, A. Gabbey et B. Rochot, 11 vols. Paris, Vrin, 1964-1974.
Aucante	René Descartes, *Écrits physiologiques et médicaux*, présentation, textes, traduction, notes et annexes de Vincent Aucante, Paris, PUF, 2000.
BL	Giulia Belgioioso (a cura di), *René Descartes. Tutte le lettere 1619-1650*, con la collaborazione d'I. Agostini, F. Marrone, F. A. Meschini, M. Savini, e J.-R. Armogathe, Milano, Bompiani 2009 [2005].
BO	Giulia Belgioioso (a cura di), *René Descartes. Opere 1637-1649*, con la collaborazione d'I. Agostini, F. Marrone e M. Savini, Milano, Bompiani, 2009.
BOp	Giulia Belgioioso (ed.), *René Descartes. Opere postume 1650-2009*, con la collaborazione d'I. Agostini, F. Marrone, e M. Savini, Milano, Bompiani, 2009.
BOS	Erik-Jan Bos, *The Correspondence between Descartes and Hernicus Regius*, Ph.D. dissertation, Utrecht, Zeno, 2002.
Clerselier I-II-III	Claude Clerselier, *Lettres de Mr Descartes*, 3 vols, Paris, Charles Angot, 1657, 1659, 1667. [Reprint ed. by J.-R. Armogathe, G. Belgioioso, Lecce, Conte, 2005; and now also in www.cartesius.net].
CSM I-II	*The Philosophical Writings of Descartes*, 2 vols, edited and translated by John Cottingham, Robert Stoothoff, and Dugald Murdoch, Cambridge-New York-Port Chester-Melbourne-Sydney, Cambridge University Press, 1984.
CSMK	*The Philosophical Writings of Descartes*, vol. III *The Correspondence*, edited and translated by John Cottingham, Robert Stoothoff, Dugald Murdoch, and Anthony Kenny, Cambridge-New York-Port Chester-Melbourne-Sydney, Cambridge University Press, 1991.
G	René Descartes, *The World and Other Writings*, ed. and transl. by Stephen Gaukroger, Cambridge, Cambridge University Press, 1998.
Shapiro	*The Correspondence between Princess Elisabeth of Bohemia and René Descartes*, edited and translated by Lisa Shapiro, Chicago, The University of Chicago Press, 2006.
Verbeek	Theo Verbeek, Erik-Jan Bos, and Jeroen van de Ven, *The Correspondence of René Descartes 1643*, with contributions of H. Bos, C. R. Palmerino, C. Vermeulen, Utrecht, Zeno, 2003.

Other Abbreviations

Acad.	Cicero, *Academica* (Eng. translation by Rackham, H.; original Latin text included) in *De Natura Deorum; Academica*, Cambridge (Ma.), Harvard University Press, 1972.
C. Acad.	St Augustine, *Answer to Skeptics* (*Contra Academicos*, transl. by D. J. Kavanagh) in L. Schopp, ed., *The Fathers of the Church: A New Translation*, vol. 5, New York, Cima Publishing Co., 1984.
CM	*Correspondance du P. Marin Mersenne religieux minime*, commencée par Mme Paul Tannery, publie et annotée par Cornelis de Waard et Armand Beaulieu, 17 vols, Paris, Editions du CNRS, 1945-1988.
De Mem.	*Aristotle, On Memory and Recollection* (Περὶ μνήμης καὶ ἀναμνήσεως, translation by Hett, W. S.; original Greek text included) in On the Soul; Parva Naturalia; On Breath, Cambridge, Harvard University Press, 1975.
De Ins.	Aristotle, On Dreams (Περὶ ἐνυπνίων, translation by Hett, W. S.; original Greek text included) in On the Soul; Parva Naturalia; On Breath, Cambridge, Harvard University Press, 1975.
M	Sextus Empiricus, *Against the Mathematicians I-VI, VII-VIII, & XI* (Πρὸς μαθηματικούς, translation by Bury, R.G; original Greek text included) in *Against the Logicians, Against the Physicists, Against the Ethicists, and Against the Professors*, Cambridge, Harvard University Press, 2000.
Meth.	Aristotle, *Metaphysics* (Τὰ μετὰ τὰ φυσικά, translation by Kirwan Christopher), Oxford, Clarendon Press, 1971 [1993].
QM	John Buridan, *Quastiones in Aristotelis Metaphysicam* (Eng. translation by Guyla Klima) in Gyula Klima, Fritz Allhoff and Anand Jayprakash Vaidya (eds.), *Medieval Philosophy: Essential Readings with Commentary*, Oxford, Blackwell Publishing, 2007
PH	Sextus Empiricus, *Outlines of Scepticism* (Πυρρώνειοι ὑποτυπώσεις, translation by Annas, Julia & Barnes, Jonathan), Cambridge, Cambridge University Press, 2002.
SQO	Henry of Ghent, *Summa Quaestionum Ordinarium*, in *The Cambridge Translations of Medieval Philosophical Texts*, vol. 3, ed. by R. Pasnau, Cambridge, Cambridge University Press, 2002.
ST	Aquinas, *Summa Theologiae*, vols II, V, IX, XI & XII (Eng. translation by McDermott, Timothy; Gilby, Thomas; Foster, Kenelm; Suttor, Timothy and Durbin, Paul T.; original Latin included), London-New York, Blackfriars, in conjunction with Eyre & Spottiswoode, & McGraw-Hill Book Company, 1964-1968.
Tht	Plato, *Theaetētus* [Θεαίτητος], in *The Theaetetus of Plato*, ed. by Miles Burnyeat, Indianapolis, Hackett Publishing Company, 1990.
Trin.	St Augustine, *On the Trinity* (*De Trinitate*, translation by McKenna, Stephen) in *On the Trinity*, Books 8-15 (ed. Matthews, Gareth B.), Cambridge, Cambridge University Press, 2002.

FABRIZIO BALDASSARRI

Introduction

Lights & Shadows in Descartes's Medicine

1. Descartes's Medicine: Lights or Shadows?

An ambivalence marks Descartes's medical enterprise. While it appears a major subject of his philosophy, and a yardstick to evaluate its success, Descartes's medicine reveals highs and lows. At the beginning of his study of medicine, in January 1630, Descartes aimed to "look for a medicine grounded on infallible demonstrations."[1] At the end of the *Discours de la Méthode* (1637), Descartes's aim consists of "deriv[ing] rules in medicine which are more reliable than those we have had up till now."[2] At various stages, Descartes suggested to his correspondents that his goals in working on medicine were to treat diseases and infirmity (of the mind and of the body) in order to have a longer and happier old age.[3] In the Letter-Preface to the French translation of the *Principia philosophiae*, published in 1647, Descartes claims that medicine is one of the branches of his natural philosophy, a discipline from which one could pick fruits to extend life and preserve health.[4] And yet, his medical project fails to achieve such goals or reach such a status.

Although Vincent Aucante has evaluated the extent of René Descartes's medical pages to be one fifth of his entire production,[5] medicine appears as a secondary discipline

---

1 Descartes to Mersenne, January 1630, AT I 106; BL 114.
2 RENÉ DESCARTES, *Discours de la Méthode* VI, AT VI 78; BO 114; CSM I 151.
3 See especially, Descartes to Huygens, 4 December 1637, AT I 649; BL 472. Cf. *Discours de la Méthode* VI, AT VI 62; BO 99.
4 See *Lettre-Préface*, AT IX-2 14-15; CSM I 186; BO 2230.
5 VINCENT AUCANTE, *La philosophie médicale de Descartes*, Paris, PUF, 2006. Here is a short list of volumes and books on Descartes's medical studies: GERRIT A. LINDEBOOM, *Descartes and Medicine*, Amsterdam, Rodopi, 1979; RICHARD B. CARTER, *Descartes' Medical Philosophy: The Organic Solution to the Mind-Body Problem*, Baltimore, The Johns Hopkins University Press, 1983; ANNIE BITBOL-HESPÉRIÈS, *Le principe de vie chez Descartes*, Paris, Vrin, 1990; FRANCESCO TREVISANI, *Descartes in Germania. La ricezione del cartesianesimo nella Facoltà filosofica e medica di Duisburg (1652-1703)*, Milano, FrancoAngeli, 1992; THEO VERBEEK, ed., *Descartes et Regius, Autour de l'explication de l'esprit humain*, Amsterdam, Rodopi, 1993; FRANÇOIS DUCHESNEAU, *Le modèle du vivant de Descartes à Leibniz*, Paris, Vrin, 1998;

Fabrizio Baldassarri • Ca' Foscari University of Venice and Indiana University, Bloomington. Contact <fabrizio.baldassarri@unive.it>

in Descartes's natural philosophy, insofar as his medical writings are scattered through various texts or manuscripts, and Descartes neither published nor completed a major work on medicine. At the same time, while he explored several different aspects of medicine, he was certainly more interested in some specific topics, such as physiology, while therapeutics was less relevant within his natural philosophical investigation.[6]

This also depended on the fact that he conceived of medicine as a section of natural philosophy. In this sense, his medical enterprise outgrows the practical concerns of physicians, and mostly concerns those of a natural philosopher (or a physicist). Yet, medicine appears to be a more central discipline in the architectonic structure of Descartes's natural philosophy than expected. As he wrote to Mersenne in 1639, the doctrine of the heartbeat is the fulcrum (together with other matters on which he wrote more than three lines) of his entire system, and if this turns out to be false, then "[his] entire philosophy is worthless."[7] As Gideon Manning has recently claimed, medicine appears at the core of Descartes's natural philosophical programme, and "can be used to illuminate the character of Descartes's physics (or natural philosophy) [...] metaphysics, unified view of knowledge and method, and his reception, among other prominent topics in Descartes studies"[8] (for a further investigation of this issue, see **Gideon Manning** in this volume).

In the *Discours*, medicine is a science of his method, and in its turn, serves to prove the correctness of his methodology, as he does through the physiological explanation of the heartbeat. Moreover, since medicine concerns both the body, the soul, and the mind-body composite, as he claimed in the project of *L'Homme* (which however remained incomplete,)[9] medical knowledge of the mind-body union boosts Descartes's exploration of the nature of the man in the *Meditationes de prima philosophia* (1641), and later composes the first section of the *Passions de l'âme* (1649).

Franco A. Meschini, *Neurofisiologia cartesiana*, Firenze, Olschki, 1998; Annie Bitbol-Hespériès, "Cartesian Physiology", in *Descartes' Natural Philosophy*, ed. by S. Gaukroger, J. Schuster, and J. Sutton, New York and London, Routledge, 2000, p. 349-382; Thomas Fuchs, *The Mechanization of the Heart: Harvey and Descartes*, trans. by Marjorie Grene, Rochester, The University of Rochester Press, 2001; Dennis Des Chene, *Spirits&Clocks: Machine and Organism in Descartes*, Ithaca, Cornell University Press, 2001; Franco A. Meschini, *Materiali per una storia della medicina cartesiana. Dottrine, testi, contesti e lessico*, Milano, Mimesis, 2015; Emanuela Scribano, *Macchine con la mente. Fisiologia e metafisica tra Cartesio e Spinoza*, Roma, Carocci, 2015; Delphine Antoine-Mahut and Stephen Gaukroger, eds, *Descartes' Treatise on Man and its Reception*, Cham, Springer, 2016; Raphaële Andrault, *La raison des corps. Mécanisme et sciences médicales*, Paris, Vrin, 2016; Gideon Manning, "Descartes and Medicine", in *The Oxford Handbook to Descartes and Cartesianism*, ed. by S. Nadler, T. M. Schmaltz and D. Antoine-Mahut, Oxford, Oxford University Press, 2020, p. 157-177; Giulia Belgioioso et Vincent Carraud, eds, *Les* Passions de l'âme *et leur réception philosophique*, Turnhout, Brépols, 2020; Fabrizio Baldassarri, *Il metodo al tavolo anatomico. Descartes e la medicina*, Rome, Aracne, 2021.

6 One should also note that the fact he died rather young raised challenges against his philosophy and medicine. See Johann van Wullen to Guillaume Pison, 11 February 1650, AT V 477-478.
7 Descartes to Mersenne, 9 February 1639, AT II 501; CSMK 134; BL 982.
8 Manning, "Descartes and Medicine", p. 157.
9 René Descartes, *L'Homme*, AT XI 119-120; BOp 362; CSM I 99. See Harold J. Cook, "Princess Elisabeth's Cautions and Descartes' Suppression of the *Traité de l'Homme*," *Early Science and Medicine* 26/4 (2021), p. 289-313.

As a result, medicine enters and substantiates his entire philosophical programme and sheds new light on several corners of his philosophy.

Still, his medicine is mostly a physiology of the body, and not of the soul, a major topic of Renaissance and early modern scholars.[10] In this sense, his medicine does not follow any traditions: neither philosophical, as his contraposition to the philosophical medicine of the scholastics clearly surfaces in his work (see **Simone Guidi** in this volume), nor medical, although a few references to classical and Renaissance physicians can be uncovered (see **Jil Muller** in this volume). Descartes was not a trained physician, although he attended a few public dissections in Leiden in the early 1630s, nor did he consider himself a professional physician or a teacher,[11] which entails that he eschewed the duties of a professor of medicine. Despite his praise of anatomy, as a way to observe the animal body directly, in his works, he mostly focused on the mechanical functioning of the body, without dealing with the anatomy of the organs as such. Moreover, in his texts, he gives no attention to a conceptualization of sanity, to the definition of diseases, or to the practice of therapeutics.

The originality (and the most significant feature, one should note) of his approach to medical knowledge surfaces in both *L'Homme* and *La Description du corps humain*, his two major medical texts, where he stressed the role of an analogy (or supposition) between the animal body and (hydraulic) machines as a way to deal with the living functions. The mechanical explanation of living functions, for which he appealed to the same principles and laws that he used to explain the whole of nature, and the reduction of bodies to matter and motion, introduced momentous changes in the early modern understanding of life and living nature. Indeed, he reduced the functioning of the body to the mechanical interactions between parts and particles, a relevant aspect of his physics. However, these texts remained incomplete, unfinished, and unpublished.[12] The absence of a major medical publication takes the form of a significant failure to produce a systematic account of medicine, especially in the light of the space this discipline occupies in both the *Discours de la Méthode* and the *Meditationes*. While medicine is a subject of his epistemological and metaphysical work, no physiology of living bodies surfaces in his physics, the *Principia philosophiae* (1644), whose fifth and sixth parts were never published — although he provided some articles on human sensation to inform the reader. The only medical reconstruction of the body appears in the first part of *Les Passions de l'âme*, a text investigating the mind-body union, somehow in continuity with the *Meditationes*.

---

10 Cf. Hiro Hirai, *Medical Humanism and Natural Philosophy: Renaissance Debates on Matter, Life and the Soul*, Leiden-Boston, Brill, 2011. Peter Distelzweig, Benjamin Goldberg and Evan R. Ragland, eds, *Early Modern Medicine and Natural Philosophy*, Cham, Springer, 2016.
11 Descartes to Mersenne, first half of June 1637, AT I 378; BL 392. Cf. Elisabeth to Descartes, 6 May 1643, AT III 662; BL 1746; Shapiro 61.
12 On the reasons Descartes left *L'Homme* unpublished, see Harold J. Cook, "Augustinian Souls and Epicurean Bodies? Descartes's Corporeal Mind in Motion," in *Descartes and the* Ingenium*: The Embodied Soul in Cartesianism*, ed. by R. Garrod and A. Marr, Leiden-Boston, Brill, 2021, p. 113-135. Cf. Daniel Garber, "The Chapters of *L'Homme* Descartes Didn't Write," in *Cartesius Edoctus*, ed. by Igor Agostini and Vincent Carraud, Turnhout, Brepols, 2022, p. 115-132.

Moreover, as is well known, Descartes's physiology mostly concerns the heartbeat and sensation. In his tentative explanation of the sensitive herb (the *Mimosa pudica*), Descartes claims this phenomenon to be consistent with his explanation of animal sensation if the same organs, namely a heart, could be detected in the plant.[13] *L'Homme* is mostly devoted to sensation; the fifth part of the *Discours* concentrates on the heartbeat; the few articles in the *Principia* deal with sensation, and the treatise on the passions focuses on the mind-body composite and its manifestations through emotions and passions. For this reason, when the Dutch Cartesian physician Henricus Regius (1598-1679) published the *Fundamenta physices* (1646) (rousing Descartes's fury,)[14] scholars such as Mersenne and Huygens welcomed its more exhaustive description of the living body (on the relationship between Regius and Descartes, see **Andrea Strazzoni** in this volume.)[15] Yet, this is not an incorrect claim. In a 1641 letter to Regius, Descartes recognized that, in the study of medicine, the former had traversed more territory than Descartes himself had. As he noted,

> there are many other things in your theses that I have ignored, and also much, so far as I have knowledge of it, that I have explained in detail otherwise than you have explained it here. This however does not surprise me; for it is much more difficult to give one's opinion on all things which concern medical matters, which is the job of a teacher [like Regius], than to choose the things that are easiest to know, and precisely to leave aside the rest, as I myself do in the sciences.[16]

In sum, while medicine plays a central role in Descartes's natural philosophy, consisting of a suitable example for understanding Descartes's willingness to enter universities,[17] and also emerging as a point of departure in the elaboration of a medical discipline in the seventeenth century,[18] Descartes's medicine reveals a restricted focus, lacunae, problems, and flaws.[19] The contributors to this volume shed new light on Descartes's

---

13 On this case, see FABRIZIO BALDASSARRI, "The Mechanical Life of Plants: Descartes on Botany", *British Journal for the History of Science*, 52/1 (2019), p. 41-63; for a Cartesian solution to this phenomenon, see FABRIZIO BALDASSARRI, "Descartes and the Dutch: Botanical Experimentation in the Early Modern Period," *Perspectives on Science*, 28/6 (2020), p. 657-683.
14 See THEO VERBEEK, "Regius's *Fundamenta Physices*", *Journal of the History of Ideas*, 55/4 (1994), p. 533-551.
15 See ANDREA STRAZZONI, "The Medical Cartesianism of Henricus Regius. Disciplinary Partitions, Mechanical Reductionism and Methodological Aspects", *Galileiana* 15 (2018), p. 181-220. ANDREA STRAZZONI, "How Did Regius Become Regius? The Early Doctrinal Evolution of a Heterodox Cartesian", *Early Science and Medicine*, 23/4 (2018), p. 362-412.
16 Descartes to Regius, November 1641, AT III 443; BL 1532. Translation is from TAD M. SCHMALTZ, "The Early Dutch Reception of *L'Homme*", in *Descartes' Treatise on Man and its Reception*, p. 71-90: esp. p. 78-79. Cf. Descartes to Regius, May 1641, AT III 371/BL 1458.
17 On this point, see the recent work of Theo Verbeek. Cf. THEO VERBEEK, "Descartes and the Classroom", in *Descartes in Classroom: Teaching Cartesian Philosophy in the Early Modern Age*, ed. by D. Cellamare and M. Mantovani, Leiden and Boston, Brill, 2023, p. 17-33.
18 Although Trevisani, Meschini, and Aucante have discussed this issue, the reception of Cartesian medicine in the seventeenth-century knowledge remains a less-explored topic.
19 I have discussed the lights and shadows of Descartes's medicine in BALDASSARRI, *Il metodo al tavolo anatomico*, p. 229-235.

medical system and enterprise at large. The first part especially concentrates on the various aspects of Descartes's physiological and medical study, dealing with his medical texts or sections of his work covering medical topics; the second part concentrates on the reception of Cartesian medicine in the seventeenth-century. Focusing on the centrality of medicine in Cartesian programme, this volume illuminates both the shadows and lights, the limitations and gaps of his study of anatomy, physiology, nosology, and therapeutics, as well as the attempts to bridge such gaps by Cartesian scholars, and the debates and responses these aspects raised in seventeenth-century culture, somehow ensuring the (academic) survival of this discipline throughout the decades.

In this introduction, I try to provide a general overview of Descartes's medical studies. In reconstructing the perimeter of medical knowledge in his philosophy, I first analyse the texts and passages Descartes devoted to medicine, highlighting the limitations of these works. Then, I deal with the topics of Descartes's medical science, namely, his physiology, following the division of the body into head, chest, and abdomen, a possible nosology, and a therapeutics. After a brief outline of the role of observation and experimentation (as well as collaborations) in Descartes's study of medicine, I finally present a few threads for investigating the reception of Descartes's medicine, and revealing its endurance in the seventeenth century.

2. Medical Texts: An Enterprise with a Restricted Focus

2.1. L'Homme

In June 1632, Descartes informed Mersenne that he aimed to include a fuller description of the living functions to complete his treatise on physics.[20] Two years earlier, Descartes had claimed to be studying medicine, combining chemistry and anatomy, and aiming to deal with diseases and remedies. Yet, of this broad programme, including a study of the structure of the body, its chemical functioning and its malfunctioning, as well as the study of diseases and remedies, there is little evidence in L'Homme. Four-fifths of this text provide a reconstruction of the mechanics of sensation and the nervous system, from the organs of sense to the brain, and little space is given to the other functions of the body, which occupy its first pages and present a very rapid overview of a few processes. Indeed, as appropriately indicated by Gabriel Alban-Zapata, L'Homme was supposed to be the final chapter of Descartes's treatise on light.[21] In this sense, it discusses man as a spectator, that is, as one who receives light and sees: major attention is paid to vision in the text, as asserted by Descartes himself (on the eye, sight and vision in Descartes, see **Tawrin Baker** in this volume.)[22] Yet, this

---

20 Descartes to Mersenne, June 1632, AT I 254; BL 234/CSMK 39.
21 Cf. GABRIEL ALBAN-ZAPATA, "Light and Man: An Anomaly in the *Treatise on Light?*", in *Descartes' Treatise on Man and its Reception*, p. 155-174.
22 *L'Homme*, AT XI 132; BOp 380; G 108.

chapter has a clear philosophical aim. Physiology helps Descartes confirm what one observes: what results from vision is a mental representation of the world, and this experience ascertains that the new world imagined (in *Le Monde*) is the actual world.

Yet, *L'Homme* contains a few important aspects of Descartes's medical system, namely the mechanization of the body and the animal-machine analogy, as well as the description of sensation and passions in a mechanical way, the physiology of the brain and the description of the circulation of blood, a recent discovery by William Harvey (1578-1657).[23] Part one of *L'Homme* starts with the supposition of the animal-machine and then describes digestion, the conversion of chyle into blood, the heating of blood in the heart, respiration, the heartbeat, nutrition, blood circulation, the production of particles from blood, and specifically animal spirits. These make the body move, the topic of Part two of *L'Homme*, which concentrates on muscles and nerves. Part three deals with a mechanical description of external sensation: touch, taste, smell, hearing, and sight. Part four concentrates on internal sensation, such as hunger, thirst, the emotions and passions, part five on the physiology of the brain. *L'Homme* goes from page 119 to page 202 of the AT edition.

What results is clear: *L'Homme* is not an exhaustive text on medicine, as its focus is a specific section concerning human nature. To this, one should add the vicissitudes of the manuscript (notoriously lost).[24] In writing to Mersenne in 1646, Descartes claimed to have "12 or 13 years ago, [...] described all the functions of the human or animal body; but the manuscript is in such a mess that I would be hard put to it to read it myself. Nevertheless, four or five years ago I could not avoid lending it to a close friend, who made a copy which was then recopied by two more people, with my permission but without my rereading or correcting the transcript…"[25] Apparently, the form of *L'Homme* changed throughout the years. Recently, Delphine Antoine-Mahut has brilliantly reconstructed the story of *L'Homme* in detail;[26] and both Daniel Garber and Harold Cook have proposed two interpretations about its nature, transformations, and the reason for it being left unpublished.[27] Yet, a lot is still to be uncovered about this text. Besides its role in Descartes's physics, the text was later copied, transcribed, probably changed, and finally corrected by its editors or someone else in-between. In 1662, Florent Schuyl (1619-1669) published a Latin translation, *De homine*, while in 1664 Claude Clerselier (1614-1684) published a French edition that includes a commentary by

---

23   Cf. Descartes to Mersenne, November or December 1632, AT I 263; BL 243.
24   One should note that, recently, Erik-Jan Bos has discovered a previously unknown manuscript of a Latin translation of *L'Homme*, likely prepared during the 1650s in Leiden, and left unpublished, and entitled *Tractatus de homine à Cartesio*. See: https://www.leidenspecialcollectionsblog.nl/articles/an-unknown-latin-manuscript-translation-of-descartes-lhomme [accessed 18 July 2022].
25   Descartes to Mersenne, 23 November 1646, AT IV 566-567; CSMK 301.
26   DELPHINE ANTOINE-MAHUT, "The Story of *L'Homme*", in *Descartes' Treatise on Man and its Reception*, p. 1-29.
27   HAROLD J. COOK, "Augustinian Souls and Epicurean Bodies? Descartes's Corporeal Mind in Motion," in *Descartes and the* Ingenium*: The Embodied Soul in Cartesianism*, p. 113-135. HAROLD J. COOK, "Princess Elisabeth's Cautions and Descartes' Suppression of the *Traité de l'Homme*", *Early Science and Medicine*, 26/4 (2021), p. 289-313. DANIEL GARBER, "The Chapters of *L'Homme* Descartes Didn't Write," in *Cartesius edoctus*.

Louis de La Forge (1632-1666). These are the versions of the text we possess — whether the French text is the one originally written by Descartes in 1632 appears unlikely.

2.2. La Description du corps humain

In the late 1640s, rather than putting the manuscript of *L'Homme* in better shape, as he probably had planned, Descartes claimed to have a better description of the animal body.[28] This text is *La Description du corps humain*, on which he worked between 1645 and 1648,[29] but more likely in 1648, as testified to in a letter to Elisabeth and in the colloquium with Burman.[30] While the original manuscript of *L'Homme* is lost, the manuscript of *La Description* was collected in the Stockholm inventory, under the item G.[31] This text was posthumously published in 1664 by Clerselier together with *L'Homme*, which has however retained primacy amongst Descartes's interpreters.[32] Yet, in comparison to *L'Homme*, *La Description* appears more autonomous and, for a few issues, more exhaustive.

This text starts with a preface, in which Descartes presents several features to improve medicine as a science: the knowledge of the bodily functions, the role of anatomy and mechanics, the rejection of the soul, and a summary of the treatise. Part two deals with the heartbeat and the circulation of blood, with a confutation of Harvey and an attack on Aristotle. Part three concentrates on nutrition and growth. Part four focuses on the formation of parts in the seed. Part five on the formation of organs, although this latter part is incomplete, as the text ends here. It goes from page 223 to page 286 of the AT edition.

While in the text Descartes presents some aspects of his embryology, the part on sensation is entirely missing. Apparently, *La Description* might have been the first section of a medical treatise, and *L'Homme* (or a re-elaboration of it) might have been another section. Whether this combination was within Descartes's aims is however impossible to state. In sum, even this second text is anything but satisfactory and complete medical work.

---

28   Descartes to X***, 1648-1649, AT V 261; BL 2612.
29   Descartes to Newcastle, October 1645, AT IV 329; BL 2099; Descartes to Elisabeth, 6 October 1645, AT IV 310; BL 2103-2105; Descartes to Elisabeth, 31 January 1648, AT V 112; BL 2513.
30   Cf. Descartes to Elisabeth, 31 January 1648, AT V 112; BL 2513: "I am in the midst of another piece of writing, one which I hope can be more agreeable to your Highness: the description of the functions of animals and of man. Since what I have had in draft for twelve or thirteen years now, and which was seen by your Highness, has come into the hands of several who have badly transcribed it, I thought myself obliged to make it more precise, that is to say, to rewrite it. I have ventured there (but only for the past eight or ten days) to want to explain the way in which an animal is formed from the beginning of its origin. I say an animal in general since I would not dare to undertake this for man in particular, as I do not yet have enough evidence for this effort." [Translation is from Shapiro, p. 168.] And *Colloquium with Burman*, AT V 170-171; BOp 1290-1292. See MATTHIJS VAN OTEGEM, *A Bibliography of the Works of Descartes (1637-1704)*, 2 vols, Utrecht, Zeno, 2002, vol. 2, p. 493.
31   Stockholm Inventory, AT X 9-10; BOp 18.
32   On the relationship between *L'Homme* and *La Description*, see ANNIE BITBOL-HESPÉRIÈS, "The Primacy of *L'Homme* in the 1664 Parisian Edition by Clerselier", in *Descartes' Treatise on Man and its Reception*, p. 33-48.

2.3. The Discours de la Méthode: the heartbeat, and La Dioptrique: sight and the eye

In Part 5 of the *Discours de la Méthode*, Descartes summarizes his earlier work on physics. Since he could not start his physiology "by demonstrating effects from causes and showing from what seeds and in what manner nature must produce them,"[33] Descartes describes the functions from a mechanical supposition. Then, he dealt with the heartbeat and the blood circulation as an example of his physiology. The text is original, and provides some important additions to *L'Homme*, in which no similar explanation surfaces. Moreover, Descartes discusses the differences between animals and men, in this part, highlighting the mechanical behavior of brutes.

Moreover, in the *Discours*, Descartes embedded medicine within his methodology. First, he rejected traditional medicine, describing the errors of physicians;[34] second, he presented a few aspects of medical knowledge; third, he claimed it was possible to draw a few rules for medicine more reliable than those possessed by traditional medicine.[35] In this sense, medicine proved the correctness of Descartes's methodology in the field.

This was a significant piece in Descartes's philosophy of nature. These few pages sparked the discussion with Plemp in the 1637-1638 correspondence, whose letters contain several important additions to Descartes's explanation of the heartbeat, as he significantly revised some aspects of the *Discours*.[36] At the end of the discussion, Plemp endorsed the circulation of blood, which he had earlier rejected. In 1643, Johannes van Beverwijck (1594-1647) contacted Descartes for a Latin version of this correspondence to be included in the *Epistolicae quaestiones* (1644). Furthermore, Regius passionately started endorsing Cartesian philosophy after his reading of the *Discours*, and later developed a physiology consistent with the philosophy of this text.[37] As a result, at the core of Descartes's natural philosophical revolution, medicine surfaces as a meaningful discipline, and scholars endorse or debate confirmation or rejection of his philosophy.

One should then note that Descartes's *Optics*, one of the essays of his method, contains several physiological claims, as he dealt with vision and the structure of the eye. In this essay, Descartes presented the role of nerves in transmitting impressions to the brain, claimed that the common sense is located in the (pineal) gland, and bolstered the notion that the soul senses, not the body.[38] Medicine intersects the

---

33 *Discours de la Méthode* V, AT VI 45; CSM I 134; BO 76.
34 *Ibid.* I, AT VI 9; BO 33; CSM I 115.
35 *Ibid.* VI, AT VI 78; BO 115; CSM I 151.
36 See BALDASSARRI, *Il metodo al tavolo anatomico*, p. 71-82. ETIENNE GILSON, "Descartes et la scolastique", in ID., *Études sur le rôle de la pensée médiévale dans la formation du système de cartésien*, Vrin, Paris, 1930, p. 51-100; MARJORIE GRENE, "The Heart and Blood: Descartes, Plemp, and Harvey", in *Essays on the Philosophy and Science of René Descartes*, ed. by Stephen Voss, New York-Oxford, Oxford University Press, 1993, p. 324-336.
37 Cf. Regius to Descartes, 18 August 1638, AT II 305-306; BL 818-820. Descartes to Regius, 20 August 1638, AT II 306-307; BL 826-828. Descartes to Mersenne, 23 August 1638, AT II 334; BL 850-852.
38 *La Dioptrique* IV, AT VI 109; BO 159.

knowledge and the location of the soul. From Libert Froidmont (1587-1653) to Lazare Meysonnier (1611-1673), debates over the seat of the soul developed after the publication of the *Optics*.³⁹

2.4. The Meditationes *and the* Passions de l'âme

Even the *Meditationes* contains several medical aspects. The First Meditation, for example, discusses the case of madmen, "whose brains are so damaged by the persistent vapours of melancholia [*atra bile*] that they firmly maintain they are kings when they are paupers...,"⁴⁰ revealing a clear medical approach to the issue. Then, in the Sixth Meditation, Descartes presents a few medical cases to prove, by means of the errors of nature, the correctness of his philosophical interpretation of the nature of man and ground the certainty of knowledge.⁴¹ This text collects several medical features: (a) instincts and the deceptions of sensation in the case of taste (see **Clément Raymond**'s contribution to this volume); (b) the case of amputations; (c) the case of dropsy (on metaphysical diseases see the contribution of **Franco A. Meschini** in this volume); and (d) the case of dreams and madness (see the contribution of **Jan Forsman** in this volume). This latter especially leads to a weakening of the brain, which possibly produces the diverse forms of insanity. As a result, the *Meditationes* uncovers a medicine of the mind, uniting both a philosophical ground for the certainty of the mind, and a medical description of the mind-body composite, which surfaces in the notion of *corpus meum* in the last meditation, where he located the seat of the soul in the brain.⁴²

The mind-body composite triggered several objections to the *Meditationes* and, amongst other things, the correspondence between Descartes and the Princess Elisabeth of Bohemia, which combined metaphysics, natural philosophy and medicine (as well as ethics and politics), ultimately resulting in the *Passions de l'âme*, published in 1649. In the *Replies* to the *Objections* (as well as in the 1640 and 1641 correspondence) Descartes dealt with a few aspects relating embryology to the explanation of the composite (see **Lynda Gaudemard** in this volume on mind-body union and its physiological interconnections). In going *à rebours* from the composite to the formation of the embryo was a meaningful physiological issue at the time. The correspondence with Elisabeth played a different role. Not only did Elisabeth call Descartes "the best doctor for my soul,"⁴³ but as Franco A. Meschini

---

39 MESCHINI, *Neurofisiologia cartesiana*, p. 30-54.
40 *Meditationes de prima philosophia* I, AT VII 18-19; BO 704; CSM II 13.
41 For an alternative interpretation, see EMANUELA SCRIBANO, "Science contra the *Meditations*: The Existence of Material Things", *The European Legacy*, 27/3-4 (2022), p. 348-360.
42 *Meditationes de prima philosophia* VI, AT VII 86; BL 794; CSM II 59-60. On several physiological issues developing from the relationship between body and soul in the *Meditationes*, and its legacy and betrayals, see the recent EMANUELA SCRIBANO, "Powers of the Body and Eclipse of the soul: From Descartes on", in *Mechanism, Life and Mind in Modern Natural Philosophy*, ed. by Ch. T. Wolfe, P. Pecere, A. Clericuzio, Cham, Springer, 2022, p. 235-258.
43 Elisabeth to Descartes, 6 May 1643, AT III 662; BL 1747; Shapiro 62.

has recently revealed, a few threads unite the exchanges in the correspondence, which developed from the metaphysical treatise, with the physiological elaboration in the *Passions*.[44] The first part of this latter text contains a physiology of the human body, in which the philosopher deals with the circulation of blood, the formation of animal spirits, the movement of muscles, sensation, and the diverse reactions to sensation in the brain and mind, ultimately discussing the passions of the soul and a way to treat them. Annie Bitbol-Hespériès has recently discussed the connection between Descartes's medical texts and the *Passions*, highlighting the importance of medicine in the study of the composite.[45] Until the publication of *De homine*, this text was the main reference in Descartes's medicine.

2.5. *The* Principia philosophiae

In 1644, Descartes published the *Principia philosophiae*, a text intended to replace Aristotelian physics at schools and universities. As is well known, the last sections on the animal body and man are missing. Still, he added a few articles on sensation, nerves, and on the seat of the soul,[46] and then detailed sensations, emotions, the affections of the soul and natural appetites, ultimately dealing with the mind-body composite.[47] What is more important to note is that Descartes reduced sensation, appetites, emotions, and passions, to the mechanics of his natural philosophy, as the movement, figure, and size of particles operate in producing the diverse sensations and passions.

2.6. *The Biomedical Manuscripts: from Embryology to Therapeutics*

Together with the correspondence, several texts collected in volume XI of AT present medical arguments. In item E of the Stockholm inventory, there are: 19 sheets with a text entitled *Primae Cogitationes circa generationem animalium* [First Reflections on the Generation of Animals]; 2 more sheets on the generation of animals; one and a half pages on animals; a sheet entitled *Remedia et vires medicamentorum* [Remedies and medical powers]; 16 sheets of observations on the nature of plants and animals; 3 pages with the title, *De partibus inferiore ventre contentis* [On the Parts Collected in the Abdomen].[48] In item G, after the pages containing *La Description du corps*

---

44 FRANCO A. MESCHINI, "Les Passions de l'âme, un testo stratificato: l'influenza di Elisabetta. Annotazioni alla lettera di Elisabetta del 25 aprile 1646 e alla risposta di Descartes del maggio 1646", in *Les* Passions de l'âme *et leur réception philosophique*, p. 101-136.
45 ANNIE BITBOL-HESPÉRIÈS, "De toute la nature de l'homme: de *L'Homme* à la *Description du corps humain*, la physiologie des *Passions de l'âme* et ses antécédents médicaux", in *Les* Passions de l'âme *et leur réception philosophique*, p. 67-100.
46 *Principia philosophiae* IV, art. 189, AT VIII-1 316; BO 2188.
47 *Ibid.*, art. 197, AT VIII-1 320-321; BO 2196-2198.
48 *Stockholm Inventory*, AT X 8-9; BOp 16-18: "*En la seconde page est ce titre*: Primae cogitationes circa generationem animalium, *en dix-neuf feuillets.*[...] *Puis deux feuillets encore de la formation des animaux.* [...] *et un feuillet et demi encore des Animaux. Six feuillets blancs. Un feuillet intitulé*: Remedia et virtus medicamentorum. [...] *il y a seize pages d'observations sur la nature des plantes et des animaux. Et après un feuillet vide, trois pages sous ce titre*: De partibus inferiore ventre contentis."

humain, there are "10 or 12 sheets [...] treating the same subject, without a clear link with the previous one."[49]

The *Primae Cogitationes* contains Descartes's observations and reflections on embryology, as he dissected calves and other animals. The *Remedia* contains a short treatise on therapeutics, dealing with both chemical and vegetal remedies. The other sheets had probably been collected in the long and non-homogeneous *Excerpta anatomica* (see **Fabrizio Baldassarri** in this volume), as these laboratory notes present a study of the structure of the body, and of several functions, namely, blood circulation, generation, digestion, nutrition, bodily formation, instincts and sensation, as well as pages on diseases and remedies. To these, one should also add *De saporibus*, a short treatise on the formation of taste in the tongue. Undoubtedly, these manuscripts reveal the richness of Descartes's laboratory studies of physiology, despite the scattered condition of such notes.

3. Anatomy and Physiology: the Abdomen, Pectus, Caput, a Nosology and a Therapeutics

In a December 1630 letter to Mersenne, Descartes asked whether the animal body is usually divided into *caput, pectus, et ventrem*, likely following the Aristotelian classification of organs by which anatomical science was accomplished.[50] Yet, Descartes did not follow this division in his medical texts. Instead of a natural historical reconstruction of the anatomy of the body, Descartes followed a mechanical functioning. This should start with the formation of the body, namely an embryology, but he was unable to follow a causal thread from the seed, as he stressed in the *Discours*, where he methodologically chose to start from a supposition, the animal-machine, and from a specific point in the chain of reasoning.[51] This starting point is the heartbeat and blood circulation, which forms the centre of the mechanical movement of the body, and a sort of principle of life grounded on its mechanics, in which the soul does not play a role in its functioning. Descartes's cardio- and hemo-centric view in physiology is well acknowledged by interpreters, and ranges from *L'Homme* to the *Passions*, and from the study of functions to the definition of life.[52] Nevertheless, I am not going to follow this thread, but aim to reconstruct the mechanization of the diverse functions and processes, following the division into areas of the body.

---

49 *Ibid.*, 10; BOp 16: "A cette liasse ont été joints dix ou douze feuillets [...] qui traitent du même sujet, mais sans qu'il paraisse de liaison avec les précédents."
50 See WILLIAM HARVEY, *Lectures on the whole of Anatomy*, ed. Ch. D. O'Malley, Berkeley, University of California Press, 1961, p. 35. ROGER FRENCH, *William Harvey's Natural Philosophy*, Cambridge University Press, Cambridge, 1994. GIANNA POMATA and NANCY SIRAISI, eds., *Historia. Empiricism and Erudition in Early Modern Europe*, Cambridge Ma., MIT Press, 2005.
51 This is consistent with his methodological rules, see *Discours de la Méthode*, II, AT VI 18-19; BO 44; CSM I 120.
52 See MANNING, "Descartes and Medicine," p. 166. FRANCO A. MESCHINI, "La dottrina della digestione secondo Descartes. Itinerari tra testi, contesti e intertesti", *Physis*, 50-51/2 (2015), p. 113-164. FABRIZIO BALDASSARRI, "Descartes' Bio-Medical Study of Plants: Vegetative Activities, Soul, and Power", *Early Science and Medicine*, 23/5-6 (2018), p. 509-529.

The abdomen contains the vegetative functions, namely (a) reproduction and generation, and (b) digestion and nutrition. A clear treatment of such operations is absent in Descartes's published works. Actually, growth, self-organization, and reproduction are difficult to apply to machines, and for this reason they put Descartes's hydraulic model at stake. Following an easier path, in the *Discours de la Méthode*, he started his physiological investigation from a specific point of the chain of reasoning, without explaining the formation of the body from seeds, but taking the move from a specific function easily reducible to a mechanical model. This text reflects the structure of *L'Homme*, where no embryology surfaces, while a few passages focus on digestion (Part I, articles 3 and 4) and nutrition (Part I, articles 8 and 9; Part III, article 33; Part 4, articles 52, 57-61). Still, in these articles, Descartes mostly connects nutrition with the circulation of blood and sensation, without investigating nutrition in its own right, although a growing attention to fermentation surfaces in Descartes's texts (see **Carmen Schmechel** in this volume). In contrast to such an absence, Descartes's biomedical manuscripts are almost entirely devoted to vegetative functions, and therefore disclose an important addition in understanding his involvement with life and living activities. In *La Description du corps humain*, part III is devoted to Nutrition, while parts IV and V concern embryology and the formation of bodies. In these texts, Descartes provided a mechanization of the basic activities of living natures, ultimately connecting vegetation with animal bodies.

The chest [*pectus*] and the head [*caput*] are more strongly connected, as the heartbeat and blood circulation produce animal spirits that govern all movements and bodily sensation, natural inclinations, emotions, and passions. Sensation is the main topic of *L'Homme*, whose last section entirely concerns the brain (see **Annie Bitbol-Hespériès** in this volume). The heartbeat is the main topic of the *Discours*, and certainly the major physiological reconstruction of Descartes's entire physiology. Discussions of the brain (and the pineal gland) and its operations, namely sensation, memory, and imagination arise in the debates on his metaphysics that surface in Descartes's correspondence of the 1640s, as the French physicians Christoph de Villiers (c. 1583-c. 1650) and Lazare Meyssonnier (1611/1612-1673) debated the nature of the pineal gland.[53] The mechanization of sensation and passions (from *La Dioptrique* to his last publication) is undoubtedly a major point in Descartes's natural philosophy, as it concerns the metaphysics of human nature and the composition of mind and body.

Although he discussed several diseases in the correspondence, no exhaustive nosology surfaces in his work. This intersects the philosophical problem of defining maladies and unhealthy bodies in a mechanical natural philosophy, as brilliantly reconstructed by Gideon Manning.[54] In some of his notes, a description of fevers

---

53 Francesco Trevisani, "Un corrispondente di Cartesio: alcune note su Lazare Meyssonnier (1611/1621-1673), medico e astrologo lionese e sulla sua *Belle Magie* (1669)", *History and Philosophy of the Life Sciences*, 1 (1979), p. 285-308.
54 Gideon Manning, "Descartes' Healthy Machines and the Human Exception", in *The Mechanization of Natural Philosophy*, ed. by D. Garber and S. Roux, Dordrecht, Springer, 2013, p. 237-262.

does however surface. Treating diseases is a further problem. In a 1639 letter to Mersenne, Descartes claims that "I do not yet know enough to be able to heal even a fever. For I claim to know only the animal in general, which is not subject to fevers, and not yet man in particular, who is."[55] Indeed, although "the preservation of health has always been the principal end of my studies,"[56] as he wrote to the Marquees of Newcastle in the October 1645, questions concerning the role and number of remedies and therapeutics upset Descartes's treatment of diseases. Accordingly, "all remedies are uncertain."[57] To Princess Elisabeth, Descartes recommends avoiding the chemical remedies of physicians.[58] At the same time, Descartes, however, developed a therapeutics, grounded on his physiology; as he wrote in *La Description du corps humain*: if one had devoted more attention to anatomy and physiology, "many reliable precepts in medicine, as much for curing illness as for preventing it, and even also to slow the course of ageing"[59] would have been found. According to Descartes, the bodily machine appears able to treat itself, as nature tends to heal. Yet, when this is not sufficient, diet and a few remedies would work, which he describes in a section of the *Excerpta anatomica* (AT XI 601-607; BOp 1170-1176) and in a short tract entitled *Remedia et vires medicamentorum* (AT XI 641-644; BOp 1216-1218).[60]

While several lacunae appear, this brief reconstruction reveals the extension of Descartes's engagement with medicine, as he tried to deal with human nature in its entirety. Indeed, he focused on generation from the seed, bodily formation, organ functioning, the principle of life, and the movements and activities of the body, ultimately disclosing the mind-body composition through the study of the passions. Once again, his medical enterprise appears as strictly connected to his philosophical programme, which in its turn is the source of the limitations of Descartes's medical investigations. Later in the century, philosophers and scholars parted from Descartes's restricted and mechanical interpretation of life, searching for an alternative explanation.

4. Anatomical Observations, Sources, and Collaborations

Descartes's attention to physiology and anatomy developed in the early 1630s as a section on human sensation would compose the last chapter of his physics (i.e., *Le Monde ou Traité de la lumière*). In this period, he worked on anatomy and chemistry, attended public anatomical dissections in Leiden, where he matriculated on 27

---

55 Descartes to Mersenne, 20 February 1639, AT II 525-526; BL 1000; CSMK 135.
56 Descartes to Newcastle, October 1645, AT IV 329; BL 2098; CSMK 275.
57 Descartes to Newcastle, April 1645, AT IV 191; BL 1988.
58 Descartes to Elisabeth, December 1646, AT IV 590; BL 2360.
59 *La Description du corps humain*, AT XI 243-244; BOp 510; G 170.
60 See FABRIZIO BALDASSARRI, "Seeking Intellectual Evidence in the Sciences: The Role of Botany in Descartes' Therapeutics", in *Evidence in the Age of the New Sciences*, ed. by J. A. T. Lancaster and R. Raiswell, Cham, Springer, 2018, p. 47-75. BALDASSARRI, *Il metodo al tavolo anatomico*, p. 209-224.

of June 1630, and dissected animals in Amsterdam.[61] At the end of 1632, he wrote to Mersenne that he was "dissecting the heads of various animals, so that I can explain what imagination, memory, etc. consist in;"[62] while in 1639 he reported to have exercised himself in dissecting animals for eleven years.[63] In the 1638 correspondence with Plemp, Descartes performed anatomical observations (and vivisection on a rabbit) to confirm his theory of the heartbeat.[64] At a certain point of the *Discours de la Méthode*, Descartes also claims that his explanation "follows from the mere arrangement of the parts [...] (which can be seen with the naked eye), from the heat in the heart (which can be felt with the fingers), and from the nature of the blood (which can be known through observation)."[65] In this sense, one could prove Descartes's theory by means of experimentation. Still, historians have debated the role of anatomical dissections in Descartes, as these appear to have a secondary aim in the philosophy,[66] though Descartes's anatomical performances remain undeniable. In *La Description du corps humain*, Descartes underlines the importance of anatomical observations to ground the understanding of the human body, therefore highlighting the role anatomy and observations played in his methodological quest for truth in the sciences (see **Benjamin Goldberg**'s contribution to this volume on a confrontation between William Harvey's and Descartes's medical experimentation).

It should be noted that, for an untrained physician, performing anatomical dissections would not be an easy task. For this reason, medicine seems to confirm the claim that "by building upon the work of our predecessors and combining the lives and labours of many, [one could] make much greater progress working together."[67] Indeed, although no proof of direct collaborations have surfaced, Descartes probably benefited from the help of experts and physicians in the Dutch provinces.[68] These were Henricus Reneri (1593-1639), Johann Elichmann (ca1601-1639), Plemp, and Regius.[69] Descartes was also friends of Adolphus Vorstius (1597-1663), who was professor of medicine and botany at Leiden University, and to whom Descartes sent

---

61 Plempius reported that, "ignored by everyone [...], like a man who did not read, nor own many books [...], [Descartes] dissected animals [in Amsterdam,] [and one may find him] just as Hippocrates found Democritus outside Abdera." Plemp, 21 December 1652, in VOPISCUS FORTUNATUS PLEMPIUS, *Fundamenta Medicinae ad scholae acribologiam aptata*, editio tertia, Leuven, 1654, p. 375-376. [Translation is mine.]
62 Descartes to Mersenne, November or December 1632, AT I 263; BL 242; CSMK 40.
63 Descartes to Mersenne 20 February 1639, AT II 525; BL 1000. Descartes to Mersenne, 13 November 1639, AT II 621; BL 1068.
64 Descartes to Plempius, 15 February 1638, AT I 526; BL 518; CSMK 81.
65 *Discours de la Méthode* V, AT VI 50; BO 82; CSM I 136.
66 See ANDRAULT, *La raison des corps. Mécanisme et science médicale*.
67 *Discours de la Méthode* VI, AT VI 63; BO 98; CSM I 143.
68 See VINCENT AUCANTE, "Les médecins et la médecine," in *La biografia intellettuale di Descartes attraverso la* Correspondance, ed. by J.-R. Armogathe, G. Belgioioso and C. Vinti, Naples, Vivarium, 1990, p. 607-625.
69 Cf. FABRIZIO BALDASSARRI, "Elements of Descartes' Medical *Scientia*: Books, Medical Schools, and Collaborations", in *Scientiae in the History of Medicine*, ed. by Fabrizio Baldssarri and Fabio Zampieri, Rome-Bristol, L'Erma di Bretschneider, 2021, p. 247-270.

a letter that appears as a short manifesto for his medicine.[70] In the debate over the conarium gland of the 1640s, Descartes describes a dissection he attended at Leiden around 1637, when "an old Professor, who performed the dissection [of a woman], named Valcher, confessed to me that he never saw it in any human body."[71] This is Adrianus Falcoburgius or van Valckenburg (1581-1650), who was a professor of anatomy and surgery.[72] Furthermore, Descartes befriended Cornelis van Hogelande (*c.* 1590-1662), a medical practitioner with whom he attended de Wilhem's daughter.[73] The relationship with van Hogelande is anything but secondary amongst Descartes's acquaintances, and should deserve more attention from historians. Descartes also met Johannes Walaeus (or de Waal, 1604-1649) in Leiden, and knew both Franciscus de le Boe Sylvius (1614-1672) and Franciscus van der Schagen. Descartes probably performed anatomical dissections with Reneri, Plemp, and Regius, and discussed anatomy and medicine with Vorstius, Falcoburgius, and the others. He was informed about remedies by Elichmann and Hogelande, although very little is known about their collaborations.

A final aspect is Descartes's confrontation with sources. The work of Annie Bitbol-Hespériès has highlighted the presence of various references in Descartes's medical investigations.[74] Although he generally dismissed books in the construction of any sciences, different sources surface in his medical study. In 1637, for example, he claimed to be studying medicine by means of observations and books,[75] and various references surface in his biomedical manuscripts. He certainly knew Galen (Aelius Galenus, CE 129-*c.* 216), and, among others, Jean Fernel (1497-1558), Jean Riolan the Younger (1577 or 1580-1657), Johannes Schenck von Grafenberg (1530-1598), Caspar Bauhin (or Gaspard, 1560-1624), Hieronimus Fabricius ab Aquapendente (1533-1619), as well as William Harvey (1578-1657), probably the only contemporary author he seriously confronted. It is unclear whether he knew the discussions of the passions of his time, such as the text of Robert Burton (1577-1640), as well as the work of Santorio Santorio (1561-1636), to name two important medical authors, or how much acquainted he was with the interconnections between medicine and philosophy at Padua University. In this sense, while this remains an issue for further investigations, it seems that Descartes used several sources to fill the gaps in his medical training, without endorsing any physiological interpretations. For example, when Regius welcomed Gaspare Aselli's (1581-1625) theory of lacteal vessels, Descartes appeared more uncertain about this issue, and failed to mention Aselli's work in his studies.

---

70 Descartes to Vorstius, 19 June 1643, AT III 686-689; BL 1772-1774.
71 Descartes to Mersenne, 1 April 1640, AT II 49; BL 1172. [Translation is mine.]
72 GERRIT A. LINDEBOOM, *Dutch Medical Biography*, Amsterdam, Rodopi, 1984.
73 Descartes to de Wihlem, 13 June 1640, AT III 91; BL 1204.
74 See ANNIE BITBOL-HESPÉRIÈS (ed.), *René Descartes. Le Monde, L'Homme*, Seuil, Paris, 1996. ANNIE BITBOL-HESPÉRIÈS, "Une source des textes biomédicaux latins de Descartes, AT XI : les *Observationes* de Johannes Schenck", *Archives de Philosophie*, 80/1 (2017), p. 152-161.
75 Descartes to X***, 30 August 1637, AT I 394; BL 406. Descartes to Huygens, 4 December 1637, AT I 649; BL 472.

5. The Reception

The second part of this volume deals with the reception of Descartes's physiology and medicine, certainly a more complex aspect and, in some cases, quite uncharted territory. This reception is anything but unproblematic. Since Descartes's more medical works have been posthumously published, the reception of Cartesian medicine reveals a major moment in the construction of this discipline. Still, a decisive step in ensuring the survival of Cartesian medicine consisted of the separation of Descartes's metaphysics from physiology, ultimately paving the way to the mechanical study of human nature.

First, there is a problem in defining Cartesian physicians, namely, those scholars who followed Descartes's metaphysical principles and mechanical physics, and applied it to physiology.[76] In the 1643 *Admiranda methodus novae philosophiae Renati Des Cartes*, Martin Schoock (1614-1669) designated Henricus Regius as a "Cartesian physician."[77] In 1669, the author of the *Nouveau cours de médecine*, likely Jacques de Roure, employed the term 'Cartesian physicians' to designate several authors, such as Hogelande, Regius, amongst others.[78] In both cases, however, being a Cartesian physician appears more a rhetorical claim, rather than a clear philosophical and physiological affiliation, and thus complicates any precise investigation of Cartesian medicine. In other cases, scholars grouped amongst the Cartesians and promoting Descartes's medicine, appeared ready to correct the latter's theory, acknowledging its obscurities and updating it to the most recent discoveries, while maintaining the general framework of his philosophy. For instance, in 1664, Louis de La Forge (1632-1666) included a series of *Remarks* in the French edition of *L'Homme* promoted by Claude Clerselier, therefore aiming to complete and correct Descartes's text at several points.[79] As Delphine Antoine-Mahut has recently shown, specifying a Cartesian canon is rather tortuous and complicated.[80]

Second, Cartesian scholars who dealt with medicine were forced to nuance it to make it consistent with the new discoveries, sometimes framing it with various

---

76 See the monumental attempt of Géraldine Caps, *Les « médecins cartésiens ». Héritage et diffusion de la représentation mécaniste du corps humain (1646-1696)*, Hildesheim-Zurich-New York, Georg Olms Verlag, 2010.

77 Martin Schoock, *Admiranda methodus novae philosophiae Renati Des Cartes*, Utrecht, 1643, Preface: "Sed quomodo tandem Theologus Medicum Cartesianum exauctorare laboravit ?" Cf. René Descartes, Martin Schoock, *La querelle d'Utrecht*, ed. by Th. Verbeek, Paris, Les impressions nouvelles, 1988, p. 167, 219, 235, 246, 250, 254.

78 Jacques de Roure, *Le Nouveau cours de médecine ou, selon les principes de la Nature et des Mécaniques, expliqués par Messierus Descartes, Hogelande, Regius, Arberius, Villis, les Docteturs de Louvain et par d'autres : on apprend le Cors de l'Home, avec les moiens de conserver la Santé, & de chasser les Maladies*, Paris, François Clousier et Pierre Aubouyn, 1669. Cf. Sophie Roux, "Une enquête sur Jacques du Roure (suite)," *Bulletin cartésien L*, in *Archives de philosophie*, (2019), p. 174-184.

79 On La Forge, see Patricia Easton and Melissa Gholamnejad, "Louis de la Forge and the Development of Cartesian Medical Philosophy," in *Early Modern Medicine and Natural Philosophy*, p. 207-225.

80 Cf. Delphine Antoine-Mahut, *L'autorité d'un canon philosophique : Le cas Descartes*, Paris, Vrin, 2021.

philosophies or traditions, as well as picking a few aspects and embedding them in a different context. Most of the Italian reception of Descartes follows this line. In this sense, the reception of Cartesian medicine appears a clear case study to understand the reception of Descartes *tout court*. For instance, the mechanization of physiology continued to be a crucial point of departure to understand living nature, but appeared more and more nuanced and transformed. From Regius to Schuyl and La Forge (just to name a few cases),[81] Descartes's medicine was transformed, reinterpreted, completed, and revised, sometimes intersecting Gassendi's atomism or the chymical traditions, neo-Platonism or stoicism, and traditional medicine (namely, Galenism). In this sense, the reception of Descartes's medicine was anything but linear, and developed as a shrub of interconnected branches, therefore revealing the riches of Descartes's thought and its malleability within early modern culture.

Third, a connection between Cartesian partisans and opponents importantly surfaces, especially as some early modern scholars who were Cartesian followers at first, became fierce critics of Descartes's philosophy in a later moment (Plemp and Regius, to name just the two most famous cases). This interconnection between supporters and opponents, echoing the connection between lights and shadows, importantly shaped the reception of Cartesian medicine. While partisans faced the challenges non-Cartesian scholars proposed to this system, opponents were forced to deal with Descartes's philosophy, a relevant presence in early modern culture.

Moving from the difficulties and obscurities of Cartesian medicine, opponents made it a privileged field to test the inconsistencies of Descartes's method and philosophy, therefore anticipating or paving the road to the reaction to Cartesianism *tout court* — as is well-known, Regius's medical disputation sparked the Utrecht crisis that resulted in utter opposition to Cartesianism. Yet, an attraction to it in society and for those scholars who remained outside universities appears significant. Cartesian medicine was indeed banned from universities, as happened in Leuven, see the Belgium *affair* against Cartesian physiology,[82] and it was rejected in Paris, while it thrived in the French *académies* (such as the *académie* Montmor, Rohault, Thévenot, Bourdelot, to name just a few) (on this context, see the contributions of **Mihnea Dobre** and **Elena Rapetti** in this volume). Similarly, it was contested in British universities, as scholars fiercely opposed Cartesianism (see **Daniel Samuel**, and Goldberg in this volume),[83] while Descartes's philosophy was an underlying

---

81 On La Forge, see EMANUELA SCRIBANO, *Macchine con la mente*. EMANUELA SCRIBANO, "Connaissance et causalité: les adversaires de Malebranche", in *Occasionalism: From Metaphysics to Science*, ed. by M. Favaretti Camposampiero, M. Priarolo, E. Scribano, Turnhout, Brépols, 2018, p. 269-288. On Schuyl, see EVAN R. RAGLAND, "Experimenting with Chymical Bodies: Reinier de Graaf's Investigations of the Pancreas", *Early Science and Medicine* 13/6 (2008), p. 615-664, and his forthcoming book.
82 LUCIAN PETRESCU, "Descartes on the Heartbeat: The Levuen Affair", *Perspectives on Science* 21/4 (2013): p. 397-428. On the Netherlands, see THOMAS PETER GARIEPY, *Mechanism Without Metaphysics: Henricus Regius and the Establishment of Cartesian Medicine*, PhD dissertation, Yale University, 1990.
83 See PETER ANSTEY, "Descartes' Cardiology and Its Reception in English Physiology", in *Descartes' Natural Philosophy*, ed. by S. Gaukroger, J. Schuster and J. Sutton, London and New York, Routledge, 2000, p. 420-444.

presence in this context. A more complex situation surfaces in the Dutch context, given the case of Regius, or the case of Czech alchemist and physician Andreas von Haberneld, who had already reacted against Descartes's work in 1637 (see **Erik-Jan Bos** and Strazzoni in this volume). In the Netherlands, Niels Steensen's (or Nicolas Steno, 1638-1686) dismissal of several Cartesian physiological theories (similar to what his peers did) significantly shaped the opposition to Descartes's medicine and the ways its supporters tried to deal with it more consistently.[84] Similarly, in Italy Cartesianism (especially through the reception of Van Hogelande's work) attracted the attention of scholars who tried to combine some aspects of Descartes's mechanical philosophy and physiology with post-Galilean science, and especially in Tuscany, at the Medici court and at the Accademia del Cimento, and in Rome (see **Stefano Gulizia** and **Maria Conforti** in this volume). A less-investigated presence of Cartesian medicine concerns Germany, despite the ground-breaking work of Francesco Trevisani, and the recent contributions of Pietro Daniel Omodeo and Mattia Mantovani.[85] In this context, Cartesian medicine paved the ground for the development of new medical and philosophical studies, as occurred at Duisburg or in other cases in German territory (see **Nabeel Hamid** in this volume). This highlights a common trend. Throughout Europe, scholars tended to reject some physiological ideas of Descartes (such as the pineal gland), while preserving the philosophical framework (such as the mechanization of living functions). In this sense, Cartesian medicine significantly intertwined with a natural philosophical re-elaboration, as happened in France with Pierre-Sylvain Régis (1632-1707) (see the contribution of **Aaron Spink** in this volume). In other cases, however, Cartesian physiology and philosophy was a mere point of departure to challenge the mechanization of life that characterized Descartes's thought, and to pave the way for an alternative understanding of living nature (see **Laurynas Adomaitis** in this volume).

As it emerges from this volume, mapping the reception and survival of Cartesian medicine (which here mostly concerns the cases of Western Europe), the ideas it conveyed, and the intersections it developed, appears as an important lens to comprehend seventeenth-century culture in general, and a path to proceed beyond the traditional canon. Both the oppositions and the supports to, and the obscurities, problems, lights, and responses emerging at the time (which developed from the reading of, and challenges planted in Descartes's medical enterprise) played, in fact,

---

84 See RAPHAËLE ANDRAULT and MOGENS LAERKE, eds, *Steno and the Philosophers*, Leiden, Brill, 2018. On the Dutch Cartesian medicine, see also DAVIDE CELLAMARE, "Medicine and the Mind in the Teaching of Theodoor Craanen (1633-1688)", in *Descartes in the Classroom*, p. 199-230.

85 TREVISANI, *Descartes in Germania*. PIETRO DANIEL OMODEO, "Lodewijk de Bils' and Tobias Andreae's Cartesian Bodies: Embalmment Experiments, Medical Controversies and Mechanical Philosophy", *Early Science and Medicine*, 22 (2017), p. 301-332; MATTIA MANTOVANI, "Descartes' Man Under Construction: The Circulatory Statue of Salomon Reisel, 1680", *Early Science and Medicine*, 25 (2020), p. 101-134. See also, PIETRO DANIEL OMODEO, "Medical and Demonological Approaches to Descartes's Psychophysical Dualism: Andreae and Brecht", in P. D. Omodeo, *Defending Descartes in Brandeburg-Prussia: The University of Frankfurt an der Oder in the Seventeenth Century*, Cham, Springer, 2022, p. 127-149.

a role in shaping not only early modern philosophy and the sciences, but also the modern understanding of human nature and life. This ultimately reveals one of the ambitions of Descartes's project, as philosophy intersected medicine insofar as it dealt with human nature in its entirety, and metaphysics grounded medicine. Still, it incorporated a contradiction, and the survival of Cartesian medicine relied on the possibility to dismember Descartes's philosophy and separate medicine and moral philosophy from physics and metaphysics, as brilliantly pointed out by Verbeek.[86]

The *Meditationes de prima philosophia* somehow testify to this contradiction, as medicine lies at the core of his metaphysical search for certainty, but the deceptions of sensation cannot find a satisfactory solution in validating the metaphysical claim,[87] and Descartes cannot but recognize that,

> since the pressure of things to be done does not always allow us to stop and make such a meticulous check, it must be admitted that in this human life we are often liable to make mistakes about particular things, and we must acknowledge the weakness of our nature.[88]

---

86 VERBEEK, "Descartes and the Classroom", in *Descartes in the Classroom*, p. 33.
87 Cf. EMANUELA SCRIBANO, "Science contra the *Meditations*: The Existence of Material Things", *The European Legacy*, 27/3-4 (2022), p. 348-360, in which the author provides a fascinating interpretation to the role of medicine (physiology) in the path of the meditator. See also EMANUELA SCRIBANO, *Descartes in Context: Essays*, Oxford, Oxford University Press, 2022.
88 *Meditationes*, VI, AT VII 90; BO 798; CSM II 62.

PART I

Descartes's Medical Philosophy

Sources and Texts, Dissections and Reflections

GIDEON MANNING

Descartes's Cartesian Medicine

*Past, Present, and Future**

▼ ABSTRACT I reflect on the past, present, and future of Descartes scholarship. By looking specifically at the place of medicine in Descartes's natural philosophical project, the manner in which Cartesian medicine has been defended, repudiated, and interpreted, and what remains to be studied and understood, I highlight not just the significance of medicine to Descartes and its role in his reception, but also the potentially misleading extremes of scholar's interpretations and the need for future archival work.

▼ KEYWORDS Descartes, Mechanics, Medicine, Harvey, La Forge, Plempius, Sylvius

1. Introduction

The legend of René Descartes (1596-1650) as the founder of modern philosophy, singlehandedly offering a wholesale replacement to what could be found in the schools, is, as we all know by now, an artifact, actively constructed by Descartes in the *Discours de la Methode* then accepted and elaborated by his friends, disciples and, in a slightly different way, by his earliest detractors. One certainly cannot doubt Descartes's ambition or that Cartesianism (the movement that came to bear his name) proved influential in the institutional and intellectual world of the seventeenth century.[1] To acknowledge this, however, is not to explain how Descartes's legend came to have the

---

* I owe a debt of thanks to Fabrizio Baldassarri, Melissa Pastrana, John Schuster and the audience at the original conference for their questions and corrections. My chapter was completed while a visitor at the Max Planck Institute for the History of Science in Berlin. I am extremely grateful to Jürgen Renn and his Department for being wonderfully supportive hosts.

Gideon Manning • Cedars-Sinai Medical Center, Associate Professor of History of Medicine and Humanities / Director: Program in the History of Medicine; Claremont Graduate University, Research Associate Professor. Contact: <gideon.manning@csmc.edu>

importance that it did (and still does). As the cultural and intellectual historian Ann Blair succinctly observes, "[i]t is not easy to explain the success of Cartesianism."[2] In a very different context the historian of medicine Anne Harrington provides what looks like an explanation: Descartes's "importance to the history of mind-body medicine [...] is less as a real philosopher and more as a symbol of modern errors, a foil against which modern champions [...] express their nostalgia for a fantasized premodern past."[3]

Among the many contentious possibilities meant to explain the success of Cartesianism there is, I believe, a shared presumption that Descartes is something other than a medical philosopher. In other words, Cartesianism is thought to be a philosophical, or scientific, or (better) natural philosophical movement, but not necessarily a medical one. Thus, historians of medicine, science, and philosophy working separately continue, by and large, to overlook the role of medicine in Descartes's project and the ways in which expectations of practical benefits, including especially those in medicine, served to create the legend of Descartes and Cartesianism, explaining the success of the latter.

In my own prior work on Descartes and his reception, I have tried to avoid this oversight and, as my title suggests, my chapter is about Cartesian medicine's past — in Descartes and the seventeenth century — its present — in our current scholarship — and its potential future, which looks bright judging from this volume. The questions

---

1 I will be making two assumptions to facilitate my discussion, though both assumptions have been defended elsewhere. First, Cartesian medicine was a major force for change in the seventeenth century, for it was Cartesian physicians who opened or stepped through the European door to innovation in institutions of learning, exposing students to new ideas and laying the groundwork for the scientific revolution (JOHN HEILBORN, "Was There a Scientific Revolution?" in *The Oxford Handbook of the History of Physics*, ed. J. Z. Buchwald and R. Fox, Oxford, Oxford University Press, 2013, p. 7-24, 15). Second, Cartesian medicine has no single essential characteristic, for even the medicine Descartes advocated for changed throughout his life, at least in emphasis, and later physicians picked and chose what to take from Descartes, thereby shaping his and Cartesian medicine's legacy (see FRANCESCO TREVISANI, *Descartes in Deutschland: die Rezeption des Cartesianismus in den Hochschulen Nordwestdeutschlands*, Münster, Lit Verlag, 2011; DENNIS DES CHENE, "Life and health in Cartesian natural philosophy," in *Descartes' Natural Philosophy*, ed. S. Gaukroger, J. Schuster, and J. Sutton, London, Routledge, 2000, p. 723-735; JOHN SUTTON, "The body and the brain" in *Descartes' Natural Philosophy*, ed. S. Gaukroger, J. Schuster, and J. Sutton, London, Routledge, 2000, p. 697-722; JUSTIN E. H. SMITH, "Heat, Action, Perception: Models of Living Beings in German Medical Cartesianism," in *Cartesian Empiricisms*, ed. M. Dobre and T. Nyden, Cham, Springer, 2013, p. 105-123; GIDEON MANNING, "Health in the Early Modern Philosophical Tradition," in *Health: A History*, ed. P. Adamson, Oxford, Oxford University Press, 2019, p. 180-221). Together these assumptions imply that we must think broadly about who counts as a Cartesian physician, i.e. as belonging to the cadre of physicians who advocate some brand of Cartesian medicine. Even today, physicians' acceptance of brain death as equivalent to the death of a person represents an inherited strand of Cartesian medicine emphasizing the separation of consciousness from the body.
2 ANN BLAIR, "Natural Philosophy," in *Early Modern Science*, ed. by K. Park and L. Daston, Cambridge, Cambridge University Press, 2006, p. 265-405, 397.
3 ANNE HARRINGTON, *The Cure Within: A History of Mind-Body Medicine*, New York, Norton and Company, 2008, p. 21.

I wish to ask as I shift from the perspective of Cartesian medicine's advocates to its scholarly and medical reception are these: (1) How was Cartesian medicine defended (and attacked) in the past? (2) How is Cartesian medicine understood today? (3) What remains to be known about Cartesian medicine?

To answer (1), I will discuss Descartes's repeated defense of his physiological conclusions by appeal to his mechanics. Often this appeal looks to be mere handwaving on Descartes's part, but not always, as I will explain.

To answer (2), I will narrow my focus to an issue on which there is still scholarly disagreement, especially, but not exclusively, between historians of medicine on the one side and historians of philosophy on the other. As we will have learned from my answer to (1), already in the early modern period there was dispute over Descartes's empiricism, i.e., his attention to particulars, medical competence, and reliance on medical authority. Today, historians of medicine tend to view Descartes as a poor observer and "hopelessly doctrinaire," someone who failed to dissect to the high standards of the day or otherwise refused to allow the senses to guide and constrain his inferences and conclusions.[4] Historians of philosophy adopt a more positive view (on which see Anne Bitbol in this volume). For my part, I believe the truth lies somewhere in between. In part two of this chapter, I will suggest we are better served to consider the shifting conceptual frameworks impacting observational evidence itself than to pick winners and losers. Indeed, conceptual frameworks are important to consider if for no other reason than because no single piece of evidence was decisive for or against Cartesian medicine, and many questions about the supposed evidence (especially in the case of generation) could not be directly tested until after the invention of the microscope.[5]

Which brings me, finally, to (3) and the future of Cartesian medicine. In the final part of the chapter, I will offer an admittedly narrow assessment of two areas that remain mostly untouched by scholars (leaving aside questions that swirl around Descartes's own texts and the authors he likely relied upon). The first area that seems to me to hold great promise relates to the spread of Cartesian medicine and the need to understand its apparent success despite manifest instances of its failure. We can still expect to find new information in the achieves of universities and scientific societies, among student notes, from the spread of manuscripts, and from lecturer's notes. I will cite the example of Louis de la Forge as my brief case study. The second area I hope to learn more about in the future relates to Descartes himself and the already much-discussed issues of his metaphysics and epistemology, even ethics, which I believe stand to benefit from more attention to the history of medicine and medicine's role in the intellectual and institutional economy of the early modern period.

---

4   DOMENICO BERTOLONI MELI, *Mechanism: A Visual, Lexical, and Conceptual History*, Pittsburgh, University of Pittsburgh Press, 2019, p. 182.
5   This approach is inspired by something I once read in the work of Ian Maclean, though I could not find the specific reference that set my thinking in this direction and so I bear all the blame if the attribution misrepresents Maclean's suggested approach.

2. Cartesian Medicine's Past

Descartes spent more than twenty years developing his views in medical theory and practice, i.e., anatomy and physiology on the one hand and preserving and restoring health on the other. This fact lies in plain sight for those willing to look.[6] In January 1630, for example, Descartes writes to Mersenne:

> I am distressed over your erysipelas, and over the illness of M.; I beg you to preserve yourself [*de vous conserver*], at least until I can determine whether there is a way to find a Medicine founded on infallible demonstrations, which is what I now seek.[7]

And, again, on 15 April of that year:

---

[6] The following passages cited as evidence for Descartes's medical interests have been noted by other scholars, but they are presented together, and in the order given here, in HOWARD STEIN, "On philosophy and Natural Philosophy in the Seventeenth Century," *Midwest Studies in Natural Philosophy* 18 (1993), p. 177-201. I follow Stein's model in part to acknowledge one of my former teachers and the impression his presentation originally made on me. I have also elected to follow Stein's translations with slight modification of the relevant passages where CSM/CSMK are not cited.

[7] Descartes to Mersenne, January 1630, AT I 105. Descartes's question of whether it is possible to find "infallible demonstrations" is noteworthy. What Descartes likely had in mind — if we offer a generous interpretation — are not purely deductive or geometrical demonstrations but something suggested in a later letter to Mersenne. He tells us a "demonstration" in the study of nature must satisfy two conditions: (1) it cannot contradict experience and (2) it must be logically consistent with other closely held principles or beliefs about the natural world. Descartes even says the assumptions attached to (2) need not be "strictly true." In his words: "You ask if I regard what I have written about refraction as a demonstration. I think it is, in so far as one can be given in this field without a previous demonstration of the principles of physics by metaphysics — which is something I hope to do some day but which has not yet been done — and so far as it has ever been possible to demonstrate the solution to any problem of mechanics, or optics, or astronomy, or anything else which is not pure geometry or arithmetic. But to require me to give geometrical demonstrations on a topic that depends on physics is to ask me to do the impossible. And if you will not call anything demonstrations except geometers' proofs, then you must say that Archimedes never demonstrated anything in mechanics, or Vitellio in optics, or Ptolemy in astronomy. But of course nobody says this. In such matters people are satisfied if the authors' assumptions are not obviously contrary to experience and if their discussion is coherent and free from logical error, even though their assumptions may not be strictly true" (Descartes to Mersenne, 27 May 1638, AT II 141-142; CSMK 103). See, for an example of a "demonstrative proof" in Descartes' medicine, the case of the circulation: "There remains the experiment in which most of the veins which go to a limb are tied, while the arteries remain free. When this experiment is performed, you say that the limb does not swell up, but rather, wastes away gradually through lack of nourishment. Surely two situations have to be distinguished here. On the one hand, as soon as the veins have been ligated as described, they will certainly swell a little, and if you open one of them above the ligature, all or practically all of the blood in the body may flow out, as is witnessed by surgeons every day. If I am not mistaken, this provides, I shall not say highly probable evidence, but rather, demonstrative proof of the circulation of the blood" (Descartes to Plempius, 15 February 1638, AT I 533; CSMK 84). Here it bears remembering that the Greek "apodeixis" (demonstration), can mean simply the "showing or making public of something" (ANDREW WEAR, "Harvey and the 'Way of the Anatomists,'" *History of Science* 23 (1983), p. 223-249, 244). Perhaps Descartes is seeking "infallible demonstration" and "demonstrative proof" more in the sense of things confirmed than in the mathematical sense of proof?

> I am now studying in chemistry and anatomy together, learning something every day that I do not find in the books. I wish I had already come to the point of research into diseases and their remedies, so that I could find one for your erysipelas, with which I am sorry you have suffered from for so long.[8]

In the concluding paragraph of the *Discours* from 1637, Descartes says:

> I have resolved to devote the rest of my life to nothing other than trying to acquire some knowledge of nature from which we may derive rules in medicine which are more reliable than those we have had up to now.[9]

And writing to the Marquess of Newcastle in October 1645 he says, "The preservation of health has always been the principal end of my studies."[10]

Similar attestations are to be found elsewhere in Descartes's correspondence and published work, but the medical topics that were of greatest interest to Descartes were longevity and the motion of the heart and blood. About longevity, on 4 December 1637 Descartes writes to Constantijn Huygens, father of the famed mathematician and physicist:

> I have never taken so much care to preserve myself as now, and whereas I used to think that death could snatch from me no more than thirty or forty years at the most, it would not henceforth surprise me if the deprivation could amount to more than a century: for I seem to see very clearly, that if we just be aware of certain mistakes that we habitually make in the conduct of our lives, we should be able without any other discovery [*invention*] to arrive at a far longer and happier old age... but because I have need of much time and many experiments to investigate everything of use for this subject, I am now working to compose a compendium of Medicine, drawn partly from the books and partly from my reasonings, that I hope to be able to use provisionally to obtain some reprieve from nature, the better afterwards to continue with my plan.[11]

There is much to comment on in this passage — about Descartes's personal character and his potential reading list — but sticking with the theme of longevity there is evidence that Descartes harbored even greater ambitions than those articulated to Huygens. According to an account first attributed to "the chevalier [i.e, Sir Kenelm] Digby," Descartes accepted that "although to render man immortal is what he would not dare to hope for [*se promettre*], he was quite certain of being able to extend his life equal to that of the Patriarchs."[12] Similarly, Descartes seventeenth-century biographer, Adrien Baillet, tells us that when the news of Descartes's death arrived in Paris, the Abbé Picot at first would not believe it and later attributed Descartes's death to the disorder in his body caused by the Northern weather, for "in the absence of such an

---

8 Descartes to Mersenne, 15 April 1630, AT I 137.
9 *Discours de la Méthode*, AT VI 42; CSM I 151.
10 Descartes to Marquess of Newcastle, October 1645, AT IV 329; CSMK 275.
11 Descartes to Huygens, 4 December 1637, AT I 649. On this letter, see Baldassarri in this volume.
12 Quoted at AT II 670-671.

alien and violent cause, [...] he would have lived five hundred years, after having discovered the art of living several centuries."[13] Descartes's medical philosophy must be judged harshly if longevity was intended to be a measure of Cartesian medicine's success (Descartes died a month short of his 54th birthday). Or, as Queen Cristina put it upon learning of his death, "his oracles have quite deceived him."[14]

Perhaps recognizing that Cartesian medicine's failure could be easily seen in the realm of practice (and licensed physicians certainly would not have been happy with the interventions of an unlicensed interloper), Descartes was cautious about the medical advice he offered to his correspondents. He was less guarded about claims in theoretical medicine. Aside from publishing on medical matters in the *Discours, Meditationes* and *Passions*, he forcefully defended his conclusions in his correspondence and vicariously through others, including Henricus Regius in the disputations the latter oversaw at Utrecht in the early 1640s. The motion of the heart and the blood were literally at the heart of Descartes's theoretical medicine, something he says in the late *Description du corps humain* when defending his position on the motion of the heart: "it is so important to know the true cause of the heart's movement that without such knowledge it is impossible to know anything which pertains to the theory of medicine."[15]

Standing against the acceptance of Descartes's cardio-centrism, at least in his own mind and in the mind of his early followers, was ignorance of two kinds of knowledge, namely, anatomy and mechanics. You need both because together they will tell you how matter is arranged, or at least some of the complex possibilities of arrangement, and then what matter so arranged can and cannot do (and according to Descartes the only thing matter cannot do, no matter how it is arranged, is produce meaningful responsive language). In his words, "the ignorance of anatomy and mechanics has contributed to this [misunderstanding of what the body can do and how it does it], for in considering only the exterior of the human body, we never imagined that it had enough organs or springs in it to move itself in all the different ways in which we see it move. And we have been confirmed in this error in judging that dead bodies have the same organs as living ones, for they lack nothing but the soul and yet there is no movement in them."[16]

This appeal to anatomy and mechanics formed part of a general defense of Cartesian medicine for Descartes and his followers, but in some instances it appears more like an impatient attempt to dismiss well founded objections. Here is one such case from 1641: "Sylvius's objections do not seem to me to be of any great importance, and they testify to nothing other than that he has an insufficient understanding of Mechanics; however, I want you to respond more gently to him."[17] Franciscus Sylvius

---

13   ADRIEN BAILLET, *La Vie de Monsieur Descartes*, Paris, Horthemels, 1691, vol. 2, p. 451-453; cited in Stein 1993, 181.
14   CHARLES ADAM, *Vie et Oeuvres de Descartes*, Paris, 1957, vol. 12, p. 552, note a; cited in Stein 1993, 181.
15   *Description du corps humain* AT XI 245; CSM I 319.
16   *Description du corps humain* AT XI 224; G 170.
17   Descartes to Regius, October 1641, AT III 440; Bos, 83; cited in EVAN RAGLAND, "Mechanism, the Senses, and Reason: Franciscus Sylvius and Leiden Debates Over Anatomical Knowledge After Descartes" in *Early Modern Medicine and Natural Philosophy*, ed. P. Distelzweig, B. Goldberg, and

(1614-1672), who had been preforming anatomical experiments at the time and was already making a name for himself as a teacher and advocate for Harvey's view of the circulation, as well as Harvey's view of the timing of cardiac motion and the pulse, was no mere amateur. In later years he would become one of Europe's premier chemical physicians, experimentalists, and university educators. In a work published 11 years after Descartes's death, Sylvius would take the opportunity to continue fighting some of the old battles from the 1640s. Specifically, Sylvius shares his judgment that "Descartes trusting more in the laws of his own Mechanics, rather than in his external Senses, suspected and judged that the Ventricles of the Heart and the Arteries were Dilated and Contracted simultaneously."[18]

Of course, Descartes was not the only one to have seen things differently from Sylvius and Harvey. Just about every physician since the second century CE sides with Descartes, so the criticism is a bit unfair.[19] Sylvius may have just as easily chided Descartes for accepting the testimony of all the other witnesses to the phenomenon. But the point I wish to make now is a different one. Just as Descartes could sometimes use mechanics as a blunt weapon to defend Cartesian medicine, his critics could cite his mechanics to indicate that he had not done enough to ascertain the truth in physiological matters. This objection is arguably the origin of the legend of Descartes that prevailed in late seventeenth-century England, as a speculative philosopher and the anthesis of a sober empiricist and careful experimentalist.

One place where we might be tempted to repeat Sylvius's objection, though I believe it would be a mistake as I explain below, is in response to Descartes's correspondence with the Dutch physician Vopiscus Fortunatus Plempius (1601-1671). In 1638, Plempius had not yet come to accept the demonstration of the circulation of the blood. At one point in the exchange between Descartes and Plempius, the latter appeals to an experiment (*experimentum*) he finds in Galen to object to Descartes's explanation for the pulse. Descartes believed the pulse to be caused by the explosive outward flow of blood from the heart's ventricle into the arteries, which were themselves already filled with blood. Aware of this, Plempius writes:

> Our Galen has taught to the contrary that the heart's motion is caused by some faculty [*facultate aliqua*] and until now this has been the teaching of all physicians [*Medici*]. My modest arguments for standing with them up till now are the following: […] [Second] If one inserts a quill or bronze tube into a cut artery, so that the blood can flow, and then binds the artery with a ligature over the tube [*super fistulam*], the artery distal to the ligature will not pulse. Therefore, the pulse

---

E. R. Ragland, Cham, Springer, p. 173-205; 177.
18 FRANCISCUS DELE BOË SYLVIUS, *Disp. med. de febribus prima*, 1661, prop. 20; reproduced in FRANCISCUS DELE BOË SYLVIUS, *Opera Medica*, Amsterdam, Daniel Elsevier and Abraham Wolfgang, 1679, p. 30-31; cited in RAGLAND, "Mechanism and the Senses," p. 193.
19 For more on the "pulse controversy," see the classic paper JEROME BYLEBYL, "Disputation and Description in the Renaissance Pulse Controversy," in *The Medical Renaissance of the Sixteenth Century*, ed. A. Wear, R. K. French and I. M. Lonie, New York, Cambridge University Press, 1985, p. 223-245.

is not caused by the force of the blood flowing into the artery but by something else which passes along the walls of the artery. This experiment [*experimentum*] is recorded by Galen.[20]

The experiment to which Plempius refers does not originate with Galen but with Erasistratus (304-250). At issue is whether we assign the cause of the felt pulse to the activity of the tunic of the artery or the material within the lumen. It is irrelevant whether the *tunica externa, media* or *intima* is the cause of the activity. Similarly irrelevant is the allied belief that the activity of the tunic might itself derive from the activity of the heart, which passes along its activity to the tunic of the artery, as if the two, heart and artery, formed a single organ. Also irrelevant is the material in the lumen, whether air or blood, which was an issue in dispute during Greek antiquity. The experiment is meant to decide between two causal explanations; it is *experimentum crucis*. Specifically, the ligated artery with a "quill or bronze tube" inside allows Galen to observe what happens when blood flows inside the artery but the activity of the tunic is impeded by a ligature. In that case, as Plempius notes, the "artery distal to the ligature will not pulse." Ergo, the flow of the blood, which continues throughout the experiment, is not the cause of the pulse. By Plempius's lights, Descartes (and Harvey) is in error about the cause of the pulse.

Descartes's response to Plempius is long. It begins with a trope we have already seen, viz. an appeal to his mechanics: "For, given the cause of the pulsation of the arteries that I have put forward [in the *Discourse*], the laws of my mechanics, i.e. my physics, imply that if we insert a quill into an artery and tie the artery above it with a ligature, the artery ought not to beat above the ligature."[21] But more than just a meaningless gesture to his mechanics, Descartes further explains:

> If a quill is inserted into the artery [...] and a ligature is tied above it, as Galen intends, the blood will be able to pass through the quill [...] but it will not strike the sides of the artery [...], at least not with any noticeable force; for when the blood passes from a narrow vessel to a more capacious one, it will lose most of its force, and what force remains will be expended more in the direction of the flow than in the direction of the walls of the artery. Hence the blood will be able to fill the artery in a continuous flow and make it bulge, but it will not make it move with distinct pulsations.[22]

The appeal to mechanics in this example is substantial and connects with claims Descartes makes outside of the correspondence. To begin with, Descartes is describing the relationship between the speed of a continuous fluid to its lateral pressure as it moves from a wider to a narrower and then to a wider container. He maintains that as the speed of the blood's motion increases as it moves through the narrower reed it exerts more pressure on the walls of the reed. But this pressure

---

20 Plempius to Descartes, January 1638, AT I 497; I have consulted the translation in GERRIT A. LINDE-BOOM, *Descartes and Medicine*, Amsterdam, Rodopi, 1978, p. 108-110.
21 Descartes to Plempius, 15 February 1638, AT I 524; CSMK 81.
22 Descartes to Plempius, 15 February 1638, AT I 524-525; CSMK 81. [Translation slightly modified.]

does not impact the arterial wall because of the presence of the reed. Moving from the narrow reed back to the larger vessel of the artery, the blood's speed is reduced and so too the lateral pressure according to Descartes. Thus, no pulse will be felt distal to the reed even as the artery fills with blood; there is simply not enough lateral pressure to cause a detectible pulse. Put another way, Descartes' position, relying on the "laws of his mechanics, i.e., physics," is that Galen's stated experimental results, as recounted by Plempius, are correct *and* to be expected given Descartes's mechanics.

As it happens, Galen and Descartes are both wrong about the experimental results; a faint pulse can be detected when this experiment is performed. But the fact remains that Descartes's mechanics is deployed to real effect in this case. Indeed, the mechanical principles involved relating speed of particle flow to lateral pressure and crowding also appear in Descartes's moon and tide theory in *Le Monde*, written in the early 1630s, and then re-presented with slight modification in the *Principia* in 1644.[23] As Descartes elaborates the results of particle flow between the moon and the earth:

> it is evident that the same force that presses the earth... must also make them [the tides] sink toward T, not only from the side 6,2, but also from its opposite 8,4, and in recompense cause them to rise in the places 5,1 and 7,3. Thus, the surface EFGH of the earth remaining round (because it is hard), that of the water 1 2 3 4 and that of the air 5 6 7 8 (which are liquids) must form an oval.[24]

Figure 1 from the *Principia* allows us to more easily visualize what Descartes has in mind, matching the text of *Le Monde* the illustration also has the advantage of showing the compression of the air and water that represents the tides. As the matter of the heavens flows from A to B to C then D, it passes between the Moon at B and the Earth's air and water at 6 and 2. This is a narrower space than on either side, both from where the matter comes and the space into which it subsequently flows. Thus, just like the case Descartes describes in his reply to Plempius, we are witnessing the relationship between particle flow and lateral pressure being used to explain a stipulated phenomenon.

The tides, of course, are a natural phenomenon, not an artificial one produced by a thought experiment, as in the exchange with Plempius, but the fundamental issues are the same. As the matter of the heavens moves from a wider space into the narrower space between the Moon and Earth, it increases its speed and exerts increased lateral pressure. This pressure pushes against the Moon and Earth. The Earth in particular moves ever so slightly toward D, that is, T moves toward D because of the pressure exerted at 6 and 2. But the air and water and not rigid like the Moon and Earth, and so they experience compression at 6 and 2. The same compression occurs at 8 and 4 because the Earth is moving toward D. The compression at 6, 2, 8, and 4 is equalized by the rise of the air and water at 7, 3, 5, and 1. Low tide occurs at the former spots and high tide at the latter. The rotation of the Earth and that of the Moon around

---

23 I thank John Schuster for pointing out this connection to me in a private communication.
24 *Le Monde*, AT XI 81; G 52.

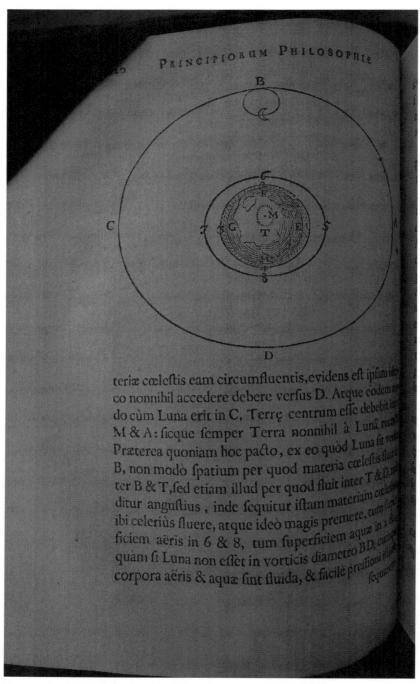

Figure 1. René Descartes, *Principia philosophiae*, Amsterdam, Elsevier, 1644, p. 220. RB 336030, the Huntington Library, San Marino, California.

the Earth from B to C, etc. are the additional factors accounting for the daily and seasonal variation of the tides.

What should we make of Descartes's appeals to his mechanics when defending his physiological views or his theory of the tides? Unity of explanation seems to be a value in favor of Descartes's position — he can explain the tides and he can explain the lack of a distal pulse when a reed is inserted into the arteries using the same principles — so we should consider his mechanism vindicated. At least this seems to be a plausible defense of Descartes's position. Returning to Sylvius then, should we accept that Descartes was simply wrong about his mechanics but not wrong, as Sylvius accused him of being, because he used mechanics in order to avoid the hard work of seeking the truth through the use of the senses? That is what I would urge us to consider. We can perhaps best answer this question, however, by turning to the present, and part two of the chapter.

3. Cartesian Medicine's Present

The dispute between Descartes and Sylvius, and the subsequent judgment of figures such as Nicolas Steno (1638-1686) and Marcello Malpighi (1628-1694) pointing out Descartes's many errors, has led historians of medicine in particular to take a negative view of Descartes's anatomical skill and the care he exercised in formulating his physiological claims. To these scholars, the historical Descartes is hard to distinguish from the speculative philosopher that members of the Royal Society in the seventeenth century found Descartes to be. Domenico Bertoloni Meli, for example, acknowledges that "Descartes played a key role in setting the agenda for a mechanistic anatomy putting forward a plethora of hypothetical structures and modes of operations." Yet Bertoloni Meli immediately qualifies his remark with: "Descartes was seen by his anatomically savvy contemporaries and immediate successors as hopelessly doctrinaire, especially with regard to his defective understanding of the heartbeat and arterial pulse, and with vivisection more broadly."[25]

I see things somewhat differently and would suggest it is misleading and slightly anachronistic to cast Descartes out of the circle of capable anatomists because of his "defective" views or because the winners of the anatomy debates disagreed with Descartes. The philosophers Marjorie Grene and David Depew's have defended Descartes: "[it] is scarcely fair to Descartes, who did after all adjure his reader to look, and even feel, what his senses told him to be the case. Moreover, he himself performed experiments."[26] But this too is not entirely satisfying because it does not acknowledge Descartes resistance to the apparent observations of his contemporaries. The disagreement between historians of medicine and historians of philosophy represented by Bertoloni Meli and Grene and

---

25 BERTOLONI MELI, *Mechanism*, p. 67. Evan Ragland's recent scholarship supporting Bertoloni Meli's conclusions appeared too late to be considered as background to some of the issues discussed in this section. I remain open to the possibility that my position may change after considering Ragland's more expansive defense and presentation of his conclusions.
26 MARJORIE GRENE and DAVID DEPEW, *The Philosophy of Biology: An Episodic History*, New York, Cambridge University Press, 2004, p. 57.

Depew may be resolved if we recall that Descartes's anatomically-able contemporaries did not always hold the same views after they performed careful experiments and live dissections. Two examples will suffice to make the point, the first of which relates to the motion of the heart and the second to the circulation of the blood and the heart's anatomy.

The dispute between Descartes and Harvey over the cause of the motion of the heart is in many ways straightforward. Roughly, the dispute relates to a choice between the heart squeezing out blood in systole (Harvey's view) or exploding out blood in diastole (Descartes's view). The difference here can just as easily be described in terms of the relaxed state of an excised heart: did such a heart have the appearance of the heart in systole or the heart in diastole? Harvey would say diastole because it was not contracted. Descartes would say systole because it was not expanded.[27] Part of what offended Harvey's partisans like Sylvius was that Descartes's view was inconsistent with what they saw as the timing of the heart's movement compared to the pulse in the artery. Harvey and Descartes agreed the pulse was caused by the lateral force of blood as it moved through the arteries. Harvey saw that systole came first and then the pulse followed while Descartes reported seeing that diastole of the heart and the pulse cooccurred, rejecting or never quite seeing what Harvey and others like Sylvius saw.

But this is not so deep a fault line as one might expect between the two camps. Views about the cause of the motion of the heart could vary. Consider George Ent, one of Harvey's most dogged defenders, responsible for the spread of his ideas to the Netherlands, and the person responsible for getting Harvey to publish his views on generation in the 1650s. One would expect Ent to share Harvey's view of the movement of the heart. He does not, at least not in 1641: "In what [...] follows, I shall offer no support to Harvey [regarding the motion of the heart], since I do not agree with him in this matter [...] [O]ne may not ascribe this movement [of the heart] to the cardiac parenchyma, but rather to the blood that is heated in the left ventricle, through whose swelling the ventricle gives way and diastole results."[28] Ent's view aligns with that of a Cartesian physician because the heart expands by virtue of an expansion of the blood.

My second example comes from the work of another early proponent of Harvey's view of the circulation, the Danish physician Thomasius Bartholinus (1616-1680). Bartholinus earned fame in his own right for his anatomical textbooks, combined interest in religion and medicine, and for his study of the lymphatic system. A prolific teacher and letter writer, Bartholinus belonged to the generation of mid-century physicians who made Harvey's demonstration of the circulation of the blood an international success story. Even so, there is at least one apparent incongruity in Bartholinus's support of the circulation

---

27 This may seem an easy observation to make but it will, in fact, depend on the orientation of the excised heart on the anatomist's table. For example, if the heart is placed on a table as it would be oriented in the body of a living person lying on their back, we would see the heart elongated in diastole. But, if placed on its base, the apex will collapse during diastole, and we would see the heart elongate in systole. Thus even this basic difference between Descartes and Harvey is not resolved by an uncomplicated observation of the excised heart.

28 GEORGE ENT, *Apologia pro circulation sanguinis*, London, Robert Young, 1641, p. 117; cited and trans. in THOMAS FUCHS, *The Mechanization of the Heart: Harvey and Descartes*, trans. by M. Grene, Rochester, University of Rochester Press, 1992, p. 159.

of the blood and Harvey's account of cardiac motion. Recall that one of the questions Harvey confronted was simply: how does the blood arrive in the arteries from the veins? There are several key assumptions in the background to this question. One is about the natural place of the blood being in the veins. Another, widely held prior to Harvey, was the belief that anastomosis took place primarily in the heart itself. Specifically, the right ventricle was filled with venous or nutritional blood from the veins and this blood seeped into the left ventricle through holes or pores in the cardiac septum. This small quantity of blood then mixed with the air drawn from the lungs into the pulmonary vein and then into the left ventricle, together producing vital spirit and arterial blood. By virtue of rejecting the existence of pores in the cardiac septum, Harvey joined with a minority of his contemporaries, but he went further by demonstrating that anastomosis takes place elsewhere in the body, and especially at the periphery of the body.

Despite supporting Harvey's conclusions, Bartholinus nevertheless continued to agree with aspects of the earlier tradition. In preparing readers for the discussion of the heart and movement of the blood in his anatomy textbook, Bartholinus wrote:

> The *left Ventricle* [...] Its *Use* is to make vital Spirit and Arterial blood, of a twofold matter, I. Of blood prepared in the right ventricle, and passed through the Septum and the Lungs. II. Of Air drawn in by the Mouth and Nostrils, prepared in the Lungs, and transmitted through the *Arteria venosa* with the blood into the left ventricle of the Heart, to kindle and ventilate the vital flame.[29]

This is all very traditional and not what one might expect from a proponent of Harvey's views. The incongruity is even more striking when the topic of anastomosis is addressed and especially so with respect to his first-person experience of the pores in the cardiac septum. In his words, that the hollows of the cardiac septum are:

> open is the opinion of the Ancients and of many Anatomists which follow them [...] I also of late found the partion of a Sows Heart, in many places obliquely perforated with manifest great Pores, which were open of themselves without the use of a Probe, so as to admit a large Pease [...] Yet are they not alwaies open in dead bodies, because in living bodies they are kept open, by the continual agitation of the Heart.[30]

To sum up, the fault lines between the Harverians and the Cartesians are not so deep, at least on this point, and the issue of reliance on the external senses for information about the natural world is not always dispositive of who is and is not an experimentalist or a capable anatomist.

We may nevertheless try to salvage some criticisms of Descartes. Perhaps the real issue here is not that Descartes was wrong since others could be wrong without being excluded from the experimentalist club. Rather, Descartes was wrong for the wrong reason. Perhaps he did not even bother to look, as opposed to looking and

---

29 THOMAS BARTHOLIN CASPER BARTHOLIN, JOHANNES WALAEUS, *Bartholinus Anatomy... In Four Books*, London, Peter Cole, 1663, p. 110.
30 *Ibid.*, p. 110-111.

being mistaken? But Descartes did bother to look. Perhaps then it is that Descartes was not just wrong here and there, or wrong for the wrong reason, but that he was wrong about so much? And he surely was wrong about many things in physiology and elsewhere in his natural philosophy. But if Descartes was wrong about more of the details than Sylvius, Ent, Bartholin, or Harvey, it was not just for being less skilled at observation. It was because Descartes also adopted views long held among physicians that Harvey and most of his followers would reject. As I have argued elsewhere, this raises challenging questions for the historian about how to characterize the relative novelty and commitment to tradition in Descartes and his contemporaries. It certainly does not follow from the details noted here that Descartes should be characterized as someone promoting a mechanical program without regard for anatomical details. Such judgments coincide with the judgment of those seventeenth-century anatomists we now look upon as harbingers of truth, but changes took place quickly in seventeenth-century anatomy and respecting this fact, and the fact that Descartes performed anatomical experiments sensitive to their causal implications, cautions against praising or faulting Descartes without great care.

4. Cartesian Medicine's Future

So much for the present. What does the future hold? My first suggestion is that we look at archives. The simple fact is that when a complicated project like Descartes's appears on the scene choices of what to accept and what to reject have to be made, and for the master's views to spread there must be disciples. Not just leaders but also foot soldiers are needed to spread ideas. In Descartes's reception history, competing interpretations were offered about topics big and small: the nature of body, mind, force, causation, the very meaning of "idea," the relevance of experimentation, and so on. Louis de La Forge's extensive commentary on the French edition of *L'Homme* in 1664 made several choices in this regard, and these choices were further cemented in La Forge's *Traitté de l'esprit de l'homme* (1666), to which he referred many times in the commentary to *L'Homme*. It had been thought that La Forge's *Traitté* was only translated into English in the twentieth century by Desmond Clarke, so that its influence was felt almost entirely among French readers and some who read a later Latin edition in the seventeenth century.[31] As I discovered at the Royal Society, however, La Forge's work was translated into English in the 1670s.

The full-length manuscript, running 272 pages not including the front matter, is by any measure a clean copy. It belongs to the library of the English experimentalist Robert Hooke (1635-1703). There is more to discover about the manuscript, and I hope to publish a closer study of the manuscript in due course. But I can report the translation was completed by a merchant named Samuel Griffith, who signed the text with the date "1673/4" and indicated his location on the island of Formosa (modern day Taiwan). The manuscript translation joins Cordemoy's *Two Treatises* from 1668

---

31 LOUIS DE LA FORGE, *Treatise on the Human Mind*, trans. by D. M. Clarke, Dordrecht, Kluwer, 1998.

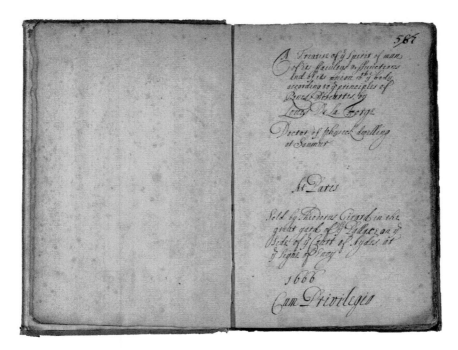

Figure 2. "Frontispiece" of a manuscript English language translation of Louis de la Forge, *Traité de l'esprit de l'homme*, MS/76, The Royal Society, London.

and 1670 and François Bayle's *The General Systeme of the Cartesian philosophy* (1670) as the earliest instances of first-generation Cartesians making their way into English; Bayle and La Forge were both physicians. There are many questions one might ask. Was this translation specifically commissioned by Hooke and if so for what purpose? Are there any additional materials related to La Forge at the Royal Society? What else can we learn about Griffith's identity and background? The La Forge translation is only one recent piece of evidence to suggest that blank spots in the canvas that is the reception history of Cartesian medicine may still be filled. There remains ample opportunity to learn more from the achieves across Europe. At least it is worth a look, you never know what you will find.

My second suggestion regarding the future of Cartesian medicine is that we consider the ways in which medicine inspired or at least contributed to Descartes's better-known claims in metaphysics and epistemology, or perhaps even his use of diagrams in his natural philosophy. There are too many questions to list here, so let me just declare that I believe there are very few parts of Descartes's project that medicine cannot help us better understand or appreciate in a new light. Take the example of longevity that I discussed in passing earlier. Descartes's interest in longevity is just one instance of a culturally resurgent movement to extend life and achieve old age coming from the sixteenth century. As I mentioned, Descartes hoped to be able to extend his life into the hundreds of years. He died in 1650, but 373 years later we are still talking about him. That's the only kind of longevity any of us can really aspire to, and in Descartes's case it was Cartesian medicine that helped to make his longevity possible.

SIMONE GUIDI

Epigenesis and Generative Power in Descartes' Late Scholastic Sources

▼ ABSTRACT What does Descartes' embryology look like, when related to the scholastic theories of his time? In order to reply to this question, the present chapter aims at sketching a portrait of the embryological epigenetics Descartes could find in his recognized scholastic sources (the Commentaries on Aristotle by Toledo, the Coimbra Jesuits, Suárez, and Rubio, as well as the *Summae* by Eustachius a Sancto Paulo and Abra de Raconis), a tradition that received and incorporated in the Aristotelian-Galenic body many novelties from Renaissance medicine, especially Fernel, Paré, and Vallès. It being impossible to deal extensively with the whole of the contents of these works, I selected three issues in particular, corresponding to the first three sections of this paper: 1) the nature of the semen, and the action of the *vis formativa*, as well as its relationship with vital heat and temperaments; 2) the problem of the real and/or rational distinction(s) between the generative, the nutritive, and the augmentative powers; 3) the epigenetic order of generation of vital organs, i.e. the right sequence over which the fundamental organs of a living body are generated and then ensouled. In the last section I integrate these reconstructions with some conclusions about Descartes' own theory.

▼ KEYWORDS Embriology, Late Scholasticism, Renaissance Medicine, Generative Power, Vital Organs

Simone Guidi • National Research Council of Italy - Institute for the European Intellectual Lexicon and History of Ideas. Contact: <simone.guidi@cnr.it>

1. Introduction

One remarkable issue in Descartes' mechanical biology is how to explain the process of generation, and how provide an account for epigenetic embryology[1] without resorting to teleological explanations.[2] Denying any vegetative and sensitive function of the soul, and limiting causation to the interaction between efficient causes, Descartes cannot indeed attribute to any specific soul faculty or final cause the role of actively shaping the body in its first stages.

Famously, Descartes dealt with the problem of generation in a significant network of texts, scattered among his scientific manuscripts: the *Primae Cogitationes circa generationem animalium*, the *Description du corps human*, and the *Excerpta Anatomica*.[3] Here he reassessed, within his mechanist framework, pivotal concepts from Galen's, Fabrici's, and Jean Fernel's embryology — for instance, the role played by innate heat and spirits in shaping the embryo.[4] Yet as Vincent Aucante stressed,[5] Descartes never reached complete and congruent conclusions on such questions, wavering, over at least three phases of his output on this matter (starting respectively in 1632, 1637, and 1648), between different accounts.

Descartes' indecision on such an important matter is significant. Jacques Roger[6] insightfully underlined that "the entire success of Cartesian 'Physics' depended

---

1 I opt for the term 'epigenesis' meaning the process in which a fetus forms gradually, by successive differentiation of its parts and their functions, starting from an amorphous initial form. See LINDA VAN SPEYBORECK, DANI DE WAELE and GERTRUDIS VAN DE VIJVER, "Theories in Early Embryology. Close Connections between Epigenesis, Preformationism, and Self-Organization", *Annals of the New York Academy of Sciences* 981 (2002), p. 7-49 and ANDREW J. PYLE, "Animal Generation and the Mechanical Philosophy. Some Light on the Role of Biology in the Scientific Revolution", *History and Philosophy of the Life Sciences* 9, (1987): p. 225-254.
2 On Descartes' mechanist account of generation see especially JACQUES ROGER, *Les sciences de la vie dans la pensée française du XVIIIe siècle: La génération des animaux de Descartes à l'Encyclopédie*, Paris, Arman Colin, 1963, translation in ID. *The Life Sciences in Eighteenth-Century French Thought*, trans. by Robert Ellrich, Stanford, Stanford University Press, 1998, p. 113-122; VINCENT AUCANTE, *La philosophie médicale de Descartes*, Paris, Vrin, 2006, p. 297-329; ROBERTO LO PRESTI, "Wissenschaftliche Revolution und Embryologie: Ablehnung oder Transformation der Antike? Ein Vergleich zwischen den Zeugungslehren Cesare Cremoninis, William Harveys und René Descartes", *Sudhoffs Archiv* 98 (2014, 1), p. 1-27; FABRIZIO BALDASSARRI, *Il metodo al tavolo anatomico. Descartes e la medicina*, Rome, Aracne, 2021, p. 183-208. See also FABRIZIO BALDASSARRI, "I moti circolari nella meccanica della vita in Descartes: embriologia e nutrizione nella medicina e nella botanica", *Physis*, 53 (2018), p. 77-93; FABRIZIO BALDASSARRI, "The mechanical life of plants: Descartes on botany", *The British Journal for the History of Science*, 52 (2019), p. 41-63. On Descartes' account of the vegetative soul see IGOR AGOSTINI, "Vegetative and Sensitive Functions of the Soul in Descartes's *Meditations*", in *Vegetative Powers The Roots of Life in Ancient, Medieval and Early Modern Natural Philosophy*, ed. by Fabrizio Baldassarri and Andreas Blank, Cham, Springer, 2021, p. 241-254, and FABRIZIO BALDASSARRI, "Descartes' bio-medical study of plants: Vegetative activities, soul, and power", *Early Science and Medicine*, 23 (2018), p. 509-529.
3 *Description du corps humain*, AT XI 252-286 BOp 552-596 CSM 321-323. *Primae Cogitationes*, AT XI 505-538; BOp 937-982. *Anatomica*, AT XI 574-579, BOp 1136-1143; AT XI 583-587, BOp 1148-1152; AT XI 595, BOp 1160-1162; AT XI 596-600, BOp 1164-1168; AT XI 608, BOp 1178; AT X 614-ff, BOp 1186-ff.
4 For instance, see *Primae Cogitationes* AT XI 507-510; BOp 939-945.
5 AUCANTE, *La philosophie médicale de Descartes*, p. 297-329.
6 ROGER, *The Life Sciences*, p. 122-123 and PYLE, "Animal Generation and the Mechanical Philosophy", p. 231.

entirely on the solution it was able to offer to the problems of generation", so that reproduction was a matter which could put a serious strain on his whole mechanistic theory. How can mechanism be a reliable model for life if it is not even able to explain the origins of living organisms? And how a purely mechanical process produces and arranges non-living parts in order for them to be constituents *of* a complete living being, performing a specific function *for* the whole organism?[7]

In this paper, I do not address such questions directly. I rather endeavour to work on the boundaries of the issue, following up with a few concluding remarks. My aim is particularly to investigate what Descartes' embryology looks like when compared with the scholastic theories of his time, and identifying more precisely which elements are peculiar of his mechanist account of generation, and which are not. This in addition to determining which components of his theory appear innovative or unorthodox when compared with the orthodoxy of his time, a tradition that had received and incorporated in an Aristotelian-Galenic body many novelties from Renaissance medicine, especially from Jean Fernel, Ambroise Paré, and Francisco Vallès[8].

In light of these premises, the aim of the present chapter is to sketch a portrait of the embryological epigenetics Descartes could find in the scholastic debates of his time. I dwell especially on Descartes' recognized sources[9], such as the Commentaries on Aristotle by Francisco Toledo, Manuel de Góis (the main writer of the famous *Cursus Conimbricensis*)[10], Francisco Suárez, and Antonio Rubio, as well as the *Summae* by Eustachius a Sancto Paulo and Charles-François Abra de Raconis.

---

7   Dissatisfaction and incredulity at Descartes' weak account is the reason why several early Cartesians (Regius, La Forge, Régis, and Schuyl) distanced themselves from Descartes on this point. See PYLE, "Animal Generation and the Mechanical Philosophy", p. 233-254; DENNIS DES CHENE, "Life after Descartes: Régis on Generation", *Perspectives on Science* 11 (2003, 4), p. 410-420, and FABRIZIO BALDASSARRI, "Failures of Mechanization: Vegetative Powers and the Early Cartesians, Regius, La Forge, and Schuyl", in *Vegetative Powers. The Roots of Life in Ancient, Medieval and Early Modern Natural Philosophy*, p. 255-275.
8   See especially CHRISTOPH SANDERS, "Medical Topics in the *De anima* Commentary of Coimbra (1598) and the Jesuits' Attitude towards Medicine in Education and Natural Philosophy", *Early Science and Medicine*, 19 (2014), p. 76-101.
9   Descartes' scholastic sources have been established especially based on the references he makes to them in a letter to Mersenne on 30 September 1640 (AT III 185; BL 1284; CSMK III 154): "I remember only Toletus, some of the Conimbricenses and Rubius. I would also like to know if there is in current use any abstract of the whole of scholastic philosophy; this would save me the time it would take to read their huge tomes. There was, I think, a Carthusian or Feuillant who made such an abstract, but I do not remember his name". The latter is likely Eustachius, knowledge of whom can be attributed to Descartes on the basis of the letter to Mersenne on 11 November 1640 (AT III 232; BL 1320; CSMK III 157): "I have bought the Philosophy of Father Eustache of St Paul, which seems to me the best book of its kind ever made". As for Abra de Raconis, see AT III 234; BL 1322: "I will also take a look at the Course of Philosophy by the Lord of Raconis…".
10 See MÁRIO SANTIAGO DE CARVALHO, *The Coimbra Jesuit Aristotelian Course*, Coimbra, Coimbra University Press & The Portuguese Mint and Official Printing Office, 2018, and MÁRIO SANTIAGO DE CARVALHO, "Manuel de Góis: The Coimbra Course and the Definition of an Early Jesuit Philosophy", in *Jesuit Philosophy in the Eve of Modernity*, ed. by Cristiano Casalini, Leiden-Boston, Brill, 2019, p. 347-372.

It being impossible to deal extensively with the whole of the contents of these commentaries, I picked up three issues in particular, which correspond to the first three sections of the present paper. The first one is the nature of the semen, and the action of the *vis formativa*, as well as its relationship with vital heat and temperaments, its instruments. The second is the problem of the real and/or rational distinction(s) between the generative, the nutritive, and the augmentative powers. The third is the epigenetic order of generation of vital organs, i.e. the right sequence over which the fundamental organs of a living body (traditionally, the liver, the heart, and the brain) are generated and then ensouled. In section four I integrate these reconstructions with some conclusions about Descartes' own theory.

2. The Semen and the *vis formativa*

2.1. The Aristotelian-Galenic Seed: Key-Elements

For the scholastics, the semen theory traces back to Aristotle and his bio-zoological works.[11] As is known, the *De Anima* is vague in describing the vegetative soul's powers, which include the generative power. Yet Aristotle provided a more detailed discussion about the process of animal generation in the *De generatione animalium*, where he assigned to semen a strategic task in the reproduction of those animals in which one can distinguish males and females.

For greater clarity in the following paragraphs, it is worth recalling a few basic points of Aristotle's theory and a few things on its re-elaboration until the Renaissance.[12] Aristotle held that the male semen is the efficient cause and the principle of motion, along with essence (final and formal cause) and matter (material cause), which is provided by the female.[13] According to a traditional reading,[14] Aristotle held that the semen is only male, and contains the vegetative soul only in potency,[15] being

---

11 I quote Aristotle's works from *Aristotelis Opera omnia. Graece et latine cum indice nominum et rerum absolutissimo*, 5 vols, Paris, A. F. Didot, 1848-1874. The English translation I quote is Aristotle, *Complete Works*, ed. by Jonathan Barnes, 2 vols, Princeton, Princeton University Press, 1984-1985.
12 On Renaissance rethinking of generation see especially HIRO HIRAI, *Medical Humanism and Natural Philosophy Renaissance Debates on Matter, Life and the Soul*, Leiden-Boston, Brill, 2011; LINDA DEER RICHARDSON, *Academic Theories of Generation in the Renaissance. The Contemporaries and Successors of Jean Fernel (1497-1558)*, Switzerland, Springer, 2018, and FABRIZIO BIGOTTI, *Physiology of the Soul. Mind, Body and Matter in the Galenic Tradition of the Late Renaissance (1550-1630)*, Turnhout, Brepols, 2019.
13 *Gen. An.* B, 3, 737a30-35; B, 4 738b15-35. See ROBERT MAYHEW, *The Female in Aristotle's Biology: Reason or Rationalization*, Chicago, The University of Chicago Press, 2004, p. 38-43.
14 Some scholars argue for the presence of a female seed in Aristotle, for instance Mayhew, *The Female in Aristotle's Biology*, p. 30-38 and 45-47; ROBERTO LO PRESTI, "Informing Matter and Enmattered Forms: Aristotle and Galen on the 'Power' of the Seed", *British Journal for the History of Philosophy*, 22 (2014, 5), p. 929-950; SOPHIA M. CONNELL, *Aristotle on Female Animals: A Study of the Generation of Animals*, Cambridge, Cambridge University Press, 2016.
15 *Gen. An.* B, 1, 735a5-10; B, 3, 736b5-15; B, 5, 741a20-25.

a hylomorphic compound.[16] The seed is indeed made of superfluous food[17] and is the material vehicle by which the male introduces into the womb a principle of animation.[18]

It is actually puzzling where, for Aristotle, such a principle comes from, given that the semen contains the vegetative and the sensitive soul just in potency, so that the souls are infused only later, and in human generation even something divine, intelligence (*nous*), "comes from the outside".[19] However, the animating principle is, according to Aristotle, cosmic heat,[20] or solar heat, which is somehow able to make the process of generation end with a complete and living animal. Yet the Philosopher stresses, about "the material of the semen, in and with which is emitted the animating principle", that there are two kinds of such a principle, one which "is not connected with matter, and belongs to those animals in which is included something divine (to wit, what is called the reason)", and another "inseparable from matter".[21]

Aristotle's theory is by itself not adamantine, and probably the Philosopher never attributed to the soul or the semen a specific formative power.[22] But the Western tradition integrated his view with another pivotal reference, Galen's *De semine*, which famously addressed harsh criticisms against Aristotle's conception of the seed.[23] Galen (re)introduced several new elements, such as the open recognition of female semen[24]

---

16 For more on this aspect see DEVIN HENRY, "Understanding Aristotle's Reproductive Hylomorphism", *Apeiron* 39 (2006, 3), p. 257-287; DAVID LEFEBVRE, "Le Sperma: Forme, Matière ou les Deux? Aristote Critique de la Double Semence", *Philosophie Antique* 16 (2016), p. 31-62. See also ABRAHAM BOS, "Aristotle on Soul and Soul-'Parts' in Semen ('GA' 2.1, 735a4-22)", *Mnemosyne*, 62 (2009, 3), p. 378-400, JESSICA GELBER, "Form and inheritance in Aristotle's embryology", *Oxford Studies in Ancient Philosophy* 39 (2010), p. 183-212 and SOPHIA M. CONNELL, "Nutritive and Sentient Soul in Aristotle's *Generation of Animals* 2.5", *Phronesis* 65 (2020, 4), p. 324-354. About physics-embryology relationship see ALAN CODE, "Soul as Efficient Cause in Aristotle's Embryology", *Philosophical Topics* 15 (1987, 2), p. 51-59.
17 Gen. An. B, 3, 736b25-30.
18 Gen. An. B, 3.
19 Gen. An. B, 3, 736b25-30.
20 Gen. An. B, 3, 736b30-737a10.
21 Gen. An. B, 3, 737a7-11. Moreover, Aristotle might have had in mind two concepts of the seed, see IGNACIO DE RIBERA MARTIN, "Seed (*Sperma*) and *Kuêma* in Aristotle's *Generation of Animals*", *Journal of History of Biology*, 52 (2019, 1), p. 87-124.
22 See DAVID LEFEBVRE, "Looking for the Formative Power in Aristotle's Nutritive Soul", in Giouli Korobili and Roberto Lo Presti (eds), *Nutrition and Nutritive Soul in Aristotle and Aristotelianism*, De Gruyter, Berlin, 2020, p. 101-126.
23 In the copious secondary literature on Galen (and Aristotle) see in particular ANTHONY PREUS, "Galen's Criticism of Aristotle's Conception Theory", *Journal of the History of Biology* 10, (1977, 1), p. 65-85; MICHAEL BOYLAN, "Galen's Conception Theory", *Journal of the History of Biology* 19, (1986, 1), p. 47-77; LO PRESTI, "Informing Matter and Enmattered Forms".
24 I quote Galen from *Claudii Galeni Opera Omnia*, ed. by Karl Gottlob Kühn, Leipzig, in officina C. Cnoblachii, 1821-1833, 19 vols. (reprint Hildesheim, Olms, 1964-1965). See *De semine* (vol. 4) I, 2, 4 and *De semine*, II, 1, 4. Cf. DEER RICHARDSON, *Academic Theories of Generation in the Renaissance*, p. 61-64.

and the role of the testicles in the production of semen.[25] One important Galenic novelty lies in the introduction of a stronger distinction between the generative and the formative powers; which, once mediated with Fernel's account, would be crucial for the late scholastic understanding of the issue. According to Galen, generative power acts through heat and physical qualities, but its task is limited to forming the homogeneous parts that constitute the body (such as bones, cartilages, nerves, and veins). By contrast, the formative power combines such parts to generate a whole and functional living body.[26] Therefore, formative power alone is that responsible for the teleological activity that, during the process of generation, intelligently combines the body, and brings it from a mere composition of parts to the status of an organic whole.

As is known, Galen himself pointed to formative power as likely revealing an intelligent cause behind generation, but he did not provide any concrete explanation for such intelligent-like behavior.[27] Closer in time to late scholasticism is Fernel, who re-elaborated Galen's framework in quite an original way. According to Fernel, even though material composition and temperaments are responsible for the formation of the fetus, they are not the causes of the integration,[28] the unification, and the organic, holistic nature of a living body. The ultimate cause of such natural phenomena is indeed the human soul, and its main instrument, the *spiritus*.[29] It is well-known that Fernel did not understand the spirit, as Galen did, as medical spirit, even if he rather tried to reconcile his account with the Galenic distinction between vital, animal, and natural spirits.[30] Fernel thinks of spirit as a subtle body, an ethereal, tenuous substance acting as the vehicle that transports throughout the body a celestial, vital heat, which is the main thing responsible for vegetative animation.[31]

According to Fernel, the action of spirit is pivotal in generation. Spirit resides as enclosed in the semen's matter, from where it finalizes the process of generation and formation of the fetus, entering throughout the body and infusing a qualitative life into it. Famously, Fernel merges this view within Galen's, arguing that while primordial elements and temperaments form the parts of the body, (i.e. the tissues), and the formative power organizes them to form true organs, spirit alone is what infuses the vital heat into the organism, making it into an organic, living whole.[32]

---

25 Galen, *De semine*, II, 4. Cf. DEER RICHARDSON, *Academic Theories of Generation in the Renaissance*, p. 65-66.
26 Galen, *De semine*, II, 5; but especially Galen, *De naturalibus facultatibus*, in *Opera Omnia*, vol. 2, I, 4. Cf. DEER RICHARDSON, *Academic Theories of Generation in the Renaissance*, p. 66-67.
27 Galen, *De foetuum formatione*, in *Opera Omnia*, vol. 4, VI, 4. Cf. DEER RICHARDSON, *Academic Theories of Generation in the Renaissance*, p. 69-70.
28 *Phys.* IV. Cf. DEER RICHARDSON, *Academic Theories of Generation in the Renaissance*, p. 224-ff.
29 *Phys.* IV, ch. 2 and 7. Cf. DEER RICHARDSON, *Academic Theories of Generation in the Renaissance*, p. 225-226.
30 *Phys.* IV, ch. 12.
31 *Phys.* II, ch. 7; *Phys.* IV, ch. 1 and 2. Cf. DEER RICHARDSON, *Academic Theories of Generation in the Renaissance*, p. 229-ff.
32 JEAN FERNEL, *De abditis rerum causis*, Paris, Chrétien Wechel, 1548, I, 4.

2.2. Scholastic Accounts for the Semen: Manuel de Góis and Francisco Suárez

Having recalled these medical premises, we can now address the early modern scholastic context, where a very influential view is obviously that of Aquinas.[33] In the wake of Aristotle, Aquinas understood semen as a mediator in the process of generation. It contains an active virtue, "derived from the soul of the generator", which he describes as "a certain movement of this soul itself" impressed in the semen. Such active force resides especially in the spirit, which in turn indwells in the semen. Once the semen is in the womb, it encounters the matter of the fetus, and finds a potential vegetative soul already there. So the semen's active power is able to shape it until fully preparing a body and, in animals, until causing the emergence of the sensitive soul.[34]

Aquinas' account is quite popular among Descartes' late scholastic sources. However, a noteworthy issue regarding especially Iberian Schools is the attack in 1554 by Gómez Pereira's *Antoniana Margarita*[35]. Gómez Pereira argued in particular against the scholastic accounts of the vegetative and sensitive soul and Aristotle's theory of generation. He accused Aristotle's doctrine of the seed of being confused and unintelligible,[36] to the extent that it put the Schools on a dead-end road. Rather, Pereira contended that the semen is just a material instrument, unable by itself to generate anything, particularly a sensitive soul.[37] This is proven also by what one can observe in processes of spontaneous generation, where the semen plays no role. Generation can rather be explained by virtue of a higher cause, which for Gómez Pereira is a celestial power, or by appealing to Augustine,[38] the direct action of God on matter. Thus, the semen's entrance in the womb is just an occasion, on which God, "the only Creator",[39] ensouls a specific piece of matter.

---

33 Thomas de Aquino, *Summa theologiae cum Supplemento et commentariis Caietani*, in *Sancti Thomae de Aquino Opera Omnia iussu Leonis XIII P. M. Edita*, vols 4-12, Rome, Typographia Polyglotta S. C. De Propaganda Fide, 1888-1906. English tr. *The Summa Theologica*, trans. by Fathers of the English Dominican Province, New York, Benziger Bros., 1947-1948, I, q. 118-119. On Aquinas' embryology (including ethical aspects) see especially the 'back and forth' by John Haldane, Patrick Lee, "Aquinas on Human Ensoulment, Abortion and the Value of Life", *Philosophy* 78 (2003), 255-278; Robert Pasnau, "Souls and the beginning of life: A reply to Haldane and Lee", *Philosophy* 78 (2003), 521-531; John Haldane, Patrick Lee, "Rational souls and the Beginning of Life: A reply to Robert Pasnau", *Philosophy* 78 (2003), 532-540. See then Jason T. Eberl, "Aquinas's Account of Human Embryogenesis and Recent Interpretations", *Journal of Medicine and Philosophy* 30 (2005), p. 379-394.
34 See Aquinas, *Summa Theologiae*, I, q. 118, art. 1, *resp.* and ad 3.
35 Gómez Pereira, *Antoniana Margarita. Opus nempe physicis, medicis, ac theologicis*, Medina del Campo, in officina chalcographica Guillielmi de Millis, 1554, eng. trans. by José Manuel García Valverde and Peter Maxwell-Stuart, *Antoniana Margarita: a Work on Natural Philosophy, Medicine and Theology*, Leiden Boston, Brill, 2019, 2 vols. On Gómez Pereira and Descartes see Gabriel Sanhueza, *La pensée biologique de Descartes dans ses rapports ave la philosophie scolastique. Le cas Gomez-Péreira*, L'Harmattan, Paris, 1997.
36 Pereira, *Antoniana Margarita* (1554 ed.), col. 393-395.
37 Pereira, *Antoniana Margarita* (1554 ed.), col. 359.
38 Pereira, *Antoniana Margarita* (1554 ed.), col. 367. See Augustinus, *De Trinitate*, III, c. 1, § 6-c. 4, § 9.
39 Pereira, *Antoniana Margarita* (1554 ed.), col. 369.

In light of Pereira's attack, it is no accident that the late scholastics dwell especially on two capital questions, being crucial doctrinal points but also expressing the need to argue against him. The first one is whether the semen is actually a living being, i.e. it already contains any soul, or not. The second problem is about the nature of the *vix formatrix*, and how it operates in the generation of the embryo.

As for these issues, a remarkable position is expressed by Góis' Commentary on the *De generatione et corruptione*,[40] which devotes to embryological questions a whole treatise. Transgressing Aristotle, the Coimbran agrees with Galen's double-seed theory (a stronger one from the father and a weaker from the mother).[41] Góis also denies that the semen is ensouled,[42] and subscribes to the Galenic[43] distinction between two sides of one same power. On the one hand, the generative power, which is responsible for the introduction of the form into matter. On the other hand, the formative power, which delineates the fetus[44] instead. What especially concerns Góis is however to establish whether the semen is able by itself to produce such teleological actions, or whether it rather has in itself a distinct virtue. Góis' lines up with the traditional solution that the formative or generative power does not reside in the semen, but rather in the generator's soul. Elaborating the semen, the parents' generative power provides it with the active virtue mentioned by Aquinas, i.e. in Góis' words, "another similar virtue, almost substitutive of it, which handles and shapes the fetus".[45]

Hence the Coimbran agrees with Aquinas on two points: 1) this virtue "represents" the generating subject in the semen, and 2) such virtue directs the ethereal heat and the vital spirit as its instruments to shape the body and to infuse life into the new organism.[46] Yet Galen's astonishment about its intelligent-like behavior remains untouched in Góis' treatise, and it goes with the echo of Gómez Pereira's attack. Indeed, how can such a virtue *know* how to act, shaping the embryo proportionally and according to the right measures? Interestingly, Góis holds that such intelligent behavior is due to the assistance of God, who even "supervises" the process.[47] An

---

40 CONIMBRICENSES, *Commentarii Colegii Conimbricensis S. J. In duos libros De Generatione et Corruptione Aristotelis Stagiritae*, Lisbon, António de Mariz, 1597.
41 CONIMBRICENSES, *De Generatione et Corruptione*, I, c. 4, q. 27, art. 2, p. 187-188.
42 CONIMBRICENSES, *De Generatione et Corruptione*, I, c. 4, q. 25, art. 2, p. 179-181.
43 GALEN, *De Naturalibus Facultatibus*, I, 4.
44 CONIMBRICENSES, *De Generatione et Corruptione*, I, c. 4, q. 26, art. 1, p. 181.
45 CONIMBRICENSES, *De Generatione et Corruptione*, I, c. 4, q. 26, art. 1, p. 182. Similarly EUSTACHIUS A SANCTO PAULO, *Summa Philosophiae Quadripartita*, Paris, apud Carolum Chastellain, 1609, *Physica*, tr. II, *De anima vegetante*, d. 4, q. 2, p. 332.
46 It is noteworthy that Góis embraces Fernel's idea that even the formative power is by itself unable to make a living being of the conjunction of the various parts of a fetus, but simultaneously he cannot accept Fernel's pneumology, and particularly the divine or metaphysical nature of the spirit. What shapes the fetus is rather the semen, and the active virtue enclosed by the father in it, whereas the spirit remains a mere instrument in this process. At the same time, what really bestows on the embryo a proper organization as a living being is actually God's remote action, which facilitates this process by infusing in the semen a specific art of correctly forming the embryo. Góis enumerates his doctrine of *spiritus* in CONIMBRICENSES, *De Generatione et Corruptione*, I, c. 5, q. 2, p. 217-220.
47 CONIMBRICENSES, *De Generatione et Corruptione*, I, c. 4, q. 26, art. 1, p. 182.

account that does not reject Pereira's preeminence of God's action in generation, but saves the active role played by the semen, which cannot be reduced to a mere instrument.

However, what does Góis really mean by talking of God's intervention in leading the semen's action? For him, God cannot indeed be the direct efficient cause of generation, as made evident by the fact that monsters exist. No irregularities should happen if God directly and personally managed the whole process of generation, though many cases bear witness to the opposite.[48] Yet, at the same time, God is directly responsible for providing the semen with intelligent-like knowledge which facilitates its formative work. He indeed introduces in the semen's power an inclination to act intelligently, and according to a formative art. Essentially, God does not instill into the semen a science, but rather a constructive technique, which explains its finalized activity as if the semen had its own mind and was intentionally aimed at producing the body.[49]

Appealing to God's disposition of the world, Góis retakes an account of final causation that came to be very popular in early modern scholasticism,[50] and which reduces teleology to 'metaphorical causation' or to the psychological intention of the agent being. According to this model, God alone is directly responsible for the dispositions of all the natural powers. Indeed, most of the early modern scholastics, including Góis,[51] think that no natural agent by itself pursues a specific end, but rather natural beings are disposed by God toward the achievement of their peculiar ends. Hence, by such a general disposition of the various elements at stake, God is also indirectly responsible for all their intelligent-like activities, including successful and unsuccessful processes of generation.[52] God cannot be the direct efficient actor who shapes the embryo in the womb (given that that process sometimes fails), but in a way he is responsible overall for all generation, being the one who disposed the natural world to act so.

---

48 CONIMBRICENSES, *De Generatione et Corruptione*, I, c. 4, q. 26, art. 1, p. 182.
49 As an Aristotelian, Góis cannot renounce Aristotle's famous idea that, whilst natural phenomena are the deterministic outcome of the overlapping of different causes, intelligent beings can act freely in the natural world, and to determine their own purposes. As it is impossible to attribute to the semen its own intelligence, it is just as impossible to think of it as a conscious and free actor. What God bestows on it is not science, which would entail the presence of an intellect, but rather an art, i.e. a set of rules finalized to the making of specific results, and whose implementation does not need a free and intelligent actor.
50 See STEPHAN SCHMID, "Suárez and the Problem of Final Causation", in *Suárez's Metaphysics in its Historical and Systematic Context*, ed. by Lucas Novák, Berlin, De Gruyter, p. 293-308 and STEPHAN SCHMID, "Finality without Final Causes? Suárez's Account of Natural Teleology", *Ergo: An Open Access Journal of Philosophy* 16 (2015, 2), p. 393-425 and GIUSEPPE CAPRIATI, "*Quid est causa?* The Debate on the Definition of 'Cause' in Early Jesuit Scholasticism", *Vivarium*, 58 (2019, 1-2), p. 111-139.
51 CONIMBRICENSES, *Commentarii Collegii Conimbricensis S. J. in octo libros Physicorum Aristotelis Stagiritae*, Coimbra, António de Mariz, 1591, II, c. 7, q. 20-21, p. 331-338.
52 See CONIMBRICENSES, *Physica*, II, c. 9, q. 5, art. 1, p. 369-376. On this point see SIMONE GUIDI, 'Errata Naturae. Cause prime e seconde del mostro biologico tra medioevo ed età moderna', *Lo Sguardo* 9 (2012), p. 65-105 and (with special attention to finalism) SILVIA A. MANZO, "Monsters, Laws of Nature, and Teleology in Late Scholastic Textbooks", in *Contingency and Natural Order in Early Modern Science*, ed. by Pietro Omodeo, Rodolfo Garau, Cham, Springer, 2019, p. 61-92.

One alternative picture to Góis' can be found in Suárez's treatise *De Anima*.[53] Suárez reckons that the semen's matter is produced by the testicles, but it remains "obscure" how and by whom vital spirits, with overall responsibility for the correct formation of the fetus, are infused into it. The most plausible account points, for him, to the heart, which is traditionally associated with vital spirits[54] and which is noble enough to be appointed for such an important task. Anyway, Suárez subscribes to the traditional view that the semen is a hylomorphic compound made up of the oleaginous matter of the semen produced by the testicles, and a formal part, i.e. the spirit. In turn, the spirit enclosed in the semen has a form playing a twofold role: it is indeed both the form of the semen's material part and the specific form of the spirit itself. Now, Suárez originally argues that, thanks to its form, the generative spirit even achieves the status of a living being.[55] A position that is probably a reaction against Gómez Pereira's criticisms enhancing the very foundations of Aristotle's account: not only is the semen active in generation, but it is even ensouled. And this should explain how it is able to let the fetus' sensitive soul spring from matter's dispositions.

Suárez argues for the ensouled semen theory by appealing to a few authorities, i.e. Johann Velcurio (Bernhardi), Iacobus Foroliviensis, and Cajetan. This quite unpopular account is nonetheless the only one explaining how the semen's action can shape the body in such an admirable way. Indeed, Suárez points out, the spirit does not act just instrumentally, given that "once the semen is separated from the living [generator], and so it is not assisted by it, it must achieve any form proportioned to the action".[56] This doctrine was however rejected by important scholastic authorities, among which are Albert and Egidius, and ancient commentators like Simplicius and Philoponus. But Suárez is concerned only with bringing Aquinas (who effectively took a position against the animation of the semen) to his side. In the Jesuit's reading, Aquinas just denied that the semen's form is any soul to be introduced in the fetus, given that the semen's matter would not be disposed to receive it. In saying so, Thomas would not have argued against the idea that "the said semen's form is higher than the forms of the inanimate beings, and to the point that it reaches the grade of an ensouled being". Indeed, the semen's soul Suárez talks about is an "imperfect one, and almost a way to another".[57]

It is also noteworthy that, affirming the semen's animation, Suárez does not make it an independent actor, able by itself to shape the fetus in an intelligent-like manner. Unfortunately, for a more detailed explanation of this point Suárez refers to his lost Commentary on the *Physics*; but one can anyway resort to his *Metaphysical Disputations*, 18, which shed a little light on his account. Here the Uncommon Doctor

---

53 Francisco Suárez, *Tractatus tertius de anima*, in *Opera Omnia*, 28 vols, Paris, Vivès, 1856-1861, vol. 3, p. 463-801. I limit quotes from Suárez to the Vivès-Álvares edition excluding Castellote's, due to chronological coherence with my aim of investigating Descartes' possible direct readings.
54 Suárez, *Tractatus de anima*, II, c. 12, § 8.
55 Suárez, *Tractatus de anima*, II, c. 12, § 9.
56 Suárez, *Tractatus de anima*, II, c. 12, § 9.
57 Such a soul would nonetheless be provided with the generative power alone, in order to explain how the ensouled semen could indwell in the testicles without being fed, more or less as it is for plants' semen. See Suárez, *Tractatus de anima*, II, c. 12, § 9 p. 105.

supposes that, even if the semen were able by itself to shape the limbs of the body, it remains surprising how it can arrange them into the right order and connection, which operation requires "another application". Such intelligent-like behavior could be explained by another natural faculty indwelling in the mother's womb, or by the celestial influx, or "any motion or direction of nature's Creator."[58]

So Suárez eventually adjusts his view to Góis', or at least he holds that an external motion, direction, or impressed art is the only possible explanation for the ability of the semen in producing the fetus. This is in accordance with the account of natural and divine teleology he provides elsewhere, quite congruent with Gois'. As Stephan Schmidt stressed, Suárez too "thinks that the operations of natural substances are, due to their indirect dependence on final causes and God, not properly *performed for the sake of* certain ends, but rather *directed towards* these ends by God".[59] At the same time, and against that metaphysical background, he adopts the middle solution that even if God is the only true creator of living beings, the semen plays a relevant role in generation.

3. Are the Generative, the Nutritive and the Augmentative Powers Really Distinct?

3.1. Nutrition, Decay and Growth

The second problem I address in this paper is the real and/or rational distinction(s) between the generative, the nutritive and the augmentative powers. Again, it is worth recalling a few distinctive elements of the main sources for the late scholastics.[60]

As is well known, in the *De Anima* Aristotle characterized "what has soul" and life as anything that displays at least one faculty among "thinking or perception or local movement and rest, or movement in the sense of nutrition, decay and growth".[61] Accordingly, he listed five main powers of the soul, i.e. "the nutritive, the appetitive, the sensory, the locomotive, and the power of thinking",[62] pointing out that "plants have none but the first, the nutritive, while another order of living beings has this plus the sensory" and the appetitive. Therefore, nutrition, decay and growth are the main powers of the vegetative soul, shared by all living beings.[63]

However, the *De Anima* delivered to posterity a vague topology of the vegetative soul's powers. The scholastic tradition thus received the need for an enquiry into the

---

58 Francisco Suárez, *Disputationes Metaphysicae*, in *Opera Omnia*, vols 25-26, XVIII, s. 2, § 33. Interestingly, Suárez applies the a likewise account to the problem of the generation of the angelic assumed bodies. See Francisco Suárez, *De angelis*, in *Opera Omnia*, 28 vols, Paris, Vivès, 1856-1861, vol. 2, IV, c. 35, § 4 and especially c. 37, § § 5-6.
59 Schmid, "Finality without Final Causes?", p. 407.
60 On late scholastic conceptions of the soul see, of course, Dennis Des Chene, *Life's Form: Late Aristotelian Conceptions of the Soul*, New York / London, Cornell University Press, 2000.
61 *De An.* II, 413a21-413a31.
62 *De An.* II, 414a29-415a12.
63 At the same time, Aristotle maintains that reproduction is a natural scope of all living beings.

nature of such powers, the only Aristotelian claim about this matter being the remark that "nutrition and reproduction are due to one and the same psychic power",[64] i.e. they are one and the same power belonging to the vegetative soul. This picture is then complicated by this topology being later accepted and refined by Galen, who famously distinguished between generation as alteration of an existing body and generation as shaping of the fetus, and associated the two of them with nutrition and growth respectively.[65]

Despite this tangled picture, among the fundamental authorities of the Schools one finds a broad agreement. Galen, Albert the Great, Aquinas and, later, Fernel maintain indeed that the three powers (nutrition, decay and growth) are really distinct. Especially for Aquinas it is a central principle that a real distinction is needed between the soul's powers, in order to deal with their different proper objects.[66] Hence, as for the power of the vegetative soul, the soul has three distinct powers enabling respectively the acquisition of the body (the task of the generative power), the acquisition of the appropriate quantity (the task of the augmentative power), and the maintenance of such appropriate dimensions (the task of the nutritive power).[67] Drawing from an Aristotelian principle, Aquinas moreover differentiated these powers into two groups, organized hierarchically. The nutritive and the augmentative power are indeed ones that cause their effects in what they inhere in, whereas the generative power, which is a higher one, produces effects in another substance, the one it generates (since no substance is able to generate itself).

3.2. The Late Scholastic Debate

About these matters the late scholastics show remarkable doctrinal confusion, revealing the existence of a still-open problem, and likely of an ongoing debate. Despite that, one could however try to reorder positions, identifying some common doctrinal currents, organized upon their assent to or dissent from a real distinction between the vegetative powers. I will try to reconstruct the views that Descartes might have found in his contemporary scholastic texts by following this principle.

One first uniform line-up is that of those who argue against the real distinction between the augmentative, the nutritive and the generative powers, following the

---

64 *De An.* II, 416a19-416b9. On this Aristotle's identification see JAMES G. LENNOX, "Most Natural Among the Functions of Living Things. Puzzles about Reproduction as a Nutritive Function", in *Nutrition and Nutritive Soul in Aristotle and Aristotelianism*, p. 1-20 and CAMERON COATES, JASON G. LENNOX, "Aristotle on the Unity of the Nutritive and Reproductive Functions", *Phronesis* 65 (2020, 4), p. 414-466.
65 GALEN, *De semine*, II, 5. See DEER RICHARDSON, *Academic Theories of Generation in the Renaissance*, p. 62-63. On Galen's account of the vegetative soul see ROBERT VINKESTEIJN, "The Vegetative Soul in Galen", in *Vegetative Powers*, p. 55-72.
66 AQUINAS, *Summa Theologiae*, I, q. 77, art. 1, *resp*.
67 AQUINAS, *Summa Theologiae*, I, q. 78, art. 2.

position of the Spanish physician Francisco Vallés[68] (openly quoted by Góis and Rubio, and whose doctrines are discussed by Suárez). Scholastics subscribing to Vallés' account are Góis — who is the forefather of this position — Antonio Rubio, and Charles-François Abra de Raconis. All of them share the idea that the three powers are not really distinct, even if they support this account from different perspectives and with different doctrinal gradients, which must be underlined.

Let us start with Góis, whose account is actually the closest to Aquinas's. Indeed the Portuguese does not identify directly the three powers, but rather associates the augmentative and the nutritive,[69] and later judges as "more probable" that the generative power is not really distinct from the nutritive one. In general, for him, the fact that the three powers have three different objects is not a sufficient reason to establish a real distinction between them, although they are formally distinct, as proven by their different definitions.[70] As for the augmentative and the nutritive powers, Góis denies their real distinction just basing on the Ockhamistic principle that there is no need to multiply the powers, especially because these two powers always act jointly.[71] As regards, by contrast, the distinction between the nutritive and the generative powers, Góis argues that nutrition is nothing but partial generation, i.e. the generation of specific parts of the body. Hence, nutrition can stem from the generative power[72] itself. Thus, Góis keeps Aquinas's hierarchy of the powers, placing the generative function at the top of the pyramid of the vegetative powers, followed by the augmentative and, lastly, by the nutritive power.

The account put forward by Góis seems to be quite popular among the late scholastics, even if in quite different forms, sometimes more radical than his. Rubio, for instance, subscribes to the same, appealing again to the principle of non-multiplication and speaking of a single power with three different tasks.[73] But he even argues that the three powers cannot be distinguished either in themselves, or by their different *modus operandi*.[74] They are just the same power, addressed to different objects. In its

---

68 Francisco Vallés, *Controversiarum Medicarum et Philosophicarum Libri decem*, Alcalá de Henares, ex officina Juan de Brocar, 1556, II, c. 20. Among the philosophers, this view belongs especially to Philoponus and Augustinus Niphus.
69 Conimbricenses, *Commentarii Collegii Conimbricensis Societatis Iesu in tres libros De anima Aristotelis Stagiritae*, Coimbra, António de Mariz 1598, II, c. 4, q. unica, art. 2, p. 128.
70 Conimbricenses, *De Anima*, II, c. 4, q. unica, art. 2, p. 129.
71 However, there is an important remark, later taken up by Charles-François Abra de Raconis, *Summa Totius Philosophiae, Tertia Pars Philosophiae seu Physica*, Cologne, ex Officina Choliniana, 1629, *Disputatio de corpore animato*, d. 2, s. 1, q. 3, p. 201. For Góis, the expression "augmentative power" does not mean that power by which a body grows until getting its proper extension, but rather the power by which an already developed body changes its quantity (for instance, it gains or loses weight). So, the augmentative power is not the one that acts in the mother's womb, but the one which is responsible for the other quantitative changes once a living being is formed and delivered. Only in this latter sense, the nutritive power constantly acts together with the augmentative (Conimbricenses, *De Anima*, II, c. 4, q. unica, art. 2, p. 128-129).
72 Conimbricenses, *De Anima*, II, c. 4, q. unica, art. 2, p. 129.
73 Antonio Rubio, *Commentarii in libros Aristotelis De anima*, Lyon, Iohannis Pillehotte, 1613, II, c. 4, q. 2, § 33.
74 Rubio, *De Anima*, II, c. 4, q. 2, § 38.

turn, Abra de Raconis holds the same view, even denying that the three powers are formally distinct, and arguing that they are distinct just by reason (*ratione ratiocinata*).[75]

The opposite line — closer to Aquinas — brings together Toledo,[76] Suárez, and Eustachius.[77] The three think that the generative power is really distinct from the nutritive and the augmentative, although the nutritive and the augmentative are not mutually distinct, if not by reason. Again in this case, despite the common doctrinal perspective, there are several disagreements between these authors, and it is especially worth taking a closer look at Suárez's approach.

The peculiarity of Suárez's account lies in reading the problem against the background of his own view, where he receives and develops Góis' arguments. As is known, Suárez is a reductionist as for the vegetative soul's powers (nutrition and augmentation[78]), which he reduces to the direct action of the soul on the food, and to the 'disposing' activity of temperaments and natural heat,[79] without any need for another specific power or specific heat. Both temperaments and natural heat prepare the food's matter to be assimilated by the soul, which acts directly on it and immediately unites itself to the nourishment prepared by temperaments and heat, to transform them into new parts of the body.[80] This entails first of all the reduction of the nutritive power to temperaments, as well as the identification of the augmentative power with the nutritive one. For Suárez, augmentative and nutritive powers are not even formally distinct, as they are just the same power seen from two different points of view.[81]

On the other hand, as for the distinction between nutritive and generative powers which remains at stake, Suárez's account is once more peculiar, and influenced by the contemporary medical tradition, especially Vallés and Fernel. The Uncommon Doctor deals with the issue by establishing a distinction between two actions in the generation of the living being: 1) the action of forming the semen from the matter of blood; and 2) the action of forming the body's limbs from the matter of the semen. Though, in the semen two different substances indwell: the material and oleaginous one, and the spiritual substance. In the light of such distinctions, the question is, for Suárez, threefold, i.e.: a) to establish if the power which forms the semen in its material and oleaginous part, is the same as the power which causes growth; b) what is the nature of the power which introduces the spirit in the semen; c) which kind of power is introduced later in the semen, allowing the semen to make up the organic body.

---

75 ABRA DE RACONIS, *Disputatio de corpore animato*, d. 2, s. 1, q. 3, *prima propositio*, p. 200-201.
76 FRANCISCO TOLEDO, *Commentaria in tres libros Aristotelis De Anima*, Venice: apud Iuntas, 1575, II, c. 4, q. 9, fol. 74, col. 3.
77 EUSTACHIUS, *De anima vegetante*, d. 4, q. 1, p. 331.
78 For more on Suárez's understanding of augmentation see the ms. *Thesaurus doctrinae circa libros Aristotelis De generatione et corruptione traditus per reverendum patrem Franciscum Suarez. Anno Domini 1575*, ed. by Salvador Castellote, d. 3 (2980-4005).
79 SUÁREZ, *Tractatus de anima*, II, c. 9, § 11.
80 SUÁREZ, *Tractatus de anima*, II, c. 9, § 4-12.
81 SUÁREZ, *Tractatus de anima*, II, c. 9, § 17.

According to this picture, Suárez argues as follows. First of all (question *a*), the power that materially forms the semen is nothing but the nutritive power itself, located in a specific part of the body.[82] Secondly (question *c*) the semen's power of shaping the body is different from the nutritive power.[83] Thirdly (question *b*), the soul's power that introduces into the semen the spiritual part, is not the nutritive power, but rather another independent one.[84] Hence, Suárez restricts the functions of the nutritive power to what is material in the generation process, but he simultaneously denies that the spiritual part one finds in the semen, which is responsible for the shaping of the body, is the nutritive power. All of these actions are specific peculiarities of the generative power alone, which is itself distinct from the nutritive.

Apart from the two opposite groups into which, for the sake of clarity, I have classed these authors, all of them abandon at least Aquinas' real distinction between the augmentative and the nutritive powers. Their mutual opposition lies essentially in some of them (Góis, Rubius, Raconis) holding that the generative power can be reduced to the augmentative-nutritive, whereas others (Toledo, Suárez, Eustachius) argue for the ontological independence of the generative power from the other two.

4. The Epigenetic Order of Generation and the Infusion of the Rational Soul

4.1. Key References

Let us now address the third problem, i.e. the epigenetic order of generation of the vital organs and the moment when the rational soul is infused in the body. As regards the problem of the order of generation, the issue is characterized by a widely known contrast between Aristotle, Hippocrates, and Galen. Famously, Aristotle supported the idea that the heart,[85] associated with the very idea of life, is the first organ generated in the embryo. By contrast, Hippocrates, followed by Galen, argued that the process of generation actually starts with the liver.[86] The reason in support of the latter view was especially that blood is the primary nutrient of the fetus, and the liver is traditionally associated with the production of it, as well as with nutrition.

As for the problem of the infusion of the rational soul, the authorities invoked by the late scholastics disagree with each other, especially about the way and the time in which such infusion happens. The debate regarding the way of infusion is strongly connected with the famous dispute about the plurality of forms, and so opposes many different perspectives presented by Góis[87] in the wake of what he

---

82 SUÁREZ, *Tractatus de anima*, II, c. 9, § 2.
83 SUÁREZ, *Tractatus de anima*, II, c. 9, § 3.
84 SUÁREZ, *Tractatus de anima*, II, c. 9, § 4.
85 *Gen. An.* B, 1, 735b20-25.
86 GALEN, *De foetuum formatione*, III, 4; See DEER RICHARDSON, *Academic Theories of Generation in the Renaissance*, p. 67.
87 CONIMBRICENSES, *De Anima*, I, q. 4, art. 1, p. 62.

found in Aquinas.[88] There are some, like Alexander of Hales,[89] claiming that vital functions appearing in the embryo are not caused by the fetus' soul but rather by the mother's. Others argue for the plurality of form, claiming that three different souls are created in the fetus and then kept in the generated human being. Some speak of a single soul evolving over three steps, from the vegetative to the rational soul. Others defend the view that the rational soul is infused from the beginning, and, throughout the generation process, it takes charge of the vegetative and sensitive soul's tasks. However, the official position remains Aquinas's, for which the embryo is generated three times, corresponding to as many infusions of a soul: the vegetative, the nutritive, and the rational.[90]

4.2. Late Scholastic Epigenesis and Infusion: Manuel de Góis and Francisco Suárez

Once again, Góis and Suárez are the most satisfactory sources for those wishing to investigate late scholastic debates. As for the epigenetic process, Góis recognizes that no particular reason pushes us to identify the liver as the living organ that is formed first. Indeed, the fetus receives its nourishment and vital heat from the mother through the umbilical cord.[91] Neither does it need any breathing faculty or a special power to breathe. This is why Góis places himself in the middle between the two traditional positions which he considers both probable and possible, even appealing to the possibility that both the heart and the liver are created first and jointly.[92]

Regarding the problem of infusion, Góis backs up Aquinas. The fetus' matter is informed threefold, i.e. by the vegetative, the sensitive and the rational soul. The process actually goes through the three phases in which the fetus is conceived and fed by the mother's blood, then (after a few days), it starts moving and reacting to stimulations from outside, and finally it is well formed and reaches the status of a human being.[93] For Góis, the rational soul definitely comes from God, as Thomas claimed, but a specific problem regards the timing of such a process. Time is the only "mediator" between the three phases, and what particularly concerns Góis is understanding when, precisely, the rational soul is informed, elevating the fetus to the status of a human being.[94] Yet the opinions of the medical sources disagree considerably on this point, and Góis opts for the most common *sententia*, according

---

88 AQUINAS, *Summa Theologiae*, I, 118, art. 2, resp.
89 ALEXANDER HALENSIS, *Summa Theologiae. Pars Secunda*, Cologne, Ioannis Gymnicis, 1622, II, q. 87, m. 3, art. 3, resp., p. 338, cols 1-2.
90 AQUINAS, *Summa Theologiae*, II, q. 87, n. 3, art. 6.
91 CONIMBRICENSES, *De Generatione et Corruptione*, I, c. 4, q. 29, art. 3, p. 196.
92 CONIMBRICENSES, *De Generatione et Corruptione*, I, c. 4, q. 29, art. 3, p. 197.
93 CONIMBRICENSES, *De Generatione et Corruptione* q. 21 p. 159; CONIMBRICENSES, *De Anima*, I, q. 4, art. 1, p. 63.
94 This issue also, of course, concerns abortion and its legitimacy within a certain span of time, as well as theological problems such as, for instance, the moment when Jesus's body is conceived in the Virgin Mary's womb.

to which men's souls are infused on about the fortieth day from the conception, whereas women's are infused on the eightieth.[95]

Besides Góis, these problems are not addressed by the late scholastics, save for Suárez again, who discusses them in his *De Anima*. Unlike the Portuguese, Suárez follows Vallés[96] and argues that the liver is the first organ generated and ensouled in an embryo. He indeed follows the Galenic principle that, in living beings, the natural, the nutritive and the sensitive powers of the soul correspond, respectively, to the liver, the heart, and the brain. Now, given that the embryo is developed over a progressive process, the liver, associated with nutrition, must be the first organ that is generated and animated, followed by the heart, and then the brain.[97]

Moreover, for Suárez — who here follows the opinion of Galen — in the case of the conception of human beings the three souls make the embryo pass through three stages: the vegetal, the animal, and the human. The vegetative soul informs the liver first, generating a non-human living embryo. Such a being is then informed by the sensitive soul, making an intermediate non-human animal[98]. Finally, into this imperfect animal, which constitutes a raw bodily being, the intellective soul is later infused by God, and so is generated a true human being.

5. Descartes' Embryology and Late Scholasticism: Concluding Remarks

In dealing with these debates, I do not want to argue any continuity between Descartes and his scholastic contemporaries. My aim is rather to contribute to shedding more light on Descartes' embryology and its boundaries, by portraying more sharply the theories he could find in works he likely knew and which represented a reference point for the authorities of his time. Despite that, a few remarks on Descartes' embryology in light of the scholastic theories circulating at his time could be of some interest.

It is worth noting that early modern schools were quite ready to accept the idea that the vegetative soul's powers are not really distinct among each other, and even that the nutritive and augmentative powers are not distinct from natural heat and temperaments. Obviously, no scholastic went as far as to embrace the idea that the generation process is entirely material or mechanical, but they did not attribute directly to the generator's soul the task of shaping the fetus. They rather used to keep the role played by the material part of the semen well separated from spirit and other spiritual principles, to which they attributed the intelligent-like process of generation. As seen, such principles are God's infusion of an art intrinsically present into the semen, or another external influx.

---

95 CONIMBRICENSES, *De Anima*, I, q. 4, art. 1, p. 64.
96 VALLÉS, *Controversiarum Medicarum et Philosophicarum*, II, c. 6, Epilogus.
97 SUÁREZ, *Tractatus de anima*, II, c. 8, § 3.
98 SUÁREZ, *Tractatus de anima*, II, c. 8, § 5-6.

In doing so, the late scholastics seem not to attribute a specific role in generation to final causes, since they rather opt for a model, very popular at the end of the sixteenth century, for which God arranges and disposes everything in the world as necessarily endowed with a specific efficient causation. This view fits quite well with the early modern scholastic tendency to dismiss or weaken the role of final causes, reducing them to metaphorical causation or to the psychological intention of the agent being. As mentioned, sixteenth-century schools tend to think that natural agents do not pursue specific ends by themselves, but rather they are disposed by God toward the achievement of peculiar ends.

From this perspective, the discrepancy between the late scholastics and Descartes is thinner than one might think, even though Descartes' own view remains very original if compared with other physicians and scientists of his time. The idea of a specific role played by divine action or final causes in the generation process was definitely still current among prominent colleagues of Descartes. One notable example is William Harvey,[99] who not unlike Suárez argued for the existence of a spiritual factor ensouling the passive material egg and leading the process of generation according to the ends prescribed by God to nature. Another is Gassendi,[100] who against Descartes defended final causes precisely based on the inexplicability of the wondrous arrangement of the parts in living bodies.

For Descartes the picture is different, even though just to some extent. On the one hand, for him there is no such thing as a vegetative or a sensitive soul, and the whole process of reproduction must be explained by efficient mechanical reactions. On the other hand, such reactions are however disposed by God to the achievement of specific goals. So, what Descartes transgresses with respect to the scholastics is mainly the idea that the very process of generation is somehow led by God, by a direct assistance or by providing the semen with an *ad hoc* constructive art.

Yet it is crucial to recall that, unlike his contemporary scholastics, Descartes' biology gives a pivotal function to the laws of physics, which are universal and common laws for whatever body, from non-living single material beings to complex apparatuses like animal-machines, or the human body-machine. As Aucante has stressed,[101] this is one of the most important features of Descartes' approach. However, his difficulty in explaining finalistic-like phenomena seems to be due exactly to his reluctance to isolate specific laws of life from the general laws of nature. This is what Descartes himself stressed in the *Anatomica*:

> Hence I expect that someone, frowning, calls it ridiculous that such an important thing as human procreation is, might derive from such meagre causes. But indeed what causes do they seek for, weightier than the eternal laws of Nature? Would they want maybe that things are done by some intelligence? But by which one?

---

99 WILLIAM HARVEY, *Disputations Touching on the Generation of Animals*, tr. by Gweneth Whitteridge, London, Blackwell Scientific Publications, p. 65.
100 PIERRE GASSENDI, *Selected Works*, ed. by Craig B. Brush, New York, Johnson Reprint Corporation, 1972, p. 226.
101 See AUCANTE, *La philosophie médicale de Descartes*, p. 302 but already ROGER, *The Life Sciences*, p. 116-120.

Perhaps directly by God? And then what is the reason why monsters sometimes are generated? Perhaps from this all-wise nature, which comes up only from unreasonable human thought?[102]

One emerging detail worth attention in this text is that for Descartes, as with the scholastics, the generation of monsters proves precisely that God does not intervene directly in the epigenetic process. But this means for him even more, i.e. that God does not intervene at all in the whole process, unlike in the (mutually different) views of the scholastics and Gómez Pereira. At the same time, Descartes rejects the very idea of an intelligent "nature", and points directly to the universal laws of physics for the shaping of the fetus. By doing so, he ends up unable to explain how the physical reactions caused by the male and female semen are directed to conceive a living being belonging to the same species as its generators, rather than to some random mechanical effect.

On the other hand, Descartes thinks of uterine generation as not essentially different from *spontaneous* generation. Spontaneous generation differs from uterine generation just by happening without a semen[103] (and outside of a womb). It is for Descartes an entirely natural and very common phenomenon, which matter and the laws of physics alone are sufficient to cause. The encounter of specific statuses in matter often leads to generating an embryo, which, once the lungs and the liver are formed, develops spontaneously — i.e. by virtue of natural forces alone — until reaching the form of a well-formed living being.[104] Somehow life (in Descartes' view, the organization of matter into a self-maintaining machine, provided with its own principle of motion, the heart) is thus an emerging property, residing in potency in any combination of matter and physical laws. And, as he remarks, for a living being to appear just a few things are required, so it is no surprise that life spontaneously comes up from putrefying matter.[105]

Nonetheless, what remains enigmatic in Descartes' theory is how in uterine generation the semen's parts[106] could be disposed by the generators as though they were prepared to cause *that* specific effect.[107] How can a mechanical generative apparatus arrange the semen's parts as if they were disposed to make another human body-machine? For Descartes a full knowledge of the parts constituting the semen and of their mutual arrangement would allow one to know the whole of its effects, and so the entire development of the fetus. Yet he also remarks that knowing the conformation of the body one could know the semen.[108]

---

102 *Primae Cogitationes* AT XI 524; BOp 964 (my translation).
103 *Primae Cogitationes* AT XI 505: BOp 936.
104 *Primae Cogitationes* AT XI 506; BOp 938.
105 *Primae Cogitationes* AT XI 506; BOp 936.
106 Both the father's and the mother's, as Descartes famously subscribes to the double-seed theory.
107 On issues related with Descartes' simultaneous rejection of teleology and leading idea of a capability of natural things of bearing internal ends, see the interesting remarks by Karen Detlefsen, "Descartes on the Theory of Life and Methodology in the Life Sciences", in *Early Modern Medicine and Natural Philosophy*, ed. by Peter Distelzweig, Benjamin Goldberg, Evan R. Ragland, Cham, Springer, 2016, p. 141-171.
108 *La Description du corps humain*, AT XI 277; BOp 585.

This claim could be read in many ways (for instance, that one can deduce the kind of semen from the conformation of the body), but it seems to mean that, for Descartes, the entire conformation of the semen can be deduced from the knowledge of the body's conformation, i.e. by a complete knowledge of the parts in charge of its production.

As is known, Descartes never drew up an account of this problem, and settled for hypotethical and general explanations, waiting for new experiments that were never carried out. Such a lack of sufficient observation is nonetheless a peculiar feature of Descartes' theory of generation, and fits in the larger picture of his tendency to formulate hypothetical, *ad hoc* explanations drawn from general metaphysical principles.[109] Like Aristotle, Descartes still conceives of science as a knowledge of universal causes, from which one can deduce specific effects and many of the difficulties raised by his mechanistic reduction of biology derive in fact from the way he understands the dependence of such machines on God. Indeed Descartes stresses how his account of living beings as machines is hypothetico-deductive, i.e. it is valid because God *could have* built, even in a better fashion, what the mechanical explanation describes.[110] Accordingly, Descartes constantly thinks of the body-machine through the hypothesis that God creates the human body on the model of a machine, but he never looks closely at how God concretely disposes such machines to produce semen able to generate a new individual in its species.

But perhaps, focusing on the semen and God's arrangement of causes and effects, we do not take into account sufficiently a distinctive element appearing in some elaborations of Descartes' theory, one that could have marked a significant distance from his contemporaries. I am referring to the function he attributes to the mother's womb in the *Primae cogitationes* (a text for which it is very hard to set a date). Here Descartes represents the uterus not just as an oven that cooks the fetus, but rather as a mold whose configuration contributes to shaping the fetus. The uterus acts indeed as a filtering system separating the semen's parts, preparing the spontaneous inflation of matter and the mutual development of pre-arranged parts.[111] Without such a setting, the inflating semen would be unable, by itself, to articulate the embryo in distinct parts, each one provided with a specific function for the development of the fetus, and later for the self-maintenance of the body-machine. Likely, the maternal environment seems strategic to explaining the determination of the embryo's sex.[112]

Hence one might argue that the fetus is for Descartes not just the outcome of matter and physical laws, but also the result of the combined interaction of the semen's fermentation and the womb's dispositions. Only the latter can handle the mechanical reactions in the embryo and push it toward the making of a well-formed animal or human being. This aspect of the uterus looks to be quite absent in the scholastic tradition, which keeps conceiving the female by analogy with passive prime matter.

---

109 This is already Roger's conclusion, see *The Life Sciences*, p. 116.
110 *L'Homme* AT XI 120; BOp 362.
111 *Primae Cogitationes* AT XI 506-508; BOp 938-940.
112 *Primae Cogitationes* AT XI 516; BOp 950-951; and see ROGER, *The Life Sciences*, p. 119.

Although they agree with the existence of female semen, having a partially active role in the process of generation, the scholastics see the womb just as a mere container, where the shaping activity of the semen's virtues takes place. So that the mother is no more than a breeding ground, tasked with feeding the fetus with her blood.

Yet, though in the *Primae cogitationes* Descartes has somehow given value to the womb in embryogenesis, it is also true that in all of his other manuscripts dealing with animal generation there is no further evidence of this theory. Aroused by natural heat, the semen develops itself independently from being or not being in the womb, and the uterus' structure. Given the difficulty of setting a definite time span for the writing of the *Primae cogitationes*, it is quite hard to say if Descartes introduced or rather abandoned over time the role of the womb. But what is clear is that he continued to think of this problem over the years, keeping the idea that generation is easy and possible once given matter, its essence and the laws of physics, and changing his mind several times about the order of generation of the fetus.

The latter is another relevant issue of Descartes' theory, and he never managed to provide a final sequence of formation of the living organs, nor did he manage to explain the infusion of the rational soul by God into the body. Of course, his bewilderment seems to result from the previous abandonment of the vegetative and the sensitive soul, which for the scholastics determined a necessary path in the generation of the associated organs. Descartes instead thinks of the living organs as the instruments for the subsequent development of the fetus, so that the latter is able to generate and even to shape itself, having in itself its own principle of motion. Accordingly, he has to identify the correct sequence that could enable such a process, but this is a sequence that he likely never found out. Over the whole of his writings Descartes actually wavers between one account and another, but maybe it is significant that, finally, he looks to the heart as the first living organ generated, and definitively for what turns on the flame of life in the body.

JIL MULLER

Ambroise Paré and René Descartes on Sensation in Amputated Limbs*

▼ ABSTRACT Ambroise Paré and René Descartes can, each in their own way, be considered pioneers in the recognition of sensation in amputated limbs. Paré is one of the first surgeons to recognize this unusual perception and to provide a kind of description of this feeling. Descartes, as philosopher and physician, goes further by giving a 'mechanical' explanation of the origin of this sensation. For Paré, when an amputated patient feels pain in a missing limb, then there must be a stimulus to the nerve endings that allows this sensation. For Descartes, the sensation of pain is explained by sensory information, due to a triggering of the nerves' ends, which send vibrations to the tubes up to the brain. These mechanical signals look like those previously associated with pain, which is why the patient thinks he feels pain. Descartes uses a mechanical understanding of the nerves functioning to explain how pain is triggered and even felt in a missing limb.

▼ KEYWORDS Paré, Descartes, Amputated Limbs, Sensation, Mechanics

1. Introduction

In 1641, in the *Meditationes de prima philosophia*, Descartes describes an extraordinary sensation, when he discusses the inner and outer senses in the Sixth Meditation:

---

* A special thanks goes to Prof. Michael Stolberg who agreed to read the first draft of this article and who was able to give me valuable advice.

> **Jil Muller** • Post-doc researcher/Assistant Professor at Paderborn University and the Center for the History of Women Philosophers and Scientists. Contact: <jil.muller@uni-paderborn.de>

Descartes and Medicine: Problems, Responses and Survival of a Cartesian Discipline,
ed. by Fabrizio Baldassarri, Turnhout, 2023 (*DESCARTES*, 9), p. 81-97
© BREPOLS PUBLISHERS   10.1484/M.DESCARTES-EB.5.132885

> And yet I had heard that those who had had a leg or an arm amputated sometimes still seemed to feel pain intermittently in the missing part of the body. So even in my case it was apparently not quite certain that a particular limb was hurting, even if I felt pain in it.[1]

For Descartes, the information coming from the senses can sometimes be erroneous, that is why one has to pay attention and verify the information they transmit. He uses the example of sensation in missing limbs in the context of the doubt he expresses concerning the sensations: if it is possible to feel pain in a missing limb, how can I be sure that I feel pain in any other part of my body? What guarantees that the sensation I feel is a) real, b) has its location in any part of my body, and c) is really pain? Sensory information can be misleading and cannot always be interpreted correctly. The sensation in missing limbs, therefore, is used to explain the special attention required for the senses and even to underline the functioning of the nerves, as we will see later.

What is most surprising about this example is, firstly, that Descartes does not deny the sensation in missing limbs (he does not qualify the sensation as imaginary) and secondly, that he presents this unusual perception as if it is well known by his readers or by the physicians and surgeons of his time. In the surgical field, the sensation in a missing limb is mentioned and described since the sixteenth century. If Descartes is certainly among the pioneers in this field of unusual perception, he is not the first to mention it. Ambroise Paré (1510-1590), one of the most famous French "battle camp" surgeons of the sixteenth century, mentioned it for the first time in 1552 in his book *La Manière de traiter les plaies faites tant par hacquebutes que par flèches*. And he repeats this idea in his *Œuvres d'Ambroise Paré*:

> Because patients long after the amputation is done, still say they feel pain in the dead and amputated parts, and complain loudly: something worthy of admiration and almost unbelievable to people who have not experienced this.[2]

The description of the perception is similar in Paré and Descartes: the patients feel pain or a kind of pain in the amputated limb. Paré does neither deny this sensation nor does not care. It is a perception "worthy of admiration", he says, and so he starts to pay more attention to it and study it as a symptom. But he also adds that this sensation is "almost unbelievable": for someone, who has not experienced this sensation, it is very difficult to understand the unusual perception, and for surgeons, it is almost inconceivable, because they do not fully understand the origin and functioning of this sensation. If Paré can "only" describe the sensation and give a mere explanation, we will see, that with Descartes, the explanation of this unusual perception becomes more sophisticated.

---

1 René Descartes, *Meditationes de prima philosophia* VI, AT VII 77; CSM II 53.
2 Ambroise Paré, *Œuvres d'Ambroise Paré*, edition from 1585, ed. by Pierre de Tartas, 1969, Book 12, ch. 28, p. 486: "Car les patients longtemps après l'amputation faite, disent encore sentir douleur dans les parties mortes et amputées, et de ce se plaignent fort : chose digne d'admiration et quasi incrédible à gens qui de ce n'ont expérience." [Translation is mine.]

History remembers Paré as an avant-garde surgeon, revolutionizing the cauterisation of wounds by firearms[3] and inventing prostheses which can work perfectly like natural limbs. He wrote a major work, in French, *Les Oeuvres d'Ambroise Paré, conseiller et premier chirurgien du Roy*, published in 1585 which brought together anecdotes, remedies, and surgical procedures, with a view of educating young surgeons. An important topic, according to the surgeon, is gangrene. Gangrene appears mostly after a war injury provoked by gunshots and requires the cutting off of the injured limb. In the sixteenth century, these amputations are done on gangrenous extremities through the dead tissues to avoid blood loss. However, this surgical intervention often provokes new gangrene and therefore a second amputation, because gangrene is already present in the healthy part of the body. Commonly the consequences are infections and haemorrhage.

Paré, therefore, recommends not to amputate too close to the gangrenous extremity, which means amputating a part of the living limb. Initially one could only cut the dead part of the body, but since the sixteenth century and above all since Paré, one could consider splitting the living part for certain precise surgical cases. Before amputation, the surgeon has to decide on the treatment of the gunshot injuries. The choice of treatments, which requires a combination of traditional knowledge and methods with new treatments,[4] depends on the surgeon's idea to consider these injuries as poisonous or not. Where gunshot wounds are considered toxic, the surgeon "recommends cautery and infusion of boiling oil",[5] if not, there are different possible treatments.

Paré abandons the idea of poison in gunshots, which considerably influences his manner of treating the wound. He takes account of the patient's pain[6] and of the evolution of the tissues of the skin at the point where the bullet entered the patient. Furthermore, he is one of the first to change the amputation method, by localizing the site of amputation well above the gangrenous area. Although he has to find a process to stop blood loss and haemorrhage, without causing a new gangrenous area.[7] To save as many lives as possible he makes sure to innovate his technique of dissection and amputation by inventing new tools to remove the bullet, or by developing artificial

---

3 Cf. PIERRE HUARD and MIRKO D. GRMEK, eds, *La chirurgie moderne, Ses débuts en Occident: XVIe-XVIIe-XVIIIe siècles*, Paris, Les Éditions Roger Dacosta, 1968, p. 29: "Paré succeeded in curing some burns by applying onion extract, a procedure recognised as effective by Soviet surgeons during the Second World War. The abandonment of boiling oil in the treatment of gunshot wounds marks a certain progress, but, contrary to what is usually claimed, Paré had many real failures." [Translation is mine.]
4 Cf. ELIZABETH LANE FURDELL, ed., *Textual Healing, Essays on Medieval and Early Modern Medicine*, Leiden-Boston, Brill, 2005, p. 80 and CYNTHIA KLESTINEC, "Practical experience in Anatomy," in *The Body as Object and Instrument of Knowledge, Embodied Empiricism in Early Modern Science*, ed. by CHARLES T. WOLFE and OFER GAL, Dodrecht, Springer, 2010, p. 33-57.
5 FURDELL, p. 85 and JEAN-MICHEL DELACOMPTÉE, *Ambroise Paré, La main savante*, Paris, Gallimard, 2007, p. 51-53.
6 Cf. on the notion of pain: RAPHAËLE ANDRAULT and ARIANE BAYLE, "Le médecin de l'Époque moderne face à la douleur", *Pour la science* N°508, 2020, p. 74-79 ; MANFRED ZIMMERMANN, "Geschichte der Schmerztherapie 1500 bis 1900 [History of pain treatment from 1500 to 1900]", *Schmerz*, 2007, p. 297-306. And https://medecin-et-douleur-16e18e.huma-num.fr.
7 Cf. PHILIPPE HERNIGOU, "Ambroise Paré II: Paré's contributions to amputation and ligature," *International Orthopaedics*, 2013, 769-772 (available online in the Springer-Verlag, Berlin Heidelberg, 2013).

limbs. Many of Paré's amputees survive but as some of them report that they feel a sensation in their missing limb, Paré becomes aware of this sensation. He is one of the first surgeons to write about the sensation in amputated limbs: patients feeling pain in the missing limb or even feeling the presence of an amputated limb. Paré locates the origin of this sensation in a kind of movement of the nerves, as we will see later. Descartes too speaks of the movement of the nerves (as the origin of sensation) and indicates the brain as the place where sensation comes into consciousness and becomes a "knowledge." In this paper, I will discuss the two positions of the anatomist and the philosopher, since the two were among the first to speak of this sensation. I try to show the evolution of the understanding of this extraordinary medical case, which is accompanied by a mechanistic idea of the human body. The most interesting point is that the information that arises from the sensation is the same, even if the place of origin is different in the case of a present member or a "phantom limb."

Descartes tries to explain this extraordinary sensation mechanically and so he not only transmits the spirit of the times, but it also seems that he supports the idea of the doctors and surgeons of the Renaissance who began to conceive the human body as if it has mechanical devices, like Paré for example. The term mechanical is here to be understood as 'machine-like'[8] rather than 'based on the laws of mechanics', even if Descartes is already interested in understanding the human body with the laws of nature and physics.[9] Thus, I will try to prove that Descartes could understand the complex sensation that is the pain in missing limbs only by considering the nervous system as 'mechanical', which is an original new thinking pathway and which is based on the mechanical conceptions of the human limbs that we can find in Paré.

The overall objective of this paper is to underline that Paré and Descartes are pioneers in the recognition of sensation in amputated limbs and that an explanation of this sensation by Descartes is only possible when the sensation is no longer localized in the limb of the body but the brain. Descartes' conception is innovative and closely linked to a mechanical conception of the human body. Paré, on the other hand, does not go so far as to find a 'mechanical' explanation of the pain in missing limbs, even if he considers the movement of the limb as 'mechanical'. However, we can consider him the first to put words on this unusual feeling and to describe it.

To comprehend the origins of Descartes' idea of the role of the nerves in the sensation of this missing arm (see Fig. 1), I will start by providing an overview of Paré's explication of gangrene and amputation techniques, before moving on to the sensation in amputated limbs. Paré's description of this sensation will later be compared to Descartes' references, to understand the links between Paré's and Descartes' thinking. Finally, I will underline Descartes' mechanism in anatomy, by highlighting the mechanical understanding of the functioning of the nervous system.

---

8   Cf. CLAUS ZITTEL, *Theatrum philosophicum, Descartes und die Rolle ästhetischer Formen in der Wissenschaft*, Berlin, Akademie Verlag, 2009 and DENNIS DES CHENE, *Spirits&Clocks: Machine and Organism in Descartes*, Ithaca, Cornell University Press, 2001.
9   Cf. DELPHINE ANTOINE-MAHUT and STEPHEN GAUKROGER, eds, *Descartes' Treatise on Man and its Reception*, Cham, Springer, 2016.

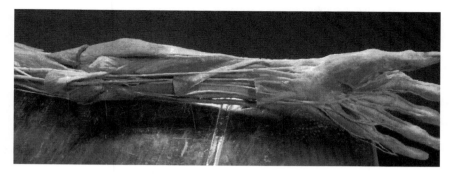

Figure 1. Nerves of the arm, photo taken at the exposition 'Bodies', hosted at the *Coque* in Luxembourg, from 8-11 October 2020.

2. Ambroise Paré: Gangrene, Amputation and Sensation in Missing Limbs

In his masterpiece, *Les Oeuvres d'Ambroise Paré, conseiller et premier chirurgien du Roy*, published in 1585, Paré dedicates the twelfth of twenty-eight books to gangrene, amputation, and the cure after amputation. This book immediately follows the book concerning the '*playes faites par hacquebutes*',[10] i.e., injuries by arquebus or gunshot injuries. This new cause of wounds necessitates a new treatment method, which Paré perfects during the years he serves in the military. The biggest concern with this new kind of wound, combined with a contusion, is the possibility of gangrene.[11] Gangrene appears because the wound is not simply located in a single place but shows continuity, i.e., it can expand or spread, and so it attacks other parts of the skin or the organs. Paré describes gangrene as the death of the injured part of the body, which is slowly decaying.[12] The decay is a slow process, which can be stopped when the surgeon provides the right treatment.

---

10 Paré's work *Dix Livres de la Chirurgie avec le magasin des instruments nécessaires à celle-ci*, published in 1564, opens with this Chapter, which proves the importance Paré dedicated to this Chapter. Cf. AMBROISE PARÉ, *Dix Livres de la Chirurgie avec le magasin des instruments nécessaires à celle-ci*, Paris, De l'imprimerie de Jean le Royer, Imprimeur de sa majesté, au vrai Pottier, 1564.
11 Gangrene for Paré was the major problem, because he abounded the idea that there was poison in the gunshots, cf. PARÉ, *Dix Livres de la Chirurgie*, Feuillet 1. The reasons of gangrene were discussed even in the seventh book of *Dix Livres de la Chirurgie*, cf. Feuillet 98: the temperament of the patient plays a role in gangrene; when there is imbalance in the four humors and temperaments gangrene progresses rapidly.
12 Cf. PARÉ, *Œuvres*, p. 480: "[…] A disposition, which tends to mortify the wounded part, which is not yet dead nor deprived of all feeling, but it is dying little by little, so that if it is not ordered soon, it will mortify itself entirely, even to the bone […]." Original: "[…] Une disposition, qui tend à mortification de la partie blessée, qui n'est encore mortes ni privée de tout sentiment, mais elle se meurt peu-à-peu, en sorte que si bientôt on n'y donne ordre, elle se mortifiera du tout, voire jusqu'aux os […]." [Translation is mine.]

Gangrene is awful: it corrupts healthy parts of the body and forces the surgeon to abandon the primary cure for the treatment of gangrene. Paré uses the image of poison which invades the whole body, or the image of a fire in dry wood: Gangrene slowly progresses through the body.[13] Only a fast intervention from the surgeon can help the patients survive. If there is already decay of one part of the skin or the limbs, then the treatment needs a delicate operation: the surgeon has to verify the loss of sensation in this part.

> If we know in the affected part blackness and coldness, coming from the extinction of the natural heat, not of the surrounding air: great softness, which if we compress cannot get up, but remains there [...] do we not feel no beating of the arteries: great stench [...], and a viscous liquor of black and green color comes out, total deprivation of feeling and movement: either one pulls, hits, presses, burns, cuts, touches, or stings: certainly will be able to conclude a perfect mortification or sphacele: however it is necessary with good judgment to explore the aforementioned deprivation of the feeling.[14]

When the surgeon concludes that the part of the body is dead, then there is only one solution: which is to amputate without hesitation.[15] Amputation is the only solution, because gangrene gains rapidly, even over the healthy parts of the body.[16] Consequently, amputation has to become a common exercise for surgeons, if they want to save their patients.

However, before amputating the gangrenous part of the body, Paré warns that other surgeons should verify if the patient has lost the sensation in this part. Very often patients still complain of pain in a dead part of the body, but this sensation is only a memory of a long-lasting pain suffered before. The surgeon should not be distracted by the complaints of his patients, because at this precise moment, the pain

---

13   Cf. Paré, Œuvres, p. 484: "[...] Such corruption travels through the whole part as venom and corrodes it as the fire does to dry wood, until finally the patients die." Original: "[...] Telle corruption chemine par toute la partie comme venin et la corrode comme fait le feu épris au bois sec, tant que finalement fera mourir les patients." [Translation is mine.]
14   Paré, Œuvres, p. 486: "Si on connaît en la partie affectée noirceur et froideur, provenant de l'extinction de la chaleur naturelle, non de l'air environnant: grande mollesse, laquelle si on comprime ne se peut relever, mais y demeure [...] ne sent-on nul battement des artères: grande puanteur [...], et en sort une liqueur visqueuse de couleur noire et verdoyante, totale privation du sentiment et mouvement: soit qu'on tire, frappe, presse, brûle, coupe, touche, ou pique: certainement pourras conclure une mortification parfaite ou sphacèle: toutefois faut avec bon jugement explorer ladite privation du sentiment." [Translation is mine.]
15   Cf. Paré, Œuvres, p. 486: "[...] It must be promptly and without delay, however small, cut and amputated." Original: "[...] La faut promptement et sans délai, tant petit soit-il, couper et amputer." [Translation is mine.]
16   Cf. Paré, Œuvres, p. 486: "[...] For contagion and corruption constantly ravish and gain the next healthy and lively parts [...] it is the only and last refuge that one must always prefer to death, which will ensue, if one seeks other means than section of the mortified part." Original: "[...] Car la contagion et corruption ravit et gagne sans cesse les parties prochaines saines et vives [...] c'est le seul et dernier refuge que l'on doit toujours préférer à la mort, laquelle s'ensuivra, si l'on cherche autres moyens que section de la partie mortifiée." [Translation is mine.]

felt is a false sensation. Paré does not deny the sensation in itself, but he wants the surgeon to understand that this sensation is no longer linked to the dead part of the body, but is only a remaining memory.

> Because I know that many have been disappointed by a feeling that patients say they have, whether one pricks, squeezes, or otherwise touches, which is totally false and disappointing. For it only comes from a great apprehension of the extreme pain, which previously was in the limb: and mainly from the continuity and consent that the dead parts still have with the living ones. [...] This false feeling will have a clear argument after the amputation of the mortified parts.[17]

Gangrene provokes a strong pain, which invades the whole limb so much that even when the part is already dead, the sensation of pain remains. Paré explains this remaining sensation by indicating the link between the living part and the dead part of the body. There is "something" between these two parts of the body, which conveys the sensation of pain. And this "something" is even present in the sensation of pain in a missing limb. After amputation, some patients continue to feel pain or the presence of a missing limb. This is because there was a link between the dead part and the living part of the body before the operation, which does not disappear with the amputation.

To understand this link or this "something" between the two parts, we should have a look at Paré's Chapter on amputation to clearly understand Paré's method of dissection and amputation and the cure he proposes. Once again, for the amputation the judgment of the surgeon is essential: the authority claims that amputation has to be prepared near the healthy part of the body to conserve the body more or less "entirely." In general, Paré agrees, but there are some exceptions. A foot is not cut near the ankle, even if the part of the lower leg is not injured, because with this cut, the leg cannot do its action. But if the leg is cut a little bit (five fingers, as Paré states in his textbook for future surgeons) under the knee, then there is a possibility to substitute the missing limb with an artificial one, while saving the functionality of the leg.[18] Amputation, due to gangrene or other causes, requires all the anatomical and medical knowledge of the surgeon, which implies the knowledge of the functionality of the limbs and the human body in general.

For Paré, amputation is a challenge: his goal is to reduce pain and to save lives. Therefore, he "made great strides in the surgical treatment for amputation; he applied ligatures to the large vessels in the limbs to staunch the bleeding following amputation and he applied tourniquets above the site of severance. As a consequence of his improved surgical techniques, more of Paré's amputees survived."[19] Furthermore,

---

17 PARÉ, Œuvres, p. 486: "Car je sais que plusieurs ont été déçus se fiant à un sentiment que les patients disent avoir, si on pique, presse, ou autrement attouche, lequel est totalement faux et deceptible. Car il ne vient que d'une grande appréhension de la douleur extrême, qui auparavant était en la partie: et principalement par la continuité et consentement qu'ont encore les parties mortes avec les vives. [...] De ce faux sentiment aura argument manifeste après l'amputation des parties mortifiées." [Translation is mine.]
18 Cf. PARÉ, Œuvres, p. 487.
19 NICHOLAS J. WADE, "Beyond body experiences: Phantom limbs, pain and the locus of sensation," Cortex 45, 2009, 243-255, p. 246. Cf. HUARD and GRMEK, La chirurgie moderne, p. 117.

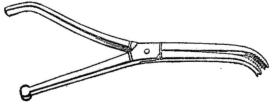

Figure 2. 'Pinces à bec de corbin', in Ambroise Paré, *Œuvres complètes d'Ambroise Paré*, edition from 1585, ed. by J.-F. Malgaigne, Paris, Baillière, 2 vols, 1840-1841, vol. 2, Book 10, ch. 22, p. 224. Source: www.gallica.fr/BNF.

"he demanded that all the soft parts were cut before sawing the skeleton, which was not always done in his time."[20] The most important step for Paré is the ligature of vessels; for this, he develops specialized tools, such as the '*pinces à bec de corbin*'.[21] (see Fig. 2) This method is crucial to saving lives because sewing the wound and not burning it, means the patient suffers less and has a better chance to heal. The burning method, on the contrary, is more common, but gangrene is frequently the consequence, which leads to a new amputation.

So Paré is innovative in his treatments, not only for amputation in itself but even in his cure. As he accompanies the patients during the healing process, he notices the need of substituting limbs with artificial limbs that perfectly mimic the functionality of the body limbs. His development of prostheses is famous and well known. In this context, Paré even notices this 'strange' sensation in missing limbs. According to him, this sensation is provoked by the retreat of the nerves to their origin.[22] This explanation differs from that Paré gave for the decay of parts of the body. For the decay, Paré speaks of a false sensation, but for amputation, he recognizes this sensation as real. However, in the first extract, Paré writes that patients say they feel the pain and, in this extract, he writes that the patients think they feel it. The sensation in the missing limb is not considered false, but Paré seems to understand it as a thought and not as a sensation. Is it an illusion of the mind? Or how can we understand this thought of a sensation?

Paré does not give more details about sensation and thought, and we can only understand this link by reading Descartes, because Paré does not go so far as to find the origin of all

---

20 HUARD and GRMEK, *La chirurgie moderne*, p. 117.
21 There were even other tools, invented by Paré, as shown in *Dix Livres de la Chirurgie*, Feuillet 4-11, which are used in ligature of vessels, and for extracting bullet residues and other intruders.
22 Cf. PARÉ, *Œuvres*, p. 492: "Now it is so that long after the amputation, the patients still think they have the whole of the limb that has been amputated, as I said, which happens to them, as it seems to me, because the nerves retreat to their origin." Original: "Or il est ainsi que longtemps après l'amputation, les patients pensent encore avoir en son entier le membre qui leur a été amputé, comme j'ai dit: ce qui leur advient, comme il me semble pour ce que les nerfs se retirent vers leur origine." [Translation is mine.]

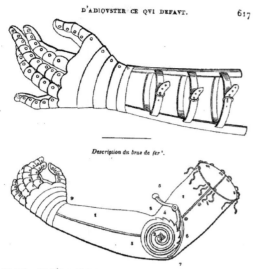

Figure 3. 'Artifical devices', in Ambroise Paré, Œuvres d'Ambroise Paré, edition from 1585, ed. by J.-F. Malgaigne, Paris, Baillière, 2 vols, 1840-1841, vol. 2, Book 17, ch. 22, p. 617. Source: www.gallica.fr/BNF.

the sensations, but only tries to explain how this sensation of pain in a missing limb can be possible. According to Paré, the nerves retreat to their origin. But in what way does this retreat or contraction provoke a sensation in a missing limb? Paré goes further in his explanation by referring to Galen (which proves that traditional medical knowledge was essential for surgeons and anatomists). According to Galen, and Paré agrees, contractions are the result of the action of the nerves and muscles. This can provoke pain, like the retractions during spasms.[23] The contraction of the nerves explains the pain, but Paré does not say, why the contraction is painful, nor why the nerves retreat to their origin when a limb is cut. The last question seems to be easily understandable: when the brain sends nerve flows to the limbs of the body and this nerve flow comes to an abrupt stop

---

23   Cf. PARÉ, Œuvres, p. 492: "For, as Galen writes [...], contraction is the true and proper action of the nerve and muscle, [...]. Now the nerves in withdrawing make great pain, and almost similar to the retractions which are made in spasms." Original: "Car, comme écrit Galien [...], contraction est la vraie et propre action du nerf et muscle, [...]. Or les nerfs en se retirant font grande douleur, et presque semblable aux rétractions qui se font aux spasmes." [Translation is mine.]

because of the missing limb, then the flow resumes in the opposite direction, i.e., to the brain. Paré, as already mentioned, does not affirm that the place of the control of the nerves is the brain because, in his time, there is no precise indication of this location. This only became an occupation for physicians and philosophers since Descartes.

However, stipulating that this place is the brain, our understanding seems consistent. The retreat of the nerves is explained by the missing limb which cannot act. This can even explain why there is pain. First, there is an abrupt stop of the nerve flow, which then has to go in the opposite direction; secondly, the intended action cannot be performed, and therefore at the end of the nerves, one feels a kind of tingling coming from this will to trigger an action. Paré seems to be incapable of explaining the origin of the pain in a missing limb, probably because he did not localize the nerve control in the brain. For him, the nerves do not find the device to complete the action, that is why they go in the opposite direction and trigger pain. But the question remains: why is there pain? Descartes will try to respond in a very mechanical way, which is influenced by the mechanical understanding of the human limbs by Paré. The latter invents artificial devices (see Fig. 3), imitating mechanically the functioning of the human limbs, but as he does not search for a first "principle" of movements and nerves, he cannot locate the origin of pain.

3. Descartes on Sensation in Missing Limbs

In the *Principia philosophiae (Principles of philosophy)*, published in 1644, Descartes describes the cure of a young girl's arm, which has to be amputated, due to gangrene, and the sensation of her missing limb:

> A girl with a seriously infected hand used to have her eyes bandaged whenever the surgeon visited her, to prevent her being upset by the surgical instruments. After a few days her arm was amputated at the elbow because of a creeping gangrene, and wads of bandages were put in its place so that she was quite unaware that she had lost her arm. However, she continued to complain of pains, now in one then in another finger of the amputated hand. The only possible reason for this is that the nerves which used to go from the brain down to the hand now terminated in the arm near the elbow, and were being agitated by the same sorts of motion as must previously have been set up in the hand, so as to produce in the soul, residing in the brain, the sensation of pain in this or that finger. And this shows clearly that pain in the hand is felt by the soul not because it is present in the hand but because it is present in the brain.[24]

From this passage, it is unclear if Descartes has read this experience in some anatomical treatises or if he has attended surgery and participated during this surgical intervention. However, in a letter to Fromondus in 1637, he already speaks about this experience,

---

24 René Descartes, *Principia philosophiae* IV, art. 196, AT VIII-1 320; CSM I 283-284.

so that it possibly occurs during his early years in the Netherlands, and that he has witnessed the surgery of amputation.

> For they know that those whose limbs have recently been amputated often think they still feel pain in the parts they no longer possess. I once knew a girl who had a serious wound in her hands and had her whole arm amputated because of creeping gangrene. Whenever the surgeon approached her, they blindfolded her eyes [...] and the place where her arm had been was so covered with bandages that for some weeks, she did not know that she had lost it. Meanwhile she complained of feeling various pain in her fingers, wrist and forearm; and this was obviously due to the condition of the nerves in her arm which formerly led from her brain to those parts of her body. This would certainly not have happened of the feeling or, as he says, sensation of pain occurred outside the brain.[25]

In this letter, Descartes confirms that he has known the young girl so that we can exclude the role of an external observer, who is the reader of anatomy treatises. Descartes has witnessed this amputation and has seen the patient afterward during the healing process. So, he reports that after the amputation she felt great pain in the missing limb. The explanation and the description of the sensation are nearly the same in the letter and in the *Principles*, where Descartes links the explanation of sensation to his theory of vision. This link to the theory of vision will be explained later, but for now: a detailed description of the young girl's sensation helps Descartes to affirm that sensation has its starting point in the brain.

As Paré, Descartes writes here, that amputated patients think they feel pain. Does Descartes, like Paré, relate sensation and thought? And how will he explain that different stimulations of the ends of the nerves cause the same sensation? As already mentioned, the letter to Fromondus seems to be more precise about the description of the sensation of pain. Differently to the text of the *Principles*, Descartes mentions here the pain in the fingers, in the metacarpus, and the elbow. These details are not mentioned in the other text, where Descartes only speaks of the pain in the fingers, which shows that in 1637, Descartes gives a lot of importance to anatomical interest and knowledge, even in a single letter. Nevertheless, the explication of this extraordinary sensation remains the same. As written by Stanley Finger and Meredith P. Hustwit, pain from an amputated limb "may be triggered by stimulation of the remaining nerves. One of the functions of these nerves is to transmit sensory information to the brain, where it is then accessible to the mind or soul in human beings."[26] All the sensory information goes to the brain so that the place of sensation is also located in the brain, namely in the soul, where sensation causes impressions or thoughts. For Descartes, pain in a missing limb is extraordinary as a sensation in itself but natural in referring to the functioning of the nerves.

---

25 Descartes to Fromondus, 3 October 1637, AT I 420; CSMK 64.
26 STANLEY FINGER and MEREDITH P. HUSTWIT, "Five early accounts of phantom limb in context: Paré, Descartes, Lemos, Bell and Mitchell", *Neurosurgery* 52 (2003), 675-686 (p. 678).

> A meaningful point is that this example of a missing limb and its sensation is linked to a discussion about vision. Colours are not in the object but in the brain; like sensation, that is in the brain and not coming from the missing limb. Let us focus on the passage of the *Optiks*, that is problematic for Fromondus.

> And we know that it is not, properly speaking, because of its presence in the parts of the body which function as organs of the external senses that the soul has sensory perceptions, but because of its presence in the brain, where it exercises the faculty called the 'common' sense. For we observe injuries and diseases which attack the brain alone and impede all the senses generally, even though the rest of the body continues to be animated.[27]

Descartes maintains that it is the soul that feels and not the body: this is because the soul is in the brain to which all the impressions are transmitted, and not in the parts of the body. The impressions are transmitted by the nerves to the brain and that is why the soul can feel. Consequently, if Descartes accepts that pain or sensation in a missing limb proceeds like the vision of colour, then he has to accept that there must be a stimulus. There must be something that provokes sensation, which also means that the organs or members of the body must still be able to receive this stimulus: the amputation does not make the possibility to feel a stimulus disappear.

> We know, lastly, that it is through the nerves that the impressions formed by objects in the external parts of the body reach the soul in the brain. For we observe various accidents which cause injury only to a nerve, and destroy sensation in all the parts of the body to which this nerve sends its branches, without causing it to diminish elsewhere.[28]

Descartes, therefore, agrees with Paré, who suggests that with amputation the nerves are not 'dead', but their flow is stopped and redirected. The example of the pain in the missing limb has to underline Descartes' position: the sensation is felt in the brain by the soul and not in the body part (which in the case of the amputated limb is missing) so that the feeling of a stimulus is still guaranteed. He repeats this idea in the Sixth Meditation:

> In similar fashion, when I feel pain in my foot, physiology tells me that his happens by means of nerves distributed throughout the foot, and that these nerves are like cords which go from the foot right up to the brain. When the nerves are pulled in the foot, they in turn pull on inner parts of the brain to which they are attached, and produce a certain *motion* in them; and nature has laid it down that this motion should produce in the mind a sensation of pain, as occurring in the foot.[29]

Descartes thinks of pain as being only in the brain[30] and communicated by the nerves. Pain is felt because nerves, functioning like cords, bind the injured part of

---

27 *La Dioptrique*, Discourse Four, AT VI 109; CSM I 164.
28 *La Dioptrque*, Discourse Four, AT VI 109; CSM I 164-165.
29 *Meditationes de prima philosophia* VI, AT VII 87; CSM II 60.
30 Cf. Descartes to Mersenne, 11 June 1640, AT III 85.

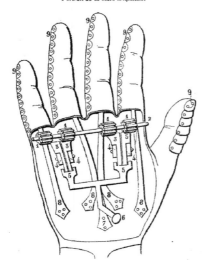

Figure 4. 'Artificial hand' in Ambroise Paré, Œuvres d'Ambroise Paré, edition from 1585, ed. by J.-F. Malgaigne, Paris, Baillière, 2 vols, 1840-1841, vol. 2, Book 17, ch. 22, p. 616. Source: www.gallica.fr/BNF.

the body to the brain: nerves, even when cut, are not dead. We see that Descartes' understanding of sensation and the functioning of the nerves in the body are explained mechanically[31], i.e., in terms of size, shape, and motions. Descartes probably recorded Paré's artificial hand (see Fig. 4). Paré's main idea is to create prostheses with artificial devices imitating the functioning of the nerves and muscles in the human body. Descartes too speaks of "branches", "filets", "tuyau" and even "cordes,"[32] which look like the devices of a machine and which guide and stimulate the nerves.

---

[31] Cf. DANIEL GARBER, "Descartes, Mechanics, and the Mechanical Philosophy", *Midwest Studies in Philosophy* 26 (2002), p. 185-204, p. 198: "[…] His point in establishing a correspondence between the artificial machine and the natural body was that we can now explain everything that happens in the natural body in exactly the same way in which we explain what happens in the artificial machine."

[32] The word "corde" is used in the description of the human heart and the nerves, linking the parts of the body to the brain. These 'cordes' are similar to the strings of a lute, of which Descartes speaks in the *Compendium musicae*. If one of these strings is touched then the others around them shake and resonate spontaneously, as do the nerves in the body too. A similar description can be found in the

However, even if the ends of the nerves cut are not dead, Descartes cannot affirm that the sensation they feel is really pain. It is much more likely that they feel only a kind of triggering, and that the brain understands this triggering as pain, remembering the pain that was in this limb before the amputation. In the First Meditation, Descartes recommends caution when dealing with the senses, whose information is always to be verified. First of all, the sensation cannot provide evidence and must be verified every time. Secondly, the memory of some sensations can alter the actual sensation or even "impose" information. This is probably what happens in the case of sensation in amputated limbs. Therefore, Descartes underlines that the patients think they feel pain, not because he is not sure about the sensation in itself, but about the denomination: it is possible that the corresponding feeling is not pain, but only a kind of triggering of stimulus. It is the stimulus that is linked in the brain to the feeling of pain, as Descartes says in the Sixth Meditation.

Descartes' mechanical reasoning about sensations concerns not only the sensation of a missing limb but all sensations. From the *Dioptrique*, and even from the Sixth Meditation, we learn that Descartes argues that the nerves are responsible not only for the sensation but even for the movement. According to him, sensation and movement are inseparably linked to each other. Domenico Bertoloni Meli correctly remarks: Descartes "[…] refers to tubes and filaments in the nerves responsible for external sensation and muscular motion; while the motions and vibrations of those filaments would transmit external sensory experiences to the brain, the tubes enclosing them would convey animal spirits to the muscles, thus explaining muscular motion in a hydraulic fashion. Thus, in this case one structure would serve a dual purpose because the same nerves would account for motion and sensation, depending on whether they convey a fluid or their inner filaments shake and vibrate."[33] And Nicholas J. Wade notes: "Descartes considered that the skin consisted of nerve endings; when these were overstimulated (as by fire), mechanical signals were transmitted via the animal spirit along the nerves to the brain, where pain was perceived."[34] Pain is perceived probably because the mechanical signals coming from the nerve endings in amputated limbs were similar to the mechanical signals of pain.

The idea of spirits is explained in the *Dioptrique*, where Descartes speaks of the spirits and little nets.[35] The spirits pass through the nerves to the muscles, which

---

Optics. The 'filets' are in the 'tuyaux', that are the nerves. These filets are so tight that if you touch one end of the rope ('corde'), the movement spreads to the other end of the rope. Descartes' description of the functioning of the nerves is therefore similar to his theory of sound and vibration in the *Compendium musicae*. Cf. on the similarity between the theory of sound and vibration and the mechanical description of the nerves: FRANÇOIS DUCHESNEAU, *Les modèles du vivant de Descartes à Leibniz*, Paris, Vrin, 1998, p. 70: "Thus Descartes compares the neuromotor system to the church organ and its pipes […]."

33 DOMENICO BERTOLONI MELI, *Mechanism A Visual, Lexical, and Conceptual History*, Pittsburg, University of Pittsburg Press, 2019, p. 61-62. Cf. DES CHENE, *Spirits&Clocks*, p. 61-64.
34 WADE, "Beyond body experience", p. 251.
35 Even Paré invokes the spirits: animal spirit is transmitted from the brain by the nerfs to cause sensation and movement. *Dix Livres de la Chirurgie*, feuillet 98.

are swelled differently and so cause the movement. And the little nets are used by the sensation.³⁶ The prevailing belief, that Descartes adopted, "was that the animal spirit flowed through the hollow nerves from the senses to the ventricles in the brain."³⁷ The spirits are responsible for the movements, by swelling the different muscles and the little nets are responsible for sensation, but both are located in the same place. This makes the instinctive reaction to a special sensation or feeling possible, such as the movement of the arm when it approaches the fire. Consequently, we understand that the feeling produced in the missing hand is a sort of triggering of the nerves, which goes back to the brain, transported by the animal spirits, which touch the brain in a certain place, with some speed, etc., and leave traces. These traces are understood by the brain as pain because they could be linked to an earlier sensation.

4. Conclusion

The analysis of Paré's and Descartes' understanding of sensation in missing limbs shows us that both were pioneers in this domain. If Paré uses the mechanical view of the human body to better understand its functioning, and that of the muscles and the nerves, Descartes goes further with this mechanical³⁸ view, by using it for the explanation of the sensation of pain. For Paré, when an amputated patient feels pain in a missing limb, then there must be a stimulus to the nerve endings that allows this sensation: nerves are cut during amputation, but they are not "dead." The nerves' "flow" is only interrupted but not removed. For Descartes, the sensation of pain is explained by sensory information, due to a triggering of the nerves' ends, which send vibrations to the tubes up to the brain. These mechanical signals look like those previously associated with pain, that is why the patient thinks he feels pain.

With this study of sensation in amputated limbs, I underline a crucial point of investigation in seventeenth century, a point that separates Paré from Descartes: while Paré is not yet looking for the origin or 'starting point' of the nerves, even if he speaks of the retreat of the nerves to their origin, from Descartes, physicians and philosophers analyse "the culmination of all nervous pathways."³⁹ Since Descartes, it is interesting for doctors and philosophers to understand how sensation is possible, and where the nerves find their origin and their final destination. The final destination is the brain, where sensory information comes into consciousness and is linked in the soul to a thought and a denomination.

---

36 Cf. *La Dioptrique*, Discourse Four, AT VI 111; this part is not translated in CSM. Here my translation: "It must be thought that it is the spirits, flowing through the nerves into the muscles, and swelling them more or less, sometimes one, sometimes another, according to the various ways in which the brain distributes them, that cause the movement of all the limbs; and that it is the little nets, of which the inner substance of these nerves is composed, that serve the senses."
37 WADE, "Beyond body experience", p. 247.
38 Cf. GARBER, "Descartes, Mechanics", p. 199.
39 HUARD and GRMEK, *La chirurgie moderne*, p. 63.

The main element of the question is to understand how Descartes, inspired by Paré's mechanical conception of the functioning of the limbs, explains mechanically how sensation is triggered and where it is "transformed" to reveal sensory information. As for Descartes, the sensation is considered as a thought, its location is the brain: all the sensory information goes to the brain, where it causes a sensation, i.e., where the mechanical signals are linked to a thought and a name. Furthermore, the missing limb anecdote proves that pain cannot, logically speaking, be in the part of the body, so it must be in the brain. Descartes uses a mechanical understanding of the nerves functioning to explain how pain is triggered and even felt in a missing limb.

A hydraulic vision of the human body is already found in Paré, who uses this image of the body as a machine to invent artificial limbs imitating the functioning of the human body. "[...] If a process could be rendered visually, then it is a candidate for a mechanistic interpretation,"[40] which is the case for example for the movement of the human hand. Consequently, for medicine, it is essential that anatomists, but even philosophers, study the human body as if it is a machine[41]: the inner functioning of organs and limbs can be virtually imagined and so can be replaced by artificial devices.

Let us come back for a little moment to the sensation in a missing body part. Both Paré and Descartes affirm that there can be a sensation of the presence of this part of the body or that there can be pain. However, neither of them already distinguishes between these different feelings. Descartes only asks in the Sixth Meditation: "Is there anything more intimate or more interior than pain?,"[42] and thus underlines that pain is something personal and subjective. Accepting that pain is personal or intimate and that it depends on the temperament of the patient is an important element in the treatment of injuries or amputation, and even Paré underlines this point. However, today we can distinguish between different sensations, also because we have the psychological background for this distinction.

Looking back on Paré's and Descartes' description, we can affirm that they probably speak of phantom sensation and phantom limb pain. "Phantom sensation is defined as any sensory perception of the missing body part with the exclusion of pain."[43] And "phantom limb pain is defined as any noxious sensory phenomenon of the missing limb or organ. [...] Pain can be immediate or delayed in onset."[44] By taking account of the patient's sensation and the description he can offer about this pain, it is possible today to classify and even distinguish different types of pain. So, the phantom limb pain differs from the stump pain, which is localized "to the site of

---

40 BERTOLONI MELI, *Mechanism*, p. 77.
41 DOMENICO BERTOLONI MELI, "Machines and the Body between Anatomy and Pathology", in *L'Automate: Modèle Métaphore Machine Merveille*, ed. by AURÉLIA GAILLARD et al., Bordeaux, Presses universitaires de Bordeaux, 2013, p. 56-63.
42 DESCARTES, *Meditationes de prima philosophia*, VI, AT VII 77; CSM II 53.
43 STEPHAN A. SCHUG and GAIL GILLESPIE, "Post-amputation Pain", in *Mechanisms of Vascular Disease*, ed. by ROBERT FITRIDGE and MATTHEW THOMPSON, Adelaide, Australia, University of Adelaide Press, 2011, p. 390.
44 SCHUG and GILLESPIE, "Post-amputation Pain", p. 390.

amputation." "Stump pain is problematic and can interfere with prosthesis use."[45] Probably Paré has heard of this kind of pain and has seen problematic prosthesis use, but he cannot name this pain. Nevertheless, the most important direction in the treatment is taking into account the personal sensation of the patient,[46] as remarked by both Paré and Descartes.

---

45 SCHUG and GILLESPIE, "Post-amputation Pain", p. 389.
46 Cf. IAN MACLEAN, *Le monde et les hommes selon les médecins de la Renaissance*, Paris, CNRS Éditions, 2006.

ANNIE BITBOL-HESPÉRIÈS

Anatomical Debates on Hearts and Brains and Philosophical Issues from Descartes' Writing of *L'Homme* to its Posthumous Publications*

▼ ABSTRACT   After describing Descartes' medical library: "Vesalius and the others" and the writing of *L'Homme*, I emphasize the importance of anatomical knowledge and of the practice of dissections.

I discuss the gap between *L'Homme* and the *Discours de la méthode*. I investigate the reasons of such a discrepancy and insist on the crucial moment of late 1632 when Descartes wrote to Mersenne about his dissections of "the heads of various animals" in order "to explain what imagination, memory, etc., consist in." In the same letter Descartes mentioned his reading of the *De motu cordis* by Harvey (AT I, 263, CSMK 40) a treatise on the movement of the heart also explaining another fundamental discovery: the circulation of the blood.

The anatomical problems Descartes had to face about hearts and brains provide the key to understanding the evolution of Descartes' thoughts. They led him to introduce new themes in the *Discours* and the *Dioptrique*. The challenge of the motion of the heart shows the entanglement of metaphysical and medical themes. The anatomy of the brain, even more than the anatomy of the heart, has given rise to medical, philosophical, metaphysical and religious considerations and controversies. Descartes' dissections of hearts and brains led to confront the problem of both the status and the location of the principle of life, and to consider the specificity of the human soul, and to pay attention to the unique mental faculties of imagination, reason and memory. These questions fitted in the framework of the *Nature on Man*, whose theme Descartes delved into in the *Discours*, the sixth Meditation, the *Passions de l'âme* and the *Description du corps humain*. The *Description* was published posthumously with *L'Homme* in

Annie Bitbol-Hespériès • Centre d'Études Cartésiennes, Paris, France. Contact: <annie.bitbol@wanadoo.fr>

1664 in Paris with a Préface (Foreword) by Clerselier and *Remarques* by La Forge.

▼ KEYWORDS Anatomy, Hearts, Brains, Principle of Life, Specificity of the Human Nature, Mechanics, Vesalius, Fabricius ab Aquapendente, Bauhin, Harvey.

Descartes became interested in medicine at the end of 1629. He had not studied medicine and he did not try to hold a degree from a medical university in those days when medical teaching was poor in its quality and unequal in its content from one university to the other. The use of human dissections was scarce. There was an exception in Europe: Padua, the University of the Republic of Venice, where the famous Girolamus Fabricius ab Aquapendente had taught for more than 40 years, with Caspar Bauhin and William Harvey among his students.

1. Descartes' Medical Library and the Writing of *L'Homme*: *"ce n'est pas un crime d'être curieux de l'anatomie"*[1]

Descartes dealt in medicine while writing an ambitious treatise in French — not in Latin — including the new cosmology and the foundation of the laws of nature. In this text combining science and metaphysics, *Le Monde (The World)*, Descartes decided to include a chapter about *L'Homme (On Man)*.

For Descartes, writing on this topic meant dealing with medicine and first of all with anatomy. He began to study anatomy in December 1629,[2] reading "Vesalius and the others" and observing "while dissecting various animals."[3]

Descartes acknowledged a debt towards Andreas Vesalius as a starting point for his knowledge of anatomy. The reference to such a name and the importance devoted to observation through dissections have to be considered seriously. In *L'Homme* as well as in *Le Monde*, Descartes wanted to draw information from the most recent sources: from Copernicus to Galileo in cosmology, from 'Vesalius' to 'the others'

---

* Many thanks to Dr Fabrizio Baldassarri for his kind invitation and for his willingness in organizing the online Pisa conference. A portion of this paper has been read at *Le cerveau cartésien: problèmes et controverses*, Paris, atelier international, 11 and 12 October 2019: « De *L'Homme* au *Discours de la méthode* et à la *Dioptrique* : Descartes face à l'anatomie du cerveau. Enjeux médicaux, anthropologiques et métaphysiques ». The illustrations in this article are from books kept in the Réserve (rare books room) of the Bibliothèque Interuniversitaire Santé, Médecine, in Paris (BIUS), where I have spent so many pleasant and fruitful hours. They are reproduced with kind permission from the BIUS. I wish to thank the Librairians Jean-François Vincent, Estelle Lambert and Stéphanie Charreaux for the illustrations kindly provided also during the conferences.

1 Descartes to Mersenne, 13 November 1639, AT II 621.
2 Descartes to Mersenne, 18 December 1629, AT I 102.
3 Descartes to Mersenne, 20 February 1639, AT II 525; CSMK 134.

in anatomy. Descartes was writing in the wake of the most recent ideas, those resulting from the famous year 1543, with the publications of both Copernicus' *De revolutionibus orbium coelestium* and of Vesalius' *De humani corporis fabrica*. Vesalius' aim was to show the "fabric of the human body" and to restore the "lost knowledge of the human body."[4] The word *fabrica* refers to a conception of the human body as an admirable work made by an *Opifex*, or by Nature associated with Providence. The superb images with articulated skeletons, with *écorchés*: flayed men revealing their muscles while standing or walking in a hilly landscape, stage the human body, a masterpiece of Nature. A body studied through human dissections, as shown in the title page of the *Fabrica*, repeated in the *Epitome* and the second edition of the *Fabrica* in 1555. And the dissection has to be performed by the anatomist himself, as Vesalius proved it by his example on the title page. This was a break with the traditional teaching based on Galen read during the lesson by the teacher of anatomy while the *prosector* was opening and showing the parts of the body. With Vesalius, the anatomy lesson aimed to show the organs and their perfect adequacy to the functioning of the human body, — and this can be associated with the Galenist tradition of admiration for the human body. The male body being the most perfect and the female one the most secret. But with Vesalius the anatomy lesson also aimed to denounce the errors of Galen who mostly dissected animals. From that moment on, emphasis was given to the sight and to the touch in anatomy. If the human body has to be admired, it is also because it holds its dignity from the soul that gives life. But where is the soul in the body? This question was based on the debate between Aristotle and Galen about the seat of the soul, either in the heart or in the brain.

Descartes associated the name of Vesalius with 'others', which means that other anatomists had followed his example.

This was the case in the Low Countries with a revival of interest towards Vesalius, as can be shown from some anatomical books inspired by Vesalius and published in small format in the seventeenth century (smaller than the *in-folio* volumes in which Vesalius's and Fabricius's works were usually published). This aspect of medical life is also shown in Rembrandt's famous *Anatomy of Dr Tulp*, painted in 1632 in Amsterdam when Descartes was writing *L'Homme*. This historical painting evokes the only one public anatomy in Amsterdam during the winter 1632, an anatomy performed by Dr Tulp[5] on a man condemned to death and who had been hanged the day before the dissection began. This painting of the members of the Anatomical guild belongs to the history of medicine and ideas in an amazing manner because what is shown is

---

4   ANDREAS VESALIUS, *De humani corporis fabrica*, Basel, Oporinus, 1543, Foreword: "emortuam humani corporis partium scientiam."
5   Nicolaes Tulp (1593-1674): Claes Pieterszoon or Nicolaus Petreus. On this painting in La Haye (Mauritshuis), see WILLIAM S. HECKSCHER, *Rembrandt's anatomy of Dr Nicolaas Tulp*, ch. VIII, New York, 1958 and my articles: ANNIE BITBOL-HESPÉRIÈS, "Connaissance de l'homme, connaissance de Dieu", *Les Études Philosophiques* (1996), p. 507-533; ANNIE BITBOL-HESPÉRIÈS, "Cartesian Physiology", in *Descartes' Natural Philosophy*, ed. by Stephen Gaukroger, John Schuster and John Sutton, London-New York, Routledge, 2000, p. 349-382. See also, RENÉ DESCARTES, *Le Monde, L'Homme*, ed. by Annie Bitbol-Hespériès, Paris, Le Seuil, 2000, Introduction.

an imaginary anatomical lesson simply because in those days no anatomy would ever begin with the arm. It would end with it. No doubt that Dr Tulp asked Rembrandt to portray him while dissecting the muscles of the forearm that allow the fingers to move, because he wanted to be seen as "The risen Vesalius," "Vesalius redivivus:"[6] Vesalius' large woodcut portrait, that is found at the beginning of the *Fabrica* shows him dissecting a forearm.

At the same moment in Europe, books were printed in the Vesalian style. This is the case for the *Theatrum anatomicum* (Frankfurt, 1605, enlarged, 1620-1621), famous all over Europe, written by Caspar Bauhin, professor of medicine in Basel. Bauhin was the most important among the 'other' anatomists read by Descartes.[7] Bauhin's smaller books than Vesalius' *Fabrica* brought together, completed and updated the anatomical drawings found in Vesalius' books. These images did help Descartes from the moment when he began to practice his anatomical experiments. In 1629, Descartes lived in Kalverstraat, street of the calves, meaning street of the butchers, who supplied him with fresh organs to dissect.[8]

Descartes' knowledge of anatomy comes from Vesalius and Bauhin, and Descartes' knowledge of embryology comes from Fabricius of Aquapendente and from Descartes' own anatomical experiments.[9] Descartes' Latin fragments, the *Primæ cogitationes circa generationem animalium (First Thoughts about the Generation of Animals)* and the *Excerpta anatomica* prove that he had read the two embryological treatises by Fabricius: *De formatione ovi et pulli (The formation of the egg and chick)* and *De formato fœtu (The formed fetus)*. These books have magnificent engraved plates showing the formation of the chick, showing a uterus, aborted human fetuses with their membranes and their umbilical cord and pregnant female animal bodies and various mammalian embryos. Fabricius' books showed that Nature does nothing in vain. According to Fabricius, the degrees of the soul — vegetative and nutritive — have to be taken into consideration in the study of generation.[10]

It has to be noted that all the physicians and surgeons in Europe agreed that the human body draws its life, that is to say its animation, its motion, from the soul or *vital principle* or *principle of life*. The human body is the "dwelling of the soul."[11] Death meant the 'departure' of that soul. Jean Riolan the Younger clearly stated: "Man is composed of two really different natures, the soul and the body. The former, which is linked with the body, is the principle of life and of all the actions, and therefore the form and perfection of the body."[12]

In June 1632, Descartes wrote to Mersenne that in *Le Monde*, he had decided not to include "how animals are generated," "because it would have taken [him]

---

6 Cf. HECKSCHER, *Rembrandt's anatomy of Dr Nicolaas Tulp*, p. 65.
7 ANNIE BITBOL-HESPÉRIÈS, *Le principe de vie chez Descartes*, Paris, Vrin, 1990.
8 Descartes to Mersenne, 13 November 1639, AT II 621.
9 Descartes to Mersenne, 2 November 1646, AT IV, 555.
10 HIERONYMUS FABRICIUS AB AQUAPENDENTE, *De formatione ovi et pulli*, Padua, 1621 part II, ch. 1, p. 111-112.
11 ANDRÉ DU LAURENS, *Historia anatomica*, Paris, 1600 (French translation by Sizé, Paris 1610).
12 JEAN RIOLAN THE YOUNGER, *Anthropographia*, Paris, 1618, 1626 (French translation 1629).

too long"¹³ and this is confirmed in the *Discourse on Method*.¹⁴ Descartes added that he "had finished all that he had planned in his treatise about inanimate bodies" and that he "only has to add something concerning the nature on man." He will then write a 'fair copy' and send it to Mersenne, though he dared not say when that will be, because he had already failed his promise.¹⁵

The question of the *Nature on man* has been a crucial one in medicine since the eponymous famous treatise in the Hippocratic corpus¹⁶ commented by Galen. This treatise became associated with the Christian anthropology and the importance of the passions of the soul, which leads to the 'obscure' question of the union of the soul to the body, to the difficult study of the senses, especially sight, and to the division of the soul into three parts in medical treatises: *naturalis or vegetativa* (in the plants), *sentiens or sensitiva* (in the beasts, *bruta*), *intelligens or rationalis* (in human beings).¹⁷

In November or December 1632, Descartes explained to Mersenne: "My discussion about man in *Le Monde* will be a little fuller than I had intended, for I have undertaken to explain all the main functions in man. I have already written of the vital functions, such as the digestion of food, the heartbeat, the distribution of nourishment, etc., and the five senses. I am now dissecting the heads of various animals, so that I can explain what imagination, memory, etc., consist in."¹⁸ In the same letter, Descartes also wrote that he had read the Latin treatise *De motu cordis*, mentioned to him by Mersenne 'previously' *autrefois*. Descartes added that his explanation of the movement of the heart "differs slightly from [his] own view, although [he] saw it only after having finished writing on this topic."¹⁹ The treatise explaining the movement of the heart is also the treatise explaining the movement of the blood in living creatures. In these two brilliant demonstrations by William Harvey, a fully qualified medical doctor, anatomy is of paramount importance as shown in the title *Exercitatio anatomica de motu cordis et sanguinis in animalibus, An Anatomical Disputation of the Movement of the Heart and the Blood in Living Creatures*. For us, the movement of the heart and blood circulation are just obvious. But both of them are Harvey's own discovery, published in 1628 in Frankfurt.

This letter to Mersenne reflects an important moment in Descartes' intellectual life as well as in his intellectual evolution. Descartes had a deep dialogue with the sciences of his time and as far as anatomy is concerned he worked a lot not only dissecting hearts and brains, foetuses, eyes, but also taking into account the text and the context of the anatomical images. It then becomes clear that the entanglement

---

13 Descartes to Mersenne, June 1632, AT I 254; CSMK 39.
14 *Discours de la Méthode*, V, AT VI, 45-46.
15 Descartes to Mersenne, AT I 254-255, CSMK 39.
16 Written by Polybus but attributed to Hippocrates by Galen.
17 See my chapter, ANNIE BITBOL-HESPÉRIÈS, "De toute la nature de l'homme: De *L'Homme* à la *Description du corps humain*, la physiologie des *Passions de l'âme* et ses antécédents médicaux," in *Les* Passions de l'âme *et leur réception philosophique*, ed. by Giulia Belgioioso and Vincent Carraud, Turnhout, Brepols, 2020, p. 67-100.
18 Descartes to Mersenne, November or December 1632, AT I 263, CSMK 40.
19 Descartes to Mersenne, November or December 1632, AT I 263, CSMK 40.

of anatomical questions with philosophical issues and religious concerns delayed the writing of *L'Homme* and forced Descartes to modify it.

After the reading of the true anatomical novelties contained in Harvey's Treatise about the movements of the heart and of the blood and after the reading of the chapters on the anatomy of the brain in the books by "Vesalius and the others," Descartes faced complex issues whose stake goes beyond medicine. He understood that he needed to modify some parts in *L'Homme*, before giving it up, while allowing copies to be made, and he also probably realized that he needed to correct and complete the *Regulæ* before he abandoned them. Descartes' silence in the following months is significant, as is the announcement to Mersenne on July 22, 1633 that *Le Monde*, which includes *L'Homme*, is "almost completed, but that he still has to correct and describe it" and that he has "trouble working on it." Descartes hoped to keep his *promise* to send it "at the end of the year."[20]

In November 1633, he learned about the condemnation of Galileo's *Dialogo sopra i due massimi sistemi del mondo*, *Dialogue on the Two Chief World Systems* by the Congregation of Cardinals established to censor books in Rome and Descartes gave up publishing his treatise.

2. From *L'Homme* to the *Discours* Together with *La Dioptrique*: Anatomy, Dissections, Anthropology and Metaphysics

Descartes took some years to publish anonymously his first book: the *Discourse on Method* with the *Essays*, including the *Optiks* (*La Dioptrique*.) In these two texts, anatomy is an important topic. In the *Discourse* published in 1637, Descartes alluded to *L'Homme*, but this is neither an abstract nor a reliable account of his work.

L'Homme is a starting point in Descartes' medical thoughts. But the *Discourse* and the *Dioprique* showed a rearrangement and a deepening of the main themes. The explanation of the movements of the heart and of the blood was extended and deepened between 1633 and 1637 and was given a major role in the fifth part of the *Discourse on Method*. Parts dealing with the explanation of sensations and especially of the sight in *L'Homme* found their definitive place in *La Dioptrique*, the first of the *Essays* of the *Method*. The explanation of pain, tackled in *L'Homme* will be developed in the *Dioptrique*, the *Sixth Meditation* and in *Principles* IV, Article 196. The same is true as regards the topic of passions, analysed in depth in *Les Passions de l'âme*, published in 1649.

But compared to *L'Homme*, the *Discourse on Method* contains two novelties of paramount importance, including for the writings that will follow:
1) The approval of the circulation of the blood with an emphasis on the anatomical proofs given by Harvey and linked with Descartes' own dissections of hearts and animal foetuses and embryos. Descartes confirmed Harvey's experiments

---

20 Descartes to Mersenne, 22 July 1633, AT I 268.

about the primacy of the heart in the embryo, the heart being the principle of life. Descartes also mentioned his disagreement with Harvey on the cause of the movement of the heart.

2) The explanation of the difference between human beings and animals. The *Discourse* aimed to resolve what Descartes qualified as "difficulties that belong to medicine." However, these difficulties and their solution by Descartes initiated a new anthropology which makes it possible to dissolve *aporia* existing in anatomy about the relations between the soul and the body of man, the singularity of the rational soul, and, as Descartes wrote, about "the difference between our soul and that of the beasts."

These themes are related to the debates found in anatomical books. I think that the anatomical problems Descartes had to face about hearts and brains provide the key to understanding the evolution of Descartes' thoughts as well as the introduction of new themes in the *Discourse* together with *La Dioptrique*.

The choice of the heart as the main subject of study was significant on interwoven major topics. The heart, *principal* organ since Aristotle, disputed the role of mediator between the soul and the body with the brain or part of the brain. Anatomists insisted that it was very difficult "to describe its admirable composition and structure," but by doing so one gains access to "marvelous secrets of Nature (Naturæ ... arcana)."[21] Trying to explain the movement of the heart without the help of suitable tools, which was the case in the seventeenth century, was a real challenge. Anatomists thought that "it was known only to Nature and to God alone."[22]. Harvey quoted this to show both how complex the question was and how daring his own explanation was.[23]

The challenge of the movement of the heart shows the entanglement of metaphysical and medical themes at the time of the reception of Harvey's treatise. I have already explained the importance of Harvey in Descartes' thought from the *Discourse on Method* to the *Passions of the Soul* and *La Description du corps humain, the Description of the Human Body*. Descartes was one of the first to approve this brilliant discovery. But Descartes never quoted the reference to Aristotle that had given birth, according to Harvey, to the resumption of the name of circulation. In an implicit but relevant manner, Descartes also focused his remarks on the eradication of Aristotelianism in medicine with the fundamental eradication of the soul 'principle of life' thanks to the distinction made between a soul known and recognized in its thinking activity (primacy of the *Cogito* to be detailed in the *Meditationes*) and a body reduced to extended matter. In the *Discourse*, Descartes wrote about the human body after having stated that the nature of the soul "is only to think," which entails its invalidation as a principle of animation and therefore of life, and that this soul is "entirely distinct from the body."

---

21 See for instance ANDRÉ DU LAURENS, (Laurentius) *Historia anatomica ...*, Frankfurt, M. Becker, 1600, p. 351. French translation in DU LAURENS, *L'Histoire Anatomique ...*, translation by F. Sizé, Paris, J. Bertault, 1610, book IX, ch. X, p. 1051 and ch. XI, p. 1062.
22 DU LAURENS, *L'Histoire Anatomique ...*, question VII, p. 1068.
23 WILLIAM HARVEY, *Exercitatio Anatomica De motu cordis et sanguinis in animalibus*, Frankfurt, 1628, first chapter.

There is nothing in the medical tradition similar to the Cartesian principle of life reduced to the "fire without light" in the heart, to the heat in the heart reduced to fermentation. Likewise, *La Dioptrique* innovates in medicine by its analysis of the senses, in particular sight, and by its study of the nerves about which Descartes claimed that "anatomists and doctors" have not "yet clearly distinguished the use."[24] With these novelties *L'Homme* became *de facto* obsolete.

I now wish to show that anatomy and especially the dissections of hearts and brains were directly linked to the evolution of Descartes' thoughts. To understand this, we must return to the end of 1632 and to the sentence, "I am presently anatomizing the heads of various animals, to explain what imagination, memory, etc. consist of." I think that this sentence has not yet received the attention it required.

This is a bold statement because the anatomy of the brain, even more than the anatomy of the heart, has given rise to medical, philosophical, metaphysical and religious considerations and controversies. Dissecting the hearts and brains of animals was not just examining an anatomical structure, trying, for instance to see in detail the valves in the heart and the 'small nerve of the heart', as well as the pineal gland and the vessels and the nerves in the brain. These dissections led to confront the problem of both the status and the seat of the principle of life, either in the heart according to Aristotle or in the brain according to Galen. Dissecting animal brains also led to consider the specificity of the human soul and to pay attention to the unique mental faculties of imagination, reason and memory, studied since Antiquity in the context of the question about the *Nature on Man*.

In Vesalius' *Fabrica*, in the chapter dealing with the function and the use (*functio et usus*) of the parts of the heart, Vesalius asked "Cor cujus animæ sedes," "Of which soul the heart is the seat."[25] When looking at the anatomical images of the brain, which are the essential tool for carrying out the dissections undertaken by Descartes and recorded in the *Excerpta anatomica*, Descartes was confronted with the questions raised by Vesalius in his study of the brain. These questions became a true obstacle to the further writing of *L'Homme*. The issues concerned not only a new method in medicine and especially in anatomy but also engaged in a decisive way both a new anthropology and a new metaphysics.

Let us come back to the main problems that Descartes encountered in his investigations of the brain, based on the Vesalian issues. This medical context linked with Descartes' dissections allows us to take the measure of the considerable innovations in the *Discourse on Method* and in the *Dioptrique*, compared to the content of *L'Homme*.

Vesalius recalled that the irascible soul sits in the heart, but he refused to admit that the hegemonic or sovereign principle of the soul could be located there. He did not agree with either the Aristotelians or the Stoics with the heart as the source of voluntary movements and nerves. He followed Galen and placed the main soul (*princeps anima*) in the brain. According to Vesalius, this *princeps anima* is that by means

---

24 *La Dioptrique*, AT VI 110.
25 VESALIUS, *Fabrica*, 1543, lib. VI, cap. XV, p. 594.

of which "we imagine, we reason and we remember." These 'functions': imagination, reasoning, memory are linked to the study of the brain. Vesalius, in agreement with theologians, distinguished a single soul endowed with three faculties.

According to Vesalius, the "life force" of the soul is contained in the heart. And Vesalius wrote that he could quite possibly know the functions of the brain with probability. On the other hand, he could not understand in a satisfactory manner "how the brain performed its function in imagination, reasoning, thought, memory, (regardless of the subdivisions of the powers of the sovereign soul according to this or that doctrine)." He quoted philosophers and mentioned the "abyss of impiety" into which fall those who "undertake to examine with their own hands into human and animal bodies."[26] In his study of the heart, Vesalius already asserted that "the physician must think of the faculties and the seat of the soul."[27] In his study of the brain, Vesalius evokes the memory of the reading of Aristotle's *De Anima* by his professor of theology in Leuven, and the thesis of the three ventricles of the brain with their position and function. Vesalius challenged this widely used anatomical division: these are "representations from those who have never observed the talent (ingenuity) of our Creator in the making of the human body."[28] Vesalius aimed at the famous image of these faculties in three cells by Gregor Reisch in his *Margarita philosophica*.

Since these opinions and representations have to be rejected, the brain has to be studied and described completely in a new way and Vesalius explained the dissection of the brain as an expert in skillfully conducted dissections: didn't he dissect with his embroidered jacket as shown in the title page and the portrait? Vesalius was the first to show pictures of human brains following the course of dissection, with a text linked to the images. He described with precision the craniectomy in order to release the dura mater, resistant meninges which protects the brain. Several anatomical plates of human brains show the hair and the ears, which allowed the head to hold better under the blows of the small saw which removes the skull box.

Vesalius knew that to describe the functions of the cerebral ventricles calling into question the powers of the sovereign soul involved "a degree of impiety," because of the very resemblance between the brains of human beings and that of quadrupeds, although we have to deny to quadrupeds "all faculty of reason and above all a rational soul, in accordance with the teaching of theologians." Indeed "the conformation of the ventricles of the brain in sheep, goats, ox, cats, monkeys, dogs" that Vesalius had dissected is not different from that of the human brain, apart from the variation in volume "in proportion to the degree of reason which seems to have been granted to them."[29] In the margins we can read: "The construction of the brain of animals does not differ from that of man: *Brutorum cerebri constructionem ab hominis non differre*."[30] As the brain convolutions appear, Vesalius added

---

26   VESALIUS, *Fabrica*, lib. VII, cap. I, p. 624.
27   VESALIUS, *Fabrica*, lib. VI, cap. XV, p. 594.
28   VESALIUS, *Fabrica*, lib. VII, cap. I, p. 623.
29   VESALIUS, *Fabrica*, lib. VII, cap. I, p. 624 and cap. IIII (IV), p. 630.
30   *Ibid.*, p. 624.

You can learn what these convolutions look like by looking at the brain of any animal, at lunch or dinner. But when it comes to considering their function, not only doctors but also philosophers take the greatest pains, arguing whether human intelligence is due to these *gyri* (convolutions) or not. And Galen, opposing the view of Erasistratus[31] stated the following view: 'Even asses have a very complex cerebrum, whereas if we consider their ignorance, their brains should be simple in all parts and uniform'.[32]

Vesalius regretted that Galen had stopped his thinking at this point. But he himself quickly stopped and he thanked God for having endowed man with the rational soul.

How to understand the functions of the brain? How to see clearly when the debates were even more lively on the intracerebral structure than on the structure of the heart? It should be remembered that the anatomical observations were in those days made only with the help of the eyes and the hands. The difficulty of the dissection of the brain has to be noted: first because of its rapid corruption. This was what made it impossible to observe the pineal gland during public anatomy lessons, which Descartes deplored. Indeed, the dissection, only in winter, proceeded according to a codified order, and the opening of the corpse began for obvious reasons of conservation, with "the lower belly" and continued with the median belly, the thoracic cavity, then with the upper belly, the cranial cavity. Descartes evoked the dissection of a female body which he attended in Leyden because he wished to observe the pineal gland, and though he knew "very well where it must have been, because [he] was used to finding it, in freshly killed animals without any difficulty, it was however impossible for [him] to recognize it." Descartes added: "And an old professor who made this anatomy, named Valcher, confessed to me that he had never been able to see it in any human body, what I believe comes from what they usually need a few days to see the intestines and other parts before opening the head."[33] Descartes' comments are accurate.

The challenge in observing the brain in order to deduce its functions also lies in the complexity of this anatomical structure, in the dissection cuts and the angles at which you observe. More than any other dissection, a successful brain dissection means doing it several times. And digging into the ventricles of the brain was in those days giving access to the generation of animal spirits, a very important question. The brain was the source of animal spirits, but where and how? What happened between the third and fourth ventricles? Which one took precedence over the other? What were the respective roles of the two small glands: the pituitary and the pineal, especially the pineal, since the pituitary secreted *pituitis* and was linked to the evacuation of the *excrementa* from the brain, through channels, especially towards the nose (nasal mucus) and into the throat (guttural mucus or catarrh)? What about the pineal and the anatomical correspondences in this complex

---

31 GALEN, *De usu partium*, VIII, 13.
32 VESALIUS, *Fabrica*, lib. VII, cap. IIII (IV), p. 630.
33 Descartes to Mersenne, 1 April 1640, AT III 49. Valcher is Adriaan van Valckenburg, Adrianus Falcoburgius (1581-1650).

intracerebral area? The brain is also the origin of motor and sensory nerves. But where? And what is the structure of the nerves, especially the optic nerve? What about the controversy over the hollow nature of the optic nerve? One thing was certain: Vesalius recommended observing the brain of an adult lamb or sheep in order to see well, because the "organs are larger and better formed." Bauhin took up the idea, put it into practice just like Descartes. Descartes had the heads of recently killed animals brought home to examine the intracerebral structure, as shown in particular by the precise dissection of a sheep's brain in the *Excerpta anatomica*, an echo of which can be found in *La Dioptrique*, Discourses V and VI. In his dissections Descartes carefully examined the intracerebral structure, especially the vessels and nerves, as well as the pituitary and pineal glands.

The nagging issue and troublesome question of the difference between animals and humans was also alluded to by Fabricius of Aquapendente and raised by Caspar Bauhin. Bauhin reorganized an anatomical treatise in his *Theatrum anatomicum* according to the order of dissection, he reorganized the images on the heart and on the intracerebral structure, added others, updated references (Columbus: Realdo Colombo, Fallopius: Gabriele Fallopio, etc.). Bauhin showed another way of dissecting the brain, with a section at the base by Constantius Varolius (Costanzo Varolio) (see Fig. 1 and Fig. 2).

All these anatomical questions arose within the more general framework of the fundamental question: since the nature of human hearts is the same as in many animals, since the brains of some animals really look like human brains, what about the human specificity? Since the proximity of human brains to that of quadrupeds is so great, is there anything more that can be learnt from anatomy "given that theologians deny all power of reason [...] to brute animals" as Vesalius wrote?

With the heart and the brain and with the question of generation he had to take up again to see the primacy of the heart in embryos, Descartes faced the most difficult anatomical issues and it took him a long time to analyse all these problems. This is all the more accurate since Descartes also proposed an explanation of the senses, of pain and even of complex medical phenomena linked with the 'obscure' question of the union of the soul to the body according to famous physicians and surgeons.

3. The Posthumous Publications of *L'Homme* and the Influence of the *Discours* and *La Dioptrique*

The innovative medical, anthropological and metaphysical issues in the *Discourse* and the *Dioptrique* were perceived by the first readers of these texts: the physician Plempius and the theologian Fromondus, who were also the first objectors to Descartes new philosophy. Among these important objections, one of them was raised about the analysis of sensations given in the *Dioptrique*, and especially the explanation of pain. Fromondus expressed surprise with the Cartesian explanation of pain taking place in the brain and he

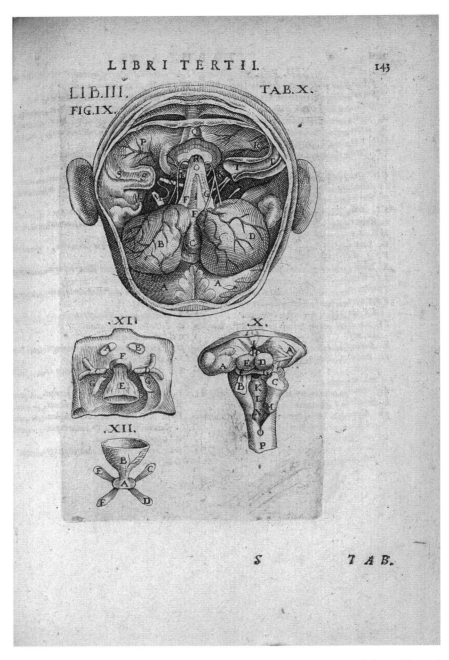

Figure 1. Brain in CASPAR BAUHIN, *Theatrum anatomicum* (ed. 1621), text followed by and bound with *Vivae imagines partium corporis humani* ex *Theatro Anatomico*, [Frankfurt and Rheinland]: J. T. de Bry publisher, 1620, Lib. II, p. 107. Published with the kind permission from the BIUS, Paris.

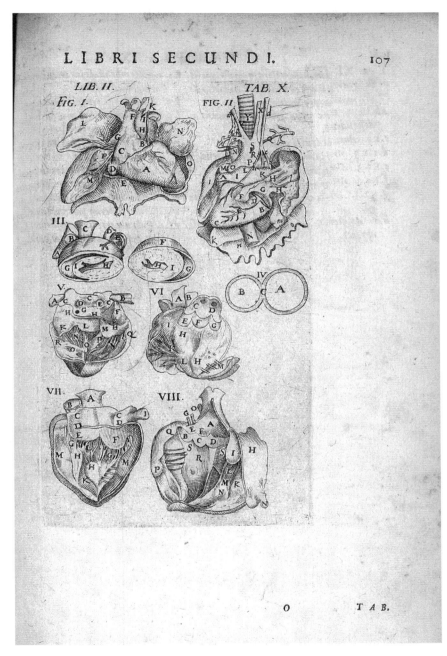

Figure 2. Heart in CASPAR BAUHIN, *Theatrum anatomicum* (ed.1621), text followed by and bound with *Vivae imagines partium corporis humani* ex *Theatro Anatomico*, [Frankfurt and Rheinland]: J. T. de Bry publisher, 1620, Lib. III, p. 143. Published with the kind permission from the BIUS, Paris.

put forward the traditional "qualitatem dolorificam" (the so-called *quality* of pain).[34] In his answer, Descartes referred to doctors and surgeons to support his conception and he quoted for the first time the example he saw of the young girl who 'had a serious wound in her hands' and did not know her arm had been amputated thanks to the bandages placed on the arm and the fact that her eyes were blindfolded during the surgeon's visits. This girl was complaining of various pains in her fingers, wrist and forearm. According to Descartes this "was obviously due to the condition of the nerves in her arm which formerly led from her brain to those parts of her body."[35] The *Sixth Meditation* referred to the phantom-limb pain and Descartes asserted that it in no way affected the unity of the soul. Descartes quoted the example of that young girl with her amputated hand in his *Principia* (Part IV, Article 196), which proved "that pain in the hand is felt by the soul not because it is present in the hand, but because it is present in the brain."[36]

This example was significant in medicine. We have to remember Rembrandt's *Anatomy of Dr Tulp* and the emphasis given on the arm. We must keep in mind that the First book of Galen's *De usu partium* is devoted to the hand, as well as the beginning of the second book. Why? Because the hand is the specific advantage of human beings thanks to its versatility. And we also have to remember that Aristotle claimed that the "hand is the *organon pro organon*," and that "it is because [man] is the most intelligent animal that he has got hands."[37] Hence the praises to the *admirable* hand in anatomical treatises and the link between the hand and the perfection of the human body. By contrast, there is no praise to the hand in Descartes' works. And some years later, in a letter to Mesland — where Descartes recalled that he had "examined the circulation of the blood" — he also wrote "we do not think that a man who has lost an arm or a leg is less a man than any other."[38] No doubt that Descartes was thinking of his friend Alphone Pollot who had lost one of his arms, but this statement was also directed against the Galenist tradition in medical and surgical books, emphasizing the importance of the hand in the human body, compared to animals.

Descartes rejected this tradition and wanted to impose a new anthropology in which God was no longer summoned in relation to the human body, the masterpiece of Creation, but evoked in relation to the union of the soul to the body. This union, assumed in *L'Homme*, described in the fifth part of the *Discourse on Method*, then deepened in the *Sixth Meditation* and in the *Passions of the Soul* constitutes the "real man."[39]

In the University of Utrecht, Henricus Regius asked his students to defend theses that contain some of these considerable innovations from the *Physiologia*. Since Regius was a physician, he understood that he had to join the fifth part of the

---

34 Fromondus to Plempius for Descartes, 13 September 1637, AT I 406.
35 Descartes to Plempius for Fromondus, 3 October 1637, AT I 420, CSMK 64.
36 *Principia philosophiae*, IV, art. 196, AT VIII-1, 320. On this aspect, see ANNIE BITBOL-HESPÉRIÈS, "La médecine et l'union dans la Méditation sixième," in *Union et distinction de l'âme et du corps: lectures de la VIe Méditation*, sous la direction de D. Kolesnik-Antoine, Paris: Kimé, 1998, p. 18-36, and Jil Muller's contribution to this volume.
37 ARISTOTLE, *On the Parts of Animals*, IV, X, 687a8-10.
38 Descartes to Mesland, 9 Februay 1645, AT IV 166-167, CSMK 243.
39 *L'Homme*, AT XI 202. See also *Discours* part V, and *Meditation* VI.

Discourse to the analysis of senses in *La Dioptrique* in order to teach a new medicine. We must remember that the novelty of the circulation of the blood, explained within the mechanist Cartesian framework by Regius, was at the origin of the famous Utrecht Affair.[40]

Descartes' attitude towards Harvey remained the same from the writing of *L'Homme* to the publication of the *Passions*, with the praises to Harvey for his demonstration of blood circulation. But in the *Passions* published in 1649, Descartes also criticized the resistance to adopting the discovery of the circulation of blood, more than twenty years after Harvey's demonstration.

At the time of writing the *Passions*, Descartes was also writing the *Description of the Human Body* (*La Description du corps humain*) and he carried out new dissections and new embryological experiments. This text sheds light on the *Passions of the soul* and Descartes refines his dialogue with Harvey's book.

Twelve years after Descartes' death, and thanks to one of the copies of Descartes' manuscript of *L'Homme* that had been circulating, a Latin translation was published in Leyden in 1662, by Florent Schuyl under the faithful title *De Homine*. This edition contains beautiful anatomical images of the heart and of the brain in a manner consistent with Descartes' illustrated anatomical sources: Vesalius and Bauhin. Schuyl added an anatomical loose sheet of the heart showing lines of incision with flaps which rise to reveal the valves in the heart, as in a skillfully conducted dissection (see Fig. 3 and Fig. 4). Following Harvey, Descartes had paid attention to these valves since they impose a direction to the blood, in other words are a proof of the circulation of the blood. Schuyl also added a foreword *Ad Lectorem* quoting many authors from Aristotle to Fabricius ab Aquapendente, some books, including the Bible and Augustine, as well as the first volume of Descartes' *Letters* published by Clerselier in 1657. Schuyl mentioned his reluctance in admitting a principle of life reduced to the heat in the heart. Schuyl also referred to the *Method* and the *Essais*.

This Foreword has been translated into French and placed at the end of the 1664 Parisian edition of *L'Homme* together with *Un traité de la formation du fœtus* (*A Treatise on the Formation of the Foetus*) by Clerselier.

While allusions to *L'Homme* were contained in some of Descartes' *Letters* dealing with medicine and published by Clerselier in the two volumes of his edition of Descartes' Correspondence (1657 and 1659), by contrast, there was no mention of the title of the second text. Moreover, there was no mention of such a title in the inventories made after Descartes' death. But the so-called Stockholm Inventory indicated a text called *La Description du corps humain*,[41] and we know that Descartes brought with him to Stockholm his most important papers. This title matches with the *Treatise on the Formation of the Foetus* and is to be found in its entirety at the

---

40   See THEO VERBEEK, *René Descartes et Martin Schoock, La querelle d'Utrecht*, Paris, Les Impressions nouvelles, 1988, and ANNIE BITBOL-HESPÉRIÈS, "Descartes et Regius : leur pensée médicale," in *Descartes et Regius, Autour de l'Explication de l'esprit humain*, ed. by Theo Verbeek, Amsterdam-Atlanta, Rodopi, 1993, p. 47-68.
41   Registered under the letter G, see Stockholm inventory, AT X 9-10.

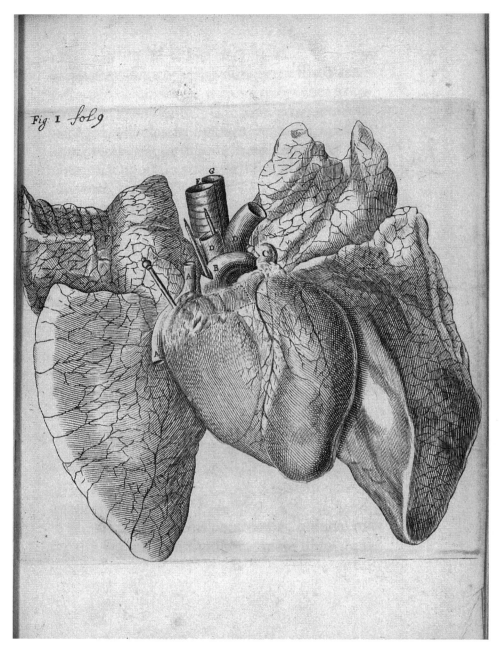

Figure 3. Heart in DESCARTES, *De Homine*, ed. F. Schuyl, Leyden, 1662 [and 2nd ed. 1664], p. 8 (the image I already present on p. 6). Published with the kind permission from the BIUS, Paris.

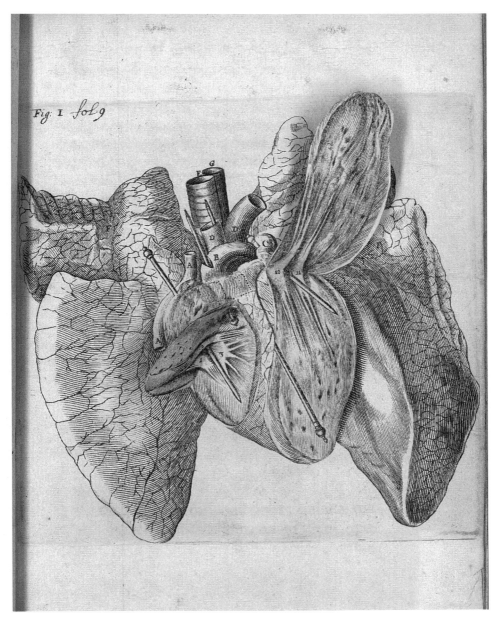

Figure 4. Heart with the valves in DESCARTES, *De Homine*, ed. F. Schuyl, Leyden, 1662 [& 2nd ed. 1664], folio between p. 8 and p. 9. [This folio is missing in many editions.] Published with the kind permission from the BIUS, Paris.

very beginning of this text: *La Description du corps humain et de toutes ses fonctions, tant de celles qui ne dépendent point de l'âme, que de celles qui en dépendent, et aussi la principale cause de la formation de ses membres*, on p. 109 in the 1664 edition. Why such a change in the title?

True, compared to *L'Homme*, *La Description* contains a new topic: the study of the formation of the foetus, a theme explicitly emphasized by Clerselier.[42] In *La Description*, Descartes was obviously trying to avoid the passive attitude of wonder of many physicians, the obscure controversies and all the prolix discussions in medical treatises. The Cartesian method stated the following principles: the existence of the two semen, male and female, and also the idea that heat and fermentation are the driving force that explains generation. What is also clearly expressed is the question of the order of the formation of the parts during the development in the womb of the mother. In the *Discourse on Method*, the heart was to become the first organ to appear, a thesis influenced by Harvey's treatise. Once the priority of the role of the heart had been checked with dissections of calves at different stages of their development and observations on incubated eggs,[43] Descartes promoted his conception of the heat in the heart which is a kind of fire, as already mentioned in *L'Homme* and in the *Discourse*. This "principle of movement and life", as mentioned at the end of *L'Homme* is a "corporeal principle" as stated in the *Passions* (Art. 8) and in some letters. This "principle of life"[44] is fully detailed in *La Description du corps humain*. The heart, its detailed structure, its movement, its cause, and its formation, and also the circulation of the blood, hence the formation of the veins and arteries, are the most important topics in *La Description*. They are more crucial than the question of generation, although the latter was emphasized by Clerselier. This text details the stated principle in *Les Passions de l'âme*: "the heart and blood, on which depend all the good of the body."[45]

Indeed "anatomy and mechanics" are of paramount importance in Descartes' Works and this connection between anatomy and mechanics is of the highest significance since it rules out the alternative connection between anatomy and finalism, and between anatomy and what will later be called vitalism. At the beginning of *La Description*, Descartes thus explicitly condemned "our ignorance of anatomy and mechanics."[46] Descartes invoked "the rules (or laws) of mechanics" in order to explain the formation of the valves in the heart, that were a traditional subject of wonder.[47] For Descartes, the body is no longer an object of admiration provoking teleological or theological considerations as in the medical tradition. It is an object

---

42   See my chapter, ANNIE BITBOL-HESPÉRIÈS, "The Primacy of *L'Homme* in the 1664 Parisian edition by Clerselier," in *Descartes' Treatise on Man and its Reception*, ed. by Delphine Antoine-Mahut and Stephen Gaukroger, Cham, Springer, 2016, p. 33-47.
43   See *Excerpta anatomica*. AT XI. On the heart, see pages: 553-564, 585-586, 599, 603, 608-614; on the incubated eggs and heart, see pages: 614-616, 619-620.
44   *Passions*, art. 107, AT XI 407.
45   *Passions*, art. 71, AT XI 381. Anonymous English translation of 1650, London, p. 56. On the British reception of the treatise on the *Passions of the Soul*, see Daniel Samuel's contribution to this volume.
46   *La Description du corps humain*, AT XI 224, CSM I 314.
47   *Ibid.*, AT XI 279-280.

of investigation of the movements which govern it, and in the first place those of the heart and the blood, and these movements have no longer any relation with the faculties connected with the division of the souls in medical books and in Regius' theses of 1641 corrected by Descartes.

With the change in the title Clerselier avoided the medical subject of the circulation of the blood, which was still rejected by the Medicine Faculty in Paris in 1664. As in the *Discourse* and in the *Passions*, in *La Description*, Descartes quoted Harvey's name in Latin. As in the *Passions*, Article 7, Descartes condemned those who still have a very prejudiced view and are unable to accept the circular movement of the blood and to distinguish "the true and certain reasons" from the false and probable ones.[48] Clerselier in his *Préface* ignored Descartes' approval of the circulation of the blood. And in his *Remarques*, La Forge commented neither the expression 'perpetual circulation' in *L'Homme* nor the detailed experimental proofs given in the so-called second Treatise. Yet La Forge referred to some "experiments" that confirm his agreement with the "truth of the circular movement of the blood,"[49] but he did not insist on this important point. What is striking in the Parisian edition is also the vanishing of the heart in the illustrations (see Fig. 5). This is all the more significant since the beautiful images of the heart with its valves by Schuyl in the *De Homine* are closer in their anatomical precision to the *Discourse* and the *Passions* and even more to the *Description* than to *L'Homme*.

The *Description* is also linked with the *Discourse* and the *Passions*, Articles 8 and 9, concerning the movement of the heart and its cause, different from Harvey's explanation. If (as Harvey asserts[50]), the expulsion of blood occurs during systole, which is the phase of contraction of the heart and thereby the phase of its diminution in volume, there must be something in the heart that is the cause of its contraction. Descartes explained: "Now if we suppose that the heart moves in the way Harvey describes, we must imagine some faculty which causes this movement; yet the nature of this faculty is much harder to conceive of than whatever Harvey purports to explain by invoking it."[51]

Among some complex questions, La Forge asked the one of the movement of the muscles, "the most difficult to understand," an echo of Clerselier's *Préface* where the movement is qualified of "the most important action for the author to describe and explain."[52] But the fundamental question of the 'principle' of all the functions performed by a living body, explained by Descartes in a new way, as confirmed in the *Passions*, Article 8, is avoided and nearly ignored by Clerselier and La Forge. Clerselier addressed this issue once praising La Forge (not Descartes) and adding "for what regards the discipline of animals it is explained without admitting in them any soul that thinks, knows or reasons, nor any other principle of life or movement except

---

48 Ibid., AT XI 240-241.
49 *Remarques*, p. 190. Taken from the original edition by Claude Clerselier, Paris, 1664.
50 HARVEY, *De motu cordis*, cap. 2.
51 AT XI, 243-244, CSM, I, 318.
52 *Préface*, np. (non paginée=no pagination). Original edition by Clerselier, Paris, 1664.

DE RENÉ DESCARTES. 9

c'est seulement ou la situation, ou la figure, ou la petitesse des pores par où elles passent, qui fait que les vnes y passent plutost que les autres, & que le reste du sang ne les peut suiure; ainsi que vous pouuez auoir veu diuers cribles, qui estant diuersement percez seruent à separer diuers grains les vns des autres.

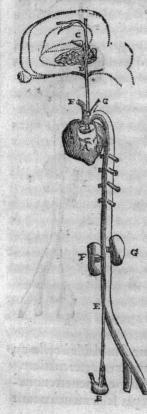

Mais ce qu'il faut icy principalement remarquer, c'est que toutes les plus viues, les plus fortes, & les plus subtiles parties de ce sang, se vont rendre dans les côcauitez du cerueau; dautant que les arteres qui les y portent, sont celles qui viennent du cœur le plus en ligne droite de toutes, & que comme vous sçauez, tous les corps qui se meuuent tendent chacun autant qu'il est possible à continuer leur mouuement en ligne droite.

Voyez par exemple le cœur A, & pensez que lors que le sang en sort auec effort par l'ouuerture B, il n'y a aucune de ses parties qui ne tende vers C, où sont les concauitez du cerueau; mais que le pas-

XII.
Que ses plus viues & plus subtiles parties vont au cerueau.

B

Figure 5. Heart in DESCARTES, *L'Homme*, ed. C. Clerselier, Paris, 1664, p. 9. [This is the only representation of the heart in this edition, and this image is also reproduced on p. 10.] Published with the kind permission from the BIUS, Paris.

the blood and the (animal) spirits moved by the heat in the heart."[53] This statement altered both the meaning of Descartes' new explanation on a fundamental topic and its context, because with Clerselier, as well as with La Forge and before them with Schuyl, it became associated to the question of the difference between humans and animals and linked to the relevant issue for them, namely the question of the soul of beasts. La Forge, Schuyl and Clerselier aimed to hide the radical Cartesian innovation in medicine: the way Descartes imposed a new conceptual framework on medical questions. It consisted in the systematization of mechanism with the heat in the heart becoming 'the principle of movement and life' as stated at the end of *L'Homme* and explained in the first part of *La Description*.

The eradication of the non-conscious or non-cogitative functions of the soul was the major philosophical reason for the Cartesian study of the *Nature on Man* and it is found at the end of *L'Homme*, in the *Dicourse on Method*, in the *Passions* and in *La Description*. The fundamental methodological challenge of dualism and the clear-cut distinction between the principle of life and the soul which breaks with the medical tradition legitimates the comparison of the body with a machine, and changed the definition of death, not linked with the fault of the soul.[54] And Descartes asserted that "our soul, in so far as it is a substance which is distinct from the body, is known to us merely through the fact that it thinks, that is to say, understands, wills, imagines, remembers, and has sensory perceptions; for all these functions are kinds of thought."[55] No doubt that Clerselier's *Préface* and La Forge's lack of comment on the last paragraph of *L'Homme* pursued the same goal, namely to expunge the strong Cartesian opposition to the traditional conception of the soul as the principle of life.

The *Description of the Human Body* is a major text in the Cartesian *summa medicinae*. First, because this text is strongly linked with the other published books by Descartes and not only with *La Dioptrique*, les *Météores*, and les *Principes de la Philosophie*, explicitly quoted in the *Description*[56]. Second, because the *Description* is dealing with the most important and most contemporaneous medical problems in the middle of the seventeenth Century, after the explanation of sensations and especially of sight already given in *La Dioptrique*. They were the questions of the movements of the body and in the body with Harvey's demonstration of the movement of the heart and of the blood, Asellius' demonstration of the lacteal veins, the question of generation, and the importance of human dissections and of animal vivisections in medicine.

Schuyl and Clerselier in their *Préfaces*, as well as La Forge in his *Remarques*, impose a different context to *L'Homme* and to *La Description*. Clerselier's *Préface* to *L'Homme* and to *La Description* stands in contradiction to three fundamental aspects of Descartes' medical ideas.

First, Descartes has rejected the view of soul as the principle of life since the writing of *L'Homme* and the publication of the *Discours de la méthode*. He has

---

53 *Préface*, np. (p. 32).
54 *La Description du corps humain*, AT XI 224-225; CSM I 314-315, and *Passions*, art. 5.
55 *Ibid.*, 224; CSM I 314, 'remembers' is an addition in *La Description*.
56 Cf. *La Description du corps humain*, AT XI 248, 255, 275.

strongly reasserted this rejection in his Letters, for instance to Regius and then to Morus [Henry More],[57] as well as in the *Passions de l'âme* and *La Description*. He advocated the systematisation of mechanism and the reduction of the principle of life and motion to the heat in the heart, an 'ordinary' heat reduced to fermentation.

Second, Descartes applied the "know yourself'" (*know thyself*)[58] principle to the body and not to the soul, as stated at the beginning of the first part (*Préface*) of *La Description*. While this point was not entirely new, Descartes' use of the Socratic precept in medicine was original, compared to the two backgrounds linked with this precept: the first one, widespread in anatomy and associated with praises to the Glory of God. Acquiring knowledge about the human body meant leading to admire Nature or/and God for the perfection of the 'fabric' of the human body. The second one linked with a moralizing context[59]. From the beginning, *La Description* is a true manifest for the new medicine, built on Cartesian principles.

Third, Descartes never mixed in his works medicine and praises to God for the human body, *i.e.* medicine and theology, and also medicine and teleology. At the beginning of *La Description*, Descartes thus explicitly condemns "our ignorance of anatomy and mechanics."[60]

For Descartes, the comparison between the body and a *machine* cannot be dissociated from the development of an original "principle of life." This "principle of movement and life," as stated in *L'Homme* is underpinned by a physical phenomenon, heat, the nature of which Descartes specifies. Its seat is the heart, whose study of movement is a direct witness to its nature. Hence, the presentation of the explanation of the movement of the heart as a privileged example of the method. The break with the medical tradition is expressed by a new demonstration on a double register, since Descartes associates the recent discovery of the circulation of the blood, which he releases from its Aristotelian context, with a radically mechanical explanation of the heat of the heart conceived as "principle of life." It is thus interesting to note the striking discrepancy between the illustrations of the *De Homine* and of *L'Homme*: the vanishing of the images of the heart in the Parisian edition of 1664 compared to the staging of its importance in the display of images in the Leyden edition. This is consistent with the *Préface* by Clerselier as well as with Clerselier's reluctance towards anatomy, which stands in opposition to the importance devoted to anatomy by Descartes. The knowledge of anatomy and the use of experiments were fundamental in Descartes' search *for truth in the sciences*. A new *Method* was required in order to establishing medicine as "une science si nécessaire," a so much-needed science.[61]

---

57 Descartes to More, 5 February 1649, AT V, 276.
58 *La Description du corps humain*, AT XI 223 (first page, at the beginning).
59 Cf. ANNIE ANNIE BITBOL-HESPÉRIÈS, "Connaissance de l'homme, connaissance de Dieu".
60 *La Description du corps humain*, AT XI 224; CSM I 314.
61 *Discours de la Méthode*, AT VI 63; CSM I 143: "an indispensable knowledge."

TAWRIN BAKER

The Medical Context of Descartes's *Dioptrique*

▼ ABSTRACT Prior anatomical investigations on the eye, along with medical ideas and practices concerning the eye and vision, were a crucial influence on Descartes's 1637 *Dioptrique*, but the precise nature of this has not been examined in fine detail. One aim of this chapter is to supply this. Moreover, the *Dioptrique* can be read as a medical work itself, at least in some respects. Descartes's description of lenses as artificial organs whose purpose is to improve and perfect vision has a direct analogue in the description, in contemporaneous surgical works, of artificial devices designed to supply what was lacking in the body due to either accident or nature. Around the middle of the seventeenth century, however, eyeglasses were only beginning to be medicalized, and thus spectacles were either missing from works on medicine and surgery or, indeed, advised against. Descartes's *Dioptrique*, therefore, seems to have contributed to the medicalization of spectacles that began to take place in the seventeenth century. Finally, in a letter to Mersenne in January 1630 he wrote that he was seeking to "discover a medicine which is founded on infallible demonstrations". Descartes believed that his work on improving and perfecting vision via lenses — including his investigations of the shape of the anaclastic — was infallibly demonstrated. Reading the *Dioptrique* from a medical point of view, then, I suggest that Descartes and others believed that he had achieved this lofty medical ambition in his *Dioptrique*.

▼ KEYWORDS René Descartes, Christoph Scheiner, Vopiscus Fortunatus Plempius, Johannes Kepler, Fabricius ab Aquapendente, Anatomy, Medicine, Surgery, Optics, Eyeglasses

Historians and philosophers of science have generally overlooked the importance of anatomy and medicine in the development of optics in the sixteenth and seventeenth

Tawrin Baker • University of Notre Dame, US. Contact: <tbaker9@nd.edu>

centuries. This is perhaps one reason why recent scholarship on Descartes's involvement in medicine and the medical aspects of his works has not considered the *Dioptrique*, which was first printed in 1637 together with the essays *La Géométrie* and *Les Météores*, all prefaced by his *Discours de la méthode*, in detail.[1] This chapter aims to supply this lacuna.

The medical context of the *Dioptrique* will here be treated in two ways. The first concerns Descartes' description of the eye. Certain details of Descartes's account of the eye were essential to his theory of vision, while others reveal his attitude towards earlier medical and philosophical understandings of the eye and its role in visual theory. His account of the eye owed a clear debt to previous anatomical and medical investigations, and the non-medical authors that influenced him — such as Johannes Kepler (1571-1630) and Christoph Scheiner (1573-1650) — were themselves clearly indebted to the medical tradition. Gideon Manning has argued that Descartes's interest in medicine and physiology was stimulated by his optical investigations.[2] It has not been fully appreciated, however, that in the first half of the seventeenth-century medical-anatomical investigations of the eye were deeply intertwined with natural philosophy and mathematics (and vice versa). As I will show, some other features of Descartes's anatomical eye also owed a debt to the practice of cataract couching by lower-status surgical specialists.

The *Dioptrique* can also be considered a medical book in itself, at least in some specific senses. In Discourse seven of the *Dioptrique* Descartes writes that optics is concerned with correcting the errors and deficiencies of vision via artificial instruments. Optics, according to Descartes, was not about understanding the nature of light and the mathematics of reflection and refraction for its own sake, but for the sake of remedying deficiencies in visual perception and perfecting vision. This can be understood as one facet of widespread early-modern ambitions to surpass nature and overcome the limitations of the human body, including restoring perfect health and longevity by remedying the corruptions which human beings were subject to after the Fall; these corruptions, moreover, were generally understood to have affected human being's perceptive and cognitive capacities. The second part of this essay will thus explore what it means to read the *Dioptrique* as a work of mechanical medicine whose aim is twofold: to correct the errors of vision due to injury, disease, and old age, and to extend and perfect humanity's visual powers.

1. The Medical and Anatomical Background to Descartes's Eye

We will go through, one by one, the key anatomical features of the eye given in discourse three of the *Dioptrique*. This account of the eye, Descartes says, "will

---

1 See, however, FABRIZIO BALDASSARRI, *Il metodo al tavolo anatomico. Descartes e la medicina*, Roma, Aracne, 2021, p. 106-121.
2 GIDEON MANNING, "Descartes and Medicine", in *The Oxford Handbook of Descartes and Cartesianism*, ed. by S. Nadler, T. M. Schmaltz, and D. Antoine-Mahut, Oxford, Oxford University Press, 2019, p. 157-177.

suffice to explain everything relevant to my subject" even while he omits a great deal of anatomical detail "with which the anatomists swell their books" that, he says, would only detract from one's understanding of how vision works.[3] He is primarily concerned with the eye as a natural instrument whose office is to cause coherent images (*images* in Descartes's French) to be imprinted on the backs of our eyes.[4] The array of impulses — light's combined linear and rotational tendencies towards motion — that constitute this image are subsequently transmitted through the fibres of the optic nerve into our brain. In the brain, Descartes says, the movements comprising the image immediately affect our soul (thus causing sensation) insofar as our soul is united to our body; these images, he later says, are "instituted by nature in order to make it [our soul] have such sensations".[5] Therefore, to understand this process of image formation it is necessary to comprehend the true nature of light, including the mathematical rules of reflection and refraction. Only once these things, along with the dioptrical properties of a healthy eye, are understood does Descartes begin his main task of the *Dioptrique*: to show the reader how to perfect vision by means of art.

Descartes's anatomy of the eye in discourse three first describes the tunics of the combined sclera/cornea, and after this the *uvea*.[6] He does not, however, refer to these tunics by the names given within works of anatomy and medicine, instead referring to the parts of his lettered illustration as one would a geometrical figure. (See Fig. 1.) This diagram of the eye is essential for Descartes's anatomical account. It is also relied upon heavily in later parts of the *Dioptrique*: it is repurposed and integrated into his accounts of the path of rays in his most famous illustration in the *Dioptrique*, the *camera obscura* model of the formation of pictures on the retina, and it is the basis for the diagrams used in his description of how to magnify the powers of sight via telescopes, of how to correct defects in vision via spectacles, and so on. This reliance on illustrations and diagrams is typical in his works. It is possible to see this as part of a general belief that diagrams can model relevant features of physical reality in an epistemically reliable way — that students of nature can trust his image to accurately convey the anatomical information needed to understand vision.[7]

---

3   "I laisse a dessein plusiers autres particularités qui se remarqent en cete matiere, & dont les Anatomists grossissent leurs livres; car ie croy que celles que i'ay mises icy, suffiront pour expliquer tout ce qui sert à mon sujet". RENÉ DESCARTES, *Discours de la Méthode pour bien conduire sa raison, & chercher la verite dans les sciences. Plus la dioptrique. Les meteores. Et la geometrie. Qui sont des essais de cete methode*, Leiden, Ian Maire, 1637, p. 29. Note that each of the four books is numbered separately; unless specified, all subsequent citations are to the *Dioptrique* specifically. AT VI 108.
4   DESCARTES, *Dioptrique*, 35; AT VI 114.
5   "institués de la nature pour luy faire avoir de tels sentimens". DESCARTES, *Dioptrique*, 51. AT VI 130.
6   Descartes's anatomy here follows his account in the *Treatise on Man*, and it is worth noting that the anatomical illustration used in discourse three of the *Dioptrique* was replicated very closely in both the 1662 and 1664 editions. RENÉ DESCARTES, *De homine figuris et latinitate donatus a Florentio Schuyl*, ed. by Florentius Schuyl, Leiden, Leffen, 1662, p. 44 ff. RENÉ DESCARTES, *L'Homme de René Descartes et Un Traitté de La Formation Du Foetus Du Mesme Autheur, Avec Les Remarques de Louys de La Forge*, ed. by Louis La Forge, Paris, Angot, 1664, p. 37 ff.
7   On this, see MELISSA LO, "The Picture Multiple: Figuring, Thinking, and Knowing in Descartes's Essais (1637)." *Journal of the History of Ideas* 78/3 (2017), p. 369-399.

Such confidence in visual depiction is not at all present in the medical tradition, where the assumption that an anatomical diagram can also serve as a mathematical diagram is problematic. Descartes is thus implicitly arguing (or assuming, based on his discussion in the *Discours de la Méthode* that introduced the *Dioptrique*) that the geometrical and mechanical features of the world, including living bodies, are the essence of material reality, and that these features can indeed be accurately represented in a diagram. All this contrasts with a common anxiety in the medical tradition that illustrations might override one's direct experience with, and understanding of, animal and human bodies. According to directives in the predominantly Galenic and Aristotelian medical tradition, one's knowledge of the body should ideally be built up via extensive and arduous observations and experiments — that is, one needs to work for a long time to acquire a robust body of experience in the Aristotelian sense. One wanders from the true pathway to *scientia* by relying on illustrations — relying, that is, on the imagination of the artist rather than nature itself.[8]

Descartes next describes the optic nerve, which he says spreads out into the retina. Again, he does not refer to the *tunica retina* by name, writing instead that the optic nerve, "extends throughout the space GHI" which is "like a third skin entirely covering the bottom of the second".[9] (See Figure 1.) He then describes the three humours: the aqueous, the crystalline, and the vitreous humours, though only the crystalline is referred to as such by Descartes. Of the crystalline he says that it "causes almost the same refraction as glass or crystal", while the other two refract similarly to water.[10] After describing the humours, Descartes mentions that the front of the first tunic — the cornea, which again Descartes does not mention by name — is transparent and bulging. He then says that the second tunic — the *uvea* — is "completely black and obscure", that it has a hole which can change in size, and that this part of the eye (the iris) "swims freely in the [aqueous] humour K".[11] There are many black fibres connecting the second humour (the *uvea*) to the crystalline lens, which "seem however like tiny tendons, by means of which this humour L becomes either more curved or flatter, according to the intention which one looks at objects close by or far away".[12] Finally, he says that there are "six or seven" muscles connecting the eye to rest of the body, allowing it to move in all directions and "and perhaps also by pressing or pulling helping to change its shape".[13]

---

8   On the epistemic worries of visual representation in medicine, see Karin Ekholm, "Fabricius's and Harvey's Representations of Animal Generation", *Annals of Science* 67/3 (2010), p. 329-352.
9   Descartes, *Dioptrique*, 26; AT VI 106: "estendent en tout l'espace GHI… laquelle est comme une troisieme peau, qui couvre tout le fons de la seconde".
10 Descartes, *Dioptrique*, 27; AT VI 106: "cause à peu prés mesme refraction que le verre ou le cristal".
11 Descartes, *Dioptrique*, 27; AT VI 107: "toute noire & obscure" and "nageant librement dans l'humeur K".
12 Descartes, *Dioptrique*, 28; AT VI 108: "semblent autant de petits tendons, par le moyen desquels cette humeur L devenant tantost plus voutée tantost plus platte, selon l'intention qu'on a de regarder des objets proches, ou esloignés, change un peu toute la figure du cors de l'oeil".
13 Descartes, *Dioptrique*, 29; AT VI 108: "& mesme aussi, peut estre, en le pressant ou retirant, ayder à changer sa figure".

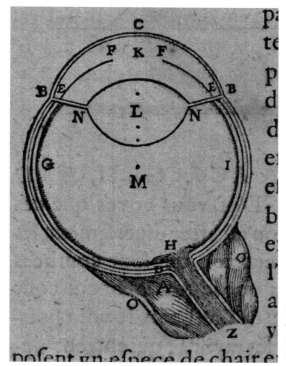

Figure 1. Descartes's anatomical eye. DESCARTES, *Dioptrique*, 26. Courtesy Bibliothèque nationale de France.

Some, but not all, of these features could have been derived from Kepler's account of the eye in his 1604 *Paralipomena*, which Descartes almost certainly read carefully.[14] Regardless, the source of this information originally comes from anatomical works written by physicians. In the sixteenth and early seventeenth centuries optics was understood as the science of sight rather than the science of the behaviour of light.[15] Crucially, it was primarily via the efforts of anatomists that optics took the eye, as revealed by careful dissection, observation, and experiment, to be the foundation of the discipline. In perspectivist optics prior to the end of the sixteenth century this was emphatically not the case. Rather, in this tradition philosophical and mathematical priors about the nature of visual rays (often understood as intromitted rays of light and colour), and about visual perception generally, necessitated a precise geometrical structure of the eye. One of the key features of this geometricized eye, given by the perspectivists from Ibn al-Haytham (Alhacen/Alhazen in Latin, *c.* 965-*c.* 1040) onwards, was that that the cornea and the anterior surface of the crystalline lens must

---

14 JOHN SCHUSTER, *Descartes-Agonistes: Physico-mathematics, Method & Corpuscular-Mechanism 1618-1633*, Dordrecht, Springer 2012, p. 153-163.
15 See especially A. MARK SMITH, *From Sight to Light: The Passage from Ancient to Modern Optics*, Chicago, University of Chicago Press, 2015. Although he gives more weight to anatomical developments than earlier scholars, even Smith undervalues the anatomical and tradition here.

be portions of concentric spherical shells.¹⁶ After arguing for the *a priori* necessity of this structure of the eye, these treatises of perspectivist optics mentioned, almost as an aside, that this structure is in accord with the books of anatomists. Despite these claims their eye was only partly in accord with anatomists prior to the sixteenth century, and by the beginning of the seventeenth century anatomists would attack key features of the perspectivist eye. Anatomists from the mid-sixteenth century worked, largely successfully, to turn their discipline into a branch of natural philosophy, and one consequence of this was that the discord between the anatomical and mathematical eye was made explicit. Anatomists began to argue that only by discovering the structure, action, and uses of the parts of the eye (in that order) via meticulous dissection can vision be properly understood, be it philosophically or mathematically.¹⁷ Kepler was influenced by this transformation in the understanding of how one ought to proceed with the science of vision, Descartes perhaps more so.

The features of the eye in Descartes's third discourse in the *Dioptrique* will be examined in turn and the influences from the fields of anatomy and medicine will be investigated. First is his description of the retina as "composed of a great number of small fibres".¹⁸ The description of the retina being the same substance as the centre of the optic nerve (the *medulla*, which term Descartes does not use) was ubiquitous, as was the knowledge that two of the meningeal layers enveloping the brain, the *dura mater* and the *pia mater*, are continued through the optic nerve and form the cornea and the *uvea*, respectively. The notion that the *pia mater* is connected with the *uvea* has since been overturned, but that the *dura mater* and the sclera are continuous still holds.

Descartes's statement that the retina consists of a great number of fibres (*filets*) was not typical for the time. For example, Vopiscus Fortunatus Plempius (1601-1671) writes:

> For when the substance of the optic nerve reaches into the eye, it softens and expands into a certain broad cloak over the vitreous humour, extending itself in front beyond the middle region of the eye up to the ciliary process. [...] It is however a soft, mucus-like tunic, white mixed with reddish, opaque and not diaphanous. It nevertheless participates in perspicuity to some degree, for the lower part of the *uvea* shines through the retina, almost in the same way that written letters are seen when exceedingly thin writing paper is placed on top. Nevertheless, it is known on exceedingly good evidence that it contains much more opacity than transparency (*perluciditas*).¹⁹

---

16 SMITH, *Sight to Light*, 186-188; 262.
17 TAWRIN BAKER, "Dissection, Instruction, and Debate: Visual Theory at the Anatomy Theatre in the Sixteenth Century", in *Perspective as Practice: Renaissance Cultures of Optics*, ed. by S. Dupré, Turnhout, Brepols, 2019, p. 123-147.
18 DESCARTES, *Dioptrique*, 26; AT VI 106: "composé d'un grand numbre de petits filets, dont les extremités s'esdentet en tout l'espace GHI".
19 VOPISCUS FORTUNATUS PLEMPIUS, *Ophthalmographia, sive Tractatio de oculi fabrica, actione, & usu*, Amsterdam, Henricus Laurentius, 1632, p. 40: "cum enim nervi optici substantia in oculum subintrat, mollescens expanditur in latum quoddam amiculum poticae vitrei humoris parti obtentum, exporrigens sese antrorsum ultra mediam oculi regionem ad ciliares processus, locus igitur eius

Plempius was born in Amsterdam and studied medicine at Leiden, Padua, and Bologna before returning to Amsterdam and practicing medicine and surgery there until 1633, when he became a professor of medicine at the University of Louvain. Today he is most well known as an early and vocal proponent of William Harvey's circulation of the blood, as one of the first physicians to adopt a version of Kepler's retinal theory of vision, and most of all as a critic of Descertes's account of the action of the heart after the publication of the *Discours de la méthode*.[20] Plempius's friendship with Descartes during his time in Amsterdam seems to have been important for the latter's anatomical investigations of the eye,[21] and Plempius's comprehensive treatment of medical and mathematical accounts of vision prior to him was important generally.

In the quote above we find Plempius deeply concerned with the exact degree of transparency/opacity, as well as colour, that the retina possesses. This was crucial for his Aristotelized retinal theory of vision. The retina needed to have sufficient transparency to be affected by light and colour, and this is because, in order to become actually illuminated and coloured, the retina must be coloured and illuminated in potency, while actually uncoloured — which is just to say that it must be transparent. But in addition, in an account derived from the perspectivist tradition, the retina must not admit light and colour in the way that air or water do; instead, it needs to delay, fix, and suffer the impressions of light and colour, and thus it must have some degree of thickness or opacity as well. His description of the retina as having just the right degree of transparency and opacity was exactly how the crystalline humour was described by the perspectivists, as well as anatomists (almost all of them prior to about 1630) who considered the crystalline humour to be the seat of vision.[22]

We should note that in the *Paralipomena*, which revolutionized visual theory by arguing that vision takes place via an inverted picture projected on the retina, Kepler denied that the *aranea* is connected to the *retina*.[23] This anatomical question had major ramifications for how vision works, and Kepler says that the fact that the *aranea* is disconnected from the retina (following, on this, the physician and anatomist Felix Platter[24]) entirely overthrows the opinion that the crystalline plays a role in fixing

---

est inter tunicam vitream & uveam. Est autem tunica mollis, mucosa, alba mixta rufedine, opaca non diaphana. participat tamen aliquatenus etiam perspicuitatem, nam uveae fundus per retinam tralucet: ad eum ferè modum, quo scriptae litterae per superimpositam tenuissimam scriptoriam chartam transparent. plus tamen multò opacitatis quam perluciditatis obtinere testatissimum".

20 J. P. TRICOT, "Vopiscus Fortunatus Plempius", *Vesalius* 6 (2000), p. 11-19; KATRIEN VANAGT, "Early Modern Medical Thinking on Vision and the Camera Obscura. V. F. Plempius' Ophthalmographia" in *Blood, Sweat and Tears: The Changing Concepts of Physiology from Antiquity into Early Modern Europe* ed. by Manfred Horstmanshoff, Claus Zittel, and Helen King, Boston, Brill, 2012, p. 569-593.
21 MANNING, "Descartes and Medicine", p. 163-164.
22 For a more detailed account of this issue just prior, see TAWRIN BAKER, "Why All This Jelly? Jacopo Zabarella and Hieronymus Fabricius Ab Aquapendente on the Usefulness of the Vitreous Humor", in *Early Modern Medicine and Natural Philosophy*, ed. by P. Distelzweig, B. Goldberg, and E. Ragland, New York, Springer, 2016, p. 59-88.
23 JOHANNES KEPLER, *Ad Vitellionem paralipomena, quibus astronomiae pars optica traditur*, Frankfurt, Marnius and heirs of Aubrius, 1604, p. 166.
24 FELIX PLATTER, *De corporis humani structura et vsu*, Basel, Froben, 1583, p. 187.

and sensing the impressions of incoming rays.[25] Descartes appropriated Kepler's retinal theory of vision, and seemingly influenced by Kepler and Platter's anatomical opinion he does not mention that the *aranea* (which today we would identify as the lens capsule) is connected to, or the same substance as, the retina. As mentioned, most medical writers prior to about 1630 located the primary seat of sensation in the crystalline humour. On this pre-Keplerian account it was typically understood that alterations in the crystalline humour were sensed by the visual spirit present in the *aranea*, either so that the faculty of seeing might judge the alterations in the eye itself and carry those judgments back, or else so that the impressions on the crystalline would themselves be carried back to the common sense in the brain to be judged there. Such anatomists made sure to stress the continuity of substance between the brain, optic nerve, retina, and *aranea*.[26] Plempius merely shifted the seat of vision from the crystalline humour to the retina, and due to this we see him, and following him Descartes, taking care to still note that the medulla of the brain and the optic nerve are of the same substance as the retina.[27]

Plempius is also typical among medical writers in describing the retina as mucus-like — seemingly the opposite of Descartes's account of it as fibrous. In his anatomical description of the retina, then, Descartes indeed omits many details given by anatomists that would "divert your attention".[28] These details, such as the texture and the specific degree of transparency of the retina, had been thoroughly accommodated to non-mechanical accounts of the reception of light and colour in the eye, but such descriptions are difficult to reconcile with a simplified mechanical account of the reception of light impulses in the retina. As we have seen, Descartes simply mentions that the fibres of the optic nerve extend and spread out through the retina. Moreover, unlike nearly all earlier adopters of the retinal theory, he describes the retina as "a kind of extremely tender and delicate flesh".[29] This fits with his rejection of both sensible species and the special powers of the visual spirit; he replaces this with an account of nervous activity occurring through local motion alone, irrespective of which sense modality is involved.[30]

Next is the corneal bulge, a feature generally absent from medieval anatomical accounts (including those of the perspectivists). This bulge was clearly described by the most famous anatomist of his day, Hieronimus Fabricius ab Aquapendente (1533-1619).[31] This was soon after taken up by Kepler (through Fabricius's student Johannes Jessenius

---

25 KEPLER, *Paralipomena*, p. 204: "Haec tota sententia... prosternitur, reflecto crystallino, à nervo & à retina, nexoque cum uvea".
26 For an influential example, see HIERONYMUS FABRICIUS AB AQUAPENDENTE, *De visione, voce, auditu*, Venice, Bolzettam, 1600, p. 9-10.
27 PLEMPIUS, *Ophthalmographia*, p. 50: "substantia medullari, quam communicavit eis cerebrum, in retiformen transformata".
28 DESCARTES, *Dioptrique*, p. 29; AT VI 108.
29 DESCARTES, *Dioptrique*, p. 26; AT VI 106: "un espece de chair extremement tendre & delicate".
30 DESCARTES, *Dioptrique*, p. 29-34; AT VI 109-114. See also CELIA WOLFE-DEVINE, "Descartes' Theory of Visual Spatial Perception", in *Descartes' Natural Philosophy*, ed. by S. Gaukroger, J. Schuster, and J. Sutton, New York, Routledge, 2000, p. 506-523.
31 FABRICIUS *De visione*, p. 5-6.

(1566-1621)) and Franciscus Aguilonius (1567-1617) in his *Opticae libri sex* of 1613. It is, moreover, present in Christoph Scheiner's 1619 *Oculus* and nearly everyone else after Scheiner concerned with both ocular anatomy and visual theory. Kepler considered this bulge important for his retinal theory of vision: that the cornea forms a portion of a sphere that is smaller than the sclera, he says, should be "carefully retained in the memory".[32] Kepler's source for this was once again Jessenius, a well-known physician, surgeon, and philosopher (among other things). Jessenius studied medicine in Padua from 1588 to 1591, and in 1600 he performed a well-publicized anatomy in Prague that formed the basis for his *Anatomiae, Pragae*, published in 1601; he then moved to Prague 1602 and lived there until 1611, returning to become the rector of Charles University in 1617.[33] Kepler, then, not only cited Jessenius's *Anatomiae, Pragae*, but interacted with Jessenius and considered him a friend during his time in Prague. For Jessenius the *utilitas* or teleological function of the corneal bulge is twofold.[34] First is so that the eye can take in more from the visual field. Jessenius here assumes one aspect of the perspectivist theory, according to which only the rays arriving perpendicular to the cornea are considered for direct vision; thus a bulging corneal surface would take in rays covering a larger solid angle. Second is so that the rays might be united more strongly within the eye.[35] This second factor is important for the new visual theory that Jessenius followed. In it, an image is first formed in the crystalline humour and judged there (by the visual faculty dispersed throughout the *aranea*), and after this the rays passing through are united into the point of a cone just beyond the crystalline humour, thereby (the theory went) dispersing and destroying the rays in the large vitreous body.[36]

We find this new visual theory from Padua in Fabricius ab Aquapendente's 1600 *De visione* as well as in the influential Aristotelian natural philosopher Jacopo Zabarella's (1533-1589) *De rebus naturalibus*, published in 1590. Jessenius acknowledges that his account of the eye was derived from his teacher Fabricius — likely from the latter's public dissections and lectures on the eye *c*. 1590.[37] Unknown to Kepler, however, is that by 1600 Fabricius was more fully aware than his pupil of the ramifications of the lack of concentricity of the cornea and anterior crystalline for traditional perspectivist optics, which he posed as a challenge to future mathematicians and other "diligent investigators of nature" wishing to trace the paths of rays in the eye and understand

---

32 KEPLER, *Paralipomena*, p. 164: "Sic ut cornea minoris sphaerae portio si, Sclerodes maioris: quod diligenter memoria retinendum est".
33 DAVID KACHLIK, DAVID VICHNAR, VLADIMIR Musil, DANA KACHLIKOVA, KRISTIAN SZABO, and JOSEF STINGL, "A Biographical Sketch of Johannes Jessenius: 410th Anniversary of His Prague Dissection", *Clinical Anatomy* 25/2 (2012), p. 149-154.
34 JOHANNES JESSENIUS, *Anatomiae, Pragae, anno M. D. C. abs se solenniter administratae historia*, Wittenberg, Laurentius Seuberlich, 1601, p. 115[v].
35 JESSENIUS, *Anatomiae*, p. 121[r]: "Rotunda item est, ut minùs laesioni foret obnoxia quatenus verò huic rotunditati extuberantia quaedam accedit, praestat, ut oculus se maiora videat, postea ut lux ingrediens impensiùs uniatur. Prior ille usus patet ex minutulis illis extuberantiis, quae in speculorum quorundam angulis cernuntur; in quibus singulis suam quisque faciem spectabat integram, cùm contrà in fragmento plano, licèt decuplo maiori, vis partem faciei videat".
36 This visual theory is outlined in BAKER, "Why all this jelly?"
37 BAKER, "Dissection, Instruction, and Debate'".

vision generally.³⁸ These empirically observable features of the eye raised serious doubts for traditional (perspectivist) optics.

As we saw, Descartes describes the pupil as formed from a hole in the *uvea*, the parts of which are swimming freely in the foremost (i.e., the aqueous) humour. His description relies on his diagram, pointing out the pupil, K, around which is depicted a good deal of space between the *uvea* or iris, EF, and the crystalline humour L. This space described in both text and image is greater than we know to exist today, and while there are many possible reasons for this one likely influence comes from the surgical practice of cataract couching. Until the beginning of the eighteenth century it was generally believed that cataracts were concretions that developed in front of, or were attached to, the crystalline lens rather than, as is known today, an opacification of the lens itself. (Opacification of the lens was at this time generally called *glaucoma*; this distinction and nomenclature goes back to antiquity and is seen in Galen.³⁹) A common operation for severe cataracts involved couching, that is inserting a special needle somewhere behind the corneal limbus (corneo-scleral junction) and then working this supposedly extraneous matter downwards, beneath the vitreous body and out of the path of visual rays. In fact, the matter that was deposited in was not a separate accumulation, but the lens itself. Some degree sight could indeed be restored by this operation, and people might be able to subsequently "find their way and path" as we read, e.g., in several patient testimonies prefacing the famous German ophthalmologist Georg Bartisch's 1583 *Ohpthalmoduleia*.⁴⁰ But this restoration of sight would scarcely be possible if the true seat of vision in the eye were, itself, pushed below the pupil. Prior to the general acceptance of the retinal theory of vision, towards which Descartes's *Dioptrique* played a significant role, the lens was typically believed to be the primary seat of visual sensation in the eye by extramissionists and intromissionists alike. Moreover, cataract couching was (and is, to the extent that it is still performed in some remote areas without access to modern surgery) a tricky operation with many potential complications, and thus learned surgeons and physicians avoided it.⁴¹ It fell to lower status surgical specialists to perform this common (and less remunerative) operation, and the disconnect between learned anatomists and those actually performing cataract couching helps explain why the centuries-old cataract theory persisted for about fifty years after the widespread acceptance of the retinal theory.⁴²

---

38 Fabricius, *De visione*, 105.
39 Christopher T. Leffler et al., "What Was Glaucoma Called Before the 20th Century?", *Ophthalmology and Eye Diseases* 7 (2015), p. 21-33. Christopher T. Leffler et al., "The History of Cataract Surgery: From Couching to Phacoemulsification", *Annals of Translational Medicine* 8/22 (2020): p. 1551. Galen, *Galen on the Usefulness of the Parts of the Body*, trans. by Margaret Tallmadge May, 2 vols., Ithaca, N.Y., Cornell University Press, 1968, p. 463-464.
40 Georg Bartisch, *Ophthalmodouleia: das ist Augendienst*, Dresden, 1583.
41 Tawrin Baker, "The Oculist's Eye: Connections between Cataract Couching, Anatomy, and Visual Theory in the Renaissance", *Journal of the History of Medicine and Allied Sciences* 72/1 (2017), p. 51-66.
42 On the transformation of the understanding of cataracts, see Maria Teresa Monti, "La Chirurgie de La Cataracte: Institutions, Techniques et Modèles Scientifiques de Brisseau à Daviel", *Revue d'histoire Des Sciences* 47/1 (1994): p. 107-127. Leffler et al., "History of Cataract Surgery".

There were two influential deviations from this accepted configuration of the eye that Descartes seemingly ignores. Both Fabricius ab Aquapendente and Christoph Scheiner describe a much reduced aqueous, and thus leave very little space between the lens and the iris, an account much closer to our modern description.[43] Fabricius also advises against cataract couching: there is so little space in the eye, he says, that the couching needle is certain to puncture either the iris or the crystalline humour.[44] Descartes gives no clues as to why he did not follow these authors who were generally regarded as authorities on ocular anatomy in the first half of the century. (Note that Descartes's illustration has the optic nerve entering the eye nasally, rather than in line with the axis of vision; this discovery was made by Scheiner and is found in both his illustrations and textual anatomical description.[45]) Descartes thus follows traditional medical opinion, and ignores recent challenges to it, in his description of the size of posterior aqueous chamber and the distance between the lens and the iris.

Turning to those who Descartes interacted with, Plempius writes that there is some debate over what disease ought to be called a suffusion or cataract, and that if the judgment were up to him the name would refer to a thickened humour persisting in the pupil, i.e., in front of the crystalline, though such a thickened humour might arise rarely in the vitreous, and even more rarely in the crystalline.[46] For treating cataracts he advises medicines first and couching only if medicines are unsuccessful. It is unclear whether Plempius followed Fabricius's and Scheiner in their estimate of the minuscule space between the crystalline and the iris, but his description of treatment is in accord with their anatomical descriptions.

Descartes's *Dioptrique* was clearly influential, and for a long time his illustrations of the eye became the model for ocular illustrations.[47] The work no doubt facilitated the acceptance of the retinal theory, yet due to the widespread use of his images of the eye as a visual model he may also have reinforced the traditional theory of cataracts. The *Dioptrique*'s influence in these respects, however, has yet to be carefully investigated.

We can now characterize Descartes's debt, in the *Dioptrique*, to the immediately preceding anatomical and medical tradition. On the shape of the cornea and the crystalline, and placement of the latter, he relied on the work of anatomists and physicians after Vesalius. Concerning the large aqueous and generous space between the crystalline and the iris compared to the authorities of Fabricius and Scheiner (not to mention modern determinations), Descartes's illustration relayed the traditional view found within learned medicine since antiquity and confirmed by the surgical practices of lower-status oculists. On the relative densities/refractive powers of the humours he

---

43 FABRICIUS, *De visione*, p. 106. CHRISTOPH SCHEINER, *Oculus, hoc est, fundamentum opticum*, Innsbruck, Agricola, 1619, p. 11, 15, 17.
44 HIERONYMUS FABRICIUS AB AQUAPENDENTE, *Opera chirurgica in duas partes divisa*, Venice, Robertus Megliettus, 1619, p. 23-24. BAKER, 'The Oculist's Eye', p. 63.
45 SCHEINER, *Oculus*, p. 4, 17.
46 PLEMPIUS, *Ophthalmographia*, p. 323, 332-337.
47 DOMINIQUE RAYNAUD, *Eye Representation and Ocular Terminology from Antiquity to Helmholtz*, Hirschberg History of Ophthalmology: The Monographs 16, Amsterdam, Wayenborgh Publications, 2020.

is consistent with Fabricius, although this opinion was found in medieval optics as well; the difference, however, is that Fabricius (and perhaps Platter) abandoned the notion that animal spirits actively intervened on the path of the rays within the eye and optic nerve. In other words, with respect to the refraction of rays Descartes's eye was a "dead eye"; this notion, which contradicted the perspectivists, was originally posited by anatomists and physicians preceding Kepler, who is often said to have instituted this break.[48] Whether Descartes in fact derived this information from these medical/anatomical sources, or merely relied upon Kepler, Scheiner, and his one-time collaborator Plempius (who knew and cited all the medical authors mentioned as well as Kepler and Scheiner) is unclear. Descartes notoriously did not mention or cite his influences.

On certain details Descartes was able to select among the work by previous anatomists and physicians, perhaps confirming them with his own dissections. He ignored many of the finer details of ocular anatomy that were either irrelevant to his account or, in the case of the consistency, colour, and degree of transparency of retina, in tension with authoritative anatomical histories. One might argue that, in some ways, Descartes engaged with the medical tradition similarly to the medieval perspectivists: a theory of light and colour was first established, and then the medical/anatomical eye was accommodated to that theory. Because of the increased status and widespread knowledge of anatomy as well as the recent consensus of key anatomical findings, however, he was under far more constraints than these medieval authors. Thus, one legacy of the efforts of sixteenth and early seventeenth century anatomy and medicine, which was acknowledged by mathematically minded polymaths such as Aguilonius and Scheiner, was that anatomy came to be (for a time) the foundation of mathematical optics.[49] Descartes combines this notion with one arising from Kepler's *Dioptrice*, namely that optics studies how vision arises due to refracting instruments generally, with the eye being one such instrument.[50]

Finally, the oculist's eye — according to which there existed a large space between the crystalline and the iris wherein cataracts were generated, a space ample enough to safely insert a couching needle without damaging the iris or crystalline lens — made its way into Descartes's illustrations of the eye, even though this account of the eye was recently challenged in both text and illustration. Descartes's depiction of the eye arguably encouraged traditional medical opinions about cataracts.

2. Reading the Dioptrique as a Medical Text

Gideon Manning has posited the following:

> The role of anatomy was circumscribed in optics. As a result, although Descartes came to be engaged in general anatomical study by 1632, in his published work

---

48 On this, see ALAN E. SHAPIRO, "Images: Real and Virtual, Projected and Perceived, from Kepler to Dechales", *Early Science and Medicine* 13/3 (2008), p. 270-312, esp. p. 310-311.
49 FRANÇOIS D'AGUILON, *Francisci Aguilonii e Societate Jesu opticorum libri sex philosophis juxtà ac mathematicis utiles*, Antwerp, Ex officina Plantiniana, 1613, p. 1-2.
50 ANTONI MALET, "Kepler and the Telescope", *Annals of Science* 60/2 (2003), p. 107-136, esp. p. 131-134.

he was more restrained, publishing only an anatomically informed optics and not a proper or easily recognizable work of medicine, as Plempius had done.[51]

I argue that, even if not "easily recognizable", there is a clear sense in which the *Dioptrique* can be considered medical work. By 1637 the role of anatomy in optics was in the midst — or, perhaps, towards the end — of a transformation. Due to this the anatomy of the eye, as revealed via first-hand, meticulous dissection, became crucial for treatises on mathematical optics. The eye became a source for rethinking accounts of light, colour, refraction, image formation, representation (and related concepts such as *imagines* or *species*), and visual perception. This process, moreover, was heavily indebted to Galenic conceptions of anatomical method and what can be gained from it. This shift is obvious in Fabricius ab Aquapendente and Christoph Scheiner, but this new emphasis on precise, empirical anatomical investigation of the eye as a necessary precondition to mathematical optics is also apparent in Kepler's *Paralipomena* and Aguilonius's *Opticorum libri sex* (the latter generally following Fabricius, the former influenced by Fabricius via the intermediary Jessenius). This contrasts sharply with the *livresque* anatomy of the medieval perspectivists from Ibn al-Haytham onwards, within which a precise geometrical anatomy of the eye was arrived at by necessity, due to constraints laid down by prior physical and geometrical postulates and demonstrations; this ocular description was only loosely coordinated with the books of the anatomists afterwards. We see, therefore, a reversal of the epistemic order for the science of vision around 1600. Only then did mathematicians hold that the structure of the eye, including its measurable, indeed geometrical, properties, had to be determined empirically. Anatomists, in a self-consciously Galenic mode, began with the assumption that Nature has foresight and thus that Nature took into account how visual/visible rays behave when she constructed the instrument of vision. Many mathematicians and philosophers treating optics followed this assumption as well, at least for a time. Consequently, only via dissection could one decipher *why* animal eyes are constructed as they are, which in turn revealed a great deal about the nature of light and colour, how rays propagate and refract, how and why images are formed in the eye, and so on.

While Descartes took for granted results stemming from this new disciplinary shift, his *Dioptrique* returned (at least in part) to a conservative order of investigation in mathematical optics. Thus, like Ibn al-Haytham, Witelo (Vitello Thuringopolonis, c. 1230-1280), and John Peckham (c. 1230-1292), Descartes begins with an investigation into the physical nature of light and the mathematics of direct and reflected rays. He next treats refraction (including his famous account of the sine rule) in Discourse two of the *Dioptroque*; although the perspectivists introduced refraction early on as well, they ignored refracted rays in their account of direct vision, and thus treated mathematical problems involving refraction only later in their treatises. In Discourse three Descartes covers the anatomy of the eye; in Discourse four he discusses the senses in general; and finally in Discourse five he combines the previous results to

---

51 MANNING, "Descartes and Medicine", p. 164.

give an account of "the images that form on the back of the eye". This allowed him to investigate the nature of vision itself — how this inverted picture on the retina results in the experience of sight — in Discourse six.

With Discourse seven, however, he begins a mechanical-medical treatise on vision. In a letter to Mersenne from January 1630 he wrote that he was seeking to "discover a medicine which is founded on infallible demonstrations",[52] and in another to Mersenne dated 25 November 1630 that, after completing his work on dioptrics, he wished to "discover something useful in medicine".[53] In 1633 he decided not to publish *Le Monde*, which contained an account of light and optics as well as an account of human physiology, including the eye; the section on physiology was published posthumously as the *Treatise on Man*.[54]

I argue that Descartes ended up investing his 1637 *Dioptriqe* with some of the medical ambitions that he mentioned in these letters. At the end of Discourse seven he describes many ways that practices of sailors, hunters, engravers, and "Indiens" have, by repeated exercise, increased the capacity of the crystalline humour to change shape (and thus better focus images) and that of the pupil to dilate and contract. Through similar practice we can correct the defects in our ability to take in light and focus images on our retina, and with bad habits we diminish these capacities. He then writes:

> But these things belong rather to Medicine, whose goal is to remedy defects in vision through the correction of the natural organs, than to Dioptrics, whose goal is only to remedy these same defects through the application of certain other artificial organs.[55]

We need not, however, take Descartes's division strictly. As he says, there are ways to remedy and prevent visual impairments via exercises of the natural organs, but also artificial remedies to visual impairments via the use of artificial organs. Both kinds of remedy were described in medical treatises. Moreover, we can interpret his investigation of artificial organs as part of his project to develop a medicine based on "infallible demonstrations", namely his demonstration of the properties of light, the sine law of refraction, and his mathematization of the eye.

Taking the *Dioptrique*'s goal to artificially correct and perfect vision as a medical goal is particularly apt given that Descartes had rejected the Galenic notion of faculties

---

52 Descartes to Mersenne, January 1630, AT I 106: "ie vous prie de vous conserver, au moins uisqu'a ce que ie sçache s'il y a moyen de trouver une Medecine qui soit fondée en demonstrations infaillibles, que est ce qui ie cherche maintenant". I am indebted here to Manning, "Descartes and Medicine".

53 Descartes to Mersenne, 25 November 1630, AT I 180: "comme de fait après la Dioptrique achevée, je suis en resolution d'étudier pour moy & pour mes amis à bon escient, c'est à dire de chercher quelque chose d'utile en la médecine".

54 See footnote 5 above.

55 DESCARTES, *Dioptrique*, 87-88. AT VI 164-165: "Mais ces choses apartienent plustost a la Medecine, dont la fin est de remedier aus defauts de la veuë par la correction des organes naturels, que non pas a la Dioptrique, dont la fin n'est que de remedier aus mesmes defauts par l'application de quelques autres organes artificiels."

as either explanatory or causal agents. Because the fundamental powers of natural and artificial organs are identical in Descartes's mechanical philosophy, the distinction between the two does not carry nearly the same weight that it would within a Galenic or Aristotelian philosophical medical framework; according to the latter the natural faculties, or capacities of organs in an ensouled body, were supposed to have powers that are in-principle beyond human artifice. While Descartes seemed to hold that God could produce things, such as animals, with capacities beyond those that mankind can generate, nevertheless for Descartes this distinction was technical rather than ontological: the powers or capacities of animals were in-principle intelligible in the sense that all matter was composed of a single substance, *res extensa*.[56] Any supposed natural faculties could thus be analyzed into a machine organized from the shape, size, number, relative motion or rest, etc. of portions of this substance.

During this time what we would today call prosthetic devices were within the scope of the art of surgery. The famous sixteenth-century surgeon Ambroise Paré (c. 1510-1590), for example, devotes book twenty-three of his *Oeuvres* to "the means and arts to supply that which is lacking naturally or by accident".[57] This, Paré says, is the fourth duty of the surgeon, the other three being to unite things in the body that become separated, to discharge the superfluities in the body, and to separate things that are united (but that ought not be). Much of this book addresses cosmetic defects, but it also covers how to improve speech by artificial aids, how to correct crookedness in the body (e.g., the spine by using iron breastplates), and the making and use of crutches and artificial legs. Notably for our account, he includes descriptions of artificial hands and arms made of iron made by a certain *serrurier* or locksmith named *le petit Lorrain*.[58] (See Fig. 2.) These complex artificial limbs are fascinating as a potential context for Descartes's account of human beings as a *machine de Terre* given that, around 1630, he was studying medicine to write *L'Homme* — but this is beyond the scope of this chapter.

Sticking to medical sources for the *Dioptrique*, it is notable that eyeglasses are absent from Paré's discussion of artificial remedies for natural defects. Paré does mention coloured spectacles at several points in his *Oeuvres* to illustrate issues about perception, but he gives no account of spectacles for near or far sightedness.[59] Yet this is typical of medical works for the time. Indeed, to the extent that reading glasses were mentioned in medical works prior to the 1630's it was typically to show the efficacy of

---

56 On the art-nature distinction in Descartes, see his remarks in the *Principia philosophiae*, IV, art. 203, AT VIII-1, 326.
57 AMBROISE PARÉ, *Les oeuvres de M. Ambroise Paré*, Paris, Chez Gabriel Buon, 1575, p. 716: "des moyens & artifices d'adjouster ce qui defaut naturellement ou par accident". This was reprinted and translated extensively, including into English in: AMBROISE PARÉ, *The Workes of That Famous Chirurgion Ambrose Parey Translated out of Latine and Compared with the French by Th: Johnson*, London, Cotes and Young, 1634. On Descartes and Paré, see Jil Muller's contribution to this volume.
58 PARÉ, *Oeuvres*, p. 723. See also HEIDI HAUSSE, "The Locksmith, the Surgeon, and the Mechanical Hand: Communicating Technical Knowledge in Early Modern Europe", *Technology and Culture* 60/1 (2019): p. 34-64.
59 PARÉ, *Workes*, p. 88, p. 184. He also recommends that either spectacles or taffety cloth be used after removing bandages the eighth day after cataract couching in order to slowly accustom the patient to light; these were almost certainly such coloured spectacles. PARÉ, *Workes*, p. 654.

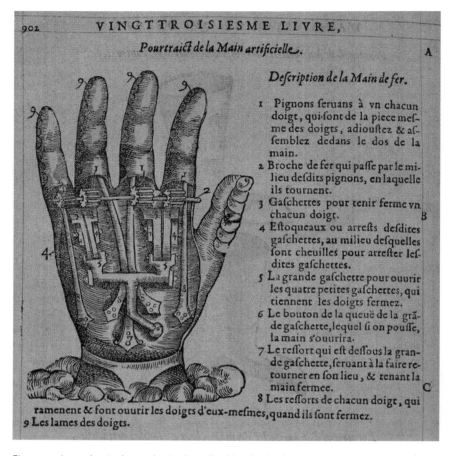

Figure 2. A mechanical prosthesis described by the barber-surgeon AMBROISE PARÉ, *Les oeuvres d'Ambroise Paré 5e edition*, Paris, Gabriel Buon, 1598, p. 902. Courtesy Bibliothèque nationale de France.

a medicament. For example, witnesses might be invoked as an assurance that, after using such and such a recipe, reading glasses were no longer required.[60] Eyeglasses themselves were typically discouraged by both physicians and surgical specialists dealing with the eye.[61] This was beginning to change in Descartes's day, however, and thus in his *Ophthalmographia* Plempius addresses the problem, "Why do convex spectacles benefit those who see remote things distinctly but nearby things in a confused way,

---

60 WALTER BALEY, *A Briefe Treatise Touching the Preservation of the Eie Sight Consisting Partly in Good Order of Diet, and Partly in vse of Medicines*, Oxford, England, Joseph Barnes, 1602, p. 7.
61 KATRIEN VANAGT, "Suspicious Spectacles. Medical Perspectives on Eyeglasses, the Case of Hieronymus Mercurialis", in *The Origins of the Telescope*, ed. by A. Van Helden *et al.*, Amsterdam: KNAW press, 2010, p. 115-128.

while those who see remote things in a confused way and nearby things distinctly are helped by concave spectacles?"⁶² This is only one page out of his 340-page treatise, however, and he does not mention eyeglasses in his discussion of diseases of the eye.

It appears that the medicalization of spectacles only truly began in the second half of the seventeenth century.⁶³ Physicians, notably, tended to subscribe to a roughly Galenic extramission theory of vision through most of the sixteenth century, and medicine as a whole only abandoned extramissionism in the seventeenth. As Katrien Vanagt has pointed out, this eventual rejection of extramission theories of vision was key for the medicalization of spectacles.⁶⁴ Also key was a broader shift in which the proper functioning of the eye, in medicine, was considered not only with respect to the body but with respect to the outside world.⁶⁵ Here I would add that the introduction in the seventeenth century of works combining ocular anatomy and dioptrics, Descartes's *Dioptrique* especially, was a pivotal moment for the medicalization of spectacles. This history is yet poorly studied, however.

While medical works prior to Descartes's tended not to do so, in the *Dioptrique* we see telescopes and eyeglasses described as what would later be called a prosthetic device.⁶⁶ In Discourse six Descartes describes catoptrical and dioptrical devices as they are traditionally presented in pre-Keplerian perspectivist optics, namely as causes of deception or illusion that are explained away via the middle science of optics. As mentioned it is in Discourse seven ("On the Means of Perfecting Vision"), in which we begin to see Descartes's medical ambitions, that he clarifies the aims of his mathematical analysis. He writes that, if we wish to perfect vision, we cannot (yet) improve the internal organs via artifice, but we can alter the eye itself, and — most importantly — we can supply artificial organs such as eyeglasses and telescopes.

> Concerning, then, the interior organs, which are the nerves and the brain, it is also certain that we do not know how to add anything to their construction by art, for we cannot make ourselves a new body, and if the doctors can help us in this respect, it does not belong to our subject.⁶⁷

---

62 PLEMPIUS, *Ophthalmographia*, 277: "Cur iis, qui remota distincte vident, propinqua confuse, perspicilla [*sic*] convexa prosunt: ii vero, qui confuse vident remota distincte propinqua iuvantur concavis perspicillis?"
63 KATRIEN VANAGT, "Aversion to spectacles and the diffusion of optical knowledge among early modern medical practitioners", *Gewina (Rotterdam)* 29/1 (2006): p. 26-40.
64 VANAGT, "Suspicious Spectacles", p. 118-125.
65 VANAGT, "Aversion to Spectacles", p. 40.
66 The earliest mention I have found in English is from 1699 (as of this writing the OED lists 1706 as the earliest instance). M. DE LA VAUGUION, *A Compleat Body of Chirurgical Operations Containing the Whole Practice of Surgery, with Observations and Remarks on Each Case, amongst Which Are Inserted the Several Ways of Delivering Women in Natural and Unnatural Labours*, London, Henry Bonwick in St Pauls Church Yard, T. Goodwin, M. Wotton, B. Took in Fleetstreet, and S. Manship in Cornhil, 1699, p. 1: "Prothesis is the adding by Art and Industry useful parts deficient, as Artificial Legs and Arms."
67 DESCARTES, *Dioptrique*, p. 70-71; AT VI 148: "Puis touchant les organs interieurs, qui sont les nerfs & le cerveau, il est certain aussy, que nous ne sçaurions rien adjouter par art leur fabrique; car nous ne sçaurions nous faire un nouveau cors; & si les medecins y peuvent ayder en quelque chose, cela n'apartient point a nostre sujet."

He next lists, given what he has determined in his prior chapters, the conditions required for vision to take place, that is, for the formation of images on the retina. He then outlines how "Nature has employed many means" for this.[68] This section is just an account of the usefulness, or teleological function, of the organs of vision; it reads as Galenic, complete with implications about the skill and foresight of nature, although this likely shouldn't be interpreted as literally as in Galen.[69] Next, he lists the defects that nature has allowed to creep into some of our organs of vision, along with artificial means of remedying them — namely, eyeglasses for either short- or far-sightedness. From this discussion about remedying natural defects he effortlessly moves to improving and perfecting vision by means of magnifying glasses — *lunetes à puces* — and telescopes.

The rest of his treatise, Discourses eight through ten, contains theoretical/mathematical discussions of the shapes of lenses that "are useful for vision",[70] how these can be combined into telescopes, and the methods of making lenses. Hyperbolic lenses in particular are key, the properties of which Descartes had demonstrated mathematically in discourse eight, and which he judges be the most useful of all lens shapes for correcting and amplifying vision. If we wish to extend our medical reading of the *Dioptrique* further, we might say that these chapters are analogous to treatises on medical simples, on compound medicines, and finally practical instructions for synthesizing a previously only hypothesized, but exceptionally powerful and desirable, medical remedy. In this analogy the hyperbolic lens can be compared to the wonders of theriac or, perhaps, even the alchemical elixir; it is a means of so perfecting vision that, as he writes in a letter from 1629, "we might see... if there are animals on the moon."[71] Notably, these chapters on correcting and perfecting vision involve mathematical demonstrations, and thus, I argue, fulfil Descartes lofty goal, stated seven years earlier, to "discover a medicine which is founded on infallible demonstrations".[72]

3. Conclusion

Jed Buchwald has noted that, "the eighth discourse in the *Dioptrique*, and the eighth in the *Météores*, are the only two that utilize geometry to produce something that was not known beforehand".[73] He is referring, respectively, to the deduction of the shape of the anaclastic in the *Dioptrique*, which brings incoming rays to a single

---

68 DESCARTES, *Dioptrique*, 71-72; AT VI 149: "Or la nature a employé plusiers moyens à pourvoir à la primiere de ces choses."
69 Cf. DESCARTES, *Dioptrique*, 72; AT VI 149: "Car nous devons supposer que la nature a fait en cecy tout ce qui est possible, d'autant que l'experience ne nous y fait rien apercevoir au contraire".
70 DESCARTES, *Dioptrique*, 89; AT VI 165: "Des figures que doivent avoir les cors transparens pour detourner les rayons par refraction en toutes les façons qui servent a la veuë."
71 Descartes to Ferrier, 13 November 1629. AT I 69.
72 Descartes to Mersenne, January 1630, AT I 106.
73 JED Z. BUCHWALD, "Descartes's Experimental Journey Past the Prism and Through the Invisible World to the Rainbow", *Annals of Science* 65/1 (2010): p. 1-46, esp. p. 2.

point, and the explanation of the colours of the rainbow in the *Météores*. Descartes demonstrates two ways of producing an anaclastic, first from a complicated series of lenses with combinations of elliptical and spherical surfaces, and then via a single lens with a flat surface on one side and a hyperbolic one on the other.[74] Buchwald then writes,

> There is, however, a marked difference between the two deductions. In the case of the anaclastic, there was no existing natural phenomenon to explain; it was instead a case of generating the specifications for an artificial object that would behave in a certain way. The rainbow on the other hand exists naturally, and its properties accordingly brought issues of observation directly into question.[75]

This is not entirely true. In the *Paralipomena* Kepler describes the shape of the crystalline humour thus:

> The crystalline, on the face that is bounded by the ciliary process and immersed in the aqueous, acquires either a spherical figure, or a portion of a lenticular spheroid, a rotated ellipse, divided by the axis, the side remaining straight. On the posterior side, which is bounded by the same ciliary process, it is immersed in the vitreous. Its figure is a hyperbolic conoid, a hyperbola rotated around the axis. For Jessenius thus relates, that it is not spherical, as Platter said, but that it protrudes markedly, and is made oblong, stretching up almost into a cone.[76]

It is certainly possible that this passage inspired Descartes in his research, and even that in his work on anaclastics he was thinking of both natural and artificial lenses. The text of the *Dioptrique* does not describe the shape of the crystalline lens with geometrical precision. His diagram instead contains a series of four points that perhaps indicate the supposed centres of curvature of the cornea, the front and rear surfaces of the crystalline, and the eye as a whole; this visual scheme was taken from the perspectivists and adopted by medical writers, such as Fabricius, in their diagrams. But the connection between this detail in the diagram and Descartes's thoughts or investigations is unclear — this ocular geometry is ignored in the text. Moreover, the tradition this depiction borrowed from considered these surfaces to be spherical, not elliptical or hyperbolic. On the other hand, in the *Treatise on Man* we read, in reference to the anatomical illustration of the eye (copied from the *Dioptrique*) "The shape of the humour marked L, which is called the crystalline humour, is like the shape of the lenses I described in the treatise on dioptrics, whereby all the rays

---

74 On the hyperbolic lens, see D. GRAHAM BURNETT, *Descartes and the Hyperbolic Quest: Lens Making Machines and Their Significance in the Seventeenth Century*, Transactions of the American Philosophical Society, v. 95, pt. 3, Philadelphia, PA, American Philosophical Society, 2005.
75 BUCHWALD, "Descartes's Experimental Journey", p. 2.
76 Translation from JOHANNES KEPLER, *Optics: Paralipomena to Witelo & Optical Part of Astronomy*, ed. and trans. by William H. Donahue, Santa Fe, New Mexico, Green Lion Press, 2000, p. 179. Original at KEPLER, *Paralipomena*, p. 167-168. See also Kepler's frustrated attempt to demonstrate the shape of an anaclastic lens at KEPLER, *Paralipomena*, p. 106-109.

that come from certain points are reassembled at certain other points".[77] The dots indicating centres of curvature are also notably lacking in the illustrations to the editions of the *Treatise on Man*. It is possible that there was a connection between, on the one hand, the proposed hyperbolic and elliptical surfaces of the crystalline lens by Kepler, and, on the other, the culmination of Descartes investigations in the *Dioptrique* — investigations which were originally to be printed in *Le Monde* prior to the *Treatise on Man*. Why the hyperbolic shape of the crystalline is implied in the *Treatise on Man* but absent in the *Dioptrique*, however, is unclear.

While there clearly is a sense in which we can read the *Dioptrique* as medical, and while doing so allows us to better understand Descartes's work and his place in seventeenth-century developments in anatomy and medicine, this reading has its limits. To discover those limits it has been necessary to at least approach them, and perhaps pass beyond into the realm of speculation. Nevertheless, we can say that medical aims, broadly understood, constituted part of the goal of "practical mastery" evident in the second half of the *Dioptrique*. While it does not resemble traditional medical genres, a fact that Descartes acknowledges several times, we can identify, in the Dioptrique, many medical aims found within those genres.

We can also say definitively that Descartes owed a great debt to the recent medical tradition in his account of the eye, and that without this the *Dioptrique* could not have existed as it stands — even though he seemed to ignore or alter certain anatomical features as he saw fit. Finally, the *Dioptrique* played a role in the gradual medicalization of spectacles over the course of the seventeenth century; understanding the extent of this, however, requires further investigation.

---

77 RENÉ DESCARTES, *The World and Other Writings*, ed. and trans. by Stephen Gaukroger, Cambridge/New York, Cambridge University Press, 1998, p. 125; AT XI 152-153.

FABRIZIO BALDASSARRI

A Medicine in the Shadows

*The Bio-Medical Manuscripts and a Compendium Descartes Never Published**

▼ ABSTRACT In this chapter, I investigate the *Observationum anatomicarum Compendium de partibus inferiori ventre contentis*, a medical compendium collected in the *Excerpta anatomica*. Likely written in 1637, this text contains a philosophical investigation of the anatomy and physiology of the organs of the abdomen, an under-studied topic in Descartes's early medical work, and possibly the subject of a letter he wrote to Huygens by the end of 1637. I contextualize the *Compendium* within Descartes's manuscript, before commenting on its text in detail and providing an English translation of it. However, although this text surfaces as a coherent description of the organs of the abdomen, it presents several problems: its relationship with contemporary medicine, with Descartes's medical *collaborators*, and, last but not least, the fact that Descartes never mentioned this text again, nor used it in his late physiology. In this sense, it emerges as an example of Descartes's problematic approach to medicine.

▼ KEYWORDS *Compendium*, Unpublished Works, Digestion, Stomach, Spleen, Pancreas, Anatomical Dissections.

« Je m'étonne pourtant, qu'il n'y a rien davantage de cette nature »

[*Leibniz on the manuscripts of Descartes*]

Fabrizio Baldassarri • Ca' Foscari University of Venice/Indiana University Bloomington. Contact: <fabrizio.baldassarri@unive.it>

Descartes and Medicine: Problems, Responses and Survival of a Cartesian Discipline, ed. by Fabrizio Baldassarri, Turnhout, 2023 (DESCARTES, 9), p. 141-160
© BREPOLS PUBLISHERS   10.1484/M.DESCARTES-EB.5.132888

1. Introduction

In a letter to Constantijn Huygens (1596-1687) of December 1637, René Descartes (1596-1650) wrote that he was working on a compendium of medicine. Accordingly, Descartes would "need more time and more observational data [...] [for] I am now working on a compendium of medicine, basing it partly on my reading and partly on my own reasoning..."[1] What these books are, what this reasoning is, and even what the compendium he mentions is, remain obscure. Descartes is probably not speaking of a mere re-elaboration of *L'Homme*, despite the fact that at this moment he had definitely detached it from *Le Monde*.[2] Left unpublished in 1633 and probably never re-worked properly, *L'Homme* mostly contains an explanation of sensation in animal bodies, describing the system of the nerves and the brain. This is a very specific section of a text on medicine, and uncovers a very restricted focus, nothing that could make a sound compendium of medicine.

Although it is unclear what this compendium is, this letter offers the reader some noticeable hints. The first is Descartes's use of medical texts to expand his work on medicine, as well as the role of reasoning to buttress such knowledge, but also the need for observations. Indeed, anatomical investigations and books appear crucial to Descartes's study of medicine, insofar as they are connected to the principles of his philosophy.[3] From August 1637, Descartes appeared immersed in the study of medicine. In an August 1637 letter to an anonymous recipient, Descartes wrote that he had "received your books [...] and start[ed] studying medicine."[4] It is possible that Descartes means he started working on a few new aspects of medicine, after what he did in *L'Homme* and in the *Discours de la Méthode*. Published in June 1637, the *Discours* contains a meaningful section on the causes of the heartbeat and blood circulation, which is the starting point for reconstructing the functioning of the human (or animal) body within his new philosophy. In the second half of 1637, the correspondence with Vopiscus Fortunatus Plempius (1601-1671) prompted Descartes's interest in expanding his physiological study and, possibly, in producing a more comprehensive work.

A solution to the question concerning the nature of the compendium is contained in a Latin bio-medical manuscript, today known as the *Excerpta anatomica*, containing a

---

* Financial support for this research was provided from the European Union's Horizon 2020 research and innovation programme under the Marie Skłodovska-Curie Grant Agreement n. 890770, "VegSciLif." I have discussed parts of this chapter in the online Conference on "Lights&Shadows in Descartes' Medicine", co-organized with Fabio Zampieri in November 2020. I must thank the participants of the conference for their precious questions, comments, and remarks. Benjamin Goldberg has importantly helped me with the translation of the *Compendium*, in Table 3.
1 Descartes to Huygens, 4 December 1637, AT I 649; BL472; CSMK 76.
2 On the nature of *L'Homme*, see "Introduction" and DELPHINE ANTOINE-MAHUT, STEPHEN GAUKROGER, eds, *Descartes' Treatise on Man and its Reception*, Cham, Springer, 2016.
3 On Descartes's anatomical studies, see FABRIZIO BALDASSARRI, "Elements of Descartes' Medical *Scientia*: Books, Medical Schools, and Collaborations," in Scientiae *in the History of Medicine*, ed. by F. Baldassarri and F. Zampieri, Rome-Bristol, L'Erma di "Bretschneider", 2021, p. 247-270. FABRIZIO BALDASSARRI, *Il metodo al tavolo anatomico. Descartes e la medicina*, Rome, Aracne, 2021.
4 Descartes to ***, 30 August 1637, AT I 394; BL407.

large note dated 1637 titled *Observationum anatomicarum Compendium de partibus inferiori ventre contentis* [Compendium on the Anatomical Observations of the Parts Contained in the Abdomen].[5] In this chapter, I aim to examine this text, the content of which is relevant to Descartes's medical investigation, and appears to be an original piece in Descartes's physiology. In section 2 of this chapter, I discuss the bio-medical notes and the reasons why they represent an attempt to proceed beyond *L'Homme*. In section 3, I provide a more detailed examination of the *Compendium*, and the first English translation of it, highlighting the novel aspects and the shortcomings of this very innovative and complex text. A turning point in Descartes's study of medicine, the second half of 1637 surfaces as a crucial period for his reconstruction of the human body as a set of functions.

2. Beyond L'Homme: The Biomedical Notes of the Manuscripts

In the Fifth part of the *Discours de la Méthode*, Descartes provides a summary of the treatises written in the early 1630s and left unfinished and unpublished, namely the *Treatise on Light*, containing an explanation about "light [...] the sun and fixed stars [...] the heavens [...] planets, comets and the earth [...] terrestrial bodies in particular [...] and finally about man, because he observers these bodies."[6] Still, in the *Discours*, while claiming that the explanation of all living functions fits his mechanical framework, he only provided an explanation of the heartbeat and arteries, and then summarized his description of the fabric of the nerves and muscles, the different senses, and described the structure and changes occurring in the brain. This is what he did in *L'Homme*, whose focus consists in describing man as a spectator of nature, as he aimed to deal with the living functions related to light, the main subject of his early treatise.

While this unearths several gaps in his early physiology,[7] it also fits Descartes's early natural philosophical aims. A fuller description of the living functions, which partially surfaces in *L'Homme*, appears beyond his goal. This is something he clarifies in June 1632, before starting writing the text. In a letter to Mersenne, Descartes claimed that, after long reflection, he decided to avoid inserting an account on the generation of animals in *Le Monde*, as it would take too long — or, as it would make the chapter too long within the Treatise, or bring him too far from its aim.[8]

However, Descartes's work in medicine goes beyond the aims of *L'Homme*. In an April 1630 letter to Mersenne, Descartes claims to be studying "chemistry and anatomy together [...]. I wish I had already started to research into diseases and their remedies,"[9] therefore suggesting a broader perspective on medicine, combining a

---

5 Cf. *Excerpta anatomica*, AT XI 587-ss; BOp 1154-1160.
6 *Discours de la Méthode*, AT VI 42; BO 72; CMS I 132.
7 See FABRIZIO BALDASSARRI, "Failures of Mechanization: Vegetative Powers and the Early Cartesians, Regius, La Forge, and Schuyl", in *Vegetative Powers: The Roots of Life in Ancient, Medieval, and Early Modern Natural Philosophy*, ed. by F. Baldassarri and A. Blank, Cham, Springer, 2021, p. 255-275.
8 Descartes to Mersenne, June 1632, AT I 254; BL234; CSMK 39.
9 Descartes to Mersenne, 15 April 1630, AT I 137; BL138; CSMK 21.

theoretical strand with a practical side (therapeutics), and uniting a study of the bodily structure (anatomy), with its functioning (chemistry), malfunctioning (nosology), and a curative system (therapeutics). Yet, his early work on physiology, i.e., *L'Homme*, has a more restricted focus that did not cover such territories.

A more enlarged focus on these features surfaces in Descartes's Latin bio-medical manuscripts. Collected under Item E of the so-called *Stockholm inventory*, several pages unearth a medical content, among others that have a very different focus. Let us see the list: (**a**) 19 sheets with a text entitled *Primae Cogitationes circa generationem animalium* [First Reflections on the Generation of Animals]; (**b**) 2 more sheets on the generation of animals; (**c**) one and a half pages on animals; (**d**) a sheet entitled *Remedia et vires medicamentorum* [Remedies and medical powers]; (**e**) 16 sheets on the observations of the nature of plants and animals; (**f**) 3 pages with the title, *De partibus inferiore ventre contentis* [On the Parts Collected in the Abdomen].[10]

Points (**a**) and (**d**) are autonomous texts, today collected with the same title in volume XI of the *Œuvres de Descartes* edited by Charles Adam and Paul Tannery. The first is the *Primae Cogitationes*, which has been firstly published in 1701 in the *Opuscula Posthuma*[11] together with a shorter text, *De saporibus* [On Flavours] of which there is apparently no mention in the Inventory.[12] The second, the *Remedia*, was published by Louis-Alexandre Foucher de Careil (1826-1891) in the 1859-1860 *Œuvres inédites de Descartes*. Indeed, Foucher de Careil had discovered these pages in the manuscripts of Gottfried Wilhelm Leibniz (1646-1716), who had copied these notes, among other material, from the manuscripts in the possession of Claude Clerselier (1614-1684) in 1676. Foucher de Careil has also published a much larger text, today known as *Excerpta anatomica*, which is probably a collection of some scattered material belonging to different parts of Item E. Indeed, it collects various notes (possibly, points (**b**), (**c**), (**d**), and (**f**) of the inventory) about the observations of the generation of animals, the nature of plants and animals, and the short compendium on the abdomen.[13]

These 4 texts are now published in the *Œuvres de Descartes*. The *Primae Cogitationes* comprises 33 pages, from page 505 to page 538 of Volume XI of the Adam-Tannery edition [AT]. *De Saporibus* follows it, ranging from page 539 to page 542. Then, *Excerpta anatomica* from page 549 to page 634, plus an appendix with the images. The *Remedia et vires medicamentorum* is collected in a section entitled *Excerpta varia* and goes from page 641 to page 644 of Volume XI. As clearly appears, *De saporibus* and the

---

10 *Stockholm Inventory*, AT X 8-9; BOp 16-18: "*En la seconde page est ce titre*: Primae cogitationes circa generationem animalium, *en dix-neuf feuillets.*[…] *Puis deux feuillets encore de la formation des animaux.* […] *et un feuillet et demi encore des Animaux. Six feuillets blancs. Un feuillet intitulé*: Remedia et virtus medicamentorum. […] *il y a seize pages d'observations sur la nature des plantes et des animaux. Et après un feuillet vide, trois pages sous ce titre*: De partibus inferiore ventre contentis."
11 RENÉ DESCARTES, *Opuscula Posthuma, Physica et Mathematica*, Amsterdam, P.&J. Blaeu, 1701, p. 1-23. See BOp 936-982.
12 *Ibid.*, p. 24-26; BOp 984-986.
13 CH. METZGER, "Descartes physiologiste et anatomiste", *Hippocrate* 4 (1936), p. 521-525. J. DANKMEIJER, "Les travaux biologiques de René Descartes", *Archives internationales des sciences* 4 (1951), p. 675-680.

Remedia are two very short tracts, though incomplete. The *Primae Cogitationes* is a more structured text dealing with embryology. It presents a series of annotations on generation from different periods, uncovering a few changes in Descartes's thought on embryology, as brilliantly reconstructed by Vincent Aucante.[14] Descartes probably started working on generation in the early 1630s, as the June 1632 letter to Mersenne acknowledges, and continued observing this aspect throughout the years. Although no notes of the text are dated, Aucante has tried to provide a date for them. Still, more work needs to be done on this text.

These four texts number 123 pages, highlighting Descartes's broader interest in medicine, and uncovering a number of features absent in *L'Homme*, such as generation, nutrition, and digestion, but also the life of plants.[15] Following the April 1630's letter, in these manuscript notes Descartes concentrated on the bodily structure, processes, and generation (in the *Excerpta anatomica* and the *Primae Cogitationes*,) on the chemical activities of the body (in the *Excerpta anatomica* and *De Saporibus*,) and on the malfunctioning of the body and the therapeutic system to treat diseases (in the *Excerpta anatomica* and the *Remedia*).

The *Excerpta anatomica* is a rather complex text. It appears as a collection of scattered and diverse notes touching a number of different features, following a non-linear timeline, rather than a more or less coherent set of annotations like the other biomedical works. At first glance, one could note that the text established by AT, who followed Foucher de Careil, unites two different sections. The first, going from page 549 to page 621 of volume XI of AT, contains the more physiological notes, while the second, going from page 621 to page 634, collects notes dealing with various aspects, or problems of a various nature, and is aptly subtitled *Problemata*.[16] In volume 8/2 of Leibniz's *Sämtliche Schriften und Briefe*, where this text is also edited, the editors have divided these two parts into two different subsections, probably following the division in Leibniz's note. The first goes from page 545 to page 589, as subsection 58, and is entitled *Anatomica*. The second part is collected in a previous section, entitled *Meteorologica*, as subsection 54, named *Problemata*.[17]

The first section of the *Excerpta anatomica*, namely the collection of anatomical notes, is what interests me more. AT divides this section into 5 parts, while this division is absent in Leibniz's works. Even in this case, the earlier notes probably belong to an earlier period, but not all of them are dated, and the few dates do not follow a linear arrangement. The first two parts mostly deal with the anatomical dissections of a young calf, especially focusing on the circulatory system. The last notes of part 2 contain the description of dissections of calf fetuses. Part 3 starts

---

14 See VINCENT AUCANTE, ed., *René Descartes: Écrits physiologiques et médicaux*, Paris, PUF, 2001.
15 One should note that both *L'Homme* and *La Description du corps humain* number 165 pages in AT.
16 I am not going to deal with this subsection. In many respects, the section echoes pseudo-Aristotle's *Problemata physica*, the book written as a collection of questions-replies. Yet, no clear connection ever surfaces, and more work should be done on it.
17 See GOTTFRIED WILHELM LEIBNIZ, *Sämtliche Schriften und Briefe*, [SSB], Darmstadt, Leipzig and Berlin, Akademie Verlag, 1923-, vol. 8/2. The part entitled *Problemata* is at p. 454-462; the anatomical part is at p. 545-589.

with a description of the anatomical dissections of the brain of a lamb, and then contains (1) a note dated November 1637 and describing the dissection of a calf fetus, and (2) the *Observationum Anatomicarum Compendium de partibus inferiori ventre contentis*, dated 1637. Part 4 starts with a note on the formation of plants and animals, a note on passions, a note on the role of food in cooling the body, and a note on the connection between the parts of the blood and the diverse fevers. These notes are also in the *Primae Cogitationes*. Then, there are a few notes entitled *De Accretione et Nutritione*, dated November 1637, and one page on generation dated December 1637. Then, a section entitled, *Partes Similares et Excrementa et Morbi*, dated 1631, ranging from page 601 to page 608 of AT. A set of notes dated 1648 concludes Part 4 of the *Anatomica*. Undoubtedly, this part contains scattered notes, following neither a clear timeline, nor a clear unity of contents. Part 5 contains a few observations on animal physiology, such as the structure of birds and fish, and the physiology of chicks and eggs. These 72 pages present Descartes's varied work on anatomy and physiology, ranging from his observations on the structure of the body, to embryology, to the brain, to sensation and passion, to nutrition [see Table 1].

Undoubtedly, these notes compose a true medical laboratory, not only because Descartes jotted down his anatomical observations, but also because he collected several issues that are absent from his main texts. For this reason, it seems possible to draw a connection between the first note of part 3, in which Descartes observed the brain of a sheep, with some of the contents of *L'Homme*, and with what Descartes wrote to Mersenne in December 1632. Accordingly, in claiming he was "dissecting the heads of various animals, so that I can explain what imagination, memory, etc. consist in,"[18] Descartes apparently referred to the description of part 3 of the *Excerpta anatomica*. Still, several differences with *L'Homme* arise, as many notes contain an original investigation of living functions, as the parts on nutrition and digestion reveal.[19] Before concentrating on the *Compendium*, let us draw some conclusions about the *Excerpta anatomica*.

This bio-medical manuscript presents several important features. The first is an editorial problem, as this is a collection of scattered notes, whose arrangement follows neither a temporal timeline nor a unity of contents. Second, in presenting Descartes's observations at the dissection table, this appears as truly a set of laboratorial notes, the style of which is far from those of a text intended for publication. Yet, other notes contain (more philosophical) reflections, such as the larger note dated 1631 uncovers, or a more structured work (such as the *Compendium*), ultimately making the *Excerpta anatomica* a very complex text. Third, in these notes Descartes sheds light on several bodily processes that he did not treat in *L'Homme*, therefore revealing a broader medical exploration of the living bodies (both animal and vegetal), such as the aspects of generation and nutrition, but also the references to specific organs

---

18 Descartes to Mersenne, November or December 1632, AT I 263; BL242; CSMK 40.
19 On a possible connection between these notes and *La Description du corps humain*, see my book and FABRIZIO BALDASSARRI, "Descartes' Bio-Medical Study of Plants: Vegetative Activities, Soul, and Power", *Early Science and Medicine*, 23/5-6 (2018), p. 509-529.

and the bodily functions. Insofar as it proceeds beyond the editorial strictures of *L'Homme*, the *Excerpta anatomica* surfaces as a complex, but crucial miscellany of diverse notes, the study of which appears to be a fundamental enterprise in dealing with Descartes's medical knowledge at large.

3. The *Compendium* on the Organs of the Abdomen

Let us now concentrate on the *Compendium* contained in Part 3 of the *Excerpta anatomica*. Although several more notes are dated 1637, this appears the most structured work, the one Descartes probably had in mind when writing to Huygens. Moreover, the *Compendium* contains several innovative features. While several other notes contain innovative reflections, the topic of the *Compendium* is new, as Descartes had never previously dealt with the organs of the abdomen in an exhaustive way. For example, in comparison to the note "On Accretion and Nutrition", which seems a philosophical reflection on the division between living and non-living bodies, the *Compendium* looks like a more anatomical and physiological reconstruction of the observations on the organs of the abdomen. One should also bear in mind that the *Stockholm inventory* contains a specific reference to the *Compendium* as an autonomous text, as it appears to be when compared to the other notes of the *Excerpta anatomica*. The fact that this was a text intended for publication (but certainly not ready to be published) reveals a more exhaustive exploration of this subject. In sum, this seems to be a clear description of the abdomen from a physiological point of view, developing from anatomical observations and medical knowledge, and combining the study of generation with the physiology of digestion and nutrition. In this sense, this text appears as a clear example of Descartes's work in the field. Let us now deal with it.

The *Compendium* raises several problems. The first is authorial. In the AT edition, Charles Adam has claimed that Descartes largely drew the text from Caspard Bauhin's (1560-1624) *Institutiones Anatomicae Corporis virilise & muliebris historiam exhibentes* (1604).[20] More recently, Franco A. Meschini has shed some light on this point, claiming that the dependence of the *Compendium* on Bauhin's work should be significantly reduced.[21] Indeed, Descartes referred twice to Bauhin, reporting two stories [*historias*], but also expressed doubts as to the veracity of such stories [*De qua re dubito*].[22] At the same time, Descartes himself referred to several books [*libri*], although he did not name any of them directly. This seems in line with the letter he wrote to Huygens, and it is rather likely that Descartes mixed his own reflections with something borrowed from medical texts. Yet, as Meschini stresses, a dependence of the *Compendium* on such other texts seems likely, but it appears unlikely to claim that Descartes copied from other sources, and the *Compendium* appears truly Cartesian.

---

20   *Excerpta anatomica*, AT XI 587, note d; BOp 1154.
21   Franco A. Meschini, "La dottrina della digestione secondo Descartes. Itinerari tra testi, contesti e intertesti", *Physis* 50-51/2 (2015), p. 113-164, esp. p. 133-135.
22   *Ibid.*, 591-592; BOp 1156. See notes 71 and 73 in BOp for the references to Bauhin.

A second issue concerns the nature of the text. Given its structure, contents, and style, the *Compendium* is rather different from the other notes collected in the *Excerpta anatomica*. First, this is a more homogeneous and autonomous set of notes. Second, as Meschini specifies, the morphology of the *Compendium* reveals a way to differentiate this text from the previous notes. Only concentrating on Part 3 of the *Excerpta anatomica* in its entirety, important differences arise. For example, the notes from page 579 to page 587 are in the first (singular or plural) person, and verbs are either (a) in the present or past tense, therefore revealing Descartes's description of the observations he performed, or (b) in the imperfect tense, as he described things as they were when he observed them. In both cases, the notes reveal a laboratorial stance, as they "contain the observations while performed, and describe the subjects of such observations in the moment they have been observed."[23] In other words, the first half of Part 3 is nothing but a collection of notes of dissections.

In contrast to this, the *Compendium* (page 587 to page 594 of AT) is mostly in the third person and the present tense. This highlights a much more structured text, which is less a report of personal observations in which the time and the person who made them is important, and not the reconstruction of very specific cases or histories. What counts in the *Compendium* is the general and universally valid description of the body as it is. For this reason, the time and person are no longer a useful variable to the contents, as this is a more systematic description of the anatomy and physiology of the organs in the abdomen. Ultimately, the focus is no longer on a specific animal, but describes the animal (brute or man) in general.[24] For this reason, in referring to two stories from Bauhin's work, Descartes underlined the fact that these are very particular, marvelous, and strange cases, which he rapidly dismissed.[25] In contrast to the tone and style of the previous notes of Part 3, the *Compendium* has the shape of a description of the lower organs of the animal body in general. However, both the references to other texts in paragraph 7 and 13 and the uses of the first singular person in paragraph 9 and 13 interrupt this general description. Yet, this is consistent with Descartes's attempt to confirm his own interpretation or specify his authorial role in performing observations to confirm the general description. In referring to particular cases collected in books, he proved the rightfulness of his observations, ultimately dismissing such cases. In using the first person, he reveals a specific observation to confirm his knowledge. This highlights Descartes's methodology at work: The observation, the role of books, and the reasoning, which takes the form of conjectures, used by Descartes to establish a certain knowledge.[26] What results is

---

23 MESCHINI, "La dottrina della digestione," p. 134-135.
24 *Excerpta anatomica*, AT XI 589; BOp 1154: "Urachus, cum in homine non sit pervius, ut in brutis, ostendit hominem minus serosi humori habere…" [The urachus, which in man is not pervious as in beasts, shows that man has less serous humor and its nature is closer to those of birds…] [Translation is mine.]
25 *Excerpta anatomca*, AT XI 591; BOp 1156: "Exstaque apud Bauhinum insignis historia cujusdam qui habebat renem sinistrum juxta vesicam locatum et alia vasa miro modo disposita."
26 See BALDASSARRI, *Il metodo al tavolo anatomico*, p. 161-162; *Regulae ad directionem ingenii* XII, AT X 424; BOp 762.

a general description of the abdomen, which is universally valid and consistent with the methodology of Descartes's natural philosophy, and grounded on observation and reasoning.[27]

Let us now move from the style to the contents of the text. The *Compendium* occupies seven pages in AT, with 13 paragraphs of different length. In these paragraphs, Descartes describes all the organs in the abdomen, namely, the peritoneum, the umbilical arteries, the bladder, the kidneys, the omentum, the intestines, the veins connecting these organs, the gallbladder, the spleen, the liver, and the stomach [see Table 2].

From this quick overview, the novelty of the *Compendium* importantly surfaces. For example, in *L'Homme*, Descartes referred to digestion and nutrition, but failed to describe the spleen, the kidneys, or the stomach, and mostly concentrated on the circulatory system developing from the liver. Moreover, digestion in *L'Homme* is a very cardiocentric process. In contrast, the *Compenium* contains several anatomical descriptions of these organs: The stomach and intestines in paragraph 13 or the list of organs in paragraph 6, where the pancreas is not just a conglomerate of lymph nodes, but an autonomous organ with a precise use, namely, to sustain the ramification of the portal vein.[28] At the same time, Descartes describes the activities of these organs in producing digestion or in transporting the chyle to the liver, highlighting a more autonomous status of such organs.

In describing the abdomen, Descartes goes from the external part to the more interior organs, as if he was following an anatomical dissection. He thus moves from the peritoneum, a membrane englobing the parts of the abdomen, to the umbilical veins and the omentum, which covers several organs and the intestines. Then, he describes the connection of the organs through the veins, which develop from the liver. At this point, he moves from the kidneys, dealing with their process of filtration, and the bladder, thus dealing with bodily excretions, to the spleen, the gallbladder, the liver, the stomach and the intestines. From the first paragraph, Descartes's attempt to connect the explanation of these parts with their formation is evident. For example, in paragraph 1 he claims that the peritoneum was formed in a later moment in the fetus, in paragraph 3 he suggests that the allantois membrane is missing in fetuses, in paragraph 4 he claims that the bladder was formed in consequence of the presence of blood.

In table 3, I provide an English translation of the *Compendium* [see Table 3]. Let us now deal with a few aspects of the text more directly. It starts with a description of the peritoneum, a very strong double membrane, one internal and one external. The peritoneum envelops the organs of the abdomen; yet, according to the text, Descartes claims that the kidneys, the vena cava and the great artery are located between these, which is anatomically incorrect. More likely, Descartes must have meant that these organs are outside the peritoneal sac. In paragraphs 2, 3, 4, and 5, Descartes describes the external parts: (2) the umbilical arteries, whose arrangement reveals the movement of blood in the formation of the fetus; (3) the urachus, which

---

27 See *Regulae ad directionem ingenii* II, AT X 365; BOp 690.
28 *Excerpta anatomica*, AT XI 590; BOP 1154.

is a fibrous remnant of the allantois, one of the tunics enveloping the fetus and easing the elimination of excretions. According to Descartes, since the human urachus is less pervious than those of beasts, it shows that the human fetus has less serous humors. The consequence of this is bizarre: The first is that the human body is closer to birds; the second is that human fetuses lack the allantois altogether. (4) The connection between the arteries, the bladder, and the kidneys. In the fetus, the blood formed the bladder and the kidneys, because together with the intestines and the liver, they stay in the frontal part of the abdomen, touching the navel and the placenta. (5) The omentum, which is a membrane covering the stomach, the spleen, and the colon, and sometimes the liver. According to Descartes, this is similar to the peritoneum.

In paragraph 6, Descartes describes the connections between the various organs of the abdomen. Accordingly, the portal vein has roots in the intestines, in the stomach, in the mesentery, in the omentum, in the pancreas, in the spleen, and in the gallbladder. In separating the mesentery and the pancreas, Descartes apparently acknowledged the latter not as a gland of the former, nor as the *pancreas Aselli*, but as a more autonomous organ, in line with Galen's interpretation. While this is an important specification, one should however note that no more clear description of the pancreas is provided, and Descartes thus appears unaware of the contemporary discussions on this organ.[29] Then, he claims a short vessel goes from the stomach to the spleen. Accordingly, in the arterial part of this short vessel, some acid blood proceeds from the spleen to the stomach, easing digestion, while in the venal part of the short vessel some digestive juice proceeds to the spleen, where it becomes an acid juice. This is an important addition to his theory of digestion. While in his early *L'Homme* he claimed digestion relies on some liquids brought from the heart, here he specifies the nature of such acid liquids, as produced by the spleen, which appears to be important in digestion. This characterizes the preparatory phase of it, making the organs of the abdomen play a central role in digestion.

Then, he claims the liver plays the role of receptacle of blood and juices, moving there through these veins. At this stage, Descartes has no knowledge of the lacteal vessels recently discovered by Gaspare Aselli (1581-1625), whose *De lactibus sive Lacteis venis* (1627), was known by Beeckman, and mostly attributed the system of the portal vein to the role of transporting the chyle to the liver.[30]

In paragraphs 7 and 8, Descartes describes the renal veins and the ureters. First, moving from the physiology of the renal veins, Descartes explains the formation of kidneys and the bladder. Within this formation moment, in which the artery ascends the vein and tends toward the bowels, the kidneys somehow float in the abdomen, which makes it possible to grow with the kidneys placed in a different position than the one usually expected, as described by Bauhin. The movement of the artery helps specify the disposition of the liver and the spleen, the one occupying the right side, the second the left side. Finally, he suggests that the Lumbar arteries and veins penetrate into the spinal cord, nuancing a connection with the brain. In the last part,

---

29 See B. ZANOBIO, "Dal dotto di Wirsung al cane spancreato del Brunner", in *Atti del convegno celebrativo di Johann Georg Wirsung*, Edizioni Universitarie Patavine, Padova 1992, p. 103-108.
30 See BALDASSARRI, *Il metodo al tavolo anatomico*, p. 170-171.

in contrast to Bauhin, Descartes claims that the valves in the renal veins prevent the blood entering the kidneys. In paragraph 8, he describes the ureters, which are composed of several glands converging into one channel. Again, a connection with the nervous system surfaces, as the ureters receive a nerve from the sixth pair; and the ureters are finally implanted into the bladder.

From paragraph 9 to 13, Descartes probed into the description of the organs of the abdomen: The spleen, the liver, the stomach and the intestines. In paragraph 9, he describes the arrangement of the spleen and the liver in the fetus, explaining why the first is placed in the left side of the body and the second in the right side. In paragraph 10, he describes the arrangement of the veins and arteries from the spleen (i.e., the short vessel or the hemorrhoid veins), especially dealing with a channel that goes from the spleen to the liver, and from there to the heart and the brain. For this reason, when some vapors, namely, the black bile, travel from the spleen to the brain at night, nightmares result.

In paragraph 11, he deals with the yellow bile. While in the fetus, the bile occupies the center of the liver, as it collects the bitter parts of the blood, then a reservoir forms. According to Descartes, this divides into two parts, a bile duct, which is probably the hepatic duct that receives the bile from the liver, and the gallbladder, which stores the bile and it is larger than the bile duct. This explanation looks insufficient, if not imprecise, as there is no mention of the role of the gallbladder in secreting the bile for digestion. In paragraph 12, he focuses on the connection of the veins to the liver.

In paragraph 13, Descartes describes the structure of the stomach, whose interior parts have straight fibers, extending from the mouth to the stomach, while the intestines have transverse fibers. This anatomical exploration of the stomach puts the stomach at the center of the abdomen, connecting the mouth, through the esophagus, to the intestines and the rectum. On the one hand, the stomach appears independent from the heart; yet on the other hand, in describing its formation, Descartes conjectures that some excretions falling from the brain have composed the mouth, the esophagus, and the stomach, therefore uncovering a connection between the stomach and the intestine on the one side, and the brain on the other side. A similar description is in *Primae Cogitationes*.[31] In his manuscript, Leibniz noted this passage as "ingeniose" [clever].[32]

On the one hand, the text follows a line of investigation, moving from the external parts and probing into the abdomen, but it also reveals a few internal threads. For example, what connects the various paragraphs is the role of blood in producing the organs or in causing their arrangement. Yet, in concluding the *Compendium*, Descartes describes the formative role of the material dripping from the brain, which produces the esophagus, the stomach, the intestines, and the rectum. A similar description of the formation of organs is in another note of the *Excerpta anatomica*, dated December 1637, and collected in Part 4.[33] Yet, the *Compendium* also presents an anatomical description

---

31   Cf. *Primae Cogitationes*, AT XI 512-513; BOp 946.
32   See LEIBNIZ, SSB 8/2, 573.
33   *Excerpta anatomica*, AT XI 599-600; BOp 1168.

of these organs, of their connections and functioning. Undoubtedly, the text uncovers a new segment of Descartes's physiological reconstruction of the body that cannot be found in his earlier notes or texts.

On the other hand, the description is generally insufficient and unclear (see Paragraph 3). Some of it seems a very general analysis of the parts of the abdomen, without a deeper investigation of these organs. The fact that the text is interspersed with a few references to books makes it even more unclear. Many of its parts could be connected with other notes of the same period, which makes the *Compendium* a Cartesian work, but reveals its lacunae. Although this is important for its novelty in Cartesian medical knowledge, the *Compendium* presents several problems and flaws, therefore remains far from being something ready for publication. It has neither the order, nor the coherence and clarity of *L'Homme* or *La Description du corps humain*.

4. Conclusions

In this chapter, I have examined a short subsection of one of Descartes's Latin bio-medical manuscripts. Collected in Part 3 of the *Excerpta anatomica*, and dated 1637, the *Compendium on the Anatomical Observations of the Parts Contained in the Abdomen* is probably the text Descartes referred to in his correspondence with Huygens. It is a rather coherent (and more cohesive than the rest of the *EA* or than the *Primae Cogitationes*), homogeneous, and well-structured text, which also reveals a new focus on a segment of physiology previously under-investigated by Descartes. Since digestion and nutrition remain two problematic activities of Descartes's physiology in general, this text proves both its importance and novelty, uncovering Descartes's anatomical observations and methodological reflections on these organs and on the related operations. Apparently, the *Compendium* bridges an important gap in Descartes's physiology.

Still, problems surface, as the text is a mere sketch of a broader work Descartes apparently never accomplished. Indeed, these pages still have a laboratorial condition, despite their style and structure differing from the other notes of the manuscripts. In any case, this text remains hard to read, even if not just a set of scattered notes, especially when compared to Bauhin and Bartholin, or even to Plemp's and Regius's works.

Moreover, the *Compendium* appears as an isolated text in Descartes's physiological studies. A couple of notes of the *Excerpta anatomica* dated 1637 parallel the issues of the *Compendium*, while a few notes of the *Primae Cogitationes* deal with the formation of the lower organs, such as the spleen, the gallbladder, the intestines, and the stomach, in a way that is not inconsistent with the *Compendium*. However, no close connections could be drawn between the *Compendium* and these other notes. Similarly, Descartes did not borrow anything from the *Compendium* in the 1647-1648 *La Description du corps humain*, whose third part on nutrition remains rather philosophical than anatomical (and then quite different from the 1637 notes of the *Excerpta anatomica*,) and whose fourth and fifth parts on generation mostly deal with the circulatory and the nervous systems. Finally, even the *Passions of the Soul*, where Descartes expounds the role of the liver, stomach, gallbladder and spleen in producing the diverse passions,[34] the text appears closer to *L'Homme*, rather than the *Compendium*.[35]

As Descartes did not use the material from the *Compendium* in his later physiological investigations, the fate of this text appears sealed as a minor source for Descartes's medical knowledge. Not only is the text difficult to read, but also useless to complete the mechanization of the living body. Despite the importance of its contents, and its originality in the picture of Cartesian medicine, this *Compendium* thus lags in the shadows, ultimately highlighting the complex condition of these studies within the Cartesian corpus.

---

34 See, for example, *Les passions de l'âme* art. 15, AT XI 340-341; CSM I 334; BO 2348.
35 See, *L'Homme*, AT XI 166-169; G 140-142; BOp 440-444. The spleen, the gallbladder, and the liver have, here, the function to purge, elaborate, transform and purify the blood. See also, ANNIE BITBOL-HESPÉRIÈS, "De toute la nature de l'homme: de *L'Homme* à la *Description du corps humain*, la physiologie des *Passions de l'âme* et ses antécédents médicaux", in *Les* Passions de l'âme *et leur réception philosophique*, ed. by G. Belgioioso et V. Carraud, Turnout, Brepols, 2020, p. 67-100; FRANCO A. MESCHINI, "Un testo stratificato: l'influenza di Elisabetta", in *Les* Passions de l'âme *et leur réception philosophique*, p. 101-136.

Table 1. The *Anatomica* divided into parts

Part n°	Pages AT	Contents	Notes
Part I	549-564	Anatomical dissections on the circulatory system of veal, plus the liver, lungs, spleen, and nerves.	
Part II	564-578	Anatomical dissections on veal, and especially on fetuses at different stages. The main focus remains the circulatory system. A first subsection contains observations on the veins and limbs of an ox. A second subsection contains observations on veal fetuses.	The first note starts with "Secta posthac", apparently implying a continuation from a previous part. A horizontal line (not reproduced in Leibniz's works) divides the two subsections.
Part III	579-594	Anatomical dissections on a sheep, especially dealing with the brain and nervous system (such as the ear). A note on a dissection on a fetus veal. The *Compendium on the lower parts of the abdomen*	This note is dated November 1637, and it appears rather structured. This subsection is dated 1637 and it is a much more structured and homogeneous text, p. 587-594.
		A first note on the formation of animals and plants. A note on passions, joy and sadness, as produced from the heart. A note on the role of food in chilling the body. A note on the parts of blood and their relation to fevers.	This note is absent from AT, as it is the copy (but not exact!) of a note from the *Primae Cogitationes*. As in the previous case, these notes are similar to 2 notes in the *Primae Cogitationes*.
Part IV	595-611	A larger note entitled *De Accretione et Nutritione*, ending with a note on diverse particles uniting to the body and composing the diverse parts of it A note on generation. A section entitled *Partes Similares et Excrementa et Morbi* A few notes on the anatomy and physiology of the body, dealing with arteries, veins, esophagus, and the stomach.	This note is dated November 1637. This note is dated December 1637. This is dated 1631. It contains descriptions of spirits, exhalations of different kinds, fires within the living body, diseases of various kinds, and possible remedies. This note is dated 1648.
Part V	611-621	Several notes on anatomical observations on animals, such as birds, fish, eggs and chicks.	This note contains his observations on eggs and the diverse stages in formation.

Table 2. The *Compendium*

Paragraph	Pages AT	Contents
1	587-589	The external parts: the peritoneum
2	589	The external parts: the umbilical veins showing the movement of blood during generation
3	589	The structure of the Urachus — similarities between men and birds.
4	589	The external parts: the arrangement of arteries and the formation of the organs, such as the bladder and kidneys.
5	589-590	The external parts: the omentum and its connection with several organs, the formation of the intestines, the kidneys, the liver.
6	590	The circulatory system in the abdomen: the portal vein connects the organs. The movement of blood and liquors between the spleen and stomach.
7	590-592	The circulatory system in the abdomen: the renal veins and the composition of kidneys. (This paragraph contains 2 references to Bauhin's text.)
8	592	The circulatory system in the abdomen: the structure of ureters and their connection to the nervous system.
9	592	The internal organs: the spleen and the liver.
10	592-593	The internal organs: The connection between the spleen and other organs, and especially the brain.
11	593	The internal organs: The gallbladder, and its connection to the liver.
12	593-594	The internal organs: The liver and the circulatory system.
13	594	The internal organs: The stomach, its structure and generation, and the intestines. The connection between the stomach and the brain.

Table 3. English translation[a] of the *Compendium*

Par.	Latin	English
1	Has omnes peritonaeum involvit, quod constat membrana satis valida duplici, interiori et exteriore, inter quas renes et arteria magna et vena cava collocantur; item productiones fecundas habet, quibus vasa spermatica, praeparantia ac deferentia, involvuntur; cumque renes natent in foetus corpore, hinc patet istam membranam nonnisi postea produci.	The peritoneum envelops all of them [i.e., the organs of the abdomen], which [peritoneum] is composed of a very strong double membrane, internal and external. The kidneys, the great artery, and the vena cava are located between these [two membranes]. Then, it has abundant prolongations, in which the spermatic, preparative and deferens vessels are enveloped; and since the kidneys float in the body of the foetus, it follows that this membrane is produced only later.
2	Arteriae umbilicales ab iliacis ad umbilicum venientes, et vena ab umbilico ad hepar, ostendunt sanguinem a corde per aortam ad ilia primum descendisse, et inde ad umbilicum placentae uteri conjunctum redisse; ubi sanguini matris se permiscens, reversus est ad hepar foetus per venam umbilicalem.	[The disposition of] the umbilical arteries, which come from the iliac arteries to the umbilicus, and [the disposition of] the vein coming from the umbilicus to the liver show that the blood first descended from the heart to the bowels through the aorta. And from there, it returned to the umbilicus connected to the placenta of the uterus where, mixing with the blood of the mother, it returned to the liver of the fetus through the umbilical vein.
3	Urachus, cum in homine non sit pervius, ut in brutis, ostendit hominem minus serosi humoris habere, et magis ad avium naturam accedere, quae non mingunt; foetusque ideo tunica allantoide etiam caret.	The urachus, which in men is not pervious, as it is in beasts, shows that men have less serous humors and its nature is closer to that of birds, which do not urinate; and so the foetus lacks the allantois tunica.
4	Connectuntur hae arteriae lateribus vesicae quae ideo videntur ex eo tantum orta, quod sanguis foetus, attingendo in placenta matris sanguinem, aliquid ibi de humiditate sua deposuerit. Renesque ibi ex eadem causa producti sunt: quippe, nondum productis vel saltem auctis intestinis, ilia, renes et hepar simul ad umbilicum, et cum illo ad placentam matris, pertingebant.	These arteries are connected with the sides of the bladder, which therefore seems to originate only because the blood of the foetus, encountering the blood of the mother in the placenta, has left some of its moisture there. Here, the kidneys are produced by the same causes. This depends on the fact that, since the intestines have not yet been produced or even increased, the bowels, kidneys and liver together extend to the navel, and with that to the placenta of the mother.

[a] Benjamin Goldberg helped me with the translation and provided some very helpful comments.

Par.	Latin	English
5	Omentum semper connectitur ventriculo, lieni, et colo, interdum etiam diaphragmati et hepati; caetera propendet veli instar supra intestinum anterius: nec videtur aliunde factum, quam ex vasis quae recipit et fulcit, ut illa in ventriculum, lienem, duodenum et colon deferat; cum enim intestina nunc vacuentur, nunc inflentur, vasa ista non potuerunt ipsis adhaerere; cumque libera starent, circa ipsa secundae membranae, ex quibus omentum componitur, eodem modo quo peritonaeum, factae sunt.	The omentum is always connected to the stomach, spleen and colon, sometimes even to the diaphragm and liver. The rest hangs like a curtain over the anterior zone of the intestine: and it seems to be made only from the vessels that it receives and supports in order to convey them into the stomach, the spleen, the duodenum and the colon. For, as the intestines are at one time empty, and at another full, these vessels will not be able to adhere to them; and since they might remain empty, around them secondary membranes are made, from which the omentum is composed, in the same manner as the peritoneum.
6	Vena portae radices educit varias ex intestinis, ventriculo, mesenterio, omento, pancreate, liene et felle; itemque exiguam ex hepate; unam etiam, nempe vas breve, educit e ventriculo per lienem. Dico autem ipsam ex omnibus illis locis radices emittere, quia in illis arterias comites habet, nempe coeliacam, vel mesentericam, superiorem vel inferiorem, quae in ejus extremitates sanguinem mittant: nempe vas breve arteriale sanguinem acidum ex splene ad ventriculum defert, et vas breve venale succum ex ventriculo in splenem, ubi acescit. Ramos autem omnes suos per hepar spargit, praecipue versus ejus concavam partem, et eo defert omnem sanguinem et succum a radicibus acceptum; ibique idcirco nullis arteriis est comitata.	The portal vein draws various roots from the intestines, the stomach, the mesentery, the omentum, the pancreas, the spleen and the gallbladder; and also a small one from the liver; and one, indeed, a truly short vessel, leads out from the stomach through the spleen. But I say that it sends out roots from all those places, because it is accompanied by arteries, namely, the celiac, or the mesenteric, superior or inferior, which [all] send blood to its extremities: for example, the short arterial vessel carries some acid blood from the spleen to the stomach, and the short vein vessel [carries] some juices from the stomach to the spleen, where it turns sour. Still, it scatters all its branches through the liver, especially toward its concave part, and carries all the blood and juice received by the roots; and on that account, it is not accompanied by any artery [in the liver].
7	Emulgentes sunt vasa latissima, quae ex aorta et cava prodeant. Videturque initio illarum finem fuisse, ibique ideo sanguinem restagnasse, atque renes et vesicam produxisse eodem tempore quo arteria ulterius pergens coepit venam conscendere et ad ilia indeque ad umbilicum per vesicae latera et in duas divisa tendere: hinc fit ut renum situs et vasorum ad illos valde varient, et in faetus corpore tanquam natantes, praesertim sinister, reperiantur. Exstatque apud Bauhinum insignis historia cujusdam qui habebat renem sinistrum juxta vesicam locatum et alia vasa miro modo	The renal veins and arteries are the widest vessels, which come out of the aorta and from the [vena] cava. And it seems that, at first, they were their final part, and for this reason the blood has overflowed there, where it produced the kidneys and the bladder. [This occurred] at the same time in which the artery, proceeding further, began to climb the vein and extended toward the bowel, and from that place towards the navel, dividing in two along [both of] the sides of the bladder. From this, it follows that the position of the kidneys and of the vessels entering them vary greatly,

Par.	Latin	English
	disposita. Quae omnia ex hoc uno videntur contigisse, quod arteria, ut venam conscenderet, per medium venae emulgentis sinistrae transiverit, venit enim semper a parte sinistra; unde puto omnem rationem petendam, cur hepar in dextro latere, lien in sinistro, etc. Item lumbares tum venae, tum arteriae, quae infra emulgentes producuntur, postquam ad spinae medullam interius penetrarunt, ramos habent qui sursum versus cerebrum reflectuntur. Quod indicat arteriam ulterius pergere conatam, in omnes partes ibi viam quaesiisse; tunc autem umbilicus totam ventris capacitatem a nothis costis ad inguina occupabat. Valvulas in venis emulgentibus dicit esse Bauhinus, quae seri refluxum impediant. De qua re dubito: contra enim potius sanguinis in renes a venis illapsum deberent impedire.	and they (especially the left one) lie as if floating in the body of the fetus. In [the writings of] Bauhin, there is a notable history of someone who had the left kidney placed near the bladder and the other vessels, arranged in a way that marvels. All these seem to have happened for this one reason: Because the artery, in order to ascend the vein, would have passed through the middle of the left renal vein, since it always comes from the left side. Whence, I think, we must look for the whole explanation concerning why the liver is in the right side, the spleen in the left, etc. Moreover, veins and lumbar arteries, which extend under the renal veins, after having entered inward to the spinal cord, have branches that fold upward toward the brain. This reveals that the artery, having endeavored to proceed further, has here sought to open a way for itself in every direction; but then the navel occupied the whole capacity of the abdomen from the spurious ribs to the groin. Bauhin says that in the renal veins there are valves, which prevent the reflux of the serum. A thing I doubt: on the contrary, in fact, they should prevent the sinking of the blood from the veins into the kidneys.
8	Ureteres autem ita ex renibus prodeunt, ut in quoque rene sint octo vel novem infundibula carne renum instar glandularum occlusa, quorum deinde duo vel tres in unum coëunt, et denique tres in unum canalem, qui est ureter, quique nervulum a sexto pari recipit, et vesicae ita implantatur, ut ab ea sine fractione separari non possit.	The ureters, on the other hand, come out of the kidneys so that in each kidney there are eight or nine infundibula enclosed by the flesh of the kidneys in the form of glands, of which the next two or three unite into one, and finally three into one channel, which is the ureter. [This also] receives a nerve from the sixth pair and is thus implanted in the bladder so that it cannot be detached from it without a rupture.
9	Mihi videtur, in embryone, lienem versus spinam in medio corporis, et hepar versus umbilicum fuisse sita, venamque umbilicalem medio hepatis fuisse implantatam; sed postea, dum inflaretur ventriculus, et aorta a sinistris cavae truncum in lumbis conscenderet, secessit hepar in dextrum latus, et lien in sinistrum.	It seems to me that in the embryo the spleen was placed towards the spine in the middle of the body, and the liver toward the umbilicus, and that the umbilical vein was implanted in the middle of the liver. Yet, afterwards, as the stomach inflated and the aorta ascended the trunk from the left of the [vena] cava into the loins, the liver has withdrawn to the right side and the spleen into the left [side].

Par.	Latin	English
10	Ex venis et arteriis per lienem transeuntibus, unae sunt vas breve dictae, quae ad fundum ventriculi transeunt, et aliae ad rectum intestinum, ubi haemorrhoïdales internas constituunt. Est autem canalis patentissimus a venis lienis per truncum portae ad hepar, et in ipso hepate a porta in cavam, et deinde a cava in cor, a corde in cerebrum. Unde fit ut nocte, liene compresso vel manu vel ob decubitum in sinistrum latus, gravia occurrant insomnia: tetri enim vapores a liene expressi in cerebrum statim ascendunt.	Of the veins and arteries that pass through the spleen, some are called short vessels, [of] which [some] cross the bottom of the stomach, while others cross the rectum, where they form internal hemorrhoids. But there is a very open channel, from the veins of the spleen through the trunk of the [portal] vein, that leads to the liver, and in the liver itself [leads] from the [portal] vein to the [vena] cava, and then from the [vena] cava into the heart, and from the heart into the brain. For this reason, when the spleen is pressed either by a hand or by lying on the left side at night, oppressive dreams occur: for the dark [or foul] vapors sent out from the spleen rise immediately into the brain.
11	Flava bilis, in embryone, videtur medium hepatis infima ejus parte occupasse: nempe partes sanguinis amarescentes eo fuisse sponte delapsas. Postea vero, crescente hepate et recedente versus dextrum latus ejus, flavae bilis receptaculum in duas partes fuisse divisum: nempe in porum bilarium, qui recipit fel a sinistra hepatis parte, et vesicam bilariam, quae recipit a parte dextra, quaeque ideo major est poro bilario.	In the embryo, yellow bile seems to occupy the center of the liver in its lowest part: that is, it seems that the bitter parts of the blood have spontaneously fallen down there. Still later, as the liver has been growing and retreating to its right side, the reservoir of yellow bile as become divided into two parts, namely, into the bile duct, which receives the gall from the left part of the liver, and the gallbladder, which receives it from the right part and is therefore larger than the bile duct.
12	In hepate notandum, quasdam venae portae extremitates (ut ajunt libri) medias venae cavae radices subire, et contra quasdam cavae medias portae radices subire. Patet autem cavam ex hepate omnino prodire; non tantum enim ejus pars ascendens ex summa ejus parte egreditur, sed etiam descendens, quae statim reflectitur, et secundum ejus posteriorem partem descendit, atque it comitatum aortam descendentem.	In the liver, one should note that some of the extremities of the portal vein (as the books say) pass under the median roots of the vena cava, and conversely some of the [vena] cava pass under the median roots of the portal vein. But it appears that the [vena] cava comes out entirely from the liver: for not only does the ascending part come out of the upper part, but also its descending part, which immediately bends back, and goes down along the posterior part, and accompanies the descending aorta.

Par.	Latin	English
13	In ventriculo, observo intus illum habere fibras rectas, quae ab ore per oesophagum eo pertingunt, intestina autem transversas. Item, illum habere multos nervos, et duos etiam esse recurrentes; item, noto historiam illius qui hepate carebat, sed omnia intestina magis carnosa; item, in pueris multa excrementa a cerebro in ventriculum delabi. Ex quibus conjicio, totum ductum ab ore ad podicem ortum habere ab excrementis e cerebro delabentibus; ipsamque oris aperturam, ab iisdem excrementis eo regurgitantibus. Restagnasse autem ista excrementa infra hepar, ibique ideo capacitatem ventriculi excavasse, dum sanguis in emulgentibus etiam restagnabat. Ex hoc autem quod ex ore in jugulum laberentur ista excrementa, viamque aëri ex aspera arteria egredi tentanti clauderent, fit, ut nares sint geminae, quia per gulae latera iste aër sursum ascendit.	In the stomach, I observe that it has straight fibers on the inside, which extend all the way from the mouth through the esophagus, while the intestines have transverse [fibers]. Next, that it has many nerves, and that two also go back; likewise, I note the history of that person who lacked the liver, but had all the fleshier intestines; next, that in children much excrescences runs from the brain into the stomach. From which I conjecture that the whole conduit from the mouth to the anus originates from the excrements that drip from the brain; and that the opening of the mouth itself originates from the same excrement that overflows into it. [I conjecture also that] these excrements overflowed under the liver, and that here they hollowed out the capacity of the stomach, while the blood also overflowed into the renal veins. From the fact that such excrements dropped from the mouth into the throat, and closed the way for the air that attempted to exit from the *aspera* artery [i.e., the trachea], it follows that the nostrils are two, since this air rises up through the sides of the throat.

CARMEN SCHMECHEL

Fermentation as 'Heat-Rarefaction' and Animal Spirits in Descartes' Medical Philosophy

▼ ABSTRACT Crucial to Descartes' physiology in general, fermentation is also at the root of muscular movement and embryo formation. I argue that in contrast to theories of fermentation popular with chymists, Descartes' own version of how fermentation happens is best described as a 'heat-rarefaction' model, whose essential components are the presence of heat and its rarefying effect on matter, resulting in an expansion in volume. This is an eminently mechanist model, which resonates most closely with certain corpuscularist medieval reworkings of ancient Aristotelian and Galenic ideas. Descartes' use of fermentation is traced across writings such as *Treatise on Man*, *Description of the Human Body*, *Passions of the Soul*, *Primae Cogitationes*, *Excerpta anatomica*, and Descartes' correspondence including some sections of the 1638 Plempius letters omitted in previous translations. By explaining the misunderstanding arising out of different ways of conceptualizing fermentation, this hypothesis sheds new light on the tensions between Descartes and some of his contemporaries, especially Plempius. It also shows how 'fermentation' is negotiated between chymists and mechanists around the middle of the seventeenth century. While both schools of thought see fermentation as a model for processes happening in the natural world, each ascribes fermentation a different manner of action in matter.

▼ KEYWORDS Fermentation, Descartes, Heat-rarefaction, Scientific Model, Animal Spirits, Muscle Movement, Generation, Innate Heat, Physiology, Aristotle

Carmen Schmechel • Institute for Philosophy, Freie Universität Berlin, Germany. Contact: <carmen.schmechel@gmail.com>

1. Introduction: The Importance of Fermentation in Cartesian Physiology

It is known that Descartes holds fermentation to be central for most physiological processes,[1] starting with digestion, the circulation and the formation of the blood, the formation of the embryo and the growth of the foetus, and even the movement of the muscles. Fermentation fuels the "fire without light" that is at the basis of life, making all physiological functions — and hence organic life[2] — possible.[3]

The importance and significance of fermentation is also a result of what it replaces, in its explanatory function. It is known that Descartes aimed to eliminate the traditional Aristotelian and Galenic[4] notions of nutritive and vegetative 'souls' in order to establish what Dennis Des Chene calls a "restrictive mechanistic ontology"[5] in biology — a framework in which living bodies were understood as moving by mechanical forces only.[6] Hence it was decisive what properties could or could not be assigned to the new element replacing the 'souls'. As the 'fire without light' of fermentation now takes over the task of making life possible (as well as sustaining it through the intertwined processes of the beating of the heart and of various physiological transformations), its nature and properties come under close scrutiny. What exactly does Descartes mean by fermentation, and how does the employment of this concept play out within a mechanistic biology?

2. Descartes' Fermentational Analogies: An Update of Ancient Ideas

Descartes supposes that God placed in the human body, more precisely in the heart,[7] a fermentational fire which works in the manner of fermenting wine or damp hay: a

---

1 See Vincent Aucante, *L'horizon métaphysique de la médecine de Descartes*, Ph.D diss., Université de Paris-Sorbonne, Paris IV, 1997, esp. ch. iv, "Les fermentations"; also Vincent Aucante, *La philosophie médicale de Descartes*, Paris, PUF, 2006; Annie Bitbol-Hespériès, *Le principe de vie chez Descartes*, Paris, Vrin, 1990.
2 On the other hand, fermentation as a criterium for life is problematic. Karen Detlefsen thinks that because fermentations and their heat also happen in the natural world, the innate heat cannot be a viable criterion of demarcating living beings from non-living forms of being: "we must dismiss the 'heat without light' candidate as a viable one for Descartes' theory of life." Karen Detlefsen, "Descartes on the Theory of Life and Methodology in the Life Sciences," in *Early Modern Medicine and Natural Philosophy*, ed. by P. Distelzweig, B. Goldberg and E. J. Ragland, Dordrecht, Springer, 2016, p. 141-173, esp. p. 147.
3 See *L'Homme*, AT XI 202; G 169.
4 On the role of the 'vegetative soul' in the physiology of Galen, see Jacques Roger, *The Life Sciences in Eighteenth-Century French Thought*, ed. by K. R. Benson and transl. by R. Ellrich, Stanford, Stanford University Press, 1997, p. 57-58.
5 Dennis Des Chene, "Mechanisms of Life in the Seventeenth Century: Borelli, Perrault, Régis," *Studies in History and Philosophy of Science Part C*, 36 (2005), p. 245-260, p. 246.
6 This refers to immediate, efficient causes. Descartes does reserve the ultimate agency for the rational soul, in humans only. This issue is, however, beyond the scope of the present paper.
7 This was an ancient location and understanding. Aristotle, too, likens the heart to a hearth (*De partibus animalium*, 170a23).

fire "without light," of the same nature as "the one which heats the hay when it has been enclosed before it turned dry, or the one which makes new wines seethe when one leaves them to mature on the lees."[8]

Thus commonly known fermentations in the natural world[9] serve as analogies[10] for how human physiology works. As Descartes will hold up until at least 1645, the fermentational fire is the "sole cause of cardiac activity"[11] and the source of all innate heat:

> Il me semble que toute la chaleur des animaux consiste en ce qu'ils ont dans le coeur une espece de feu, qui est sans lumiere, semblable à celuy qui s'excite dans l'eau forte, lors qu'on met dedans assez grande quantité de poudre d'acier, & à celuy de toutes les fermentations.[12]

This alleged similarity goes beyond a convenient analogy. Firstly, I argue that Descartes systematically employs fermentation (or more precisely, what he understands by it) as a descriptive model[13] for physiological processes at the micro-level of particles. Fermentation thus performs an explanatory function, in the sense of generating hypotheses about how bodily processes happen. Secondly, beyond serving as models for unobservable phenomena inside the body, certain fermentations are literally carried over from the natural world into the human body. Because many of the foods we ingest are the ones in which fermentations occur, physiology itself continues the work of nature. This is not a metaphor. Descartes writes of bread, beer, wine, "from

---

8   *Discours*, AT VI 45-46: "que je ne concevois point d'autre nature que celuy qui échaufe le foin, lorsqu'on l'a renfermé avant qu'il fust sec, ou qui fait bouillir les vins nouveaux, lorsqu'on les laisse cuver sur la rape." [Translation is mine.] CSM I 134 renders this as "no different from that of the fire which heats hay when it has been stored before it is dry, or which causes new wine to seethe when it is left to ferment from the crushed grapes." However, I here distance myself from this translation insofar as Descartes does not use the verb "ferment"; Descartes' "cuver" is, in my view, best rendered as "to mature". For more on this terminological issue see CARMEN SCHMECHEL, "Descartes and fermentation in digestion: iatromechanism, analogy and teleology," *The British Journal for the History of Science* (2021), p. 101-116, here p. 107-108.
9   Importantly, while Descartes makes use of fermentation analogies, he rejects the analogy of innate heat with solar heat, in order to avoid association with Fernel and others in the idea of the origin of innate heat being divine. Cf. ANNIE BITBOL-HESPÉRIÈS, "Cartesian Physiology," in *Descartes' Natural Philosophy*, ed. by S. Gaukroger, J. Schuster, and J. Sutton, London and New York, Routledge, 2000, p. 349-382, p. 363-364.
10 For the particular analogy of innate heat with external heat, see EVERETT MENDELSOHN, *Heat and Life*, Cambridge, Harvard University Press, 1964, p. 3-4.
11 THOMAS FUCHS, *The Mechanization of the Heart: Harvey and Descartes*, transl. by Marjorie Grene, Rochester, University of Rochester Press, 2001, p. 127; Fuchs refers to the *Description*, AT XI 228, as well as to the *Discours* 5, AT VI 46-47.
12 Descartes to the Marquis de Newcastle, April (?) 1645, AT IV 189.
13 I rely on the concept of an explanation model in science, and especially in biology, as exposed by the following sources: MANFRED LAUBICHLER and GERD MÜLLER, ed., *Modeling Biology: Structures, Behavior, Evolution*, Cambridge, Mass., MIT Press, 2007; LINDLEY DARDEN, "Mechanisms and Models," in *The Cambridge Companion to the Philosophy of Biology*, ed. by D. L. Hull and M. Ruse, Cambridge and New York, Cambridge University Press, 2007, p. 139-159; JAY ODENBAUGH, "Models," in *A Companion to the Philosophy of Biology*, ed. by S. Sarkar and A. Plutynski, Malden, Blackwell Publications, 2008, p. 506-524. See also, for descriptive models, ROMAN FRIGG and STEPHAN HARTMANN. "Models in Science," in *Stanford Encyclopedia of Philosophy*, Stanford: The Metaphysics Research Lab, 2020, p. 19-20.

which a great part of our blood arises [is made]."[14] Hence, what happens *in* the body is a continuation and/or a reiteration, under new environmental conditions, of what happens outside of it. Food thus becomes the literal and direct source of the fermentational fire and heat. This point is important because it serves to distance[15] Descartes from the claim of coeval chymical theories about the origin of innate heat being celestial and/or divine (such as with Fernel and his followers.)[16] It also marks the beginnings of thinking about physiology in terms of literal chemical reactions conceptualized mechanistically, an approach continued by Borelli.

Descartes' ideas on heat coming from food resonate with a line of ancient authors such as the Hippocratic writers, Galen and even — in part, and controversially — Aristotle. A relationship between nutriment and the innate heat[17] was established already in the Hippocratic corpus. The text on "Nutriment" claims that "[p]ower of nutriment reaches to bone and to all the parts of bone, to sinew, to vein, to artery, to muscle, to membrane, to flesh, fat, blood, phlegm, marrow, brain, spinal marrow, the intestines and all their parts; it reaches also to heat, breath and moisture."[18] As for Aristotle, while a famous passage[19] courted by Renaissance Neoplatonists seems to suggest that innate heat may be celestial[20] due to being analogous with solar heat, several other Aristotelian passages either state or at least imply that the heat comes from food.[21]

---

14 Descartes to Plempius, 15 February 1638, AT I 530; this part is not translated in CSMK.
15 For Descartes' positioning towards coeval chymistry, the most helpful resource remains BERNARD JOLY, *Descartes et la chimie*, Paris, Vrin, 2011. See also JEAN-FRANÇOIS MAILLARD, "Descartes et l'alchimie: une tentation conjurée?," in *Aspects de la tradition alchimique au XVIIe siècle: actes du colloque international de l'Université de Reims-Champagne-Ardenne*, ed. by F. Greiner, Paris, SEHA [u.a.], 1998, p. 95-109.
16 For Fernel's position on this issue see HIRO HIRAI, "Alter Galenus: Jean Fernel et son interprétation platonico-chrétienne de Galien," *Early Science and Medicine* 10 (2005), p. 1-35, p. 26 *et passim*.
17 On innate heat see MENDELSOHN, *Heat and Life*; FRIEDRICH SOLMSEN, "The Vital Heat, the Inborn Pneuma and the Aether," in *The Journal of Hellenic Studies* 77 (1957), p. 119-123; for a recent short overview, ELISABETH MOREAU, "Innate Heat," in *Encyclopedia of Renaissance Philosophy*, ed. by M. Sgarbi, Cham, Springer, 2015, DOI: 10.1007/978-973-319-02848-4_399-391.
18 HIPPOCRATES, *Ancient Medicine; Airs, Waters, Places; Epidemics I and III; The Oath; Precepts; Nutriment*, translated by W. H. S. Jones. Vol. 1. Loeb Classical Library, London, Heinemann, 1958, p. 345.
19 ARISTOTLE, *De generatione animalium*, 736a-737a: "the semen contains within itself that which causes it to be fertile — what is known as 'hot' substance, which is not fire nor any similar substance [...] this substance is analogous to the element which belongs to the stars;" also later "the heat which is in animals is not fire and does not get its origin or principle from fire."
20 However, there was pushback from other commentators underlining that Aristotle had only made an analogy, not stated an identity. Joachim Cureus, a German theologian and an old-school Aristotelian, writes: "Non fuit ita incogitans Aristoteles, ut aeterna & incorruptibilia misceret cum caducis & corruptibilibus, sed facit collationem ex analogia, sicut manifeste ostendunt verba." CUREUS, *Lib. Ph.*, p. 264-265, quoted after D. P. WALKER, "The Astral Body in Renaissance Medicine," *Journal of the Warburg and Courtauld Institutes* 21 (1958), p. 119-133, esp. p. 129: "Aristotle was not as thoughtless as to mix up eternal and incorruptible things with those that are perishing and corruptible; instead he made a comparison by analogy, as [his] words explicitly reveal" [my translation.]
21 ARISTOTLE, *De partibus animalium*, 650a1-5; *De sensu*, 442a4; *De respiratione*, 473a10: "Further, how are we to describe this fictitious process of the generation of heat from the breath? Observation shows rather that it is a product of the food."

Galen, on the other hand, explicitly and repeatedly endorsed a vision of food as a source of heat in the body: "All nutriment [...] increases the heat of the animal [...] and likewise it truly heats the body which it nourishes;"[22] food also serves as fuel for physiological processes: "Whatever in the blood is fatty, light, and tenuous, becomes in the warmer bodies a kind of fuel for heat, in the colder it is stored [...] but in the parts warmer by nature such as the fleshy ones, it is taken up by the heat itself and carried off."[23]

While not directly derivative from these Ancient sources, Descartes' own project remains largely compatible with them. For Descartes, the fire in the heart comes from the blood, which in turn is a distilled and fermented form of chyle, meaning that the fire comes ultimately from food; additionally, the fire comes from the air by means of respiration. Thus while Descartes explains the micro-process differently, the larger contours of his theory follow Ancient sources including in the issue of the origin of fermentational heat.

3. The 'Heat-Rarefaction' Model: A Mechanist Version of Fermentation

Beyond being the source of all innate heat, this fermentation is also the efficient cause of the beating of the heart, by driving the expansion of the blood matter: "it is this rarefaction of the blood alone that is the cause of the movement of the heart."[24] Descartes exposes this in most detail in *La description du corps humain*, Part Two ("Concerning the Motion of the Heart and Blood").[25]

Without dwelling here on the debate about the movement of the heart as it relates to the circulation of the blood,[26] I will focus on how exactly Descartes claims that fermentation works at a microscopic level to further the physiological processes necessary for the beating of the heart. This approach will reveal the main features of Descartes' model of how fermentation happens, and will shed light on his 1638 disagreement with Plempius. The reason I understand this as an analogical scientific model is because Descartes uses it to explain not just everyday fermentations, but also processes in the body, transferring onto physiology the blueprint of how he understands everyday fermentations to be working. This will be explained in detail in the following.

---

22 Galen (Kühn), I, 660.
23 Galen (Kühn), I, 606.
24 *La Description du corps humain*, AT XI 244; G 182.
25 For Descartes, the issue of what causes the movement of the heart is not a marginal debate, but one that he considers central to the whole of medicine, since "without it, we cannot know anything about the theory of medicine, because all the other functions in the animal depend on it." Ibid., AT XI 245; G 182.
26 This has received much attention, mainly due to the Descartes-Harvey controversy; see, among others: FUCHS, *The Mechanization of the Heart*; LUCIAN PETRESCU, "Descartes on the Heartbeat: The Leuven Affair," *Perspectives on Science* 21 (2013), 397-428; FABRIZIO BALDASSARRI, *Il metodo al tavolo anatomico. Descartes e la medicina*, Rome, Aracne, 2021, esp. p. 74-82; BITBOL-HESPÉRIÈS, "Cartesian Physiology".

In the *Description*,[27] Descartes argues that the undoubtedly existing heat in the heart is of the same nature as "that which is caused by the addition of some fluid, or yeast, which causes the body with which it is mixed to expand."[28] It is this fermentative expansion at micro-level which holds the key to the circulation of blood, in Descartes' view. The blood expands, growing in volume and becoming rarefied as its particles move away from each other. In addition, the mechanical movement is imparted to adjacent particles. Thus, even a small quantity of such rarefied blood can animate an incoming larger quantity into the same expansion behaviour:

> the small amount of rarefied blood that remains in these ventricles, mixing straightaway with the fresh blood coming in, is like a kind of yeast [*comme vne espece de leuain*], which causes it to heat and expand immediately, and by these means the heart swells, hardens, and becomes a little squatter in shape [...][29]

The analogies regarding this phenomenon had been laid out more explicitly and vividly in the 1638 correspondence with the physician, Plempius,[30] where Descartes claimed that the small quantity of blood that remains in the heart "performs a fermentation" much like the fermentations observable in nature:

> we see that certain liquids, when mixed with certain others, by this very act they heat up and inflate; in the same way, indeed in the recesses of the heart some humour could reside, like a ferment [*instar fermenti*], whose admixture causes another incoming humour to swell up.[31]

Since he knew that Plempius was suspicious of how this rarefaction happens, Descartes explains in more detail:

> As the blood swells up in the heart, indeed the larger part of it exits violently through the aorta and the arterial vein, yet another [part] in fact remains inside, which, filling the inner ventricles of the heart, through a new degree of heat takes over, as it were, the nature of ferment (*veluti fermenti naturam adipiscitur*); and immediately afterwards, as the heart deflates, anew the blood that glides in through the vena cava and the arterial vein mixes itself up quickly, in order to

---

27 The text, said to have been composed around 1647-1648, was published posthumously by Clerselier in 1664. See the Introduction to this volume.
28 DESCARTES, *La Description du corps humain*, AT XI 228; G 172.
29 *La Description du corps humain*, AT XI 231; G 174.
30 For the debate with Plempius see also ETIENNE GILSON, *Études sur le rôle de la philosophie médiévale dans la formation du système cartésien*, Paris, Vrin, 1951, p. 84-91; BALDASSARRI, *Il metodo al tavolo anatomico*, p. 74-82.
31 Descartes to Plempius, 15 February 1638, AT I 523. Original Latin is "denique vt videmus quosdam liquores quibusdam alijs admistos hoc ipso incalescere atque inflari, sic forte etiam in recessibus cordis nonnihil humoris instar fermenti residere, cuius permistione alius humor adueniens intumescit." Cf. existing translation at CSMK 80 which renders "instar fermenti" as *"yeast-like"* although such a term is absent in the original ('yeast' usually translates the French *levain* or the Latin *levamen*, both terms used by Descartes in other places).

quickly grow in volume and depart for the arteries; yet another part of it is left behind, which acts like a ferment (*fermenti vice*).³²

Descartes is here showing caution when mentioning the ferment — he never says it *is* a ferment, but that the liquid 'acts like', or 'serves as' a ferment, or is endowed with 'the nature of a ferment'. This caution is indicative of Descartes distancing himself in this respect from the coeval chymical philosophy. He does not mean the fermentation such as the chymists understand it, but he means something *similar* or *analogous* to it as to the manner of action. He does believe that these processes are actual fermentations, but he lays stress on the precise manner in which he conceptualizes them, and which is different from the understanding that was current among chymical philosophers.

But Plempius' response is unexpected. He fears that the ferment may be a 'figment' of Descartes' scientific imagination: "Confugis deinde ad fermentum cordiale, quod rarefaciet sanguinem, quod fermentum vereor ne figmentum sit. Et vt non sit, quomodo, inquam, tam celeriter rarefaciet?"³³ The disagreement concerns the issue of how the rarefaction of the blood in the heart happens; Plempius doubts that fermentation could effect such a powerful motion by itself. Descartes in turn expresses that he is "extremely surprised" that no one had hitherto had the insight that it is "this rarefaction of the blood alone that is the cause of the movement of the heart,"³⁴ including Aristotle. He is attempting to draw attention away from the ‚ferment' issue, and onto his own ideas about the rarefaction of blood. The 'ferment' is in fact secondary, he suggests.

The key to understanding the stakes of this passage is that Descartes employs here a mechanistic model of fermentation which I will call the 'heat-rarefaction' model. Fermentation, in this Cartesian version, uses heat as a means to increase space between particles of matter, hence to 'rarefy' and 'subtilize' it, leading to the mass of matter taking up more space and hence its parts being propelled through various channels as are available (such as the vein structure in the case of the blood). This model is ontologically different from how coeval chymists understood fermentation to be working. Chymists relied on a medieval tradition which saw fermentation as the process through which a 'ferment' transforms a given mass into the ferment's own nature.³⁵ This tradition, which reached the Latin West along

---

32 Descartes to Plempius, 15 February 1638, AT I 530; CSMK 83 omits this fragment. Original: "Cum sanguis in corde intumescit, maxima quidem eius pars per aortam & venam arteriosam foras erumpit, sed alia etiam intus manet, quae intimos eius ventriculorum recessus replens, nouum ibi caloris gradum & quamdam veluti fermenti naturam adipiscitur: statimque postea, dum cor detumuit, nouo sanguini per venam cauam & arteriam venosam illabenti celerrime se admiscens efficit, vt celerrime turgescat, in arteriasque discedat; sed relicta rursus aliqua sui parte, quae fermenti vice fungatur." [Translation is mine.]
33 Plempius to Descartes, March 1638, AT II 54.
34 *Description*, AT XI 244; G 182.
35 For an excellent treatment of 'ferment' in medieval alchemy and medicine see SÉBASTIEN MOUREAU, "Elixir atque fermentum: New investigations about the link between Pseudo-Avicenna's alchemical 'De anima' and Roger Bacon: Alchemical and medical doctrines," *Traditio* 68 (2013), p. 277-325.

lines of transmission from medieval Islamic medicine and alchemy, emphasized the qualitative[36] change of the nature of matter, as opposed to a simple dilution or expansion. For example, in Pseudo-Avicenna's influential treatise *De anima*, the ferment is said to be that which transforms the thing into the nature of the ferment itself: "Fermentum non est aliud nisi hoc quod revertaris causam de illa natura de qua est ad naturam fermenti;"[37] it acts like the leaven in bread (*levamen* being used as a synonym for *fermentum* in this work). While *levamen*, by way of its etymology, does suggest 'rising' (a term used in baking until today), the focus was not on the rarefaction of existing matter (and consequent increase in volume) as much as on the transformation of its nature. For Descartes, however, there seems to be no question of a qualitative transformation of matter at microscopic level; it is a *rearrangement of particles* at microscopic level, which *only apparently* leads to a transformation at macroscopic level. In other (Aristotelian) words, fermentation for chymists was a substantial change, while for Descartes it could be subsumed under accidental change.

Descartes' fermentation hence creates heat and an agitation[38] of particles, promoting further movement and rarefaction. As Justin Smith also emphasizes, the change taking place is solely quantitative: "it is clear that Descartes conceives fermentation as a straightforwardly microstructural process, and that he conceives the changes it brings about not in terms of the emergence of new forms but in terms of the quantitative alteration of preexisting corpuscles."[39] Marina Banchetti-Robino argues similarly: "the Cartesian account would not accept that chemical qualities are higher-level properties that have any causal power unto themselves, since all causal efficacy was attributed only to mechanistic properties and to primary causes."[40] In the case of fermentative processes, these primary causes acted at the level of particles; whatever happened macroscopically was a result of microscopic rarefaction. Hence, with fermentation, Descartes employs a bottom-up (or: upward) model of causation.[41]

At this point an objection might be raised. When it comes to the blood remaining in the heart which 'acts like a leaven' or a 'ferment,' Descartes would seem to be using the old fermentation model, because the remaining drop of blood confers its 'nature' to the incoming blood. Yet I argue that what exactly it conveys in Descartes' understanding is not a different *nature*, but a *property*: heat and agitation of particles

---

36   In the sense in which we understand 'qualitative' now. For the scholastics this would have been a change of substantial form.
37   PSEUDO-AVICENNA, *De anima*, 363; apud MOUREAU, "Elixir atque fermentum," p. 292.
38   For an explanation of how for Descartes the expansion by heat occurs through violent motion, see J. R. PARTINGTON, *A History of Chemistry*, London, Macmillan St Martin's Press, 1969, vol. II, p. 435.
39   JUSTIN E. H. SMITH, *Divine Machines: Leibniz and the Sciences of Life*, Princeton, Princeton University Press, 2011, p. 78-79.
40   MARINA PAOLA BANCHETTI-ROBINO, "Mechanism and Chemistry in Early Modern Natural Philosophy," in *Encyclopedia of Early Modern Philosophy and the Sciences*, ed. by D. Jalobeanu and Ch. T. Wolfe, Cham, Springer, 2020, p. 3. DOI: 10.1007/978-973-319-20791-9_145-141.
41   For more on causation, including in Descartes, see Jaegwon Kim's work, esp. JAEGWON KIM, "Mental Causation in a Physical World." *Philosophical Issues* 3, Science and Knowledge (1993): 157-176.

(motion). The matter remains the same: blood. This means that Descartes interprets mechanistically even those fermentations which at first glance seem to be working after a chymical model. This mechanist functionality of Cartesian fermentation as 'heat-rarefaction' is focused on processes that, in their macroscopic manifestations in the natural world (as opposed to inside the human body), can be observed and even measured externally (such as ebullition or effervescence, as well as thermal changes). It is an instrumental model of fermentation: fermentation serves a certain goal of transforming matter, but it does not have its own mysterious agenda. Therefore, this model is incompatible with any occult powers, hidden virtues, or other types of obscure agencies that elicited caution on the part of more hardline mechanist philosophers. The 'heat-rarefaction' model of fermentation will have some success with followers such as Borelli, before merging with its chymical counterpart in the work of English physicians such as Thomas Willis or William Simpson.

My hypothesis, hence, is that in their letters of 1638 Descartes and Plempius are in fact talking about different things. What Plempius understood by fermentation was not what Descartes meant. While Descartes makes use of analogies with common fermentations, his underlying stance still entails that such fermentations act by 'heat-rarefaction'. Plempius, however, reads quickly and assumes that Descartes has in mind the fermentation of the chymists, and *this is what he refutes*. The matter is not helped by the fact that Descartes does in fact say that chymistry ('Chymia') provides many examples of the processes he discusses.[42] Left unconvinced, Plempius accused Descartes of a suboptimal choice of words as regards 'fermentation'; the debate, which turned rather sour,[43] is likely to have contributed significantly to Descartes' later avoidance of the term fermentation.[44] Descartes never stopped employing his comparisons with (fermentative) wine and hay, but ceased to call them explicitly fermentations, resorting instead to describing the phenomena every time in what looks like contrived paraphrases of 'fermentation' ("such as happens with new wines when they are left to mature"). As for the noun 'ferment,' the word later virtually disappeared from his vocabulary, being replaced by 'yeast' (*levain*) which was functionally identical but rhetorically a better option, since as a term in everyday usage it was less likely to conjure alchymical associations.

Fermentation for Descartes, therefore, is a process of heating, rarefaction and subtilization of matter. When blood ferments repeatedly, due to its rarefied state it becomes prone to generating animal spirits which are a more subtle form of matter. In this transformation Descartes claims that there is, again, no qualitative change involved. In Aristotelian terms:

---

[42] Descartes to Plempius, 15 February 1638, AT I 530 (absent in CSMK): "At quid opus est alienis exemplis, quorum magnam multitudinem Chymia posset suppeditare…"

[43] Plempius mounted an attack at Descartes and petitioned to exclude his teachings from the university. See Descartes to Plempius, 15 February 1638, AT I 534-535; also PETRESCU, "Descartes on the Heartbeat," p. 421.

[44] In "Descartes and fermentation in digestion," I show how (and why) Descartes grew reluctant to use both fermentation and concoction, all the while still employing the images of natural processes which were, then as now, classified as fermentations.

there is a change in qualities or properties (ἀλλοίωσις, *alloiosis*, alteration) but no *substantial* change (γένεσις, *genesis*, coming-to-be).⁴⁵ As Descartes insists in *Passions de l'ame*, "elles [*les Esprits animaux*] n'ont besoin à cet effect de recevoir *aucun autre changement* dans le cerveau, sinon qu'elles y sont separées des autres parties du sang moins subtiles."⁴⁶

To trace back some of the heritage of Descartes' ideas of medical spirits, it is worth making a short incursion into the medieval philosophies of spirit and medical spirits.

4. Descartes' 'Animal Spirits' and their Medieval Historical Background

For Descartes, the 'animal spirits' in human bodies were "a certain very fine wind, or rather a very lively and very pure flame"⁴⁷ produced by the parts of blood that "penetrate as far as the brain," thanks to being particularly volatile; these were the "most agitated and most active parts of this blood."⁴⁸ Such 'spirits' enter the nerves, and from there, they move the limbs of the body-machine.⁴⁹ The production of spirits presupposes the rarefying action of heat;⁵⁰ yet their engendering from the most subtle parts of blood is not a qualitative (substantial) transformation of blood, but a mechanical sieving.⁵¹

Descartes employed his version of the 'animal spirits' in *L'Homme, A Description of the Human Body*,⁵² as well as in the *Passions*. In a comparison of the nerve system of the human body, in this respect, with the mechanical pipe system of the "grottoes and fountains in the royal gardens,"⁵³ the 'animal spirits' corresponded to the water moving through these pipes.

---

45 ARISTOTLE, *De generatione et corruptione* (On Coming-to-Be and Passing-Away), 319b6-320a5. However, because the process of generating animal spirits as an elevated form of matter is clearly teleological, this poses a problem for Descartes' system; on teleology in Cartesian physiology see: KAREN DETLEFSEN, ed. *Descartes' Meditations: A Critical Guide*, Cambridge, Cambridge University Press, 2013, chapter "Teleology and natures in Descartes' Sixth Meditation;" also DETLEFSEN, "Descartes on the Theory of Life and Methodology in the Life Sciences;" PETER M. DISTELZWEIG, "The Use of *Usus* and the Function of *Functio*: Teleology and Its Limits in Descartes's Physiology," *Journal of the History of Philosophy* 53/3 (2015), p. 377-399.
46 *Passions de l'âme*, art. X, AT XI 335, my emphasis.
47 *L'Homme*, AT XI 129; G 104-105.
48 *Description*, AT XI 227; G 172.
49 *L'Homme*, AT XI 134; G 107.
50 *Passions*, X, AT XI 334: "toutes les plus vives & plus subtiles parties du sang, que la chaleur a rarefiees dans le coeur, entrent sans cesse en grande quantite dans les cavitez du cerveau."
51 *L'Homme*, AT XI 130: "ainsi, *sans autre preparation, ny changement*, sinon qu'elles sont separées des plus grossieres, & qu'elles retiennent encore l'extreme vitesse que la chaleur du coeur leur a donnée, elles cessent d'auoir la forme du sang, & se nomment les Esprits animaux," my emphasis. See also *Passions*, X, AT XI 334: "a cause qu'il n'y a que des passages fort estroits, celles de ses parties qui sont les plus agitees & les plus subtiles, y passent seules, pendant que le reste se respand en tous les autres endroits du corps. Or ces parties du sang tres-subtiles composent les esprits animaux."
52 *Description*, AT XI 227; G 172.
53 *L'Homme*, AT XI 131; G 107.

Importantly, Descartes' animal spirits retain a material nature: "ce que je nomme icy des esprits, ne sont que des corps, & ils n'ont point d'autre proprieté, sinon que ce sont des corps tres-petits, & qui se meuvent tres-viste, ainsi que les parties de la flame qui sort d'un flambeau."[54] They are immanent in living matter — not divine, celestial, or otherwise occult. In animals, including humans, they are transmitted from mother to foetus through the umbilical cord, and while they do not interfere with the rational soul in humans, they act rather as its instruments. A certain time after digestion is achieved, "le mesme sang, ayant passé & repassé plusieurs fois dans le coeur, est deuenu plus subtil."[55] As the blood is passed repeatedly through the heart, it undergoes every time a process of fermentation, which includes rarefaction. As an effect, the animal spirits, too, become stronger as the blood from which they are produced becomes more purified.[56] Hence the repeated fermentation leads to production of purer animal spirits. Together with the fermentation in the heart, the 'animal spirits' — ultimately the most refined[57] form of blood — replace the Aristotelian vegetative and sensitive souls.[58]

I argue that Descartes' 'spirits' and the operations correlated with them (such as the fire of fermentation) are modelled after the 'spirits' of a medical tradition rooted in antiquity and transmitted throughout the Middle Ages.[59] In particular, Galen had posited very similar spirits of an airy, subtle nature, that originate in respiration and in the blood.[60] As James Bono notes, Galen's *pneuma* is 'of a corporeal, that is material, nature, though the matter in question is of an exceptionally fine and rarified sort, rather like hot vapor'.[61] Much like Descartes' fire in the heart, this Galenic pneuma has a double source in air and blood.[62] Such spirits were active in all areas where a more subtle, rarefied type of matter was called for, such as in the nerves and the brain.

Throughout the Middle Ages, the idea of *spiritus* underwent gradual changes along different schools of thought. One strand in medieval Arabic medicine brought

---

54 *Passions*, art. X, AT XI 335.
55 *L'Homme*, AT XI 168, see also AT XI 199.
56 *L'Homme*, AT XI 199: "cependant ces esprits se trouuent estre plus forts, d'autant que le sang qui les produit, s'est purifié, en passant & repassant plusieurs fois dans le cœur," see also AT XI 168.
57 *L'Homme*, AT XI 128.
58 See *Description*, AT XI 202; G 169.
59 For a detailed history of medical spirits, from Antiquity throughout the Middle Ages, see JAMES BONO, "Medical Spirits and the Language of Life," *Traditio*, 40 (1984), p. 91-130. In what follows in this section I am highly indebted to Bono's work. Another notable account of spirit from Antiquity into the seventeenth century is that of MARIELENE PUTSCHER, *Pneuma, Spiritus, Geist: Vorstellungen vom Lebensantrieb in ihren geschichtlichen Wandlungen*, Wiesbaden, Franz Steiner Verlag, 1973.
60 BONO, "Medical Spirits," p. 92.
61 BONO, "Medical Spirits," p. 92. On Galen's pneuma see, among others: OWSEI TEMKIN, "On Galen's Pneumatology," *Gesnerus* 8 (1951): p. 180-189; L. G. WILSON, "Erasistratus, Galen, and the Pneuma," *Bulletin of the History of Medicine* 33 (1959): p. 293-314; JULIUS ROCCA, "Chapter 11 Pneuma as a Holistic Concept in Galen," in *Holism in Ancient Medicine and Its Reception*, ed. by C. Thumiger, Leiden: Brill, 2020, p. 268-291; PHILIP VAN DER EIJK, "Galen on Soul, Mixture and Pneuma," in *Body and Soul in Hellenistic Philosophy*, ed. by B. Inwood and J. Warren, Cambridge: Cambridge University Press, 2020, p. 62-88.
62 BONO, "Medical Spirits," p. 92, adding on p. 97 that "[t]here is some question whether Galen considered spirits to have an origin which is internal (derived from the blood) or external (derived from the air)."

it from a fine sort of matter to representing a divine essence. This line harked back to some ideas of Stoic and Neoplatonic heritage. Another school constituted itself along a medieval corpuscular tradition rooted in Aristotle. Within the latter, the spirits retained their material character and medical role, while the immortal soul was retained as transcendent; this forms the contours of a dualism that survived until and beyond Descartes. Costa ben Luca (Constantinus Africanus), in *De animae et spiritus discrimine*,[63] claims that the spirits are material while the soul is incorporeal.[64] He also differentiates between two kinds of corporeal spirits: vital (in the heart), related to respiration and circulation — this one being the source of life; and animal (related to the soul, *anima*), which resides in the brain and feeds on the vital spirit. The *animal* spirit operates the thinking, memory, and the nerves and movement of the muscles.[65] How exactly the *vital* spirit, on the other hand, functions as a cause of life — whether it has inherent activity or whether it is moved by an external principle — remains unclear; Constantinus does not address this.[66]

This ontological ambiguity is present with Descartes as well. Descartes posits only one type of spirits (the animal spirits), which derive from the fermentational fire in the heart. But while we know that this fire comes to the heart from nutriment via blood, its ultimate origin is shrouded in some obscurity. Descartes does not address the final cause of fermentations in the natural world (presumably, it belongs to the inscrutable will of God). He relies on them as analogies to explain physiology, and explains how he believes that they happen at a microscopic level (which is a speculative hypothesis). But the ultimate question of why fermentations happen at all remains largely beyond the scope of the mechanist endeavour.

These tensions are relevant for Descartes' positioning in terms of the debate regarding the role of the soul (or of other agents, internal or external) in moving the body. While in Aristotle's more immanent biology and teleology, soul and body had been inseparable,[67] for the medieval scholastics a rift took shape between mortal matter (flesh) and a divine, transcendent soul. The distance between them was connoted

---

63 Costa ben Luca, "De animae et spiritus discrimine liber" in Constantinus Africanus, *Opera*, Basel, 1536, p. 308-317. See the reprint in Putscher, *Pneuma, Spiritus, Geist*, p. 145-150.
64 "Dicamusque quod prima differentia haec est, videlicet, quod spiritus est corpus. Anima vero res incorporea est." -Putscher, *Pneuma, Spiritus, Geist*, p. 150.
65 Costa ben Luca, in Putscher, *Pneuma, Spiritus, Geist*, p. 147: "In humano corpore sunt *duo* species: Unus, qui vocatur *vitalis*, cuius nutrimentus vel sustentatio est aer, et eiusdem animatio [*sic: for* emanatio] est ex corde, et mittitur per pulsus ad reliquum corpus, et operatur vitam, pulsum atque anhelitum. Est et alter, qui ab anima, dicitur *animalis*, qui operatur in ipso cerebro, cuius nutrimentum est spiritus vitalis, et eius emanatio est ex cerebro, et operatur in ipso cerebro cogitationem, et memoriam, atque providentiam, et ex eo mittitur per nervos ad caetera membra, ut operetur sensum, atque motum."
66 See Bono, "Medical Spirits," p. 95.
67 For Aristotle soul and body formed a whole; Aristotle, *De anima* 412a28-29; "neither the soul nor certain parts of it, if it has parts, can be separated from the body" (413a4-5). However, 429b-430a may be (and was) taken as a suggestion that the rational soul is, after all, separable from the body. See also Katharine Park, "The Organic Soul," in *The Cambridge History of Renaissance Philosophy*, ed. by C. B. Schmitt et al., Cambridge, Cambridge University Press, 2007, p. 468.

morally. Under these auspices, spirits, which had started out in Galenic tradition as a rarefied, subtler form of matter, gradually were reconceptualized to fit the dichotomy between the material body and the more transcendent component that had begun to take hold; within this dichotomy, on the one side, spirit(s) approached the soul and its incorporeal nature, and on the other side might still be found performing physiological functions (hence retaining material character). Alain de Lille, for example, found the compromise of positing two kinds of spirit: rational (incorporeal, immortal) and physical (natural and perishing with the body):

> There is in fact in man a double spirit, the rational and incorporeal spirit, which does not perish with the body; and another one, which is called physical or natural, by whose mediation the rational soul is united with the body, and this spirit is more subtle than air and even than fire, and it mediates sense perception and imagination: and that [spirit] perishes with the body.[68]

As Bono shows, the issue at hand was the transition of the human being from its mortal condition in the flesh towards a more spiritualized state (the eschatological narrative). In other words, at the more 'spiritual'[69] end of this continuum salvation had to be possible, while at the more corporeal end (where spirits were still understood as material) the natural philosophy had to provide medical explanations about how the human body works.

Regarding Descartes, my thesis is that while the sixteenth century's revival of Renaissance Neoplatonism and of natural magic would later blur these differences, Descartes, interestingly, reverted in part to earlier medieval traditions of thought in which spirits were still entirely corporeal (material) and fulfilled medical and physiological functions. The rationale for this might have been that if Descartes had wished to uphold the dichotomy between the body and the rational soul, another non-corporeal item (of the type of Alain de Lille's *spiritus incorporeus*) would have been in the way.[70] Thus with regard to this particular issue Descartes replaced Aristotle's framework of 'souls' with an updated version of Galenic *pneuma* in the form of 'animal spirits.' It is to be noted that such 'animal spirits' are, in principle, compatible with both Descartes' more restricted mechanist view, and with the new

---

68 ALAIN DE LILLE, *Contra haereticos* I, 28, in M.-D. CHENU, "Spiritus: Le vocabulaire de l'âme au XIIe siècle," *Revue des Sciences Philosophiques et Théologiques* 41 (1957), p. 209-232, p. 215: "Est namque in homine duplex spiritus, spiritus rationalis et incorporeus, qui non perit cum corpore; et alius qui dicitur physicus sive naturalis, quo mediante anima rationalis unitur corpori, et hic spiritus est subtilior aere, et etiam igne, quo mediante fit sensus et imaginatio: et ille perit cum corpore." [Translation is mine.]
69 I here use 'spiritual' rather anachronistically, in a modern sense, which is itself the result of this historical process of semantic transformation.
70 Descartes will have been aware of the troubles into which Fernel had run due to positing two kinds of immortal agents in the body. Criticizing the doubling of soul and spirit in Fernel's embryology, Cureus had written: "since the heavenly bodies are exempt from the mutability of generation and corruption, you will have to imagine that the heat from the heavens is infused into bodies by a miracle, as St Thomas wished for the soul, and thus in man there will be two immortal bodies, the soul and the innate heat; which everyone, I think, will admit is absurd." CUREUS, *Lib. Ph.*, p. 262, in D. P. WALKER, "The Astral Body," p. 130.

chymical philosophy; the difference lies in the explanation of the cause of movement of particles, but the particulate nature and the role of these spirits in physiology is preserved in both versions.

One position not too far from Descartes' in this particular regard was that of Alfred of Sareshel (Alfredus Anglicus), a thirteenth century monk (active between 1180 and 1217) and one of the earliest commentators of Aristotle in the medieval Latin West. In his work *De motu cordis*,[71] which treats of medical spirits, the heart plays a central role as the site of such spirits.[72] As the seat of life, the heart also imparts life throughout the body by means of its motion, the heartbeat: "Virtus cordis in motu est; motu enim vitam distribuit."[73] But for Alfred, the source of the heartbeat, a violent motion, had to be an *external agent* — which he located in an external heat, as opposed to the innate heat of the Ancients. The heat did reside in the heart, but its ultimate source was extrinsic and divine — the soul: "exterius est principium [...] Extrinseco igitur principio [...] movetur."[74] However, the heat was nevertheless for him the immediate, efficient cause of the heartbeat, which it produced by means of the dilation and rarefaction of the blood. Thus it is possible that Alfred ascribes to a similar model of 'heat-rarefaction.' There are, however, two main differences to consider. First, Alfred does not call this principle 'fermentation,' nor does he write of a ferment. Second, for Descartes, the heat-rarefaction process (which he understands as a fermentation) is a wholly inherent principle, not an extrinsic one. The fermentation in the heart creates its heat spontaneously, and does not need heat from an external source, just as in the natural world where the fermenting masses normally heat up of their own accord: "neither beer, nor wine, nor bread, from which a great part of our blood arises [is made], require intense heat in order to ferment, but indeed they spontaneously warm up of their own accord."[75] Descartes claims that the process of rarefaction effected in the body by this immanently generated heat is, if not identical, very similar to the analogous processes in the natural world: "I am not maintaining that the rarefaction of the blood that takes place in the heart is similar in all respects to the rarefaction which is brought about by artificial means. All the same, to be quite frank, I do think it comes about in that way."[76] In more than one sense, this echoes Aristotle's discussion of 'concoction by boiling' in the *Meteorology* IV, where the Stagirite had argued that "it makes no difference whether it takes place in an artificial or a natural vessel, for the cause is the same in all cases."[77] Though what Descartes envisages in the blood is a fermentation, Descartes' idea of fermentation

---

71 See the complete edition by C. BAEUMKER, *Des Alfred von Sareshel (Alfredus Anglicus) Schrift De motu cordis* (BGPhMA 23.1-2), Münster, 1923. On Alfred see the bibliography in BONO, "Medical Spirits," p. 112, note 63.
72 Cf. BONO, "Medical Spirits," p. 113.
73 *De motu cordis*, cap. 5 (Baeumker p. 17). [Paraphrase is mine.]
74 *De motu cordis*, cap. 9 (Baeumker p. 36 f.): "the principle is external ... Hence, it is moved by an extrinsic principle." [Translation is mine.]
75 Descartes to Plempius, 15 February 1638, AT I 530. [Translation is mine.]
76 Descartes to Plempius, 15 February 1638, AT I 530; CSMK 83.
77 ARISTOTLE, *Meteorology* IV, 381a9-12.

parallels Aristotle's 'boiling' (ἕψησις) firstly in a functional sense (fermentation, just as boiling, could happen in different kinds of vessels) and secondly, in content: Since Aristotle's boiling included the natural processes undergone by milk and must, it makes sense to consider it related to fermentation.[78]

Another point in which Descartes' project exhibits some similarity with that of Alfred is the *spiritus*. For Alfred, the spirit was ontologically intermediate between the organic body and the soul (anima). Although it was ultimately the soul from whence all motions in the body, as well as life, originated, the soul itself remained an external principle. It lived in the heart conceptually but not physically. But how could the soul then act on and from the heart, and perform actions like moving the limbs? The answer is that this happened with the help of spirit, which played the role of instrument of the soul. The (vital) spirit was a 'virtue' distributed (irradiated, as Alfred writes) throughout the body from its center, the heart. But while the ultimate cause remained the soul, the local efficient cause of this movement of irradiation was heat. In a similar way, for Descartes, the fermentational fire in the heart drives the production of animal spirits,[79] which in turn play a key role in muscle movement. A salient difference, however, is that Descartes' spirits are material, while Alfred's tended towards preternaturality.

Another significant voice in medieval natural philosophy, Albert the Great, sides with Alfred as to the heart being the domicile of the soul in the body, as well as to the spirits performing physiological functions. Yet Albert does not mention any celestial origin for such spirits,[80] promoting a view of spirit as a fine vapor[81] (thus closer to Galen). Albert defines the spirit, which is found in the bodies of the animals, as the "vehicle of life," adding that "that which is the seminal moisture in the bodies of the living should be more mixed in with the airy, spiritual moisture and a heat should be in it, making the spirit in it frothy.[82] For otherwise, this moisture would not be rendered the principle of life."[83]

However, the Albertian spirit functions, like for Alfred, as a mediator between the soul and the body and as the direct instrument of the soul. Only that instead of an ontological mediator, it is a functional one, whose own nature remains material.

Descartes, I believe, is to be seen as a heir of this tradition, which from his own vantage point is an older one when compared to the more recent developments of the sixteenth century. Unlike for Renaissance Neoplatonists such as Fernel or Severinus,[84] Descartes' animal spirits are not produced in the stars, but wholly immanent to the

---

78 However, while boiling has some overlap with fermentation in terms of how it works on matter, the concept of concoction (πεψις, *pepsis*) may be even more closely related to fermentation.
79 For Alfred, the spirits "irradiated" from the heart were vital spirits which were close to the very principle of organic life. Alfred also posited animal spirits which were more concrete. We shall not delve into detail here.
80 See Albertus. *On Animals: A Medieval Summa Zoologica*. Translated by Kenneth F. Kitchell and Irven Michael Resnick. Vol. 2. Baltimore: Johns Hopkins University Press, 1999, here Chapter XX, 1.4.
81 See BONO, "Medical Spirits," p. 121, p. 124 f.; cf. ALBERT, *On Animals* XX.1.7.
82 This is likely an Aristotelian reference, see *De gen. anim.* 3.11, 762a13-27.
83 *On Animals*, XX 1.1 (p. 1358).
84 See D. P. WALKER, "The Astral Body," *passim*.

body and purely material. In this respect, other aspects of Descartes' heritage may also be traced back to one particular "corpuscular theory" which, as William Newman has noted, was derived from Aristotle's *Meteorology* IV's "corpuscular proclivities".[85] This version of Aristotelian corpuscularism later "became a mainstay of medieval alchemy,"[86] only to merge, in the seventeenth century, with Paracelsianism and iatrochemistry. In my view, this tradition supplies another apt framework of thought for Descartes' 'heat-rarefaction' model of fermentation. Notably, Descartes does not join the step of merging corpuscularism with iatrochemistry. He reverts to the older, medieval version, exemplified by writers such as Albert the Great; while this tradition itself was not without affinities with chemistry, the stage that Descartes is most closely related to is the one *before* this tradition's definitive "marriage," as Newman calls it, with Paracelsian iatrochemistry. This is not to say that Albert was a foreigner to alchemy,[87] only that, as Newman notes, he was "willing to entertain corpuscular ideas when framing his explanations of phenomena."[88] Thus Albert's ideas on the microstructure of matter turn out more compatible with Cartesian mechanism than later mergings which included occult forces, pulsific faculties, or other formative powers or virtues.

Descartes' animal spirits do replace the Aristotelian vegetative and nutritive souls, which were immanent faculties. Importantly, however, they do not replace all the souls — the *âme*, rational soul,[89] remains; but this soul is transcendent, divine, and put into the body by God. Descartes hence solves the dilemma by positing a dualism in which the transcendent soul stays, while matter itself moves fueled by fermentation, which becomes the most prominent efficient cause of physiology: the force that fuels the production of blood, its circulation, and hence also the production of animal spirits. This dualism is not unlike some of the solutions found to this problem by medieval physician scholars — like Alfred of Sareshel — who preferred to keep the 'soul' as an external principle while at the same time having to account for how the body performs the motions of living, but crucially, without granting matter an intrinsic moving agency.

The final cause of fermentation, however — and the origin of the motion which it produces — must be said to rest with divine causation. In other words, why the fermentational fire exists at all in bodies — which is the same as asking 'why is there organic life' — is, for the medievals, left to God. That does not mean that the fire itself has a literal celestial origin; as argued in the previous section, heat could very well constitute a local, efficient cause of movement. Descartes' fermentation, too, is a 'heat-rarefaction' process with no occult powers partaking in it.

---

85 NEWMAN, "Corpuscular Alchemy," p. 145.
86 *Ibid.*
87 See, among others, ROBERT HALLEUX, "Albert le Grand et l'alchimie," *Revue des Sciences philosophiques et théologiques* 66/1 (1982), p. 57-80.
88 WILLIAM R. NEWMAN, *The Summa Perfectionis of Pseudo-Geber: A Critical Edition, Translation and Study*, Leiden-New York, Brill, 1991, p. 189.
89 The rational soul remains the ultimate *movens* of the body. For how the mind moves the body as an occasionalist cause see DANIEL GARBER, "Mind, Body, and the Laws of Nature in Descartes and Leibniz," in DANIEL GARBER, *Descartes Embodied: Reading Cartesian Philosophy through Cartesian Science*, Cambridge, Cambridge University Press, 2010, p. 133 ff.

We shall now take a look at how Descartes implements his theory in two physiological realms: muscle movement and generation.

5. Animal Spirits and Fermentation in Muscle Movement

For Descartes, both animal spirits[90] and fermentation (as their driving force) play a role in muscle movement.[91] From the brain, the animal spirits travel along the nerves, descending and ascending[92] across a network compared with trees and their branches.[93] Through their movements, they "have the power to change the shapes of the muscles into which these nerves are embedded, and in this way to move all the limbs."[94] The mechanism through which this happens entails the contraction and inflation of muscles and their opposites, due to a higher or lower quantity of spirits entering the muscles and combining with spirits that are already present.[95] While spirits are in movement all the time, even a small differential quantity suffices in order to move a certain muscle.[96]

The direction into which the animal spirits move is determined by two factors, both geometrical: the size and shape of the animal spirit particles themselves, and the size and shape of the pathways they take.[97] The pathways are predetermined by God;[98] the movement of the animal spirits, while fueled by the fire in the heart, obeys the predetermined rules of geometry. The spirits' own shapes cause an "unequal agitation"[99] (*inegale agitation*) due to differences such as in speed or force: the smaller, subtler ones move faster. The causes of these inequalities may be either in the "diverse dispositions" of the organs which contributed to their generation, or in the "diverse types of matter of which they are composed;"[100] an example of the latter case are 'vapours of wine', which, after drinking, convert into stronger and more abundant spirits[101] which "move the body in several strange ways" — perhaps as a result of wine already being a fermentative liquid, hence, containing the principle of movement.

Descartes' account is reminiscent of Plato's account of the structure of matter in *Timaeus*. For Plato, the subtlest particles of matter were those of fire, whose shape

---

90 For an account of the workings of Cartesian animal spirits, see also BALDASSARRI, *Il metodo al tavolo anatomico*, p. 106-110.
91 For an overview of the philosophies of muscular movement, see DOROTHY M. NEEDHAM, *Machina Carnis: The Biochemistry of Muscular Contraction in Its Historical Development*, Cambridge, Cambridge University Press, 1971, esp. p. 1-27 for early developments.
92 *Primae Cogitationes*, AT XI 530.
93 *Primae Cogitationes*, AT XI 532.
94 *L'Homme*, AT XI ; G 106-107; see also *Description*, AT XI 227; same idea in *L'Homme*, AT XI 132; *Passions*, AT XI 332; *Passions*, AT XI 335.
95 *Passions*, art. XI, AT XI 335-336.
96 *Primae Cogitationes*, AT XI 518.
97 *L'Homme*, AT XI 189-190.
98 *L'Homme*, AT XI 192.
99 *Passions*, art. XIV, AT XI 339.
100 *Passions*, art. XV, AT XI 340.
101 *Passions*, art. XV, AT XI 340.

was a pointy tetrahedron endowed with a "cutting quality."[102] This is compatible with the rarefaction role of heat in Descartes' natural philosophy.

Importantly, the *movens* of the spirits is an immanent principle in the body — the heat in the heart.[103] In fact, the fire from the heart constitutes the corporeal principle of fermentation and of muscle movement. "For as long as we live," Descartes writes, "there is a continual heat in our heart, which is a kind of fire maintained by the blood in the veins, and this fire is the corporeal principle of all the movements of our limbs."[104] Hence movement of muscles is indirectly owed to the fermentational fire, through the mediation of animal spirits.

Later mechanical philosophers largely adopted Descartes' explanation, further emphasizing fermentation as a chemical reaction at particle level.[105] Many of them did, however, employ a less restrictive version of mechanism in which mechanical laws were acknowledged but the animal spirits were considered the instruments of souls, including in non-human animals.[106] As regards muscular movement, a common modification was that they claimed fermentation happened locally, in the muscle, as a swelling that provoked the movement directly, in addition to having been triggered by the animal spirits traveling along the nerves. Such is the case in the works of Giovanni Alphonso Borelli (1608-1679), who, like Descartes, employs fermentation analogies from the natural world as well as from chemical experiments to account for physiological processes. For Borelli, as for Descartes, fermentation was a process or mechanism defined by heat and a subsequent expansion in volume. Noting that "all acid spirits mixed with fixed salts suddenly boil by fermentation," he concludes that "in muscles some similar mixing may occur," entailing a "sudden fermentation and ebullition which fill and expand the pores of the muscles, resulting in turgescence and contraction"[107] — a mechanism "not different from that of common fermentation."

Many other seventeenth-century thinkers similarly held that fermentation triggered muscle movement by happening locally, in the muscle. For some, such as William Croone[108] (1633-1684), the animal spirits had a character similar to

---

102 Cf. PLATO, *Timaeus*, transl. by Donald J. Zeyl, Indianapolis/Cambridge: Hackett Publishing Company, 2000, p. 47 (56a6-56b2): "the body with the sharpest edges belongs to fire, the next sharpest to air, and the third sharpest to water. Now in all these cases the body that has the fewest faces is of necessity the most mobile, in that it, more than any other, has edges that are the sharpest and best fit for cutting in every direction."
103 *Passions*, XVI, AT XI 342: "les esprits excitez par la chaleur du coeur".
104 *Passions*, art. VIII, AT XI 333: "pendant que nous vivons, il y a une chaleur continuelle en nostre coeur, qui est une espece de feu que le sang des venes y entretient, & que ce feu est le principe corporel de tous les mouvemens de nos membres." [Translation is mine.]
105 For instance Borelli; see GIOVANNI ALFONSO BORELLI, *De Motu animalium, Jo. Alphonsi Borelli,... opus posthumum*, Rome, ex typographia Angeli Bernabo, 1680-1681; English translation in GIOVANNI ALFONSO BORELLI, *On the Movement of Animals*, transl. by Paul Maquet, Berlin, Heidelberg, Springer 1989.
106 See DES CHENE, "Mechanisms of Life," p. 251.
107 BORELLI and MAQUET, *On the Movement of Animals*, 232.
108 See L. G. WILSON, "William Croone's Theory of Muscular Contraction," *Notes and Records of the Royal Society of London* 16 (1961), p. 158-178, esp. p. 160.

wine — again, likely related to wine being itself already a fermentative liquid, hence carrying over the fermentative expansion force into the body. Croone understood animal spirits as a "subtle, active and highly volatile liquor of the nerves, in the same way as we speak of spirit of wine or salt or others of this kind."[109] Like Borelli, he presumed that animal spirits travel along the nerves, but that they also produce a local fermentation in the muscles by their interaction with blood. For John Mayow (1640-1679), similarly, muscle contraction was the result of a local fermentation or ebullition in the muscle; interestingly, this fermentation is caused by a different chemical reaction. Instead of indigenous animal spirits and blood, Mayow here presumes a mixing of 'nitro-aërial spirits' derived from air through respiration, with a locally extant sulphureous fuel; the reaction provokes contraction. Somewhat later along a similar pathway of reasoning, oxygen would be discovered.[110] While this is far from anything Descartes himself imagined, his model of fermentation as 'heat-rarefaction' may have been one of the factors that nudged his followers into this direction of thinking.

6. Fermentations in the Formation of the Embryo

In his theory of generation,[111] Descartes reserves for fermentation two kinds of roles. The first one refers to the fermented, i.e. heated and rarefied animal spirits, the second subtlest blood particles (after the first ones going to the brain)[112] flowing to the vessels of reproduction[113] prior to generation. The second one refers to the fermentative mixing of seeds which gives rise to the embryo; here fermentation plays a direct role, non-mediated by any animal spirits. In broad lines, Descartes claims that the male and female[114] seed mixing together in the uterus engender a fermentation, which, as expected, entails heat;[115] the heat then pushes the seeds

---

109 Quoted after WILSON, "Muscular contraction," p. 160, note 11. Wilson notes that the analogy between *spiritus animae* or *spiritus vitae* and the spirit of wine is supported by both van Helmont and Sylvius. See JAN BAPTISTA VAN HELMONT, *Ortus medicinae*, Leyden, 1655, p. 122, and FRANS DE LE BOË (FRANCISCUS SYLVIUS), *Disputationem medicarum* 4. 29 in SYLVIUS, *Opera medica*, Coloniae Allobrogum, 1680, p. 8.
110 SIDNEY OCHS, *A History of Nerve Functions: From Animal Spirits to Molecular Mechanisms*, Cambridge, Cambridge University Press, 2004, p. 81, note 50.
111 For an account of Cartesian generation see also BALDASSARRI, *Il metodo al tavolo anatomico*, p. 191-197.
112 *L'Homme*, AT XI 128; *Primae Cogitationes*, AT XI 507.
113 *L'Homme*, AT XI 128; G 104. Original: "apres celles qui entrent dans le cerveau, il n'y en a point de plus fortes ny de plus vives, que celles qui se vont rendre aux vaisseaux destinez à la generation."
114 For the background of the contribution of the female seed to generation in Antiquity see SOPHIA M. CONNELL, *Aristotle on Female Animals: A Study of the* Generation of Animals, Cambridge, Cambridge University Press, 2016, Chap. 3, "Menstrual blood and female semen," p. 93-120; and Chap. 4, "Matter," p. 121-160.
115 For the role of heat in generation in Ancient theories, see GIANNA POMATA, "Innate Heat, Radical Moisture and Generation," in *Reproduction*, ed. by N. Hopwood, R. Flemming, and L. Kassell, Cambridge, Cambridge University Press, 2018, p. 195-208.

upwards, leading to the formation of the individual organs — first of all the heart, afterwards the brain, and so forth.

But how does this fermentation work? It seems like a fermentation without a ferment, in the sense that no external element has to be added. Here, too, fermentation acts as 'heat-rarefaction.' The formation of the embryo is, of course, a qualitative transformation (in the sense of substantial); and yet there is no process in which an 'embryo ferment' would transform an amorphous mass into itself. Instead, the two seeds serve as 'a kind of yeast' to one another. Because it is not a chymical type of fermentation, none of the seeds has to impose its own nature upon the other one; instead they propel each other into agitation, "heating one another so that some of the particles acquire the same degree of agitation as fire, expanding and pressing on the others, and in this way putting them gradually into the state required for the formation of parts of the body."[116] Central to this process is a kind of heat that Descartes compares, again, to fermentations of wine or hay (which he cautiously refers to by paraphrase in order to avoid the loaded term):

> Or ie croy que la première chose qui arriue en ce mélange de la semence, & qui fait que toutes les goutes cessent d'estre semblables, c'est que la chaleur s'y excite, & qu'y agissant en mesme facon que dans les vins nouueaux lors qu'ils bouillent, ou dans le foin qu'on a renfermé auant qu'il fust sec, elle fait que quelques-vnes de ses particules s'assemblent vers quelque endroit de l'espace qui les contient, & que là se dilatant, elles pressent les autres qui les enuironnent; ce qui commence à former le coeur.[117]

Heat making an appearance in the process of generation is very common in the medical literature up to Descartes. Following Galen, this heat used to be ascribed to the menstrual blood of the mother.[118] Yet Descartes assigns its origin elsewhere: namely, in the mutual fermenting of the seeds. Because it leads to the formation of the embryo's heart, this process is likely also the source of the fire in the heart of the offspring individual.

Annie Bitbol-Hespériès writes that Descartes' use of fermentation at this juncture of the argument "amounts to a total rejection of the previous medical tradition,"[119] explaining it as a break from Fernel and the divine origin of heat.[120] I agree that Descartes' fermentation, and the heat that it is correlated with, is not Fernelian i.e. does not have a divine origin; I have tried to show that it comes instead, along

---

116 *Description*, AT XI 253; G 187.
117 *Description*, AT XI 253-254. Cf. English translations in G 187 and CSM I 322. Note that the verb 'ferments,' introduced both in the CSM and in Gaukroger's version, is markedly absent in the AT original, though the comparison is essentially about fermentation.
118 On this topic more extensively, see LINDA DEER RICHARDSON, *Academic Theories of Generation in the Renaissance*, ed. by B. Goldberg, Cham, Springer, 2018, p. 61-64. For a recent account of Galen's theory of generation see REBECCA FLEMMING, "Galen's Generations of Seeds," in Hopwood, *Reproduction*, 95-108.
119 ANNIE BITBOL-HESPÉRIÈS, "Monsters, nature, and generation from the Renaissance to the Early modern period: The emergence of medical thought," in *The Problem of Animal Generation in Early Modern Philosophy*, ed. by J. E. H. Smith, Cambridge, Cambridge University Press, 2006, p. 47-62, p. 61.
120 BITBOL-HESPÉRIÈS, "Monsters, nature, and generation," p. 41.

Ancient lines, mainly from nutriment. Far from being divine, the spirit, for Descartes, is transmitted from mother to child through the umbilical cord: "Spiritus autem transit per arterias umbilicales."[121]

In the *Excerpta anatomica*, Descartes explains how the mixture of the seeds is performed by means of the rarefaction within the heat-rarefaction model:

> animals are generated first from the seeds of the male and the female, which, mixed together and rarefied by heat, engender from one part the matter of the windpipe and of the lungs, and from the other part the matter of the liver; hereafter from the encounter of these two, the fire is enkindled in the heart.[122]

The seeds need rarefaction in order to be able to mix ("sine rarefactione permisceri non possunt").[123] On the other hand, they do not need to be much different from one another:

> And *these two liquids need not be very different from one another* for this purpose. For, just as we can observe how old dough can make new dough swell, and how the scum formed on beer is able to serve as yeast for making more beer, so we can easily agree that the seeds of the two sexes, when mixed together, serve as yeast to one another.[124]

This might be another Cartesian departure from the ancient tradition. In Aristotle's theory of mixture, elements which combine have to be opposed to each other, or else one would speak of an increase and not a mixture: "only those agents are combinable which involve a contrariety, for these are such as to suffer action reciprocally."[125] While the analogy with dough and beer prompts the question of how exactly this reciprocal action is possible, the answer might be found in the same idea of a heated agitation of particles. The moving particles would impart their motion to adjacent particles until the whole quantity would be encompassed by this agitation. From the particles that have fermented from the mixed seeds, some turn into blood, some into animal spirits; depending on the path taken, and on their own constitution, they engender the individual organs.[126] The very first one is the heart, the future seat of innate heat and fermentational fire. This was an Aristotelian idea, exposed in *De generatione animalium*[127] where Aristotle argued that this is because the heart functions as the seat of the nutritive soul. The next organ to be formed is the brain,[128] made from the subtler particles of blood: "les plus subtiles,

---

121 *Primae Cogitationes*, AT XI 511.
122 *Excerpta*, AT XI 599 (Dec. 1637): "animalia generentur primo ex eo quod semina maris & foeminæ permista & calore rarescentia excernant ex una parte materiam asperæ arteriæ & pulmonum, ex altera materiam hepatis; deinde ex harum duarum concursu accenditur ignis in corde." [Translation is mine.]
123 *Primae Cogitationes*, AT XI 507.
124 *Description*, AT XI 253; G 187 (my emphasis).
125 ARISTOTLE, *De generatione et corruptione*, 328a32-328a33. The secondary literature on Aristotle's theory of mixture abounds and is beyond the scope of this paper.
126 *Primae Cogitationes*, AT XI 508. See also *Description*, AT XI 260.
127 *De generatione animalium* II 4 (esp. 740a).
128 *Description*, AT XI 261.

qui composent les esprits, s'auancent vn peu dauantage, & se mettent en la place ou doit estre apres le cerueau."[129] Yet the animal does not yet have an existence ("nondum est animal"[130]); its life only begins with the enkindling of fire into the new heart: "Hicque incipit animal esse, quoniam ignis vitae accensus est in corde."[131] In other words, it is only with (and through) the fire in the heart that the new animal comes into being as such. This seems problematic, as the very juncture when the fire is enkindled may not be explainable by the fermentative heat-rarefaction motions that preceded this moment.

Briefly, in his embryology Descartes employs broadly the same model of fermentation as 'heat-rarefaction,' yet this time within the potentially problematic framework of a non-Aristotelian theory of mixture. Though his description of how the male and female seed serve as yeast to one another may also be interpreted mechanistically, it remains difficult to uphold that transformations of motion and heat alone may result in a new being. At the point where the fire is enkindled in the heart, a metaphysical dimension enters the stage. The fermentation of seeds in embryology is hence a process of substantial transformation, which possibly goes one step beyond the heat-rarefaction model that Descartes uses in all other instances. After Descartes, mechanist philosophers continued to ascribe a similar role to fermentation in their embryologies.[132]

7. Conclusion

I have argued that when Descartes uses the term 'fermentation,' he does so in a purely mechanist manner, or at least as pure as he can achieve.[133] Reconceptualizing fermentations as processes of 'heat-rarefaction,' as opposed to their chymical version entailing qualitative (substantial) change, Descartes employs analogies with the natural world to describe human physiology. The 'heat-rarefaction' model of fermentation would later be taken up by Borelli and other continental mechanists. The more chymical one would be adopted in England by the chemical physicians who tended to integrate mechanism with occult powers such as that of a ferment. As Des Chene succinctly put it, in the aftermath of Descartes "[m]echanism as ontology failed, but mechanism as method succeeded."[134]

Even if later conceptualizations of fermentation in physiology departed from the Cartesian perspective, it remains the case that Descartes gave a decisive impetus to the use of the fermentation concept within the mechanical medical philosophy of

---

129 *Description*, AT XI 261.
130 *Primae Cogitationes*, AT XI 508.
131 *Primae Cogitationes*, AT XI 509.
132 For instance Borelli; see BORELLI AND MAQUET, p. 375-380.
133 In "Descartes and fermentation in digestion," I attempt to describe an inherent problem with Descartes' otherwise mechanist account of fermentation. Whether they act chymically or by 'heat-rarefaction,' fermentations do yield ameliorated products, thus entailing a natural teleology which poses a problem for Descartes' philosophical system.
134 DES CHENE, "Mechanisms of Life," p. 249.

the seventeenth century. It can be argued that he turned a controversial concept with alchemical overtones into something that more restrictive mechanists such as Borelli were more likely to adopt.[135] This in turn opened up the way for further discoveries related to respiration, circulation, digestion, and metabolism.

---

[135] This accords with Antonio Clericuzio's argument about the circle of Hartlib which reinterpreted chymical theories in a corpuscular framework. See ANTONIO CLERICUZIO, *Elements, Principles and Corpuscles*, Dordrecht, Springer Netherlands, 2000, p. 90.

LYNDA GAUDEMARD

What Descartes's Embryology Tells Us about his Dualism*

▼ ABSTRACT According to the separatist interpretation of Descartes's substance dualism, the nonphysical mind can exist without the body. In this article, I argue that, according to Descartes, the mind is a non-material substance created by God which emerges through a particular arrangement of material particles. This interpretation is based on texts suggesting that the mind cannot be created by God without a properly configured body. Firstly, I will begin to show that, factually, the mind does not begin to think before being united to the body, and that the body enables the mind to have its first thoughts. Secondly, I develop Descartes's account of embryology showing that God is not the immediate cause of the mind's first thoughts. Thirdly, I address several objections to my emergentist reading of Descartes's view of mind. This will enable me to show that the mind does not only begin to think without being united to body: the mind cannot begin to think (or exist) without the body. This emergentist view is consistent with the claim that a mind can continue to exist separately from body when it perishes.

▼ KEYWORDS Substance Dualism, Embryology, Mind, Emergentism, Creationism

1. The Rise of the Fetal Thought

To understand what is the origin of the mind according to Descartes is crucial for our understanding of his version of substance dualism. According to the separatist

---

* I would like to thank Fabrizio Baldassarri for his help and his careful read. I also thank the anonymous reviewers of Brepols.

Lynda Gaudemard • Law Theory Laboratory, Aix-Marseille University, Aix-en-Provence. Contact: <lynda.gaudemard@univ-amu.fr>

interpretation of Descartes's substance dualism,[1] the nonphysical mind is created by God and can exist without the body. However, several texts show that Descartes's conception of the mind-body relationship should be more balanced. In this first section, I will start by demonstrating through the use of various texts that, for Descartes, the mind does not begin to think before being united to the body.

Descartes considers that animals begin to live when the heart begins to beat;[2] however, we cannot know when exactly the first heartbeat occurs, as Descartes writes in the *Primae Cogitationes circa generationem animalium*.[3] Since this phenomenon is not observable by dissection, we do not know when the first heartbeat occurs; for Descartes, this issue remains pending. He believed that the primary cause of the formation of organs, blood and vessels, was the fermentation of the male and female semen. As the beating heart is the principle of life for him,[4] to explain mechanically the cause of the formation of animals is crucial. Indeed, in the *Fourth set of replies*, Descartes writes that he does consider "no principle of movement in animals apart from the disposition of their organs."[5] Any mechanical function of the body depends on "the heat of the fire burning continuously in its heart,"[6] like a fire burning in a lamp.[7] Descartes's physics denies qualities and substantial forms. He rejects the hylomorphic view that a form organises matter and is the principle of life.[8]

In the Middle Ages, the soul was considered to be in the embryo[9] either forty days or three months later after the conception, mainly because the unborn baby started to move at this stage.[10] The organism of the embryo has to be sufficiently developed to move and to have a soul. From the seventeenth century, the question of when the fetus receives a soul from God began to be controversial. No stage was

---

1   This interpretation is supported by many scholars. See for example HENRI GOUHIER, *La Pensée métaphysique de Descartes*, Paris, Vrin, 1962; MARTIAL GUÉROULT, *Descartes selon l'ordre des raisons*, 2 vols., Paris, Aubier, 1968; MARGARET D. WILSON, *Descartes*, London/Henley/Boston, Routledge and Kegan Paul, 1978; DANIEL GARBER, *Descartes's Metaphysical Physics*, Chicago, Chicago University Press, 1992.
2   *Primae Cogitationes circa generationem animalium*, AT XI 506.
3   *Ibid.*. AT XI 509-510. This note of *Primae Cogitationes* was likely written between 1630 and 1632, but posthumously published in 1692. See Fabrizio Baldassarri's contribution to this volume.
4   For an illuminating detailed study of Descartes's theory principle of life, see ANNIE BITBOL-HESPÉRIÈS, *Le principe de vie chez Descartes*, Paris, Vrin, 1990.
5   *Meditationes de prima philosophia*, AT VII 230-231; CSM II 161-162.
6   *L'Homme*, AT XI 202; CSM I 108.
7   *Primae Cogitationes circa generationem animalium*, AT XI 509-510.
8   *La Description du corps humain*, AT XI 245; CSM I 319. Descartes to Mersenne, 9 February 1639, AT II 501; CSMK I 13.
9   As Descartes does not distinguish them, I will use "embryo' and 'fetus" interchangeably to refer to the unborn child.
10 According to Hippocrates and Galen, the male fetus receives the soul forty days after conception, while the female fetus receives it thirty days after. Aristotle thought the opposite. Aquinas thought that, first, the vegetative soul was in the semen, and that sensitive soul appeared during fertilization; and, finally, rational soul. For Van Foreest the fact that a fetus begins to move during the third month of pregnancy means that it has a mind. For a detailed survey of ensoulment, see N. N. FORD, *When did I begin?*, Cambridge, Cambridge University Press, 1991, and R. E. JONES and K. H. LOPEZ, *Human reproductive biology*, Amsterdam, Elsevier, 2013.

determined because life was supposed to begin at least at fertilisation, and that to be alive implies having a mind. As Descartes refused to consider the soul as a principle of life, he was very careful of not predicting when life begun. The origin of biological life, which is a physical issue, must be distinguished from the issue of the origin of the mind which is conceptually different. However, the origin of life and the origin of thought are connected for Descartes.

Indeed, a few years later, in 1641, Descartes claims that the mind "begins to think" when it is infused in the human embryo:

> In view of that I do not doubt that the mind begins to think (*cogitare*) as soon it is implanted (*infusa*) in the body of an infant, and that it is immediately aware of its thoughts (*cogitationis conscis sit*), even though it does not remember this afterwards because the impressions of these thoughts do not remain in the memory.[11]

The soul is not what gives life to the human body.[12] Life begins when the body is well disposed. Once the body lives, that is when the body parts are properly disposed or properly function, then the soul is created in it. While the physical events do not directly cause mental events, the body must be well disposed to be united to a soul. This passage from the *Fourth Set of Replies* suggests that the mind does not begin to think before being infused by God in the embryo; this suggests that the mind does not exist before union. According to Descartes, the first thoughts of an embryo are confused thoughts (sensations and passions), thoughts which cannot be instantiated without body. The embryo has also pure intellectual thoughts such as self-awareness; it can be aware that it is the subject of mental states (although it will not remind its first thoughts).

Furthermore, in 1641, Descartes also wrote to Hyperaspistes that the mind does not think before being united to the body:

> …it seems most reasonable to think that a mind newly (*recenter*) united to an infant's body is wholly occupied in perceiving in a confused way or feeling the ideas of pain, pleasure, heat, cold and other similar ideas which arise from its union and, as it were, intermingling with the body.[13]

This passage suggests that the mind does not think before being united to a human body. To be able to be united to the mind, the body has to be well disposed, that is, to be sufficiently heated to cause heart's beating and blood circulation. Union does not occur and the mind does not begin to think if the embryo's body is not alive. This means that, factually, the mind depends on the body to begin to exist and think. We shall discover that this factual dependence does not entail that the mind is material or that it cannot continue to exist without the body.

Another later passage in the *Passions of the Soul* also suggests that the mind-body union, (which coincides with creation) depends on a suitable disposition of the body:

---

11 *Fourth set of replies*, AT VII 246; CSM II 171-172.
12 *Les Passions de l'âme*, art. 5, AT XI 330; CSM I 329; and art. 6, AT XI 330-331; CSM I 329.
13 Descartes to Hyperaspistes, August 1641, AT III 424; CSMK 190.

the soul takes its leave when we die only because this heat ceases and the organs which bring about bodily movement decay.[14]

Descartes claims that the mind 'takes its leave' from the body when the body no longer functions. This means that the mind can exist apart from the body. Death does not occur because the mind leaves the body (as the scholastics thought), but because the heart stops beating.[15] Indeed, for Descartes, the body's movements are not caused by mind.[16]

Without a certain arrangement of parts of matter that causes movement in the body, the body's unity is compromised and it cannot be united to a soul. A suitable body's disposition relies on a physical unity (the kind of unity material particles have when they share a common movement). However, this kind of unity is not sufficient to make the body suitable for a union. Physical particles have to be arranged in a suitable way. A dispositional unity (the unity material particles have when they are disposed in such a way that the whole fulfills a function) is also required for a mind-body union.

Other texts also show that for Descartes the body disposes a soul in order to have its first thoughts, which are mainly confused. In the letter to Chanut on 1 February 1647, Descartes reaffirms that a suitable bodily disposition is a necessary and sufficient condition for the soul to be created by God in the body, and to make union happen:

> I think that the soul's first passion was joy, because it is not credible that the soul was put into the body at a time when the body was not in a good condition; and a good condition of the body naturally gives us joy.[17]

According to Descartes, it is inconceivable that a soul is united to a body which is not sufficiently well organised. This particular organisation is what makes a certain quantity of matter able to be united to a soul, and what, in return, disposes a soul to be affected. This letter indicates that joy is probably generated for the first time in the soul through body.[18] More precisely, when the blood absorbed by the embryo is properly fed, it keeps its heart warm; this suitable arrangement provides the embryo the ability to feel joy.[19] When an embryo feels joy for the first time, its heart's holes are more open allowing the subtlest blood's particles (called 'animal spirits') to pass through the nerves and cause bodily movements. That is why, according to Descartes, bodily movements follow from joy. On the contrary, when the maternal blood lacks nutrients, the embryo's blood temperature will low, and its development will be compromised.

The passion of joy felt for the first time by the embryo's soul will then prompt it to keep its union to the body. As more suitable blood flows, the heart of the embryo is better

---

14 *Les Passions de l'âme*, art. 5, AT XI 330; CSM I 329.
15 *Les Passions de l'âme*, art. 6, AT XI 330; CSM I 329.
16 *La Description du corps humain*, AT XI 225; CSM I 315.
17 Descartes to Chanut, 1 February 1647, AT IV 604-605; CSMK 307.
18 While joy is chronologically the first passion according to Descartes, admiration arises logically first.
19 *Les Passions de l'âme*, art. 109, AT XI 409; CSM I 366.

kept heated. As the embryo wants[20] to absorb blood, it joins maternal blood; in doing so, the passion of love arises for the first time. The embryo begins to feel love for the maternal blood, as Descartes explains in the *Passions of Soul*.[21] For him, love is a voluntary union with something that provided joy to the soul. Love prompts the soul to keep its union with the body.[22] If the heart does not receive thick blood (this keeps 'fire' in the heart and rarefaction), the body is not well-disposed[23] and union does not occur. Therefore, the mind-body union depends, at least factually, on a suitable disposition of the body.

Moreover, in the *Passions of the Soul*, Descartes writes that the soul gains new psychological powers caused by the brain:

> In consequence the spirits going to the brain also have very strangely. As a result they strengthen the ideas of hatred which are already imprinted there, and they dispose the soul to have thoughts which are full of acrimony and bitterness.[24]

Animal spirits strengthen brain patterns (which Descartes calls 'ideas' because those patterns give rise to confused thoughts) printed on the pineal gland. These patterns dispose the mind to feel such or such passion. The many prints caused by the animal spirits allow the mind to gain new psychological dispositions such as the capacity to feel bitterness and acrimony.[25]

These passages about the genesis of passions deal with the genesis of union. They suggest that Descartes believed that the first thoughts do not appear without the body. It also suggests that the body can change, in some way, the structure of the mind by generating new kinds of thoughts.

In this section, I have tried to show that in several texts Descartes suggests that the soul, *de novo* created by God, does not begin to think without a union with a well-disposed body. God does not create souls that think before being infused in a body. However, several exegetical difficulties arise. First, the claim that the body is well-disposed enough to receive the union suggests that it needs some physical properties to make both the union and thought occur. If the soul is said to be always

---

20 This means that the first actions of the soul are caused by passions.
21 *Les Passions de l'âme*, art. 107, AT XI 407; CSM I 365-366. See also Descartes to Chanut, 1 February 1647, AT IV 605; CSMK 308.
22 The question arises to know whether the soul decides to maintain its union to the well-disposed body; see PIERRE GUENANCIA, *L'intelligence du sensible. Essai sur le dualisme cartésien*, Paris, Gallimard, 1998, p. 202, who adresses this issue : "Certes l'âme ne « choisit » pas, semble-t-il, d'être unie avec le corps, c'est Dieu bien sûr qui met une âme dans nos corps, mais en éprouvant de la joie de cette union l'âme ne la rend-elle pas sienne et par là-même volontaire?"
23 *L'Homme*, AT XI 124, 5-7.
24 *Les Passions de l'âme*, art. 103, AT XI 405; CSM I 364.
25 However, Descartes also suggests that the mind can on its own give rise to new passions by applying itself to the corporeal imagination. Due to its direct impact on blood, corporeal imagination can modify our passions (Descartes to Elisabeth, May or June 1645, AT IV 219-220; CSMK 250). When the soul imagines, it can act on the arrangement of brain's parts (Descartes to Hyperaspistes, August 1641, AT III 425; CSMK 190). In his work, Desmond Clarke explains that imagination is a cognitive and an affective function; due to its location in the brain, it can directly affect blood and cause different emotional states. See DESMOND CLARKE, *Descartes's theory of mind*, Oxford, Oxford University Press, 2003.

united to a well-disposed body, then one could be led to admit that the human body ought to be united to a soul, or that the body itself potentially contains a soul. The two claims are problematic for a philosopher like Descartes who officially rejected forms and final causes. Second, if the mind-body union is a mechanical phenomenon requiring some physical dispositions to occur, then the role of God in the rise of thought should be reconsidered.

2. Embryology and the Naturalization of the Mind-Body Union

What Descartes says about the mind-body relationship is puzzling. According to God's laws, the body is disposed to feel, to imagine, to move and to be affected by the body, and not only to know, judge or will. Contrary to God and angels's mind, the human mind is the sole mind which is disposed to be united to a body. While Descartes never writes that the soul ought to have properties in order to be united to the body, several texts seem to suggest the contrary.

Indeed, in 1648, Descartes writes to Arnauld that "if we count as corporeal whatever belongs to a body, even though not of the same nature as body, then even the mind can be called corporeal, in so far as it is made to be united (*apta corpora uniri*) to the body."[26] This letter suggests that Descartes admits that the mind is created by God in order to be united to a body.

Yet, Descartes wrote to Henricus Regius in 1641 that nothing in the mind appeals to a union with the body, and that nothing in the body appeals to a union with the mind:

> because when we consider the body alone we perceive nothing in it demanding union with the soul, and nothing in the soul obliging it to be united to the body.[27]

In 1641, at the University of Utrecht, Regius led one of his students to claim that, for Descartes, a human being is an *ens per accidens*.[28] According to Regius, Descartes's real distinction argument found in the *Sixth Meditation* concluded that a human being is an *ens per accidens*.[29] According to the scholastic traditions, the mind and body are incomplete substances whereas their union is a complete substance. Incomplete substances are really distinct from each other but they can compose together an *unum per se*. While the vegetative and sensitive part of the soul cannot function without the body (as Aquinas thought)[30], the rational part of the soul does not require a body in order to operate. The mind-body union is not stronger than the substance-accident union. Consequently, for Regius, Descartes's real distinction argument proves either

---

26 Descartes to Arnauld, 29 July 1648, AT V 223; CSMK 358.
27 Descartes to Regius, mid-December 1641, AT III 461; CSMK 200.
28 For a very informative study on the Utrecht crisis, see RENÉ DESCARTES and MARTIN SCHOOK, *La querelle d'Utrecht*, ed. by Theo Verbeek, Paris, Les impressions nouvelles, 1988, p. 41.
29 Besides *La querelle d'Utrecht*, see also GENEVIÈVE RODIS-LEWIS, ed., *Lettres à Regius et Remarques sur l'explication de l'esprit humain*, Paris, Vrin, 1959.
30 THOMAS AQUINAS, *Summa Theologiae*, 60 vols,. New York, Blackfriars and McGraw-Hill, 1964- , I.89.1 (part, question and article).

that the mind is an accident of the body (which means that it is not its substantial form), or that the mind is a kind of platonic mind existing separately from the body. If the soul and the body are really distinct, how could both compose an accidental union? Descartes had condemned this interpretation.

In a letter to Regius of mid-December 1641, Descartes agrees with the view that, while nothing in the soul requires its union to the body, and that nothing in the body requires its union to the soul, the body is nevertheless disposed to receive a soul:

> It may be objected that it is not accidental to the human body that it should be joined to the soul, but its very nature; since, when the body has all the dispositions required to receive the soul, without which it is not a human body, it cannot be without a miracle that the soul is not united to it. And also that is not accidental to the soul to be joined to the body.[31]

Descartes claims in this letter that a body not disposed to be united to a soul is not a human body. Additionally, a body suitably disposed will always be (at least in our world), united to a soul, unless a miracle happens. Descartes admits that a union can also not occur "par miracle",[32] although God's nature would be unwilling to change the laws of nature. Despite the fact that it is a substance, the soul is also disposed to be united to a properly disposed body.[33] While the mind and the body are two substances of distinct natures, they are disposed to be substantially united. The latin terms *dispositiones* and *apta*, that Descartes uses in both letters, strongly refer to a function and an end. Both of these letters suggest that the mind and the body are disposed in such a way as to produce a particular effect; namely that they must be united in order to compose a whole human being.

For Descartes, as nothing belonging to the mind resides in the body, the mind can subsist *per se*, without being a mode of body or being itself extended. No mode of thought is a mode of extension (including modes such as sensations and imaginations). This claim entails that the soul is not the form of the body. This is contrary to the religious doctrine of the Lateran Council of 1514. Descartes replies to Regius that if we consider the nature of the soul apart from the body, we will find nothing which requires its union to the body. Indeed, we can clearly and distinctly conceive that the soul can exist without being physical. And we can clearly and distinctly conceive that the body can exist without being nonphysical.

As no mode of thought (including sensation and imagination) is a way of being extended, the mind and body can be called *accidental substances* and the human being can be considered as an *ens per accidens*. But since the capacity to be united to the soul belongs to the nature of the body (it has all the dispositions to be united to the mind), the mind-body union is not an accident. Without these dispositions, the body would not be specifically human since the mind provides its numerical identity.[34] In this

---

31 Descartes to Regius, mid-December 1641, AT III 460-446; CSMK 220.
32 Descartes to Regius, December 1641, AT III 460-461; CSMK 200, "because if the body has all the dispositions required, to receive a soul, which it must have to be strictly a human body, then short of a miracle (*miraculo*) it must be united to a soul."
33 Descartes to Arnauld, 29 July 1648, AT V 223; CSMK 358.
34 Descartes to Mesland, February 1645, AT IV 166; CSMK 242-243.

reply to Regius, Descartes seems to assume that without the particular dispositional properties in the body, the creation of the mind in the body would not occur. If the human body has all suitable physical dispositions, God will usually create the mind in it. Without particular physical dispositional properties, a union with a non-material mind will not occur. With the exception of heat, Descartes writes nothing about the physical dispositions required to be united to the soul. On the one hand, the fact that Descartes does not indicate which particular dispositions a body must have in order to be united to a soul may be problematic. One could object that animals's bodies can also receive a soul (a claim that Descartes rejects several times). On the other hand, one could also think that Descartes deliberately underlies this element to avoid appealing to teleological notions. However, to know whether body disposition is suitable or not, one has to appeal to a normative criterion. We cannot know whether a body is well disposed if we do not know the purpose of this body (that is health for Descartes). But for Descartes, no immaterial *intentio* exists in the physical world.[35]

However, Descartes does not need to postulate final causes or substantial forms to prove that mind-body union is not accidental. If the mind and body are always disposed to be united together, according to the laws of nature decided by God, any time the body's dispositions are actualized, a mind-body union will occur. Thus, this union is not accidental. This interpretation is consistent with Descartes's reply to Arnauld on 29 July 1648 where he claims that the mind is in some way extended because it is disposed to be united to a body.

Several texts from Descartes's embryology can also help us understand that although God creates everything, God is not the immediate cause of a mind's first thoughts. Indeed, Descartes appeals to embryology to explain how the mind can affect the body and be affected by it, without God's intervention and Aristotelian final causes.[36] For example, he explains how a mother's passions are the primary causes of angioma (that Descartes calls 'marques d'envie', translated in English as 'birthmarks')[37] printed on the infant's body. Imagination is the secondary cause of birthmarks. Passions are confused ideas that have physiological correlates printed on the mother's corporeal imagination. These correlates impregnate the mother's

---

35 See DENNIS DES CHENE, *Physiologia: Natural philosophy in late Aristotelian and Cartesian Thought*, Ithaca, Cornell University Press, 2000.
36 See REBECCA WILKIN, "Descartes, Individualism, and the Fetal Subject", *Differences: A Journal of Feminist Cultural Studies*, 19 (2008), p. 96-127; and also "Essaying the Mechanical Hypothesis: Descartes, La Forge, and Malebranche on the Formation of Birthmarks", *Early Science and Medicine*, 13 (2008), p. 533-567. JUSTIN E. H. SMITH, "Imagination and the Problem of Heredity in Mechanist Embryology", in *The Problem of Animal Generation in Early Modern Philosophy*, ed. by Justin E. H. Smith, Cambridge, Cambridge University Press, 2006, p. 80-100. LYNDA GAUDEMARD, "Les Marques d'Envie: Métaphysique et Embryologie chez Descartes", *Early Science and Medicine*, 17 (2012), p. 309-338.
37 For Descartes's account of birthmarks, see *La Dioptrique*, AT VI 129; Descartes to Meyssonnier, 29 January 1640, AT III 20-21; CSMK 144. Descartes to Mersenne, 1 April 1640, AT III 49; CSMK 146; *L'Homme*, AT XI 174; *Primae cogitationes circa generationem animalium*, AT XI 538; *Excerpta anatomica*, AT XI 606. For a historical survey of the relationship between the maternal imagination and birthmarks, see B. BABLOT, *Discours Sur le Pouvoir de l'Imagination des Femmes Enceintes*, Paris-Geneva, Champions Slatkine, 1989 [1803].

blood, and affect the embryo. When a pregnant woman feels a violent passion (such as desires, or aversions), her imagination can cause disabilities in the embryo.[38]

According to Descartes, angiomas are caused by instances of maternal imagination,[39] and by the sympathy (which is a physical disposition consisting in a mechanical movement produced by both the mother's and the embryo's heartbeat). Sympathy, as *causa proxima*,[40] allows a union between the embryo and its mother, without Aristotelian final causes or God's direct intervention. As imagination provides sympathy by affecting the heartbeat, it is the *causa principalis*[41] of the union between the mother and her unborn child. Imagination implements the actualisation of the disposition of sympathy. Due to physical dispositions, the mother can affect the embryo through a purely mechanical relation, without the direct intervention by God.

As it is the case for the formation of organs,[42] and for the relation between the mother and the fetus, the mind-body union is mainly caused by the mechanical laws of movement decided by God. In *The World*, written around 1629, Descartes explains that matter is created and conserved by God; any change is governed by the laws of nature he created.[43] Changes occurring in the disposition of material particles are not efficiently caused by God because his nature does not change. Instead, any material change is efficiently caused by the matter itself,[44] according to the laws of nature that are freely decided by God.[45] Any physical change can be explained by the secondary causes,[46] which depend on a primary and main cause, God's immutable free will. Nature changes but always according to the laws decided by God. God does not know these laws before establishing them, as Descartes writes to Mersenne in 1630. Instead, for Descartes God knows and wills at the same time.[47]

Descartes's account of birthmarks enables us to understand how the mind-body union occurs without God. God does not directly intervene in the embryo's development. This development is merely explained by mechanical laws and properties. The union between the mother and the unborn child requires a well-disposed human body, with physical dispositions that are actualised by some mechanical laws. A body whose parts are arranged in a certain way makes it suitable for a union. The claims that God creates substances, and laws of nature that allow a union between certain

---

38 Descartes to Meyssonnier, 29 January 1640, AT III 20-21; CSMK 144.
39 Descartes to Mersenne 27 May 1630, AT I 153; CSMK 26.
40 The *causa proxima* is the last efficient cause in a causal chain, which is itself caused. Cf. *Les Passions de l'âme*, art. 25, AT XI 347; CSM I 296; art. 29, AT XI 350; CSM I 339; art. 51, AT XI 371; CSM I 349; Descartes to Chanut, 1 February 1647, AT IV 616; CSMK 313; *Notae in Programma*, AT VIII-2 360; CSM I 305.
41 The *causa principalis* (or ordinary cause) is the first cause that operates by itself, and carries out other causes Descartes to Elisabeth, 18 May 1645, AT IV, 201; *L'Homme*, AT XI 180 1-3.
42 Descartes to Mersenne, 20 February 1639, AT II 525; CSMK II 134.
43 *Le Monde*, AT XI 36-37; CSM I 92-93.
44 However, in other texts, Descartes claims that matter is causally inert.
45 Descartes to Mersenne, 20 February 1639, AT II 525; CSMK 134.
46 The secondary causes are the causes that have been caused.
47 Descartes to Mersenne, 15 April 1630, AT I 145-146; CSMK 23; Descartes to Mesland, 2 May 1644, AT IV 11; CSMK 235.

physical and nonphysical substances, are consistent with the view that God is not the *causa proxima* of the mind-body union.[48] Similarly, while God creates a soul as soon as the human body is well disposed, neither the mind-body union, nor the rise of thoughts, are directly caused by him. Like birthmarks and the formation of organs, the mind-body union is a natural phenomenon governed by God's laws of nature.

As we shall see in the next section, the interpretation that the mind does not begin to think without a union with a well-disposed body echoes to the contemporary emergentist theories of mind claiming that mental properties are instantiated only if the brain has the suitable physical properties.

3. Descartes's Emergent Creationist Substance Dualism

Emergence is commonly understood as a relation according to which new non-reducible entities arise from more fundamental entities. A phenomenon is said to be emergent when it cannot result from the sum of the effects of the fundamental properties constituting it. This theory was very popular at the beginning of twentieth century. Emergentism claims that organism parts are disposed in such a way that they share a common activity ultimately leading to the existence of a new entity. Emergentists argue that the realisation of material dispositional properties enables the rise of consciousness. Emergentist dualists mostly claim that mental properties supervene on physical properties, that mental properties are not reducible to physical properties, and that mental properties are causally efficacious. According to Hasker's substance dualism (1999), a new nonphysical substance (the soul) naturally emerges from the brain when it is properly configured.[49] The ability to give rise to a soul potentially exists in the brain which generates it.

As emergentist views, several of Descartes's writings also suggest that the soul begins to think *through* the body. However, emergentism assumes that the mind potentially exists in the body. Thus, emergentism seems to be inconsistent with Descartes's creationist view that God creates the soul.[50] I do not argue that for Descartes the mind emerges *from* the body in the sense that the mind exists potentially in the body. I do not think that, for Descartes, the mind cannot exist without the body. Instead, I have previously demonstrated that, for Descartes, at least in our world, the soul emerges

---

48 A passage in the letter to Regius of June 1642 seems to threaten this interpretation: "So even if God conjoins (*conjugat*) and unites (*uniat*) them as much as he can, he cannot thereby divest himself of his omnipotence and lay down his power of separating them; and hence they remain distinct." (Descartes to Regius, June 1642, AT III, 567; CSMK 214). Here Descartes seems to claim that God directly causes the mind-body union. However, he could have also merely referred to God's laws of nature allowing the mind-body union and their separability.
49 William Hasker, "The Dialect of Soul and Body," in *Contemporary Dualism: A Defense*, ed. by Andrea Lavazza and Howard Robinson, New York, Routledge, p. 204-219 (see especially 215-216).
50 See William Hasker "Souls Beastly and Human" in *The Soul Hypothesis: Investigations into the Existence of the Soul*, ed. by Mark C. Baker and Stewart Goetz, New York, Continuum, 2011, p. 202-217. The author claims that, for this reason, Descartes is creationist (cf. p. 209-211).

through the body (not from the body). The view I attribute to Descartes is that the mind cannot be created by God without an intermediary that is a particular physical configuration. This soft version of emergentism (emergent creationist substance dualism) I attribute to Descartes is consistent with his claims that God creates *de novo* the human souls, and that the soul can continue to exist without the body after death. Descartes's writings help us understand that to produce directly something is a way of understanding the notion of emergence. But this is not the only way.

In addition, the standard theories of emergence do not assume that emergence is immediate. They mostly consider that consciousness arises from several levels of properties. From the arrangement of categoric properties, emerge physical causal powers and the consciousness emerges from these powers. Emergence is not necessarily immediate. We can assume that, according to Descartes, the categoric properties of the body share a common movement grounded on a physical unity. Then, the dispositional physical properties supervene on the basic properties. These dispositional properties allow the body to fulfill its functions (heartbeat for example); this is dispositional unity. Their common activity brings something new into existence. Once the human body lives, God's laws of nature enable a creation of the soul through the well-disposed body. After the union, the lower properties can continue to exist.[51]

Yet, what I argued in the previous sections is not sufficient to support a metaphysical emergentist reading claiming that, for Descartes, the mind *cannot* begin to think without a body. The fact that the mind is factually disposed to be mechanically united to the body (and vice-versa) does not entail that the mind could not begin to think without the body. It only asserts that, factually, at least in our world, and according to God's laws of nature, a union with a soul occurs if a certain configuration of the body's particles occurs. But, in another world, God could create a soul without it being united to a body. A world where souls can begin to exist before being united to the bodies. In several texts, Descartes seems to endorse the view that the mind can think independently from the brain. If, for Descartes, the soul thinks or can think without the brain, why would it need a body to begin to think? At least three objections can be raised against the emergent creationist dualist view I attribute to Descartes.

One may object to my interpretation that the concomitance between the soul's creation and the union's creation does not entail that God cannot create the soul independently from the body. The fact that both occur simultaneously only shows that a suitable disposition of the body is a sufficient and necessary condition that enables God to infuse the soul in it. It is not because, *de facto*, the soul thinks only once it is united to the body, that the soul could not think without a body, or that

---

51 To know whether emergence is groundless or not is significant to understand the relation of emergence. However, this question goes beyond the scope of this article. On this issue, see for example MARK H. BICKHARD and DONALD T. CAMPBELL, "Emergence", in *Downward Causation: Minds, Body and Matter*, ed. by Peter Bøgh Andersen, Claus Emmeche, Niels Ole Finnemann, and Peder Voetmann Christiansen, Aarhus, Aarhus University Press, 2000, p. 322-348; and MICHEL BITBOL, "Ontology, Matter and Emergence," *Phenomenology and the Cognitive Sciences*, 6 (2007), p. 293-307.

the soul essentially depends on the body. The claim that before being created in the body the soul does not think does not entail that before being created in the body, the soul cannot think. God could create the soul before its union with the body (although that is not what usually happens in our world). Descartes's writings seem to be consistent with the claim that God can create souls that begin to think separately from the body. As seen above, the passage from the letter to Chanut on 1 February 1647 supports this interpretation:

> I think that the soul's first passion was joy, because it is not credible that the soul was put into the body at a time when the body was not in a good condition; and a good condition of the body naturally gives us joy.[52]

In our world, it is unlikely for the soul not to be united to a body that is well-disposed; this does not mean that God cannot create a soul without a body.

Let me reply to this objection. Firstly, Descartes never mentions the possibility for the soul to be able to think before being united to the body. We may assume that, for him, the soul could instantiate volitions or pure perceptions; but Descartes says nothing about this possibility. Additionally, Descartes writes to Chanut that "it is not credible that the soul was put in the body at a time when the body was not in a good condition."[53] This sentence suggests that, at the time the soul is created in the well-disposed body, it is simultaneously united to it. Descartes also writes to Regius in January 1641 that God creates the soul "immediately" in the body.[54] This creation-union occurs as soon as the human body lives. Descartes does not only factually establish a relation of dependence between thought and body; he sets a logical impossibility ("it is not credible"), that is, for him, a metaphysical impossibility; the soul cannot begin to think without being united to a suitable body:

> …I do not doubt that the mind begins to think as soon as it is implanted in the body of an infant, and that it is immediately aware of its thoughts[55]

Descartes points out that it is inconceivable that the soul "begins to think" before being united to a portion of the properly configured extended matter. One could argue that the soul can at least instantiate pure thoughts before being united to the body. According to this text, the soul is not supposed to have (pure) thoughts before its union with the body. If the soul cannot exist without thinking (according to Descartes, the soul does not think before being united to the body), then the soul cannot begin to exist and so cannot be created without the body. Thus, an emergentist reading of Descartes is plausible.

The second objection is that if, for Descartes, the soul is generated through the body, then it would cease to exist once the body perishes (since the soul ontologically

---

52 Descartes to Chanut, 1 February 1647, AT IV 604-605; CSMK 307.
53 Descartes to Chanut, 1 February 1647, AT IV 604-605; CSMK 307.
54 Descartes to Regius, January 1642, AT III, 505, 18-19; CSMK, 208. Note that neither the latin, nor the English translation add "in the body"; this addition was made by GENEVIÈVE RODIS-LEWIS, *L'Individualité selon Descartes*, Paris, Vrin, 1950.
55 *Fourth set of replies*, AT VII 246; CSM II 171.

depends on the body). If the soul emerges from the body in the sense that God cannot create it except if it is united to a well-disposed body, then the soul essentially depends on the body for its existence. Several of Descartes's texts threaten this interpretation. A well-known passage in the *Synopsis* mentions that while the human "body can very easily perish, the mind is immortal by its very nature."[56] Although the human body perishes, the human mind continues to exist (except if God decides to destroy it). This means that the mind can exist without the body. In a letter to Elisabeth of 15 September 1645, Descartes asserts that the soul "subsists apart from the body."[57] In another letter to Reneri for Pollot of March 1638, Descartes writes that once the soul is separated from the body, it can continue to think.[58] These passages are inconsistent with the emergentist view I attribute to Descartes. In the *Second Set of Replies*,[59] Descartes writes that if two substances are really distinct, they can exist ("potest existere") independently of each other. This passage is generally understood to mean that the mind and the body can exist apart from each other. This separatist interpretation of Descartes's real distinction argument, supported by many scholars,[60] is based on several texts. The thought experiment found in the *Second Meditation* leads us to conclude that we can clearly and distinctly conceive that the soul can exist without the body. In the letter to Gibieuf of 29 January 1642, Descartes writes that the non-separability between the mind and body entails a logical inconsistency.[61] In the *Fourth Set of Replies*, Descartes argues that if we can clearly and distinctly conceive two things as being complete, then they are really distinct from each other.[62] The mind and body are really distinct from each other since God can separate them.[63] That is why the real distinction argument in the *Sixth Meditation*[64] is mostly interpreted as meaning that the mind and body do not essentially depend on each other for their existence. For Margaret Wilson, the real distinction argument means that the mind and body can exist apart from each other.[65] These texts confirm that the soul can exist without body, which is inconsistent with an emergentist interpretation of Descartes's conception of mind.

I will reply to this second objection into two parts. Firstly, this objection relies on some controversial readings of Descartes's texts. The passage in the *Synopsis* ("body can very easily perish, the mind is immortal by its very nature"[66]) can also mean that

---

56 *Meditationes de prima philosophia*, AT VII 14; CSM II 10.
57 Descartes to Elisabeth, 15 September 1645, AT IV 292; CSMK 265.
58 Descartes to Reneri for Pollot, March 1638, AT II 38; CSMK 99.
59 *Second set of replies*, AT VII 162; CSM II 114.
60 See for example HENRI GOUHIER, *La Pensée métaphysique de Descartes*, Paris, Vrin, 1962; MARTIAL GUÉROULT, *Descartes selon l'ordre des raisons*, 2 vols., Paris, Aubier, 1968; MARGARET D. WILSON, *Descartes*, London/Henley/Boston, Routledge and Kegan Paul, 1978; DANIEL GARBER, *Descartes's Metaphysical Physics*, Chicago, Chicago University Press, 1992.
61 Descartes to Gibieuf, 19 January 1642, AT III 478; CSMK 203.
62 *Fourth set of replies*, AT VII 223; CSM II 157.
63 *Principia Philosophiae*, AT VIII-1 29; CSM I 213.
64 *Meditationes de prima philosophia*, AT VII 78; CSM II 54.
65 MARGARET D. WILSON, *op. cit.*, p. 191-198 and 206-207.
66 *Meditationes de prima philosophia*, AT VII 14; CSM II 10.

since the soul is a pure substance, it can only be created and destroyed by God. In this sense, the soul is immortal or non-corruptible; nothing but God can annihilate the soul. In the *Synopsis*, Descartes does not write that the soul can exist without body broadly understood (a pure substance). He claims can the mind can continue to exist without the "human body" that is not a pure substance. The immortality of the soul echoes to its non-corruptible essence that makes it a substance, by contrast with the substantial forms that can change. Descartes points out that a demonstration of the immortality of the soul (that he did not undertake) must be grounded on mechanist physics deprived of substantial forms.[67] This passage shows the strong relationship between the immortality of the soul and Descartes's new characterisation of souls as substances.

Contrary to what Margaret Wilson claims, the passage in the *Fourth Set of Replies* about the completeness of substances can also mean that if the mind can be clearly and distinctly conceived without bodily attributes, then it is a complete thing. Thus, the mind is a substance. According to Descartes, a complete thing is something that possesses enough properties to recognize that it is a substance.[68] A substance needs nothing else to exist.[69] To be a substance, in a weak sense, is to be able to exist without the main attribute of another substance, and to be able to exist without inhering in something else. If the thought is the principal attribute of the mind, and if no bodily properties inhere in the mind, the mind can be clearly and distinctly conceived as a complete thing.[70] Therefore, the real distinction argument is consistent with the claim that the mind exists without being extended. As Paul Hoffman argues,[71] for Descartes, to exist apart from x can also mean to actually exist without the attribute of another substance. Hoffman's argument can be summarized as follows. If the real distinction consists of a separability regarding existence, and since, for Descartes, the mind and the body cannot exist without God's support, then God would be modally distinct from his creation. The mind would be also modally distinct from the body. These views are inconsistent with Descartes's metaphysics. On the contrary, an emergentist interpretation of Descartes's dualism is consistent with the claim that the existence of the soul depends on God's support, and that it can survives the human body.

The third objection is that, in the *Fourth Set of Replies*, Descartes claims that the mind can think independently of the brain.[72] The soul can instantiate pure intellectual thoughts such as willing for example. When it is united to a body, the soul gains new mental capacities such as emotions, sensations, imaginations etc. When it dies, it loses these dispositions. Indeed, in the letter to More of August 1649, Descartes argues that the human mind separated from the body cannot feel ("I reply that the human mind separated

---

67 *Meditationes de prima philosophia*, AT VII 13; CSM II 10.
68 *Fourth set of replies*, AT VII 222; CSM II 156.
69 *Principia Philosophiae*, AT VIII-1 24; CSM I 210.
70 *First set of replies*, AT VII 120-121; CSM II 85-86; *Fourth set of replies*, AT VII 221-223; CSM II 156-157.
71 PAUL HOFFMAN, *Essays on Descartes*, Oxford, Oxford University Press, 2009.
72 *Fifth set of replies*, AT VII 358; CSM II 248.

from the body does not have sense-perception strictly so-called").⁷³ But when Descartes claims that the soul can "operate" without the body, he does not necessarily mean that thought does not need the brain to occur. He can also mean that the mind can think without necessarily imagining. A passage in the *Fifth Set of Replies* supports this reading:

> I also distinctly showed on many occasions that the mind can operate (*operari*) independently of the brain; for the brain cannot in any way be employed in pure understanding (*nullus cerebri usus esse potest ad pure intelligendum*), but only in imagining or perceiving by the senses.⁷⁴

At first reading, it seems that Descartes claims that someone does not need a brain to instantiate pure thoughts. But to argue that we can think without imagining does not entail that we can think without the brain. A few lines later, Descartes admits that every thought, including the pure thought, is ineluctably accompanied by imagination:

> Admittedly, when imagination or sensation is strongly active (as occurs when the brain is in a disturbed state), it is not easy for the mind to have leisure for understanding other things. But when the imagination is less intense, we often have the experience of understanding something quite apart from the imagination. When, for example, we are asleep and are aware that we are dreaming, we need imagination in order to dream, but to be aware (*advertamus*) that we are dreaming, we need only the intellect.⁷⁵

In this text, Descartes does not write that a pure perception is a kind of thought that can be instantiated without the brain. Instead, he admits that imagination is always present when we think ("But when the imagination is less intense"), even when we are aware that we are aware. Self-awareness is related to an imaginative thought, not to a pure thought. This relationship raises the question of whether, for Descartes, the mind can really think independently from body. It seems that he would agree with the idea that we cannot experience what it is like to think without a body because the temporal continuity of the thought requires brain activity.⁷⁶ The pure and reflexive perceptions can be instantiated without thinking about corporeal things. We can understand something without imagining it. This does not mean that these thoughts occur without brain's support.

This factual claim is consistent with the view that when the human body perishes, the mind can continue to exist. But without the body the mind will not feel pain. It will merely receive the information that something happens to the body. Without imagination, the

---

73 Descartes to More, August 1649, AT V 402; CSMK 380. For Descartes, imagination and sensation are faculties that belongs to the soul as united to the body. If the human body ceases to exist, the mind cannot perform these cognitive functions. See also Descartes to Gibieuf, 19 January 1642, AT III 479; CSMK 203.
74 *Fifth set of replies*, AT VII 358; CSM II 248.
75 *Fifth set of replies*, AT VII 358-359; CSM II 248.
76 I agree with Kambouchner who sheds doubt on the possibility for the soul to think without the body. See DENIS KAMBOUCHNER, *Descartes n'a pas dit*, Paris, Les Belles Lettres, 2015 and "Descartes et l'indépendance de l'esprit", *Intellectica*, 57 (2012), p. 55-67.

mind will have difficulties in evaluating distances. It will not love because, according to Descartes, imagination gives rise to the passion of love. This faculty enables us to imagine our union with somebody as if we were a part of him/her.[77] Concerning the other kind of love similar to sexual desire only due to a natural inclination, imagination plays the same role.[78] Imagination also enables us to rectify some behaviors, to focus attention, to extend the duration of a thought, to make a decision, or to know that something is harmful.[79] Imagination plays an important role for our emotional life because it impacts directly on the animal spirits, and that these spirits control and regulate our passions. Descartes writes to Elisabeth that imagination enables us to experience certain emotional states.[80] As it can change the disposition of material particles in the brain, imagination enables us, with memory, to anticipate the consequences of some events.[81] Imagination can also control the agitation of animal spirits that cause surprise.[82] Without imagination, the disembodied mind would know nothing about the "conduct of life".

4. Conclusion

What the mind can think without the brain is a question left open by Descartes. Perhaps Descartes considered that the question whether the mind can think without the body had to be distinguished from the issue of whether it can exist without the body. This distinction is found in Eustachius of St Paul's *Summa Philosophiae*, that Descartes knew well. For Eustachius, the soul depends on the body, not because thz former needs the latter to exist. Without the body, the functions of the soul could not be actualised.[83] The soul could not correctly think without the body. Descartes would also have thought that while the soul can continue to exist without the body, this soul would not be able to think correctly without the brain. Perhaps Descartes did not want to point out the defects of a disembodied soul because he was afraid of being in conflict with his own characterisation of the soul.

However, to argue that, for Descartes, the soul cannot begin to think without the body does not entail that the soul cannot continue to exist once it is separated from the body. While the soul cannot begin to think without being created through the body, God could maintain its existence after death. For Descartes, the soul is not a mode of the body, but a substance opposed to it. Therefore, an emergentist interpretation is

---

77 *Les Passions de l'âme*, art. 80, AT XI 387; CSM I 356.
78 *Les Passions de l'âme*, art. 90, AT XI 395-396; CSM I 360. Deborah Brown provides an illuminating account of Descartes's conception of love; see DEBORAH BROWN, *Descartes and the passionate mind*, Cambridge, Cambridge University Press, 2006 (especially p. 23 and 161-164).
79 See Kambouchner's analysis in DENIS KAMBOUCHNER, *L'Homme des passions. Commentaires sur Descartes*, 2 vols, Paris, Albin Michel, 1995, II, p. 345. The author shows that without body, the soul would have disabilities.
80 Descartes to Elisabeth, May or June 1645, AT IV 219; CSMK 249-250.
81 Descartes to Elisabeth, 6 October 1645, AT IV 312-313; CSMK 271.
82 Descartes to Elisabeth, May 1646, AT IV 411; CSMK 287.
83 EUSTACHIUS OF ST PAUL, *Summa philosophica quadripartita*, 4 vols, Paris, Carolus Chastelain, 1609, III, p. 417.

consistent with Descartes's claim that the soul is immortal. Furthermore, according to several physical theories, a magnetic field can continue to exist, even when the magnet is destroyed.[84] Why this could not be the case for the soul?

Contemporary emergentism can be reconsidered through the perspective of Descartes's embryology. While this theory is usually associated with potentiality and opposed to creationism, Descartes's writings reveal that emergentism is consistent with creationism. Furthermore, an external transcendent cause such as God avoids some objections addressed to the emergentists. For example, the combination problem (how the unconscious particles of matter can be combined to produce unconscious mental states or a nonphysical substance?) is avoided. Finally, the causal psychophysical relations and the individuation of immaterial minds are not mysterious: they can be explained through the action of God on matter.

---

84 See W. HASKER, *The emergent self*, Ithaca, Cornell University Press, 1999, p. 232.

CLÉMENT RAYMOND

From the Animal Instinct to the Mind's Acknowledgement of the (In)Commoda in Descartes

▼ ABSTRACT This chapter studies the relationship between the animal instinct and the human soul. If instinct is sufficient to ensure the preservation of the body, why should it be necessary for nature to institute a way to signify to the mind the disadvantages that the body to which it is united suffers, thanks to the perceptions of the senses? To answer, I first analyse the concept of (in)commodum, mobilised both in the physiological texts and in Descartes's first philosophy. I then show that, in the first case, it is mobilised in connection with the survival of the body, while in the second it intervenes to describe the preservation of health. The conclusion is therefore twofold. There is, in Descartes, a concept of *commodum* that is derived from his physiology and transposed into his metaphysics as well as a demanding conceptualization of the notion of "health".

▼ KEYWORDS Animal Instinct, Health, Survival, (In)commodum, Mens, One's Own Doctor

1. The Preservation of the Body: Animal Instinct and the Problem of the *Mens*

The starting point of this research lies in the concept of *animal instinct* that Descartes developed in his early physiological work. It is a strictly mechanical tendency to pursue the advantages (*commoda*) of the body and to flee the disadvantages

Clément Raymond • IHRIM-Université Jean Moulin Lyon 3. Contact: <clement.raymond1@univ-lyon3.fr>

(*incommoda*).¹ The challenge, in a Cartesian context, is to account for this instinct or impulsive action by appealing only to elements that are themselves physiological or corporeal. This is the reason why Descartes mobilizes the notion of *disposition of the brain* to define it.²

According to him, the brain is indeed nothing else than a tissue made up in a particular way:³ its different *dispositions* concern the small threads that build up the brain's substance. These threads have many features: they originate in the inner surface of the brain (*L'Homme*)⁴ or in its innermost part;⁵ they make up the brain⁶ as well as the medulla of the nerves.⁷ They are certainly very loose,⁸ but they extend from the brain to the limbs:⁹ Their extremities end on one side at its inner surface which is turned towards its concavities, and on the other at the skins and flesh against which the tube which contains them ends.¹⁰ A disposition of the brain is therefore a disposition of its threads. It is a certain size of the interval between them, their folding, and their placing in a certain place, as well as the fact that they are tight or loose.¹¹ The concept of *disposition of the brain* makes it eventually possible to thematize animal instinct. When an advantage or disadvantage comes into contact with the sense organs, they move the little threads of nerves in these organs, that "tirent au même instant les parties du cerveau d'où ils viennent, et ouvrent par même moyen les entrées de certains pores, qui sont en la superficie intérieure de ce cerveau (pull the parts of the brain from which they come, and thereby open the entrances to certain pores in the internal surface of the brain.)"¹² The role of the natural (namely: independent of the changes that are imposed by circumstances)¹³ disposition of the brain is in this context very precise. It allows the animal spirits, which are moved by a particular action, to be led to all the nerves where they have to go¹⁴ in order to produce the movements of flight from the disadvantages and of pursuit of the advantages. The shaping of the nets that compose the substance of the brain determines between them intervals,

---

1 See: Descartes to Mersenne, 16 October 1639, AT II 599, l. 5-12; *Primae Cogitationes circa generationem animalium*, AT XI 520, l. 14-15.
2 I addressed this problem specifically and at length in a lecture given at the International Workshop 'The Cartesian Brain: Problems and Controversies' (org. by Denis Kambouchner, Damien Lacroux and Ruidan She in the University of Paris (Paris 1, Panthéon-Sorbonne), 11 and 12 October 2019.
3 See *L'Homme*, AT XI 170, l. 6-8.
4 *Ibid.*, AT XI 142, l. 23-26.
5 *Ibid.*, AT XI 141, l. 19.
6 *Ibid.*, AT XI 174, l. 18-19.
7 *Ibid.*, and AT XI 143, l. 28-29.
8 *Ibid.*, AT XI 143, l. 7; i.e.: thin.
9 *Ibid.*, l. 7-8.
10 *Ibid.*, AT XI 133, l. 9-12.
11 E.g. *L'Homme*, AT XI 177, l. 29-30.
12 *L'Homme*, AT XI 141, l. 16-19; CSM I 101.
13 On the difference between acquired and natural brain dispositions, see *L'Homme*, AT XI 192, l. 13-25. French Cartesian studies have already dealt at length with this point (see GENEVIÈVE RODIS-LEWIS, *L'Individualité selon Descartes*, Paris, Vrin, 1950, p. 86-88 and DENIS KAMBOUCHNER, *L'Homme des passions*, 2 vols., Paris, Albin Michel, 1995, vol. 1, p. 170.
14 *L'Homme*, AT XI 192, l. 21-23.

through which the spirits flow from the interior of the brain to the pores. The natural disposition of the brain is therefore a purely corporeal intermediary between the sensory stimulation and the setting in motion of the external movements serving the preservation of life. It impels certain movements in the sense that it imposes on the animal spirits a single path which they cannot transgress — namely: it can be equated to the animal instinct itself.

However, and this is a well-known point, the Cartesian analysis of the pursuit of advantages and the flight from disadvantages does not end with the mention of the animal instinct. Although human beings share this instinct with beasts,[15] their behaviour cannot be reduced to it, since its understanding implies the consideration of the spirit (*mens*) that is united to the body. More precisely, the *Meditatio Sexta* introduces the mind into the very analysis of the movements of flight and pursuit of what is bad or good for the body. The issue I intend to raise is to question the implications, from a medical point of view, of the addition to the animal instinct of the human *mens*. Of particular importance in this respect are the texts of the *Sixth Meditation* in which Descartes uses the vocabulary of *commoda* and *incommoda*[16] to examine the relationship between the senses and the preservation of the body, and mentions the *valetudo*[17] or health (*santé*) of the human being, as well as *homo sanus*.[18] If the bodily instinct, which the human being shares in common with animals, aims to avoid the disadvantages of the body and to pursue the advantages, what role remains to the mind, in the human composite, relatively to the search of the good of the body?

Let's go deeper into the problem. The introduction of the mind in the analysis adds the fact that the perceptions of the senses *signify*[19] the presence of (dis)advantages to the mind, and thus the fact that the mind is able to recognize or notice them. As Descartes himself says: "il n'y a personne, qui ait un peu d'esprit, qui ne puisse mieux remarquer ce qui est utile à sa santé, pourvu qu'il y veuille un peu prendre garde, que les plus savants docteurs ne lui sauraient enseigner (anybody who has any intelligence, and who is willing to pay a little attention to his/her health, can better observe what is beneficial to it than the most learned doctors)".[20] But if a strictly corporeal process is able to make us avoid disadvantages and on the contrary pursue advantages, it seems that the addition of the mind is in this respect perfectly superfluous. If, as a body, the human being can by instinct flee from disadvantages and pursue advantages, how can we understand that nature has given the human being sensitive perceptions *so*

---

15 See Descartes to Mersenne, 16 October 1639, AT II 599, l. 5-12.
16 *Meditatio Sexta*, AT VII 74, l. 21-23; 81, l. 26; 83, l. 18-19.
17 *Ibid.*, AT VII 88, l. 18 and 89, l. 3. For the French term "santé", see AT IX-1 67, 70, and 71.
18 *Ibid.*, AT VII 84, l. 13-14.
19 This term appears twice in the *Meditatio Sexta*. Thus, for example, Descartes argues that the *perceptiones sensuum* "proprie tantum a natura datae sunt ad menti significandum quaenam composito, cujus pars est, commoda sint vel incommoda / [were] given me by nature [...] simply to inform the mind of what is beneficial or harmful to the composite of which the mind is a part" (AT VII 83, l. 16-19; CSM II 57).
20 Descartes to the Marquess of Newcastle, October 1645, AT IV 330, l, 1-5; CSMK 276 [Translation slightly modified].

that the mind can be signified the disadvantages or advantages encountered by the compound of which it is a part?

2. Animal Instinct and Health Conservation

First, there is a concept of *animal instinct* in the Cartesian texts of the 1630s relative to physiology. I propose to elaborate it, as well as the notions of *(in)commodum* and *health* which are attached to it.

The explanation of the animal instinct, and more broadly of all the movements of animals and human beings as bodies, is based on a fundamental relationship: *commoditas*. The effort required to define it is neither trivial nor easily successful. It is indeed not enough to substitute for the Latin *(in)commodum* a name or a couple of names that would alone, arguably, exhaust its meaning (useful/harmful, convenient/ disconvenient, good/evil). In Descartes's work, it is possible to distinguish several meanings to the vocabulary of *commode-incommode* (in both French and Latin). In the broadest sense, an advantage (*commodum*) is anything that facilitates an action; a disadvantage (*incommodum*), on the contrary, is what hinders the performance of an action[21]. There is also a use of this notion in a strictly physical context.[22] I propose first of all to distinguish between inert and living bodies. *Commodité*, for a given inert body,[23] seems to designate the absence of resistance of the surrounding bodies to the fact that it perseveres in its same state.[24] What does *commode-incommode* mean for a living body? First, let's underline that, insofar as Descartes claims to explain

---

21   Thus, for example, Descartes writes to Henri Reneri for Alphonse Pollot about French spelling: "s'il faut ici que j'en dise mon opinion, je crois que si on suivait exactement la prononciation, cela apporterait beaucoup plus de commodité aux étrangers pour apprendre notre langue / if I am to give my own view, I think it would be much more advantageous for foreigners to learn our language if the spelling followed the pronunciation exactly; it would outweigh the inconvenience to them and us which would be caused by the ambiguity of some expressions" (Descartes to Reneri for Pollot, March 1638, AT II 46, l. 13-17; CSMK 102) [Translation is slightly modified].

22   In the physical context, the concept of *commodum* raises two difficulties which it is not for me to discuss in detail here. Firstly, insofar as this term can designate what is favourable to the realisation of a goal that one has set oneself, there is a risk, by using it in physics, of reintroducing a form of teleology into the consideration of bodies. On another level, one can physically question the use of a single term to think about the good of a living body and what is favourable to an inert body remaining in its state.

23   Let's take the example of the vapours. Descartes defines them as "those small parts which are thus raised into the air by the sun, [and which] must for the most part have the figure [...] of water" ("ces petites parties, qui sont ainsi élevées en l'air par le soleil, [et qui] doivent pour la plupart avoir la figure [...] de l'eau", *Les Météores*, II, AT VI 239, 20-22 [My translation]. He then speaks of the "movement of vapours which, as the expand, pass from the place where they are to some other place where they find it more convenient to expand" ("mouvement des vapeurs qui, en se dilatant, passent, du lieu où elles sont, en quelque autre où elles trouvent plus de commodité de s'étendre", *Les Météores*, IV, AT VI 265, l. 14-17, my translation).

24   According to the formulation of the first *law of nature* (*Principia philosophiae*, II, 37: "in eodem statu [perseverare]", AT VIII-1 62, margin).

inert and living bodies according to the same principles, the term should not be that equivocal. In the first approach, it can therefore be said that, for a living body, something is (in)*commode* that comes into contact with it and is (de)favourable to the conservation of its life.

But this is still saying too little and Descartes is more precise. First of all, on the subject of the advantages and disadvantages of nature (*commoda* naturae vel incommoda**)[25] that affect animals, Descartes says that they can refer "vel singulis partibus vel toti (either to singular parts or to the whole)"[26] of the body. He notes that:

> Cum sensus exhibent aliquid commodum toti, protinus ista motio, quae efficit sensum, efficiat etiam motus omnes in aliis membris ad fruendum istis commoditatibus; si exhibent aliquid commodum uni parti tantum, et alteri incommodum, motio illa quae sentitur, determinet spiritus animales ad efficiendos omnes motus possibiles in una parte, per quos fruatur isto commodo, et in alia, per quos fugiat istud commodum. (When the senses show something advantageous to the whole, the movement which produces the sense immediately produces all the movements in the other limbs to enjoy these advantages; if they show something advantageous to one part only, and disadvantageous to another, this movement which is felt determines the animal spirits to make all the possible movements in one part, by which one enjoys this advantage, and, in the other, all the movements by which one flees from this disadvantage.)[27]

Descartes also states that animals have been exposed, when they were in the uterus,[28] to advantages and disadvantages by which they grew up and which impelled them to certain movements,[29] and that whenever something similar happens to them afterward,[30] they carry out these same movements. Finally, it should be noted that the concept of (in)*commodum* is not accompanied, in the physiological texts, by the concept of "health" — in other words: Descartes does not think of the health of the body through the concept of (dis)advantage. The term "santé" is absent from *L'Homme*;[31] the terms *sanitas* and *valetudo* are absent from *Primae cogitationes circa generationem animalium*. The last lexical point we can make in this respect is that Descartes — unlike some of his contemporaries or predecessors[32] — only raises

---

25 *Cogitationes circa generationem animalium*, AT XI, 519, 10-11. Vincent Aucante dates this fragment from 1637 (RENÉ DESCARTES, *Écrits physiologiques et médicaux*, ed. by Vincent Aucante, Paris, PUF, 2000, p. 88-89).
26 *Primae Cogitationes circa generationem animalium*, AT XI 519, l. 11.
27 *Primae Cogitationes circa generationem animalium*, AT XI 519, l. 12-20. [Translation is mine.]
28 *Ibid.*, AT XI 520, 13-14: "in utero existentibus obvia fuerunt". V. Aucante dates this fragment from 1630-1632 (*Écrits physiologiques et médicaux*, p. 56-57).
29 *Primae Cogitationes circa generationem animalium*, AT XI 520, l. 14-15: "quorum ope creverunt, et a quibus ad certos motus impulsa sunt".
30 *Ibid.*, AT XI 520, l. 15-16: "quoties illis postea simile quid occurrit".
31 This word is not to be found either in a later text (1647): *La Description du corps humain*.
32 One thinks both of veterinary medicine and of certain scholastic reflections on the concept of 'health' (e.g. THOMAS AQUINAS, *De veritate*, q. 21, a. 4, arg. 2, where we find mention of *sanitas* animalis*). Descartes will in fact write late to More that "dicere licet sanitatem soli homini competere / one

the question of health in relation to the human being (possibly considered only as a body or machine),[33] but never in relation to the animal.[34] This is all the more paradoxical since he does speak of the health of the human *body* and indicates that certain diseases have strictly physiological causes[35] — two elements that seem to imply that the non-human animal should not be excluded from their examination. What can we learn from all these textual elements?

Commodité is a relationship that involves contact of the living body with some of the bodies that surround it. No body is objectively and without exception an (dis)advantage for any living creature. The same flame can be disadvantageous for a hand if it is already hot or simply too close to the fire and it can be advantageous for it if the hand is cold and at a good distance.[36] By this same example, one can understand that the (dis)advantage cannot be reduced to that which directly (attacks) preserves the "principle of life", namely the warmth of the heart.[37] It can in fact concern the whole body or some of its parts, without any exclusivity being reserved for the heart by Descartes. Something will be *incommodum* for a living body if it threatens to destroy or damage one of its parts, or to attenuate the warmth of the heart. On the contrary, a thing will be *commodum* for a living body if it is capable of maintaining the warmth of the heart, the "bonne constitution des [...] membres (good condition of the [...] parts of the body)"[38] or of "la structure | de toute la machine (the structure of the whole machine)"[39]. But insofar as they are exhibited by the senses, the *commoda* and *incommoda* are also differentiated by a certain type of action on the nerves of the sense organs. For the former, the movement is temperate or moderate; it is strong or

---

can say that health refers to the human being alone" (Descartes to More, 5 February 1649, AT V 270, l. 25-26) [Translation is mine.]

33 See, on this point, GIDEON MANNING 'Descartes' Healthy Machines and the Human Exception', in *The Mechanization of Natural Philosophy*, ed. by Daniel Garber and Sophie Roux, Dordrecht & New York, Springer, 2013, p. 237-262 (in particular p. 251-260), and GÉRALDINE CAPS, 'La conservation de la santé chez René Descartes (1596-1650): une mise à distance des thérapies somatiques', *Dix-septième siècle*, 245 (2009), p. 735-747 (in particular p. 735-740).

34 I looked for, but could not find, occurrences of the following terms associated with the examination of the non-human animal: "health", "healthy" (and its derivatives), "disease", *valetudo*, *valetudinarius*, *sanitas*, and *morbus* (and their declensions).

35 Descartes famously discuss with Mersenne the diseases that are caused by the heat of the air (Descartes to Mersenne, 13 November 1639, AT II 623, l. 29).

36 *L'Homme*, AT XI 192, 26-193, l. 20.

37 About the warmth of the heart, see the now classic study by ANNIE BITBOL-HESPÉRIÈS, *Le Principe de vie chez Descartes*, Paris, Vrin, 1990; in particular: Part Two: Chapter 2: "La chaleur du cœur, principe de vie chez Descartes", p. 55-102.

38 *L'Homme*, AT XI 144, l. 10-11; CSM I 103.

39 *Ibid.*, AT XI 143, 31-144, 1 (my translation). In an interesting article (Barnaby R. Hutchins, "Does Descartes Have a Principle of Life? Hierarchy and Interdependence in Descartes's Physiology," *Perspectives on Science*, 24 (2016), p. 755-769), Barnaby R. Hutchins asserts that the living bodies are defined, in Descartes, by the interdependency of their organs and limbs. I do not fully subscribe to the undermining of the 'principle of life' in the explanation of physiological phenomena. However, insofar as (dis)advantage does not directly concern the warmth of the heart, I can suggest that it is with regard to such interdependence that it plays its role (by being relative not necessarily to the whole body, but to one of its parts).

violent in the case of the latter.⁴⁰ For example, food that is advantageous for a living body only tickles the tongue moderately.⁴¹ On the other hand, a disadvantage can stimulate the nerves so intensely that the small threads which "composent la moelle (make up the marrow)"⁴² will be broken.

To conclude the effort to determine the relation of *commoditas*, note that it is understandable that the *commoda* encountered in extrauterine life are only similar (and not perfectly identical) to those of intrauterine life. In the uterus, the *(in)commoda* are undifferentiated foods (not separate objects) which are directly assimilated by the body *via* the umbilical cord and which directly (threaten) promote the warmth of the heart. In extrauterine existence, the *(in)commoda* to be (shunned) pursued are exterior to the living body, with which the contact is therefore external. But if they are similar, it is because the survival of the concerned body is at stake.⁴³ Finally, it must be stressed that *(in)commodum* does not primarily concern health or disease, but the survival of the living body. The undeniable absence of the vocabulary of health in Descartes's examination of *(in)commodum* in its relation to animal movements shows that there can be no question of reducing health to the mere preservation of life.

3. The Status of the *(in)commoda* and the *valetudo* in the 'Sixth Meditation'

So far, the notion of animal instinct and its correlative concept, the *(in)commodum*, have been clarified. The latter designates a fundamental relationship between every living body and some of the bodies that surround it. The textual fact on which I would now like to insist is Descartes's use of the same vocabulary of *(in)commodum* in the examination of the union of soul and body that he proposes in the *Meditatio Sexta*.

One of the important theses of the *Sixth Meditation* is well known. The senses do not teach me the essence of the bodies around me, but, on the one hand, that there is a variety in the bodies that responds to the variety of perceptions that one has of them⁴⁴ and, on the other hand, that "meum corpus, sive potius me totum, quatenus ex corpore et mente sum compositus, variis commodis et incommodis a circumjacentibus corporibus affici posse (my body, or rather my whole self, in so far

---

40 A study that would be focused on the short Cartesian work *De Saporibus* would show this in detail, for the sense of taste (see: AT XI, 539-542).
41 *L'Homme*, AT XI 146, l. 24-25.
42 *Ibid.*, AT XI 143, l. 28-29. [Translation is mine.]
43 In my attempt to define the *(in)commodum*, my remark is analogous to the analyses of Kambouchner about some of Descartes's later texts on the relation of *convenance* (KAMBOUCHNER, *L'Homme des passions*, vol. I, p. 264-266).
44 *Meditatio Sexta*, AT VII 81, l. 17-22: "Et certe, ex eo quod valde diversos sentiam colores, sonos, odores, sapores, calorem, duritiem, et similia, recte concludo, aliquas esse in corporibus, a quibus variae istae sensuum perceptiones adveniunt, varietates iis respondentes, etiamsi forte iis non similes".

as I am a combination of body and mind, can be affected by the various beneficial or harmful bodies which surround it)".[45] Descartes rephrases it:

> Sensuum perceptionibus, quae proprie tantum a natura datae sunt ad menti significandum quaenam composito, cujus pars est, commoda sint vel incommoda, et eatenus sunt satis clarae et distinctae, utor tanquam regulis certis ad immediate dignoscendum quaenam sit corporum extra nos positorum essentia, de qua tamen nihil nisi valde obscure et confuse significant. (The proper purpose of the sensory perceptions given me by nature is simply to signify to the mind what is beneficial or harmful for the composite of chich the mind is a part; and to this extent they are sufficiently clear and distinct. But I misuse them by treating them as reliable touchstones for immediate | judgements about the essential nature of the bodies located outside us; yet this is an area where they provide only very obscure information.)[46]

Why signify to the mind the advantages and disadvantages, when the human body can by itself, instinctively, pursue the former and flee the latter? The risks are multiple. First of all, the gift of nature appears to be redundant in relation to what the body can do on its own. More radically, it looks like a potential source of danger: it entails the possibility of misinterpretation and, by the same token, of error.

Descartes's use of the same term of *(in)commodum*[47] is striking, for it was already employed in a strictly physiological context. Are we dealing with the same *concept*? A reticence could arise, when one considers Descartes himself seems to hesitate: he first asserts that it is my body that can be affected by advantages or disadvantages because of the bodies that surround it, before saying that it is rather *me as a whole*, as a compound of mind and body. This hesitation can also be found in the French translation of the Duke of Luynes, who does not always render the vocabulary of the *(in)commoda* using terms from the French lexical family of "commode". For example, he translates "sensique hoc corpus inter alia multa corpora versari, a quibus variis commodis, vel incommodis affici potest, et commoda ista sensu quodam voluptates, et incommoda sensu doloris metiebar"[48] without any fear of reproducing in French the repetitions of the Latin text, as he writes:

> J'ai senti que ce corps était placé entre beaucoup d'autres, desquels il était capable de recevoir diverses commodités et incommodités, et je remarquais ces commodités par un certain sentiment de plaisir ou volupté, et les incommodités par un sentiment de douleur.[49]

45　*Ibid.*, AT VII 81, l. 24-27; CSM II 56.
46　*Ibid.*, AT VII 83, l. 15-23; CSM II 57-58. [Translation slightly modified.]
47　The concept of *(in)commodum* appears nine times: four times in AT VII 74, l. 21-23, twice in AT VII 81, l. 26, twice in AT VII 83, l. 18-19, and once in AT VII 89, l. 13. The French word *(in)commodité* appears four times in AT IX-1 59, twice in AT IX-1 65, and twice in AT IX-1 71.
48　*Ibid.*, AT VII 74, l. 20-23.
49　*Sixième Méditation*, AT IX-1 59. CSM II 52 translates: "I also perceived by my senses that this body was situated among many other bodies which could affect it in various favourable or unfavourable ways; and I gauged the favourable effects by a sensation of pleasure, and the unfavourable ones by

But while his translation from the Latin *commodum* into the French "commode" seemed systematic, he finally chooses to mobilize the French adjective "convenable" (AT XI-a 66), at the moment when Descartes formulates his proper thesis in the Sixth Meditation!

Has *commoditas* ceased to characterize an exclusively corporeal relationship? It does not seem so. Just a few lines before mentioning *myself as a whole*, Descartes refused, with regard to the union of soul and body, the image of the pilot in his ship. Damage to the body is not seen from the outside by the spirit, as is damage to the hull by the pilot, but is instead felt by the soul, through unpleasant feelings.[50] Thus, the mind is well engaged as part of the compound when (dis)advantages occur, not in the sense that it is affected as such, but in the sense that they manifest themselves to it in a particular way. Moreover, let us add that if a part of the compound is affected by an (dis)advantage, this also applies to the whole compound. It must therefore be said that the *Meditatio Sexta* contains the same concept of *(in)commodum* that the one that was used in physiology. The human body to which a spirit is united is affected by an *(in)commodum* in the sense we have previously outlined; this is manifested to the mind by means of particular feelings. In this respect, a definitive certainty has been reached. It is true that the commentators often point at the medical knowledge that arises in the *Meditatio sexta*: it breaks up the *ordo meditandi* insofar as it is a knowledge that was not previously attained in the course of Cartesian metaphysical meditation. Though this is a well-known point in the secondary literature, I claim to have reached an additional certainty: the very concept of *(in)commodum* is also a notion of Cartesian physiology that was transposed into metaphysics.[51]

However, there is an important discrepancy with the use of the concept of *(in)commodum* in physiology: in the *Meditatio Sexta* there is a massive presence of *health* vocabulary.[52] We need to drink for the preservation of our health;[53] Descartes also says that perceptions of the senses that cause pleasant or unpleasant feelings in the

---

a sensation of pain".

50 *Sexta Meditatio*, AT VII 81, l. 1-14; IX-1 64; CSM II 56.

51 In this respect, and contrary to certain interpretations of the Cartesian text, it is not certain that the relation of (in)commodity can best be grasped through the categories of phenomenology — and in particular of Heideggerian philosophy. (1) First of all, the relation of (in)commodity is not identified at first by the *philosophia prima*, but taken over by the latter from anatomy. From this point of view, a historical elucidation of this notion would involve looking at Descartes's medical sources, which deal with the affection of the human body by external bodies. (2) It is true that the Sixth Meditation questions the relation of (in)commodity in order to discuss the way it appears to the *mens*, the way it is signified to it. However, the fact that it was first mobilized in an anatomical context, and that it thus designates above all a relation between *bodies*, allows to demonstrate that it is not enough, in order to understand it, to reduce the analysis to its appearance to the mind. For a different interpretation, see: JEAN-LUC MARION, *Sur la pensée passive de Descartes*, Paris, PUF, 2013, ch. II, § 10: '*In/commoda*: le moment heideggérien', p. 78-87.

52 *Valetudo* appears in AT VII 88, l. 18; 89, l. 3. The adjective *sanus, a, um* appears in AT VII 84, l. 13-14; 85, l. 13; 87, l. 24. The word *santé* appears four times (AT IX-1 67, 70 (two occurrences), 71). The adjective *sain* appears in AT IX-1 l. 68.

53 *Sexta Meditatio*, AT VII 88, l. 17-18: "*potu ad conservationem valetudinis egemus**". In general, drinking is beneficial for the health of the body (*ad corporis valetudinem potus conducit**, *ibid.*, AT VII 89, l. 3-4).

mind are useful for the preservation of a healthy man.⁵⁴ We saw that, in contrast, the term *health* did not appear in strictly physiological texts involving the notion of *(in)commodum*. What conclusions can be drawn from this appearance for the analysis of the relationship of the human being, as a compound of soul and body, to the bodies that surround him or her? The most convincing way to answer is to say that the *valetudo-sanitas-santé* mentioned in the *Sixth Meditation* cannot be reduced to the enjoyment of advantages and escape from disadvantages, although such enjoyment and escape are undoubtedly necessary conditions for it. Two remarks can be made:

(1) First of all, if nature has instituted the perceptions of the senses in such a way that they signify present *(in)commoda* to the mind, it is not so that the latter can compete for the survival of the body — perhaps the body would do better on its own. The mind is indeed, in this respect, a source of error.⁵⁵ In fact, survival presupposes (almost) immediate flight reactions when encountering bodies that are dangerous to our own. Since the human being as a body shares with animals an instinct that enables such evasive movements, it must be said that the addition of the mediation of the mind is not particularly effective in this respect.

(2) The preservation of health, as opposed to survival, implies a relationship to the *(in)commoda* that goes beyond the immediate reaction to their presence and the impression they make in the body. It implies that one must be prepared in advance for the encounter of disadvantages and not just turn away from them when they occur.

The role of the mind in determining how to deal with the advantages and disadvantages of the body is now clearer. The action of the (animal or human) body in the face of *(in)commoda* depends on their impulse on the nerves of their sense organs; this action is thus necessarily a *reaction*. Conversely, the introduction of the *mens* allows for a considerable enrichment of the temporal relationship that human beings have with the *(in)commoda*. It is at least twofold. (a) Firstly, it is a form of planning, prospection, or forecasting turned towards the *future*.⁵⁶ Human beings do not simply try to react to the presence of *(in)commoda*, but to favour good encounters and avoid bad ones. This is what Descartes himself says in his *Conversation with Burman*, when he comments admittedly not on the *Sixth Meditation*, but on the developments in

---

54 *Ibid.*, AT VII 87, l. 23-24: "ad hominis sani conservationem."
55 Thus, to illustrate to Pierre Gassendi the fact that in error the will extends further than the understanding, Descartes takes the example of an error related to what is advantageous to us: "cum pomum, quod forte venenatum est, judicas tibi in alimentum convenire intelligis quidem ejus odorem, colorem, et talia grata esse, non autem ideo ipsum pomum tibi esse utile in alimentum sed quia ita vis, ita judicas / when you judge that an apple, which by chance is poisoned, will be good for you, you conceive that its smell, its colour, and even its taste is pleasant, but you do not conceive that this apple should be useful to you if you make it your food; but because you want it so, you judge it so" (*Quintae Responsiones*, AT VII 377, l. 4-7. [Translation is mine.] It should also be remembered that, in the letter to the Marquess of Newcastle of October 1645 quoted above, Descartes adds a condition for knowing the (dis)advantages: the mind must be attentive.
56 The *mens* allows us to look *in futurum* (*Conversation with Burman*, AT V 179) and to know from now what we *will* have to protect ourselves from, an what we *will* have to pursue.

the sixth part of the *Discourse on Method* about medicine.[57] The past experience of consuming a food, for example, teaches us for the future "an idem et eodem modo et ordine rursus assumendus sit necne (whether we should take the same again, in the same way and in the same order, or not)".[58] This forward-looking dimension indeed corresponds to an achievement of the compound of soul and body as opposed to the animal, in Cartesian thought. (b) Secondly, in order to play as an experience, the *past* encounters of the compound of soul and body with bodies that were favourable or harmful to it must be mobilized in the present moment or to plan the future, by means of *memory*. We are not talking here of the mere bodily memory, by means of which animal spirits, when stimulated in the present, take up paths previously traced in the brain substance on the occasion of similar encounters,[59] but of a memory which presupposes the *mens*.[60]

This twofold enrichment, compared to the rest of the animals, of the temporal relationship of the human being with regard to the good and bad things for his body allows to make several final considerations. First, by emphasizing the irreducibility of human behaviour to a reaction to present *stimuli*, it explains why health is only mentioned in the examination of the human being and not in the strictly physiological texts on (in)commodity. Maintaining health is always more than conserving life — namely: survival. Secondly, this allows to build a bridge between the *Sixth Meditation* and Descartes's later texts that defend the possibility of the human being to become his or her own doctor.[61] Although this theme is not explicitly developed in the *philosophia prima*, it is inscribed there in filigree and, above all, it finds part of its conditions of possibility there.[62]

4. Conclusions

This chapter took as its starting point the Cartesian concept of animal instinct, i.e. a strictly physiological explanation of unlearned corporeal movements of escape from disadvantages (*incommoda*) for the body and of pursuit of advantages (*commoda*). It was motivated by the surprise of finding this same vocabulary of (in)commodity

---

57 See AT V 178-179, about *Discourse on Method*, VI, AT VI 61, l. 28-63, l. 17.
58 *Conversation with Burman*, AT V 179. [Translation is mine.]
59 See *L'Homme*, AT XI 174, l. 4-185, l. 6.
60 On the two kinds of memories, see the remarkable article by XAVIER KIEFT, 'Mémoire corporelle, mémoire intellectuelle et unité de l'individu selon Descartes', *Revue Philosophique de Louvain*, 104 (2006), p. 762-786. Let us note that the validity of this memory regarding (*in*)*commoda* admits a prerequisite: it supposes a relative stability of what harms or benefits our body, through its variations.
61 *Conversation with Burman*, AT V 179: "*sibi medicus esse.*" See also: Descartes to the Marquess of Newcastle, October 1645, AT IV 329, l. 16-330, l. 5. For more information on this thesis, see: ÉVELYNE AZIZA-SCHUSTER, *Le Médecin de soi-même*, Paris, PUF, 1972; and CLAUDE ROMANO, 'Les trois médecines de Descartes', *Dix-septième siècle*, 217 (2002), p. 675-696.
62 We are thinking here, though this paper is not the accurate place to demonstrate it, of the identification of the *natura* that teaches us what is good or bad for us with the compound of soul and body, or *whole self*, of which the *Sixth Meditation* explored certain modalities.

in a text belonging to the Cartesian metaphysics, namely the *Sixth Meditation*. This text did not take any longer as its object the behaviours that are common to human beings and the rest of the animals, but the specificity of the human being as a compound of soul and body. There were, however, many discrepancies. (1) Given the explanatory power of the body alone in relation to the movements that occur within it, the mind ran the risk of appearing potentially redundant, even useless, in relation to human reactions to (dis)advantages. (2) The notion of *health*, which could have arguably be correlated to the (dis)advantages encountered by the body, was in fact only present in the Cartesian texts when the human being was examined and not in the physiological ones. (3) These two discrepancies could only invite the question of whether the relation of (in)commodity retained a real univocity in both of these contexts.

In order to answer these questions, I clarified the Cartesian concept of animal instinct, which had been developed in the 1630s, while at the same time proposing a journey through Descartes's texts mentioning *commoditas*, from the physiological works of the 1630s to the *Meditatio Sexta* of 1641. In this way, I have reached a series of results that I hope will be definitive in Cartesian studies. (3) There is no need to assume a change of meaning from physiological texts to metaphysics, regarding the relation of (in)commodity. On the contrary, it is an achievement of Descartes's medical studies that he transposes into the *philosophia prima* — in the same way, for example, as the description of the structure of the nerve.[63] (2) The Cartesian conception of health, i.e. in a philosophy in which the illness of the animal is never mentioned, consists in distinguishing between the reaction to present *stimuli* relating to the survival of the body and a set of planned, anticipated actions, which, after all, aim at preventing rather than curing. (1) All of these considerations allow to understand, *in fine*, the role of the *mens* in relation to the (*in*)*commoda*. If one accepts the difference I have made between the preservation of life (survival) and the preservation of health, then the mind intervenes in the context of the latter. It allows to account for the considerable temporal enrichment of the human relationship to the (*in*)*commoda*, compared to the mere reaction to the present that characterizes animal behaviour.

---

63 *Meditatio Sexta*, AT VII 86, l. 24-87, l. 18 and IX-1 69.

JAN FORSMAN

Madness and Dream in Descartes's *First Meditation**

▼ ABSTRACT At the beginning of the First Meditation, Descartes's meditator considers not only the famous scenarios of dreaming and deceiver but also a third scenario: that she might be insane. This *madness scenario* is apparently rejected in favor of dreaming. I analyze the scenario of madness, drawing from Descartes's comments about insanity as a medical condition, and compare it with the dreaming scenario. Overall, the scenario of madness has been generally neglected, receiving only minor discussion in the literature, most of which I take to be misguided, without well-driven attempts to place it in the narrative of the First Meditation or contrast it with Descartes's more medical analysis of defects in the brain. However, the scenario deserves to be discussed more as it serves an important argumentative turning point in the narration of the First Meditation. I view the role of the madness scenario to be acting as a *transitional* passage between the *natural* common-sense attitude, used in practical everyday life, and the *unnatural* metaphysical doubt. These two should be considered two different *states of mind*, with the latter being the metaphysical attitude required for the Cartesian suspension of judgment.

▼ KEYWORDS Descartes, Madness, Dreaming, Skepticisim, Doubt

---

* I want to thank all the participants at the online conference "Lights & Shadows in Descartes' Medicine", organized by Fabrizio Baldassarri and Fabio Zampieri.

Jan Forsman • University of Iowa, US. Contact: <jan-forsman@uiowa.edu>

Descartes and Medicine: Problems, Responses and Survival of a Cartesian Discipline,
ed. by Fabrizio Baldassarri, Turnhout, 2023 (*DESCARTES*, 9), p. 215-228
© BREPOLS PUBLISHERS   10.1484/M.DESCARTES-EB.5.132892

1. Introduction

At the beginning of the First Meditation, Descartes's meditator considers not only the famous scenarios of dreaming and deceiver but also a third scenario: that she might be insane. This *madness scenario* is apparently rejected in favor of dreaming. But why is the scenario turned down and why is dreaming favorable to it as a reason for doubt? Better yet, if madness is immediately rejected, what purpose does it serve in the narrative of the First Meditation?

In this chapter, I analyze the scenario of madness, drawing from Descartes's comments about insanity as a medical condition, and compare it with the dreaming scenario. Overall, the scenario of madness has been generally neglected, receiving only minor discussion in the literature, most of which I take to be misguided, without well-driven attempts to place it in the narrative of the First Meditation or contrast it with Descartes's more medical analysis of defects in the brain. However, the scenario deserves to be discussed more as it serves an important argumentative turning point in the narration of the First Meditation. I view the role of the madness scenario to be acting as a *transitional* passage between the *natural* common-sense attitude, used in practical everyday life, and the *unnatural* metaphysical doubt. These two should be considered two different *states of mind*, with the latter being the metaphysical attitude required for the Cartesian suspension of judgment.

Reading the madness scenario alongside Descartes's other comments on madness as a physiological defect brings out important differences between Descartes's handling of dreaming and lunacy, which make madness *unconvincing* and *unreasonable* as a skeptical scenario. Thus, madness fails as a reason for doubt, but it is included in the First Meditation because of its transitional role.

The article is divided into four parts. In the first part, I detail how the madness scenario follows from the previous scenario of Occasional Sensory Errors (OSE). The second part discusses madness further, comparing it with Descartes's other writings about madness as a medical condition. Third part then examines the role that the madness scenario is intended to play in the *Meditations*' narrative. Finally, the fourth part compares madness with the dreaming scenario, detailing what the latter accomplishes better than the former.

2. 'Tis But a Madness

Descartes begins the First Meditation with a brief questioning of particular sensory perception: 'From time to time I have found that the senses deceive, and it is prudent never to trust completely those who have deceived us even once'.[1] The senses occasionally deceive and provide erroneous testimony. The first step in the meditative project for avoiding error is then not to trust them on each occasion.

---

[1] René Descartes, *Meditationes de prima philosophia*, I, AT VII 18; CSM II 12.

Aristotelians, who are typically taken to be the main target of the *Meditations*'s sensory access critique, however, would not have been very impressed by this first counter measure. It was widely acknowledged in the Medieval Scholastic discussions that senses can deceive from time to time, typically referring to cases inherited from the ancient skeptical tropes, such as large objects seeming small in the distance, islands seeming to be in motion when passed by in a ship, and sweet things tasting bitter when sick. The common remedy for such doubts was to refer to sense perception in normal circumstances. Take, for example, Henry of Ghent (*c.* 1217-1293): '[I]n a case in which the one sense is deceived in one condition, in another [...] it indicates what is true'.[2] The Scholastics had what has been called an *epistemologically optimistic* attitude towards sensory perception, viewing that human perception is fundamentally veridical and reaches reality in a reliable fashion in the common course of nature. They admit that misperceptions, like illusions, do occur but are exceptional cases, required to be evaluated against the background of normal, veridical perceptive acts.[3]

In fact, the meditator will not swallow the first level sensory doubts hook, line, and sinker either:

> [A]lthough the senses occasionally deceive with respect to objects which are small or in the distance, there are many other beliefs about which doubt is quite impossible, even though they are acquired through the senses — for example, that I am here, sitting by the fire, wearing a winter dressing-grown, holding this piece of paper in my hands and so on.[4]

Unlike sometimes accused, Descartes does not question the whole testimony of sense perception just because some sense data is deceptive.[5] That senses sometimes deceive does not mean they would not accurately testify reality in optimal cases. Despite certain occasional mishaps, the meditator finds that the senses report reality fairly well as a norm, especially when the circumstances are optimal. So called Occasional Sensory Error (OSE) cases need to be evaluated against this background of perception in normal, optimal situations. As an example, the meditator offers her present state of sitting *here* by a fireplace and writing on a piece of paper.[6]

---

2   Henry of Ghent, *SQO*, a. 1, q. 1, IV. Cf. St Augustine, *C. Acad.* 3.11.26; *Trin.* 15.12.21-22, Thomas Aquinas, *ST* I, Q.85, a. 6, and Jean Buridan, *QM* II, 1: 8rb. See Jack Zupko, "Buridan and Skepticism," *Journal of the History of Philosophy* 31/2 (1993), p. 191-221.
3   Hans Thomas Adriaenssen, *Representation and Scepticism from Aquinas to Descartes*, Cambridge, Cambridge University Press, 2017, p. 241. Cf. Robert Pasnau, *After Certainty: A History of Our Epistemic Ideals and Illusions*, Oxford, Oxford University Press, 2017, p. 70-94.
4   *Mediatationes de prima philosophia*, I, AT VII 18; CSM II 12-13.
5   See Nicholas Rescher, "The Legitimacy of Doubt," *The Review of Metaphysics* 13/2 (1959), p. 230-231; W. H. Walsh, *Metaphysics*, New York, Harcourt, Brace & World, Inc., 1963, p. 91. The accusation was already raised by Pierre Gassendi, *Disquitiones metaphisica, seu dubitationes et instantiaea adversus Renati Cartesii metaphysicam, & responsa*, Amsterdam, Johannes Blaev, 1644, I, i, 5.
6   Cf. René Descartes, *La recherche de la vérité par la lumière naturelle*, AT X 510; CSM II 407: "[T]he senses are sometimes deceptive if they are in poor condition [...] or, in general, whenever they do not act freely in accordance with their natural constitution. But such defects [...] do not prevent me from being quite sure [...] that everything which ordinarily appears to my senses is genuine."

Unlike with the famous scenarios of dreaming and deception, there is a sense of casuality and normalcy, even naturalness, related to the OSE. Sensory errors are fairly common and while they can make the meditator perform double-checks when the circumstances are not optimal, perhaps even suspend judgment in certain particular cases, they do not make her doubt her perception to be *systematically* in error. The issue is driven home in the French translation: '*il s'en recounter peut-être beaucoup d' autres desquelles on ne peut pas* raissonablement *douter*'. Particular sense-error doubt is clearly reasonable and occurs in an unlabored fashion merely from the experience of seeing a square tower rounded from afar or a straight oar bent in water. Meanwhile, the meditator finds no reasonable room for doubting these being her hands holding the paper and this being her body sitting near a fire ([*m*]*anus verò has ipsas, totumque hoc corpus meum esse*).[7]

Descartes's gambit with the dreaming doubt is to suggest that instead of being reliable, senses systematically failing to grasp what is real might be the norm. However, since the meditator resists such a general doubt, Descartes cannot just seamlessly flow into the systematic error by dreaming. In order to succeed in the general doubt, Descartes must guide the meditator from the naturally occurring occasional doubts to the *metaphysical* doubt, making her recognize, despite initial resistance, that it is fully possible and reasonable for the senses to be systematically in error as a norm.

I read this transition fulfilled by the scenario of madness. Like the OSE, madness has received only minor discussion in the literature without well-driven attempts at placing it in the larger narrative. Even when separation between everyday life and metaphysical inquiry is given attention, the role that the discussion of madness plays in the exercise has been missed.[8]

The scenario of madness takes places in the fourth paragraph, between the OSE cases and the dreaming doubt, and has its origin in the meditator's resistance. She wonders how she can find reason for doubt that the hand holding the paper and the body wrapped in a dressing-gown are hers:

> [P]erhaps I were to liken myself to madmen (*insanis*), whose brains are so damaged by the persistent vapours of melancholia that they firmly maintain they are kings when they are paupers, or say they are dressed in purple when they are naked, or that their heads are made of earthenware, or that they are pumpkins, or made of glass.[9]

The meditator considers that she might be insane, maintaining wearing a dressing-gown and holding a paper due to physiological defect (unbalanced vapor-levels in the brain), whereas in reality she could be naked and not holding a paper at all. The examples of madmen's delusions mentioned were common in the medical literature of the

---

[7] *Meditationes de prima philosophia*, I, AT VII 18; CSM II 13.
[8] See DAVID MACARTHUR, "The Seriousness of Doubt and Our Natural Trust in the Senses in the First Meditation," *Canadian Journal of Philosophy* 33/2 (2003), p. 159-181. Carriero notices a similar heuristic value in the paragraph but does not take madness as an attempt at a skeptical scenario, considering the search for such a scenario as "overreading". JOHN CARRIERO, *Between Two Worlds: A Reading of Descartes's* Meditations, Princeton University Press, Princeton, 2009, p. 38-39.
[9] *Meditationes de prima philosophia*, I, AT VII 18-19; CSM II 13.

time, their source traceable to André du Laurens's (1558-1609) *Discours des maladies mélancoliques* (1594), the most famous of them being the *glass delusion*, the maintenance, or fear, of being made of glass.¹⁰ The madness scenario is then seemingly rejected, as the meditator considers insane people unfit to be equated with herself due to their condition. "But such people are insane (*amentes*), and I would be thought equally mad (*demens*) if I took anything from them as a model for myself."¹¹

3. Madness as a Physiological Defect

It seems that both the madness scenario's placement before the dreaming doubt and its appearing rejection have resulted in neglect and lack of interest. Many readings simply treat it as uninteresting and unworthy of analysis because the meditator seemingly does so. Often it is also confusingly piled up with the dreaming doubt, as a mere version or projected draft of the latter. Classic readings of the First Meditation not even mentioning the madness scenario include for example Martial Gueroult, Bernard Williams, and John Cottingham.¹² Other classic readings do mention the madness doubt, but seem uninterested in analyzing it further, usually dismissing the scenario of madness without offering a clear reason for this dismissal, merely observing that Descartes seems to dismiss it. These readings include Anthony Kenny, Edwin Curley, Margaret Wilson, and Williams, having more recently been followed by José Luis Bermúdez.¹³

A typical way to read the scenario is to see madness dismissed because if the meditator were to be insane it would demolish the whole enterprise of proper reasoning which Descartes is aiming at. This way of reading would mean that madness is not even intended as a skeptical scenario (or at least not as a serious one), but instead it is brought up specifically so that it can be rejected, for example, in order to emphasize the meditator's rationality. Harry Frankfurt famously takes this stand and later followers include for example Fred Ablondi, Michael Williams, and Andrea Christofidou.¹⁴

---

10 See Elena Fabietti, "A Body of Glass: The Case of *El Licenciado Vidriera*," *Symplokē* 23/1-2 (2015), p. 327-340. See also Robert Burton, *Anatomy of Melancholy*, London, 1621, Pr. I, Sec. 3, p. 386, 403, 410.
11 *Meditationes de prima philosophia*, I, AT VII 18-19; CSM II 12-13.
12 Martial Gueroult, *Descartes: selon l'ordre des raisons, vol. I & II-L'ame et Dieu, L'ame et le corps*, Paris, Aubier Éditions Montaigne, 1953; Bernard Williams, *Descartes: The Project of Pure Enquiry*, London & New York, Routledge Classics, 2015 (1978); John Cottingham, *Descartes*, Oxford, Basil Blackwell Ltd, 1986.
13 Anthony Kenny, *Descartes: A study of his philosophy*, New York, Random House, 1968; Edwin Curley, *Descartes against the Skeptics*, Cambridge (Ma.), Harvard University Press, 1978; Margaret Wilson, *Descartes*, London, Routledge, 1978; Bernard Williams, "Descartes's Use of Scepticism", in *The Skeptical Tradition*, ed. by M. Burnyeat, Berkeley & Los Angeles, University of California Press, 1983, p. 337-352. José Luis Bermúdez "Cartesian Skepticism: Arguments and Antecedents" in *Oxford Handbook to Skepticism*, ed. by J. Greco, Oxford, Oxford University Press, 2008, p. 53-79.
14 Harry G. Frankfurt *Demons, Dreamers, & Madmen*, Princeton, Princeton University Press, 2008 (1970), p. 51-54; Fred Ablondi "Why it Matters that I'm Not Insane: The Role of the Madness Argument in Descartes's First Meditation", *International Philosophical Quarterly* 47/1 (2007), p. 79-89; Michael Williams, "Descartes' transformation of the skeptical tradition" in *The Cambridge Companion to Ancient Skepticism*, ed. by R. Bett, Cambridge, Cambridge University Press, 2010, p. 309; Andrea

Descartes does not propose that the meditator seriously consider, as a ground for doubt, the possibility that she is mad. In equating doubt about things seen up close in good light with madness, he is offering her a reason to dismiss such doubts. The *Meditations* is constructed for sane readers who are willing to accept the reason given for undertaking the process of doubt — to gain lasting knowledge — and engage the process accordingly.[15]

By raising the possibility of madness, Descartes then intends to separate the skeptical exercise from sheer lunacy. Lunatic mind would not be able to distinguish right judgment from wrong and would, therefore, not be able to build the strong validation for reason that Descartes is claimed to be after.[16]

Yet, reading madness as contrasted against rational thinking is not really supported by the text. There is nothing in the passage which implies madmen having difficulties with e.g., mathematics or understanding that their essence is to think. In fact, Descartes seems perfectly willing to grant that madmen can have clear and distinct perception: "[E]verything that anyone clearly and distinctly perceives is true, although the person in question may from time to time doubt whether he is dreaming or awake, and may even, if you like, be dreaming or mad."[17] Comparing the madness paragraph to Descartes's other discussions of madness and its cause conveys that the madmen have a disability in their sensation and imagination, not in rationality.

> [M]admen and those who are asleep often see, or think they see, various objects which are nevertheless not before the eyes [because] certain vapours disturb their brain and arrange those of its parts normally engaged in vision exactly as they would be if these objects were present.[18]

> [M]elancholic individuals who think themselves to be vases [...] will swear that what they see and touch is just as they imagine it to be. To be sure, a good man would be indignant if you told him that his beliefs cannot have any more rational basis than theirs, since he relies, like them, on what the senses and imagination represent to him.[19]

The description of madness in the First Meditation and the *Search* follows the theory of unbalanced bodily fluids that was still popular in the medical practices of early 1600s,

---

CHRISTOFIDOU, *Self, Reason, and Freedom: A New Light on Descartes' Metaphysics*, London, Routledge, 2013, p. 35-36. Cf. MARJORIE GRENE, "Descartes and Skepticism", *The Review of Metaphysics* 52/3 (1999), p. 561-562; KURT BRANDHORST, *Descartes' Meditations of First Philosophy: An Edinburgh Philosophical Guide*, Edinburgh, Edinburgh University Press, 2010, p. 32-36. See also MICHEL FOUCAULT, *History of Madness* (*Folie et Déraison: Histoire de la folie à l'âge classique; Histoire de la Folie à l'âge classique*, trans. by J. Murphy & J. Khalfa), Taylor & Francis e-Library, 2006 (1972; 1961), p. 44-45.

15 GARY HATFIELD, *Routledge Philosophy Guidebook to Descartes and the* Meditations, London & New York, Routledge, 2007 (2003), p. 75-76.
16 *Cogito* of a lunatic mind would not be very stable, nor is it certain that a lunatic would even reach the *cogito*-moment.
17 *Meditationes de prima philosophia*, 7th Replies, AT VII 461; CSM II 310.
18 RENÉ DESCARTES, *La dioptrique*, AT VI 141; CSM I 172.
19 *La recherche de la vérité par la lumière* naturelle, AT X 511; CSM II 407.

although aspects of it had already been challenged by Andreas Vesalius (1514-1564) and William Harvey (1568-1657). The theory is based on Hippocrates's (c. 460-c. 370 BC) doctrine of four essential humors of the human body: blood, phlegm, black bile, and yellow bile (comparable to the four classical elements of air, water, earth, and fire), which Galen (129-c. 216 AD) later adopted and developed, cementing the idea of illnesses being caused by imbalance of these humors for later medical theories.

Humor	Element	Organ	Qualities	Temperament
Blood	Air	Liver	Warm and Moist	Sanguine
Yellow Bile	Fire	Gallbladder	Warm and Dry	Choleric
Black Bile	Earth	Spleen	Cold and Dry	Melancholic
Phlegm	Water	Brain/Lungs	Cold and Moist	Phlegmatic

According to the First Meditation description, the meditator assigns the madmen's state to be due to unbalanced amount of *melancholia* (black bile, gr. μέλαινα χολή, *melaina chole*), causing physiological damage to the brain.[20] Madmen do not think their head is a vase because they are irrational but because of an unbalanced distribution of vapors in their brains. Their faulty judgment is to do with defective causal capacities, which corrupts cognitive mechanisms and can introduce systematic error in some people's beliefs. Just as I may have an occasional sensory error with viewing a straight branch as bended in water, madman may have a more systematic error in viewing himself to be clothed in purple even if he is naked. And, as the next part in the paragraph alludes, a dreamer may similarly view that he is sitting by a fire, even if he is sleeping in his bed.[21] All of these scenarios include also a causal nature.[22]

---

20 Descartes himself, though, was not a strong supporter of the humor theory, being more influenced by Harvey's account of human anatomy and blood circulation. *Discours de la Méthode*, V, AT VI 50-52; CSM I 136-137. (A probably apocryphal story has Descartes, lying ill in Stockholm, telling the local doctor coming to perform bloodletting to "spare French blood".) The humor theory is included in the First Meditation and the *Search* most likely due to its commonality, being familiar to most readers.
21 According to Charles Larmore, the overall structure of the First Meditation is that of a *dialogue*, staged by Descartes between "the empiricist and the skeptic". Reconstructing the doubts in this way would then guard against misconceptions on why madness is not taken seriously in the discussion. The one who dismisses this doubt is not Descartes, but rather the empiricist, and rightly so since "the possibility that we might be mad forms no part of the perspective of someone following the natural inclination to trust in the senses", and it is not until the skeptic raises the possibility of dreaming that the empiricist's position is truly threatened. CHARLES LARMORE, "Descartes and Skepticism", in *The Blackwell Guide to Descartes'* Meditations, ed. by S. Gaukroger, Oxford, Blackwell Publishing, 2006, p. 19-23; "The First Meditation: skeptical doubt and certainty", in *The Cambridge Companion to Descartes'* Meditations, ed. by D. Cunning, Cambridge, Cambridge University Press, 2014, p. 56-59. This reading, however, has the disadvantage of being rather forced. Even if I agree on separating Descartes from the character of the text, I find the reading to run much more smoothly by having only one narrative character in the writing.
22 *Principia philosophiae*, IV, § 196, AT VIIIA 319-320; CSM I, 283. Cf. JOHN CARRIERO "First Meditation" in *Descartes's* Meditations: *Critical Essays*, ed. V. Chappell, Lanham, Rowman & Littlefield Publishers, Inc., 1997 (1987), p. 4; JANET BROUGHTON, *Descartes's Method of Doubt*, Princeton, Princeton University Press, 2002, p. 64-66; "Dreamers and Madmen", in *Early Modern Philosophy: Mind, Matter, and Metaphysics*, eds by C. Mercer & E. O'Neill, Oxford, Oxford University Press,

In fact, Descartes makes use of two words in the madness passage, *amentes* and *demens*. The former designates a temporary attack of madness, whereas the latter is a more permanent state. The meditator would then be unwilling to follow those who from time to time suffer from a defect in the brain in order not to be permanently insane.[23]

4. Method in Madness

Despite it all, then, madness fails to create a sufficient reason for doubt and the meditator disregards it quickly. To make systematic doubt of the senses possible, the meditator needs to be convinced that senses failing to perceive reality in the normal course of events might be more typical than she originally considered. However, madness is still an exceptional case — as a physiological impairment, madness is not a normal or natural state and implies a background of physically defectless minds. Thus, madness is unconvincing as a systematic scenario.[24]

If madness is an unconvincing scenario, what is it doing in the First Meditation? It feels strange that Descartes would waste space in such a short text for raising a scenario that fails. As I read it, madness is raised to transition the meditator from the practical life context to the metaphysical context of suspension of judgment, preparing her thinking for the upcoming dreaming scenario. Madness bridges the narrative, paving the way for moving from the First Level of doubt to the Second.[25]

2005, 12; STEPHEN I. WAGNER, *Squaring the Circle in Descartes's* Meditations*: The Strong Validation of Reason*, Cambridge, Cambridge University Press, 2014, p. 52. The dream scenario's causality is noticeably less detailed. Yet, one can assume it having a similar physiological basis. For a detailed picture of the physiological character of madness and dreaming scenarios, as well as on the physiology of Descartes's doubts in general, see KRISTEN BESHEER, "Descartes' doubts: Physiology and the First Meditation", *Philosophical Forum* 40/1 (2009), p. 55-97.

23 *Meditationes de prima philosophia*, I, AT VII 19; CSM II 13. Cf. ROBERT IMLAY, "Descartes and Madness", in *René Descartes: Critical Assesments, vol. II*, ed. G. J. D. Moyal, London & New York, Routledge, 1991, p. 90. In the so-called Toulouse Manuscript (an unpublished draft of the *Meditations*) the term for insanity is *furiosis*, which likewise suggests a stronger physiological link.

24 Cf. R THOMAS M. LENNON & MICHAEL W. HICKSON, "The skepticism of the First Meditation", in *Descartes' Meditations: A Critical Guide*, ed. by K. Detlefsen, Cambridge, Cambridge University Press, 2013, p. 14-15. Some read madness creating a genuine reason for doubt, which is not turned down but assimilated into the dreaming scenario, influenced by Broughton (*Descartes's Method of Doubt*; "Dreamers and Madmen") and followed by e.g., DAVID SCOTT, "Descartes, Madness and Method: A Reply to Ablondi", *International Philosophical Quarterly* 49/2 (2009), p. 153-171; ANDREW RUSSO, "Why It Doesn't Matter I'm Not Insane: Descartes's Madness Doubt in Focus", *Southwest Philosophy Review* 27/1 (2011), p. 157-165, and Wagner (*Squaring the Circle in Descartes's* Meditations).

25 Madness, of course, was one of the traditional weapons of the ancient skeptics, often found paired with dreaming. Madness and dream are also paired in Galen, JULIA ANNAS & JONATHAN BARNES, *The Modes of Scepticism: Ancient Texts and Modern Interpretations*, Cambridge, Cambridge University Press, 1985, p. 86; PLATO, *Tht.* 158b-d; ARISTOTLE, *Met.* 4.5-4.6., 1010b8-101127; Augustin, *C. Acad.*, 2.5.11, 3.11.2; *Trin*, 15.12.21 and MICHEL DE MONTAIGNE, *Apologie de Raimond Sebond*, in *Essais de Montaigne, Texte et Traduction*, ed. by Michaud, Paris, Libraire de Paris, 1907, p. 404, 410; English translation by M. A. Screech, *The Complete Essays*, London, Penguin Books, 1991, p. 674, 677-678. Broughton (*Descartes's Method of*

This need for transition is motivated by Descartes's careful distinction between the meditative inquiry and practical life matters.

> [W]e must note the distinction which I have insisted on in several passages, between the actions of life and the investigation of the truth. For when it is a question of organizing our life, it would, of course, be foolish not to trust the senses, and the sceptics who neglected human affairs to the point where friends had to stop them falling off precipices deserved to be laughed at. Hence I pointed out in one passage that no sane person ever seriously doubts such things. But when our inquiry concerns what can be known with complete certainty by the human intellect, it is quite unreasonable to refuse to cast aside (*rejicere*) these things in all seriousness as doubtful and even as false; the purpose here is to come to recognize that certain other things which cannot be cast aside in this way are thereby more certain and in reality better known to us.[26]

The meditator's thinking needs to be altered from the everyday context to the skeptical context of the general suspension of judgement, driven by the search for metaphysical certainty. Thus, a transition is required for moving from the naturally occurring particular doubts to the metaphysically charged systematic doubt, and from the common-sense naïve conviction of 'teaching of nature' to the meditative skeptical exercise, where perception of reality and reality itself might be cut off.[27]

The above is a lot to ask and Descartes seemingly recognizes it. The meditator is expected to seriously consider that not only is her sensory cognition limited, it might not even access reality regularly and systematically (not just exceptionally and occasionally). Descartes hints with madness that this sort of doubt is extremely difficult. From the meditator's perspective, it seems initially *insane*, going against what nature has taught us. To an extent, it is an *unnatural* doubt. As Descartes points out in the Synopsis, to deny our everyday trust in the senses is quite mad and something which "no sane person (*sanae mentis*)" has ever seriously doubted.[28]

The meditator's decision not to take the mad as an example also works as a warning not to expand the metaphysical doubts to the everyday situation of practical living. Reading the madness discussion in this fashion likewise allows us to see in it an

---

Doubt, 65-66; "Dreamers and Madmen") and Russo ("Descartes, Madness and Method: A Reply to Ablondi") suggest following this tradition as a sufficient motivation for Descartes to include madness into the discussion. However, this reasoning comes off as ungenerous towards Descartes.

26 *Meditationes de prima philosophia*, 5th Replies, AT VII 350-351; CSM II 243. Translation modified.
27 *Meditationes de prima philosophia*, III, AT VII 38-39; CSM II 26-27. Due to the work's meditative nature, it would be expected of Descartes to make this separation in the beginning of the First Meditation. Indeed, this is what he does in the *Discours de la Méthode*, III, AT VI 25, 31; CSM I 123, 126, and the *Principia philosophiae*, I, art. 3, AT VIII-1 5; CSM I 193. However, the First Meditation surprisingly does not include a similar distinction before the very end. *Meditationes de prima philosophia*, I, AT VII 22; CSM II 15. On the other hand, the *Discours* and the *Principia* do not include madness.
28 *Mediationes de prima philosophia*, Synopsis, AT VII 16; CSM II 11. Cf. *Meditaiones de prima philosophia*, 7th Replies, AT VII 460; CSM II 309, and Descartes to Hyperaspistes, August 1641, AT III 422-423; CSMK 188-189.

inherent critique of the ancient skeptics. In the previous quote, Descartes contrasts the practical doubts of the ancients with insanity, which is deservedly laughed at. The meditator's decision not to follow the mad can then be likewise understood as a statement not to take the ancients as a model for skepticism.[29]

5. Madness and Dream

Leading up to the fifth paragraph, the meditator is willing to side with the sane crowd and is, thus, resistant to considering herself a lunatic. However, while tentatively considering madness as the only way to succeed in the systematic doubt, she now realises a much more likely scenario:

> A brilliant piece of reasoning (*preclare sane*)! As if I were not a man who sleeps at night, and regularly has all the same experiences while asleep as madmen do when awake — indeed sometimes even more improbable ones. How often, asleep at night, am I convinced of just such familiar events [...] when in fact I am lying undressed in bed![30]

Insanity is not a convincing reason for doubting the background norm of reliable sensory cognition because it is a defect of our natural capacities, affecting only *some* people for some of the time. One cannot make this same objection against dreaming, with the meditator sarcastically declaring how *sane* the earlier objection appears when compared with it.[31] Dreaming, a feature of human cognition, just like occasional sensory errors, is something we all experience some of the time. Dreaming enables the meditator to consider that her senses might not work as she thought, allowing for the possibility that sense perception is unreliable as a norm even if the meditator's (and everyone else's) brain was physically defectless. Thus, it offers a more convincing challenge to the background of epistemic optimism than madness.[32] The meditator, by considering madness, is able to ease into the attitude of sensory doubt and discover dreaming as a possible way to find their connection to the world as suspect, temporarily casting aside her naïve realist conviction of sensation.

However, when sketching the dream scenario, the meditator is still struggling with the systematic doubt of the senses. Comparing the case of dreaming to her own sensory experience, she finds that at the moment she is "certainly wide awake" and does a series of tests to prove this to herself.

> All this would not happen with such distinctness to someone asleep. Indeed! As if I did not remember other occasions when I have been tricked by exactly similar thoughts while asleep! As I think about this more carefully, I see plainly that there

---

29 Cf. Christofidou, *Self, Reason, and Freedom*, p. 18.
30 *Mediationes de prima philosophia*, I, AT VII 19; CSM II 13.
31 Cf. *La recherche de la vérité par la lumière naturelle*, AT X 511; CSM II 407-408: 'But you cannot take amiss if I ask whether you are not, like all men, liable to fall asleep...'.
32 Cf. LENNON & HICKSON, "The skepticism of the First Meditation", p. 14-15.

are never any sure signs by means of which being awake can be distinguished from being asleep. The result is that I begin to feel dazed, and this very feeling only reinforces the notion that I may be asleep.³³

Systematic doubt proves to be difficult even with dreaming as indicated by the meditator's insistence that she is awake, and the description of being 'dazed (*obstupescam*)' when concluding that she might be asleep. This is to be expected. The dreaming scenario is meant to suggest that the meditator's senses might not generally access the reality in the ordinary common course of nature, as she thought they do. Cartesian suspension of judgment as an attentive meditative exercise is not intended to be easy for humans, ingrained with well-established habits and belief systems. Compare with Jean Buridan (*c.* 1301-1362), who views dreaming as an unfavourable state: '[T]he species of sensible things can be preserved in the sense organs in the absence of these things, as it is stated in [Aristotle's] *On Sleep and Waking*. And then we judge that which is not there to be there'.³⁴ Dreaming is simply uninteresting for Buridan. He offers no criteria for distinguishing between waking and dreaming states and gives no direct answer to dream-based skepticism. He merely does not take it as a serious argument, because he views sensory perception as working reliably in the natural order of things, this being sufficient for scientific and moral certainty.³⁵

Descartes, in contrast, compares the waking experience to errorless sensory cognition and the dream experience to sensory cognition that has been disrupted by error in some way, and suggests that dream experiences cannot be distinguished from wake experiences with any *inherent features* of sensation. In the paragraph from the *La dioptriques* quoted above, Descartes considers dreamers to have causal hindrances similar to the madmen's, which arranges errors in cognitive mechanisms.³⁶ When I assume I am looking at a frozen lake from my balcony, due to a causal error in my perception, there might be no balcony, no lake, and no cat seeking to be caressed. Just as a naked madman may erroneously view himself to be clothed in purple due to the causal effects in his brain, I may have a similar systematic error that I am sitting by the fire writing on a piece of paper — or on the balcony, writing on my laptop — due to a causal error like dreaming.

Descartes's account of dreaming differs not only from Buridan's but also from certain ancient considerations. Specifically, Sextus Empiricus (*c.* 160-210 AD), our main source to ancient pyrrhonistic skepticism, describes how "different appearances" occur depending on whether one is dreaming or awake. "[W]hen asleep we will see things which are unreal in waking life, not unreal once and for all. For they exist in sleep, just as the contents of waking life exist even though they do not exist in sleep".³⁷ Sextus contends that one cannot be sure whether waking contents are truer than dream contents, satisfying the Pyrrhonian contrast of impressions. However, for Descartes, the difference between erroneous and errorless sensation cannot be pointed out by

---

33 *Meditationes de prima philosophia*, I, AT VII 19; CSM II 13.
34 *QM* II, 1: 8rb.
35 *QM* II, 1: 94a.
36 *La Dioptrique*, AT VI 141-142; CSM II 172-173. Cf. *L'Homme*, AT XI 173-174, 198-199; CSM I 104-105).
37 SEXTUS EMPIRICUS, *PH* I, 104.

inherent criteria in the sensory experience. Senses failing to reach the reality might be more akin to the natural order than is assumed by epistemological optimism.[38]

The dream scenario in the First Meditation is infamously sketchy and unclear, though, which has led to disagreement on the consequences of the indistinguishability. The text does not offer a clearly worked out argument, so many commentators have relied on their own resources and Descartes's other texts to squeeze the argument out.[39] An earlier common reading was to take Descartes as suggesting that we might be dreaming in every instance, our lives a continuous dream.[40] Since *continuous dream* reading proved difficult to maintain, many took Descartes to mean that we might simply be dreaming at any given instance, because dream experiences are sometimes indistinguishable from waking ones.[41] However, if Descartes's intention is to suggest that the meditator might have never perceived reality as it is (and neither has anyone else), the *any-instance* reading seems insufficient. Some have then questioned whether the scenario has to do with distinguishing dreaming and waking at all but, rather, whether even waking experience should be taken as providing reliable cognitive access to the world.[42]

However, the simplest way to grasp the dreaming scenario in the *Meditations* is to look at its resolve. What most take as the resolution of dreaming comes at the end of the Sixth Meditation: 'I now notice that there is a vast difference between [dream and awake], in that dreams are never linked by memory with all the other actions of life as waking experiences are'.[43] This resolve is seen by many as *ad hoc*[44], and it would surely be such, if it was the only resolution to the dreaming doubt. However, by this point the meditator has discovered her true cognitive nature and has full use of her intellect, memory, and free will. Metaphysical knowledge of her epistemic

---

38 Cf. SEXTUS EMPIRICUS, *M* VII, 403-408. However, see CICERO, *Acad.* 2.28.90. Cicero does not generalize that our whole cognitive experience might be false but offers a version of the dream argument that is close to Descartes's, though still running dreaming and madness together. Of course, Cicero's argument is directed at the Stoic doctrine of cognitive impressions, which claims there *to be* inherent criteria to distinguish between veridical and non-veridical impressions. Note that in both Cicero and Descartes, the interlocutor does view dreaming as epistemically *unreliable* compared to being awake.
39 Cf. CARRIERO, *Between Two Worlds*, p. 44. Focusing on other instances of dreaming, Descartes's willingness to experiment with the scenario comes apparent. He phrases the doubt as the indistinguishability of dreaming and waking in the *Principia philosophiae*, I, art. 4, AT VIIIA 6; CSM I 194, as a possibility of continuous dreaming in *La recherche de la vérité par la lumière naturelle*, AT X 511; CSM II 408, and as a comparison between dream and waking experiences in the *Discours de la Méthode*, IV, AT VI 32, 28; CSM I 127, 130, approaching Sextus's account of dreaming.
40 WALSH, *Metaphysics*, p. 91; KENNY, *Descartes*, p. 16; MICHAEL WILLIAMS, "Descartes and the Metaphysics of Doubt", in *Essays on Descartes' Meditations*, ed. by A. O. Rorty, Berkeley & Los Angeles, University of California Press, 1986, p. 128.
41 FRANKFURT, *Demons, Dreamers, and Madmen*, p. 70-72; HATFIELD, *Routledge Philosophy Guidebook to Descartes and the* Meditations, p. 76.
42 WILSON, *Descartes*, p. 17-31; JAMES D. STUART, "The role of dreaming in Descartes' *Meditations*", *Southern Journal of Philosophy* 21/1 (1983), p. 97-108.
43 *Meditationes de prima philosophia*, VI, AT VII 89; CSM II 61.
44 *Meditationes de prima philosophia*, 3rd Objections, AT VII 195-196; CSM II 137; cf. KENNY, *Descartes*, 30.

character allows her to recognize the cause of her errors, which removes the reason for the dreaming doubt (inability to distinguish between reliable and non-reliable sensory cognition). She realizes that in relation to natural habits, senses do reliably access reality more often than not.[45]

The meditator is not searching for an epistemic criterion to distinguish between dreaming and waking. Rather, her inquiry is about delving into the causes of her errors in order to know whether she can reach errorless cognition. Dream experiences are clearly false; they do not reach a cognitive access to reality as it is.[46] The dream scenario demonstrates that we are incapable of knowing whether we reach such errorless sensory access, because we cannot distinguish between those experiences that are veridical and those that are not. Reading the dream scenario as based on the indistinguishability of erroneous and errorless cognition, Descartes does not take the epistemic stand of dreaming and waking experience being the same.[47] Dreaming is intended to make us consider that things might not be as they appear and question the background of veridical sensation as a norm. Descartes then does not have to make the meditator consider that there have been actual cases of errorless sensation nor that she is dreaming all the time. It suffices that she is unable to tell whether her cognition is bereft of error and her experience of objects comes from outside or not.[48]

Dreaming suggests that erroneous sensation might be the natural order, undermining the meditator's cognitive foundation and providing a reason to put aside her naïve convictions regarding access to reality. It prepares the meditator to distinguish between sensation and imagination, which was touched on in the madness paragraph

---

45 *Meditationes de prima philosophia*, VI, AT VII 89; CSM II 61. Cf. *Meditationes de prima philosophia*, 3rd Replies, AT VII 195-196; CSM II 137: "An atheist can infer that he is awake on the basis of memory of his past life [but not] that he is not mistaken, if he does not know that he was created by a non-deceiving God." One has to be aware of the author of one's nature and the reasons for one's errors before the dreaming doubt can be resolved.
46 Cf. *Meditationes de prima philosophia*, 3rd Replies, AT VII, 195-196; CSM II, 137: "[E]veryone admits that a man may be deceived in his sleep. But afterwards, when he wakes up, he will easily recognize his mistake."
47 Cf. CHRISTOFIDOU, *Self, Reason, and Freedom*, p. 21-22. Descartes seems to give a new version of the scenario in the Sixth Meditation: "[E]very sensory experience I have ever thought I was having while awake I can also think of myself as sometimes having while asleep; and since I do not believe that what I seem to perceive in sleep comes from things located outside me, I did not see why I should be any more inclined to believe this of what I think I perceive while awake". *Meditationes de prima philosophia*, VI, AT VII 77; CSM II 53. This rephrasing, along with the version in the *Discours de la Méthode*, have been taken as evidence for the reading of whether we should take even wakeful experience as veridical data. Wilson, *Descartes*, p. 24; Stuart, "The role of dreaming in Descartes' *Meditations*", p. 99-101. However, we can also read the rephrase to support the indistinguishability reading: We do not take dream objects to be located outside of ourselves; thus, we should withhold judgment on sensory objects that we think we perceive while awake but could just as well be perceiving while asleep.
48 Cf. WAGNER, *Squaring the Circle in Descartes's* Meditations, p. 54-56. Wagner though suggests that Descartes's "strong validation of reason" project means that he must always raise the strongest possible doubt; thus, that no external objects exist, and the meditator is dreaming all the time. However, I take the meditative exercise as not requiring the strongest doubt at every level due to its gradual process.

and is brought up in full form in the later analogy between dreaming and painting.[49] The meditator, thus, moves from questioning some sensory beliefs at certain times to questioning all sensory cognition at any given time, temporarily putting aside the common-sense view of everyday naïve realism.

6. Conclusion

In this chapter, I have analyzed the madness scenario in the *Meditations*, comparing it with Descartes's other writings about madness and the dreaming scenario that follows it. I argue that the madness scenario is not intended to question the meditator's rational capacities, nor is it turned down in order to emphasize her rationality. Instead, the madness, like the dreaming, has a physiological basis, that places the madmen's errors in the senses and imagination, causing hindrances in the use of cognitive capacities as they are intended. However, the madness scenario is turned down due to its non-general nature: madness is a fault in our capacities and suggests the existence of non-faulty individuals. Dreaming, meanwhile, is a feature of our physiological capacities, affecting all the people some of the time, instead of just some people some of the time. Thus, it works better for the more systematic scenario of suggesting our cognitive grasp to be at fault as a norm. Madness is nevertheless included in the meditative narrative due to its transitive nature: it helps us in accepting what is suggested by the dreaming doubt, changing our attitude from everyday natural life to the skeptical meditative inquiry for locating metaphysical certainty. Thus, the madness scenario plays a crucial role in the meditative exercise.

---

49 Cf. *L'Homme*, XI 174; CSM I, 105, and the *Principia philosophiae*, I, art. 5, AT VIIIA 6; CSM I 194. See also CHRISTOFIDOU, *Self, Reason, and Freedom*, p. 22; Wagner, *Squaring the Circle in Descartes's Meditations*, p. 49, 52-53, 58. It is natural for the meditator to take the dream images as the result of her imagination. Likewise, Aristotelian tradition draws a difference between external and internal senses, with dreaming, imagination, and memory belonging to the internal ones. See e.g., ARISTOTLE, *De Ins.* I, 459a23; *De Mem.* I, 450a24.

FRANCO A. MESCHINI

Malattie e metafisica

*La prova patologica**

▼ ABSTRACT In this chapter, Franco A. Meschini lists the diseases discussed by René Descartes, and then explores their role within Descartes's philosophy, and especially his metaphysics. This is a clear example of a missing spot in Descartes's medicine, as the philosopher failed to produce any treatise on pathology, and the text devoted to therapies is a very short manuscript today collected in Volume XI of AT, namely, the *Remedia et vires medicamentorum*. Despite this striking absence, as pathology (and therapeutics) were major subjects in any medical study, several diseases surface in Descartes's texts, and the philosopher himself repeated several times the ultimate goal of his medical philosophy consists of treating diseases. Yet, Meschini reconstructs the importance of this claim, listing the diseases Descartes discussed throughout his entire *oeuvre*. The chapter contains an important, and by far more complete, very large table containing all the occurrences of diseases in Descartes's works, and their location in the Adam-Tannery edition. The table reveals how much Descartes's involvement with diseases was not merely rethorical or casual, or just forced by Princess Elisabeth of Bohemia, but uncovers his attempt to encompass any specific disease within his natural philosophical approach to medical knowledge. Insofar as he speaks of diseases, Descartes did it in a philosophical way. The second part of the chapter especially deals with some metaphysical diseases. Accordingly, there are at least 3 kinds of metaphysical diseases: madness (i.e., the troubles in the pineal gland), amputation, and dropsy. Meschini thus reconstructs how much the physical issue of any of these diseases later affects the mind in its capability. In this sense, from madness to dropsy, Descartes's uses of diseases acquire a metaphysical stance, insofar as he discusses the limitations of human condition as a strong composition of mind and body, and not a mere aggregation of two substances, and verifies human metaphysical certainty. While diseases surface as borderline

Franco A. Meschini • Università del Salento, Lecce. Contact: <francoaurelio.meschini@gmail.com>

condition that reveals the weakness of the human nature, they also help clarify its nature, as the conclusive lines of the *Meditationes de prima philosophia* shows: "From the fact that God is not a deceiver it follows that in cases like these [namely, when one has no doubt] I am completely free of error. But since the pressure of things to be done does not always allow us to stop and make such a meticulous check, it must be admitted that in this human life we are often liable to make mistakes about particular things, and we must acknowledge the weakness of our nature" (*Meditationes*, VI, AT VII 90; CSM II 62).

▼ KEYWORDS Metaphysical Diseases, Dropsy, Amputation, Pineal Gland, Therapy, Human Nature

a Marta Fattori.
In memoriam

1. Premessa

Nell'ambito degli studi cartesiani dedicati alla medicina, quelli relativi alla malattia sono ancora rari. Ciò non meraviglierà giacché manca pressoché del tutto, tra gli scritti di Descartes, un testo che lasci intravedere una patologia vera e propria[1]. Eppure, la malattia ha attirato fin dagli anni giovanili l'attenzione di Descartes, che non è poi mai venuta meno, con ampie testimonianze anche nel carteggio. Basterà qui ricordare alcune tappe significative lungo l'arco della sua produzione: il 1630

---

* Un primo ringraziamento va a Fabrizio Baldassari, organizzatore del convegno online e curatore di questo volume. Più volte ho fatto ricorso alla sua invidiabile competenza bibliografia. Come in altre circostanza la disponibilità e la sapienza di Giulia Belgioioso mi hanno permesso un confronto proficuo, sempre in grado di aprirmi nuove prospettive, questa volta poi la sua generosa rilettura del testo ha contribuito a renderlo notevolmente più chiaro. Nel ringraziarla per un sodalizio intellettuale che dura da tanti anni devo tuttavia sollevarla dagli eventuali errori e omissioni, la cui responsabiltà è ovviamente solo mia. Un ringraziamento va all'amico e collega Igor Agostini, che generosamente continua a coinvolgermi nelle sue iniziative scientifiche. Flavia Antico, Mattia Galati e Carmine Taddeo, per le ricerche bibliografiche, sono stati preziosi, a loro va l'augurio di proseguire sulla strada dello studio che hanno intrapreso, con la stessa passione che ora li anima. Non posso più ringraziare Marta Fattori che ci ha lasciato il 17 luglio 2021. Alla sua memoria dedico questo testo con il rammarico di non poter più fare tesoro delle sue acute osservazioni e dei suoi insegnamenti.

1 VINCENT AUCANTE (*La philosophie médicale de Descartes*, Paris, PUF, 2006), che rappresenta in questo ambito di studi una delle poche eccezioni, accenna a un'embrionale spiegazione patologica in *Excerpta Anatomica* (AT XI 603/BOP 1172) in cui il filosofo tenta di spiegare le cause dei fuochi non naturali (flemmoni, erisipela, accessi, pleurite), contrapposti a quelli naturali nel cuore, nel cervello e nello stomaco (p. 348) e, non meno interessante, a una patologia fetale, la quale pur non essendo stata sviluppata «a bien été esquissée» (p. 347).

(le lettere a Mersenne del gennaio[2] e aprile[3]); il 1637 (la sesta parte del *Discours*[4]); 1648/1650 (l'*incipit* e la conclusione della prima parte de la *Description du corps humain*[5]). In ognuno di questi scritti la cura e la prevenzione delle malattie figurano sempre per Descartes come principale scopo della medicina e dei suoi interessi medici.

Descartes, tuttavia, non ha relegato il suo interesse per quest'aspetto invero singolare della macchina vivente – la sola (macchina) ad esserne affetta (con differenze anche nell'ambito del vivente stesso, tra *macchine con la mente*[6] e macchine che ne sono prive[7]) – alla sola medicina, ma se n'è servito anche per porre o rispondere a questioni decisive fin nel cuore della sua metafisica e, più in generale, della sua filosofia meccanica e, infine, della sua filosofia morale. Di fatto Descartes non ha mai cessato di confrontarsi con la malattia, le *Meditationes* sono al riguardo emblematiche: nella prima, fa la sua comparsa la follia, nella sesta, l'idropisia e, infine, le meditazioni

---

2 «Je suis marri de votre érysipèle, et du mal de M. M.; je vous prie de vous conserver, au moins jusqu'à ce que je sache s'il y a moyen de trouver une Médecine qui soit fondée en démonstrations infaillibles, qui est ce que je cherche maintenant» (Descartes a Mersenne, gennaio 1630, AT I 105-106; BL 114).

3 «[…] mais je ne désire pas qu'on le sache, afin d'avoir toujours la liberté de le désavouer; et j'y travaille fort lentement, parce que je prends beaucoup plus de plaisir à m'instruire moi-même, que non pas à mettre par écrit le peu que je sais. J'étudie maintenant en chimie et en anatomie tout ensemble, et apprends tous les jours quelque chose que je ne trouve pas dedans les livres. Je voudrais bien être déjà parvenu jusqu'à la recherche des maladies et des remèdes, afin d'en trouver quelqu'un pour votre érysipèle, duquel je suis marri que vous êtes si longtemps affligé» (Descartes a Mersenne, 15 aprile 1630, AT I 137; BL 138).

4 «Il est vrai que celle qui est maintenant en usage, contient peu de choses dont l'utilité soit si remarquable; mais, sans que j'aie aucun dessein de la mépriser, je m'assure qu'il n'y a personne, même de ceux qui en font profession, qui n'avoue que tout ce qu'on y sait n'est presque rien, à comparaison de ce qui reste à y savoir, et qu'on se pourrait exempter d'une infinité de maladies, tant du corps que de l'esprit, et même aussi peut-être de l'affaiblissement de la vieillesse, si on avait assez de connaissance de leurs causes, et de tous les remèdes dont la nature nous a pourvus» (*Discours de la méthode*, VI, AT VI 62; BO 98).

5 «Il n'y a rien à quoi l'on se puisse occuper avec plus de fruit, qu'à tâcher de se connaître soi-même. Et l'utilité qu'on doit espérer de cette connaissance, ne regarde pas seulement la morale, ainsi qu'il semble d'abord à plusieurs, mais particulièrement aussi la médecine; en laquelle je crois qu'on aurait pu trouver beaucoup de préceptes très assurés, tant pour guérir les maladies que pour les prévenir, et même aussi pour retarder le cours de la vieillesse, si on s'était assez étudié à connaître la nature de notre corps, et qu'on n'eût point attribué à l'âme les fonctions qui ne dépendent que de lui, et de la disposition de ses organes» (*Description du corps humain*, AT XI 223-224; BOP 510-512); e così si legge nella conclusione: «Voilà, sommairement, toutes les choses que j'ai ici à décrire, afin que, connaissant distinctement ce qu'il y a en chacune de nos actions qui ne dépend que du corps, et ce qu'il y a qui dépend de l'âme, nous puissions mieux nous servir, tant de lui que d'elle, et guérir ou prévenir leurs maladies» (*Description du corps humain*, AT XI 227; BOP 514-516).

6 Per riprendere la felice espressione di Emanuela Scribano, *Macchine con la mente. Fisiologia e metafisica tra Cartesio e Spinoza*, Roma, Carocci, 2015.

7 Su questa differenza mi permetto di rinviare a Franco A. Meschini, *Considerazioni sulla malattia in Descartes*, in *Sapientia veterum. Scritti di storia della filosofia dedicati a Marta Fattori*, a cura di Massimo L. Bianchi e Riccardo Pozzo, Firenze, Olschki, 2017, p. 141-152: 149.

sono suggellate da un richiamo all'*infirmitas* della natura umana, *infirmitas*, che è più propriamente una malattia ontologica e che Descartes aveva chiamato in causa già nella quarta meditazione.

Nella sua ottima sintesi del pensiero medico cartesiano, *La philosophie médicale de Descartes*, Vincent Aucante ci ha fornito una tavola delle malattie menzionate nel *corpus* cartesiano[8], che con alcune integrazioni e aggiustamenti può costituire uno sfondo per il nostro discorso. Si tratta di integrazioni in parte mie, in parte suggerite dagli studi di Annie Bitbol-Hespériès[9], di Fabrizio Baldassarri[10], infine di indicazioni, tratte dalla stessa *Philosophie medicale* di Aucante, di malattie da lui esaminate analiticamente (cap. VIII), ma non inserite nell'elenco, che in realtà può considerarsi un'appendice e completamento del capitolo VIII. Rispetto alla tavola redatta da Aucante, ho utilizzato, per il lemma, il solo lessico cartesiano, laddove lo studioso francese ha preferito ridurre anche la nomenclatura latina a quella francese e, nella scelta dei lemmi, non ho proceduto ad alcuna riduzione nosografica, per intenderci al lemma figurano anche verbi e aggettivi (al plurale se Descartes usa solo il plurale, al singolare maschile negli altri casi). Come ha già fatto Aucante ho inserito in alcuni casi malattie presenti bensì nel *corpus* cartesiano, ma non negli scritti di Descartes, se, invece, di una malattia parlano sia Descartes sia qualcuno dei suoi interlocutori mi sono per lo più limitato ai luoghi cartesiani. Nondimeno, nonostante le aggiunte e queste accortezze, questo elenco non va inteso come un *index terminorum*, ma come uno strumento di lavoro *in fieri*, non ha infatti pretesa di completezza, si tratta per ciò che riguarda le occorrenze dei singoli lemmi di una scelta e, per ciò che riguarda le malattie, di una ricognizione, che in alcuni casi potrà anche apparire troppo larga e, in altri (anche per questo) lacunosa. Per non appesantire troppo questa tavola delle malattie, ho proceduto ad una semplificazione dell'apparato citazionale con delle abbreviazioni o acronimi per gli scritti cartesiani (v. tav. 1), mentre i rinvii alle edizioni AT e Bompiani sono dati con la sola indicazione delle pagine (la prima indicazione di pagina sarà sempre riferita ad AT e la seconda a Bompiani) e senza l'indicazione del volume, che sarà possibile recuperare con la tav. 2; solo per le lettere verrà indicato anche il numero del volume per AT, non per Bompiani in quanto le lettere sono tutte contenute in un volume. Rispetto alla tavola di Aucante, infine, non ho inserito le indicazioni bibliografiche di opere mediche coeve, cosa che avrebbe portato ad una dilatazione dei tempi non possibile in un lavoro collettaneo come il nostro, sicché la tavola di Aucante anche sotto questo aspetto resta riferimento necessario.

---

8 AUCANTE, *Philosophie médicale*, p. 349-351.
9 ANNIE BITBOL-HESPÉRIÈS, *Sur quelques* errata *dans les textes biomédicaux latins de Descartes, AT XI*, "Bulletin cartésien" XLIV ["Archives de philosophie" 78], 2015, p. 161-168; Eadem, *Une source des textes biomédicaux latins de Descartes, AT XI: les* Observationes *de Johannes Schenck*, in "Bulletin cartésien" XLVI ["Archives de Philosophie" 80], 2017, p. 152-159.
10 FABRIZIO BALDASSARRI, *Il metodo al tavolo anatomico. Descartes e la medicina*, Canterano (Roma), Aracne, 2021, p. 209-224.

Tav. 1

Discours	Dsc	Dioptrique	Dpt	Meditationes	Med
Objectiones	Ob	Responsiones	Resp	Meditations	Medfr
Principia	Princ	Passions	Pass	Excerpta Anatomia	EA
Cogitationes Privatae	CP	Primae cogitationes	PC	Regulae	Reg
Recherche de la vérité	RV	Monde	M	L'Homme	H
Description du corps humain	DCH	Compendium musicae	CM	Notae in programma quoddam	NP
Ep. a Dinet	ED	Ep. a Voetius	EV	Coll. con Burman	CB
Naissance de la paix	NdP	Remedia	Rm	Cartesius	Cart
Lett. a Beeckman	aBk	Lett. a Condren	aCn	Lett. a Debaune	aD
Lett. a Elisabetta	aE	Lett. da Elisabetta	dE	Lett. a Mersenne	aM
Lett. a Regius	aR	Lett. da Regius	dR	Lett. a Plempius	aP
Lett. a Newcastle	aN	Lett. a Vorstius	aV	Lett. a Hyperaspistes	aH
Lett. a Arnauld	aA	Lett. da Arnauld	dA	Lett. a Reneri per Pollot	aRnxPl
Lett. a Picot	aPc	Lett. a More	aMr	Lett. da More	dMr
Lett. a Meyssonnier	aMs	Lett. a Huygens	aHg	Lett. a Chanut	aCh
Lett. a Balzac	aB	Lett. a Villebressieu	aVill	Lett. a Wilhem	aW
Lett. a Pollot	aPl	Lett. a Colvius	aCl		

Tav. 2

Lettere	AT I-V	BL	CM	AT X	BOP
Dsc	AT VI	BO	CP	AT X	BOP
Dpt	AT VI	BO	Reg	AT X	BOP
Med	AT VII	BO	RV	AT X	BOP
Ob	AT VII	BO	M	AT XI	BOP
Resp	AT VII	BO	H	AT XI	BOP
ED	AT VII	BO	DCH	AT XI	BOP
Princ	AT VIII	BO	Pass	AT XI	BO
EV	AT VIII-2	BO	EA	AT XI	BOP
Medfr	AT IX	—	Rm	AT XI	BOP
			PC	AT XI	BOP
			Cart	AT XI	BOP
			CB	AT V	BOP
			NP	AT V	BOP
			NdP	AT V	BOP

Tavola delle malattie

abscessus	EA 603/1172
abscissus	aP (3 ottobre 1637) I 420/430; Med 77/782; Princ 320/2196; Cart 649/1396
accidents: on voit divers accidents, qui, ne nuisant à rien qu'à quelque nerf, ôtent le sentiment…	Dpt 109/158
affaiblir le cerveau	aM (23 novembre 1646) IV 565/2342
affaiblissement de la vieillesse	Dsc 62/98
alterer: le poumon	aE (maggio o giugno 1645) IV 219/2020
alterer: les humeurs	aE (1 settembre 1645) IV 283/2076
amentes	Med 19/704; 4Ob 204/954; 4Resp 228/988
amputatus (v. abscissus)	aP (3 ottobre 1637) I 420/430; aP (23 marzo 1638) II 66/600; Pass 351/3260; Cart. 649/1396
angina	aV (19 giugno 1643) III 689/1774
apoplecticus	aA (29 luglio 1648) V 219/2576
apostème	dE (29 novembre 1646) IV 579/2354; aE (dicembre 1646) IV 589/2358; dE (21 febbraio 1647) IV 618/2398; dE (11 aprile 1647) IV 630/2412
asciticus	aR (novembre 1641) III 440/1530
asthmaticus	EA EA 606/1176
aveugle	Dpt 84-876/ 122-126
aveugle (né)	dE (10 ottobre 1646) IV 523/2312; Dpt 84/122
blessure d'un boulet	aM (28 ottobre 1640) III 210/1304
blessure dans l'oeil	Dpt 131/188
blessures et maladies qui, n'offensant que le cerveau seul, empêchent généralement tous les sens	Dpt 109/158
boiteux (nés)	Pass 465/2498; dE (10 ottobre 1646) IV 523/2312
borgne	Pass 465/2498
bossus (e bossus nés)	Pass 465/2498; dE (10 ottobre 1646) IV 523/2312
caecus, caecus natus (a nativitate caecus)	aP (3 ottobre 1637) I 417/426; aX*** (agosto 1641) III 432/1524; Reg 438/780
calculus	NP 358/2272
calculus in vesicis renibusque	Rm 643/1218
castrati: barbam non habeant, et sint imbecilliores, et vocem habeant acutiorem	PC 525/964
catarrheuse (cervelle)	dE (29 novembre 1646) IV 581/2356
cerveau troublé et offusqué	Medfr 14
ceux qui n'ont pas le cerveau bien rassis	aE (22 febbraio 1649) V 281/2628
ceux qui ont été mordus par des chiens enragés	aMs (29 gennaio 1640) III 20/1146
cicatrice v. eccroissement de chair	aM (30 luglio 1640) III 122/1230
circulatio sanguinis: impedita circulatione (v. gangraena)	aR (dicembre 1641) III 458/1544
colique; morbus cholicus	dH (14 marzo 1644) IV 772/1900; EA 605/1176
contusion	aRnxPl (aprile o maggio 1638) II 44/654

convulsion des nerfs du visage	aE (maggio 1646) IV 410/2200
convulsion/convulsio	aM (11 marzo 1640) III 42/1164; aR (dicembre 1641) III 459/1546; DCH 225/512; EA 603/1172
corps défecteux	Pass 351/2360
corrompre: quelqu'une des principales parties du corps se corrompt (v. mort)	Pass 330/2336
corruptio sive putrefactio (v. gangraena)	aR (dicembre 1641) III 458/1544
coupé [le reste du bras] v. amputation	aM (11 giugno 1640) III 84/1200
coupure	aRnxPl (aprile o maggio 1638) II 44/654
defaillance: v indispositions du corps	Pass 419/2442
défauts de la vue / defauts de l'œil, defaut de ceux qui ne voient pas bien les objets un peu éloignés que les proches, ou les proches que les éloignés	aCl (5 ottobre 1646) IV 518/2302; Dpt 84/122; Dpt 150/212; Dpt 164-165/230; 198/274
delirus/deliro	5Ob 271/1044; 7Ob passim; 7Resp 461/1260
demens	Med 19/704
dementia: laetum dementiae genus	aBk (17 ottobre 1630) I 162/160
désordenner [se]: mon corps	dE (22 giugno 1645) IV 234/2034
désordres: qui arrivent dans le corps	aE (maggio 1646) IV 411/2200
difficulté de respirer	dR (ottobre-novembre 1639) I 54/1064
dispositio sive facultas ad morbos contrahendos: infantes nascantur cum quadam dispositione sive facultate ad illos [morbos] contrahendos.	NP 358/1598
disproportion entre les parties solides et les fluides (v. vieillesse)	DCH 250 / 546
dolor	aB (17 ottobre 1630) I 164/ 165; Med 74-88/778-798; Princ 32-35 / 1758-1762; Princ 320/2196
dolores capitis	aR (dicembre 1641) III 459/1544
douleur	aE (6 ottobre 1645) IV 310-312; 315 / 2102;-2104 2106; aE (gennaio 1646) IV 355 / 2138; aE (22 febbraio 1649) V 282 /2628; Dpt 131/188; Pass 338/2346; 398-399/2418; H 144 /402; M 6 / 218
douleur a l'oeil	Pass 424/2448
douleur proprement dit	aM (11 giugno 1640) III 85/1200
éblouissement de la vue	aM (4 marzo 1630) I 126/130
éblouissement, ou vertige, qui trouble les fonctions de l'imagination	H 172/452
eccroissement de chair qui [sort] par le trou de la cicatrice (histoire de la soit qui croît au front d'une fille)	aM (30 luglio 1640) III 122/1230
empêchement de l'urine	aM (4 gennaio 1643) III 611/1694
enflure: au bras	dE (30 giugno 1648) IV 195/2558
enragés	aM (1 aprile 1640) III 20/1146
épilepsie	aM (23 novembre 1646) IV 565/2342; aPc (8 giugno 1647) II 324/2476
érysipèle	aM (15 aprile 1630) I 137/138; EA 603/1172

estropié	NP 621/1420
excrescentiæ: carnium excrescentiæ non naturales	EA 522/960
faiblesse ou indisposition du corps	aPl (1648) V 557/2510
febris ephemera: ephemeram febrim	PC 536/980
febris intermittentis	dP (gennaio 1638) I 499/494; aP (15 febbraio 1638) I 532s/524
febris quartana	PC 537/980
febris quotidiana	PC 536/980
febris tertiana	PC 537/980
fièvre /febris	(*passim*) cf. soprattutto: aP (15 febbraio 1638) I 533/524; aR (dicembre 1641) III 458/1544; aN (aprile 1645) IV 190-191/1986-1988; aE (18 maggio 1645) IV 201/2008; aE (22 febbraio 1649) V 282/2628; Pass 479/2516; Pass 486/2524; PC 536-537/978-980; EA 602s/1172s
fièvre lente	aE (18 maggio 1645) IV 201/2008; dE (24 maggio 1645) IV 208/2014
fluxions [les] et les autres maux de tête	aPc (2 novembre 1646) IV 563/2340
folie [sempre con significato metaforico]	Dsc 15/40; RV 503/834
fou	Medfr IX 14; aN (23 novembre 1646) IV 574/2350; 4Obfr IX 159; 4Resfr IX 177
frénetiques	Dpt 141/201
gangraena, gangrène	aP (3 ottobre 1637) I 420/430; aR (dicembre 1641) III 458/1544; Princ 320/2196; aM (28 ottobre 1640) III 210/1304
goutte	aCn (2 dicembre 1630) I 188/182; aD (30 aprile 1639) II 542/1014; aPc (29 luglio 1644) II 217/1924; aM (23 novembre 1646) IV 565/2342; aPc (8 giugno 1647) II 324/2476
hébéte / hébét /hebetus	aMs (29 gennaio 1640) III 20/1144; Dsc 57/90; Pass 386/2402; Reg 425/764
hémicrânie [AT: haemorrhagia][11]	EA 607/1178
hermaphroditus	EA 584/1148; PC 524/962
humor febrilis	aP (gennaio 1638) I 499/494
hydrops, hydropicus; hydropiques	Med 84/792; Med 85/792; Med 89/798; 2Resp 143/870; 2Resp 145/872; 4Resp 234/994; RV 500/830
ictericus	Med 145/872; 2Resp 145/872; Reg 423/762
ictericus morbus	Reg AT X 423/762
idiopathia	aR (dicembre 1641) III 457/1542
ignes non naturales (phlegmones, erysipelates, abscessus, pleuritides, etc.)	EA 603/1172
imbecillis: v. castrati; semen.	PC 525/964; PC 508/940

---

11 Seguo la correzione del tutto convincente di BITBOL-HESPÉRIÈS, *Sur quelques* errata …, op. cit. p.. 167; ovviamente alle pagine di ATe BOP, indicate nella tabella, si trova haemorrhagia.

imbecillitas: aurium imbecillitas	CM 98/42
indisposition: souvent l'indisposition qui est dans le corps empêche que la volonté ne soit libre	aE (1 settembre 1645) IV 282/2074
indisposition… naturelle	aE (marzo o giugno 1645) IV 221/2020
indispositions du corps, qui peuvent faire qu'on tombe ainsi en défaillance	Pass 419/2442
indispositions, qui ne troublent pas | tout à fait les sens, mais altèrent seulement les humeurs	aE (1 settembre 1645) IV 283/2076
infantes morbis istis in utero matris laborent	NP 358/2272
infecte [une certaine rosée] les passants	dE (23 agosto 1648) V 226/2584
infecter: le reste du corps par ses vapeurs	dE (24 maggio 1645) IV 208/2014
infirmitas	Med 62/762; Med 90/798; Princ 13/1726; Princ 92/1852
infirmité	Medfr 7; Pass 453/2484
insani: insani[s], quorum cerebella tam contumax vapor ex atra bile labefactat	Med 18/704
insensé	Dsc 57/90
jaunisse	Dsc 39/68; Dpt 142/202
laesa imaginatione, ut melancholicis accidit	Reg 423/726
laesa matris imaginatione	PC 518/954
laesa… (nervis) medulla	EA 605/1176
laesio	Med 81/788; Princ 318/2192
le corps cesse entièrement de croître, et même aussi qu'il ne peut plus se nourrir (v. vieillesse)	DCH 250/546
lethargia	dA (3 giugno 1648) V 186/2548
lethargicus / léthargique	aA (29 luglio 1648) 219/2576, aM (1 aprile 1640) III 49/1172; sRep 356-357/1156
mal aux yeux [ceux qui ont]	Dpt 353/470
mal de poumon [mère qui mourut d'un]	aE (marzo o giugno 1645) IV 121
malade: nos matelots ont été malades depuis peu à cause de la mauvaise odeur des espagnols qu'ils avaient prisonniers dans leurs navires	aHg (12 dicembre 1639) II 695/1084
malades d'esprit	aVill (estate 1631) I 261/204
maladie [de la glande]/maladie […] dues à une alteration de la g.p.	aM (30 luglio 1640) III 123/1230
maladie de ceux qui sont aveuglément curieux	Pass 386/2402
maladie de l'esprit	Dsc 62/96-98
maladie de l'humeur cristalline	aM (30 luglio 1640) III 123/1228
maladie universelle	aCh (maggio 1648) V 183/2546; RV 500/830
maladie: il retient en lui une humeur chagrine qui le tourmente toujours en son intérieur. Cela se doit, ce me semble, plutôt appeler maladie que vice,	aHg (17 dicembre 1639) II 704/1094

maladie: la maladie de Mr de Clairsellier m'a davantage surpris, et toutefois elle n'est pas sans exemple, et, selon ce que vous m'en écrivez, je ne la juge aucunement mortelle ni incurable.	aM (23 novembre 1646) IV 565/2342
maladie: quelque grande maladie	H 172/452
maladies [qui sont] fort longtemps à s'en aller	aW (24 giugno 1640) III 93/1206
maladies [causées par] la chaleur de l'air	aM (13 novembre 1639) II 624/1072
maladies du corps	Dsc 62/96; aE (settembre 1646) IV 492/2286
[maladies] qui se passent en peu de jours	aW (24 giugno 1640) III 93/1206
maladies qui ont été plusieurs années à se former	aW (24 giugno 1640) III 93/1206
maladies qui ôtent tout à fait le pouvoir de raisonner	dE (16 agosto 1645) IV 269/2064; aE (1 settembre 1645) IV 282/2074
maladies qui viennent fort vite	aW (24 giugno 1640) III 93/1206
manum gravi morbum affectam	Princ 320/2196
marques d'envie	aM (1 aprile 1640) III 49/1172; aM (30 luglio 1640) III 120/1228; Dpt 129/186
materia febrilis, materia febrium, febris	dP (gennaio 1638) I 499/494; aP (15 febbraio 1638) I 532-533/524; aR (dicembre 1641) III 458/1544
mauvais temperament du sang qui causent la tristesse	aE (maggio o giugno 1645) IV 220/2018
mauvaise disposition des organes	aRnxPl (aprile o maggio 1630) II 38/650
maux de tête (v. fluxions)	aPc (2 novembre 1646) IV 563/2340
mélancoliques qui ... pensent avoir quelque partie du corps d'une grandeur énorme [dismorfismo corporeo]	RV 511/842
mélancoliques/melancholici; mélancolie	aE (18 agosto 1645) IV 276/2070; aE (novembre 1646) IV 532/2318; RV 511/842; Reg 423/762; dE (22 giugno 1645) IV 233/2032; dMr (23 luglio 1649) V 378/2712
mola: [non generatur animal, sed mola]	PC 508/940
monstrosa membra [fœtus] (ex laesa matris imaginatione fœtus monstrosa membra sortitur)	PC 518/954
monstrum: cur aliquando fiunt monstra	PC 524/964
morbi animi	CP 215/1062
morbi corporis	aX*** (1628) I 10/36; CP 215/1062; Cart 653/1402
morbi mentis	CP 215/1062; Cart 653/1402
morbi varii, solum cerebrum afficientes, omnem sensum tollant, vel perturbent	Princ 319/2194
morbus	Med 84/792; 3Resp 172/908
morbus: fieri potest ut, morbo lapsis crinibus, ista cuticula densetur, crisisque renascantur, cum prius fuissent plane recti; quod in quodam observavi.	EA 633/1210
mort [par vieillesse v.]	DCH 250/546
mort: la mort n'arrive jamais par la faute de l'âme, mais seulement parce que quelqu'une des principales parties du corps se corrompt	Pass 331/2336

[mort]: elle [l' âme] s'en sépare entièrement [du corps], lorsqu'on dissout l'assemblage de ses organes.	Pass 351/2360
mourir: ils meurent plutôt à cause que l'urine ne peut entrer en la vessie, qu'à cause qu'elle n'en peut plus sortir.	aM (4 gennaio 1643) III 611/1694
mourir: on meurt lorsque le feu qui est dans le coeur s'éteint tout à fait	Pass 418/2440
muet	aN (23 novembre 1646) IV 574-575/2350-2352
nain	aM (2 novembre 1646) IV 548/2328
obstructions (temperament sujet aux) ; partie du sang qui causent des obstructions	dE (24 maggio 1645) IV 208/2014; aE (maggio o giugno 1645) IV 220/2020
obstructions [de la vessie]	aM (4 gennaio 1643) III 611/1694
opiler: la rate	dE (24 maggio 1645) IV 208/2014; aE (maggio o giugno 1645) IV 219/2020
ôter [...] le pouvoir de raissonner: v. maladies	dE (16 agosto 1645) IV 269/2064; aE (1 settembre 1645) IV 282/2074
ôter l'appétit	aE (maggio 1646) IV 409/2198
ôter l'appétit: causes qui ôte l'appétit aux malades	aN (ottobre 1645) IV 327/2096
ôter la vie	DCH 250 / 546
ôter: le mouvement sans ôter le sentiment	Dpt 110/160
ôter: le sentiment	Dpt 109/158
palpitatio	aR (dicembre 1641) III 458/1544
pâmoison /pâmer	Pass 418/2440; 486/2524
paralysie / paralysis	Dpt 110/160; EA 605/1176
peste /pestis	aB (5 maggio 1631) I 204/198; EV 40/1536; EA 606/1176
petit mal [ce]	aE (dicembre 1646) IV 589/2358
phlegmon	EA 603/1172
phreneticus	aA (29 luglio 1648) V 219/2576
phthisicus	EA 606/1176
pleurésie: fausse pleurésie	dR (ottobre-novembre 1639) I 54/1064
pleuritides	EA 603/1172
podagra	NP 358/2272
poison/venin; empoissonné	Med 83-84/790-792; a Pl (1648) V 558/2510
pus	aM (30 luglio 1640) III 142/1244
pustula	EA 598/1168
putrefactio: corruptio sive putrefactio (v. gangraena)	aR (dicembre 1641) III 458/1544
qui hepate carebat: noto historiam illius qui hepate carebat, sed omnia intestina magis carnosa	EA 594/1158
rabies	aV (19 giugno 1643) III 689/1774
rejeter (v. vomir)	Pass 402/2422
renis: exstatque apud bauhinum insignis historia cujusdam qui habebat renem sinistrum juxta vesicam locatum et alia vasa miro modo disposita.	EA 591/1156
rheumatisma (v. catarrheuse)	aM (1635-1636) IV 698/324 [AUCANTE: a Bloswel]?

ris [...] sardonienne (v. convulsione des nerfs)	aE (maggio 1646) IV 410/2200
sanguinis per nares profluvium	aM (1635-1636) IV 698/324
sarcomata	EA 522/960
scorbutus	EA 607/1178
semen imbecillum: ex parentibus semen sit ita imbecillum	PC 508/940
sourd	dE (10 ottobre 1646) IV 523/2312
sourds et muets	aN (23 novembre 1646) IV 575/2352; Dsc 57/92
stupide	Dsc 57/90; Pass 385/2402
stupidi et mente capti: maxime stupidi et mente capti	aMr (5 febbraio 1649) V 278/2624
sublata [una parte corporis]	Cart 649/1396
tempérament du sang [...] corrompu	aN (ottobre 1645) IV 327/2096
tête monstreuse	aM (2 novembre 1646) IV 548/2330
tomber en defaillance	Pass 418/2442

toux: qui à la long serait fort à craindre	aE (maggio o giugno 1645) IV 219/2020
toux sèche	aE (18 maggio 1645) IV 201/2008; aE (maggio o giugno 1645) IV 221/2020
tristesse [v. mauvais temperament du sang; fièvre lente]	aE (maggio o giugno 1645) IV 220/2018; aE (18 maggio 1645) IV 201/2008; dE (24 maggio 1645) IV 208/2014
trouble [qui]les fonctions de l'imagination (v éblouissement)	(H) 172/452
troubler: la digestion	aE (21 luglio 1645) IV 252/2050
troubler: la santé	dE (30 novembre 1645) IV 335/2118
troubler: les sens, la raison (v. indisposition)	aE (1 settembre 1645) IV 282-283/2074-2076
troubles de l'esprit dus aux vapeurs de bile noir.	Med 19/44
troubles du cerveau	Dsc 58/92
tussis	EA 606/1176
valetudinarius	CB 179/1306
valetudo	aH (agosto 1641) III 423/1514
varices	ED 565/1428
ventre [...] percé d'un coup d'épée	aM (30 luglio 1640) III 140/1242
vérole	dBr (4 dicembre 1647) V 93/2496
vertige (cf. éblouissement)	H 172/452
vieillesse [cf. affaibblissement]	Dsc 62/98; DCH 224/510; DCH 250/546; aHg (4 dicembre 1637) I 649/472
vieillesse: la vieillesse seule ôte la vie (v. disproportion)	DCH 250/546
vomir: l'estomac cesse de faire son office, et est enclin à vomir et rejeter les viandes qu'on a mangées, ou du moins à les corrompre et convertir en mauvaises humeurs	Pass 402/2422; Pass 408/2430

Questo elenco, pur nella sua provvisorietà ed eterogeneità, può fornirci alcune prime indicazioni su come Descartes si riferisce alle malattie, indicandole in vari modi:
a) in base al nome della malattia stessa: abcès, angina, apostème, blessure, convulsion/ convulsio, epilepsie, eresypele, fievre, gangraena/gangrène, goutte, hémicrânie, hydrops, idiopatie, jaunisse, laesio, léthargie, morbus cholicus, palpitatio, pâmoison, paralysie/paralysis, peste/pestis, phlegmon, pleuritides, podagra, pustula, rabies, sarcomata, scorbutus, tussis / toux, vulnus.
b) In base alla denominazione di colui che è affetto dalla malattia: amentes, apoplecticus, asciticus, asthmaticus, aveugle, boiteux, borgne, bossus, caecus natus, caecus, castrati, delirus, demens, hébéte/hébét/hebetus, hydropicus, insensé, lethargicus, mélancoliques/melancholici, mentecapti, monstrum, muet, nain, phreneticus / frénetiques, phthisicus, sourds et muets, stupide.
c) In base all'organo o parte o funzione colpiti dalla malattia o malformazione: capitis dolores; défauts de la vue; éblouissement, ou vertige, qui trouble les fonctions de l'imagination; maladie de la glande; maladie de l'humeur cristalline; monstrosa membra; semen imbecillum; tête monstreuse; troubles du cerveau.
d) In base all'azione che caratterizza un malessere o una malattia (verbo più organo colpito): affaiblir, altèrer, careo, couper, empêcher, laedo, opiler, ôter, pamer, rejeter, tomber, troubler.
e) In base al verbo specifico che definisce uno stato patologico o mortale: mourir, se corrompre, vomir.
f) In base alla causa delle malattie: [maladies causées par la] chaleur de l'air, troubles de l'esprit dus aux vapeurs de bile noir.
g) In base agli effetti delle malattie: maladies qui ôtent tout à fait le pouvoir de raisonner; divers accidents, qui [...] ôtent le sentiment; ôter l'appétit aux malades; la vieillesse seule ôte la vie.
h) In base al decorso della malattia: maladies qui vient fort vite; maladies qui ont été plusieurs années à se former; maladies [qui sont] fort longtemps à s'en aller; [maladies qui] se passent en peu de jours.
i) In base alle due sostanze che compongono l'uomo: maladie du corps, morbi corporis, morbi mentis, morbi animi, troubles de l'esprit.
j) In base a termini generali come: accidents, affaiblissement, defaillance, imbecillitas, indisposition, infirmitas / infirmité, mal, maladie, mauvaise disposition, morbus, obstructions, trouble, valetudo (a volte usati assolutamente a volte specificati).
k) In base all'eziologia della morte: parce que quelqu'une des principales parties du corps se corrompt; lorsqu'on dissout l'assemblage de ses organes; lorsque le feu qui est dans le coeur s'éteint tout à fait; ils meurent plutôt à cause que l'urine ne peut entrer en la vessie, qu'à cause qu'elle n'en peut plus sortir; par la vieillesse.

Una prima conclusione che si può già trarre dalla semplice considerazione della nomenclatura è che in Descartes, pur a fronte di una notevole messe di dati, manca un qualsiasi tentativo di classificazione, ciò che sembra confermare il poco interesse di Descartes per la nosologia propriamente detta, anche se è plausibile che il filosofo avesse una conoscenza di testi come la *Pathologia* di Jean Fernel, visto che la cita con precisione (*Path*. l. 4, c. 9), a proposito delle febbri,[12] e le *Observationes medices rariores* di J. Schenck[13]. Peraltro, questo disinteresse non è bilanciato da un suo interesse clinico, Descartes non è un medico (lo ribadisce egli stesso[14]) e, al di là di alcuni consulti in favore di amici[15] e di visite di cortesia[16], non emette diagnosi e non prescrive se non raramente terapie[17]. Un caso a parte è rappresentato dal carteggio con Elisabetta a beneficio della quale si spinge a esprimere giudizi sulle prescrizioni dei medici di corte e a dare consigli e spiegazioni circa precisi stati patologici della principessa stessa[18]. Non solo, è proprio in quel carteggio che il filosofo accennerà ad una teoria generale della malattia[19] e alle sue conseguenze sull'uomo, in quanto composto di anima e corpo.

D'altro lato, come si dirà più precisamente in seguito, *le malattie* non sono viste (o non sono solo viste) come oggetto di indagine eziologica o terapeutica, non costituiscono in altre parole elementi pensati per una futura patologia *cartesiana*, ma sono introdotte spesso (se si fa eccezione per gli *Excerpta anatomica*), come strumenti di indagine esse stesse, quasi che il patologico rappresenti un potenziamento conoscitivo, nel senso di un'estenuazione del fisiologico, così da configurarsi in diversi casi come *prova patologica*. Potremmo anche dire che il patologico rappresenta per Descartes un esperimento della natura[20] così come l'indagine vivisettoria è non solo un'osservazione della natura viva, in movimento, ma anche un esperimento, una forzatura della natura, per ottenerne risposte[21].

---

12 Nella lettera a Plempius, del 15 febbraio 1638, AT I 53; BL 524).
13 Cf. ANNIE BITBOL-HESPÉRIÈS, *Une source des textes biomédicaux latins de Descartes, AT XI: les Observationes de Johannes Schenck*, in "Bulletin cartésien" XLVI ["Archives de Philosophie" 80], 2017, p. 152-159.
14 Cf. Descartes a Mersenne, 1635/1636, AT IV 698; BL 323-325; a Mersenne, 23 novembre 1646, AT IV 565; BL 2343.
15 Cf. Descartes a Mersenne, 1635/1636, AT IV 698-899; BL 323-325; a Mersenne, 12 settembre 1638, AT II 361; BL 865; a Debeaune 30 aprile 1639 AT II 542; BL 1013-1015; a Mersenne, 11 marzo 1640, AT III 42; BL 1165; a Wilhem, 13 giugno 1640, AT III 91; BL 1205; a Wilhem, 24 giugno 1640, AT III 92-93; BL 1207; a Mersenne, 23 novembre 1646, AT IV 565; BL 2343.
16 «... nous avons aussi eu ici plusieurs malades, et je n'ai été occupé tous ces jours qu'à en visiter, et à écrire des lettres de consolation» (Descartes a Mersenne, 21 gennaio 1641, AT III 283; BL 1380).
17 Cf. Descartes a Mersenne, 1635/1636, AT IV 699; BL 324, sempre a Mersenne, lettera del 23 novembre 1646 AT IV 565; BL 2342. Tra gli scritti cartesiani non destinati alla pubblicazione occorre però ricordare a questo proposito un'eccezione costituita dai *Remedia et vires medicamentorum*, e da alcuni rimedi in *Excerpa Anatomica* (AT XI 606-607; BOP 1176). Sulla terapeutica oltre alle pagine dedicatele da AUCANTE, *Philosophie médicale*, p. 375-416, si vedano ora interessanti considerazioni in BALDASSARRI, *Il metodo al tavolo anatomico*, p. 209-224.
18 Descartes a Elisabetta, 8 luglio 1644, AT V 64; BL 1920); a Elisabetta, maggio o giugno 1645, AT IV 220; BL 2020.
19 Cf. Descartes a Elisabetta, 1 settembre 1645, AT IV 281; BL 2075.
20 In questo senso EMANUELA SCRIBANO, "Descartes on Error and Madness", *Rivista di storia della filosofia*, n. 4, 2016, p. 599-613, parla a proposito della follia, nella *Dioptrique* (discorso IV), di esperimento cruciale (cartesiano) per comprendere la fisiologia della percezione. Per più aspetti questo mio contributo è debitore a questo lavoro della studiosa veneziana, in particolare per quanto riguarda la sottolineatura dell'aspetto euristico della follia e in generale della malattia nella fisiologia e metafisica cartesiana.
21 Sono numerosi gli esperimenti fisiologici di Descartes, cf. Descartes a Plempius, 15 febbraio 1638, AT I 527; BL 518, Descartes a Plempius, 23 marzo 1638, AT II 63; BL 596, Descartes a Mersenne, 30 luglio 1640, AT III 139-140; BL 1242; *Description*, AT XI 243; BOP 243.

Infine, quanto al rapporto che s'instaura tra malattia e filosofia, diciamo in via preliminare che esso verte soprattutto sulla relazione tra il cervello o una sua parte e l'anima (*esprit/âme; mens*) e tra il cervello (o una sua parte) e il resto del corpo. Delle malattie o menomazioni conseguenti a traumi che rientrano in questa tipologia esamineremo qui di seguito in particolare le malattie della ghiandola pineale, le amputazioni e l'idropisia[22].

2. La ghiandola pineale

2.1. ... des personnes deviennent troublées d'esprit...

Tra il gennaio del 1640 e i primi mesi del 1641 Descartes mette a punto una dottrina della ghiandola pineale, che aveva già abbozzato ne *L'Homme*, allora inedito, e appena lasciata intravedere nella *Dioptrique*[23]. Sarà nel carteggio che il filosofo darà un'articolata esposizione della dottrina della ghiandola pineale. Lo farà per rispondere ad alcuni interlocutori, Lazare Meyssonier, Cristopher Villiers e Mersenne che si era fatto portavoce di questioni sottopostegli da Jean Cousin[24], oltre a fare da intermediario per Villiers e, in parte di Meyssonier. Proprio nel mezzo di questo fitto scambio epistolare, almeno quindici lettere (non tutte pervenuteci) prendendo lo spunto da un'obbiezione sollevata da Villiers (e riferitagli da Mersenne), Descartes accennerà a un'embrionale patologia della ghiandola pineale:

> Pour la lettre de ce docte Médecin [scil. Villiers], elle ne contient aucune raison pour impugner ce que j'ai écrit de la glande nommée *Conarium*, sinon qu'il dit qu'elle peut être altérée comme tout le Cerveau. Ce qui n'empêche point qu'elle ne puisse être le principal siège de l'âme: car il est certain que l'âme doit être jointe à quelque partie du corps; et il n'y en a point qui ne soit autant ou plus sujette à altération que cette glande, qui, bien que fort petite et fort molle, toutefois est si bien gardée au lieu où elle est, qu'elle n'y peut quasi être sujette à aucune maladie, non plus que l'humeur vitrée ou cristalline de l'oeil. Et il arrive bien plus souvent que des personnes deviennent troublées d'esprit, sans qu'on en sache la cause, auquel cas on la peut attribuer *à quelque maladie de cette glande*, qu'il n'arrive que la vue manque par quelque maladie de l'humeur cristalline; outre que toutes les

---

22 Ciò che segue è stato letto nel convegno online del novembre 2020, "Lights&Shadows in Descartes Medicine", organizzato da Fabrizio Baldassarri e Fabio Zampieri, ed è stato ripresentato e discusso, con delle aggiunte, nella seduta del 20 maggio del seminario "Une science si nécessaire. Médecine et morale à l'époque cartésienne" (gennaio-giugno 2021), organizzato dagli amici Igor Agostini, Fabio A. Sulpizio e dal sottoscritto, presso l'Università del Salento. Sulle amputazioni, si veda il contributo di Jil Muller in questo volume.
23 *Dioptrique* V, AT VI 129; BO 188.
24 Su Jean Cousin mi permetto di rinviare al mio *Neurofisiologia cartesiana*, Firenze, Olschki, 1998, p. 47-54.

altérations qui arrivent à l'esprit, lorsqu'on dort après qu'on a bu etc., peuvent être attribuées à quelques altérations qui arrivent à cette glande.[25]

La risposta di Descartes all'obiezione mossagli da Villiers è sia tesa a neutralizzarne l'obiezione, sia, in secondo luogo, a volgere a proprio favore l'argomento stesso dell'obiettante. Il primo obiettivo lo raggiunge in due passaggi: ribadendo l'assunto di fondo (*il est certain que l'âme doit être jointe à quelque partie du corps*) e negando la validità di ciò che sosteneva l'obiettante. Il *conarium*, scriveva, è sì soggetto ad alterazioni, ma nessuna parte del cervello lo è di meno, semmai di più. Il secondo obiettivo, osservando che, proprio in quanto il *conarium* è passibile di malattie, risulta ora possibile trovare e indicare la causa del perché «des personnes deviennent troublées d'esprit», causa che risiede, appunto, sostiene il filosofo, in «quelque maladie de cette glande». A completare il discorso circa il nesso individuato tra malattia della ghiandola e offuscamenti dell'*esprit*, Descartes pone in relazione tutte le alterazioni che *arrivent à l'esprit*, come l'assopimento dopo aver bevuto, con qualche alterazione della ghiandola (*toutes les altérations qui arrivent à l'esprit, lorsqu'on dort après qu'on a bu etc., peuvent être attribuées à quelques altérations qui arrivent à cette glande*). Ovviamente Descartes usa a ragion veduta *altération* in questo secondo caso, giacché a differenza del caso precedente qui si tratta non di malattie vere e proprie ma di malesseri passeggeri[26].

Le considerazioni svolte qui da Descartes sulla malattia che *trouble l'esprit* interessano non da ultimo perché, mentre risponde a Villiers (la lettera è del 30 luglio 1640), il manoscritto delle *Meditationes* è ancora sul suo tavolo[27] e, quindi, ancora in qualche modo suscettibile di cambiamenti, soprattutto nel momento in cui l'obiezione sollevata da Villiers porta Descartes a considerare (di nuovo) le malattie del cervello. Le attese dello storico, qualora pensasse di trovare dei contatti, restano, però, deluse. Una sinossi tra i due testi mostra, infatti, una loro indipendenza. Detto in altre parole, da un testo all'altro non sembra esserci stato alcun passaggio: Descartes in effetti, (a) risponde a Villiers senza tener conto di ciò che aveva scritto nella prima meditazione (M1) non ancora data alle stampe e (b) non recepisce nel testo a stampa nulla della risposta fatta pervenire al medico di Sens il 30 luglio 1640 per il tramite di Mersenne da Leyda (L1640). Ciò mi pare che si possa affermare alla luce del dato di fatto che i due testi (M1 e L1640) sono tra loro diversi. Per il momento si deve tener fermo che non ci sono tracce di *cambiamenti* in M1 a favore di L1640 e *dipendenze* di L1640 da M1. Ma, allo stesso tempo, nei due testi l'argomento trattato è pressoché lo stesso.

---

25 Descartes a Mersenne, 30 luglio 1640, AT III 123; BL 1230.
26 Definizione di *alteratio* nella lettera di Descartes a Regius di metà dicembre 1640. AT III 461; BL 1548.
27 Nella stessa lettera in cui risponde a Villiers, Descartes comunica a Mersenne d'aver terminato da tempo la Metafisica, ma di non averla ancora data alle stampe (Descartes a Mersenne, AT III 126-127; BL 1232.

Meditatio I	Lettre1640 (AT III 126-127/BL 1232)
me forte comparem nescio quibus insanis, quorum cerebella tam contumax vapor ex atra bile labefactat, ut constanter asseverent vel se esse reges, cum sunt pauperrimi, vel purpura indutos, cum sunt nudi, vel caput habere fictile, vel se totos esse cucurbitas, vel ex vitro conflatos; sed amentes sunt isti, nec minus ipse demens viderer, si quod ab iis exemplum ad me transferrem.	Et il arrive bien plus souvent que des personnes deviennent troublées d'esprit, sans qu'on en sache la cause, auquel cas on la peut attribuer à quelque maladie de cette glande, qu'il n'arrive que la vue manque par quelque maladie de l'humeur cristalline

Dunque, abbiamo due testi contemporanei, quanto alla loro redazione, che si presentano come differenti e indipendenti, ma che sono, tuttavia, analoghi. Analoghi, fino a che punto? Gli *insani*, di cui si parla in M1, che Descartes definisce come *amentes* (e nello stesso luogo è pronto a qualificare l'*ego* meditante come *demens* qualora scegliesse di condividerne il delirio o la stravaganza), sono le *personnes... troublées d'esprit* di L1640? Sembra, come cercherò di corroborare anche con testi paralleli, che la risposta debba essere positiva, e ciò nonostante che la spiegazione causale sia, almeno apparentemente, diversa.

Nel *corpus cartesianum* (CC) sono presenti i corradicali *troubler* (*troublé* p.p.), *trouble* agg., *trouble* sost.; *perturbation*, e quelli latini: *turbo, turbatus, turbator, turbatrix, turbolentia, turbulentus, turba, turbo-inis, turbinatus; disturbo, interturbo, perturbo, perturbatio*[28]. Non è questa la sede per esaminare analiticamente quest'ampia famiglia di termini francesi e latini, qui sarà sufficiente notare in primo luogo, a proposito dei quattro termini francesi, quanto segue: 1) il verbo *troubler* (44 occ.) è usato da Descartes in ambito fisico (fisiologico, ottico, meteorologico, metallurgico), politico, morale, gnoseologico e soprattutto nell'ambito dell'unione di anima e corpo; 2) il sostantivo *trouble* (6 occ.) è usato in ambito politico, morale, dell'unione di anima e corpo; 3) l'aggettivo *trouble* (6 occ.) è usato in ambito fisico (ottico e fisiologico) e gnoseologico; l'unica occorrenza di *perturbation* (*perturbations*) è in una lettera di Elisabetta (*perturbations de l'âme*). Si può dire, dunque, che nel CC i tre termini e soprattutto il verbo assumano quella *polisemanticità* che è loro propria nella lingua francese (i lessicografi dovrebbero dirci se Descartes, nell'ampia gamma di significati registrati nei dizionari, ha solo preso o non invece è anche in credito, ma i lessicografi

---

28 Ho utilizzato l'edizione AT che comprende anche le traduzioni delle opere (*Meditations, Reponses, Principes, Specimina*), i testi degli interlocutori (lettere, colloquio con Burman, *Notae*), i testi degli obiettanti (le *Objectiones /Objections* nel *corpus* delle meditazioni) nonché i testi riportati (nei testi polemici come l'*Epistola ad Voetium* e ai Magistrati). Per l'interrogazione dei testi ho usato <Œuvres Complètes de René Descartes CONNAUGHT DESCARTES PROJECT, ed. by André Gombay assisted by Calvin Normore, Randal Keen and Rod Watkins>, verificandone sempre la corrispondenza con AT. Per la traduzione latina di *Discours* e *Essais*, non presente nell'edizione elettronica del Connaught Descartes Project, ho utilizzato una versione elettronica dell'ottima edizione critica a cura di Corinne Vermeulen, non comprensiva della *Geometria*. L'interrogazione di questi ultimi due testi ha evidenziato la presenza dei seguenti lemmi: *turbo, turba, turbo-inis*.

non hanno mai posto, mi pare, molta attenzione alla lingua di Descartes, salvo e solo marginalmente per il *Discours*).

Almeno 18 sono le occorrenze di *troubler* nel CC relative all'unione di anima e corpo. Eccone alcune: quando l'anima è congiunta al corpo «elle puisse être troublée en ses opérations par la mauvaise disposition des organes»[29]; non c'è alcuna cosa che possa impedirci di essere felici «pourvu qu'elle ne trouble point notre raison»[30]; «pour faire que l'âme ne soit pas troublée[31]»; «... une forte agitation des esprits animaux, qui pourrait entièrement troubler l'imagination de ceux qui n'ont pas le cerveau bien rassis[32]»; nell'ambito delle passioni: «les plus violents efforts des Passions n'ont jamais assez de pouvoir pour troubler la tranquillité de son âme»[33]. Ne *L'Homme*: «un *éblouissement*, ou *vertige*, qui trouble les fonctions de l'*imagination*»[34]; nel *Discours*: «n'ayant d'ailleurs, par bonheur, aucuns soins ni passions qui me troublassent»; e ancoraa: «un enfant des plus stupides, ou du moins un enfant qui aurait le cerveau troublé»[35]. Infine, nella traduzione delle *Meditationes* e delle *Obiectiones et Responsiones*.

Cominciamo dal passo della prima meditazione ove il Duca de Luynes per tradurre «cerebella tam contumax vapor ex atra bile labefactat» fa ricorso a *troublé*[36]:

> ... si ce n'est peut-être que je me compare à ces insensés, de qui *le cerveau est tellement troublé et offusqué par les noires vapeurs de la bile,* qu'ils assurent constamment qu'ils sont des rois, lorsqu'ils sont très pauvres; qu'ils sont vêtus d'or et de pourpre, lorsqu'ils sont tout nus; ou s'imaginent être des cruches, ou avoir un corps de verre[37].

De Luynes traduce, dunque, *cerebella ... labefactat* con *le cerveau est ... troublé et offusqué*. *Labefacio* (mutata la diatesi verbale) è tradotto con *troublé et offusqué*, che formano un'endiadi in cui il secondo membro specifica il primo, giacché un effetto del *troubler* è proprio l'offuscamento e, potremmo dire, è un prestito (di ritorno) dell'esperienza ottica del *troubler*, quasi che il traduttore tenga presente più che l'effetto immediato del vapore proveniente dall'*atra bile*, che è quello di *guastare*[38] il cervello,

---

29 Descartes a Reneri per Pollot, aprile/maggio 1638, AT II 38; BL 650.
30 Descarte a Elisabetta, 1 settembre 1645, AT IV 283; BL 2076.
31 Descartes a Elisabetta, maggio 1646, AT IV 411; BL 2200.
32 Descartes a Elisabetta, 22 febbraio 1649, AT V 281; BL 2628.
33 *Passions*, art. 148, AT XI 442; BL 2470.
34 *L'Homme*, AT XI 172; BOP 452.
35 *Discours de la Méthode*, AT VI 58; BO 92.
36 La definizione di *insani* come *amentes* è, d'altro lato, decisiva, in quanto ci permette, come diremo, di trovare un medio per stabilire un'analogia tra i due casi.
37 Si veda anche la *Recherche de la vérité* in cui parla di *mélancoliques*: «je veux passer outre, pour savoir si vous n'avez jamais vu de ces mélancoliques, qui pensent être cruches ou bien avoir quelque partie du corps d'une grandeur énorme; ils jureront qu'ils le voient et qu'ils le touchent ainsi qu'ils imaginent» (*Recherche de la vérité*, AT X511; BOP 844), ove, per inciso, non si mancherà di notare come qui Descartes faccia riferimento al cosiddetto dismorfismo corporeo, di cui parla solo in questo luogo.
38 Così è ottimamente tradotto *labefacio* in BO 704.

la conseguenza che ciò ha sul vedere, ove il vedere è, però, non tanto una funzione degli occhi quanto della *mens*. Se questa scelta traduttiva appare soddisfacente, corroborata anche dal *cerveau troublé* del *Discours*[39], non altrettanto si può dire per la resa di *contumax vapor ex atra bile*, de Luynes, infatti, tralascia *contumax*, che qui, nel testo latino, misura l'intensità, la persistenza del vapore, in sé stesso non nocivo, ma nocivo proprio perché resistente a rarefarsi[40], laddove il traduttore sembra attribuire l'effetto nocivo piuttosto all'atrabile in quanto tale. Anche la traduzione di *cerebella* merita una riflessione. Si tratta del plurale di *cerebellum*, e in quanto tale rappresenta un *hapax* nel C.C., le altre 10 occorrenze di *cerebellum* sono tutte al singolare. È qui necessario precisare che il plurale latino ha finito con l'essere sentito probabilmente come un singolare[41] e che da esso, in francese, deriva *cervelle* (come in italiano *cervello*[42]) e pertanto non sarà azzardato supporre che in una retroversione di un testo latino scritto da un autore francese *cerebella* lasci intravedere non *cerveau* ma piuttosto *cervelle*, col quale andava forse tradotto, anche perché non in contrasto con l'*usus scribendi* di Descartes, che in due circostanze ricorre a questo termine e proprio per indicare l'essere o l'uscire fuori di senno[43]. In una lettera a Mersenne: «En une 3ᵉ lettre du 20 Sept., vous m'avertissez de celui qui dit qu'il croit que ma Philosophie a bien aidé à troubler la cervelle etc.»; e in un testo particolare come il balletto composto per la regina Cristina, *La Naissance de la Paix*, ove, precisamente nella settima entrata, dedicata ai soldati *estropiés*, Descartes scrive, a proposito di chi pensa che la guerra è bella o migliore della pace, che costui *est estropié de cervelle*: «Qui voit comme nous sommes faits / Et pense que la Guerre est belle, / Ou qu'elle vaut mieux que la Paix,/ Est estropié de cervelle»[44].

Se ora passiamo ad esaminare il versante latino, andrà detto che delle 61 occorrenze dei corradicali in turb*, di cui ben 14 sono nell'*Epistola* a Voetius, solo alcune interessano il nostro tema. A cominciare dal *turbatus sum* con cui l'*ego* meditante descrive il proprio stato d'animo *all'indomani* della radicale eversione provocata dal dubbio: «In profundum gurgitem ex improvviso delapsus, ita turbatus sum, ut nec possim in imo pedem figere, nec enatare ad summum». Anzitutto *delapsus*: il verbo che Descartes usa per esprimere la situazione che segue alla rinuncia di ogni conoscenza indica la caduta, che legittima un confronto con la caduta dei progenitori, lo *status naturae lapsae*. Ciò va detto perché occorre immaginare la drammaticità del momento: l'io si sta incamminando su una strada che era stata interdetta ai progenitori, per di più lo fa rinunciando a Dio. La traduzione francese (*je suis tellement surpris*) rende solo in parte la forza del verbo latino (*turbatus sum*), giacché la sorpresa non è che un aspetto di quella situazione, l'*ego* va qui pensato piuttosto come confuso, agitato, disorientato e la misura di tale disorientamento è manifestata dallo stato

---

39 *Discours*, AT VI 58; BO 92.
40 Cf. Descartes a Plempius, 3 ottobre 1637, AT I 426; BL 434.
41 Cf. *Tresor de la langue Française, sub voce* "cervelle", consultato nella versione informatizzata: *Trésor de la langue Française informatisé*, http://www.atilf.fr/tlfi, ATILF-CNRS & Université de Lorraine.
42 La cui alternativa *cerebro* è termine obsoleto o parte di composti.
43 Una terza occorrenze di *cervelle* in C. C. è della principessa Elisabetta.
44 Descartes, *Naissance de la paix*, AT V 621; BOP 1420.

d'incertezza, giacché l'io è come intorbidito e irretito (*inter inextricabilis tenebras*) «ut nec possim — così dice l'*ego* — in imo pedem figere, nec enatare ad summum». Ma questo stato d'animo è presto superato, il *turbatus sum* cede il posto ad un nuovo tentativo di riprendere la strada intrapresa il giorno prima: «Enitar tamen et tentabo cursus eandem viam quam heri fueram ingressus...». La figura della follia evocata nella prima giornata non offusca, dunque, questo nuovo tentativo. Per un attimo se ne affaccia, però, un'altra: quella dell'irresolutezza (tuttavia non nominata) che può condurre all'inazione. Una malattia (passione) della volontà verrebbe da dire. L'io, può contare, ora, solo sulla sua volontà. A sottolineare la forte tonalità voluntaristica del percorso meditativo. L'io che non conosce ancora l'art. 170 delle *Passions* ha, tuttavia, alle sue spalle il *Discours*, in cui la seconda massima mette proprio in guardia dalle conseguenze dell'irresolutezza.

C'è un altro testo o, meglio, una serie di testi, tra loro strettamente connessi da una forte intertestualità, che ci permettono di ritornare ai due passi da cui siamo partiti. Si tratta di un passo delle quarte *responsiones*, in cui Descartes risponde a una obiezione di Arnauld: «Difficultatem auget, quod illa cogitandi vis corporeis organis affixa videatur, cum in infantibus sopita, in amentibus extincta judicari possit; quod impii animorum carnifices potissimum urgent»[45].

L'obiezione che Arnauld muove a Descartes è, come si sa, rivolta a mettere in dubbio la validità della distinzione reale di anima e corpo, la quale è, a dire di Arnauld, niente più che un'astrazione e, d'altro lato, aggiunge Arnauld, la difficoltà nel concepire tale distinzione aumenta perché la *vis cogitandi* sembra *affixa* agli organi corporei, dal momento che si può ritenere che essa sia sopita nei fanciulli e *morta* (*extinta*) nei dementi (*in amentibus*).

L'obiezione di Arnauld permette a Descartes di ritornare sugli *amentes* (della prima meditazione), con una precisazione questa volta ontologica (che diventerà poi una prova *patologica* dell'alterità tra uomo e animale), in una sintesi in cui è perfettamente rappresentato lo statuto conoscitivo dell'unione e della distinzione ed anche il loro rapporto, successivamente sviluppati nel carteggio con Elisabetta.

> Nec denique ex eo quod vis cogitandi sit in infantibus sopita, in amentibus non quidem extincta sed perturbata, putandum est illam organis corporeis ita esse affixam ut absque iis existere non possit. Ex eo enim quod experiamur sæpe ab ipsis eam impediri nullo modo sequitur ab iisdem produci; neque hoc ulla vel minima ratione probari potest. Verumtamen non inficior arctam illam mentis cum corpore conjunctionem, quam sensibus assidue experimur, in causa esse cur realem ejus ab ipso distinctionem non sine attenta meditatione advertamus[46].

---

45 *Quartae Responsiones*, AT VII 204; BO 954.
46 *Quartae Responsiones*, AT VII 228-229; BO 988. Cf. anche: «Quæ opiniones cum plurimum different ab iis, quas prius de iisdem rebus habueram, cœpi deinde considerare quas ob causas aliter antea credidissem; præcipuamque esse animadverti, quod primum ab infantia varia de rebus Physicis, utpote quæ ad vitæ, quam ingrediebar, conservationem conferebant, judicia tulissem, easdemque postea opiniones, quas tunc de ipsis præconceperam, retinuissem. Cumque mens, illa ætate, minus recte organis corporeis uteretur, iisque firmius affixa nihil absque ipsis cogitaret,

Qui interessa sottolineare l'intervento di Descartes sull'affermazione di Arnauld, che è anche caratterizzato dall'assunzione del lessico dell'interlocutore: *vis cogitandi, sopita, affixa* (termine che Descartes non usa mai in proprio per indicare il modo dell'unione), non tuttavia *extinta*; non si tratta, ovviamente, solo di sfumature. Descartes respinge l'idea di Arnauld secondo cui nell'*amens* la *vis cogitandi* sia estinta, non c'è più, come dire che il folle è privato del pensiero. A suo giudizio, al contrario, la *vis cogitandi* è solo *perturbata*. *Perturbata*, sconvolta, più del *turbatus sum* della seconda meditazione, ma non *extinta*.

Non si tratta, come vedremo, solo di sfumature. Torniamo ora alla domanda che ci siamo posti più sopra, se cioè tra gli *insani* (M1) e le *personnes troublées d'esprit* (L1640) ci sia un'analogia. Avevamo stabilito che non c'è un passaggio dall'uno all'altro testo; avevamo anche accennato al fatto che ci potesse essere una differenza quanto alla causa. Ora, alla luce della risposta di Arnauld (R4) possiamo dire che tra M1 e L1640 effettivamente c'è un'analogia ed è possibile stabilirla grazie all'implicita definizione di *insani*. Possiamo, infatti, affermare che gli *insani* sono *amentes*, e che in essi la *vis cogitandi* è *perturbata*, quindi *troublée*. È così del resto che Clerselier traduce il passo di R4: la facoltà di pensare «est assoupie dans les enfants, et [...] dans les fous elle est, non pas à la vérité éteinte, mais *troublée*»[47]. Torneremo a breve su questo punto, ora dobbiamo fermarci a considerare più da vicino che cosa Descartes afferma in R4 che non abbia già affermato in M1 o in L1640.

... *vis cogitandi* ... [est] *in amentibus non quidem extincta sed perturbata*: il folle che *sragiona* non perde la *vis cogitandi*, il pensiero, pur nella consapevolezza del filosofo che l'anima possa cadere completamente in balia del corpo[48]. Dunque, rispetto a M1 in R4 si precisa un qualcosa in più sulla natura degli insani, che ora sappiamo non essere privi di *vis cogitandi*.

Se poi, accanto al passo di R4 leggiamo la lettera a Newcastle del 23 novembre 1646 (L1646), troviamo la conferma di ciò che abbiamo detto all'inizio, ossia che una situazione di malattia e alterazioni del nostro corpo può trasformarsi in una prova 'patologica' dell'alterità dell'uomo rispetto agli animali:

> Enfin il n'y a aucune de nos actions extérieures, qui puisse assurer ceux qui les examinent, que notre corps n'est pas seulement une machine qui se remue de soi-même, mais qu'il y a aussi en lui une âme qui a des pensées, excepté les paroles, ou autres signes faits à propos des sujets qui se présentent, sans se rapporter à aucune passion. Je dis les paroles ou autres signes, parce que les *muets* se servent de signes en même façon que nous de la voix; et que ces signes soient à propos,

---

res tantum confusas advertebat; et quamvis propriæ suæ naturæ sibi conscia esset, nec minus apud se ideam cogitationis quam extensionis haberet, quia tamen nihil intelligebat, quin simul etiam aliquid imaginaretur, utrumque pro uno et eodem sumebat, notionesque omnes, quas de rebus intellectualibus habebat, ad corpus referebat» (*Sextae Objectiones*, AT VII 440-441; BO 1234-1236).

47 *Objections et résponses* IXa 177.
48 Cf. per esempio la lettera di Descartes a Elisabetta del 1° settembre 1645 già citata. Sulla follia in Descartes, si veda anche il contributo di Jan Forsman in questo volume.

> pour exclure le parler des perroquets, *sans exclure celui des fous, qui ne laisse pas d'être à propos des sujets qui se présentent, bien qu'il ne suive pas la raison* [...]⁴⁹

Come dire che il grado zero di ragione non annulla il pensiero e che il pazzo (*fous*) continua ad essere altro rispetto all'animale⁵⁰. Detto in altre parole, Descartes fornisce la prova più forte dell'alterità dell'uomo rispetto all'animale, estenuando l'umano fino al *grado zero* della sua *vis cogitandi*, che è la perdita della ragione e della comunicazione verbale. Se la sua capacità espressiva è affidata alla parola, alla voce che si fa parola, allora laddove tale capacità comunicativa non c'è sotto questa forma, nel mutismo, essa tuttavia si manifesta con dei segni. Il che significa che il pensiero, la *vis cogitandi*, può essere completamente condizionata dal corpo e, tuttavia, non può mai cessare del tutto. Descartes ne fornisce una prova sperimentale: la capacità di produrre segni, di tradurre in segni e ciò in modo appropriato agli oggetti cui si riferiscono. Diversamente dall'animale che non traduce in segni né ciò per cui è passivo (ma ciò non lo possiamo dimostrare, possiamo solo palesarne la plausibilità), né le proprie *eventuali* rappresentazioni, quell'ente composto di anima e corpo che è l'uomo ha quella capacità sia nel grado zero della comunicazione verbale o vocale (è il caso dei sordomuti), sia nel grado zero della comunicazione razionale (il parlare dei folli). Ciò era stato espresso da Descartes in modo già compiuto, nella quinta parte del *Discours*⁵¹.

---

49 La lettera al Marchese di Newcastle così prosegue: «et j'ajoute que ces paroles ou signes ne se doivent rapporter à aucune passion, pour exclure non seulement les cris de joie ou de tristesse, et semblables, mais aussi tout ce qui peut être enseigné par artifice aux animaux; car si on apprend à une pie à dire bonjour à sa maîtresse, lorsqu'elle la voit arriver, ce ne peut être qu'en faisant que la prolation de cette parole devienne le mouvement de quelqu'une de ses passions; à savoir, ce sera un mouvement de l'espérance qu'elle a de manger, si l'on a toujours accoutumé de lui donner quelque friandise, lorsqu'elle l'a dit; et ainsi toutes les choses qu'on fait faire aux chiens, aux chevaux et aux singes, ne sont que des mouvements de leur crainte, de leur espérance, ou de leur joie, en sorte qu'ils les peuvent faire sans aucune pensée. Or il est, ce me semble, fort remarquable que la parole, étant ainsi définie, ne convient qu'à l'homme seul. Car, bien que Montaigne et Charron aient dit qu'il y a plus de différence d'homme à homme, que d'homme à bête, il ne s'est toutefois jamais trouvé aucune bête si parfaite, qu'elle ait usé de quelque signe, pour faire entendre à d'autres animaux quelque chose qui n'eût point de rapport à ses passions; et il n'y a point d'homme si imparfait, qu'il n'en use; en sorte que ceux qui sont sourds et muets, inventent des signes particuliers, par lesquels ils expriment leurs pensées. Ce qui me semble un très fort argument, pour prouver ce qui fait que les bêtes ne parlent point comme nous, est qu'elles n'ont aucune pensée, et non point que les organes leur manquent. Et on ne peut dire qu'elles parlent entre elles, mais que nous ne les entendons pas; car, comme les chiens et quelques autres animaux nous expriment leurs passions, ils nous exprimeraient aussi bien leurs pensées, s'ils en avaient» (Descartes al Marchese di Newcastle, AT IV 574; BL 2350).

50 Su questo punto andrà esaminata anche l'obiezione di Gassendi.

51 *Discours de la Méthode*, AT VI 57-59; BO 90-94; cf. anche la lettera di Descartes a Reneri per Pollot, aprile o maggio 1638, AT II 40; BL 653. Il discorso sarà poi ripreso nella citata lettera a Newcastle del 23 novembre 1646. Si veda inoltre la lettera a H. More del 5 febbraio 1649: «Hæc enim loquela unicum est cogitationis in corpore latentis signum certum, atque ipsa utuntur omnes homines, etiam quam maxime stupidi et mente capti, et lingua vocisque organis destituti, non autem ullum brutum; eamque idcirco pro vera inter homines et bruta differentia sumere licet» (AT V 278; BL 2624).

Si potrebbe forse intravedere un modo del pensiero, pensiero che è attributo della *res cogitans*, coessenziale al pensiero stesso, che è quello di comunicare per segni (anche le parole sono segni)[52]. Un modo, giacché se è vero che l'uomo in quanto composto non può pensare se non per segni, nell'universo cartesiano il pensiero non è solo del composto, ma anche delle anime dopo la morte e degli angeli, per i quali la comunicazione, come la conoscenza è solo intuitiva. Sicché chi ha sottolineato (negativamente) come in Descartes il linguaggio resti subalterno al pensiero ha visto giusto, ma non ha visto tutto[53].

Dopo aver esaminato le analogie tra L1640 e M1 e i guadagni che derivano dalla considerazione di malattie/infermità come il sordomutismo e la pazzia (la prova patologica) ecc. possiamo ora tornare alle differenze tra L1640 e M1.

Una prima strutturale differenza, a ben guardare, gira attorno (ancora una volta) al ruolo della ghiandola pineale. Ebbene, se nel testo della prima meditazione ancora non dato alle stampe e nella lettera a Mersenne contemporaneamente parla della stessa cosa e cioè della follia (meglio, forse, dei folli), come si spiega allora che Descartes fornisca due spiegazioni diverse attribuendone la causa in M1 alla resistenza del vapore dell'atrabile e in L1640 a qualche malattia della ghiandola detta *conarium*.

Ora, non si andrà lontano dal vero supponendo che la malattia della ghiandola pineale dipenda per Descartes da un eccesso di atrabile, e che quindi i due testi siano sì differenti, ma complementari. La domanda diventa allora: perché Descartes non ha unito le due spiegazioni, inglobando nella spiegazione organicista quella umorale?

La risposta al perché Descartes abbia tenuto distinte le due spiegazioni va cercata non tanto in sede fisiologica, ma piuttosto nelle circostanze in cui compone il testo delle meditazioni. Le circostanze sono conosciute, in parte quelle cui abbiamo accennato sopra: Descartes scrive le meditazioni tra il novembre del 1639 e il marzo del 1640, nel dicembre del '39 Meyssonier lo coinvolge nel dibattito sul *conarium*, che si protrae, con l'intervento di Jean Cousin fino all'aprile del 1641. Ebbene, perché nelle *Meditationes*, laddove pure avrebbe potuto, Descartes non parla della ghiandola pineale? E, si badi bene, non solo non ne parla nel passo della follia, ma neppure nella sesta meditazione che è poi il luogo (come aveva fatto già nella *Dioptrique*) in cui lascia trapelare in modo enigmatico (e dubitativo: *forte*) la sua dottrina della pineale:

> Deinde adverto mentem non ab omnibus corporis partibus immediate affici, sed tantummodo a cerebro, vel forte etiam ab una tantum exigua ejus parte, nempe ab ea in qua dicitur esse sensus communis; quae, quotiescunque eodem modo est disposita, menti idem exhibet, etiamsi reliquae corporis partes diversis interim modis possint se habere, ut probant innumera experimenta, quae hic recensere non est opus. (Med. VI, AT VII 86).

---

[52] Sull'importanza del segno in Descartes mi limito a segnalare l'ottimo e utilissimo studio, con ampio apparato bibliografico e antologico, di CLAUDIA STANCATI, *Cartesio. Segno e linguaggio*, Roma, Editori Riuniti, 2000.
[53] Un accenno alla questione in STANCATI, *Cartesio*, p. 17.

Non c'è alcun motivo di dubitare che Descartes qui si stia riferendo alla ghiandola pineale, basterà confrontare questo testo con *L'Homme*, con la *Dioptrique*, con i *Principia* (IV, 189) e poi con le *Passions* (art. 32). Semmai qui può destare una certa meraviglia che la responsabilità dell'identificazione di questa parte come sede del senso comune sia lasciata da Descartes nel vago: «[exigua pars] in qua *dicitur* esse sensus communis», diversamente dai luoghi sopra citati. Descartes, infatti, rivendica sempre questa identificazione come sua. La traduzione del duca de Luynes sembra rimettere le cose a posto, lasciando trapelare un intervento diretto dell'autore:

> Je remarque aussi que l'esprit ne reçoit pas immédiatement l'impression de toutes les parties du corps, mais seulement du cerveau, ou peut-être même d'une de ses plus petites parties, à savoir de celle où s'exerce cette faculté qu'*ils appellent* le sens commun, laquelle, toutes les fois qu'elle est disposée de même façon, fait sentir la même chose à l'esprit, quoique cependant les autres parties du corps puissent être diversement disposées, comme le témoignent une infinité d'expériences, lesquelles il n'est pas ici besoin de rapporter[54].

In conclusione, se è fuor di dubbio che nei due testi Descartes parli della stessa malattia (di *maladie*, come si ricorderà parla nella lettera a Mersenne) e che tale malattia sia quella che colpisce i folli, perché ne dà due spiegazioni differenti? Non contrapposte, sia ben chiaro, probabilmente complementari e, tuttavia, non uguali. La risposta va cercata probabilmente fuori dal testo, nella preoccupazione (poi caduta con le *Passions*, ma ancora operante nei *Principia*) che una dottrina come quella della pineale avrebbe finito con l'aprire un altro fronte di discussioni. Cosa che puntualmente accadrà dopo la pubblicazione delle *Passions*, il filosofo era ormai scomparso, a partire dalla *Anatomia... tertium... reformata* (1651) di Thomas Bartholinus[55].

Sempre nel carteggio del 1640 affiora per due volte una considerazione su un'altra disfunzione della ghiandola pineale, è appena un accenno in risposta a Meyssonnier, una prima volta nella lettera allo stesso Meyssonnier del 29 gennaio del 1640 e la seconda volta, ancora una risposta al medico lionese, contenuta nella lettera a Mersenne del 1ᵉ aprile 1640, in cui Descartes riprende, con qualche modifica, ciò che aveva già scritto il 29 gennaio[56]. Si tratta del rapporto tra la ghiandola pineale e le specie della memoria: la disfunzione della ghiandola è causata in questo caso da un sovraccarico di tracce

---

54 *Meditations*, AT IX 69. Il corsivo è mio. Si vedano gli altri passi, in cui Descartes allorché parla del senso comune rinvia sempre ad un *si dice*: «... ad aliam quamdam corporis partem, *quae vocatur sensus communis*» (*Regulae*, AT X 414; BOP 750); «faculté *qu'ils appellent le sens commun...*» (*Dioptrique*, AT VI 109; BO 158); «ubi illam facultatem exercet, quam *nuncupant sensum communem*» (*Dioptrice*, AT VI 597); «sensu externo, vel saltem *sensu communi, ut vocant...*» (*Meditationes*, AT VII 32; BO 722); «ou à tout le moins du *sens commun, ainsi qu'ils appellent...*» (*Meditations*, AT IX 25); «sed ea tantum facultate, quae *sensus communis vocari solet*» (*Notae*, AT VIII 357; BO 2270). Il corsivo è mio (salvo in AT IX 25, in cui sensu communi è corsivo nel testo).
55 THOMAS BARTHOLINUS, *Anatomia [...] tertium [...] reformata*, Lugduni Batavorum, apud Franciscum Hackium, 1651, lib. III, cap. 6, p. 336-337.
56 Cf. BL 1144.

mnestiche, che impediscono alla ghiandola di esercitare in modo appropriato la sua funzione immaginativa. Riportiamo i due testi in modo sinottico:

Descartes a Meyssonnier, 29 gennaio 1640	Descartes a Mersenne, 1 aprile 1640
[...] je crois qu'elles [les espèces qui se conservent dans la mémoire] sont principalement reçues en toute la substance du cerveau, bien que je ne nie pas qu'elles ne puissent être aussi en quelque façon en cette glande, surtout en ceux qui ont l'esprit plus hébété: car pour les esprits fort bons et fort subtils, je crois qu'ils la doivent avoir toute libre à eux et fort mobile; comme nous voyons aussi que dans les hommes elle est plus petite que dans les bêtes, tout au rebours des autres parties du cerveau. Je crois aussi que quelques-unes des espèces qui servent à la mémoire peuvent être en diverses autres parties du corps, comme l'habitude d'un joueur de luth n'est pas seulement dans sa tête, mais aussi en partie dans les muscles de ses mains, etc.[57]	[...] pour les espèces qui servent à la mémoire, je ne nie pas absolument qu'elles ne puissent être en partie dans la Glande nommée *Conarium*, principalement dans les bêtes brutes, et en ceux qui ont l'esprit grossier; car, pour les autres, ils n'auraient pas, ce me semble, tant de facilité qu'ils ont à imaginer une infinité de choses qu'ils n'ont jamais vues, si leur âme n'était jointe à quelque partie du cerveau, qui fût fort propre à recevoir toutes sortes de nouvelles impressions, et par conséquent fort malpropre à les conserver. Or est-il qu'il n'y a que cette Glande seule, à laquelle l'âme puisse être ainsi jointe; car il n'y a qu'elle seule, en toute la tête, qui ne soit point double. Mais je crois que c'est tout le reste du cerveau qui sert le plus à la mémoire, principalement ses parties intérieures, et même aussi que tous les nerfs et les muscles y peuvent servir; en sorte que, par exemple, un joueur de luth a une partie de sa mémoire en ses mains; car la facilité de plier et de disposer ses doigts en diverses façons, qu'il a acquise par habitude, aide à le faire souvenir des passages pour l'exécution desquels il les doit ainsi disposer.[58]

Già ne *L'Homme* Descartes aveva localizzato la memoria al di fuori della ghiandola H, sede del senso comune e dell'immaginazione, indicando come sua sede la parte interna del cervello: «Mais je me contenterai de vous dire encore, comment elles [les traces de ces idées] s'impriment en la partie intérieure du cerveau marquée B, où est le siège de la *Mémoire*»[59].

Nelle due risposte a Meyssonnier, Descartes precisa come il confliggere tra le due facoltà, quella immaginativa e quella della memoria, impedisca una loro coabitazione, possibile è vero, ma patologica (o tendente al patologico); possibile, perché la memoria corporea è una facoltà che potremmo definire *diffusa* sicché non si può escludere che le sue specie, le sue tracce si trovino anche nella ghiandola detta *conarium*,

---

57 Descartes a Meyssonnier, 29 gennaio 1640, AT III 20; BL 1146.
58 Descartes a Mersenne, 1 aprile 1640, AT III 47; BL 1172.
59 *L'Homme*, AT XI 177; BOP 462 (nella citazione il riferimento alla lettera B rinvia alla figura), poco sopra aveva parlato della ghiandola H come sede del senso comune e dell'immaginazione («... della ghiandola H, *dove è la sede dell'immaginazione e del senso comune*»).

tuttavia patologica perché il sovraccarico di tracce mnestiche nella pineale contrasta con un corretto funzionamento dell'immaginazione (di cui la ghiandola pineale è propriamente la sede). Tale disfunzione determina una situazione che Descartes non riconduce ad una categoria nosologica vera e propria (che potremmo individuare nell'ebetismo). Il filosofo si limita invece a indicare coloro che ne sono affetti, i quali sono «ceux qui ont l'esprit plus hébété» o «ceux qui ont l'esprit grossier», gli stessi che in altri testi chiamerà «hommes… hébétés et… stupides»[60], «maxime stupidi et mente capti»[61], «esprits… si grossiers… si tardifs»[62], «hébétés et stupides»[63]. Costoro non sono *insani*, diversa è l'eziologia (un eccesso di atrabile per gli *insani*, un sovraccarico di tracce mnestiche per gli altri), sebbene ad essere colpito sia lo stesso organo, la pineale, appunto.

Anche in questo caso, l'estensione del fisiologico fino al suo limite, il patologico, qui rappresentato dall'avere *l'esprit grossier*, porta Descartes a chiamare in causa l'altra macchina vivente, l'animale, nella quale è, per così dire, normale ciò che nell'uomo è patologico: «pour les espèces qui servent à la mémoire, je ne nie pas absolument qu'elles ne puissent être en partie dans la Glande nommée *Conarium*, principalement dans les bêtes brutes, et en ceux qui ont l'esprit grossie»[64].

Questo è quanto Descartes afferma nella seconda risposta a Meyssonnier, che trova la sua giustificazione anatomica nella lettera precedente, del 29 gennaio, nella quale si era limitato a comparare la ghiandola pineale nell'uomo e nei bruti: «comme nous voyons aussi que dans les hommes elle est plus petite que dans les bêtes, tout au rebours des autres parties du cerveau»[65].

La diversa dimensione della pineale, più piccola nell'uomo rispetto agli animali, e ciò contrariamente alle altre parti del cervello, appariva a Descartes, probabilmente, valida base anatomica di due caratteristiche che egli attibuiva alla pineale, l'estrema mobilità (ciò che permette alla pineale di intercettare le specie sensibili trasportate dagli spiriti animali provenienti da varie direzioni e con diversa intensità) e la piccolezza, che evidentemente favorisce la mobilità e al tempo stesso rende la ghiandola, in condizioni normali, meno esposta, per così dire, alle tracce mnestiche. Nella lettera del 29 gennaio, Descartes non va al di là della comparazione, senza trarre alcun'esplicita conclusione in merito al rapporto tra memoria e ghiandola pineale negli animali bruti ed è probabile che Meyssonnier, nella lettera di risposta indirizzata a Mersenne per Descartes, abbia chiesto ulteriori delucidazioni alle quale Descartes risponde: 1) non negando che anche nella pineale possano trovarsi tracce della memoria; 2) mettendo sullo stesso piano, a questo riguardo, coloro che hanno *l'esprit grossier* e gli animali bruti.

---

60 *Discours*, AT VI 57; BO 90.
61 Descartes a More del 5 febbraio 1649, AT V 278; BL 2624.
62 *Lettre preface à la traduction française des* Prinpia philosophiae (AT IX-2 12.)
63 *Passions*, art. 77, AT XI 386; BO 2402.
64 Per ciò che riguarda più in particolare la dottrina della ghiandola pineale, le risposte a Meyssonnier, oltre alle precisazioni sulla memoria locale, permettono a Descartes di rilevare una differenza anatomica, relativamente alla dimensione, tra animali e uomo: nell'uomo, infatti, la pineale è più piccola.
65 Descartes a Meyssonnier, 29 gennaio 1640, AT III 20; BL 1146.

3. Gli amputati

L'esperienza degli amputati (la cosiddetta sindrome dell'arto fantasma) serve a Descartes come prova (patologica) per dimostrare la centralità della sensazione localizzata nel senso comune. La prima menzione si trova nella lettera a Plempius del 13 settembre 1637. Descartes vi risponde ad un'obbiezione di Fromondus, trasmessagli da Plempius, sulla *Dioptrique*.

Ci troviamo difronte a tre testi in sequenza. Fromondus critica il passo del quarto discorso della *Dioprique* in cui Descartes ricostruisce il tragitto della sensazione, dai sensi esterni, al cervello, all'anima ponendo nel cervello e precisamente nel luogo in cui l'anima esercita quella facoltà «qu'ils appellent les sens commun»[66] la sensazione vera e propria, si tratta del passo che precede la descrizione dei nervi:

> On sait déjà assez que c'est l'âme qui sent, et non le corps: car on voit que, lorsqu'elle est divertie par une extase ou forte contemplation, tout le corps demeure sans sentiment, encore qu'il ait divers objets qui le touchent. Et on sait que ce n'est pas proprement en tant qu'elle est dans les membres qui servent d'organes aux sens extérieurs, qu'elle sent, mais en tant qu'elle est dans le cerveau, où elle exerce cette faculté qu'ils appellent le sens commun: car on voit des blessures et maladies qui, n'offensant que le cerveau seul, empêchent généralement tous les sens, encore que le reste du corps ne laisse point pour cela d'être animé[67].

Nel passo sono dunque precisati due aspetti della sensazione: 1. è l'anima a sentire. Lo dimostra il fatto che, nei casi di estasi o forte contemplazione, il corpo rimane senza sentimento anche se viene toccato da diversi corpi; 2. l'anima sente nel cervello, tanto è vero che se il cervello non è in grado di ricevere le impressioni provenienti dagli organi dei senti non si dà sensazione alcuna. Due situazione, quindi, quella in cui l'anima si estranea dal corpo; quella in cui il cervello è affetto da una malattia o subisce una ferita, e per questo motivo tutti i sensi sono impediti nonostante il corpo non cessi d'essere animato.

Fromondus non si sofferma su questa distinzione, ma fa appello alla nostra immagine interiore che ci presenta la qualità dolorifica come inerente all'operazione dei sensi, in questo caso del tatto. Per rispondere al professore di Lovanio, Descartes fa ricorso ad un'esperienza diversa da quella che aveva invocato nel quarto discorso della *Dioptrique*, dove, per dimostrare la centralità della sensazione, aveva richiamato genericamente una patologia cerebrale (quando il cervello è malato o ferito ecc.). Ora per rispondere all'obiezione mossagli da Fromondus mette in campo un'esperienza particolare, quella della fanciulla amputata:

> 9. Ad pag. 30 miratur me non agnoscere aliam sensationem, quam eam quæ exercetur in cerebro. Sed juvabunt me, ut spero, medici omnes et chirurgi

---

66 *La Dioptrique*, IV, AT VI 109; BO 158. Sul senso comune in Descartes cf. JEAN-MARIE BEYSSADE, *Le sens commun dans la Règle XII: le corps et l'incorporel*, in "Revue de Metaphysique et de Morale", an. 96/4, 1991, p. 497-514.
67 *Dioptrique* IV, AT VI 109; BO 158.

> ad hoc ipsi persuadendum: sciunt enim illos quibus membra nuper fuerunt abscissa, dolorem sæpe in iis partibus quibus carent putare adhuc se sentire. Novique olim puellam cui, cum grave vulnus haberet in manu, velarenturque ejus oculi, quoties chirurgus accedebat, ut facilius se ab eo tractari pateretur, totum brachium ob gangrænam serpentem fuit amputatum, pannique in ejus locum ita substituti, ut per aliquot postea hebdomadas eo se privatam esse ignorarit: cum tamen interim varios dolores nunc in digitis, nunc in metacarpio, nunc in brachiali, quibus carebat, se sentire quereretur: affectis scilicet adhuc in brachio iis nervis qui prius a cerebro ad illas partes descendebant. Quod procul dubio non contigisset, si doloris sensus sive, ut loquitur, sensatio extra cerebrum perageretur[68].

Rispetto alla *Dioptrique*, dunque, Descartes propone qui una nuova prova patologica rovesciando completamente il punto d'osservazione, non il cervello, questa volta, ma una mano o un braccio. Il processo è inverso, non si tratta in altre parole di considerare il caso in cui è il cervello a bloccare la sensazione, ma piuttosto di giustificare una sensazione in assenza dell'arto in cui il soggetto sente quella sensazione. Ciò che è identico è l'esperienza del dolore. Inoltre la prova patologica (la sindrome dell'arto fantasma) viene presentata non solo come una conoscenza acquisita dalla lettura di testi medici[69], ma anche come un fatto occorso a una fanciulla di sua conoscenza, così come nella sesta meditazione riporta la stessa esperienza riferita a persone anch'esse di sua conoscenza («audiveram aliquando ab iis, quibus crus aut brachium fuerat abscissum, se sibi videri adhuc interdum dolorem sentire in ea parte corporis qua carebant»)[70]. L'esempio della fanciulla, ma riferito ormai in modo generico, viene riproposto anche nell'articolo 196 della quarta parte dei *Principia*. Diverso è il caso, che a volte capita di vedere avvicinato ai testi qui menzionati, di cui Descartes parla nel primo capitolo del *Mondo* (AT XI 6 / BOP 219), dove non si tratta tanto della localizzazione del dolore, ma piuttosto della differenza tra le sensazioni e le cose che le producono.

4. L'idropisia

Nella sesta meditazione il meditante (e il lettore) vengono posti di fronte ad una malattia insidiosa e ingannatrice, l'idropisia. Insidiosa perché si presenta per ultima nel percorso meditativo, quando l'io sa ormai che le percezioni dei sensi «propriamente sono state date dalla natura soltanto per dire alla mente cosa sia vantaggioso o svantaggioso al composto di cui essa è parte[71]» e tanto più insidiosa perché ingannatrice proprio a questo riguardo:

---

68 Descartes a Plempius del 3 ottobre 1637, AT I 420; BL 420.
69 Un riferimento può essere AMBROISE PARÉ, *Dix livres de la chirurgie: avec le magasin des instrumens necessaire à icelle*, Paris, 1564, p. 116b.
70 Cf. anche *Meditationes*, VI, AT VII 77; BO 782.
71 *Meditationes* VI, AT VII 83; BO 791.

Sed nova hic occurrit difficultas circa illa ipsa quae tanquam persequenda vel fugienda mihi a natura exhibentur [...] At vero non raro etiam in iis erramus ad quae a natura impellimur: ut cum ii qui aegrotant, potum vel cibum appetunt sibi paulo post nociturum[72].

È in questo contesto che cade il discorso sull'idropico[73]. Descartes non si dilunga a parlare dell'idropisia, la malattia era ben presente (e riconoscibile) nella società e nella cultura[74] oltreché considerata ampiamente dalla medicina del

---

72 Ibid., AT VII 83-84; BO790-792.
73 Nelle *Meditationes* le occorrenze sono *hydrops* (2 occ., entrambe all'ablativo dipendente dal verbo *laboro*) e l'aggettivo (sostantivato) *hydropicus* (1 occ.); nelle *Responsiones*: *hydropicus* (3 occ., due nelle seconde, una nelle quarte: sempre sostantivato).
74 Senza voler qui aprire un problema di fonti, ma piuttosto fornire alcuni elementi di contesto, si può indicare, quale testimone importante della utilizzazione anche simbolica di questa malattia nella cultura del tempo, un testo come l'*Iconologia* di Cesare Ripa, che ebbe grande fortuna europea, in cui all'idropico si fa riferimento a proposito dell'avarizia, quasi a sancire il perdurare di un *topos* antichissimo. Nella prima edizione francese (1636), dell'idropico si parla alle p. 34 e 35 (Iconologie, ou Explication nouvelle de plusieurs images, emblèmes et autres figures hyérogliphiques des vertus, des vices, des arts, des sciences ... Tirée des recherches et des figures de César Ripa, desseignées et gravées par Jacques de Bie et moralisées par J. Baudoin, Paris, 1636). In questa edizione (come nella successiva del 1643) manca il riferimento ad Orazio, presente invece nelle edizioni italiane precedenti (1593, 1603, 1611, 1613): «Crescit indulgens sibi dirus idrops Nec sitim pellit, nisi caussa morbi Fugerit venis et aquosus albo Corpore languor» (p. 56 dell'edizione 1613), citazione, tratta dalla seconda ode del secondo libro dei *Carmina*, che, a sua volta, possiamo ipotizzare abbia avuto un ruolo di rilievo nella fortuna filosofica e letteraria della idropisia. In Montaigne, per menzionare un autore che intesse le sue pagine di continui riferimenti e citazioni, costituendosi quasi come un repertorio della letteratura classica, l'idropisia compare sorprendentemente solo in due luoghi (II, 3; II, 37), sorprendentemente perché essa è invece presente esplicitamente o implicitamente in molte delle sue fonti, a cominciare da Plutarco (cf. *Magna Moralia*: 11, 25-26; 28, 18-19; 40, 3; 44, 14; 57, 8; 74, 11-12; 75, 5, 16; *Vitae: Crassus*, 33,8; *Antonius*, 49,6) e, poi, Aristippo (fr. 4 A 73 G = Plut. *De cup.* 524a-b), Antistene (Xen. *Smp.* 4.37), Diogene di Sinope (Stob. 3.10.45), Cicerone (*De officiis*, III, 92), Ovidio (Fast. 1, 215), lo stesso Orazio (che oltre al passo citato *supra* allude all'idropisia in *Epistolae*: 1, 2, 34; 2, 2, 146), Seneca (*Ad Lucilium Epistulae Morales*, 95, 16-22; *Consolatio ad Helviam matrem*, 11, 3), Gaio Lucilio (v. 764), Persio (III, 63-65; 88-106), Svetonio (*De Vita Caesarum*, VI, 5), Diogene Laerzio (*Vitae philosophorum*, IX 3; 5). In uno dei due luoghi in cui accenna all'idropisia, Montaigne ne parla narrando l'incontro di Speusippo, sofferente perché affetto da idropisia, con Diogene il Cinico, incontro che troviamo riferito anche da Diogene Laerzio, che, tuttavia, non parla di idropisia a proposito di Speusippo, ma genericamente di paralisi; di idropisia Diogene Laerzio parla invece a proposito di Eraclito sostenendo che ne sarebbe morto (IX 3), riferendo anche un'altra tradizione secondo cui Eraclito sarebbe guarito dall'idropisia (IX 5). Tra gli altri autori che parlano o alludono alla idropisia si possono ancora citare Sereno Sammonico (vv. 493-513) e Marco Aurelio (*Pensieri*, III, 3). Un discorso a parte va fatto per i medici, a cominciare dal *corpus Hippocraticum*, che è disseminato di riferimenti alla idropisia e ai malati affetti da idropisia:124 le occorrenze dell'intera costellazione dei corradicali ὑδρωπίαω, ὑδρωπικός, ὑδρωπιώδης, ὑδρωποειδής, ὕδρωψ (cf. *Concordantia in Corpus Hippocraticum*, editée par Gilles Maloney et Winnie Frhon, Hildestein, Zürich, New York, Olms-Weidmann, 1986); la rilevanza, della idropisia in Ippocrate, ancorché i dati ora riportati andrebbero analizzati, la si può comunque provare anche *a parte lectoris* solo che si scorra l'*index in Hippocratem* dell'edizone di Girolamo Mercuriale (1588), che conta non meno di settanta lemmi. Ugualmente importante, almeno a livello di fortuna, è l'idropisia in Galeno, soprattutto perché si combina in modo più sistematico con la dottrina degli umori (cf. *Hippocratis Aphor. et Gal. in eos*

tempo[75] e dunque un accenno era sufficiente. E, in effetti, la questione posta in questo punto della sesta meditazione è prettamente una questione filosofica ed

---

Commentarius IV: XI; *Definitiones medicae*, CCLXXIX, CCLXXX, CCLXXXI; *De locis affectis* V, 7; *De causis morborum*, cap. 3). Altra fonte importante per la medicina moderna è il *De medicina* di Celso, che dedica all'idropisia una vera e propria, sia pur concisa, trattazione (*De medicina*, 3, 21, 1-17), più didascalica di quanto non fosse il testo di Alessandro di Tralles, anch'esso disponibile (*Alexandri Tralliani Medici libri duodecim* [...] Joanne Gunterio Andernaco interprete et emendatore, Basileae, per Henricum Petrum [1556]. Varrà la pena, infine, ricordare come anche negli scritti aristotelici ci siano riferimenti all'idropisia (cf. l'*Index Aristotelicus* di H. Bonitz), sia nei *Problemata* (871b24; 887a23) sia nel *De generatione animalium* (789b14). Una scheda sull'idropisia nella medicina greca e romana si trova in Innocenzo MAZZINI, *La medicina dei greci e dei romani. Letteratura, lingua, scienza*, 2 voll., Roma, Jouvance, 1997, vol. II, p. 315-320; allo stesso studioso si deve un esame di come l'idropisia sia stata trattata nella poesia latina, in particolare in Orazio:"La descrizione delle malattie nei poeti e nei medici", in *Maladie et maladies dans les textes latins antiques et médiévaux*, Actes du Ve Colloque International "Textes médicaux latins" (Bruxelles, 4-6 septembre 1995), Carl Deroux (éd.), Bruxelles, Latomus, 1998, v + 458 p. (Collection Latomus, 242), pag. 14-28 (sono debitore a questo articolo dei passi di Ovidio, Lucilio, Sereno Sammonico); v. anche: Idem, "La malattia conseguenza e metafora del peccato nel mondo antico, pagano e cristiano", in *Cultura e promozione umana. La cura del cuerpo e dello spirito nell'antichità classica e nei primi secoli cristiani. Un magistero ancora attuale?*. Atti del I Conv. Intern. (Troina, 29 ottobre-1 novembre 1997), E. Dal Covolo e I. Gianetto (edd.), Troina, Oasi Editrice, 1998, p. 159-172; Valentina GAZZANIGA, "La malattia del corpo e i mali dello Stato. La metafora satirica di Persio", in "Medicina nei secoli", 3 (1990), p. 331-346; per la tradizione cinica, utili considerazioni (e bibliografia) in Barbara DEL GIOVANE, *Seneca, la diatriba e la ricerca di una morale austera*, Firenze, Firenze University Press, 2015; per un'indagine sulla presenza della idropisia nel mondo antico sono preziosi l'approccio e la documetazione di Mirko GRMECK, Danielle GOUREVITCH, *Les maladies dans l'art antique*, (Collection Penser la médecine), [Paris], Fayard, 1998.

75 Dell'idropisia la medicina moderna trattava regolarmente. Jean Fernel, tra gli altri, ne parla diffusamente nel cap. VIII del sesto libro della sua *Pathologia* (uso l'edizione sesta della *Universa medicina*, [...], Francofurti apud Claudium Marnium et haerede Ioan. Aubrii, 1607, p. 582-590) a proposito delle malattie del fegato e della milza e ne ricorda tre specie l'anasarca, l'ascite e la timpanite, la prima, la più grave, riguarda tutto il corpo ed è un accumulo di liquido sieroso; la seconda è un gonfiore dell'addome causato da un versamento di un umore acquoso e sieroso, la terza, la timpanite, riguarda sempre l'addome, ma consiste in un rigonfiamento dovuto ad un eccesso d'aria; tripartizione che si trova anche in Bartolomeo Castelli, *Lexicon graecolatinum ex Hippocrate et Galeno desumptum*, Venetiis apud Nicolaum Polum, et Franciscum Bolzettam, 1607 *sub voce*. E in genere, di idropisia, si parla nei trattati di medicina pratica o di osservazioni anatomiche, tra i quali merita una menzione particolare Ioannes Schenckius, *Observationum medicarum, rararum, novarum, admirabilium et monstrosarum*, Fribourg en Brisgau, Johannes von Grafenberg, 1596 e numerose riedizioni, (le pagine dedicate alla idropisia sono 411-436), su cui si veda BITBOL-HESPÉRIÈS ("Une source des textes biomédicaux latins de Descartes, AT XI", cit.), che ha indicato nel medico tedesco una fonte dei testi biomedici di Descartes. A testimonianza dell'interesse medico per l'idropisia nella prima modernità si possono portare anche le *Quaestiones medicae*, discusse presso la scuola di medicina di Parigi; se prendiamo come termine a *quo* il 1539 (anno dal quale prendono il via le *Quaestiones* registrate dal Baron cf. *infra*) e come tremine *ad quem* il 1650 (anno della morte di Descartes), sono almeno sedici le tesi che vertono proprio sull'idropisia: An hydropi paracenthesis? neg. (1572: sostenuta da Pet. De la Mer); An ut ab inflammato jecore icterus, ita a refrigererato hydrops? aff. (1575: sostenuta da Petr. Des Monts.); An hepatis scyrrhum necessario sequatur hydrops? (1577: sostenuta da Sim. le la Croix); An hydropi ab hepate phlebotomia et paracenthesis? neg. (1584: sostenua da Joan Duret); An ut ab inflammato jecore icterus, sic a refrigerato hydrops? aff. (1597: sostenuta da Math. Chevallot); An in omni hydrope jecur ατονόν? aff. (1601: sotenuta da Petr. De la Boissiere); An Hydropicis potus parcitas salubris? aff. (1609: sostenuta da Philb. Guybert); An

è una questione cruciale che l'idropico (il suo stesso esserci) pone alla teodicea: «ideoque hic remanet inquirendum, quo pacto bonitas Dei non impediat quominus natura sic sumpta sit fallax[76]». Questa nuova battuta d'arresto (nel percorso meditativo) si colloca a livello dell'unione di anima e corpo, alla luce della quale viene introdotto un concetto *strictius* di natura («hic naturam strictius sumo») e solo a questo livello poteva porsi giacché solo ora si affaccia una possibilità di errore della natura, la quale è colta in fallo non perché violi delle leggi (di natura), ma perché entra in contrasto con il finalismo, che qui è legittimo in quanto non siamo più sotto il solo dominio della fisica, ma del composto di anima e corpo. Non per nulla questo testo è l'ennesimo in cui Descartes pone una netta distinzione tra l'animale (macchina) e l'uomo (composto: macchina con la mente) e, questa volta, tra meccanicismo e finalismo. O anche, detto in altri termini, ma non meno efficaci, tra natura fisica e natura antropologica[77]. Ed è proprio avendo in mente questa distinzione che Descartes non può liquidare l'idropisia come un semplice fatto, come un orologio rotto, che pur derogando dallo scopo per cui è stato costruito, segnare le ore, non risponde meno alle leggi di natura[78]. Studiosi come M. Gueroult[79], G. Canziani[80] e S. Landucci[81] hanno approfondito e chiarito quest'aspetto perché qui sia necessario richiamarlo. Qui bastava ricordare come ancora una malattia venga usata da Descartes, come prova da superare, nel suo percorso metafisico.

Ma l'idropisia non è solo una malattia del corpo, Descartes lo sa tanto è vero che nella *Recherche de la Verité* la figura dell'idropico è evocata nel dialogo tra Epistemone ed Eudosso:

> Eudoxe. Est-il possible, Epistemon, qu'étant savant comme vous êtes, vous vous puissiez persuader, qu'il y ait une maladie si universelle en la nature, sans qu'il y

---

hydropi ιδρωτίκα? neg. (1611: sostenuta da Franc. Le Sage); An hydropi sectio? aff. (1613: sostenuta da Guil. De Vailly); An diarrhaerea hydropi? aff. (1614: sostenuta da Mich. Francier); An hydrops κατα απόφασιν sanabilis? aff. (1617: sostenuta da Petr. Robynet); Utrum in thoracis quam in abdominis hydrope paracentesis tutior? aff. (1624: sostenuta da Jac. Adam); An praecavendo hydropi venae sectio? aff. (1628; sostenuta da Nic. Brayer); An epilepsia hydropi superveniens lethalis? aff. (1629: sostenuta da Dion. Bazin); An hydropi siccantia? aff. (1635: sostenuta da Nic. Richard); An a frequenti venae sectione hydrops? neg. (1646: sostenuta da Lud. le Noir). L'elenco delle tesi è in [H. T. BARON], *Quaestionum Medicarum, quae circa medicinae theoriam et praxim, ante duo saecula, in Scholis Facultatis Medicinae Parisiensis, agitatae sunt et discussae, Series Chronologica* [...], Parisiis, apud Joannem-Thomam Herissant, 1703.

76 *Meditationes*, VI, AT VII 85; BO 794. Cf. SERGIO LANDUCCI, *La teodicea nell'età cartesiana*, Napoli, Bibliopolis, 1986.
77 Mutuo questa distinzione da GUIDO CANZIANI, *Filosofia e scienza nella morale di Descartes*, Firenze, La Nuova Italia, 1980, p. 245.
78 Cosa che fa, invece, in *Primae Cogitationes* a proposito della nascita dei mostri (AT XI 524; BOP 964).
79 MARTIAL GUEROULT, *Descartes selon l'ordre des raisons*, 2 vols, Paris, Aubier, 1991 [1968], vol. II, p. 122-218.
80 CANZIANI, *Filosofia e scienza*, p. 245-247.
81 Cf. LANDUCCI, *La teodicea*, p. 17-25.

ait aussi quelque remède pour la guérir? Quant à moi, il me semble que, comme il y a en chaque terre assez de fruits et de ruisseaux pour apaiser la faim et la soif de tout le monde, il y a de même assez de vérités qui se peuvent connaître en chaque matière, pour satisfaire pleinement à la curiosité des âmes réglées, et que le corps des hydropiques n'est pas plus éloigné de son juste tempérament, que l'esprit de ceux-là qui sont perpétuellement travaillés d'une curiosité insatiable[82].

Di fatto l'*hydropisia* è anche vista nella tradizione, soprattutto patristica, come una *inflatio animi*, un gonfiamento dell'animo, un peccato di superbia, di avarazia[83].

È probabile che Descartes avesse presente la guarigione miracolosa narrata in Lc. 14, 2-4: «Et ecce homo quidam hydropicus erat ante illum. Ipse verum apprehensum sanavit eum ac dimisit». È certo, tuttavia, che il filosofo non invoca il miracolo; la conclusione della sesta meditazione torna a mettere di fronte al meditante — che pure può confidare ormai nella somma bontà di Dio e che quindi non deve temere d'essere ingannato su ciò che avrà esaminato accuratamente (con tutti i sensi, con la memoria e con l'intelletto) — l'*infirmitas* della natura umana: «Sed quia rerum agendarum necessitas non semper tam accurati examinis moram concedit, fatendum est humanam vitam circa res particulares saepe erroribus esse obnoxiam, et naturae nostrae infirmitas est agnoscenda»[84]. Se la sesta meditazione va letta fino all'epilogo non annunciato nel titolo[85], l'epilogo andrà letto non dimenticando questa conclusione.

---

82 *Recherche de la vérité*, AT XI 500; BOP 830, ringrazio l'amico Baldassarri che ha richiamato la mia attenzione su questo passo; BALDASSARRI, *Il metodo al tavolo anatomico*, p. 33-35. Descartes parla di idropisia, precisamente di ascite, anche in una lettera a Regius, novembre 1641, AT III 440; BL 1530.

83 Cf. J. M. Poinsotte, "La présence des poèmes antipaïens anonymes dans l'oeuvre de Prudence", in REAug, 28 (1982), p. 33-58: 54. Della idropisia parlano, tra gli altri, Giovanni Crisostomo (*In Epistulam ad Philippenses homiliae*, 7, 5: PG 62, 236); Girolamo (Epistola CVIII, *Ad Eustochium virginem*, 34, PL 22: 878-906); Agostino (*Sermones de Scripturis, Sermo LXI*, 3, 3: PL 38, 410; *Sermo CLXXII*: PL 38, 956); Prudenzio (*Perist.* 2, 237ss; *Cath.* 8, 62-63); Isidoro di Siviglia (*Etimologiae sive origines*, IV, 7, 23). La tradizione patristica, relativamente all'idropisia, spesso congiuntamente a quella classica e a quella medica si prolunga nella trattatistica e omiletica medievali ed ha uno dei momenti più alti nell'*Inferno* dantesco, con il canto XXX, 49-129, in cui è descritta la pena inflitta al falsario Maestro Adamo, di soffrire, appunto, di *idropesi*, si veda in proposito Vittorio BARTOLI, "L'idropisia di maestro Adamo in Inferno XXX. Importanza della dottrina umorale di Galeno nel Medioevo" (in "Tenzone", 8 (2007), p. 11-29), che fornisce anche un'utile rassegna (p. 16-19) di autori medievali che definiscono l'idropisia o la descrivono indagandone cause ed effetti: Costantino Africano, Taddeo Alderotti, Avicenna, Pietro d'Abano, Bartolomeo Anglico, Guido da Pisa.

84 *Meditationes*, VI, AT VII 90; BO 791.

85 È stato Sergio Landucci a notare questa eccedenza rispetto a quanto annunciato nel titolo «Una sorta di fuor d'opera, aggiunto a quel che soltanto ci si attenderebbe, sulla base del titolo» (LANDUCCI, *La teodicea*, p. 18).

PART 2

Reception And Opposition

Cartesian Medicine and Cartesianism

ERIK-JAN BOS

Mercurius Cosmopolita alias Andreas of Habernfeld

The Hermetic Response to Descartes[*]

▼ ABSTRACT In 1640 a curious book appeared at The Hague which vehemently attacked Descartes' *Discours de la Méthode*. The identity of the author, evidently an adherent of Paracelsian and Hermetic philosophy, remained unknown, until a clear indication was found in the Hartlib Papers. This article discloses the name of the person hiding behind the pseudonym Mercurius Cosmopolita, and sketches his life and works, including the book against Descartes: *Pentalogos*.

▼ KEYWORDS Descartes, Rosicrucianism, Hermetic philosophy, Paracelsian Medicine, Alchemy

One of the first printed reactions to Descartes in the Dutch Republic was a curious book entitled *Pentalogos in libri cujusdam Gallico idiomate evulgati quatuor discursuum: De la methode, Dioptrique, Meteorique, & Geometrique* (The Hague, 1640), that is, a *Pentalogue*, or a conversation between five, on Descartes's *Discours de la méthode*

---

[*] The draft of this article was first presented at the British Society for the History of Philosophy Annual Conference, Rotterdam, March 2007, and again at a conference organised by Roger Ariew, *Descartes on Shaky Grounds (Once Again)*, Tampa, October 2016. I thank the participants of these conferences for their helpful comments, and Han van Ruler, Theo Verbeek and Vladimír Urbánek for their critical remarks. I thank Nicolette Mout and Vladimír Urbánek for their interest in my findings and their encouragement to publish them, and I appreciate the acknowledgements in their publications (see note 41).

Erik-Jan Bos • Erasmus University Rotterdam. Contact: <erik-jan.bos@xs4all.nl>

(Leiden, 1637) and the three appending essays.[1] According to Descartes, the author, who called himself Mercurius Cosmopolita, was a Bohemian chemist living in The Hague, but his real name was never revealed. The editors of the standard edition of Descartes's works, Charles Adam and Paul Tannery, did not discover a copy of the pamphlet written by Mercurius Cosmopolita, and thus the work, and its author, remained a mystery. Cornelis de Waard located a copy of *Pentalogos* in the library of the Pulkovo Astronomical Observatory (Russia), and sketched its contents in the *Correspondance de Mersenne*.[2] Theo Verbeek unearthed two other copies (in Amsterdam and London) but despite further investigations the author's identity remained elusive.[3] Below I finally disclose the identity of Mercurius Cosmopolita, and sketch the life and works of this colourful person. He was indeed a Bohemian exile living in The Hague, and a doctor of medicine from the Paracelsian school, as well as an adherent of Hermetic philosophy. We will then have a closer look at *Pentalogos*, and consider the possibility that its author is responsible for another anti-Cartesian book. However, let us first recall how Descartes himself reacted to the Hermetic response.

1. Descartes and *Pentalogos*

Descartes received a copy of *Pentalogos* in October 1640. On 5 October he wrote the following to his friend David de Wilhem (1588-1658), who had sent him the book:

> Ie vous remercie du beau livre que Mr Hesdin [Johann Eding] m'apporta dernierement de vostre part. I'y ay trouvé tant de belles choses que, si St[ampioen] estoit aussy sçavant en latin, en Hebreu, en Philosophie, en Chymie et en Medecine,

---

[1] The complete title reads: *Pentalogos in libri cujusdam Gallico idiomate evulgati quatuor discursuum: De la methode, Dioptrique, Meteorique, & Geometrique: Partem de Meteoris peregrinam quandam doctrinam exhibet, rationi et naturae repugnantem, academiarum & universitatum scholas omnes contemnentem, utpote errorum nutriculas.* 56 p. in-12°. The printer, Franck van der Spruit, was active between 1640 and 1642 (the Short Title Catalogue Netherlands lists 15 titles); his widow continued the press until 1645 (5 titles in STCN). Their main author was Caspar Streso, an orthodox Calvinist minister at The Hague, and an acquaintance of Habernfeld (see note 38). On Streso, see ROBIN BUNING, "Scholarly Communication between England, the Netherlands and Central Europe: Samuel Hartlib's Dutch Agent Caspar Streso (1603-1664)", in *The Practice of Scholarly Communication: Correspondence Networks between Central and Western Europe, 1550-1700*, ed. by Vladimír Urbánek and Iva Lelková, Leiden, Brill, forthcoming.

[2] Descartes to Mersenne, 3 December 1640, *CM* X 297-298, and note *l*. 26, p. 300-301; cf. AT III 249; BL 1336.

[3] THEO VERBEEK, *Descartes and the Dutch: Early Reactions to Cartesian Philosophy, 1637-1650*, Carbondale and Edwardsville, Southern Illinois University Press, 1992, "Appendix 1: Mercurius Cosmopolita and Others", p. 93-95. In my doctoral dissertation I was able to be more precise on some details; see ERIK-JAN BOS, *The Correspondence between Descartes and Henricus Regius*, Utrecht, Zeno, 2002, p. 170-171. The Amsterdam and London copies of *Pentalogos* are nowadays found on Google Books.

qu'il est en Mathematique, ie ne douterois point qu'il n'en fust l'autheur; mais ie n'en connois point d'autre que luy qui ait l'esprit assez relevé pour cela.⁴

In other words, Descartes would like to know the name of the author. Just one candidate springs to Descartes's mind, namely Johan Stampioen the Younger (1610-1653). In 1638, Descartes got entangled in a violent dispute with this Dutch mathematician, a dispute that had been decided in favour of Descartes earlier in 1640.⁵ However, the author of this new publication cannot be Stampioen, according to Descartes, because Stampioen has no knowledge of Latin, Hebrew, philosophy, chemistry or medicine. So who can it be?

A few days later, Descartes received a letter from Constantijn Huygens (1596-1687), telling him that his brother-in-law De Wilhem will reveal the identity of the author of, as Huygens puts it, 'that funny book composed by a charlatan here in The Hague'.⁶ Unfortunately, neither *Pentalogos* nor the question of its authorship are mentioned again in the extant correspondence between Descartes, Huygens and De Wilhem, but Descartes must have been informed about the author's identity. Indeed, two months later Descartes could write to Mersenne that the author was a Bohemian chemist living in The Hague. In his letter Descartes has to satisfy the curiosity of Mersenne, who obtained a copy of *Pentalogos*, although not from Descartes himself. Irritated the philosopher complains that books produced by madmen attract as much attention as any other. However, in a way the author has done him great honour, Descartes adds, for he claims to have said the worst possible things of him, but in fact he has said nothing that could touch him.⁷

The theologian André Rivet was responsible for sending a copy of *Pentalogos* to Mersenne. Mersenne replied Rivet that he found it 'very spicy', and that much insulting, that he assumes there must be a personal row of some kind between the author and Descartes. Mersenne asks Rivet to tell him who is hiding behind the name of Mercurius Cosmopolita, and what might have happened between Descartes and him.⁸ Unfortunately, Rivet's answer is lost.

---

4 AT III 201. 'Mr Hesdin' is probably Johann Eding (c. 1611-1651), a German diplomat in the service of the Danish Crown.
5 On Stampioen and the Stampioen affair, see THEO VERBEEK, 'The Stampioen Affair', in *The Cambridge Descartes Lexicon*, ed. by L. Nolan, New York, Cambridge University Press, 2016, p. 695-697, and THEO VERBEEK, ERIK-JAN BOS and JEROEN VAN DE VEN, *The Correspondence of René Descartes: 1643*, Utrecht, Zeno, 2002, p. 299-303. The printer of *Pentalogos*, Van der Spruit, bought his press from Stampioen on 7 September 1640; *Pentalogos* was one of his first publications. For the sale contract, see Haags Gemeentearchief (HGA), Notarieel archief (0372-0301), inv. no. 132, fol. 95.
6 Huygens to Descartes, 8 October 1640, AT III 760-761: "I'espere qu'elles vauldront un peu mieux voz peines, que le joly traicté qu'un charlatan vient de publier icy contre vous. Mon beau frere de Wilhem le cognoit, et me promit hier de vous le nommer. Son beau stile m'en avoit faict doubter". For De Wilhem's acquintance with Habernfeld, see section 7 below.
7 Descartes to Mersenne, 3 December 1640, AT III 249; BL 1336: "En effet, ie voy que, si ceux des petites Maisons faisoient des livres, ils n'auroient pas moins de lecteurs que les autres; car ie ne tiens pas l'autheur du *Pentalogos* en autre rang. C'est un Chymiste Boémien, demeurant à la Haye, qui me semble m'avoir fait beaucoup d'honneur, en ce qu'ayant témoigné vouloir dire de moy tout le pis qu'il pouvoit, il n'en a rien sceu dire qui me touchast".
8 Mersenne to Rivet, 25 November 1640, in *CM* X 293, and 14 December 1640 in *CM* X 335-336.

Descartes mentions *Pentalogos* a few more times in his letters to Mersenne, but only as a yardstick to judge other works published against him. Repeatedly he assures Mersenne that the *Admiranda methodus novae philosophiae Renati des Cartes* (Utrecht, 1643) by Voetius and Maarten Schoock is on a par with *Pentalogos* and does itself not merit a reply.[9]

In sum, the attack itself by Mercurius Cosmopolita appears to be of no concern to Descartes. However, he is very annoyed by the fact that others show a keen interest, and seem eager to spread the news in the Republic of Letters, even to the point that he has to explain the case to Mersenne in Paris.

2. Mercurius Cosmopolita Identified

The news of a Hermetic response to Descartes travelled rapidly. Rivet had told Mersenne about *Pentalogos* and sent him a copy of the book, but the theologian was not the first to bring it to Mersenne's attention. The first report on the anti-Cartesian attack came to Paris from across the English Channel.

In the late 1630s, Theodore Haak started a correspondence with the learned Minim in an attempt to connect Mersenne's network with that of the Hartlib circle. In the first half of November 1640 Haak must have written Mersenne on the subject of *Pentalogos*, for we know Mersenne's reply: 'I have not seen the chemical booklet against Descartes, nor heard about it. I would like to have it, although I do not believe that it is scientifically any match'.[10] A few weeks later Mersenne wrote to Haak that he had seen *Pentalogos*, but did not believe Descartes would reply to it, and that, in any case, Descartes is a subtler philosopher than all those chemists.[11]

Another member of the Hartlib circle spread the news of the publication of *Pentalogos* as well. From London Joachim Hübner wrote to Jan Amos Comenius that Descartes's attempt at restaging the doctrine of atomism was unsuccessful, as would appear from an anonymous booklet published against him.[12]

Next to Haak and Hübner, Samuel Hartlib was aware of the publication against Descartes. At first he seems to have had no better idea about who was hiding behind

---

9 Descartes to Mersenne, 7 December 1642, AT III 598; BL 1682-1684. Descartes to Mersenne, 4 January 1643, AT III 608; BL 1690. Descartes to Mersenne, 23 March 1643, AT III 643; BL 1728. *Epistola ad Voetium*, AT VIII-2 189; BO 1686.
10 Mersenne to Haak, 16 or 23 November 1640, in *CM* XI 419: "Je n'ay point aussi le livret chymiste contre M^r des Cartes, ni ouy parler. Je voudrais bien l'avoir, qouyque je ne croye pas qu'il soit égal en science".
11 Mersenne to Haak, 13 December 1640, in *CM* XI 435.
12 Hübner to Comenius, 7 December 1640: "Ita Democriteam de atomis doctrinam in theatrum nostra tempestate reducere coepit Cartesius, sed non prospero admodum successu, ut ex brevi quodam Anonymi cujusdam scripto adversus ipsum apparet". *Korrespondence Jan Amosa Komenského*, ed. by Jan Kvačala, vol. 1, Prague, Česká Akademie pro vědy, slovesnost a umění, 1898, p. 101. Members of the Hartlib circle showed a keen interest in Descartes, whom they probably knew through Henricus Reneri; see ROBIN BUNING, *Henricus Reneri (1593-1639): Descartes' Quartermaster in Aristotelian Territory*, Utrecht, Zeno, 2013, p. 181-198.

the name Mercurius Cosmopolita than the other members of the circle. The question of the author's identity was important enough for Hartlib to jot it down in his *Ephemerides* or private notebook after receiving the necessary information. Hartlib's private notebooks have been preserved among the Hartlib Papers, which collection of manuscripts proved to be crucial in identifying the author and in providing more details on the author's life.[13] In 1641 Hartlib wrote down the following remark:

'Dr Haverfeld is the Author of the Tr. C. Meteor. Cartes. Figulus.'[14]

What exactly does this note say? 'Cartes' is Descartes; the '*Treatise Contra* Meteora' is, as I assume, *Pentalogos*, which deals almost exclusively with Descartes's essay on meteorology, *Les Météores*. 'Figulus' is probably Hartlib's source. Peter Figulus (1619-1670) was a Bohemian exile, who accompanied John Dury on his travels as secretary. Figulus and Dury arrived in the United Provinces in early 1641, visiting Groningen, Amsterdam, Leiden and, finally, The Hague, calling upon the Bohemian court in exile.[15] It must have been during his stay in The Hague that Figulus discovered the identity of Mercurius Cosmopolita, and presumably met the author.

Who then is this 'Dr Haverfeld'? His first name is nowhere mentioned, but on the basis of various references in the Hartlib Papers (see below, section 6) he can be identified as Andreas Habervešl of Habernfeld, a Bohemian chemist living in The Hague.[16]

3. Andreas Habervešl of Habernfeld (1587-before 1660)

Habernfeld enjoys some fame as the author of a work entitled *Bellum Bohemicum*, published in 1645.[17] It is an account of the Bohemian war with as dramatic climax the Battle of White Mountain. If we have to rely on the *Bellum Bohemicum*, Habernfeld brought the word of the battle's disastrous outcome to King Frederick in person.

---

13 The Hartlib Papers (HP), kept in the library of the University of Sheffield, are accessible online <https://www.dhi.ac.uk/hartlib/>.
14 Hartlib, Ephemerides, 1641, HP, 30/4/74A. The transcription offered by the Hartlib Papers-project gives 'Havenfeld' but I read 'Haverfeld'.
15 Figulus's travels can be reconstructed with the help of his *album amicorum*. His album has over 400 entries, among others by Queen Elisabeth of Bohemia and her daughters, including princess Elisabeth. Descartes contributed to the album too: on 18 July 1641, in Leiden, he wrote "Philosophandum sed cum paucis!". See ERIK-JAN BOS, "Descartes and Comenius: New Insights-Old Errors", *Comenius-Jahrbuch*, 11-12 (2003-2004), p. 83-95. For Figulus, see also MILADA BLEKASTAD, "Peter Figulus. Letters to Samuel Hartlib", *Lychnos* (1988), p. 201-245, and VLADIMÍR URBÁNEK, "Comenius, the Unity of Brethren, and Correspondence Networks", *Journal of Moravian History*, 14 (2014), p. 30-50, here p. 45-47.
16 His name occurs in many variations. His Czech name reads Ondřej Habervešl z Habernfeldu. In Latin we come across Hoberweschel ab Hobernfeld, or Haberweschel ab Habernfeld; in Dutch and English sources the 'b' in the toponym is often substituted by a 'v': Havernfeld. I will use Habernfeld throughout this chapter.
17 *Bellum Bohemicum recensente Andraea ab Habernfeld ab anno MDCXVII*, Leiden, Warnerus à Tuernhout, 1645. The publisher is otherwise unknown.

The King and his household fled from Prague, and eventually put up their court in exile at The Hague.

Further bits of information on Habernfeld are scattered over various publications; most authors complain about the lack of biographical data. In fact, besides his publications, little else was known of him before 2005.[18] His date of birth was unknown, as was his marital status, and one even had no clue about the year of his death. I have been able to find two sources that resolve various biographical questions regarding Habernfeld. I have already made use of the first one, the Hartlib Papers, and I will turn to them again later on. The second source is a nineteenth century Czech publication on the Habernfeld family with special focus on the author of *Bellum Bohemicum*.[19]

This publication seems to have escaped the attention of scholars until recently, probably due to the fact that it was published in an archaeological journal. The author bases his information on a sixteenth century Czech calendar that once belonged to the Habernfeld family.[20] In this calendar, family members, among whom our Andreas, wrote down important family events, and these provide us with the following family history.

Andreas's father, Albrecht Haberweschel (d. 1604), was an administrator at the court of Rudolf II in Prague. In 1594 the King ennobled him, granting him the title 'of Habernfeld'. In 1586 Albrecht married Anna Žlutická (d. 1644), and the next year, on January 17, 1587, at half past six in the afternoon, their first child, Andreas, was born, under the zodiacal sign of Capricorn, his 'Lord' being, or so the family calendar adds, the planet Mercury. The next event regarding Andreas is his marriage with Magdalena Skálová of Zhoř in 1614; the calendar moreover reveals he was a doctor of medicine. Between 1615 and 1619, Andreas and Magdalena had five children, but none of them

---

18 Since 2005, several studies appeared that greatly enlarged our understanding of Habernfeld, especially by Nicolette Mout and Vladimír Urbánek: NICOLETTE MOUT, "Ondřej Haberwešl of Habernfeld and the Thirty Years' War: His writings, the war and international politics", in *Mezi Baltem a Uhrami. Komenský, Jednota bratrská a svět středoevropského protestantismu*, ed. by V. Urbánek and L. Řezníková, Prague, Filosofia, 2008, p. 149-165; MOUT, "Exil, Krieg und Religion: Erwartungen und Enttäuschungen gelehrter böhmischer Exulanten im Dreissigjährigen Krieg", *Historisches Jahrbuch*, 132 (2012), p. 249-275; VLADIMÍR URBÁNEK, "The Idea of State and Nation in the Writings of Bohemian Exiles after 1620", in *Statehood Before and Beyond Ethnicity: Minor States in Northern and Eastern Europe, 1600-2000*, ed. by Linas Eriksonas and Leos Müller, Brussels, Lang, 2005, p. 67-83. Urbánek moreover wrote extensively (in Czech) about Habernfeld in his book *Eschatologie, vědění a politika: Příspěvek k dějinám myšlení pobělohorského exilu* [*Eschatology, Knowledge and Politics: On the Intellectual History of the Post-White-Mountain Bohemian Exiles*], České Budějovice, Jihočeské univerzity, 2008, p. 145-207. This is the most comprehensive study on Habernfeld available, also paying attention to the various references to the Bohemian doctor in the Hartlib Papers. Urbánek prepared an entry on Habernfeld in the Czech biographical dictionary as well (*Biografický slovník českých zemí*, vol. 21, Prague, Academia, 2018, p. 31-33). Mention must also be made of Govert Snoek's helpful and detailed study of Dutch Rosicrucians including Habernfeld, see GOVERT SNOEK, *De Rozenkruisers in Nederland, voornamelijk in de eerste helft van de 17e eeuw, een inventarisatie*, Haarlem, Rozekruis pers, 2006, p. 88-98.

19 JAN BOHUSLAV MILTNER, "Habrvešlové z Habernfeldu", *Památky archeologické*, 8 (1868), p. 46-56. I thank Dr Ton van den Beld (Utrecht University) for translating the relevant parts of the article for me.

20 DANIEL ADAM OF VELESLAVÍN, *Kalendář historický*, Prague, 1578 and 1590, an overview of European history.

survived infancy. The notes in the calendar and the information in Andreas's work *Bellum Bohemicum* make it clear that he had close ties to the royal court, possibly practising as a court physician. After the Battle of White Mountain, Andreas's goods were confiscated.[21] He fled from Prague, and joined the Bohemian court in exile at The Hague in the early 1620s. The calendar remained in Prague, with Andreas's mother, who had remarried Pavel Rosenberger (d. 1629) in 1608.

4. Academic Studies

Andreas Habernfeld started his academic studies at the University of Helmstedt, where he matriculated on 27 September 1604.[22] In 1607 he moved to Heidelberg, enrolling at the university on October 19.[23] In Heidelberg Habernfeld witnessed the dissection of a human body by professor Johannes Jodocus Lucius.[24] Subsequently he went to Basel in early 1609, where he graduated in medicine in towards the end of the same year.[25] According to Tillman Walter, the Faculty of Medicine in Basel was one of the most frequented in the German speaking realm, owing its 'modernity' not only to the teaching of anatomy and botany by Felix Platter (1525-1614) and Caspar Bauhin (1560-1624), but also to the openness towards chemical medicine initiated by Theodor Zwinger (1533-1588). In fact, 'a whole generation of influential Paracelsian physicians grew up under these three professors'.[26] The case of Habernfeld, however, is a curious one in that respect. In his doctoral thesis on the medical art of uroscopy, Habernfeld judges that the teaching of Paracelsian physicians, who are eager to disagree with Galenus, is partially in line with Galenus (and hence superfluous), but in other

---

21 See URBÁNEK, *Eschatologie*, p. 157, 162, and MOUT, "Habernfeld and the Thirty Years' War", p. 149.
22 PAUL ZIMMERMANN, ed., *Album Academiae Helmstadiensis*, Band I, *Album Academiae Juliae, Abteilung 1, Studenten, Professoren etc. der Universität Helmstedt von 1574-1636*, Hannover, Selbstverlag der historischen Kommission, 1926, p. 176; in 1606 Habernfeld is listed as a student of medicine (p. 187). Habernfeld defended a logical disputation presumably in December 1605, but the original titlepage being lost, the exact date, the title, and the dedication are unknown. Habernfeld's disputation is the fourth one in NICOLAUS ANDREAE GRANIUS, *Logicae disputationes decem*, Helmsted, Lucius, 1606; URL to the digitised copy at the Herzog August Bibliothek, Wolfenbüttel, <https://diglib.hab.de/drucke/0-231-4f-helmst-5s/start.htm?image = 077>.
23 'Andreas Haberweschel de Habernfeld Pragensis', Heidelberg, Universitätsarchiv, UAH M4: 1579-1662, fo. 113v (https://doi.org/10.11588/diglit.17558#0230). The personal name 'Johannes' found in the printed edition is mistaken (G. TOEPKE, ed., *Die Matrikel der Universität Heidelberg*, vol. 2, Heidelberg, Winter, 1886, p. 237).
24 HABERNFELD, *Theoremata de uroscopia in genere*, p. [9]; see note 27. On J. J. Lucius (1576-1613), see DAGMAR DRÜLL, *Heidelberger Gelehrtenlexikon 1386-1651*, Berlin and Heidelberg, Springer, 2002, p. 362.
25 Habernfeld matriculated at the University of Basel in January 1609, and graduated MD on 21 November 1609, see *Die Matrikel der Universität Basel*, III, ed. by H. G. Wackernagel, Basel, Verlag der Universitätsbibliothek, 1962, p. 97.
26 TILMANN WALTER, "New Light on Antiparacelsianism (*c.* 1570-1610): The Medical Republic of Letters and the Idea of Progress in Science", *Sixteenth Century Journal*, 43 (2012), p. 700-725 (esp. p. 720-721).

respects their ideas are most obscure, and any physician unworthy.²⁷ Then again, in the short preface to the disputation Habernfeld does speak of urine as a general microcosm, which was, admittingly, an ancient and common notion in medicine, but as such very typical for Paracelsian medicine as well. In any case, Habernfeld, who in the remainder of the text displays an extensive knowledge of Paracelsian medicine, showed himself to be a Paracelsist physician a few years later. The question whether Habernfeld was very critical of only some aspects of Paracelsian medicine, or that he presented views that were in accordance with the views of his professors, cannot be answered at present. That Paracelsian medicine could be favourably discussed in a doctoral thesis is shown in the case of Ole Worm (1588-1654) — professor of medicine in Copenhagen from 1624 onwards — who graduated MD in Basel in 1611 (his promotor being Platter).²⁸

Exercising his right to preside over academic disputations, Habernfeld delivered at least one medical disputation in April 1610, and presents himself as the author of the text.²⁹ There is nothing Paracelsian about the main text of the disputation, but in the introductory remarks the author dwells (again) upon the microcosm — macrocosm analogy, a key concept in Paracelsian, Hermetic and Neo-Platonic philosophy. Remarkably, one of Habernfeld's own study books has been preserved: a copy of the Greek Aphorisms of Hippocrates, with Latin translation and commentary by Johannes Heurnius, shows Habernfeld's ex libris.³⁰

5. Early Publications

Habernfeld's first known publication outside academia is an open letter dated Prague, September first, 1614. It is written in reply to the famous *Fama confraternitatis* by the secret members of the Rosicrucian Order. As is well known, the members of this order asked their audience to openly react to their manifesto, and Habernfeld

---

27 *Theoremata de uroscopia in genere* [...] *publico examini proponit Andreas Hoberweschel ab Hobrfeld. Boh. Ad diem ... Octobr. horâ et loco solitis*, Basel, Genathus, 1609. On the title page the exact date of the disputation is intentionally left blank, but the day is added in handwriting; see <http://dx.doi.org/10.3931/e-rara-17828>. The official graduation took place in November (see note 25); the printed invitation has been preserved and indicates Petrus Ryff (1552-1629) as Habernfeld's promotor. See Basel University Library, UBH EJ I 26:149.
28 See JOLE SHACKELFORD, "Paracelsianism and the Orthodox Lutheran Rejection of Vital Philosophy in Early Seventeenth-Century Denmark", *Early Science and Medicine*, 8 (2003), p. 210-252, esp. p. 240-241. For Habernfeld's studies at Basel see also URBÁNEK, *Eschatologie*, p. 151-156.
29 *Disputationem* [...] *physico medicam de medicamentorum facultatibus in genere: Consensu Spectabilssimi Decani Clariss. Dn. D. Caspari Bauhini* [...] *Praesidente Andrea Hoberweschel ab Hobrnfeld* [...] *exercitii causa placide vellicandam praebet Joannes Jacobus Frisius Tigurinus*, Basel, Waldkirch, 1610. Date: 16 April (the day is added in handwriting, only the month being printed). The dedication is signed 'Praeses Auctor etc.'. See <https://doi.org/10.3931/e-rara-17843>.
30 *Hippocratis Coi Aphorismi*, ed. by Johannes Heurnius, Leiden, Plantin/Raphelengius, 1601. Graz University Library, shelf mark: Rara 2-I 35775. The book entered the personal library of a certain Karl Bohuslaus Felix before *c.* 1625, see <http://sosa2.uni-graz.at/sosa/druckschriften/druckschriften/g-feliciana.php> (last accessed 5 October 2021).

enthusiastically obeyed. In his letter he refers to an earlier and anonymous reply of his, to which he had not received an answer.[31] So he now vigorously restates his application as member of the Rose-Cross, with the full mention of his name.

The original and undoubtedly Latin publication appears to be lost. For reasons still unresolved, Habernfeld's letter was reprinted in a Dutch translation, appended to the Dutch translation of the *Fama fraternitatis*, which saw the light in 1615.[32] The title of Habernfeld's contribution reads *Discovery of an anonymous reply to the Fama Fraternitatis of the Rose-Cross, by an author dedicated to Hermetic medicine [...] Andreas Hoberveschel of Hobernfeld, Doctor of medicine, lover of chemical medicine*.[33]

The following passage from Habernfeld's writing illustrates his dedication to Hermetic and chemical medicine. Habernfeld recognises in the *Fama* a programme for universal knowledge, a programme, which, according to Habernfeld, can only be carried out by the morally pure and god-fearing Christian. Taking the light of nature as his guide, Habernfeld states that:

> by the number of four he will obtain perfect knowledge of the trinity, and he will learn what the earth carries in her lap, what the sea contains at its centre, what the quick air, and what the unlimited chaos. Then the true and inner anatomy of animal and mineral spirits will be revealed to him; the magical harmony between heaven and earth, as well as the magnetic attraction, will be opened up for him. What else? He will learn that all these things are endowed with one and the same moving spirit, from whom, by whom and [through] whom all things exist, and he is everything in all. Thus, [...] being firmly taught in this way, he will subsequently attain knowledge of himself, and understand how he, as if in a small world and a mirror, is a small-worldly globe.[34]

In this passage Habernfeld enumerates a number of closely related concepts. Working our way up through the passage, we first of all encounter the concept

---

31 As *Fama fraternitatis* was published in Kassel in 1614, it seems likely that Habernfeld read the manifesto in manuscript.
32 *Fama Fraternitatis, oft Ontdeckinge van de Broederschap des loflijcken Ordens des Roosen-Cruyces* (s.l., s.n., 1615). The book is unpaginated. Habernfeld's letter is in the last quire, on K3-[K6r°]. Cf. the discussion of this writing in URBÁNEK, *Eschatologie*, p. 181-182. See also SNOEK, *Rozenkruisers*, p. 59-62.
33 *Ontdeckinghe van een onghenoemde Antwoorde op de Famam Fraternitatis des Rosen-Cruyces van een Autheur der Hermetischer Medicijn-konst toeghedaen [...] Andreas Hoberveschel van Hobernfeld etc. Doctoor der Medicijne, Liefhebber der Chymische Genees-konste*. For some doubts whether Habernfeld's letter appeared in 1615 or 1617, see SNOEK, *Rozenkruisers*, p. 59-61.
34 "[C]rijght hy door 't getal van vieren een gantsch volcomen kennisse van de dryheyt, ende leert wat het aertrijck in synen schoot voert, wat de Zee in haer middelpunct, wat de snelle locht, ende het ongemeten Chaos in sich begrijpt: daer na werdt hem de | ware ende innerlijcke ontledinge der dierghelijcke roerende ende minerale gheesten bekent: de Magische overeenstemminghe der hemelsche ende aertsche dinghen, midtgaders hare Magnetische toebuyginghe tot malcanderen, wordt hem gheopent. Wat meer? Hy leert dat alle dese dingen ghedreven worden van eenen ende densleven bewegenden gheest, uyt wien, door wien, ende wt wien alle dinghen zijn, ende hy is alles in allen. Hier door dan, [...], grondelick onderwesen zijnde, comt hy aldernaest tot kennisse van hem selven, waer in hy als in een cleyne werelt ende spiegel dese cleyn-wereltschen Cloot". *Fama Fraternitatis, oft Ontdeckinge*, [K4r°-v°].

of two worlds: the macrocosm or the universe, and the microcosm or man. Man is a small replica of the great universe and within him are represented all parts of that universe.[35] Consequently, knowledge of the macrocosm will, according to Habernfeld, result in self-knowledge. Next we come across the concept of a World-Soul pervading the universe, being 'everything in all'. There is, furthermore, a magical harmony between heaven and earth, which unites the two worlds and may point to the influence of the stars on the terranean world. Furthermore, minerals and living creatures have a hidden anatomy or an internal essence, which resembles the so-called doctrine of signatures, the idea that God had 'signed' all things on earth. Finally, at the beginning of the text, Habernfeld offers a brief account of his theory of elements. I presume that 'the number of four' refers to the four Aristotelian elements, the firm grasp of which would lead to the understanding of a more fundamental division in three principles. Being 'dedicated to chemical medicine', Habernfeld must refer to the chemical principles salt, sulphur and mercury.

We recognize elements of Neo-Platonism, Hermetic philosophy and alchemy. These elements were put into a more or less coherent system by the sixteenth century physician Paracelsus. On the basis of the text just considered, we can characterise Habernfeld as a follower of Paracelsus, or, in his own words, a 'lover of chemical philosophy'. In the remainder of his letter Habernfeld maintains that chemical wisdom is among the most ancient of all wisdom, and he expresses his hope that the fraternity of the Rose-Cross will fully reveal all the treasures of the divine-magical, or chemical philosophy.

Next to being a Paracelsian physician and a would-be member of the Rosicrucian Brotherhood, Habernfeld shows himself a chiliast in his next publications. In 1620 he polemised on the meaning of the comet that had appeared in 1618.[36] Using corrosive irony against his opponent, a professor of physics at the University of Prague who offered an Aristotelian explanation of the phenomenon, Habernfeld placed the appearance of the 'hairy star' in an apocalyptic framework. The new star would be a sign of the second coming of Christ, whose forerunner, Frederick of the Palatinate,

---

35 ALLEN DEBUS, *The Chemical Philosophy: Paracelsian Science and Medicine in the Sixteenth and Seventeenth Centuries*, vol. 1, New York, New York Science History Publ., 1977, p. 99.
36 *De asterisco comato magico theosophica consideratio [...] Currenti calamo depicta per H. F. C. M. A. D. C. R. H. Anno MDCXIX*. Anonymous, no place; actual date of publication is presumably 1620, not 1619, given that one of the laudatory poems is dated February 1620. For the identification with Habernfeld and the historical context of the pamphlet, see VLADIMÍR URBÁNEK, 'The Comet of 1618: Eschatological Expectations and Political Prognostications during the Bohemian Revolt', in *Tycho Brahe and Prague: Crossroads of European Science*, ed. by J. R. Christianson and others (Frankfurt a. M.: Deutsch, 2002), p. 282-291. The initials on the title page are printed in a circle with HAH on its vertical axis, which probably denotes, as Urbánek suggests, "Andreas Haberweschel ab Habernfeld"; if so, 'MD' on the horizontal axis is "Medicinae Doctor", and the remaining initials could mean "Fraternitatis Christianae Rosae Crucis". The copy of this work in the Czech National Library (available on Google Books) shows a handwritten note on the title page saying "Ex dono auctoris possidet Ioachimus [?] Strasburg mense april. a. 1620". If the reading "Ioachimus" is correct, could it be Joachim Morsius (see section 7 below)?

elected King of Bohemia in August 1619, is predestined to crush the Catholic forces. The defeat at White Mountain must have come as a shock to Habernfeld, but once in Holland he published yet another visionary work, entitled *Jerusalem Restored, or the Age of the firy Holy Spirit*, now proclaiming that the 'Roman Beast' would be destroyed and the Palatine House restored towards the year 1624.[37]

However, the year 1624 came and went by, without a political or religious revolution. In his private life, however, Habernfeld suffered another blow: having tragically lost all his children before he went into exile, he also lost his wife shortly after his arrival in the Dutch Republic. He remarried in 1635, and his second wife bore him several children.[38]

6. Habernfeld's Further Political Enterprises

In the autumn of 1643 Peter Figulus travelled from Sweden to The Hague carrying with him instructions of the Swedish High Chancellor Oxenstierna for the Bohemian community in The Netherlands. Oxenstierna asked Figulus to assure the Bohemians that Sweden aimed at restoring the political situation from before 1618, and would not to lay down the weapons before Bohemia was liberated. The High Chancellor urged the Bohemians in exile to substantiate their claims in print.[39] In October 1643, Figulus wrote to Oxenstierna that a certain Dr Habernfeld, attending the Bohemian court, was delighted to hear the Swedish promises and will follow his directions.[40] Habernfeld subsequently composed two works in favour of the Bohemian cause, his *Bellum Bohemicum* (1645) being the most well-known. It is a remarkably balanced historical account of the Bohemian Revolt, in which the author cites and uses many historical documents. Habernfeld's intention is to show that the Bohemian Estates had always enjoyed the freedom to elect their king and to resist any monarch who infringed their rights. He is particularly hostile to the Jesuits, and blames them for

---

37 HABERNFELD, *Hierosolima restituta, sive Seculum Spiritus Sancti igneum*, The Hague, Meurs, 1622. Habernfeld dedicated the pamphlet to the Dutch States General. For more details of this work, see Urbánek, *Eschatologie*, p. 189-193.
38 The intended marriage with Catharina Pumbeke (Pumbeek) van Crabin was announced on 20 May 1635. See SNOEK, *Rozenkruisers*, p. 92-93, and MOUT, "Habernfeld and the Thirty Years' War", p. 150. Three children are mentioned in the The Hague baptismal records, but there have been more: 1. Johanna Haberffvelt (13 February 1639); 2. Johannes Havervelt (23 June 1641); 3. Haversfelt (no first name, 6 September 1643). One of the witnesses of the baptism of Johannes was Caspar Streso (cf. note 1), see SNOEK, *Rozenkruisers*, p. 93. The third child must be Catharina Elisabeth, born 3 September, who married into the Utrecht noble family Van Reede tot Nederhorst (MOUT, *Habernfeld*, p. 150; *De Navorscher*, 17 (1867), p. 61). Habernfeld's wife is called Catharina Havervelt, 'widow of doctor Havervelt, aged around 67 years,' in a notary deed from 1667; she signed as Katarina Haberffelt (HGA, Notarieel archief (0372-0301), inv. no. 518, fol. 490).
39 MILADA BLEKASTAD, *Comenius: Versuch eines Umrisses von Leben, Werk und Schicksal des Jan Amos Komenský*, Oslo and Prague, Universitetsforlaget and Academia, 1969, p. 376.
40 MILADA BLEKASTAD, *Unbekannte Briefe des Comenius und seiner Freunde 1641-1661*, Ratingen, Henn, 1976, p. 107-108.

executing a devious plan to abolish the Bohemian liberties. Habernfeld's second writing, a pamphlet equally published in 1645, is an attempt to put the Bohemian cause on the agenda of the peace talks at Osnabrück.[41]

However, Habernfeld deployed more activities in support of the Palatine family and the Bohemian cause. As it turns out, he also excelled in the art of plotting. Indeed, one of the plots to murder the English King carries his name, and although the Habernfeld Plot is not as famous or important as the Gunpowder Plot (1604), it became widely known and the documents relating to the plot were reprinted several times during the seventeenth century.

The history of the plot is briefly as follows. In August 1640 the English ambassador at The Hague, William Boswell, wrote in distress to the Archbishop Laud about a plot against the King's life and Laud's own.[42] Boswell was informed about the plot from 'a friend of good quality and worth in this place', namely Andreas of Habernfeld. The ambassador took the information seriously, as did Laud. According to the information provided by Habernfeld, the plot was already in full swing, being planned by the Jesuits, carried out by countless Jesuit spies in England, including many intimates of the King 'corrupted with a foreign pension'. According to Habernfeld, the Scots were moved into action against the Anglican Church and the King by the Jesuits, who at the same time encouraged the English to support the Scots, in order to force the King into an alliance with the papists, under strong popish conditions. If the King refused these conditions, he would be assassinated.

Habernfeld wrote to Laud himself, supplying all the details of the plot, including the names of the persons involved. Laud in his turn informed the King, who at first seemed disposed to believe in the plot. But upon hearing that nearly all his courtly intimates were supposedly corrupted by the Jesuits, he soon lost his interest in the plot. However, when Laud's enemies discovered the Habernfeld documents, they seized the opportunity to publish them with their own strained interpretation, depicting Laud as one of the traitors. The publication fuelled the sentiments against the Archbishop, who was executed for treason in 1645.

The Habernfeld plot differs in one important respect from other Popish plots against Charles I, because it came from a party that was not hostile to the royal court. It is argued that the Habernfeld plot reflects the views of the circle of Charles' sister, Elisabeth Stuart, Queen of Bohemia. Indeed, the aim of the discovery of the plot was to convince Laud's opponents that they had fallen victim to popish agitators, and to persuade the King that his true enemies were not found on the British Isles, but on the Continent. If the plot was an invention by the Bohemian court at The Hague,

---

41 HABERNFELD, *Ad exceptiones contra Bohemos a suae Caesareae Majestatis Ferdinandi Tertii ad pacificationem publicam Monasteriensem, plenipotentiario legato, objectatas Responsum* (no place, no publisher, 1645). For Habernfeld's political views, see MOUT, "Habernfeld and the Thirty Years' War"; MOUT, "Exil, Krieg und Religion", *Historisches Jahrbuch*, 132 (2012), p. 249-275; URBÁNEK, "The Idea of State and Nation"; URBÁNEK, *Eschatologie*, p. 195-202.

42 See CAROLINE M. HIBBARD, *Charles I and the Popish Plot*, Chapel Hill, University of North Carolina Press, 1983, "The Habernfeld Plot", p. 157-162, and URBÁNEK, *Eschatologie*, p. 167-172, who also worked with the manuscript material from the Public Record Office.

as seems likely, its goal was to turn England's attention to the protestant war against the Spanish-Habsburg rule.

It is improbable that the plot was entirely Habernfeld's own invention, but the experience made him develop a taste for plotting. In 1642 he convinced John Dury that in Germany, Hungary and Bohemia a secret party was being formed to liberate Bohemia. Dury informed Hartlib of the existence of this secret party, which would show itself as soon as the Prince Elector would cross the Channel to lead the party into battle. Dury urged Hartlib to pass the information on to the members of parliament who favoured the Bohemian cause.

In the following year, Hartlib received various reports that two strangers from the far east were lodging with Habernfeld. These 'Indies', as they are called, would be representatives of a powerful Christian commonwealth, who were sent out to investigate the fate of the protestants in Europe. Having been informed of the current state of affairs, the Indies promised to supply all the protestants' needs in their battle against the Habsburgs. This news seemed too good to be true, but exactly because it was such a wonderful story, it could, according to Hartlib, be real. To one of his correspondents Hartlib confided his view that the Indies might be one of the lost Jewish tribes. And isn't it true, Hartlib wrote, that the Lord will call the Jews home, and it cannot be long before that time comes.[43]

Seeking confirmation of the reports, Hartlib wrote to Dury at The Hague. Strangely enough, Dury knew nothing about the matter, but immediately started an investigation. Dury's reply to Hartlib has been preserved among the Hartlib papers:

> The Businesse which yow desire to know concerning Dr Haberfelds Indies is a thing which hee will not take any notice of towards me; hee will not owne any such matter; nor indeed can hee with a good Conscience owne many thinges which hee giveth out, & I have beene informed (what I in part beleeve, & am loath to relate) that hee hath trickes to give informations [grounded] upon nothing but fancies, & chimeraes.[44]

Remembering what he had written on Habernfeld's secret army to Hartlib the previous year, Dury is reluctant to admit that Habernfeld's credibility is not undisputed. Now his eyes are opened, he reconsiders the story of the party 'underdecks', writing in one of his next letters to Hartlib that it was a plot of Habernfeld to raise an expectation.[45]

7. Habernfeld's Medical Tracts and Practice

During the early 1620s Habernfeld made at least one journey to the German countries. In the spring of 1623 he was in Hamburg, where he met Joachim Morsius (1593-1643/4)

---

43 Hartlib to [Sir J? Hobart?], 6 July 1643 (HP, 7/27/25A). For more source evidence of this story and its eschatological context, see URBÁNEK, *Eschatologie*, p. 176-178. Cf. BLEKASTAD, *Comenius*, p. 337-338.
44 Dury to Hartlib, The Hague, 6 August 1643 (HP, 2/10/9B).
45 Dury to Hartlib, The Hague 12 April 1644 (HP 3/2/14B).

in whom he must have recognised a kindred spirit.[46] Like Habernfeld, Morsius had replied to the Rosicrucian call in print, and from 1618 he travelled extensively throughout the north-west of Europe, pursuing his interest in the fraternity and esoteric wisdom. In 1625 Morsius published a short pseudo-Paracelsian text using the pseudonym Anastasius Philaretus Cosmopolita.[47] He dedicated the short tract to Andreas Habernfeld, urging him to publish the posthumous manuscripts of Paracelsus in his possession, as well as those of the Danish Paracelsian physician Petrus Severinus (1542-1602), and his own works.[48] Habernfeld never published any text of Paracelsus or Severinus, but he did comply to Morsius's request regarding his own works. He published two medical tracts that will have been to Morsius's liking, one on potable gold, and another on the plague and its cure.

Aurum potabile, or potable gold, was, together with the philosopher's stone, the highest aim of any alchemist. It is the elixir for the prolongation of life, and a universal medicine, much esteemed by Paracelsus and his followers, who were trying to establish a magical and alchemical healing art. During the seventeenth century various authors claimed to possess the secret method of manufacturing potable gold and published their discoveries using the veiled language of alchemy. In 1631 Habernfeld published his *Golden elixir or potable Gold, communicated for public use*.[49] After a theoretical account of the elixir, in a mixture of Hermetic, Paracelsist and alchemical concepts, Habernfeld describes the process to produce the potable gold. He subsequently offers a catalogue of diseases to be cured by the medicine: diseases of the head, thorax, lungs,

---

46 Habernfeld contributed to Morsius' *album amicorum* in Hamburg on 7 April 1623 (URN: <https://nbn-resolving.org/urn:nbn:de:gbv:48-41-631642/fragment/page = 347>). The very rich album is kept in the Bibliothek der Hansestadt Lübeck. Beneath Habernfeld's entry Morsius (?) wrote "Serenissimi Regis Bohemiae Medicus". Two years earlier, Habernfeld appears to have been in Strasbourg, see note 36.

47 ANASTASIUS PHILARETUS COSMOPOLITA [J. MORSIUS], *Magische Propheceyung aureoli Philippi Theophrasti Paracelsi*, Philadelphia [Amsterdam?], no printer, 1625. Next to Habernfeld and Morsius, Descartes too showed an interest in the Rosicrucian Brotherhood around 1620. He intended to publish a work entitled *Thesaurus mathematicus*, using the pseudonym "Polybius Cosmopolitanus", with a dedication to the "distinguished Fraternity of the Rosy Cross in Germany" (see *Cogitationes privatae*, AT X 214; BOp 1060). Descartes's choice of a pseudonym, in line with that of Morsius, and Habernfeld's in 1640, is not coincidental; for the "cosmopolitan vocabulary", see LEIGH PENMAN, *The Lost History of Cosmopolitanism: The Early Modern Origins of the Intellectual Ideal*, London, Bloomsbury, 2021. Descartes's interest in Rosicrucianism seems to have been short-lived; Didier Kahn debunked much of the stories Adrien Baillet relates in his biography (see note 68) about Descartes and the Rosicrucian Brotherhood in DIDIER KAHN, "The Rosicrucian Hoax in France (1623-1624)", in *Secrets of Nature: Astrology and Alchemy in Early Modern Europe*, ed. by A. Grafton and W. Newman, Cambridge, MA, MIT Press, 2001, p. 235-344.

48 The salutation reads "Nobilissimo & Excellentissimo Domino D. Andreae Hoberweschelio ab Hobernfeld, Politico, Philosopho & Medico celeberrimo". See J. BRUCKNER, *A Bibliographical Catalogue of Seventeenth-Century German Books Published in Holland*, The Hague and Paris, Mouton, 1971, p. 30.

49 HABERNFELD, *Elixir aureum seu aurum poatabile. Publico usui communicatum*, The Hague, Breeckevelt, 1631. The text has 32 p. in-8°. On 6 January 1631, at The Hague, Habernfeld contributed to the *album amicorum* of Johann Elichmann (*c.* 1600-1639), a Silesian physician, chemist, and orientalist, who befriended Descartes not much later (London, Wellcome Library, MS 257, fo. 30). For Elichmann, see JOHANN FÜCK, "Elichman(n), Johann" in: *Neue Deutsche Biographie* 4 (1959), p. 440.

heart, liver, intestines, genitals, and joints. Moreover, a monthly dose mixed with a generous amount of beer or wine will protect the human body against all infirmities.

In 1635, when the plague ravaged the Dutch Republic, Habernfeld published a short treatise on the disease and its cure: *Treatise on the plague from the quintuple Entia, containing the true anatomy of the plague from the foundations of Hermetic Wisdom, and its cure*.[50] Following the writings of Paracelsus, Habernfeld distinguishes the five powers or *entia* which cause the pest. He starts with the *Ens Divine*: the plague as God's wrath for the sins of mankind.[51] According to Paracelsian theory, the true origin of the plague are men themselves. By their sins, impure thoughts or bad passions, men corrupt the heavens, which subsequently mirror these bad influences, sending back the plague. Habernfeld then discusses the other four *entia*: the *Ens astrale*, the *Ens venene*, the *Ens naturale*, and finally the *Ens spirituale*. After summing up the signs and symptoms of the plague distinguished after each of the five different *entia*, Habernfeld sets out to offer cures to the various types of the disease. Of course, there is no natural cure against God's retribution, but remedies against the other types do exist. Habernfeld supplies various recipes, based upon the doctrines of Paracelsus and Hermetic philosophy, and to be chemically prepared.

These publications widened Habernfeld's name and fame as a Paracelsist physician. He practised in the higher societal circles of The Hague, including the Bohemian Court and the court of the Prince of Orange. Sources mentioning his capabilities as a physician are, however, scarce, and the two we have offer opposing views on his qualities. John Dury was about to send Habernfeld's remedy for kidney stones to Hartlib, when he was told that it was a very dangerous medicine, which had almost ruined the health of Sir Robert Honeywood.[52]

The second report regarding Habernfeld as a physician comes from David de Wilhem, who had revealed the identity of Mercurius Cosmopolita to Descartes in 1640. Some historical background is needed to understand the passage of a letter cited below. In 1642 the Prince of Orange, Frederik Hendrik, invited the famous wonder doctor Andreas Cnoffelius (d. 1658) to treat him. After much effort, the Polish Royal physician finally agreed to visit the Prince who was campaigning in Flanders. Cnoffelius could cure the Prince, or so he claimed, but in order to manufacture his legendary tincture, the potable gold, he needed to visit the apothecaries in Amsterdam. In The Hague Cnoffelius had a row with the royal Bohemian physician, who also served the Orange family, Christian Rumpf (or Romph, 1580-1645). Because of this

---

50 HABERNFELD, *Tractatus de peste ex quintuplici ente, continens, ex fundamentis Hermeticae sapientiae, veram pestis anatomiam, et ad illius curationem*, The Hague, Breeckevelt, 1635. The work, dedicated to the Dutch States General, has 88 p. in-4°. On this work see also URBÁNEK, *Eschatologie*, p. 193-195.
51 The theory of the five *entia*, the origin of all diseases and especially the plague, is found in PARACELSUS, *Volumen medicinae paramirum*, Eng. transl. by Kurt Leidecker, Baltimore, Johns Hopkins University Press, 1949. Recent articles studying Paracelsus' views on the plague are CHARLES GUNNOE, "Paracelsus, the Plague, and *De Pestilitate*", *Early Science and Medicine*, 24 (2019), p. 504-526, and DIDIER KAHN, "*De Pestilitate* and Paracelsian Cosmology", *Daphnis*, 48 (2020), p. 65-86.
52 See Dury's letters to Hartlib from 9 October 1642 and 2 February 1643 (HP, 2/9/37A, 60/4/1B). Robert Honeywood (c. 1601-1686) held offices at both the Bohemian and the Orange courts.

row and some further unpleasantness, Cnoffelius did not go to Amsterdam but left the Dutch Republic. The Prince's retinue now eagerly searched for someone else capable of preparing the tincture. Huygens, at the army, and De Wilhem, at The Hague, corresponded about this matter, and about Maurits Huygens, Constantijn's brother, who became seriously ill in September 1642 — he died on September 24. On September 17, 1642, De Wilhem wrote to Huygens:

> Dr Havervelt has a good understanding of the particular cures of diseases and has many rare secrets. He does not work in the usual way. He even boasts that he has the tincture of Dr Cnoffelius, which I find hard to believe even though he says so himself. Nevertheless, I have ordered more to be made and I will send you a flask to be compared with the one used by colonel Ysselstein.[53] Tomorrow or the day after tomorrow it will be ready. In any case, he has successfully cured my wife, whom Rumpf and all the other scoundrels had abandoned after having reduced her to an unspeakable exhaustion. I have recommended him to your brother but he will have none of it. When he treated my wife he ordered nothing without Mr Rumpf's approval and he bravely admitted that he never contradicted him. But when he is alone he scorns everybody and thinks he knows it all.[54]

Contrary to Dury (and Honeywood) De Wilhem has a favourable opinion of Habernfeld, and how could he not? Habernfeld cured his wife, Constantia Huygens (1602-1667), after Rumpf and others had aggravated her condition and given up on her. Habernfeld, according to De Wilhem, does not work like other, more common doctors, and has 'many rare secrets'. Unsurprisingly, given his 1631 publication, the Bohemian doctor claims he can reproduce the potable gold to cure the Prince, but De Wilhem is doubtful.[55] De Wilhem's final remark reveals Habernfeld's position: he is secunary to doctor Rumpf and in no position to openly disagree with him. De Wilhem recognises some weaknesses in Habernfeld, but he is clear as to which of the two physicians is to be preferred. To illustrate his view, he tells him in the remainder of the letter an anecdote showing Rumpf's bad faith.

---

53 Presumably Vincent van IJsselstein (d. 1656), Governor of Orsoy and colonel in the States' army. He had Cnoffelius' tincture at his disposal and used it (cf. J. A. WORP, ed., *De briefwisseling van Constantijn Huygens*, 6 vols, The Hague, Nijhoff, 1911-1914, III (1914), p. 328, 346).

54 De Wilhem to Huygens, 17 September 1642: "Le docteur Havervelt entend fort bien les cures particulieres des maladies et a quantites de secrets rares. Il ne s'occupe pas tant aux facons ordinaires. Voire il se vante d'avoir la teincture du Dr Cnoffelius, ce que j'ay de la peine de croire selon son recit mesmes. Neantmoins plus en ay commandé d'en faire et vous en enverray une ampoulle pour la conferer avec celle qu'use M. le Colonnel Ysselstein. Demain ou apres demain elle sera faicte. Tant y a qu'il a guairy heureusement ma femme, laquelle Romph et toute cette autre canaille avoit abandonné apres l'avoir reduict a une extenuation indicible. Je l'ay recommandé a vostre frere mais il n'en veut rien faire. Quand il traitta ma femme il n'ordonna rien que par l'approbation de M. Romph et il se faisoit advouer bravement que jamais il ne luy a contredit. Mais quand il est seul il blasme tout le monde et fait l'entendu". A summary is in WORP, *Briefwisseling*, III, 351; original letter: <http://resources.huygens.knaw.nl/briefwisselingconstantijnhuygens/brief/nr/3156>.

55 Habernfeld's name does not reappear in Huygens' correspondence. In any case, the Prince's health problems persisted, and in 1645 he paid 2500 guilders to Cnoffelius to visit him again. See Thymen van Volbergen to Huygens, 15 August 1645, in WORP, *Briefwisseling*, IV 193; <http://resources.huygens.knaw.nl/briefwisselingconstantijnhuygens/brief/nr/4077>.

The question whether Habernfeld cured Constantia Huygens before or after the publication of *Pentalogos* (1640) is interesting but impossible to answer now. We also do not know if Habernfeld's success influenced De Wilhem's opinion about Paracelsian medicine, or Hermetic philosophy, but De Wilhem acknowledged in any case that the Bohemian chemist knew things others did not. Presumably he did not share Huygens's and Descartes's view that Habernfeld was a charlatan. Remarkably, in 1640 De Wilhem sought Descartes's advice in the treatment of his little daughter, who apparently suffered from rickets.[56] While the attending physician was Cornelis van Hogelande, assisted by a surgeon, Descartes was presumably asked to advice on the fabrication and adjustement of the splints. Tellingly, Descartes also talks about powders prepared by Van Hogelande, who indeed took an interest in alchemy.[57]

8. Habernfeld's Demise

I will now quickly bring my biographical account of Habernfeld to an end so that we can turn our attention to *Pentalogos*. It is not known when exactly Habernfeld died; before 2008, it was generally assumed that he died in the second half of the 1640s, because he did not to publish anything after 1645. Once again, Hartlib's notebook proves to be of great value. In Hartlib's notes over the year 1659, we find the following entry:

> Dr Haberfield's Widdow hath left unto her by her Husband the Receipt and Medecin of perfectly curing Cancers Ulcers. etc. In a Word, A Universal Chirurgical Medecin.[58]

The note indicates that Habernfeld died before 1660. The recipe of the 'universal medicine' the widow refused to impart, seems not to have been lost but published in one of the posthumous recipe books by Sir Kenelm Digby, who apparently had received it from Habernfeld himself.[59]

One last quote from Hartlib's diary notes regarding Habernfeld needs to be mentioned. It reveals the sad circumstances of Habernfeld's last years. The note is dated 1655.

---

56 See Descartes to De Wilhem, [13 June 1640], AT III 91, and H. J. WITKAM, "Jean Gillot (Een Leids ingenieur)", *Jaarboekje voor geschiedenis en oudheidkunde van Leiden en omstreken*, 59 (1967), p. 29-54, esp. p. 35-36, 46-53.
57 Descartes to De Wilhem, 24 June 1640, AT III 92-93. On Van Hogelande and alchemy, see SYLVAIN MATTON, "Cartésianisme et alchimie: à propos d'un témoignage ignoré sur les travaux alchimiques de Descartes", in *Aspects de la tradition alchimique au XVIIe siècle*, ed. by F. Greiner, Paris and Milan, SEHA/Arché, 1998, p. 111-184.
58 Hartlib, Ephemerides, 1659, HP, 29/8/9B. The note is written towards the end of 1659.
59 KENELM DIGBY, *A choice collection of rare chymical secrets and experiments in philosophy [...] Collected and experimented by [...] Sir Kenelm Digby*, London, 1682, p. 232-233: "Doctor Havervelt his Remedy, wherewith he cured the Evil o[f] Scrofulaes, Cancers, and Old Ulcers. [...] The said Doctor Communicated this Remedy to Sir K. D". Snoek discovered two more recipes in a manuscript kept at Cambridge University Library (SNOEK, *Rozenkruisers*, p. 96).

[Habernfeld] Plaid the bankrupt, leaving his daughters behind him at the Hague, spending the money which was given him towards Chymical Experiments upon whores.[60]

According to the information received by Hartlib, Habernfeld went bankrupt, abandoned his children, and surely his wife as well. He would have cheated upon his benefactors, spending their money not on chemical experiments, but for his own carnal pleasures. He ran off, which may explain why his name is not found in the burial registers of The Hague. There seems to be some truth in these rumours, for apparently Habernfeld was forced to leave his house at the Denneweg in The Hague in 1655.[61] Moreover, in October 1654, a certain Catherine Smiellen made a statement before a notary that the gossip that she bore a child from doctor Habernfeld was false.[62] Quite a sad and humiliating end of the life of this Bohemian physician and Hermetic philosopher.

9. *Pentalogos*

Pentalogos starts as a conversation between five, namely, between *Hermetis Filius*, or the Son of Hermes, *Apolonii nepos*, or Apollo's grandson, *Natura*, Nature, *Mercurius filius Naturae*, or Mercurius the son of Nature, and finally, *Naturalista gloriosus*,[63] or the boasting Naturalist. After the introduction, *Pentalogos* continues as a dialogue between Mercurius and the braggart naturalist, in whom we easily recognize the two opponents, the first submitting the views of Mercurius Cosmopolita, or Habernfeld, the second being Descartes.

The conversation takes place in a bookshop, where *Apollonii nepos* runs into the son of Hermes, examining a certain book. *Apollonii nepos* asks the son of Hermes his opinion about the book, and the latter answers that the author is an utter fool excelling in absurdities. Speaking of the devil, the swaggering Descartes appears at the scene:

> Good day, Mylords, good day. Oho, I see that you are nosing in my stuff, how does this book look to you, isn't it to your liking, as it explains to you the principles and enumerates the causes? I am its author: am I not a learned man? What do you think of me?[64]

This is a cheerful Descartes, vainglorious and full of himself, and throughout the conversation he stays that way. While the others throw the worst insults at him,

---

60 Hartlib, Ephemerides, 1655, HP, 29/5/45A. According to Urbánek (*Eschatologie*, p. 180) Hartlib's note may indicate that Habernfeld was dead by then, which is indeed possible.
61 See a notary deed dated 27 August 1655, HGA, Notarieel archief (0372-0301), inv. no. 306, fol. 340, executing a decree by the Court of Holland.
62 HGA, Notarieel archief (0372-0301), inv. no. 83, fol. 190.
63 Allusion to Plautus' *Miles gloriosus* ("The braggart warrior").
64 *Pentalogos*, 5: "Bona dies, Domini, bona dies. O ho, video vos meas vertere plumas, quid vobis videtur de hoc libro, invenistisne librum ad palatum, qui rerum vobis declaret principia, causas enumeret. Hujus ego auctor sum: nae ego sum homo doctus? Quid sentitis de me?".

Descartes remains in high spirits, and is not easily put off. There is certainly a comical element to it. Of course, in the end, Descartes is portrayed as a dim-witted idiot, who continues to be cheerful only because he hardly understands what is being said to him.

Once Nature has heard Descartes boasting over his great new science abolishing all previous knowledge, she orders her son Mercurius to deal with the braggart, to show him his errors, revealing the true nature of nature. Descartes and Mercurius agree that they will focus on the *Météores*, and the philosopher subsequently summarises the ten chapters of his work, each time followed by Mercurius's rejoinder.

The fundamental differences between Descartes and Habernfeld become clear straight away in the first chapter, where Descartes discusses the structure of bodies. For Descartes, water, air and earth, as well as the bodies in it or on it are composed of small particles of diverse size and shape; the gaps between these particles are filled with a fine subtle matter. Habernfeld smirks at this literally superficial explanation of nature, and accuses Descartes of reviving the ancient doctrine of atomism. He brings forward the Paracelsian doctrine of the four elements air, water, earth and fire. None of these elements are elements in the sense of a pure substance; water, for example, is not a 'simple' but a composite body in itself. Consequently, Habernfeld states, if one judges by what one sees, one does not see the elements, but 'elemented' bodies, *corpora elementata*. Each element is in fact an admixture of all four elements. Next to the elements, we may distinguish the three principles, salt, sulphur and mercury. These principles confer some faculty or condition to natural objects: salt is that what makes an object solid; sulphur makes an object more or less combustible, and mercury is responsible for fluidity. Every principle is present in every object. The real essence of objects is, however, spiritual: a 'signature' implanted by the Creator.

Armed with these Paracelsian notions, Mercurius/Habernfeld offers a chemical alternative for Descartes's explanation of winds, clouds, rain, and so on, occasionally collapsing in an alchemical frenzy.[65] Constantly Mercurius Cosmopolita refers Descartes to his book *Herminia trismegiston*, which contains further elucidations on every topic discussed — but no work with that title seems ever to have been published. In any case, there is no real dialogue between the two worldviews, and no serious attempt is made to refute Cartesianism; instead, negative qualifications, to put it mildly, appear to be Mercurius's strongest counter-arguments.

Habernfeld's worries about Cartesianism are clear enough: it represents a de-deified picture of the world, a denial of the fundamentally spiritual nature of nature; a reduction to matter in motion, which, governed by mechanist laws, destroys the harmony between macrocosm and microcosm, and ultimately between God and man. It is no coincidence that in the rebuttal of Descartes's explanation of the rainbow, without question the highlight in the *Météores*, Mercurius observes with

---

65 The discussion on the structure of snowflakes is the subject of the only reference in contemporary literature to *Pentalogos* found so far; see GEORG PHILIPP HARSDÖRFFER, *Deliciae mathematicae et physicae: Der Mathematischen und Philosophischen Erquickstunden, Zweyter Theil*, Nuremberg, Dümlern, 1651, p. 309. The author offers Descartes' account regarding snowflakes, referring the reader to the *Meteora* (Latin translation of *Les météores*, 1644) and *Pentalogos* by Mercurius Cosmopolita, who disagrees with Descartes, Harsdörffer adds.

horror that the naturalist fails to interpret the rainbow as the covenant between God and mankind.

Descartes will have considered the text of *Pentalogos* as its own refutation. However, the sting of the book is in its tail, and it is perhaps the last part which irritated Descartes most. In a corollary Habernfeld urges the universities to speak up and give their judgement of Descartes's doctrines. It is impossible that the universities remain silent, Habernfeld argues, because Descartes has shown his utter contempt of all schools and universities, describing them as breeding places of errors. The professors should speak out and the boards of universities cannot close their eyes. For the university is a palace of wisdom, and it is, according to Habernfeld, obvious that Descartes has never seen it from the inside. Indeed, let him prove that he ever went to school, and learned the Latin language, which alone lends lustre to a man of learning. This appeal to the Dutch universities will certainly have annoyed Descartes, because his philosophy was just gaining attention at the University of Utrecht.

10. Theophilus Cosmopolita

I am now nearing the conclusion of my chapter. I will finish by having a quick look at another anti-Cartesian work, which, as I suspect, was composed by Habernfeld as well. The title reads: *In primam philosophiam cartesianam notae, auctore Theophilo Cosmopolita*. Year, publisher and place are not mentioned, but it is in all likelihood published in 1643 in The Hague.[66] According to the editor of Descartes's *Notae in programma quoddam* (Amsterdam, 1648), Mercurius and Theophilus Cosmopolita are twin brothers, implying that both pamphlets have the same author.[67] And indeed, like Mercurius, Theophilus shows himself to be an admirer of Hermetic philosophy. Descartes himself never spent a word on the book, but his biographer Adrien Baillet attributes it to Voetius.[68] However, this is very unlikely for several reasons, not in the least because it is written in the same Paracelsist frame as *Pentalogos*. Moreover, Voetius himself lists the work among the refutations of Cartesianism, suspecting that the author is a physician at The Hague.[69]

An indication that it may indeed be Habernfeld's second work against the French philosopher, is found at the very end of the book. Theophilus offers Descartes the friendly advice, that if he considers to publish more rubbish in the future, he should use the French language, because he is ignorant in Latin. Now, in *Pentalogos* it was doubted if Descartes had received any proper education, because he wrote the

---

66 According to Paul Voet, the publisher was Aert Meuris at The Hague (VOET, *Pietas in parentem, contra Ultimam Impotentiam Samuelis Maresii*, Utrecht, Strick, 1646, [124]). However, STCN lists no publications by Meuris after 1642. Meuris published Habernfeld's *Hierosolima restituta* in 1622.
67 AT VIII-B, 337.
68 ADRIEN BAILLET, *La vie de Monsieur Des-Cartes*, 2 vols, Paris, Horthemels, 1691, II, p. 204.
69 GISBERTUUS VOETIUS, *Exercitia et bibliotheca studiosi theologiae*, Utrecht, Strick, 1644, p. 687: "Anonymus, professione, uti videtur, Medicus tractatu in 4° Hagae-comitis anno 1643".

Discours in French. Theophilus is able to fill in Mercurius on this point: Descartes has no command of the Latin language; ergo: he is an illiterate peasant.

The pamphlet against Descartes was not the first publication to appear under the pseudonym Theophilus Cosmopolita. In 1640 Spruyt printed *In libellum de absoluto reprobationis decreto* [...] *notae*,[70] a reply to *De absoluto reprobationis, versio ex Anglico*, anonymously published by Blaeu in Amsterdam in 1640. The latter work is a shortened version, in Latin, of Samuel Hoard's (anonymously) published *Gods love to mankind: Manifested, by dis-proving his Absolute Decree for their Damnation* (1633).[71] In the 1640 pamphlet Theophilus strongly defends the Calvinistic doctrine of reprobation and predestination, but unlike the *Pentalogos* and the 1643 pamphlet there is no hint that the author adheres to Hermitic philosophy. However, having the same surname, and given that the title pages of both 1640 booklets have the same lay-out, and each ends with a corollary text (*Corollarium*), it seems that they have the same author, who, when writing in defence of Hermetic philosophy, calls himself Mercurius, and when defending the Calvinist doctrine, Theophilus.

11. Conclusion

In his *Discours* Descartes promised a completely new philosophy and a reform of medicine. These claims attracted a great number of opponents for various reasons. Nowadays we usually list the theologians, such as Voetius, Revius, and Bourdin; philosophers, such as Hobbes, Gassendi, and More; physicians like Plemp and Primrose, and of course mathematicians, Fermat, Roberval, and so on. These persons have one thing in common, namely that Descartes allowed them to be his opponents; he took their objections seriously, in greater or lesser degree, and replied to them accordingly. One could argue that, in a way, Descartes staged the reception of his philosophy. However, some philosophical currents were to be excluded, in particular the adherents of the theories Descartes calls 'the false sciences' in his *Discours*: alchemy, astrology, and magic. Undoubtedly, these included Paracelcian medicine and chemical philosophy as well.[72] This is where, perhaps not so much the importance, but the interest of Habernfeld's publications come in. They show that within Paracelsist circles Descartes's philosophy was seen as a threat. And rightly so: Paracelsus, who rejected Aristotle and Galen, and proposed a fundamental reform of medicine and natural philosophy, was now being outflanked by a boasting naturalist.

---

70 THEOPHILUS COSMOPOLITA, *In libellum de absoluto reprobationis decreto, versionis ex Anglico, ubi articulus de electione divina, qua Deus alios ad salutem aeternam alios ad interitum praedestinavit, impugnatur, et impia Arminianismi deliramenta extolluntur, Notae*, The Hague, Spruyt, 1640.
71 For the discussion in which the pamphlet participates, see P. MOLHUYSEN, B. MEULENBROEK, P. WITKAM, H. NELLEN, AND C. RIDDERIKHOF, eds, *Briefwisseling van Hugo Grotius*, 17 vols, The Hague, Nijhoff, 1928-2001, XI, p. 323, 540.
72 For Descartes' view on chemistry and chemical philosophers, see BERNARD JOLY, *Descartes et la chimie*, Paris, Vrin, 2011.

BENJAMIN GOLDBERG

The Rules of Anatomy: On the Empiricisms of Descartes and Harvey*

▼ ABSTRACT In this chapter, I explore the similarities and differences in the empiricisms of René Descartes and William Harvey as viewed through the lens of their conceptions of anatomical method. While Descartes has long been labelled a Rationalist, I argue here, following the work of Desmond Clarke and others, that Descartes' methods show a fundamental commitment to empirical experiment and observation. I begin by connecting Descartes' empiricism to the concept of theory-ladenness in the context of the cardiological dispute between Descartes and Harvey. I argue for a similarity between Descartes' understanding of reason and Harvey's characterization of experience, as both concepts relate to an idea of *long experience*, a kind of wisdom gained through practice. Thus there is, in both thinkers, a commitment to deep familiarity with nature's operations, familiarity gained by direct experience. Behind this similarity, however, is an important difference regarding their ideal scientific observer. For Descartes, the ideal is of an untutored, ordinary observer, while for Harvey this observer must have technical, anatomical expertise. I conclude by comparing their empiricisms in terms of a specific anatomical method, what physicians called *"historia"*, collections of observations, demonstrating the important ways by which their ideas of experience affected their rules for anatomical inference. In particular, by tracing the philosophical history of Harvey's concept of the "rule of Socrates [*regula Socratis*]", I show that Harvey's preoccupation with collecting especially comparative anatomical observations stems from

---

* I would like to thank Fabrizio Baldassarri for his inspiration and help throughout the writing process. This paper was also greatly improved through the comments and criticisms of Gideon Manning and Justin Begley.

Benjamin Goldberg • Department of Humanities and Cultural Studies, University of South Florida. Contact: <big@usf.edu>

Descartes and Medicine: Problems, Responses and Survival of a Cartesian Discipline, ed. by Fabrizio Baldassarri, Turnhout, 2023 (DESCARTES, 9), p. 285-314
© BREPOLS PUBLISHERS   10.1484/M.DESCARTES-EB.5.132895

his humanist background and conception of technical experience. Meanwhile, Descartes' relative neglect of anatomical comparison is due to his desire to abandon the categories and worthless learning of the Scholastics. In the end, the differences in anatomical method for these two thinkers can be boiled down to how they chose to focus on their respective strengths: Harvey on (meticulous) observation, Descartes on (mechanical) explanation.

▼ KEYWORDS René Descartes, William Harvey, Anatomy, Method, *Historia*, Empiricism

Scholars have long conceded that there are empiricist tendencies in Descartes, especially in his correspondence.[1] Thus, in 1945, Jean Laporte writes,

> To adjust in all things, to what one sees; to register it as we see it, to whatever category it may belong, without mixing anything from our own sensibility [*Se plier en toutes choses, à ce qu'on voit; l'enregistrer comme on le voit, à quelque ordre qu'il appartienne, sans rien y mêler de sa sensibilité propre*]: that is the Cartesian attitude as it manifests itself in the theory of method as well as in the *Cogito* and the steps that precede it [...] if we must characterize the philosophy of Descartes with a name, the one that would best fit would be — all paradox set aside — that of empiricism, radical and complete empiricism.[2]

The key phrase is: "To adjust in all things, to what one sees [...] without mixing anything from our own sensibility." Taking my inspiration from Laporte, I compare Descartes' empiricism with William Harvey's, concentrating on their ideas of experience in anatomy.

I begin by connecting Descartes' empiricism to the concept of theory-ladenness, explaining it in the context of the dispute between Descartes and Harvey on the motions of the heart and the blood. I argue that Descartes' understanding of reason is similar to Harvey's characterization of experience: both concepts relate

---

1   Or, in a different way, if one looks instead to the development of the Cartesian *tradition*: *Cartesian Empiricisms*, ed. by MIHNEA DOBRE and TAMMY NYDENN, Dordrecht, Springer, 2013; see also EVAN RAGLAND, "Between Certain Metaphysics and the Senses: Cataloging and Evaluating Cartesian Empiricisms," *Journal of Early Modern Studies*, 2 (2014), p. 119-139.
2   JEAN LAPORTE, *Le rationalism de Descartes*, Paris, PUF, 1988 [1945], p. 477. Unless noted, all translations are my own. Laporte's is a complex work, and I do not claim my views align with his. There are also empiricist readings of Descartes in English as well, for example: RALPH BLAKE, "The Rôle of Experience in Descartes' Theory of Method Part I," *The Philosophical Review*, 38/2 (1929), p. 125-143; and "Part II", p. 201-218; and ALAN GEWIRTZ, "Experience and the non-mathematical in the Cartesian method," *Journal of the history of Ideas*, 2 (1941), p. 183-210. Also essential is DESMOND M. CLARKE, *Descartes' Philosophy of Science*, Manchester, Manchester University Press, 1982, p. 1-2.

to the idea of *long experience*, a kind of wisdom gained through practice.³ Behind this similarity, however, is an important difference regarding their ideal scientific observer. Descartes' ideal is an untutored, ordinary observer, while, on the contrary, Harvey's must have technical, anatomical expertise.⁴ I conclude by comparing their empiricisms in terms of a specific anatomical method, what physicians called *"historia"*, collections of observations, demonstrating the important ways by which their ideas of experience affected their rules for anatomical inference.

1. Theory-ladenness and Background Assumptions in Anatomy

Gideon Manning points us to an idea helpful for understanding Descartes' anatomy: what philosophers call the "theory-ladenness of observation."⁵ Theory-ladenness is the idea that scientific observations are not neutrally described, but instead partake of the terms of the theoretical background assumed by the experimenter.⁶ As Erik-Jan Bos and Theo Verbeek argue, "Descartes is one of the few philosophers of the early modern period to have clearly grasped the point that experiments and 'special observations' become useful only against the background of a general theory."⁷ This has, in fact, been suggested by several scholars.⁸ Desmond Clarke, for instance, argues

---

3 Wisdom as in understanding, as described in MILES BURNYEAT, "Aristotle on Understanding Knowledge," in *Aristotle on Science: The Posterior Analytics*, ed. by Enrico Berti, Padua, Editrice Antenore, 1981, p. 97-139. This sense of wisdom relates to the idea that wisdom is knowledge that leads to the good. During the Renaissance, the idea of wisdom was often analogous to Aristotle's prudence, necessitating the collection of practical knowledge of things to be sought or avoided. See EUGENE F. RICE, *The Renaissance Idea of Wisdom*, Cambridge, Harvard University Press, 1958.
4 There is a difference, however, between the ordinary experiencer and the unpracticed experiencer, as Descartes thought of his method as both requiring practice and as practical: Descartes to Mersenne, March 1637, AT I 349; *Discours*, AT VI 61.
5 GIDEON MANNING, "Descartes and Medicine," in *The Oxford Handbook of Descartes and Cartesianism*, ed. by Steven Nadler, Tad M. Schmaltz, and Delphine Antoine-Mahut, Oxford, Oxford University Press, 2019, p. 157-177, p. 164 n. 13.
6 The literature on theory-ladenness is too large to summarize, but I think the best formulations are those related to underdetermination, for which see especially: HELEN LONGINO, *Science as Social Knowledge*, Princeton, Princeton University Press, 1990, Chapters 2-3, p. 16-61. For an application of underdetermination in early modern science, see my, "William Harvey's Rejection of Materialism: Underdetermination and Explanation in Historical Context", in *Eppur si muove: Doing History and Philosophy of Science with Peter Machamer*, ed. by Marcus Adams, Zvi Biener, Uljana Feest, and Jacqueline Sullivan, Dordrecht, Springer, 2017, p. 1-19.
7 BOS and VERBEEK, "Conceiving the Invisible", p. 177. Relevant here are ideas of holism, often found in discussion of empiricisms; see, e.g., DELPHINE BELLIS, "An epistolary lab: the case of Parhelia and Halos in Descartes' correspondence (1629-1630)", in *The Circulation of Science and Technology*, ed. by Antoni Roca-Rosell, Barcelona: Societat Catalana d'Història de la Ciència i de la Tècnica, 2012, p. 372-377.
8 CLARKE, *Descartes' Philosophy of Science*, p. 37-38 and p. 147; SPYROS SAKELLARIADIS, "Descartes's Use of Empirical Data to Test Hypotheses," *Isis* 73.1 (1982), p. 68-76, p. 74 n. 17; DANIEL GARBER, "Descartes and Experiment in the *Discourse* and *Essays*," in. *Descartes Embodied: Reading Cartesian philosophy through Cartesian science*, Cambridge, Cambridge University Press,

that Descartes invokes something like theory-ladenness as a means of insulating his theories from refutation.[9] Descartes has been branded "cavalier" on this account,[10] but I hope to interpret Descartes as instead offering a cautious empiricism that considers how background assumptions affect scientific observation, warning against unthinking acceptance of observations and experiments.

Consequently for Descartes, the truth of these assumptions affects whether one accepts or rejects some observation or experiment. In the *Discours*, Descartes notes two such assumptions:

> And as for the experiments [*expériences*] that others have already made, even if they were willing to communicate them [...] (something which those who call them secrets would never do), they involve, for the most part, so many circumstances, or superfluous ingredients, that it would be very difficult for him to decipher the truth; besides this, he would find nearly all of them quite badly explained, or even quite false [*si mal expliquées, ou mesme si fausses*], because those who did them strove to make them appear to conform to their own principles.[11]

Descartes' reference to "secrets" likely refers to chymists or artisans in the secrets tradition,[12] for whom experimental practices were meant to be hidden. Such experiments involved complex preparations of obscure ingredients, implemented through obliquely described procedures. Descartes here is arguing that to accept these kinds of experiments is to accept a host of assumptions, e.g., about how the results were not affected by the complexity of the experiment, or by the superfluity of ingredients. Desmond Clarke and Spyros Sakellariadis describe this as an interference argument: the assumption that experimental or observational complexities do not interfere with the results.[13] The second assumption concerns motivated reasoning: experimenters interpret their results according to their preconceptions, again throwing doubt upon these observations. Accordingly, Descartes questions both assumptions to reject various experimental results and interpretations.

2001, p. 85-110, p. 109; Theo Verbeek and Erik-Jan Bos, "Conceiving the Invisible. The Role of Observation and Experiment in Descartes's Correspondence, 1630-1650," in *Communicating Observations in Early Modern Letters (1500-1675): Epistolography and Epistemology in the Age of the Scientific Revolution*, ed. by Dirk van Miert, Turin-London, Nino Aragno-The Warburg Institute, 2013, p. 161-178, p. 177; and Manning, "Descartes and Medicine," p. 164. See also, William Shea, *The Magic of Numbers and Motion the Scientific Career of René Descartes*, Canton, Science History Publications, 1991, p. 235-235. Theory-ladenness is also briefly discussed in a review and discussion of Shea's book: Maurice Gagnon, "Métaphysique, théorie scientifique et expérience chez Descartes: ambiguités et difficultés", *Philosophiques* 22/2 (1995), p. 371-383, esp. p. 374.

9 Clarke, Descartes' Philosophy of Science, p. 39.
10 Ernan McMullin, "Conceptions of Science in the Scientific Revolution," in *Reappraisals of the Scientific Revolution*, ed. by David Lindberg and Robert Westman, New York, Cambridge University Press, 1990, p. 27-92, esp. p. 43.
11 *Discours de la Methode*, VI, AT VI 73.
12 On secrets of nature, see: William Eamon, *Science and the Secrets of Nature: Books of Secrets in Medieval and Early Modern Culture*, Princeton, Princeton University Press, 1996.
13 Clarke, *Descartes' Philosophy of Science*, p. 200-201; Sakellariadis "Descartes' Use of Empirical Data", p. 74.

We see another example of assumptions and theory-ladenness in Descartes' debate with William Harvey over the motions of the heart and the blood. This has been illustrated in a paper by Geoff Gorham, who argues that the disagreement here is not a difference between empiricism and rationalism, nor a difference in observation, but is, in fact, a complex dispute resulting from divergent theoretical assumptions about fundamental issues of causation, explanation, and metaphysics.[14] I will briefly summarize the debate to show how theory-ladenness obtains.

Harvey's picture is that the venous blood moves during the contractive phase of the heart's movement.[15] He argues that the blood is driven via the aorta into the arteries, what he calls the forceful systole, later compared to a spout or fire-engine.[16] This systolic action is the motive (efficient) cause of the blood's circulation, and this action explains the arterial pulse's synchronicity with the dilation of the pulmonary artery; thus diastolic action is the relaxation of the contractions.[17] Harvey's explanations of these motions lay in the fundamental suppositions of the traditional Galenic-Aristotelian system of natural philosophy and anatomy, where the functions of the body are explained by reference to the powers of the soul. This is a basic (which is not to say simple) medical picture, stemming from a tradition of natural inquiry arising from (among other things) Aristotle's *De anima*, and Galen's *De naturalibus facultatibus* and *De usu partium*. As Aristotle defined it in *De anima*, the soul is the formal, final, and efficient cause of the body, and thus, in the medical tradition, the soul became the primary cause and explanation of the various parts and processes of living bodies. The soul is the set of capacities or faculties that accomplish those things necessary for life, e.g., nutrition, generation, movement, and sensation. The soul *literally* organizes the body according to these ends, that is, each part of the body, each organ, is created for some purpose that needs to be accomplished, e.g., the liver

---

14 I rely on GEOFFREY GORHAM's "Mind-body dualism and the Harvey-Descartes controversy", *Journal of the History of Ideas* 55/2 (1994), p. 211-234. The literature here is large, but see: ETIENNE GILSON, "Descartes, Harvey et la scolastique", in *Etudes sur le role de la pensee medievale dans la formation du systems cartesien*, Paris, Vrin, 1975, p. 51-100; CLARKE, *Descartes' Philosophy of Science*, p. 148-154; MARJORIE GRENE, "The Heart and Blood: Descartes, Plemp and Harvey", *Essays on the Philosophy and Science of Descartes*, ed. by S. Voss, Oxford, Oxford University Press, 1993, p. 324-336; PETER ANSTEY, "Descartes' cardiology and its reception in English physiology", in *Descartes' Natural Philosophy*, ed. by Stephen Gaukroger, John Schuster, and John Sutton, London and New York, Routledge, 2000, p. 432-456; ANNIE BITBOL-HESPÉRIÈS, "Cartesian physiology", in *Descartes' Natural Philosophy*, p. 349-382; and LUCIAN PETRESCU, "Descartes on the heartbeat: The Leuven affair", *Perspectives on Science* 21/4 (2013), p. 397-428.
15 WILLIAM HARVEY, *Exercitatio anatomica de motu cordis et sanguinis in animalibus*, Frankfurt, 1628, p. 25-26.
16 WILLIAM HARVEY, *Exercitatio altera ad Jean Riolan*, in *Exercitationes duae anatomicae de circulatio sanguinis ad Jean Riolanum*, Rotterdam, 1649, p. 13, 51, 72, and 108. The word Harvey uses is "*sypho*", which has a variety of meanings, including a tube-like spout of water or a pump-driven fire-engine. See PETER DISTELZWEIG, "'Mechanics' and Mechanism in William Harvey's Anatomy: Varieties and Limits", in *Early modern medicine and natural philosophy*," ed. by Peter Distelzweig, Benjamin Goldberg, and Evan Ragland, Dordrecht, Springer, 2016, p. 117-140.
17 GORHAM, "Mind-Body Dulaism", p. 212-213.

and stomach realize the end of nutrition.[18] Thus in his second letter to Riolan, Harvey attributes the heart's motion to a pulsific faculty (*facultas pulsifica*) that is cause of the heart's contractile motion (thus the forceful systole's ejection of blood and etc.), and which itself is ultimately caused by the innate heat (*calidus innatus*).[19] In *De motu*, the heart, as the seat of the soul and furnisher of this heat, is thus responsible for the various faculties that accomplish the activities necessary for the life of a living thing. Later, in his letters and the work on generation, Harvey locates this heat not in the heart, but in the blood itself.[20]

Meanwhile, and despite his embrace of circulation, Descartes retains much of the traditional Galenic anatomical picture.[21] But Descartes' anatomy, unlike Harvey's, starts *a priori*, that is, from the causes. In this case, Descartes proposes a mechanical reinterpretation of the same cause as Harvey's, the traditional heat-based explanation. For Descartes, the ebullition of the blood is powered by *un de ces feux sans lumière*, a fire without light, burning continually in the heart.[22] When the blood enters the right chamber drop by drop, the heart's heat instantaneously rarefies it into tiny particles, increasing its volume, and, for purely mechanical reasons, the heart swells, closing the atrioventricular valves, forcing the blood through the semi-lunar valves and causing the arteries to swell.[23] Here too there is synchronous movement on the left side of the heart, caused by the blood's rarefaction. For Descartes it is when the heart is distended due to the expansion of the blood that the blood moves into the arterial system. As the blood cools, we see the process of contraction, starting the cycle anew. The active stage of the heart's motion takes place when it expands, inverting Harvey's order.

Both Harvey and Descartes, then, agree on circulation, disagreeing on its causes and the sequence of motions of the heart and blood. The point here is not that observation is *irrelevant*; on the contrary, both thinkers constantly appeal to observations and experiments (though not often to the same ones). The point is rather that observations are not *decisive*. Not only do many of their observations differ, but, even when they seem to agree, they involve different conceptual frameworks and vocabularies: theory-ladenness affects description. For instance, though both Harvey

---

18 The parts of the body are thus the instruments of soul: DON BATES, "Machina Ex Deo: William Harvey and the meaning of Instrument", *Journal of the History of Ideas* 61/4 (2000), p. 577-593.
19 HARVEY, *Exercitationes duae anatomicae*, p. 51.
20 WILLIAM HARVEY, *Exercitationes de generatione animalium*, Ex. 71, London, 1651, p. 245.
21 For more on the traditional and non-traditional aspects of Descartes' cardiology, see: GORHAM "Mind-Body Dualism", p. 214-215; and ANSTEY, "Descartes' cardiology", p. 421-423; on his physiology more generally, see: GARY HATFIELD, "Descartes" physiology and its relation to his psychology", in *The Cambridge Companion to Descartes*, ed. by John Cottingham, Cambridge, Cambridge University Press, 1992, p. 335-370. Descartes work here and on generation owes much Galenic thinkers, like Jean Fernel; see VINCENT AUCANTE, "Descartes's Experimental Method and the Generation of Animals" in *The Problem of Animal Generation in Early Modern Philosophy*, ed. by J. E. H. Smith, Cambridge, Cambridge University Press, 2006, p. 65-79.
22 *La traité de L'Homme*, AT XI 123; see also *Discours* AT VI 48.
23 *L'Homme*, AT XI 123; *La Description du corps humain*, AT XI 244. On rarefaction (and much else) see Descartes to Plempius, 15 February 1638, AT I 529 (for whole letter, see: 521-534).

and Descartes locate in the heart a kind of heat that ultimately explains physiological processes, how this heat is conceptualized is quite different. For Descartes, the heat causes rarefaction, causing the blood to be turned into tiny particles, understood through various kinds of mechanisms (swelling, pushing, etc.). But for Harvey, the blood's heat signifies the presence of certain kinds of teleologically organized causal faculties that accomplish the soul's operations.[24] And while both insist on the special nature of the heat in the body, what makes its unique is understood differently: for Descartes the heat's interesting property is that it has no light associated with it, but is otherwise of the *same kind* as a normal fire, causing rarefaction, etc. For Harvey, this heat is *different in kind*, as, unlike a normal fire, it acts to create and grow.[25] Their disagreements reveal not just divergent observations, but also differences in background assumptions that affect the very nature of their observations.

Consider the only experiment mentioned here by both philosophers, involving excised eel hearts. Both philosophers make claims about what happens to such hearts, focusing upon the observation that eel hearts continue to pulsate after they are extracted, even once all the blood has been drained. This latter observation would seem — and indeed, was seen in the period itself — as decisive in undermining Descartes' theory, which, after all, relied on the expansion of rarefied blood to power the movements of heart and blood.[26] But, as Gorham notes, this is *only* decisive if Descartes cannot account for this observation in his own theory. And, in fact, Descartes *does* think he can so accommodate postmortem eel heart movements, by pointing out that the observation assumes that the heart has no heat remaining. He then argues that the heat of the heart lies its walls, and thus lasts after death, causing vapors to be emitted that continue to power the heart's movements.[27] Their disagreement cannot be resolved by a single observation or experiment:

> Descartes claims [...] to have observed an excised heart actually increase in volume as it hardens, contrary to Harvey's contraction model. Harvey answers that Descartes has mistaken the simple relaxation of the heart after the systolic contraction for full-blown diastole. [...] Harvey does not claim that Descartes saw something that did not happen [...] he suggests that Descartes is confused about

---

24 As in ARISTOTLE, *De Partibus animalium*, lib. I, cap. v., *Aristotelis libri omnes, ad animalium cognitionem attinentes, cum Averrois Cordubensis variis in eosdem commentariis*, Venice 1552, p. 67. I cite an edition of Aristotle likely used by Harvey, the Venice Aristotle-Averroes.
25 As noted, Harvey moves this heat from the heart to the blood in his work on generation (see HARVEY 1651, Ex. 52 and Ex. 71). His conception of the heat, though different in some ways, is not so far removed from his contemporaries: cf.: JEAN FERNEL, *On the hidden causes of things: forms, souls, and occult diseases in Renaissance medicine*, bk. II, ch. 6, edited and translated by John Forrester, Brill, 2005 [1551], p. 477.
26 In England, this observation was taken quite seriously as an argument against Descartes, and by the 1640s few natural philosophers working there subscribed to Cartesian explanations in cardiology: ANSTEY "Descartes' cardiology", p. 438-439.
27 Descartes to Plempius, 27 March 1638, AT II 266-268; on rarefaction in the heart and elsewhere, see: Descartes to Plempius, 15 February 1638, AT I 528-531; see also: GORHAM, "Mind-Body Dualism", p. 222.

which movements of the heart correspond to the systolic and diastolic phases. The real source of the confusion, according to Harvey, is Descartes's ignorance of the fact that relaxation, diastole, and systole all have different causes [...] Harvey's answer [...] amounts to nothing more than a brief lesson in (his own) anatomical terminology together with a restatement of his own theory.[28]

This is a case of theory-ladenness, wherein differing assumptions cause Harvey and Descartes to use different vocabularies: they are, in effect, talking past each other. As Gorham notes, Harvey is but redescribing the experiment in his own terminology. But did Descartes recognize something like theory-ladenness? What does this mean for his empiricism? To answer these questions, I turn to contrast his method of experiencing with Harvey's.[29]

2. Experience, Theory-Ladenness, and Methodology

Let's start with similarity: Descartes and Harvey agree that it is only through the *combination* of reason and experience that we arrive at the truth. Few thought that these two modalities were independent, but instead, various debates turned on questions about the degree to which one or the other should be favored, and, given that mixture, what precise methods should be used. The necessity of both reason and experience was a veritable commonplace in the medical tradition,[30] stated unequivocally by Galen, Mondino de Luzzi, Berengario da Carpi, Niccolò Massa, Fabricius ab Aquapendente, not to mention Harvey himself.[31]

Harvey was a partisan of the empirical, of *autopsia*: "seeing for oneself."[32] But he was also careful to affirm two relevant points: first, that reason and experience are inextricable, and second, that experience refers not usually to a specific instance of

---

28 GORHAM, "Mind-Body Dualism", p. 223-224. For readability, I have here excised citations to primary sources.
29 The word method, its various terms in Latin and French, *methodus, méthode*, etc., refers to a complex concept. For some relevant background, focusing on Descartes, see: TIMOTHY REISS, "Neo-Aristotle and method: Between Zabarella and Descartes" in *Descartes' Natural Philosophy*, p. 207-239; and DANIEL GARBER, "Descartes, the Aristotelians, and the Revolution that did not happen in 1637," *Monist* 71 (1988), p. 471-486; and DANIEL GARBER, "J.-B. Morin and the Second Objections," in *Descartes embodied*, p. 33-51.
30 Note, however, that there had long been a question among physicians about the status of medicine and anatomy: was it *scientia* or *ars*? While all argued that both reason and experience were necessary, only the rational aspect of medicine, that is, *theoria* and its causal explanations, count as science. Cf. NANCY SIRAISI, "Medicine, Physiology and Anatomy in Early Sixteenth-Century Critiques of the Arts and Sciences", in *New Perspectives on Renaissance Thought*, ed. by John Henry and Sarah Hutton, London, Duckworth, 1990, p. 217-229.
31 See: CYNTHIA KLESTINEC, *Theaters of Anatomy*, Baltimore, Johns Hopkins University Press, 2011, p. 9-10, p. 30-32 and *passim*.
32 In the *Dedicatio* to *De motu cordis*, Harvey writes that he would never have proposed his findings if he had they had not been "proved through personal experience [*per autopsiam confirmassem*]" (Harvey, *De motu cordis*, p. 6).

witnessing, but rather to *long experience*, accumulated wisdom or expert judgment. In connection with the first point, as Vivian Nutton has noted, there is a particular marginal note in Harvey's copy of Theodore Goulston's edition of Galen's works, made in response to Galen's *De sectis*. Harvey affirms that the dispute between the empiricist and rationalist is beside the point because, "investigative reasoning makes a doctor by experience".[33] Although Harvey emphasizes experience in a way that Descartes does not, he always regards reason to function in concert with sensation. So, e.g., in *De motu cordis*, Harvey argues that blood flows into the right ventricle and passes out from the left, noting that this is, "obvious to both reason and sense [*& ratione & sensu patet*]" and thus blood moves continually from the vena cava into the aorta.[34]

The second methodologically important point, that experience for Harvey is *long experience*, is something I have argued at length.[35] Take the *Proem* of Harvey's *De motu cordis*:

> It profits one who is reflecting upon the movement, pulse, action, use and usefulness of the heart and arteries, to order those things which have been written by others, to unfold and to take note of the things which have been commonly discussed and taught, so that what has been rightly said might be proved [*confirmentur*], and what is false might be corrected by anatomical dissection, by manifold experience, and by diligent and accurate observation [*quae falssa dissectione anatomica, multiplici experientia, diligenti, & accurata observatione emendentur*].[36]

Experience is not the same as sensation, it is separate from both anatomical dissection and observation. Harvey here also insists upon the profitability of considering other's opinion, to which I will return to below. What I have here translated as "manifold experience" is, in Latin, "*multiplici experientia*", a singular noun in the ablative, which might be literally rendered as "experience having many folds". Given the grammar, the sense here cannot refer to many discrete experiences but rather to a compound set of such experiences, a complex multiplicity rendered into a unity under the singular term *experientia*. This unity, this manifold, is the source of a kind of wisdom that allows one to judge true and false, good and bad, in anatomy. We might reasonably translate *experientia* in this context as *expertise*. Similar ideas of long experience are found not just in anatomy, but in pharmacy as well. For example, this idea is often invoked in discussions where a medicine's efficacy is assured by noting that something is "an experienced Cure."[37] For Harvey, then, and in some of the medical traditions

---

33 Quoted in Vivian Nutton, "Harvey, Goulston and Galen" in *From Democedes to Harvey*, London, Variorum Reprints, 1988, p. 116-117.
34 Harvey, *De motu cordis*, cap. VIII, p. 40.
35 Benjamin Goldberg, "William Harvey on anatomy and experience", *Perspectives on Science* 24/3 (2016), p. 305-323.
36 Harvey, *De motu cordis*, Proemius, p. 10.
37 Aletheia Howard, *Natura Exenterata*, London, 1655, p. 208. For more on recipe book and experience, see: Benjamin Goldberg, "Concepts of Experience in Royalist Recipe Collections," Journal of Early Modern Studies 11.1 (2022), p. 37-68.

of early modernity, experience signifies expertise: skill and knowledge gained by "investigative reasoning".

Like Harvey, Descartes is quick to invoke personal experience. Although he does not use the term *autopsia*, he expresses similar sentiments, as in a letter to Huygens: "I do not trust experiments that I have not made myself".[38] In fact, his reasons for preferring personal experience are somewhat like Harvey's but expressed quite differently (which we ought to expect given theory-ladenness). So let us turn to consider what Descartes means by *"ratione"* or *"raison"* and other terms relating to reason and inference, such as "deduction" and "intuition". These do not signify exactly what they do for us. I will return to the signification of reason below, but consider deduction: for Descartes, this often includes what we would call induction, explanation, or proof, depending on the context. Descartes understood deduction as an inference made up of a sequence of propositions, each step guaranteed by the light of reason via clear and distinct ideas.[39] Intuition, meanwhile, is the basis for all deduction, the limiting case where the use of clear and distinct ideas relates two propositions.[40]

What do these terms have to do with experience? In fact, experiment and observation are an important part of the process here, as they essential for finding the *correct deduction*, that is, the *true explanation*.[41] Experience, as Descartes emphatically argues in the *Meditationes*, is important, but it only deduction establishes a phenomenon and its causes in a scientific sense.[42] Descartes is arguing with those enamored of the material world, who thought their senses were unproblematic grounds for finding the truth.[43] Of course, in the *Regulae*, Descartes often refers to our "fluctuating faith in the senses."[44] But this attack on the senses is not an rejection of it, but rather an argument that sensation has to be guided by the "pure and attentive mind, which arises from the light of reason alone".[45] Here we find that Descartes' notion of reason,

---

38 Descartes to Huygens, 18 or 19 February 1643, AT III 617. The only use of *"autopsia"* I can find in Descartes' corpus occurs in a letter from Plempius to Descartes, again in the context of his debate with Harvey: Plempius to Descartes January 1638, AT I 499.
39 STEPHEN GAUKROGER, "Descartes' Conception of Inference," *Metaphysics and Philosophy of Science in the Seventeenth and Eighteenth Centuries*, ed. by Roger Woolhouse, Dordrecht, Springer, 1988, p. 101-132, esp. p. 115-116. Cf. CLARKE, *Descartes' Philosophy of Science*, p. 179. DANIEL GARBER, "Science and Certainty in Descartes," in *Descartes: Critical and Interpretive Essays*, ed. by Michael Hooker, Baltimore, Johns Hopkins University Press, 1978, p. 114-151, esp. p. 116-123, and GARBER, "Descartes and Experiment", p. 91 and 103-104. Cf. DANIEL GARBER, "Descartes and Method in 1637," in *Descartes Embodied*, p. 33-51.
40 As Gaukroger argues, the shared meaning inherent in Descartes uses of *deducere, demonstrare, deduire*, and *demontrer*, "is no more specific than the comparison of one item with another" (STEPHEN GAUKROGER, "Descartes' Conception of Inference", in *Metaphysics and Philosophy of Science in the Seventeenth and Eighteenth Centuries*, ed. by Roger S. Woolhouse, Dordrecht, Springer, 1988, p. 101-132, esp. p. 116). See: *Regulae* XIV, AT X 439-440.
41 GARBER, "Descartes and Experiment", p. 93, 109.
42 *Ibid.*, p. 109.
43 See, for instance, the wax argument in *Meditationes de prima philosophia* II; GARBER, "Descartes and Experiments", p. 45.
44 *Regulae* III, AT X 368.
45 *Ibid.*

is, in fact, surprisingly similar to Harvey's idea of experience. Descartes understands reason as a discursive faculty of judgment that allows the mind to make inferences. He identifies reason with "good sense", the power to "judge well" and distinguish true from false, sometimes also called "universal wisdom".[46] In the *Replies* to the sixth set of objections, Descartes argues with those asserting the fundamental reliability of the senses:

> when we say that the certitude of the intellect is much greater than the certitude of the senses, that only means that those judgments which we make in our mature years on account of some new observations are more certain than those we first formed in our infancy, without any contemplation. And this is obviously the case.[47]

The certainty of reason is the result of our increased ability to critically reflect on our thoughts and sensations. Taking the stick that looks bent because of refraction in the water as an example, Descartes argues that we cannot merely use our empirical sense of touch to correct our visual impression, since we need a reason to prefer this tactile evidence over the visual.[48] What is the difference, then, in how time affects our judgments? The answer must be experience, in the sense of *long experience*, the accumulated wisdom earned by repeated use of our intellect, an ability to make correct judgments. Harvey expresses this in terms of *multiplici experientia*, and Descartes in terms of *ratio* and *intellectus*. This, then, is an important similarity between the empiricisms of Descartes and Harvey, for they both understand an idea of wisdom as correct, practiced judgment to be central to scientific inference.

But lurking below this similarity is a profound difference. This difference returns us to the issues of assumptions and theory-ladenness and concerns how they think about the ideal observer whose witnessing counts as reliable evidence. Whereas Descartes privileges untutored experience, Harvey depends on expert investigating.[49] In his pedagogically focused notes for the Lumleian lectures, the *Prelectiones anatomie universalis*, Harvey states that, "Anatomy is a skilled ability [*facultas*] that teaches the uses and actions of the parts by ocular inspection and dissection".[50] To properly observe and judge in anatomy, one must have the requisite training: long experience

---

46 *Discours de la Méthode*, I AT VI 1-2; *Regulae* VIII, AT X 360. Harvey, unlike Descartes, does not take wisdom to imply the unity of science; JEAN-FRANÇOIS GAUVIN, "Artisans, machines, and Descartes's organon," *History of science* 44/2 (2006), p. 187-216.
47 *Sextae Responsiones*, AT VII 438; *Principia Philosophiae*, AT VIII 39. I do not claim that Descartes' reason and Harvey's experience are identical.
48 *Sextae Responsiones*, AT VII 439. See also: CLARKE, *Descartes' philosophy of science*, p. 71. This is another example where Descartes' seems sensitive to assumptions.
49 Harvey and Descartes thus disagree on the origin of the wisdom in the ideal scientific observer.
50 WILLIAM HARVEY, *Prelectiones anatomie universalis*, edited and translated by Gweneth Whitteridge, London, Royal College of Physicians, 1964 [1616], p. 4. "Anatomia est facultas quae occulari inspectione et sectione partium usus et actiones". For the reasons for translating "*facultas*" as skilled ability, see GOLDBERG, "William Harvey on Anatomy". While I cite Whitteridge's edition for ease of reference, my interpretation has been guided by my reappraisal of the original notes, for which see: British Library, Sloane MS 230a. Whitteridge's translation is faulty, interpreting "*facultas*" as "branch of learning".

in the art of dissection. This is traditional, at least by the sixteenth century, and here Harvey follows Galen's arguments in *De placitis hippocratis et platonis* that the relevant kind of experience to understand the body is technical, anatomical experience.[51] As I have argued: "Far from being something shared by all human beings, *experientia* was the result of long training and specialized ability — one has to work hard to develop a *facultas*".[52] To make correct judgments about anatomical structure and function (to judge wisely), one must be deeply immersed in anatomical learning, as passed down in books, as well as be intimately acquainted with the body though personal experience.

Desmond Clarke argues that Descartes advocates instead for "ordinary experience [*ordinaria/quotidiana experientia*]".[53] I noted above that Descartes points to two assumptions to rebut experimental disconfirmation of his theories, and these map onto his reasons for preferring ordinary experience. The first concerned interference, involving the complexity of experiments and the possibility for unacknowledged assumptions to interfere with results. As he argues in the *Discours*, non-ordinary observations, including complex experimental setups, are problematic. Thus,

> it is better to make use only of those which present themselves to our senses, and which we do not know how to ignore, provided we give them some thought, than to seek out rarer and more studied ones [*plus rares & estudiées*]: the reason for this is that these rarer ones often deceive us when we do not yet know the causes of the more common ones, and that the circumstances on which they depend are almost always so particular and so small [*si particulieres & si petites*] that it is very difficult to notice them.[54]

Descartes' preferred observations or experiments are simple ones, as these, combined with reflection, are more certain than those that depend on complex experiment or technical experience.[55] In the *Regulae* and *Discours*, Descartes has a two part strategy:

---

51 GOLDBERG, "William Harvey on Anatomy", p. 314. See GALEN, *De placitis Hippocratis et Platonis*, lib. I, cap. 3 (cap. 6 in modern editions) in *Galeni Peragameni…opera quae nos extant omnia*, vol. 1, Basel, 1549, p. 883. I cite this early modern *omnia* of Galen, with which Harvey was likely familiar.
52 GOLDBERG, "William Harvey on Anatomy", p. 314.
53 CLARKE, *Descartes' Philosophy of Science*, p. 37. See also the discussion on this term in Descartes, see: JEAN-ROBERT ARMOGATHE, "Sémantèse d'experientia/experimentum/expériences dans le corpus cartésien", in *Experientia*, ed. by Marco Veneziani, Florence, Leo S. Olschki, 2002, p. 259-271, esp. p. 263. Armogathe gives an example of "*ordinaria*" supposedly located in the *Principia* AT VIII-1 568, but this page number is incorrect, as the first part of this volume does not even reach 400 pages. For "*quotidiana*" see, e.g., *Principia*, AT VIII-1. 61. According to Armogathe, and quite differently from Bacon, when experience is (rarely) modified by an adjective, it is by: "long [*longa*]", "certain/reliable [*certa*]", "ordinary [*ordinaria, quotidiana*]", or "apparent/evident [*evidens*]". There is some relation here to what Peter Dear calls "Aristotelian experience", which he understands as those basic facts that everyone would assent to; see: PETER DEAR, "The Meanings of Experience," in *The Cambridge History of Science*, ed. by Katherine Park and Lorraine Daston, Cambridge, Cambridge University Press, 2006, p. 106-113. For a different view on experience in the case of Harvey, see my, "William Harvey on Anatomy".
54 *Discours de la Méthode*, VI, AT VI 63.
55 CLARKE, *Descartes' Philosophy of Science*, p. 37.

in the reductive part, one seeks to move from the complex and obscure to the simple and obvious (that is, to intuitions), and, in the constructive part, one moves in the opposite way.[56] Intuitions, in part because they are simple, are indubitable and grasped via clear and distinct perceptions, able to serve as an epistemological foundation. Ordinary experience, too, insofar as it is simple, is more certain, and can be trusted to help us reach these intuitions.

There other reason Descartes prefers ordinary experience relates to the assumption about motivated reasoning noted above. This has to do with Descartes' self-construction as a man overcoming all previous learning, whatever the truth of the matter.[57] Here Descartes contrasts the illusions of the learned with the certainty of the regular person, noting that a person appears less wise if they have a false opinion than if they claim to not know at all. Thus,

> it is better never to study at all than to occupy ourselves with objects which are so difficult that we are unable to distinguish what is true from what is false, and are forced to take the doubtful as certain [...] Men of learning [*litterati*] are perhaps convinced that there is very little indubitable knowledge, since, owing to a common human failing, they have neglected to reflect [*reflectere neglexerunt*] upon such truths, taking them to be too easy and obvious to everyone.[58]

In fact, this statement also considers the kind of complexity referenced above that Descartes finds problematic, insofar as this complexity makes it difficult to distinguish true from false. Descartes' rational inquirer has not "neglected reflecting" upon simple truths, and they do so in a way that is "natural."[59] As Descartes writes in the *Discours*, he came to believe that,

> book learning [*les sciences de livres*] [...] having been composed & enlarged little by little by the opinions of several different persons, is not so close to the truth as the simple reasoning which a man of good sense can naturally make concerning the things that he considers [*que les simples raisonnemens que peut faire naturellement un home de bon sens touchant les choses qui se préfèrent*].[60]

Given this rhetoric against book-learning, Descartes argues that those most suitable to science are people of "good sense" who have not yet been corrupted by the learned.

There is a kind of naivety that characterizes the ideal observer, a contrast between the learned pedant, too full of complex preconceptions to see things as they are, and the unburdened common person, able to see clearly without those prejudices:

---

56 See his description in *Regulae*, 5, AT X 379. See also: GARBER, "Descartes and Method", p. 35.
57 This is a huge subject, but see: ROGER ARIEW, *Descartes among the Scholastics*, Leiden, Brill, 2011; and, DENNIS DES CHENE, *Physiologia: Natural philosophy in late Aristotelian and Cartesian thought*, Ithaca, Cornell University Press, 2000.
58 *Regulae* Regula 2, AT X 362-363; CSM I 10-11. [Translation slightly modified.]
59 This has to do with the *lumen naturalis*, central to the *Meditationes*; see: *Meditationes* III, AT VII 40 and 42; *Mediation* IV, AT VII 53-54 and 59-60. Cf. REISS, "Neo-Aristotle and Method", p. 212-213, where he notes some connections to Zabarella as well as Descartes' pre-*Meditationes* writing.
60 *Discours* II AT VI 12-13.

This contrast is repeatedly invoked in favour of peasants and the common man. It also underlies Descartes' reservations about experiments, in so far as they are not easy to interpret, they depend on a variety of factors which can interfere with results, and they demand a level of theoretical and technical expertise which renders any conclusions one might hope to draw at least uncertain [...] In this respect, Descartes is a naive empiricist.[61]

Our judgments would be superior if, instead of learning from books, we were born with good sense.[62] For Descartes, the ability to determine the truth by means of recognition of clear and distinct ideas is a fundamental feature of the human mind, but one that improves over time with practice. This is an ecumenical view as this power is available to all human beings, as all have the "same natural light."[63] Methodologically speaking, this light is meant to critically oversee, "inferences from observation to observational judgment and thereby exploit the valid resources of sensory experience."[64] And here again we come back to the issue of background assumptions and theory-ladenness.

Recall Laporte's statement above, an image of Descartes' philosophy as adjusting to observations "without mixing anything from our own sensibility". Descartes uses interference and motivated reasoning assumptions to dispute experiments and technical expertise, arguing instead for untutored, ordinary observation. Descartes worried about the extent to which natural philosophers "mixed their own sensibilities" into their observations, assuming explanations that would seem dubious to an untutored mind with good sense. Hence observations and experiments must always be accompanied by the *correct* explanation. Descartes notes in his discussion of Maurolicus' incorrect measurement of the angle of elevation of the primary and secondary bows of the rainbow that this experiment, "demonstrates the little trust one should place in observations which are not accompanied by the true explanation [*vraye raison*]."[65] That is to say, observations and experiments are theory-laden, and so experiments and observations are useful only when explained by the *correct* theory. Until they are so deduced, observations can assist in but two ways. First, they help the scientist better define the phenomenon they are attempting to explain.[66] Second, experiment and observation help us understand how natural phenomena are embedded in a web of dependent relations, e.g., refraction depends on light moving through different media, refraction is important for color, but reflection is not, etc.[67] This web of relations is helpful for determining explanations, and Descartes suggests in a letter to Mersenne that it would be profitable for celestial science if someone made a

---

61 CLARKE, *Descartes' Philosophy of Science*, p. 200-201. Clarke here refers to Descartes to Mersenne, 20 November 1629, AT I 81-82: "Now I believe that this language is possible and that one could discover the science on which it depends, by means of which peasants could better judge the truths of things than philosophers do now."
62 *Discours* Seconde Partie, AT VI 13.
63 Descartes to Mersenne, 16 October 1639, AT II 597-598.
64 CLARKE, *Descartes' philosophy of science*, p. 34-35.
65 *Meteors*, AT VI 340. See also: CLARKE, *Descartes' Philosophy of Science*, p. 35-36; p. 45 n. 50.
66 GARBER, "Descartes and Experiment", p. 101.
67 *Ibid.*, p. 101-102.

Baconian history of astronomical dependencies "without reasons and hypotheses".[68] As Garber has noted in exactly this context, a-theoretical histories and experiments are used in early stages of inquiry to better define the problem and determine the set of correlations and correspondences that will be essential in determining its proper deduction and explanation, thus guiding us to the correct theory.[69] I return to histories in the following section, as this idea helps distinguish the empiricisms of Descartes and Harvey.

In sum, only the ability to deduce or explain observations from one's theory counts as confirmatory for Descartes. This conception of scientific theorizing is motivated in part by his recognition that scientists make assumptions when observing and experimenting, and these assumptions affect not only how experimental results are described, but whether we can trust these results as true. Descartes thus has a sophisticated view about the relation between our existing ideas and our experiments, distinctly resembling theory-ladenness. On the one hand, indicated by his mention of Baconian histories, Descartes seems to think that in the initial stages of inquiry (and for the right kind of observer), it is possible to observe in a way that avoids the pitfalls of theory-ladenness, of assuming "reasons and hypotheses". On the other hand, in later stages of inquiry, Descartes argues for a return to those observations to ensure their veracity, something that can only be done by showing how they are deduced by the correct theory. Theory-ladenness is thus both a problem and a solution, something that can avoid vicious circularity by paying attention to when and how it is used. Of course, Descartes' ideas here are not identical to contemporary notions of theory-ladenness and background assumptions, as modern accounts emphasize that *many* possible explanations are observationally consistent. Descartes, meanwhile, seems to think that *only* the true explanation will be so consonant, and so he believes that having the true theory will thus guarantee the truth of our observations. Still, understanding Descartes in terms of theory-ladenness is helpful for making sense of his empiricism insofar as these ideas help us understand his preference for untutored observers, his reticence concerning complex experiments, as well as his conviction that observation can only be trusted once we are in possession of the correct explanation.

Harvey, quite to the contrary, is unaware and unconcerned with Descartes' skeptical worries, and thus his rules of anatomy are quite different.

3. *Historia* and the Rules of Anatomical Inference

Because of background assumptions, Descartes thinks we cannot achieve deductions merely by gathering experiences, what anatomists called *"historia"*.[70] This matter,

---

68 Descartes to Mersenne, 10 May 1632, AT I 251.
69 GARBER, "Descartes and Experiment," p. 109.
70 Descartes' critiqued Mersenne for his "curiosity", which in this period is closely connected to the practices of natural history and collection: Descartes to Huygens, 12 March 1640, AT III, p. 746. See also FABRIZIO BALDASSARRI, "[P]er experientiam scilicet, vel deductionem: Descartes' battle for scientia in the early 1630s", *Historia Philosophica* 15 (2017), p. 115-133 (p. 118-119 and 128-130).

as Manning points out, pushes him in a different direction from many physicians and anatomists, as it diminished his, "enthusiasm for the mass accumulation of observational and experimental results, particularly when those results were inconsistent with a well-established theory (especially one he endorsed)".[71] I now consider these histories.

Historiae are accumulations of empirical information. These are often exactly what Descartes doubted, that is, they are collections of things "rarer and more studied", not to mention having been collected by various people, not necessarily directly experienced by their author.[72] Further, Renaissance anatomy, in its humanist guise in places like Padua, was deeply textual, modelled on the ideal of the well-read, eloquent scholar.[73] Paduan anatomists like Harvey, famous for their dependence on sense, were yet steeped in book learning, and their practices must be understood in terms of humanist medicine.[74] Indeed, Harvey is careful never to reject book learning altogether, but only insofar as it is thought the *only* method of learning:

> Because I do not think it possible to reach the truth from other men's opinions, whether they be given out on bare authority or even confirmed by probable arguments, without adding also the help of diligent experience [*nisi diligens quoque experientia accesserit*]; and by the help of clear observations [*perspicuis observationibus*] I will expound from the book of Nature [...].[75]

Thus, for Harvey, experience is a necessary *compliment* to book learning. Descartes, meanwhile, rejects this tradition of learned eloquence.[76]

Turning to anatomical *historiae*, it is important to appreciate how early modern medicine understood anatomical explanation. This tradition explained the body in terms of a complex set of hierarchically organized, teleological causes: *action*: the basic movements and processes of a part; *usus*: the larger functions of that part within the system of the whole body; and *utilitas*: explanations of what the overall "good" of the

---

71 MANNING, "Descartes and Medicine", p. 164. See especially *Discours*, AT VI 64-65, where Descartes opines about the variety of particulars that overwhelm the mind, that is, natural histories. Concerning such *historia*, see: GIANNA POMATA and NANCY SIRAISI (eds), *Historia: Empiricism and erudition in early modern Europe*, Cambridge (Ma.), MIT Press, 2005.
72 Harvey reports as fact what we might call a folktale, namely housewives' "daily test [*quotidie experiantur*]" to check if a hen will lay an egg; see: HARVEY, *De generatione*, Ex. 11, p. 28.
73 JEROME BYLEBYL, "The School of Padua: humanistic medicine in the sixteenth century", in *Health, Medicine and Mortality in the Sixteenth Century*, ed. by Ch. Webster, Cambridge, Cambridge University Press, 1979, p. 335-370.
74 In his *William Harvey's Natural Philosophy*, Cambridge, Cambridge University Press, 1994, ROGER FRENCH often opposes Harvey's work with strict humanism of some of his opponents, such as Plempius or Riolan. While Harvey's practices are not identical to every humanist physician, we can see them as part of a humanist spectrum.
75 HARVEY, *De generatione*, Ex. 45, p. 202.
76 Descartes method of reading, and his (purported) rejection of this tradition, are examined in: FABRIZIO BALDASSARRI, "Libri inutili, compendi e libri 'primarii'. Descartes tra lettura e scrittura della filosofia", *Giornale critico della filosofia italiana* XII (2016), p. 324-342. Cf. RICHARD OOSTERHOFF "Methods of Ingenuity: The Renaissance Tradition behind Descartes's Regulae", in *Descartes and the Ingenium*, ed. by Raphaële Garrod and Alexander Marr, Leiden, Brill, 2020, p. 163-183.

part is, how it is designed in the best way.⁷⁷ For Harvey, to reach knowledge of these causes, *historiae* have to be carefully organized, e.g., each part must be considered in terms of its position, shape, quantity, motion, and division.⁷⁸ That is, there are certain norms that structure historical accounts of anatomy. For Harvey, *historiae* must be both broad and comparative, including a staggering array of observed particularities. Such histories offer a telling distinction between Harvey and Descartes, signaled by Descartes when he argues that we should place little trust in observations not accompanied by the true explanation.

In fact, a *historia* is often just such a collection of observations not guided by theory, unable to overcome Descartes' worries about assumptions. That is, the wrong explanation is assumed (traditional anatomical book learning), or the history contains observations guided not by the trustworthy sensibilities of an ordinary person, but by the too-learned categories of the university physician. We might thus distinguish here two different rules for anatomical inference. Harvey's rule is not bottom-up, but rather a conception of causal inference grounded in broad technical experience, one that I will characterize below as needing to be organized in a meticulous manner. Descartes' rule for inference is not top down, but rather concerned about background assumptions, where truth is ensured only if the order of reason is followed, and if observations are corrected by means of the true explanation. Thus, as Fabrizio Baldassarri has argued, Descartes is skeptical of natural history on account of its uncertainty and confusion.⁷⁹ That is not to say that natural histories have no role, since Descartes did write that it would be good, "if someone [...] wanted to write the history of celestial phenomena, according to the method of Verulamius [...] without putting in any reasons or hypotheses".⁸⁰ The important part here is that Descartes' understanding of Bacon's method as *sans* reasons equates it with ordinary experience, and it must ultimately be guaranteed by means of the correct explanation. And, even then, Descartes has little patience for the collection of all the particularities necessary for such a Baconian history.⁸¹

---

77 GOLDBERG, "William Harvey on Anatomy", p. 316-318. In fact, this is an oversimplification, as there are other terms like "*officio*", but I leave aside these complications.
78 HARVEY 1616, p. 20. Not all *historiae* are understood in the same way, and Harvey's method of careful organization is related to his training at Padua. *Historiae* are discussed in detail in the case of Harvey in GOLDBERG, "William Harvey on Anatomy"; and JAMES LENNOX, "The Comparative Study of Animal Development" in *The Problem of Animal Generation*, p. 21-46. For a wider discussion, see: GIANNA POMATA, "*Praxis Historialis*: The Uses of *Historia* in Early Modern Medicine", in *Historia: Empiricism and Erudition in Early Modern Europe*, ed. by G. Pomata and N. Siraisi, Cambridge, MIT Press, 2005, p. 105-146.
79 FABRIZIO BALDASSARRI, "Between Natural History and Experimental Method. Descartes and Botany" *Societate si politica* 8/2 (2014), p. 43-60 (p. 46). Cf. *Regulae* II, AT X 362, and *Regulae* III, AT X 367.
80 Descartes to Mersenne, 10 May 1632, AT I 251. In an earlier letter to Mersenne (1 March 1638, AT II 26), he writes that he did not cite those who had written before on optics, since his "purpose was not to write a history [*histoire*]".
81 See Descartes to Mersenne, 23 December 1630, AT I 196. In this letter he understands Baconian histories as necessitating "general Collections of all the most common things [*Recueils generaux de toutes les choses les plus communes*]", something he seems to not enthusiastic about since, "For the most particular ones, it is impossible that one should not have many superfluous ones, & even

For Harvey one cannot determine in advance which particular observations will prove useful, but only that certain *kinds* of observations will be needed. Descartes part ways here:

> I have purposely left out several other particulars [*particularités*] which are noticeable in this matter, and with which the Anatomists swell their books; for I believe that those which I have put here will suffice to explain all that serves my purpose, and that the others which I could add to them, in no way aiding your intelligence, would only entertain your attention.[82]

Unlike Harvey, Descartes doesn't have worked-out rules for dissection or a conception of a specific rational organization for anatomical experience. Descartes' *regulae* are rules for a singular, unified science,[83] one which is based on the ability to recognize clear and distinct ideas, a science guided by simple natures that have been intuited (e.g., the nature of body as extension).[84] Importantly, comparative dissections are one kind of particularity that often "swell" anatomical *historiae*. Descartes' anatomy is grounded not in comparative anatomy, but in comparisons or analogies between anatomical parts/processes and mechanisms, allowing for explanation in terms of corpuscles, motions, and even whole systems.[85] Descartes, in arguing for the unity of science and its method, opposes Harvey's Aristotelian practice of dividing sciences by subject, each science having different principles.[86] One might describe Descartes' rule for anatomy (as elsewhere) as "explanation first, experience later", as it depends upon the theoretical (causes) to make sense of the historical (observations). That is, the exceptionally deep acquaintance with animal bodies upon which Harvey's anatomy is founded is replaced in Descartes with a more targeted approach to dissection, and a universal (mechanical) approach to explanation. Harvey's approach, on the contrary, is "experience first, explanation later".

I have left aside Bacon to focus on Harvey. Briefly, however, note that Harvey saw in Bacon a reflection of his own Galenic-Aristotelian idea of science: in the twenty-fifth exercise of Harvey's *De generatione*, he signals the transition from *historia*

---

false ones, if one does not know the truth of things before doing them".
82 La Dioptrique, AT VI 108.
83 See *Regulae* I, AT X 360, where he writes that all the sciences are nothing but "human wisdom [*humana sapientia*]", which makes all sciences uniform (cf. *Regulae* II, AT X 362); ROBERT MCRAE, "The Unity of the Sciences: Bacon, Descartes, and Leibniz", *Journal of the History of Ideas* (1957), p. 27-48. On the *Regulae* and *scientia*, see: FABRIZIO BALDASSARRI, "Descartes' Battle for *Scientia*", p. 116-119.
84 There are, however, relevant intellectual attributes like *perspicacitas* and *sagacitas* whose practice breeds skill: GAUVIN, "Artisans, machines, and Descartes", p. 189-191. On the relation between Descartes' rejection of qualities in favor of reducing them to modifications of extension, etc., see: BALDASSARRI, "Descartes' Battle for *Scientia*", p. 126-128.
85 Regarding the use of systems in Descartes' explanations of living things, see: BARNABY R. HUTCHINS, "Descartes, corpuscles and reductionism: Mechanism and systems in Descartes' physiology", *The Philosophical Quarterly* 65 (2015), p. 669-689.
86 GEWITZ, "Experience and the non-mathematical", p. 209; and GAUVIN, "Artisans, machines, and Descartes". On Aristotelian science, see: JAMES LENNOX, *Aristotle on Inquiry: Erotetic Frameworks and Domain-Specific Norms*, Cambridge, Cambridge University Press 2021.

to causal investigation by citing Bacon's idea of a "second vintage".⁸⁷ To my knowledge, Bacon never mentions a *second* vintage, but the idea is clear enough: from historical harvesting one might ferment the fruits of one's labors, producing causal wine. *Pace* Harvey, however, Bacon and Descartes are not interested in the tradition of *historia* founded upon curiosity and knowledge of the variety of nature, Bacon writing that "now men have put a great deal of hard and careful work into noting the variety of things and minutely explaining the distinctive features of animals, herbs and fossils; most of which are more sports of nature than real differences of any use to the sciences".⁸⁸ In contrast to Bacon and Descartes, Harvey's conception of *historiae* turns upon *just* this idea of learning about nature's variety.

Yet Bacon and Harvey are united *against* Descartes in focusing not just on certain kinds of mechanical or physical analogies, but upon similarity, as Bacon continues in the passage just cited that, "we must turn all our attention to seeking and noting the resemblances and analogies of things, both in wholes and in parts".⁸⁹ Descartes' method of comparison is more akin to model building than it is to historical resemblance seeking.⁹⁰ Thus Descartes analogizes to ordinary things, not to "sports of nature" or "rarer and more studied things": the heart's heat is compared to that of a normal fire, the blood to other heated fluids, the micro-world of invisible corpuscles to that of visible macro-world objects like tennis balls.⁹¹ Histories might allow for comparison, but in the absence of the true explanation, they are of limited use.⁹²

Descartes is certainly aware of anatomical histories, referring directly to Bauhinus' "*historia*" concerning the valves of the veins.⁹³ As Vincent Aucante explores, Descartes

---

87 Harvey, *De generatione*, Ex. 25, p. 75.
88 Francis Bacon, *Novum organum* II.27, ed. by Lisa Jardine and Michael Silverthorne, Cambridge, Cambridge University Press, 2000, p. 146. For Descartes on curiosity, see his criticism of Mersenne: Descartes to Huygens, 12 March 1640, AT III, p. 746. See also: Mădălina Giurgea and Laura Georgescu, "Redefining the role of experiment in Bacon's natural history: How Baconian was Descartes before emerging from his cocoon?" *Early science and medicine* 17/1-2 (2012), p. 158-180; and Baldassarri, "Descartes' Battle for *Scientia*", p. 118-119.
89 Bacon, *Novum organum* II.27, p. 146.
90 On comparison, see: *Regulae* VI, AT X 381-387. Cf. Jean-Luc Marion, "Ordre et relation. Sur la situation aristotélicienne des Regles V et VI", *Archives de Philosophie* 37/2 (1974), p. 243-274; and Massimiliano Savini, "Comparatio vel ratiocinatio. Statuto e funzione del concetto di comparatio/comparaison nel pensiero di R. Descartes", in *DesCartes et des Lettres: Epistolari e filosofia nell'età cartesiana*, ed. by Francesco Marrone, Florence, Le Monnier, 2008, p. 132-169. Neither of these papers specifically discusses anatomical comparison.
91 See: *Dioptrique* AT VI 94 and 96; and *Regulae* VIII, AT X 395; also, the "model universe" in the fable of *Le monde*, AT XI 31. For another example of the correspondence between visible and invisible, see: *Discours* AT VI 238. See also: Peter Galison, "Descartes's Comparisons: From the Invisible to the Visible", *Isis* 75 (1984), p. 311-326; and Clarke, *Descartes' Philosophy of Science*, p. 122-123.
92 See also: Baldassarri, "Descartes' Battle for *Scientia*", p. 131.
93 *Excerpta anatomica*, AT XI 590-591. This is a reference to one of the books Descartes consulted, Bauhinus' *Theatrum Anatomicum*, Frankfurt, 1605. As Baldassarri points out, the case described by Descartes is contained in Bauhin's *Anatomica corporis virilis et muliebris historia* (Lyon, 1597) as well as the later collection of the *Theatrum*; see: Fabrizio Baldassarri, "Elements of Descartes' Medical Scientia: Books, Medical Schools, and Collaborations", in *Scientia in the History of Medicine*, ed. by Fabrizio Baldassarri and Fabio Zampieri, Rome-Bristol, L'Erma di Bretschneider, 2021, p. 247-270.

often refers to contemporary manuals that use the term *"historia"*, like Laurentius' *Historia anatomica*.⁹⁴ Indeed, despite his preference for ordinary experience, and despite his rhetorical opposition to book learning, Descartes' anatomy is essentially "bookish".⁹⁵ But, whatever his familiarity with anatomical writing, his use of the Latin *"historia"* and the French *"histoire"* does not map onto the use by physicians generally, let alone to Harvey's specific kind of *historiae*. By my count,⁹⁶ Descartes uses history words only 54 times: mostly in correspondence (21 times), but also numerous times in the *Epistola ad Voetium* (10), the *Discours* (4), *De methodo* (4), the *Principiorum* (3) and the *Principes* (2), the *Excerpta anatomica* (2), the *Recherché de la verité* (2), and the *Lettre apologetique de Mr Descartes* (2), with a single instance in the *Querla Apologetica*, the *Replies*, the *Traité de la Lumiere*, and the *Regulae*. The vast majority of these uses are meant either in the sense of a narrative story, or in the sense of writing about the past.⁹⁷ And, of course, he uses the term synonymously with "fable" in the *Discours*: "let us propose this writing only as a story [*histoire*], or, if you prefer, as a fable."⁹⁸ When he does use the term to mean something close to the idea of an anatomical *historia*, it is often in connection with Francis Bacon.⁹⁹ So, although he must have been familiar with the term as used by physicians, he almost never uses it in that sense, perhaps, as mentioned above, equating it with the swelling of anatomical texts overstuffed with "rarer and more studied" perceptions.

Descartes was an enthusiastic anatomist, and he worked closely with several physicians who had studied at Padua, the very place Harvey learned about *historiae*.¹⁰⁰ Indeed, Descartes read Harvey's teacher Fabricius' egg experiment.¹⁰¹ Fabricius opened an egg across subsequent days to see how the chick embryo develops, an experiment also performed by Aristotle and Harvey. In fact, Descartes indulges here in a rare instance of comparative anatomy:

> And as for the formation of chickens in the egg, it has been more than 15 years since I read what Fabricius ab Aquapendente wrote about it, & even I have sometimes

---

94 Vincent Aucante, *La philosophie médicale de Descartes*, Paris, PUF, 2015, p. 214 n. 1, referring to Andreas Laurentius' *Historia anatomica humani corporis*, Paris, 1600. Aucante also mentions here Vesalius' *Tabulae anatomicae*, Venice, 1544. For another source, see: Annie Bitbol-Hespériès, "Une source des textes biomédicaux latins de Descartes, AT XI: Les *Observationes* de Johannes Schenck", *Archives de Philosophie* 80 (2017), p. 152-161.
95 Aucante, *La philosophie médicale*, p. 71; "livresque".
96 I did this by hand, and then checked using an OCR'd version of the AT volumes. It is quite possible I missed a few instances, but I think the point holds regardless.
97 For a "story" meaning, see e.g., Descartes to Mersenne, 1 March 1638, AT II 25, discussing the "true story [*l'histoire au vray*]" that had been related to him regarding Beaugrand; for "writing about the past", see any of the instances in the *Epistola ad Voetium*, AT VIII-2 30 and 87-88.
98 *Discours* AT VI 4.
99 Descartes to Mersenne, 10 May 1632, AT I 251-252. See also his other references to *historia* (though he doesn't use that term) in the sense being elaborated, and which also mentions Bacon: Descartes to Mersenne, January 1630, AT I 109; and Descartes to Mersenne, 23 December 1630, AT I 196.
100 Plempius, Vorstius, and Regius all studied there; see: Baldassarri, "Elements of Descartes' Medical Scientia", p. 260.
101 Hieronymus Fabricius ab Aquapendente, *De formatione ovi et pulli*, Padua, 1621.

broken eggs to see this experiment [*expérience*]. But I was more curious; for I had once had a cow killed, which I knew I had conceived a short time before, in order to see the fetus. And having learned, afterwards, that the butchers of this country often kill some that come back pregnant, I had them bring me more than a dozen bellies in which there were small calves, some as big as mice, others as rats, and others as small dogs, where I was able to observe much more than in chickens, because the organs are larger and more visible.[102]

Besides cows, and the eels noted above, Descartes dissected hares,[103] sheep, codfish, and hake.[104] But Descartes' use of comparison is often opportunistic, based on the availability of, e.g., pregnant cows, the larger size of parts a bonus. Descartes' comparisons and the animals chosen are haphazard, having less to do with comparison itself, and more to do with responding to criticism, or in reaction to other's observations. While Descartes seems aware of the way that non-human anatomy could lead one astray when attributing it to humans,[105] he seems not to be interested in the collection of information about variety. So, while Descartes does argue that there is need of "particular observations",[106] this is not equivalent to observing a variety of particulars, that is, observing similarities and differences within and between animal kinds, something fundamental to Harvey's approach.[107] For Harvey, histories *had to be* comparative. To understand how different Descartes is from Harvey and traditional physicians and anatomists, I must explain in detail Harvey's philosophy of *historiae*.

For Harvey *historiae* could be trusted only if the person has the requisite technical, anatomical experience. *Pace* Descartes, Harvey argues that those without the requisite experience are incapable of anatomical judgment, even anatomical *learning*:

> How hard and difficult it would be to teach those having no experience [*nullam experientiam habentes*], indeed, they have no experience or sensible acquaintance in anything [*experientiam aut sensibilem cognitionem non habent*]; and how foolish and unteachable, how inexperienced, are these listeners to true knowledge:

---

102 Descartes to Mersenne, 2 November 1646, AT IV 555.
103 Descartes to Plempius, 15 February 1638, AT I 526-527; Descartes to Plempius, 23 March 1638, AT II 66.
104 *Excerpta anatomica* AT XI 617-618; BALDASSARRI, "Elements of Descartes' Medical Scientia", p. 256.
105 See Descartes to Mersenne June 6(?) 1637, AT I 378, where Descartes notes differences between a sheep's and a man's cerebral ventricles.
106 See *Discours*, AT VI 64-65, and Préface to the *Principes de la philosophie*, AT IX-2 20, where Descartes' targeted method of observing is discussed.
107 *Comparatio* were part and parcel of much Renaissance natural philosophy, beyond biological concerns and spurred (in part) by the rediscovery of ancient mathematics as well as commentators like Alexander of Aphrodisias; see: SAVINI, "Comparatio vel ratiocinatio", p. 141-143. Mersenne, in connection with Bacon, thought that this was the way to proceed, constructing knowledge from comparing experiments, and was criticized by Descartes. See: MARIN MERSENNE, *La Verité des sciences* I, Paris, 1626, p. 212-216; and BALDASSARRI, "Descartes' Battle for *Scientia*", p. 124-125. See also: CLAUDIO BUCCOLINI, "Mersenne Translator of Bacon?", *Journal of Early Modern Studies* 2 (2013), p. 33-59.

> they clearly show the judgments of the blind about colors, and of the deaf about harmonies [...] One inexperienced in anatomies [*Inexpertus in Anatomicis*] [...] is thought to be blind in some way, and is unsuitable to instruction.[108]

Inexperienced judgments about nature are as faulty as the judgments of the blind about geometry.[109] Therefore, lack of experience is a serious deficit, as experience teaches not only the nature of the world and its objects, but also the ability to make wise judgments in anatomy. This is part of how Harvey responded to his largest difficulty in the reception the *De motu cordis*, namely, that he had not provided the "correct explanation", that is, that he had not provided the final cause of the circulation.[110] Harvey's failure to convince his fellow physicians of the circulation can be keenly sensed in his 1649 work, where he argues that these other scientists misunderstand the nature of anatomical experience, since one must first inquire "that something is [*Quod sit*]" before we ask "why something is [*Propter quid*]."[111] For Harvey, the unwillingness of physicians to accept circulation prompted a thought opposite to Descartes', namely, that expert observation is logically *prior* to explanation: to put it in Aristotelian terms, *hoti* (what is the case) precedes *dioti* (why it is the case).[112]

What are these expert observations? Consider Harvey's *Prelectiones*, under the heading of "*historia anatomica*":

> In each part, [one should consider it] according to age, sex, disease, and its customary use (bringing in, putting out, or carrying away) within the same kind [of animal], [and one should consider the part] in different kinds [of animals] that also have those parts, such as winged creatures of the shore, land, and water, in fish and snakes, in oviparous and viviparous quadrupeds.[113]

Harvey's comparative anatomizing is part of his method, such comparisons a norm for organizing anatomical inference. Harvey argues for a wide field of comparison across *kinds of animals*, far beyond the haphazard comparisons of Descartes. This is an

---

108 HARVEY, *Exercitationes duae anatomicae*, p. 99-100. See also GOLDBERG, "William Harvey on Anatomy", p. 315-316.
109 This is, in fact, a non-sequitur, as blind mathematicians are often geometers or topologists, e.g., Louis Antoine (1888-1971) and Lev Semyonovich Pontryagin (1908-1988).
110 In England at least, Harvey's work was quickly accepted, and the search for the purpose of the circulation began a research program in anatomy, see: ROBERT FRANK, *William Harvey and the Oxford Physiologists*. Berkeley, University of California Press, 1980. On Descartes and teleology, there is now a vast literature, but see: PETER DISTELZWEIG, "The Use of *Usus* and the Function of *Functio*: Teleology and Its Limits in Descartes's Physiology," *Journal of the History of Philosophy* 53/3 (2015), p. 377-399.
111 HARVEY, *Exercitationes duae anatomicae*, p. 76. Roger French incorrectly separates the search for causes from the establishment of facts, in part because of his focus on the *De motu cordis*; see also GOLDBERG, "William Harvey on Anatomy".
112 This is found in the relation between ARISTOTLE's *Historia animalium* and explanatory works like *De partibus animalium* or *Generatione animalium*. For the Renaissance, see POMATA "Praxis Historialis", p. 111.
113 HARVEY, *Prelectiones*, p. 20-22. Because this text is a set of lecture notes, one must interpolate to make sense of the passages. Further, the arrangement of this page is helpful for making sense of it; see BL Sloane MS 230a.

Aristotelian paradigm: each part must be understood in terms of its differences *within* its kind, also attending to the differences *between* kinds.[114] Such comparisons are so important that Harvey describes them using a special phrase: the *regula Socratis*.[115]

The phrase first occurs in Harvey's *"Canones anatomae generalis"*, a set of heuristics for anatomy, emphasizing the pedagogical context of these lecture notes. In the fifth canon, Harvey exhorts students:

> To examine one's own and others' observations to prove your own opinion, or in the strictest form, deal with other animals according to the rule of Socrates: where it is farer written. Whence exotic[116] observations:
> 1. about the causes of disease: chiefly useful to the physician
> 2. about the variety of Nature: [chiefly useful] to the philosopher
> 3. for the purpose of refuting errors and solving problems
> 4. for the purpose of discovering uses and actions, excellences, and thus also on account of these, their classifications.
>
> The end of an anatomy is knowledge of a part, its purpose, its necessity and use. Its [anatomy's] chief purpose for Philosophers is to learn which [parts] are required for each action insofar as it is excellent. Likewise [its chief purpose] for Physicians is [to learn] the natural constitution [of the parts], [that is] the standard by which they must classify those who are sick, and then what they must do in diseases.[117]

Harvey here is careful not to reject the book learning Descartes (at least rhetorically) dispensed with, a more general norm of his scientific practice. The rule of

---

114 See the following sections in JAMES LENNOX, *Aristotle's Philosophy of Biology*, Cambridge, Cambridge University Press, 2001: "Divide and Explain: The Posterior Analytics in Practice", p. 7-38; "Matter, Form, Kind (Introduction to Part II)", p. 127-130; and, "Kinds, Forms of Forms, and the More and the Less in Aristotle's Biology", p. 160-181.

115 Harvey only uses this phrase twice in the *Prelectiones*, and never again in any writing we have available to us now. The reasons for this are obscure.

116 Although the reading of this word, *exoticas*, is reasonably sure, its meaning is not. I interpret this as that observations are "exotic" insofar as they involve other animals; it would be no stretch to say that at least Harvey's own use of animals was rather exotic, ranging from parrots to dogs to deer to eels and beyond.

117 HARVEY, *Prelectiones*, p. 16. I note the following changes from Whitteridge's transcription based upon my own archival work (see BL Sloane MS 230a): (1) I read as *confirmandam* and not as *considerandum*; (2) as *varietatem* and not as *veritatem*; (3) I read as *dignitates* and not *dignitatem*; and (4) I read as *inde* and not as *idem*. Further, I have chosen to render "*diducendum*," which means more literally "to divide", as "classify".

"Observationes proprias et alienas recensere ad confirmandam propriam opinionem vel obsignatis tabulis in aliis animalibus agere secundum Socratis regulam: where it is farer written. Unde observationes exoticas:

1. ob causas morborum: medicis praecipue utilis
2. ob varietatem Naturae, philosophicis
3. ad refutandos errores et problemata solvenda
4. ob usus et actiones inveniendas dignitates et propter inde colectanea

Anatomae enim finis partis cognitio, propter quod, necessitas et usus. Philosophicis praecipue qui inde sciant ad umamquanque actionem quae requiruntur quod praestat. Medicis item qui inde constiutionem naturalem, regulam, quo diducendum aegrotantes, et inde quid agendum morbis."

Socrates is a sort of specific version of this, where one compares observations not to other *authors* but to observations in *other animals*. This rule is central to *historiae* because it allows another way to determine anatomical definitions and causes. These observations have various important uses, e.g., some are useful to physicians insofar as they assist in determining the causes and seats of diseases. For instance, in a section titled "Affections of the viscera", Harvey lists a variety of observations of the viscera of patients suffering from various maladies, e.g., "in melancholics and those who are thin, [the spleen] is larger and more loosely textured, reddish-yellow or dark in color".[118] One thus finds Harvey using exotic comparisons to understand diseases.

Another use of the *regula* is particularly beneficial to the natural philosopher: understanding the variety of nature. But why should this be helpful? Later in the *Prelectiones* we find a clue (and another difference from Descartes): namely, a humanist mode of inquiry that depends upon familiarity with the classics. In discussing the function of the *caecum*,[119] Harvey makes his second and final mention of the rule of Socrates:

> [Called "*caecum*"] since its office [*officio*] is obscure. The size of a worm. In man, it is [counted] among the great [guts] for the sake of classification, as with the nipples. Conversely [in] hoggs, hare[s], oxen, ratt[s], etc., it is almost like another belly [in size]. In man it is sometimes large, as in the foetus WH, [as] Salomon Albertus [says], it is sometimes entirely absent. Thus the rule of Socrates through similarity in a great print [*Hinc Socratis regula per similitudinem in a great print*].[120]

Notice, first, that this is a sentiment strikingly similar to Descartes' justification for (an instance of) comparative anatomy, noted above. However, Harvey's methodology here goes further than Descartes' *ad hoc* justification. The end of the above passage refers to part of the *Republic*, wherein Socrates suggests that, since,

> we are no great wits, I think that we had better adopt a method which I may illustrate thus; suppose that a short-sighted person had been asked by someone to read small letters from a distance; and it occurred to someone else that they might be found in another place which was larger and in which the letters were larger, if they were the same and he could read the larger letters first and then proceed to the lesser, this would have been thought a rare piece of good fortune.[121]

The nature of justice in the soul is obscure, so one should look to the *Polis*, the soul writ large, and consider justice at this larger scale. Analogously, in certain animals, and especially in human beings, the actions and uses of the parts are obscure. But if the anatomist begins to look at other animals, on the assumption that, like the city and soul they are related by a fundamental similarity,[122] then the anatomist will often find that understanding is more easily achieved because the parts there

---

118 Harvey, *Prelectiones*, p. 144.
119 Literally "the blind part", the end of the colon.
120 Harvey, *Prelectiones*, p. 86.
121 Plato, *Republic* bk. 2, 368d, translated by Benjamin Jowett, accessed via: classics.mit.edu.
122 Recall the importance of such similarity, or resemblance, in Bacon's histories, noted above.

are "writ larger," that is, the parts are more easily observable. Observations should also be performed across time (that is to say, at different developmental stages), a technique Harvey uses to great effect in the *De motu cordis*.[123] When anatomists begin to mark patterns of variation in their organized *historiae*, they begin to understand a part's actions and uses. *Pace* Descartes' dismissal of those "rarer and more studied" observations, the view that anatomists "swell their books" with needless particularities and varieties, for Harvey, the collection of such variety is central to philosophical anatomy. Thus, e.g., Harvey notes the various features of the kidney's shape, location, etc., adding that,

> In some animals there are no hollows but the kidney is divided into lobes as in oxen and calves, in bears, and note that Eustachius saw it twice in a foetus... In the seal the cake-like mass of the kidney is made of an agglomeration of small pieces as if it were a haul of fish and it is thought that it is [for the sake of] the spleen, X but this is not so as is shown by the fact that the ureters derive from it; in another female it was not made of an agglomeration.[124]

Here is just what the rule suggests is useful for philosophers: understanding the variety of nature, or, better, *understanding how the nature of a thing varies*. Harvey compares his own observations, performed across animals, to observations from other anatomists, and, on account of this variation, he can redefine the use of the kidney. In each case (seal, oxen, etc.) because the ureters don't derive from the spleen connected to the kidney, but from the kidney to the bladder, he can conclude that the kidney's primary use cannot be to assist the spleen.

The use of the *regula Socratis* in the *De motu* follows this pattern. In his discussion of the use and purpose of the valves of the veins, Harvey notes that

> The discoverer of these doors did not understand the use of them, nor others who have said that the blood by its own weight should fall downward: for there are in the jugular vein those that look downwards and which hinder the blood to be carried upwards. I (and others likewise) have found in the emulgent branches of the Mesenterie, those which did look towards the vena cava and vena porta; add to this further that there are no such in the arteries, and it is to be seen that dogs and cattle have all their portals in the dividing of the crural veins at the beginning of the os sacrum, or in the branches near the coxendix, in which there is no such thing to be feared on account of the upright stature in man.[125]

It is clear here that Harvey's broad, comparative *historiae* are the basis for his account of the use of the valves. The discoverer of the valves, Harvey's teacher Fabricius, argued that the use had to do with preventing the blood from falling downwards. But Harvey, having collected observations about the distribution and structure of

---

123 See HARVEY, *De motu cordis*, cap. 6, p. 33, p. 35-36; cap. 9, p. 46. Observing across time is also important in Harvey's work on generation.
124 HARVEY, *Prelectiones*, p. 166.
125 HARVEY, *De motu cordis*, cap. 13, p. 55.

valves in various sorts of animals, found that their use cannot have anything to do with the blood falling because of the upright stature of humans, for he had seen the very same structures located in similar places in other creatures that do not have an upright posture.[126]

This conception of the *regula* is close to Roger French's argument that Harvey's,

> anatomical knowledge was incomplete without a knowledge of function, which could be found only in animals. Many animals had to be investigated to form a comprehensive composite term for the thing being investigated, in this case the heart. *Per similtudinem* is the search for similarity of function; in Aristotelian terms, the what-it-is-to-be-a-heart.[127]

This anatomical rule is used to great effect by Harvey:

> Next, it is not difficult to see the same thing in all animals that have but one ventricle, or as it were but one, as toads, frogs, snakes and lizards, which, although they are said in some manner to have lungs [...] yet it is plainly to be seen from personal experience that in them the blood is transferred in the same way from the veins into the arteries by the pulsation of the heart [...] For in these animals the case is as it might be in man were the septum of his heart perforated or taken away or one ventricle made out of the two; that done, I believe no man would then doubt by which way the blood could pass out of the veins into the arteries.[128]

Harvey collects observations on animals without lungs, with the idea that, since the pulmonary transit of the blood makes its movements difficult to follow, by looking in creatures without lungs, and in animals with only one ventricle, he will be able to more easily witness the transit of the blood from the veins to the arteries via the heart, just as Socrates could observe the city more easily than the soul. Furthermore, and getting to the core of the *regula*, by understanding how hearts, veins, arteries, and blood vary, Harvey can come to find the true essence of the heart by abstracting to what is in common between all these kinds. This is both an important method for determining the nature of a part or kind, as well as essential to the training that is necessary to gain the *experientia* needed to properly judge things anatomical. By following the rule of Socrates, Harvey can conclude that since,

> there are more creatures which have no lungs than there are which have them, and more which have but one ventricle of the heart than there are which have two, it is easy to conclude that in animals *by the more and the less* [epi to polu], usually and generally, the blood is sent from the veins into the arteries by an open way through the cavity of the heart.[129]

---

126 The *regula* is on display throughout the *De motu cordis*; see especially cap. 17.
127 FRENCH, *William Harvey's Natural Philosophy*, p. 85.
128 HARVEY, *De motu cordis*, cap. 6, p. 33.
129 Ibid.

Notice the concern not just with the existence of the circular path of the blood, but also with the distribution of this feature across different kinds of animals, with attention to how it varies, as Aristotle would say, by the more and the less — indeed Harvey even uses here the curious Greek phrase, *epi to polu*.[130] With the accumulation of yet more evidence, Harvey concludes that the heart is for the sake of the circulation of the blood, its action the forceful systole.[131]

While French is right that the rule of Socrates is supposed to help the anatomist obtain knowledge of uses and actions, this does not fully explicate *regula Socratis* — and in fact French misunderstands the details. Harvey, following Aristotle, thinks that it is important to look at how the part varies along all sorts of properties in order to determine its function, as knowledge of the function is the *goal* and not the *method*. Harvey's method is not the search for similarity in function, but rather, it is the discovery of certain kinds of similarity that allows Harvey to establish the function of a part in the first place — similarity relations are fundamental to the *regula Socratis*. Importantly, the relevant variation for determining function is often variation among those features I noted above from Harvey's conception of *historia anatomica* (and, indeed, even to Bacon's conception of natural history),[132] and so this method *per similitudinem* is a central feature of anatomical experiencing in general. The goal of anatomical experience is not just to learn the function, but, indeed, to learn the true essence and nature of the part of the body in question, both its formal and material nature. To understand this, one must first understand in more detail why Harvey calls this the "*regula Socratis*" beyond the allusion to the Republic.[133]

In Plato's *Phaedrus*, Socrates argues that some things are easily known, others under dispute, because how they are classified is obscure — one must therefore be trained to recognize the forms of things. The method Socrates uses is one that, by interrogating various interlocutors, one can come to the definition of that thing. Noting that rhetoric and medicine proceed alike. Socrates says that,

> Until a man knows the truth of the several particulars of which he is writing or speaking, and is able to define them as they are, and having defined them again to divide them until they can be no longer divided, and until in like manner he is able to discern the nature of the soul, and discover the different modes of discourse which are adapted to different natures, and to arrange and dispose them in such a way that the simple form of speech may be addressed to the simpler

---

130 See ARISTOTLE's *De partibus animalium*, lib. I, cap. 4. See also: JAMES LENNOX, *Aristotle on the Parts of Animals*, Oxford, Clarendon Press, 2001, p. 168-169; and: JAMES LENNOX, "Aristotle on genera, species, and 'the more and the less'", *Journal of the History of Biology* 13/2 (1980), p. 321-346.
131 HARVEY, *De motu cordis*, cap. 17, p. 70-71.
132 Lisa Jardine connects Bacon's natural history with humanist doctrines, including the commonplace book, see LISA JARDINE, *Francis Bacon: Discovery and the Art of Discourse*, Cambridge, Cambridge University Press, 1974. Cf. ANN BLAIR, "Humanist Methods in Natural Philosophy: The Commonplace Book", *Journal for the History of Ideas* 53/4 (1992), p. 541-551.
133 Descartes' project has a different goal, not so much to determine action and use but to explain them mechanically. For the medical background and Descartes' relation to it, see: BITBOL-HESPÉRIÈS, "Cartesian physiology".

nature, and the complex and composite to the more complex nature-until he has accomplished all this, he will be unable to handle arguments according to rules of art, as far as their nature allows them to be subjected to art [...].[134]

Now, set aside Plato's specific method of division and definition, which Aristotle criticizes.[135] What is important is that this method of definition by differentiation is part of Aristotle's Platonic inheritance, and is at the core of his method. Indeed, as Aristotle argues in the *Metaphysics*, there are two things that he owes to Socrates: the two starting points of science, namely, inductive arguments and universal definitions.[136] Since *historiae* are the inductive basis for one's inferences in anatomy, the *regula*, as the method for collecting *historia*, combines induction and definition: in order to be able to define something, one must come to know its nature through "several particulars". The *regula Socratis* is a method of experiencing, allowing the formation of a true concept of the nature of a thing, and especially its variation and definition. This brings us to the anatomical method of Galen, who also takes seriously the Socratic/Platonic background to medical method.

In *De placitis hippocratis et platonis*, Galen argues that science requires finding proper premises, and thus anyone,

> who tries to demonstrate anything, must first have learned the differences in the premises themselves; then he must have undergone long training [...] Suppose someone wishes to become [an arithmetician]: he first learns all the numbers which those people call "square" and those others called "oblong"; then he spends a very long time in the contemplation of multiplication and division [...].[137]

Galen here connects the method of anatomy to that of geometry. We hear an echo of this in Harvey, insofar as Galen also uses *historiae* to determine universal definitions.[138] In the case of anatomy, one must learn the differences in living animal bodies and their parts. One does this through training, which includes reading learned books, but, importantly, it also necessitates the cutting and observing of many animal bodies in order to become familiar with their variation and nature. Galen (and Harvey following him) understands this process as one of coming to recognize similarity and dissimilarity in what the anatomist perceives, determining animal natures based on how things in the world are alike and unalike.[139]

In Book IX of *De placitis*, Galen identifies similarity as a key culprit in mistaken ideas about the body, as something that Hippocrates admitted could mislead and perplex even good physicians. In order to succeed in medicine, then, Galen argues

---

134 PLATO, *Phaedrus*, 277c, translated by Benjamin Jowett, accessed via: classics.mit.edu/.
135 On Aristotle's method of division and explanation, see LENNOX, "Divide and Explain".
136 ARISTOTLE, *Metaphysicorum*, lib. XIII, cap. 4, in *Aristotelis libri omnes, ad animalium cognitionem attinentes, cum Averrois Cordubensis variis in eosdem commentariis* Volume 8, Venice, 1552, 61^v.
137 GALEN, *De placitis*, lib. II, cap. 3.
138 HARVEY, *Exercitationes duae anatomicae*, p. 97-98. "We would surely admit no knowledge, if faith through the senses were not most certain, and stabilized by reasoning [*ratiocinando stabilita*] (as the Geometers are accustomed to do in their constructions) [...]".
139 GALEN 1549, *De placitis* lib. IX, cap. 2, p. 1079-1082.

that one must learn to discriminate similarity and difference within the natural world,[140] which is precisely what *historiae* are for. At this point in the chapter, Galen then quotes both the passages noted above from Plato's *Republic* and *Phaedrus*, and points to these as encapsulating the idea that the training of anatomical ability is fundamentally about the power to distinguish similarity and dissimilarity in things. Echoing the passage from the *Phaedrus*, Galen concludes that any general method divorced from training in many particulars is insufficient to produce a true physician.[141]

Given this contrast with the anatomical tradition and Harvey's rule for dissection, and the traditional nature of his anatomy, we can conclude that Descartes' anatomical method departs greatly from tradition on precisely the importance and use of comparison and variation in anatomical method.

4. Conclusions

Harvey, following in this hybrid Galenic-Aristotelian-Platonic method, understands long experience using the rule of Socrates as the means by which we discriminate similarity and difference, the very key to anatomical judgment and the basis for the development of expertise. To do so, one must use this rule in the construction of *historiae*. Harvey's empiricism is one that is based upon a very particular notion of experience, involving exceptional and broad acquaintance with varying animals' anatomies. This is a kind of technical experience, one not common to all inquirers, but instead the result of a specific humanist educational background and regimen of practice in the pursuit of skill. Descartes' empiricism is quite different. Even if both thinkers are certain that autoptic, personal experience is key, even if they agree on the importance of both reason and experience, they disagree upon who is capable of such experiencing. Descartes' is an ecumenical view, an ideal of the scientific observer whose lack of technical background is, in fact, what allows them to offer epistemically trustworthy observations. Because Descartes is concerned with how observation and experiment can mislead due to assumptions, he is wary of the ways by which the theory-ladenness of observations based on incorrect theories can cause us to think something is true when it is not. Harvey, not so similarly burdened, still in thrall to humanist modes of natural philosophy, finds no problems on this account.

In sum, these two thinkers have different rules for achieving anatomical knowledge. Above, I contrasted these two approaches as being ordered, as it were, by different priorities, and resulting in different strengths: Harvey prioritizes deep acquaintance with the phenomena, with an eye to explanation only after the facts have been established. Descartes' science, on the contrary, is predicated upon our intuitive ability to construct mechanical explanations for any sort of natural phenomenon, observation and experimentation seen as a means of ensuring we have characterized the phenomena correctly, an aid to find the right deduction. The kind of skepticism

---

140 *Ibid.*
141 *Ibid.*, 1081. See also HIPPOCRATES' *De officina medici*.

prompted by Descartes' understanding of theory-ladenness is a different kind of skepticism than that found in the *Meditationes*, but it is no less important for understanding his natural philosophy. His preference for ordinary experience, his suspicion of rare and learned observations, all stem from his conviction that what we observe is a function of how we understand and explain the world, derived from our background theories. If this is the case, thinks Descartes, one must begin by determining the true theory, thus prioritizing explanation. Of course, Descartes' belief that he could (and had) found the uniquely correct theory is almost comically optimistic. But this does not impugn his anatomy. Descartes did not make mistakes concerning the heart because he was a bad or uniformed anatomist; rather, his conception of science, his set of assumptions, and his ideas of how to do science were quite far removed from that of physicians like Harvey.

When assessing his importance to the history of medicine, there is a tendency to criticize Descartes' anatomy for getting things wrong. But notice that Harvey's shine is dimmed by the fact that his *explanations* — the very thing Descartes prioritized — did not fare well among the increasingly mechanical world views that begin to dominate European natural philosophy. If Descartes' cardiological picture is quickly abandoned in favor of the Harveian one, we must observe that Harvey's work on generation suffered a similar rejection, embodied in a 1674 compendium of his *De generatione* which excised the explanatory and theoretical parts, leaving only those empirical — nay, historical — parts.[142] That is, we must recognize that their contributions are of different kinds, whose nature is dictated by divergent rules for anatomy, by differing empiricisms: one explanatorily focused, the other historically. Despite his naivety on some matters, and his mistakes on others, Descartes' empiricism is a sophisticated one that takes seriously how our own "sensibilities" might lead us astray. There is thus an interesting duality here. Harvey tended to get his observations right, but his explanations wrong, and Descartes the reverse. Their priorities, it seems, dictated their successes and failures.

---

142 JUSTUS SCHRADER, *Observationes et Historiae*, Amsterdam, 1674. This work also contains material not from Harvey, including a variety of post-mortem examinations conducted by various physicians, including Sylvius, Swammerdam, and others. See POMATA, "*Praxis Historialis*", p. 121-122.

ANDREA STRAZZONI

The Lost *Dictata* of Henricus Regius*

▼ ABSTRACT In this chapter, I discuss the contents of the now lost academic *dictata* of Henricus Regius, embodying one of the first comprehensive teachings of natural philosophy inspired by René Descartes at a university. These contents are partially extant in Martin Schoock's *Admiranda methodus* (1643), and can be reconstructed from Regius's early texts and correspondence with Descartes. They reveal that Regius was original with respect to Descartes especially in his account of magnetism, which was functional to his medical physiology, and discussion of the powers of plants, out of which he developed such a physiology.

▼ KEYWORDS René Descartes, Henricus Regius, *Dictata*, Magnetism, Plants

1. Introduction

Henricus Regius (1698-1679) was the first expert who systematically adopted the contents of the *Discours de la méthode* and *Essais* (1637) by René Descartes (1596-1650) for university lectures, using such texts for his teaching of medicine and natural philosophy at Utrecht from 1638 onwards, as well as in his first lengthy series of disputations in medicine, the *Physiologia sive Cognitio sanitatis* (1641-1643). While his and Descartes's

---

* The research leading to this publication has received funding from the European Union's Horizon 2020 research and innovation programme under the Marie Skłodowska-Curie grant agreement No 892794 (*READESCARTES*), and, previously, from the Swiss National Science Foundation-SNF, Spark grant number CRSK-1_190670 (*Testing a Multi-Disciplinary Approach to an Unexplored Body of Literature: The Case of Cartesian Dictations*). A special thank you goes to the Forschungszentrum Gotha der Universität Erfurt.

Andrea Strazzoni • Marie-Skłodowska-Curie Fellow, Ca' Foscari University of Venice.
Contact: <andrea.strazzoni@unive.it>

friend Henricus Reneri (1593-1639) only sporadically inserted Cartesian ideas into his disputations,[1] Regius became at first associated with Descartes's 'new philosophy'. Later (1645), however, he entered into a quarrel with Descartes over the nature and functioning of the mind, about which Regius held a materialist and 'radically empiricist' standpoint, and over his own originality and plagiarisms with respect to Descartes. While most of the secondary literature has focused on such topics, as well as on the 'pre-Cartesian' influences on Regius,[2] little attention has been devoted to the contents of his early lectures at Utrecht, embodying not only a medical physiology (i.e. the first part of medicine, devoted to the explanation of the conditions of health) but also natural-philosophical theories as such (though intertwined with physiology itself),[3] and taking place before the appearance of Descartes's complete treatise in natural philosophy, namely his *Principia philosophiae* (1644). In what follows, I will provide a reconstruction and discussion of the contents of Regius's early teaching, by considering some fragments of his now lost academic *dictata*, namely the contents he dictated during his lectures, constituting a textbook in natural philosophy. After having presented some indirect evidence on the contents of his teaching (section 2), in section 3, I provide a discussion of the extant fragments of Regius's lectures, which have survived in the *Admiranda methodus* (1643) by Martin Schoock (1614-1669). In section 4, I then focus on Regius's most original theory extant from such fragments, namely his theory of magnetism, pre-dating the one Descartes put into his *Principia philosophiae* and being kindred to that developed by Isaac Beeckman (1588-1637). Eventually (section 5) I reconstruct the overall contents and originality of Regius's early teaching, showing the importance of his theory of plants in it, and how he developed his theory of medical physiology on its grounds.

2. Early Evidence for Regius's Textbook (1637-1642)

In his *Epistola ad Patrem Dinet* (May 1642) Descartes reported that

> a certain doctor of medicine [...] read my *Dioptrique* and *Météores*, when they were first brought to light. [...] Diligently studying them, and deducing other [things] from them, [he] was [of] such a sagacity, that within a few months [he] thence prepared a

---

1 ROBIN BUNING, *Henricus Reneri (1593-1639): Descartes's Quartermaster in Aristotelian Territory*, Utrecht, Zeno: The Leiden-Utrecht Research Institute of Philosophy, 2013.
2 THEO VERBEEK, "Regius's *Fundamenta Physices*," *Journal of the History of Ideas*, LV (1994), p. 533-551; DELPHINE BELLIS, "Empiricism without Metaphysics: Regius' Cartesian Natural Philosophy," in *Cartesian Empiricisms*, ed. by Mihnea Dobre and Tammy Nyden, Dordrecht-Heidelberg-New York-London, Springer, 2013, p. 169-172; ANDREA STRAZZONI, "How Did Regius Become Regius? The Early Doctrinal Evolution of a Heterodox Cartesian," *Early Science and Medicine*, XXIII/4 (2018), p. 362-412.
3 On the different concepts of physiology in the early modern age, see VIVIAN NUTTON, "*Physiologia* from Galen to Jacob Bording," in *Blood, Sweat, and Tears: The Changing Concepts of Physiology from Antiquity into Early Modern Europe*, ed. by Manfred Horstmanshoff, Helen King, and Claus Zittel, Leiden-Boston, Brill, p. 27-40.

complete physiology, which, having been seen privately by some [students], [it] pleased them so [much], that [...] they asked the magistrate for a post in medicine for him.⁴

Descartes refers to the years 1637-1638, when Regius was appointed as extraordinary professor of theoretical medicine and botany at Utrecht (11/21 July 1638), after the creation of a second chair in medicine at the University: a position which was assigned to him thanks to two supporters of Descartes, namely Reneri and of one of the mayors of Utrecht, Gijsbert van der Hoolck (1598-1680), curator of the University.⁵ In fact, according also to a letter of Regius to Descartes of 8/18 August 1638 and to a letter of Descartes to Marin Mersenne (1588-1648) of 23 August 1638, Regius was appointed as he had already successfully lectured to private students in Cartesian philosophy, which he learnt from Reneri and, upon their publication in June 1637, from Descartes's own *Discours de la méthode* and *Essais*.⁶ So that his appointment to a medical chair was undoubtedly related to his being a Cartesian. Moreover, at that time (8/18 August 1638) Regius sent to Descartes some *Essais de Médecine* or "very short notes" of his on Vittore Trincavelli (1496-1588), now lost, in order to show Descartes that he was a follower of his ideas,⁷ while earlier that year he imparted private teaching to Antonius Mudenus (c. 1618-1675), who was to dedicate to him, in March 1638, a disputation with a notably physiological i.e. medical character (which I discuss in section 5). So that we can suppose (even if Descartes's judgment as given in his *Epistola ad Dinet* might have been based on later writings by Regius, as I discuss

---

4   "Doctor quidam medicinae [...] legit Dioptricam meam et Meteora, cum primum edita sunt in lucem [...]. Quae colligendo diligentius, et alia ex iis deducendo, ea fuit sagacitate, ut intra paucos menses integram inde physiologiam concinnarit, quae, cum privatim a nonnullis visa esset, eis sic placuit, ut professionem medicinae [...] pro illo [...] a magistratu petierint," RENÉ DESCARTES, *Epistola ad Patrem Dinet*, in AT VII 582-583; BO 1450. [All translations are mine.]
5   As discussed in BOS 8-9.
6   "Afin de ne pas rendre sa modestie ou sa timidité suspecte d'ingratitude, il prit la liberté de lui écrire le XVIII d'Août [*i.m.*: Lettre I de Regius MS.] pour le remercier d'un service qu'il lui avait rendu sans le savoir. Il lui demanda la grâce d'être reçu au nombre de ses serviteurs, avantage qu'il avait recherché et qu'il croyait avoir mérité depuis qu'il s'était rendu son disciple. Et pour ne lui point faire un mystère d'une chose qu'il ne pouvait savoir, c'est-à-dire de la manière dont il prétendait que M. Descartes l'avait fait Professeur dans l'Université, il lui fit un détail de la connaissance qu'il avait acquise de sa méthode et de sa philosophie, premièrement par la bouche de M. Reneri, qui l'avait amplement informé des qualités héroïques de son esprit, et ensuite par la lecture des Essais qu'il avait publiés l'année précédente. Il lui marqua ensuite comment il s'était heureusement servi de cette méthode pour enseigner sa philosophie à quelques particuliers suivant ses principes; et il lui apprit que le grand succès de cette entreprise avait porté les Magistrats de la ville et les Professeurs de l'Université à le choisir pour remplir la chaire de nouvelle érection," Regius to Descartes, 8/18 August 1638, in BOS 5; AT II 305-306; BL 818 and 820; Descartes to Mersenne, 23 August 1638, in AT II 334; BL 850-852.
7   "Il lui protesta que de son côté il ferait tout ce qui dépendrait de lui pour ne rien faire qui fût indigne de la qualité de son disciple qu'il préférait à tous les autres avantages de sa vie; et qu'il suivrait les pas de M. Reneri le plus près qu'il lui serait possible. Pour se mettre d'abord en possession des droits attachés à cette qualité, il prit la liberté de lui envoyer ses *Essais de Médecine*, qui n'étaient autre chose que des notes assez courtes sur Trincavel, et le pria de les examiner avec toute la sévérité d'un maître," Regius to Descartes, 8/18 August 1638, in BOS 5-6; AT II 306; BL 820. The medical works of Trincavelli were posthumously published in 1586, 1592, and 1599, and included commentaries on Galen and Avicenna.

in section 5), that at the time of his appointment, Regius was privately teaching both natural philosophy and medicine: if not all the parts of medicine, at least physiology.

References to such teachings and manuscripts (the chronology of which is somewhat tentative, I summarize in the following table) recur in the next years.

June 1637-August 1638	Physiology
August 1638	*Essais de Médecine* or short notes on Trincavelli
May 1639	Short propositions touching physiology (unfinished)
May 1640	Physics
May 1639-March 1641	*Compendium physicum*
May 1641	*Novae philosophiae prodromus*
May 1641-February 1642	*Physica fundamenta*
August 1638-May 1642	*Cogitata physica*
May 1641-July 1642	*Dictata physica*[8]

In May 1639, indeed, Regius was finishing some "short propositions [...] touching physiology" and asked Descartes to review them when they were completed,[9] while in May 1640 he reported that his students pressed him to publish his "physics," having in the meantime started to publicly lecture on physical topics as such, being allowed to teach Aristotle's *Problemata* since April.[10] Eventually, in April 1641 Descartes wrote to Regius that

> I remember that I read many things, in your *Compendium physicum*, completely alien to the common opinion, which are barely proposed there, without any

---

8   On Regius's *Cogitata physica* and *Dictata physica* see, respectively, sections 5 and 3.
9   "Après s'être assuré des bontés de M. Descartes, il continua le dessein qu'il avait entrepris de renfermer dans des propositions courtes tout ce qu'il croyait savoir touchant la physiologie. Il était presque sur la fin de cet ouvrage, lorsqu'il en écrivit à M. Descartes [...] pour lui communiquer les difficultés qu'il y trouvait; [...] Il le pria par avance [...] de prendre la peine de le revoir quand il l'aurait achevé," Regius to Descartes, 17 May 1639, in Bos 20; AT II 548-549; BL 1024.
10 "Ses écoliers le pressaient, dit-il, [*i.m.*: Lettr. XI de Regius, MS.] incessamment de faire imprimer sa physique, afin d'exposer aux yeux de tout l'univers une philosophie qui ne faisait encore bruit que dans quelques provinces," Regius to Descartes, 5/15 May 1640, in Bos 38; AT III 61; BL 1180. Around April 1640 Regius asked Gysbertus Voetius and other professors to be allowed to teach physics as such, or at least that part of physics more kindred to medicine ("ad professionem physicam vel totam, vel saltem partem eius specialem (quae maxime affinis esset medicinae)," GYSBERTUS VOETIUS et al., *Testimonium Academiae Ultraiectinae, et Narratio historica qua defensae, qua exterminatae novae philosophiae*, Utrecht, Ex typographia Wilhelmi Strickii, 1643, p. 12), albeit without success. Hence, he asked Voetius to be allowed to teach, once a week, on Pseudo-Aristotle's *Problemata*, namely on topics such as optics or mechanics. This was granted him on 17/27 April 1640, when the Utrecht Vroedschap increased Regius's salary (VOETIUS et al., *Testimonium*, p. 12-13; Bos 39-40). In any case, he imparted this kind of teaching, privately, well before April 1640. He was forbidden to teach on physical topics in March 1642, during the *querelle d'Utrecht*, given the heterodox contents of his disputations, *dictata*, and lectures. See VOETIUS et al., *Testimonium*, p. 12-18; ARNOLDUS C. DUKER, *Gisbertus Voetius*, Leiden, Brill, 1897-1915, vol. II, p. 141 and 146-147, and appendices LV-LVI.

reasoning added [to them], by which they can be made probable to the reader. I deemed that these can be tolerated in theses, where often paradoxes are gathered in order to give a broader matter of disputing to the adversaries. However, in a book, which you seem to want to propose as a *Novae philosophiae prodromus*, I deem that is to be done completely the opposite: namely reasons have to be provided, by which you persuade the reader of those [things] you want to conclude are true, before you expound such things, in order that [they] do not offend him with their novelty.¹¹

Indeed, Regius had in the meantime (from 17/27 April 1641) started to preside over his series of disputations *Physiologia sive Cognitio sanitatis*, taking place until December 1641, and then completed in March-June 1643.¹² As reconstructed by Theo Verbeek, Regius held these kind of disputations in partial fulfillment of the *desiderata* of Gysbertus Voetius (1589-1676), who became rector on 11 March 1641. At the time of his rectorship Voetius suggested that Regius publish a book — or textbook — on natural philosophy instead of giving disputations (preferred by Descartes, as seen above, and by Regius himself accordingly), which could give rise to problems within the University, given the fact that Regius was professor of medicine, and not of natural philosophy. Upon Regius's insistence, Voetius allowed him to preside over disputations on medical topics, with the occasional insertion of natural-philosophical considerations concerning physiology, allowed by the fact that this was intertwined with physics, if not synonymous with it.¹³

---

11 "[...] meminerim me multa legisse in tuo compendio Physico, a vulgari opinione plane aliena, quae nude ibi proponuntur, nullis additis rationibus, quibus lectori probabilia reddi possint, toleranda quidem illa esse putavi in Thesibus, ubi saepe paradoxa colliguntur, ad ampliorem disputandi materiam adversariis dandam; sed in libro, quem tanquam novae Philosophiae Prodromum videbaris velle proponere, plane contrarium iudico esse faciendum: nempe rationes esse afferendas, quibus lectori persuadeas quae vis concludere vera esse, priusquam ipsa exponas, ne novitate sua illum offendant," Descartes to Regius, April 1641, in Bos 57; AT IV 239-240; BL 2036.
12 Regius's *Physiologia* was preceded by the *Disputatio medico-physiologica pro sanguinis circulatione* (1640), the defensive booklet *Spongia* (1640) against the criticisms of James Primrose (1598-1659) of the *Disputatio*, and concomitant with his *De illustribus aliquot quaestionibus physiologicis* (November-December 1641), a short series of disputations with a more notable natural-philosophical and metaphysical character, notoriously prompting the *querelle d'Utrecht*: see René DESCARTES and Martin SCHOOCK, *La Querelle d'Utrecht*, ed. by Theo Verbeek, Paris, Les Impressions nouvelles, 1988.
13 "Paulo post cum ab inclyto urbis Senatu munus Rectoris Theologo impositum esset, 16. Martii anno 1641, aliquot post diebus convenit eum Medicus et praemisso proemio de benevolentia et favore eius erga se, de eiusdem in Academia auctoritate, et quae istius erant farinae, aperuit nunc demum sub ipsius Rectoratu affulgere pulcherrimam occasionem Academiae huic industriam suam probandi, eamque pro virili illustrandi: quod ille fore putabat evulgatione suae philosophiae. In quem finem postulabat consilium et auxilium Theologi, tunc Rectoris, sine cuius auctoritate nihil se tentaturum dicebat. Consultabat vero utrum satius esset sententiam suam libro edito, an thesibus academicis in lucem proferre. Cumque posterius libi potissimum arridere ostenderet, Theologus conabatur persuadere, li omnino statuisset, meditationes suas in publicum edere, priorem modum potius amplecteretur neque enim posse collegium disputationum, praesertim paradoxarum, de tota physica ordine proponi a Professore Medicinae, sine praeiudicio Professorum Philosophiae, atque [...] academicae perturbatione. Cumque Medicus obtenderet partim autoritatem Rectoris, partim lectionem problematicam, cuius respectu, etiam esset Professor Philosophiae, Theologus utrumque diluebat, additis rationibus rei et tempori tunc convenientibus. Tandem cum videret Theologus eum a proposito dimoveri non posse,

Moreover, besides sending to Descartes a *Compendium physicum* (certainly after May 1639, when he announced to Descartes to be still preparing some "short propositions [...] touching physiology," and probably before meeting Voetius in March 1641, Descartes's preference for theses being a likely reason motivating Regius to insist on presiding over disputations), and announcing to him a *Novae philosophiae prodromus* before or during May 1641 (when Regius apparently reverted to his idea of publishing a textbook), in February 1642 Regius published a *Responsio* against the criticisms Voetius and his student Lambertus vanden Waterlaet (*c.* 1619-1678) moved against the 'new philosophy', during the so-called *querelle d'Utrecht*.[14] In his *Responsio*, Regius refers both to Descartes's *Le monde* (the manuscript of which was received by Regius in May 1641 c.,[15] and about which he could nevertheless have had insights from Reneri even earlier),[16] and to his own *Physica fundamenta* (which has to be dated after the *Prodromus*, namely to May 1641-February 1642) as sources of explanations in a broad number of natural-philosophical topics, largely exceeding physiology intended as the first part of medicine:

> [...] even if we cannot yet specifically explain all the mysteries of nature with our principles, the matter is however as such (as is manifest to those who saw the *Monde* of the prince of our philosophy, or who are acquainted with our *Physica fundamenta*) that heaven and earth, fixed stars, planets, comets, tides, salt, meteors, the magnet, the operations of plants and animals, light, luminary, colors and innumerable other qualities of natural things are already perfectly understood by us.[17]

Notably, this list includes topics not dealt with in Descartes's at that time published texts, as in his *Discours de la méthode* and *Essais* he treated (with regard to the topics of this list) the nature of salt, meteors, light and colors, as well as a theory of blood circulation. Moreover, if Descartes treated in his *Le monde* the topics of the heavens, planets, stars, comets, tides, and light (and in fact Regius used this text in preparing

---

consilium suggessit, ut totam medicinam disputationibus publicis ventilandam proponeret, quaeque haberet [...] paradoxa primae parti sc. physiologiae sive per appendices et corollaria (quod maxime suadebat) sive ipsis thesibus insereret," VOETIUS *et al., Testimonium*, p. 17-18. See VERBEEK, "Regius's *Fundamenta Physices*," p. 538-539; DUKER, *Gisbertus Voetius*, vol. II, p. 144-145.

14 The *Responsio* was written with the supervision of Descartes and was directed against Voetius's *Appendix ad Corollaria theologico philosophica nuperae Disputationi de Iubilaeo Romano, de rerum naturis et formis substantialibus*, held with Vanden Waterlaet as *respondens* on 23-24 December 1641 (Julian calendar). Voetius and Vanden Waterlaet reacted (mostly) to Regius's *De illustribus aliquot quaestionibus physiologicis*.
15 As demonstrated in VERBEEK, "Regius's *Fundamenta Physices*," p. 543-544. See also BOS 67.
16 See *infra*, n. 104.
17 "Etiamsi omnia naturae arcana nondum specifice ex nostris principiis [...] possimus explicare, eo tamen res iam pervenit (ut iis constat, qui principis nostrae philosophiae Mundum viderunt, aut Physica nostra Fundamenta sunt edocti) ut coelum et Terra, stellae fixae, planetae, cometae, aestus maris, sal, meteora, magnes, stirpium et animalium operationes, lux, lumen, colores, et innumerae aliae rerum naturalium qualitates a nobis iam perfecte intelligantur," HENRICUS REGIUS, *Responsio, sive Notae in Appendicem ad Corollaria theologico-philosophica* [...] *Gisberti Voetii*, Utrecht, Apud Joannem a Doorn, 1642, p. 20.

his lectures, as he deals with the cosmological theories presented in it in his *De illustribus aliquot quaestionibus physiologicis*, November-December 1641), he did not deal with magnetism or plants, which therefore have to be traced only to Regius's *Physica fundamenta*, and are absent even from his *Physiologia*, while they return in his *Fundamenta physices*, clearly an evolution of his *Physica fundamenta*. In particular, the explanation of magnetism was at the center of Regius's teaching natural-philosophical theories between the late 1630s and early 1640s, as I show in the next sections, where I also provide some remarks on Regius's theory of plants.

3. Direct Insights on Regius's *Dictata* (1642)

The only direct insights on the contents of Regius's handwritten treatise are to be found in the *Admiranda methodus novae philosophiae Renati Des Cartes* (1643), in which some extracts from Regius's *Dictata physica* dating — as I clarify below — to c. May 1641-July 1642 (so that we can presume that the contents of these *dictata* were roughly the same as his *Physica fundamenta*) are reported and commented. The book had a complex genesis: its first part was written, under the pressure of Voetius and Vanden Waterlaet, by Schoock (professor at Groningen) in July-August 1642, during the Summer holidays which he spent at Utrecht. Upon his return to Groningen, he interrupted his work: after a reminder by Vanden Waterlaet to supply the rest of the book, such a part had nonetheless begun to be printed in October-November. Probably after having been completed also by Voetius and Vanden Waterlaet, eventually, the whole book was published, without reporting the name of any author, in March 1643, causing Descartes to request, through the French Ambassador (Gaspar de Coignet de La Thuillerie, 1594-1653), the prosecution of Schoock by the States of Groningen. Being then summoned by the Groningen academic senate, in April 1645 Schoock eventually claimed that the actual author of the book was Voetius.[18] At that point, a lengthy intellectual and legal quarrel arose between Schoock, Voetius and Carlous de Maets (1597-1651), taking place in Utrecht: first at the council of Aldermen (1645-1649), and afterwards at the higher provincial court (c. 1649-1652) — apparently with a settlement between the parties (as no documents of the latter trial are extant).[19]

It was Vanden Waterlaet who, in the morning of 18 July 1642 (the day after a dinner during which Voetius and Vanden Waterlaet himself pressed Schoock for the first time to prepare a refutation of Cartesian philosophy), personally handed to Schoock the "excerpts from the [...] *dictata* and theses of Regius, [...] written by Waterlaet's hand," and afterwards kept by Schoock, namely "*dictata* from his lectures, of someone addicted to Cartesian philosophy" (i.e. an unknown private student of Regius, as I show

---

18 As reconstructed in THEO VERBEEK, *Descartes and the Dutch: Early Reactions to Cartesian Philosophy, 1637-1650*, Carbondale, Southern Illinois University Press, 1992, p. 30-31; RENÉ DESCARTES, *The Correspondence of René Descartes 1643*, ed. by Erik-Jan Bos, Theo Verbeek, and Jeroen van de Ven, Utrecht, Zeno: The Leiden-Utrecht Research Institute of Philosophy, 2003, p. 185-189.
19 DUKER, *Gisbertus Voetius*, vol. III, p. 243-244 and appendices XXXII-XXXIII; vol. II, appendix LVII; DESCARTES, *The Correspondence 1643*, p. 295-296.

below) — according to a *Corte memorie* given by Schoock to the Utrecht major Johan van Weede (1584-1658) in July 1645 in an attempt to defend himself against the forthcoming lawsuit by Voetius, and to his *Necessaria et modesta defensio* (1646).[20] Unfortunately, such *dictata* are now irretrievable. Probably, Schoock produced them to the Utrecht Aldermen in May 1647, together with the letters of Voetius (both Gysbertus and his son Paul, 1619-1667) and Vanden Waterlaet as evidence that Voetius was the real author of the *Admiranda methodus*.[21] However, of such a trial only the proceedings are extant.[22] Later, Schoock probably used these *dictata* in his appeal to the higher provincial court: but the proceedings of the trials from the years 1641-1657 are missing from the Utrecht city archives,[23] which, besides the proceedings of the first trial, preserve today only the *Corte memorie* and some letters of Gysbertus and Paul Voet (probably acquired by the archives at the end of the nineteenth century).[24] Therefore, we can rely today only on the excerpts from his *Dictata physica* provided by Schoock in his *Admiranda methodus*, and tracing to Regius's private lectures taking place no later than July 1642.[25]

In the following tables, I compare the fragments of Regius's *dictata*, as they are extant in Schoock's *Admiranda methodus*, with Regius's printed texts up to his *Fundamenta physices*, by highlighting in bold, in the latter texts, their textual agreements. The tables reveal that most of the extant contents of Regius's *dictata* were also used in

---

20 "V. Seijt dat Waeterlaet hem uijt raet van Voetius heeft gebracht versceijden excerpten uijt de boecken Cartesii, dictatis et thesibus Regii, om in sijne boecken te gebruijcken: Sulx blijct uijt diergelicke papieren Waterlaets handt beschreven, bij Schoockium wel bewaert," and in margin, by Voetius's hand: "Ambiguum, et ex parte mendacium," ERIK-JAN BOS, "Epistolarium Voetianum II," *Nederlandsch Archief voor Kerkgeschiedenis*, LXXIX/1 (1999), p. 39-73: p. 70. See also ERIK-JAN BOS, "Epistolarium Voetianum I," *Nederlandsch Archief voor Kerkgeschiedenis*, LXXVIII/2 (1998), p. 184-215. This passage is absent in the Latin version of Schoock's *Corte memorie*, dating to *c.* 1646: SAMUEL DESMARETS, *Bonae fidei sacrum, sive Documenta omni exceptione maiora veracitatis et innocentiae Samuelis Maresii theologi, in causa Schoockio-Voetiana*, Groningen, Apud Iohannem Nicolai, 1646, p. 26-28. "Waterlaet, qui suppeditaturus esset praeter dictata cuiusdam ex suis collegiis Cartesianae philosophiae addicti, varia personalia [...]," MARTIN SCHOOCK, *Necessaria et modesta defensio pro veritate ac innocentia sua, in caussa inter eum ac rever doctorem voetium controversa*, Groningen, Typis Johannis Nicolai, 1646, p. 28 (it is unclear whether Schoock uses the Julian or Gregorian calendar in his account). See also DESMARETS, *Bonae fidei sacrum*, p. 4-5. In turn, in his disputationes Voetius attacked the 'new philosophy' at a more general level, without directly criticizing Regius's *dictata*: GYSBERTUS VOETIUS, *Selectarum disputationum theologicarum pars prima*, Utrecht, Apud Joannem a Waesberge, 1648, *Praefatio*, p. 13-14 (unnumbered).
21 BOS, "Epistolarium Voetianum II," p. 47-49.
22 DUKER, *Gisbertus Voetius*, vol. III, appendices XXXII-XXXIII.
23 DUKER, *Gisbertus Voetius*, vol. III, p. 244, n. 3.
24 BOS, "Epistolarium Voetianum II," p. 48-49. A copy of a letter by Vanden Waterlaet to Schoock of 13 June 1643, which was one of the attachments of Schoock's *Corte memorie* and was certainly used during the trial(s), is now extant in Schoock's *Commercium epistolicum*, preserved at the University Library of Tartu, which however does not contain any reference to Regius's *dictata*: Tartu, University Library, Mscr 51, *Commercium epistolicum Martini Schoockii, professoris Groningensis*, fol. 260. A transcription of the letter can be found in DESMARETS, *Bonae fidei sacrum*, p. 31-33.
25 VOETIUS *et al.*, *Testimonium*, p. 18. See also Schoock's text accompanying fragment 1, quoted below. Dictations usually took place during private lectures, rather than during the often noisy public ones: GERHARD WIESENFELDT, "Academic Writings and the Rituals of Early Modern Universities," *Intellectual History Review*, XXVI/4 (2016), p. 1-14.

his printed texts, and that their *terminus post quem* was May 1641, given the fact that they present (fragment 9) a theory of tides developed upon Descartes's *Le monde*, to which Regius had direct access around that month (while of course the *terminus ante quem* is July 1642, when they fell in Schoock's hands). Moreover, even if it is unclear whether the texts already put into print before July 1642 (i.e. fragments 2, 3, 5, 6, and 7) were first conceived for his *dictata*, and then re-used in his printed texts or vice-versa, we can in any case assume that the overall contents of his *dictata* can be inferred from those of his published texts, in particular, from his *Fundamenta physices*. In other words, the backbone of the latter treatise was most probably constituted by Regius's *Dictata physica*, which in turn coincided, in content, with Regius's *Physica fundamenta*. Not surprisingly, indeed, Descartes himself was to note, in commenting upon a draft of Regius's *Fundamenta physices* in July 1645, that such a text was circulating among Regius's students.[26]

Fragment 1

Dictata physica (May 1641-July 1642)	*Fundamenta physices* (1646)
[...] redivivum Pythagoram suspicit, ut non dubitarit lepidae physiologiae, quam privatim adolescentibus aliquibus dictavit ac praelegit, carmen hoc Academico professore indignissimum, mox pag. 1, post laudes scientiae naturalis propriasque, praescribere: *si vestigiis et principiis nobilissimi viri Renati des Cartes libere insistens, hic plusculum a receptis quorundam opinionibus recessero, amor antiquae et charissimae veritatis, qua haec a me extorquet, apud aequos rerum aestimatores, me, ut spero, a calumniis vindicabit.*[27]	Si vero **vestigiis viri nobilissimi** et vere incomparabilis philosophi, **Renati des Cartes, insistens**, vel propria sectans, vel alia via procedens, **a vulgaribus quorundam opinionibus**, eam solam ob causam, quod principiis, quae occulta et a se non intellecta fatentur, ac proinde nil nisi cimmerias tenebras, loco quaesitae lucis, exhibere possunt, tamquam ruinosis tibicinibus innitantur, hic pro libertate philosophica, quae iubet, ut *Nullius addictus iurare in verba magistri, Quid verum atque decens curem, et rogem, et omnis in hoc sim,* nonnihil **recessero. Antiquissimae et charissimae veritatis amor**, aliosque iuvandi studium, mihi iustam, **apud aequos rerum aestimatores**, excusationem, **ut spero**, invenient. [...] [H]anc votivam tabellam [...] itaque, ut benignus accipias, et a malignis livoris et **calumniarum** morsibus tutam **vindices**, supplex rogat, Illustrissimae Celsitudini tuae devotissimus Henricus Regius.[28]

---

26 "Si scripta ista in malevolorum manus incidant (ut facile incident cum ab aliquot discipulis tuis habeantur) [...]," Descartes to Regius, July 1645, in Bos 188; AT IV 249; BL 2038; CSMK 255.
27 MARTIN SCHOOCK, *Admiranda methodus novae philosophiae Renati Des Cartes*, Utrecht, Ex officina Joannis van Waesberge, 1643, p. 36-37. Italics by Schoock.
28 HENRICUS REGIUS, *Fundamenta physices*, Amsterdam, Apud Lodovicum Elzevirium, 1646, *Frederico Henrico dedicato*, p. 2-4 (unnumbered); HORACE, *Epistulae*, book 1, epistle 1, verses 11 and 14.

Fragment 2

De illustribus aliquot quaestionibus physiologicis (November-December 1641)	*Dictata physica* (May 1641-July 1642)	*Fundamenta physices* (1646)
III. **Constitutio** autem **coeli** secundum dogmata **Ptolomaei et Tychonis, adversatur mechanicae, quae** est verum et fere **unicum physicae** fundamentum.[29]	Ita [...] Cartesianus medicus in dictatis physicis, sub finem capitis De mundo: *caeli Ptolemaici et Tychonici constitutio adversatur mechanicae, quae sola est physica nostra.*[30]	[...] ita ut non opus sit fingere incredibilem coeli stelliferi ab ortu in occasum, 24 horarum spacio, raptum [...] innumeraque alia non intelligibilia com comminisci, quae in **Ptolomaica et Tychonica mundi constitutione** fingi solent.[31]

---

29 HENRICUS REGIUS, *De illustribus aliquot quaestionibus physiologicis*, Utrecht, Ex officina Aegidii Roman, 1641, disputation 3, thesis 16.
30 SCHOOCK, *Admiranda methodus*, p. 132-133. Regius's *dictata* are also briefly mentioned at p. 139 and 244.
31 REGIUS, *Fundamenta physices*, p. 76.

Fragment 3

De illustribus aliquot quaestionibus physiologicis (November-December 1641)	Responsio (February 1642)	Dictata physica (May 1641-July 1642)	Fundamenta physices (1646)
Unde iam constat veram formarum materialium originem natura sua **quam maxime esse manifestam**: dum dicimus materiam varie moveri et per motum illum certam magnitudinem, figuram et situm partium rebus naturalibus convenientes resultare, in quibus forma earum consistit. Eductione **vero** formarum substantialium e potentia materiae, quae excogitata est ab iis, qui veras formas ignorarunt, nos non amplius indigere.[32]	Reiicimus [...] omnes formas substantiales, [...] ac quamvis **statuantur** incognitae et inexplicabiles, dicuntur tamen omnium actionum et proprietatum atque affectionum esse causae. Quandoquidem haec omnia ex eo collabuntur, quod alia dentur rerum naturalium **principia**, clara ac facilia, et **quam maxime intelligibilis** formarum materialium iam suppetat origo: contra **vero** materia ista prima et forma substantialis omnium rerum per illas explicandarum tenebras inducant.[33]	[I]n dictatis physicis sub finem doctrinae de principiis: *haec principia a me iam explicata, quam maxime sunt intelligibilia, quae vero ab aliis statuuntur, captum humanum superare videntur.* [...] [I]deam philosophus in dictatis physicis habet, sub quorum vestibulum ita pro loquitur: *haec principia a me iam explicata, quam maxime sunt intelligibilia, quae vero ab aliis statuuntur, captum humanum superare videntur.*[34]	Videntur etiam reiici posse omnes formas substantiales, [...] ac quamvis **statuantur** incognitae et inexplicabiles, dicuntur tamen omnium actionum et proprietatum atque affectionum esse causae. Quoniam haec omnia ex eo collabuntur, quod alia, quae iam **explicuimus**, dentur rerum naturalium **principia**, clara ac facilia, et **quammaxime intelligibilis** formarum materialium iam suppetat origo: contra **vero** materia ista prima, et forma substantialis, omnium rerum per istas explicandarum tenebras, sua obscuritate, inducant.[35]

Fragment 4

Dictata physica (May 1641-July 1642)	Fundamenta physices (1646)
Positura, per quam intelligunt situm, qui a medico in dictatis definitur: *ipsa corporis inter corpora positio*. [...] Ex principiis per somnium excogitatis sola *figura* superest, quae, medico in dictatis teste, nihil aliud est, quam *ipsius extensionis terminatio*. [...] Medicus [...] dicit: *magos figuras considerare sine materia, se vero cum materia*.[36]	**Figura** est **extensionis terminatio**. Haec quam sit efficax, docet vel solum ferrum, in gladium vel cultrum figuratum, quibus durissima corpora discinduntur. **Situs** est **ipsa corporis inter corpora positio**. Huius efficacia patet ex sola aequipondii in statera positione varia.[37]

---

32 REGIUS, *De illustribus aliquot quaestionibus physiologicis*, disputation 3, thesis 7.
33 REGIUS, *Responsio*, p. 10-11.
34 SCHOOCK, *Admiranda methodus*, p. 142 and 199.
35 REGIUS, *Fundamenta physices*, p. 30.
36 SCHOOCK, *Admiranda methodus*, p. 209-211.
37 REGIUS, *Fundamenta physices*, p. 28-29.

Fragment 5

Phyisiologia (1641)	De illustribus aliquot quaestionibus physiologicis (November-December 1641)	Responsio (February 1642)	Dictata physica (May 1641-July 1642)	Fundamenta physices (1646)
Omnes enim formae, **praeter animam rationalem,** sunt tantum accidentariae, vel potius modales quaedam qualitates. [...]. Ab omni enim absurditatis metu nos liberamur etiamsi ipsius formae e nihilo productionem, et annihilationem statuamus: cum forma nihil aliud revera sit, quam comprehensio motus vel quietis, item magnitudinis, situs et figurae partium materiae seu corporis, **rebus naturalibus** conveniens; in qua nihil substantiale seclusa ingenerabili et incorruptibili materia continetur.[38]	Formae itaque nihil aliud sunt quam accidentariae quaedam qualitates. **Quicquid** autem, **praeter mentem, substantiale in rebus naturalibus** invenitur, **est a materia; quae est substantia corporea,** in longum, latum, et profundum se extendens.[39]	Quicquid **autem** substantiale praeter mentem humanam in rebus naturalibus existit, totum illud a materia seu substantia corporea originem ducere **existimamus.**[40]	[I]nter alia oracula medicus in vestibulo dictatorum physicorum hariolatur: *quicquid in rebus naturalibus praeter mentem humanam est substantiale, totum illud a materia, sive substantia corporea originem ducit.* [...] Recolamus vero medici verba modo ad partes vocata: *quicquid in rebus naturalibus praeter mentem humanam est substantiale, totum illud a materia sive substantia corporea originem trahit.*[41]	[...] intelligimus, illam in corporibus coelestibus et terrestribus esse unam eandemque: nam in omnibus est una eademque extensio. Estque substantia: per se enim potest subsistere, et **quicquid praeter mentem in rebus naturalibus est substantiale, illud totum**, non aliunde, sed hinc **originem ducit**, cum nihil substantiale praeter haec in rerum natura dari possit.[42]

---

38 HENRICUS REGIUS, *Physiologia, sive Cognitio sanitatis. Tribus disputationibus in Academia Ultraiectina publice proposita*, Utrecht, Ex officina Aegidii Roman, 1641-1643, p. 18-19.
39 REGIUS, *De illustribus aliquot quaestionibus physiologicis*, disputation 1, thesis 3.
40 REGIUS, *Responsio*, p. 10.
41 SCHOOCK, *Admiranda methodus*, p. 213 and 214.
42 REGIUS, *Fundamenta physices*, p. 3.

Fragment 6

Phyisiologia (1641)	De illustribus aliquot quaestionibus physiologicis (November-December 1641)	Dictata physica (May 1641-July 1642)	Fundamenta physices (1646)
[...] Estque vel **insensibilis** vel **sensibilis. Insensibilis** est, quae ob suam exiguitatem, **vel motus sui celeritatem sensum fugit.** Haec non est indivisibilis, **nec semper eiusdem magnitudinis aut figurae sed, quantum ad talia, idem de ipsa, quod de reliquis corporibus est putandum.** Et quamvis ad istas insensibiles **particulas** alii medici vel philosophi non multum attendere consueverint; nos tamen ex illis innumera naturae mysteria pendere arbitramur. Quia sine his nec acrimoniae, nec lenitatis, nec subtilitatis, nec crassitiei, nec infinitarum aliarum qualitatum ratio reddi potest: his autem positis, omnium intelligibilis est explicatio.[43]	IX. **Dividitur** autem **haec materia in partes, tum sensibiles, tum insensibiles.** X. **Partes insensibiles, ob exiguitatem vel motus celeritatem sensus fugiunt.** XI. **Hae non sunt atomi,** sed indefinite divisibiles, **nec semper eiusdem sunt magnitudinis aut figurae, sed quantum ad talia, idem de ipsis, quod de reliquis corporibus, est dicendum.** XII. **Quamvis autem ad illas particulas alii philosophi non multum attendere soleant, nos tamen ex illis plurima naturae mysteria pendere arbitramur: sine his enim nec acrimoniae, nec lenitatis, nec subtilitatis, nec crassitiei, nec infinitarum aliarum qualitatum ratio reddi potest. His autem positis, omnium intelligibilis est explicatio.**[44]	Medicus in dictatis physicis pergit: *materia haec divisa est in partes insensibiles et sensibiles: partes insensibiles sunt, vel [ob] motus sui celeritatem fugiunt sensus. Hae itaque non sunt atomi, verum indefinite divisibiles: nec semper eiusdem sunt magnitudinis aut figurae, sed quantum ad talia, idem de ipsis, quod de reliquis corporibus est dicendum. Quamvis autem ad illas particulas alii philosophi non multum attendere soleant, nos tamen ex illis plurima naturae mysteria pendere arbitramur: quia sine his nec acrimoniae, nec lenitatis, nec subtilitatis, nec infinitarum aliarum qualitatum ratio reddi potest: his autem positis, omnium intelligibilis est explicatio.* [...] Si dicant crassitiem oriri ex magnitudine insensilium partium (ut innuit idem medicus in iisdem dictatis) ridiculos se praebent.[45]	**Haec divisa est in partes**, tum **insensibiles, tum sensibiles. Insensibiles sunt,** quae, propter exiguitatem aut parvitatem **sensus fugientes**, solo intellectu in omnibus rebus naturalibus observantur. [...] Hae ex **subtilitate, crassitie, acrimonia, lenitate**, fluiditate, oleaginositate, aquositate, salsadine, aliisque innumeris corporum qualitatibus, postea explicandis, manifeste **colliguntur. Nam his positis, clara et distincta illarum est explicatio**; quae iis negatis est obscura, vel confusa. **Hae non sunt atomi, sed indefinite divisibiles**, utpote extensae: **nec semper eiusdem sunt figurae, vel magnitudinis.** Cum enim ipsis semper aliquid addi vel detrahi, vel quidpiam aliter in iis disponi queat, **idem de ipsarum, quod de reliquorum corporum** magnitudine et figura, **est dicendum**.[46]

---

43 REGIUS, *Physiologia*, p. 1.
44 REGIUS, *De illustribus aliquot quaestionibus physiologicis*, disputation 2, theses 9-12.
45 SCHOOCK, *Admiranda methodus*, p. 215-216 and 218.
46 REGIUS, *Fundamenta physices*, p. 3-4.

Fragment 7

Spongia (1640)	*Phyisiologia* (1641)	*Dictata physica* (May 1641-July 1642)	*Fundamenta physices* (1646)
Quod vero **ex insensibilibus**, fiant **sensibilia**, apparet **in filis sericis**, quorum **singula filamenta** seorsim visa **non apparent ullius coloris**, simul autem iuncta **componunt filum** aut **flavum**, aut **album**, aut **alio colore tinctum**.[47]	Quod vero **ex insensibilibus**, fiant **sensibilia**, apparet **in filis sericis**; quorum **singula** filamenta seorsum visa **non apparent illius coloris**, simul autem iuncta **componunt filum** aut **album**, aut **flavum**, aut **alio colore tinctum**.[48]	[D]ocet medicus ita philosophans in dictatis suis physicis: *partes sensibiles, quae ex multis insensibilibus compositae sub sensum cadunt, quemadmodum ex. gr. ex filamentis pluribus sericis, quae nullum colorem singula habere videntur, componitur filum, albo, flavo, vel alio colore tinctum*.[49]	Quomodo autem **sensibiles** partes **ab insensibilibus constitui** possint, apparet **in filamentis sericis, quae quamvis singula nullum colorem habere videantur**, *multa tamen coniuncta* **componunt filum album, aut alio colore tinctum**.[50]

Fragment 8

Dictata physica (May 1641-July 1642)	*Fundamenta physices* (1646)
Medico teste, qui in dictatis physicis ita de admiranda illius attractione philosophatur: *inter lapides opacos admirandus est magnes, cuius operationes non fiunt per attractionem, sed circumpulsione corporum magneticorum vi exhalationis magneticae e tellure versus septentrionem vel austrum exhalantis*.[51]	**Inter** omnes **lapides**, tam **opacos**, quam alios, viribus **praecellit magnes**; quae ut recte intelligantur, ante omnia partium eius constitutio, unde eae profluunt, explicanda venit. Is itaque constat plurimis particulis ramosis et crassis, nec tamen, ad transitum impediendum, nimis solidis; quae **ab** interiore **Terra**, maximam partem **magnetica**, in superiorem evectae, dum cum reliqua eius materia miscebantur, a gemina et diversimode contorta materia striata, Terram a septentrione **in austrum**, et ab austro **in septentrionem** circa eius polos perpetuo ingrediente, et, post vorticem in superiore Terra factum, eam rursus transeunte.[52]

---

47 HENRICUS REGIUS, *Spongia qua eluuntur sordes Animadversionum quas Jacobus Primirosius [...] adversus Theses pro circulatione sanguinis in Academia Ultraiectina disputatas nuper edidit*, Leiden, Ex officina Wilhelmi Christiani, 1640, p. 7.
48 REGIUS, *Physiologia*, p. 30.
49 SCHOOCK, *Admiranda methodus*, p. 222.
50 REGIUS, *Fundamenta physices*, p. 4.
51 SCHOOCK, *Admiranda methodus*, p. 228.
52 REGIUS, *Fundamenta physices*, p. 130-131.

Fragment 9

Dictata physica (May 1641-July 1642)	Fundamenta physices (1646)
[...] in dictatis aperto capite hunc in modum philosophatur: *quantum ad aestum maris attinet, hic oritur ex eo, quod coelum nostrum peculiare (clauso illo circulo quem Luna singulis mensibus peramit [sic]) circumraptu suo circum Terram et interfluxu inter Terram et Lunam ipsam Terram ad aliquot pedes extra centrum sui caeli deturbat. Hinc enim oriuntur duae angustiae in illo caelo sibi mutuo diametraliter oppositae, una inter Lunam et Terram, altera inter Terram et illam peculiaris caeli extremitatis partem, versus quam ipsa Terra ab interfluxu subtilis materiae sive caeli fuit propulsa. Dum itaque torrens peculiaris nostri caeli istas angustias interfluit, aquas maris in istis partibus premit et versus littora attollit. Cum autem ob diurnum Terrae motum illa pars maris, quae Lunae erat obversa, a Luna paulatim avertatur, sensim etiam cessat in illis partibus aëris et maris pressio, quo a littoribus versus altum relabentes refluxum maris efficiunt.*[53]	[Q]uantum ad aestum maris attinet, hic oritur ex eo, quod caelum nostrum peculiare, (clausum illo circulo ABCD, quem Luna L singulis mensibus percurrit) suo, circum Terram T, raptu, et inter Lunam et Terram celeriori, quam alibi, **interfluxu,** Terram ad aliquod spatium extra centrum sui caeli deturbet. Hinc enim oriuntur duae angustiae, in illo coelo seu vortice sibi mutuo diametraliter oppositae, una inter Lunam et tellurem, altera inter tellurem et illam oppositam peculiaris caeli extremitatis partem, versus quam tellus, ab interfluxu subtilis materiae, sive caeli, celeriori, fuit propulsa. Dum itaque torrens nostri caeli, utrasque **illas angustias** celerius, quam alibi, **interfluit,** premit ille vehementius aërem et **aquas maris in istis partibus** exsistentes, easque inde abigit, **et versus litora attollit,** fluxumque facit. **Cum autem ob diurnum Terrae motum,** qui 24 horis peragitur, **illa pars maris, quae Lunae erat obversa, a Luna paulatim avertatur, sensim etiam cessat, in illis partibus, aëris et maris pressio, quo** aquae, **a litoribus versus** altum **relabentes, refluxum maris faciunt.**[54]

Let us now concentrate on the fragments.[55] Fragment 1 was to be re-used by Regius in his preface to his *Fundamenta physices*: in particular, Regius used, with some variants,

---

53 SCHOOCK, *Admiranda methodus*, p. 234-235.
54 The references are to the figure used by Descartes in his *Principia philosophiae* (RENÉ DESCARTES, *Principia philosophiae*, Amsterdam, Apud Ludovicum Elzevirium, 1644, p. 185; AT VIII-1 197; BO 2006) and by Regius in his *Fundamenta physices* (REGIUS, *Fundamenta physices*, p. 91): in fact, Regius's *Fundamenta physices* was printed by re-using the same woodcuts already used for the printing of Regius's treatise.
55 Moreover, other fragments from Regius's sayings are reported by Schoock, even if he does not ascribes them to Regius's *dictata*: (A) "[Regius] saepissime publice privatimque discipulis suis inculcarit, *terminos metaphysicae* (quorum in omnibus prope dogmatibus antiquae philosophiae maximus usus est) *corruptelam esse omnium disciplinarum*"; (B) "[...] possitque citra ruborem de cathedra proclamare (audita in Academia vox est): *audeo meam experientiam omnium mathematicorum experientiae opponere*"; (C) "dato insensibilium particularum variae agitationi quid circa caloris negotium deferendum esse, non tamen agitatio illa formaliter ipsa calor erit, sed potius efficiens caloris caussa. Iutphasiana mola (quam medicus aliquando pro exemplo adducit) agitatione sua aëra frangit, non tamen aut ipse aër, aut illius fractio est," SCHOOCK, *Admiranda methodus*, p. 102, 115-116, and 226. Fragment A embodies an overt attack on Scholastic metaphysics as a source of error in philosophy: a topic which was a leitmotiv among Dutch Cartesians (and deriving from the criticism of Scholastic philosophy by Francis Bacon, 1561-1626), but which in Regius's case

the text already included at the beginning of his *dictata* (as reported by Schoock), instead of a text, planned to be used as a preface, which is extant to us in an extract from a letter of Regius to Descartes of 6 July 1645. Such a letter is a reply to a now lost first, negative judgment of Descartes on a draft version of Regius's *Fundamenta physices*. In his letter to Descartes, Regius, not willing to change the contents of his book, nonetheless submitted to him the text of a preface announcing that his *Fundamenta physices* did not just reflect Descartes's ideas, and asked him to suggest further contents for the preface itself.[56] However, in two subsequent letters of his to Regius, Descartes, criticizing both Regius's order of exposition and his very theories, just warned him not to publish his book.[57] Probably as a consequence of such a reaction, in his published 1646 preface Regius reverted to the text of his *dictata*, just adding the following words to it: "[by] following my way, or proceeding by another [one]" ("[...] vel propria sectans, vel alia via procedens"), probably in the attempt not to discontent too much, if not Descartes, the *desiderata* of the Dutch Cartesian

---

can barely be found (see, for instance, REGIUS, *Responsio*, p. 9). As to fragment B, it is absent from Regius's extant texts, even if it is somehow in line with his overall empirical approach to natural philosophy (see BELLIS, "Empiricism without Metaphysics"). Fragment C, concerning Regius's explanation of heat (on this, see HAN VAN RULER, *The Crisis of Causality. Voetius and Descartes on God, Nature and Change*, Leiden-New York-Cologne, Brill, 1995, p. 117-129), reports a sample not given by Regius in his extant texts, but used to scorn him by his enemies at Utrecht, in some now lost pamphlet appearing after his *Pro circulatione sanguinis* (1640): LAMBERTUS VAN VELTHUYSEN, *Bewys dat noch de leere van der sonne stilstant, en des aertryx bewegingh*, Utrecht, Gedruckt by Dirck van Ackersdijck, en Gijsbert van Zijll, 1656, *Voor-reden*, p. 9 (unnumbered); LAMBERTUS VAN VELTHUYSEN, *Opera omnia*, Rotterdam, Typis Reineri Leers, 1680, p. 1043 (unnumbered); CASPAR BURMAN, *Traiectum eruditum, virorum doctrina inlustrium, qui in urbe Traiecto, et regione Traiectensi nati sunt, sive ibi habitarunt, vitas, fata et scripta exhibens*, Utrecht, Apud Jurianum a Paddenburg, 1738, p. 290. Also Schoock uses elsewhere the sample of the mill of Jutphaas (which no longer exists: Molen Database, Ten Bruggencate-nr. 15359, https://www.molendatabase.org/molendb.php?step=details&tbnummer=15359 (accessed on 24 December 2021)), in order to criticize Regius's idea that the source of movement of clocks is internal to them (this being in fact a strawman thesis): SCHOOCK, *Admiranda methodus*, p. 138. Moreover, Schoock reports a fragment from a poem allegedly adorning the first disputation on physiology (it being unclear if Schoock refers to Regius's *Physiologia* or *De illustribus aliquot quaestionibus physiologicis*): SCHOOCK, *Admiranda methodus*, p. 58. Such a poem could not be found in the printed text of this series of disputations.

56   "[...] pour éviter les inconvénients dont M. Descartes l'avait averti, il lui envoya ce modèle d'avertissement au lecteur, pour être mis au bout de sa préface: «Pour détromper ceux qui s'imagineraient que les choses qui sont contenues dans cet ouvrage seraient les sentiments purs de M. Descartes, je suis bien aise d'avertir le public qu'il y a effectivement plusieurs endroits où je fais profession de suivre les opinions de cet excellent homme; mais qu'il y en a aussi d'autres où je suis d'une opinion contraire, et d'autres encore sur lesquels il n'a pas jugé à propos de s'expliquer jusqu'ici. C'est ce qu'il sera aisé de remarquer à tous ceux qui prendront la peine de lire les écrits de ce grand homme, et de les confronter avec les miens.» Pour tâcher de prévenir le désaveu public dont il croyait que M. Descartes le menaçait, il lui fit offre d'ajouter encore, dans sa préface, tout ce qu'il jugerait à propos [...]. Mais il ne parla point de retoucher au fond de son ouvrage," Regius to Descartes, 6 July 1645, in BOS 185; AT IV 241; BL 2042.

57   Descartes to Regius, July 1645, in BOS 187-188 AT IV 248-250; BL 2038-2041; CSMK, 254-255; Descartes to Regius, late July or early August 1645, in BOS 192-193; AT IV 256-258; BL 2040-2043. See also *supra*, n. 11, and *infra*, n. 93.

faction, with which he certainly shared his initial intention to provide a preface substantially recognizing his debts to Descartes.[58]

Fragment 2, in turn, also appears in the third of Regius's disputations *De illustribus aliquot quaestionibus physiologicis*, and anticipates Regius's foundation of natural philosophy on mechanics as it is presented in chapter 1 of his *Fundamenta physices*. Such a fragment was probably taught by Regius for the first time in the Summer, after having read Descartes's *Le monde*, which he received in May 1641 (though he might have had some access to its contents even before), as it deals with cosmological topics. Moreover, such topics were also included in his *Physica fundamenta*, dating to May 1641-February 1642.

Fragment 3 is echoed in many printed texts by Regius, while fragment 4, concerning Regius's first explanatory principles (the subject also of fragment 3), partially recurs in his *Fundamenta physices*. Regius's first principles were nothing but those expressed in his *Physiologia*, in his famous distich "Mens, mensura, quies, motus positura, figura / Sunt cum materia cunctarum exordia rerum." But while in his *Physiologia* Regius only defines measure (*mensura*) intended as any quantity, and movement (*motus*) as local motion,[59] in his *dictata* he also deals with the idea of *situs* or *positura*, which was nothing but Aristotle's category of being-in-a-position, or κεῖσθαι, usually intended, however, not as the reciprocal position of a body with respect to other ones, but rather as the position of a part of a body with respect to its other parts.[60] A re-interpretation of this category probably derived from the idea that, in a Cartesian framework, there are not individual bodies, but rather parts of the one material substance. Moreover, Regius defines figure in quite traditional terms,[61] and remarks that he considers it as a quality of matter, while the 'magi' considered figure without matter.[62] A remark which disappears in his *Fundamenta physices*, where nonetheless Regius defends the causal role of figure and *situs*, which was in fact criticized by Schoock in his *Admiranda methodus*, where these notions are

---

58   As evident from a letter of Constantijn Huygens to Mersenne of 21 August 1646: MARIN MERSENNE, *Correspondance*, ed. by Cornelis de Waard, René Pintard, Bernard Rochot, and Armand Beaulieu, Paris, PUF/CNRS, 1933-1988, vol. XIV, p. 413. Later, Huygens was in any case displeased that Regius omitted such a preface from his book; contrary to Descartes's judgment, in any case, he deemed Regius's *Fundamenta physices* as a book generally faithful to Descartes's philosophy: Huygens to Samuel Johnson Johnson (1603-1661), 27 September 1646, in CONSTANTIJN HUYGENS, *De briefwisseling van Constantijn Huygens, 1608-1697*, ed. by Jacob Adolf Worp, The Hague, M. Nijhoff, 1911-1917, vol. IV, p. 354.
59   REGIUS, *Physiologia*, p. 5.
60   Cf. the definition given by Franco Burgersdijk (1590-1635): "situs est ordo partium corporis inter se," FRANCO BURGERSDIJK, *Institutionum logicarum libri duo*, Leiden, Apud Abrahamum Commelinum, 1634 (first edition 1626), p. 48.
61   Cf. BURGERSDIJK, *Institutionum logicarum libri*, p. 34: "figura est qualitas orta ex terminatione magnitudinis."
62   The reference is to the so-called 'image magic' typical of Renaissance authors like Marsilio Ficino (1433-1499) and Cornelius Agrippa (1486-1535): see FRANK F. KLAASSEN, *The Transformations of Magic: Illicit Learned Magic in the Later Middle Ages and Renaissance*, University Park, The Pennsylvania State University Press, 2013.

deprived of the status of causal principles, as *situs* is merely an accident, and figure has no role in the substantial alterations of bodies.[63]

Fragments 5, 6 and 7 widely recur in Regius's works: indeed, they concern the most basic ideas in Regius's natural philosophy, namely his Cartesian idea of material substance, as well as the differentiation between perceptible and imperceptible particles, which had a medical origin and has been widely discussed by historians.[64] Eventually, fragments 8 and 9 concern two more advanced natural-philosophical topics, namely magnetism and tides, and were put into print for the first time only in his *Fundamenta physices*. Nonetheless, these two topics were discussed, during the *querelle d'Utrecht*, also before the appearance of Schoock's *Admiranda methodus*, as they are variously mentioned in Voetius's *Appendix ad Corollaria theologico philosophica nuperae Disputationi de Iubilaeo Romano, de rerum naturis et formis substantialibus* (discussed on 23-24 December 1641, Julian calendar),[65] in Regius's *Responsio* (February 1642), where Regius used them as examples of his rejection of occult qualities in natural philosophy,[66] in Vanden Waterlaet's *Prodromus sive Examen tutelare orthodoxae philosophiae principiorum* (April 1642),[67] in Descartes's *Epistola ad Voetium* (May 1643),[68] and in the correspondence of Mersenne and Constantijn Huygens (1596-1687).[69] In fact, they were not dealt with by Descartes in his published texts until the appearance of his *Principia philosophiae* (1644) — as I discuss in the following section.

---

63 SCHOOCK, *Admiranda methodus*, p. 209-211. On Regius's principles, see STRAZZONI, "How Did Regius Become Regius?".
64 BELLIS, "Empiricism without Metaphysics," p. 172-173.
65 Mentioning magnetism: VOETIUS et al., *Testimonium*, p. 46 (see thesis 5). As reported later by Schoock, the *opponens* in the discussion of the *Appendix*, namely a student of Regius whose identity could not be ascertained, was dared by Vanden Waterlaet to provide an explanation of magnetism and tides without recurring to substantial forms: at that point, the *opponens* could do nothing but to claim that an explanation was forthcoming with the publication of Descartes's physics: SCHOOCK, *Admiranda methodus*, p. 70 (unnumbered). See also REGIUS, *Fundamenta physices*, p. 97.
66 Mentioning both topics: REGIUS, *Responsio*, p. 29.
67 Mentioning magnetism: LAMBERTUS VANDEN WATERLAET, *Prodromus sive Examen tutelare orthodoxae philosophiae principiorum*, Leiden, Excudebat W. Christiani, 1642, part 2, p. 31-34.
68 "[...] transitis ad physica, de quibus nullum vel minimum verbum ex meis scriptis profertis; sed pauca tantum ex Regii dictatis desumpta: 1. de principiis; 2. de particulis insensibilibus; 3. de calore; 4. de magnete; 5. de aestu maris. Atque in illa tanquam Andabatae nugamini, adeo ut non opus sit ut quidquam respondeam, nisi quod insignis impudentia calumniae vestrae in eo possit notari, quod prolixe de magnete ac de aestu maris tanquam contra me disputetis, quamvis nullum plane verbum de istis quaestionibus in meis scriptis hactenus editis reperiatur," AT VIII-2 168; BO 1664.
69 Mersenne was eager to read Regius's *Fundamenta physices*: "[q]uand vous me demandez des a cest heure comment il explique le flux et reflux, l'Aymant et que vous faictes proprement le françois qui a accoustumé, disons nous, de demander quelle heure va sonner à l'Horologe, sans vouloir avoir la patience de le compter. Attendez donq; dans peu vos desirs seront satisfaicts," Constantijn Huygens to Mersenne, 12 September 1646, in CHRISTIAAN HUYGENS, *Œuvres complètes*, ed. by Johan Adriaan Vollgraff et al., The Hague, Martinus Nijhoff, 1888-1950, vol. II, p. 548. No previous mentioning of tides and magnetism could be found in their extant correspondence.

4. Regius's Theory of Magnetism: Pre-Dating Descartes

Concerning the explanation of tides, Regius's theory is evidently based on Descartes's *Le monde* — either on its very text or on the insights on it Reneri might have provided Regius before May 1641. Such an explanation reveals above all Regius's eagerness to incorporate Cartesian ideas into his own teaching: indeed, the theory proposed by Regius relies on a vortex theory of planetary motion, and perfectly matches Descartes's explanation.[70] The explanation of magnetism, however, was devised by Regius in a way certainly independent from Descartes, who before 1643 did not put his theory on paper, and made it public only in his *Principia philosophiae*. Regius, on the contrary, had probably developed and taught a theory of magnetism at least since 1639. Indeed, on 3/13 or 9/19 July 1639 he was the protagonist in a clash which occurred during the *pro gradu* disputation of Florentius Schuyl (1619-1669) — at that time a student of the Aristotelian professor Arnold Senguerd (1610-1667) at Utrecht. The text of the disputation is now lost; however, the *Narratio historica* (1643) of the *querelle d'Utrecht* reports that during the disputation the *opponens* attacked Schuyl's explanation of magnetism as reverting to an occult quality. The *opponens*, certainly a student of Regius, did so on the basis of the "new philosophy." At that point Regius himself attacked Senguerd, and declared the triumph of the *opponens* even before Schuyl's reply. Yet — according to all the professors — Schuyl then successfully rebutted all the objections.[71] Hence, in May 1641 Descartes expressed his disagreement with an explanation he found in the now lost manuscript draft of the disputation *De actionibus naturalibus, Pars prior* of Regius's *Physiologia* (discussed in May-June of the same year), labelling it as "still not fully certain" and discouraged Regius to include it in the final, printed text,[72] where Regius rejects the idea that the

---

70 Cf. the text of fragment 9, quoted above, and ch. 12 of Descartes's *Le monde*. Regius aimed at providing or mentioning an explanation of tides in a corollary to his *De illustribus aliquot quaestionibus physiologicis*, as revealed in a letter of Descartes to him of November 1641, where he was discouraged to do so: "[i]n his autem adiungis corollarium de maris aestu, quod non probo; non enim rem satis explicas, ut intelligatur, nec quidem ut aliquo modo probabilis fiat," Bos 88; AT III 445; BL 1534.
71 "Problematum vero praelectionem ita instituebat D. Regius, ut in explicaarcanorum philosophiae liberius evagaretur, et in receptae ac communis philosophiae principia nimis quam acerbe grassaretur, eaque contem[p]tui haberet et exploderet. [...] Quae hactenus semina contentionum sub glebis deliuisse videbantur, primum erumpere coeperunt, occasione disputationis D. Florentii Schuilii, pro obtinendo philosophiae magisterio publice institutae 9 Jul. anno 1639, ubi cum opponens, secundum sententiam novae philosophiae, omnes qualitates attractrices et qualitatem occultam magnetis oppugnaret, medicus stans in subselliis D. Senguerdio, ordinario philosophiae professori et promotori, satis indecore insultavit, et contra doctiss. candidatum, D. Senguerdii discipulum, triumphum ante victoriam cecinit; cum tamen, omnium professorum iudicio, candidatus perquam solide et dextre omnia obiecta dilueret, et non inconcinne opponentem perstringeret, atque ad terminos revocaret," VOETIUS *et al., Testimonium*, p. 13-14. For a discussion, see Bos 24. See also DUKER, *Gisbertus Voetius*, vol. II, p. 142-143.
72 "In chartulis quas misisti [...] [p]agina 5, quae habes de magnete, mallem omitti; neque enim adhuc plane sunt certa," Descartes to Regius, second half of May 1641, in Bos 72-73; AT III 455; BL1542. In his *Epistola ad Voetium* (1643), Descartes was to claim that he had not published anything on magnetism and tides, therefore Regius's ideas on these topics had not to be attributed to him himself: AT VIII-2 168 (quoted *supra*, n. 68) (BO 1664-1665).

parts of the human body 'attract', by a magnetic force, the parts of the blood capable of restoring their substance.[73] A magnetic force the explanation of which Regius, in his *De morborum signis* (15/25 December 1641), was to announce as forthcoming.[74] Eventually, his explanation of magnetism was made public in fragment 8 published by Schoock (quoted above in Latin), according to which

> among opaque stones the magnet is admirable, the operations of which do not take place by attraction, but by the circular thrust of magnetic bodies, due to the force of a magnetic exhalation, which exhales from the earth towards north or south.

A source of such an explanation, as revealed by Regius himself in his *Fundamenta physices*, was Plato's *Timaeus*, which Regius read via Galen's commentary. In chapter 7 of this treatise, Regius proposes a more complete Cartesian theory of magnetism, viz. one at that point certainly indebted to Descartes's *Principia philosophiae*, based on the idea of screwed particles flowing from one pole to the other.[75] In presenting it, Regius nonetheless vindicates his overall originality on this topic, by remarking that

> [...] from these it is evident, that it is true that [theory] of Plato, saying, according to our Galen on the *Timaeus*, that the magnet does not act by attraction but by circular thrust. This, to say things as they are, first gave me the occasion to investigate and to propose the cause of magnetic operations, already many years ago.[76]

Actually, in his *Timaeus* Plato does not provide a theory of magnetism as such. Rather, he claims that the phenomena of magnetism and attraction can be explained through the principle of circular thrust. Such a principle is chiefly used by Plato — shortly before his discussion of magnetism — to explain respiration: according to this theory, when we dilate the thorax, we push some external air which cannot move but towards our lungs though mouth and nose, as every external place is a plenum.[77] Notably, such an explanation was employed by Regius as well, in his account of respiration given in his *Pro circulatione sanguinis* (1640),[78] so that Plato could have been Regius's

---

73 "Hepar itaque alias partes non alit, quia vim alimentum in illas impellendi non habet; nec partes alendae quidquam possunt attrahere per vim magneticam, vel aliam quamlibet, qualis dicitur esse fuga vacui, similitudo substantiae, calor, dolor, etc.; nec partes habent intellectum bonum a malo discernendi," REGIUS, *Physiologia*, p. 17. See also p. 30.

74 "Interim moneo ne quis inani labore hic se fatiget, magnetica enim operatio non est tractoria, sed pulsoria: quod data occasione evidenter demonstrabitur," REGIUS, *Physiologia*, p. 98.

75 See fragment 8 (quoted above), and below in this section, where I discuss Descartes's theory. Notably, in his *Fundamenta physices* Regius presented his explanation with some of the woodcuts already used by the Amsterdam Elzeviers (who also published Regius's treatise) for the printing of Descartes's *Principia philosophiae*.

76 "[...] ex his patet, verum esse illud Platonis, apud Galenum nostrum in Timaeo dicentis, magnetem non per attractionem sed circumpulsionem agere, quod, ut dicam quod res est, mihi iam ante multos annos occasionem, veram magneticarum operationum causam investigandi et proponendi, primum dedit," REGIUS, *Fundamenta physices*, p. 141-142.

77 PLATO, *Timaeus*, 79a-80c.

78 HENRICUS REGIUS, *Disputatio medico-physiologica pro sanguinis circulatione*, Utrecht, Ex officina Aegidii Roman, 1640, theses 9-10.

source also in this regard.⁷⁹ The same idea of circular thrust, in any case, had also been expressed by another key source of Regius, namely Lucretius,⁸⁰ according to whom when a magnet is close to a piece of iron the magnetic exhalations emanated from it expel the air in between the two bodies: this generates a circular thrust of air, and the two bodies come close to each other.⁸¹

However, neither Plato nor Lucretius provided an explanation of terrestrial magnetism based on the idea of particles exhaling from the body of the Earth. Back to Regius's times, William Gilbert (1544-1603), who availed himself of the idea that the whole Earth is a magnet, criticized Plato's idea of circular thrust in the second book of his *De magnete* (1600), and explained magnetism in terms of animation of nature.⁸² The idea of circular thrust was also rejected by Niccolò Cabeo (1586-1650) in his *Philosophia magnetica* (1629),⁸³ and by Athanasius Kircher (1602-1680) in his *Ars magnesia* (1631), namely, in the chief works on magnetism which appeared in the early seventeenth-century.⁸⁴ In fact, in order to find a theory of magnetism kindred to Regius's and Descartes's in the early seventeenth century we need to revert to Beeckman. In entries of his *Journal* dating to 1614-1627 he repeatedly avails himself of the explanation of magnetic 'attraction' by the idea of circular thrust, in discussing which he overtly refers to Lucretius.⁸⁵ Moreover, in an entry dating to

---

79 A partial commentary of Galen on the *Timaeus* can be found in the works of Galen published by the Giunti in nine editions between 1641 and 1625, namely, the *Fragmentum ex quatuor commentariis de iis quae medice dicta sunt in Platonis Timaeo*. In it, nineteen *textus* from Plato's *Timaeus* are reported: the last three *textus* are devoted to respiration (on which Galen provides a discussion of the idea of circular thrust), and to magnetism (on which Galen rejects Plato's explanation). Plato's treatment of magnetism is not dealt with in any other place of the *Corpus Galenicum*, so that the *Fragmentum* was certainly Regius's source. The fact that Galen discusses here both respiration and magnetism (following the order of Plato's discussion), makes probable the idea that the *Timaeus* (via Galen's commentary) was also the source of Regius as to respiration. See GALEN, *Prima classis naturam corporis humani: hoc est elementa, temperaturas, humores, structurae habitudinisq[ue] modos, partium dissectionem, usum, facultates et actiones*, Venice, Apud Iuntas, 1550 (first edition 1541), fols 289ᵛ-290ʳ, reporting the text from PLATO, *Timaeus*, 79a-80c.
80 STRAZZONI, "How Did Regius Become Regius?" p. 378.
81 LUCRETIUS, *De rerum natura*, book 6, verses 1002-1009.
82 WILLIAM GILBERT, *De magnete, magneticisque corporibus, et de magno magnete tellure*, London, Excudebat Petrus Short, 1600, p. 30; CHRISTOPH SANDER, *Magnes: der Magnetstein und der Magnetismus in den Wissenschaften der Frühen Neuzeit*, Leiden-Boston, Brill, 2020, p. 662-663.
83 NICCOLÒ CABEO, *Philosophia magnetica, in qua magnetis natura penitus explicatur et omnium quae hoc lapide cernuntur causae propriae afferuntur*, Ferrara, Apud Franciscum Succium, 1629, p. 103 (see *infra*, n. 88). Cabeo adopts an Aristotelian-inspired theory of magnetism, according to which it is a primary quality of bodies, besides hot, cold, wet, dry, heavy and light: MARK A. WADDELL, *Jesuit Science and the End of Nature's Secrets*, Farnham, Ashgate, 2015, p. 66-75.
84 ATHANASIUS KIRCHER, *Ars magnesia, hoc est Disquisitio bipartita-emperica seu experimentalis, physico-mathematica de natura, viribus, et prodigiosis effectibus magnetis*, Würzburg, Typis Eliae Michaelis Zinck, 1631, p. 3. Kircher then presented his theory of magnetism in his *Magnes sive De arte magnetica* (1641).
85 ISAAC BEECKMAN, *Journal tenu par Isaac Beeckman de 1604 à 1634*, ed. by Cornelis de Waard, The Hague, Martinus Nijhoff, 1939-1953, vol. I, p. 36 (April 1614-January 1615), 101-102 (6 February-23 December 1616), and 309 (4-10 June 1619); vol. II, p. 119 (26-31 August 1620), 229 (22 January-21 February 1623), and 387 (18 December 1626-1624 March 1627); vol. III, p. 26 (30

1623 he explains the orientation of a magnet towards north (or south) by assuming that the particles or spirits causing the phenomena of magnetism exhale from the body of the Earth — which is a "big magnet" — and impact on a magnet: as soon as such particles do not fit its pores unless it is disposed in a certain direction, they move the magnet until it reaches the right position, i.e. heading towards north. At that point, the pores of the magnet are disposed exactly as the pores of the Earth, through which the magnetic particles pass.[86] This account is consistent with the essential explanation given in the *dictata* of Regius — who had no demonstrable relation with Beeckman, and certainly developed his theory independently from him — as well as with Descartes's one, traces of the development of which date to 1643 at the earliest.

Descartes's theory of magnetism, expounded in articles 133-183 of the fourth part of his *Principia philosophiae*, is based on the idea of screwed particles (*particulae striatae*) coming from the heavens, entering into the body of the Earth through a pole, following the direction of its pores, exiting from another one, and then coming back through the atmosphere to the first pole — forming a sort of vortex. As these particles pass through magnets, they can orient them to the north or to the south in accordance with the disposition of their pores. Also, these particles can make magnets apparently attract each other or other bodies, like pieces of iron. They do so by expelling the air between magnets and other bodies, so that these are pushed towards each other by the surrounding air — namely by a process of circular thrust, given the *plenum*.[87] Such a theory was put on paper by Descartes from January to December 1643, and was communicated by him for the first time in a letter to Huygens of 24 May 1643.[88] Descartes had consulted Beeckman's *Journal* as early as

---

October-4 November 1627).

86 "Magnetis polus semper spectat polum mundi, quia spiritus ex magno magnete Terrae ascendens et occurrens partibus ejus circa polum, non respondet poris qui ibi sunt, Unde fit ut illas partes repellat à se seque insinuando intra proximos poros, unâ sui parte nihil tangit. Atque ita removet id latus quod tangitur, non aliter ac si baculum obliquè in foramen immittamus; id enim foramen jam obliquè baculo respondens, mox directè ei opponetur. Tam diù igitur spiritus à se repellit ac movet mobilem magnetem, donec ei pori magnetis respondeant atque is eundem situm obtineat quem magnus ille magnes obtinet sub Terrâ," BEECKMAN, *Journal*, vol. II, p. 231 (22 January-21 February 1623); see also vol. III, p. 17-18 (8 October 1627).

87 See especially articles 133, 149-150, 170, and 171. On Descartes's explanation of magnetism, which is built upon his vortex theory of planetary motion (as the *particulae striatae* are a sub-set of Descartes's first matter, i.e. the subtlest one, shaped by its passing through the globular particles of second matter), see JOHN SCHUSTER, *Descartes-Agonistes. Physico-mathematics, Method & Corpuscular-Mechanism 1618-1633*, Dordrecht-Heidelberg-New York-London, Springer, 2013, ch. 12. For a discussion of the similarities and differences between Descartes's and Beeckman's accounts, see KLAAS VAN BERKEL, "Descartes' Debt to Beeckman," in *Descartes' Natural Philosophy*, ed. by Stephen Gaukroger, John Schuster, and John Sutton, London-New York, Routledge, 2000, p. 46-59; RICHARD ARTHUR, "Beeckman, Descartes and the Force of Motion," *Journal of the History of Philosophy*, XLI/1 (2007), p. 1-28.

88 Descartes declared that he had started to work on the articles of the *Principia philosophiae* concerning magnetism in a letter to Huygens of 5 January 1643 (AT III 799-801; BL 1694-1697); he completed its treatment only one year later, as stated in a letter to Pollot of 1 January 1644, where he declares:

in 1628-1629, though, he never acknowledged any debt towards him, and discouraged him from publishing his writings (as he planned around the same years),[89] as he did with Regius both with regard to magnetism and to his textbook, which for him lacked the due demonstrations.[90] For sure, Descartes had theoretical reasons in dissuading Regius from his publishing plans — which he did also in 1645, after the publication of his *Principia philosophiae* — and he published his *Principia* well after 1641 (when Regius's *Compendium physicum* was ready, and when he announced to Descartes his plan to publish a *Novae philosophiae prodromus*).[91] So we can exclude that Descartes engaged in a 'race' with Regius in publishing a treatise in natural philosophy. And yet, as suggested by Verbeek, "Descartes's main reason for opposing Regius's plans [...] was probably because, if they had come to pass, Regius would have cut the ground from under Descartes's feet,"[92] as he had already done with Beeckman. The very case of magnetism — a topic absent from Descartes's *Le monde* — shows in fact that Regius, too, and not only Beeckman could have exerted a certain influence on Descartes.

5. The Contents and Structure of Regius's *Dictata*

In the light of this evidence, it is worth attempting a possible reconstruction of the overall contents and structure of Regius's *dictata* across time, and to provide some

---

"[j]e n'ai jamais fait de traité de l'aimant; mais la troisième partie de ma philosophie, que j'écris en latin, en contient les principes, et j'en explique les propriétés à la fin de la quatrième, laquelle j'achève maintenant, en sorte que j'en suis à cet endroit-là," AT IV 76-77; BL 1874. See, moreover, his letter to Huygens of 24 May 1643 (AT III 669-672; BL 1754-1757; CSMK 220), and his letter to Mersenne of 30 May 1643 (AT III 673; BL 1756-1759). Descartes already considered the problem of magnetism in his *Regulae ad directionem ingenii* (without providing any explanation: AT X 427 and 430-431; BOp 766-767 and 770-773; CSM I 52), as well as in his correspondence prior to 1643. See, for instance, his letter to Mersenne of 4 November 1630, where he declares that the experiences with the magnet are consistent with the theories of his *Le monde*, but no insights are provided (AT I 176; BL 172-173), and his subsequent letter to him of 25 November 1630, where Descartes declares not to be interested in reading the *Philosophia magnetica* (1629) by Niccolò Cabeo (AT I 180; BL 176-177; CSMK 29; see also *supra*, n. 83). Ten years later, he was to repeat the same sort of statements, still without providing more insights: "[j]'ai su, il y a longtemps, toutes les Expériences de l'Aimant dont vous m'écrivez, et puis aisément donner raison de toutes dans mon Monde; mais je tiens que c'est une extravagance de vouloir expliquer toute la Physique par l'Aimant," Descartes to Mersenne, 29 January 1640, in AT III 8; BL 1136-1137; "[p]our l'aimant, ce ne peut être que la seule matière subtile qui lui donne ses qualités, et je ne les puis bien expliquer l'une sans l'autre, ni toutes dans une lettre," Descartes to Mersenne, 15 September 1640, in AT III 177; BL 1278-1279. The genesis of Descartes's *Principia philosophiae* is reconstructed in Desmond M. Clarke, *Descartes: A Biography*, New York, Cambridge University Press, 2007, ch. 10.

89 This publication plan was eventually accomplished by Beeckman's brother Abraham in 1644, when he published Isaac's *Mathematico-physicarum meditationum, quaestionum, solutionum centuria*, containing a theory of magnetism. For a thorough discussion, see VAN BERKEL, "Descartes' Debt to Beeckman."
90 See *supra*, n. 11.
91 See *supra*, nn. 11 and 57.
92 VERBEEK, "Regius's *Fundamenta Physices*," p. 542.

remarks on Regius's originality with respect to Descartes. This issue at the center of the quarrel between Descartes and Regius, which started once Regius shared with Descartes a draft of his *Fundamenta physices* in 1645, and exploded with its publication in 1646, when Descartes accused Regius of having appropriated the contents of his works (including his still unpublished *Traité de l'homme*, from which Regius plagiarized Descartes's theory of muscular movement) and of having misused them, ignoring their correct order of exposition and providing them without the due demonstrations.[93] In the midst of this quarrel, the contents of Regius's early lectures at Utrecht became important to vindicate his originality.

In the following table, I compare the contents of (1) Regius's *Physica fundamenta* (provided in his *Responsio*),[94] (2) his *dictata* (as revealed by the fragments provided by Schoock), (3) his *Fundamenta physices* (on whose succession of chapters the table itself is structured), and (4) the contents of Regius's lectures expounded by Petrus Wassenaer (d. 1680) in his introductory letter opening Regius's *Brevis explicatio mentis humanae* (1648), referring to the overall contents of Regius's lectures in the years 1637-1641, but probably tracing to a later period (as discussed after the table).

Regius, *Physica fundamenta* (May 1641-February 1642)	Regius, *Dictata physica* (May 1641-July 1642)	Regius, *Fundamenta physices* (1646)-order of chapters	Regius, lectures (1637-1641/1644-1648)
	Laudes scientiae naturalis (fragment 1)	Preface	
	Vestibulum (fragment 5) *De principiis* (fragments 3, 4, and probably 6 and 7)	1. *De principiis rerum naturalium*	"Formam et materiam rerum naturalium in extensione motu quiete situ figura et magnitudine partium consistentem, […] leges motus, […] vires machinarum."
"Coelum et Terra, stellae fixae, planetae, cometae."	*De mundo* (fragment 2)	2. *De aspectabilis mundi fabrica*	"Coelorum vortices; solem; stellas fixas; planetarum annuum et diurnum motum, […] cometas."
		3. *De aqua, terra, aëre et igne*	"[Naturam] mineralium."
"Aestus maris."	Fragment 9.	4. *De aestu maris, et motu aëris et aquae ab oriente versus occasum*	"Aestum maris."
		5. *De generatione, corruptione, mixtione, temperamentis et qualitatibus*	

---

93 Descartes to Elisabeth of Bohemia, March 1647, in AT IV 625-626; BL 2402-2405; CSMK 314-315.
94 See *supra*, n. 17.

Regius, *Physica fundamenta* (May 1641-February 1642)	Regius, *Dictata physica* (May 1641-July 1642)	Regius, *Fundamenta physices* (1646)-order of chapters	Regius, lectures (1637-1641/1644-1648)
"Sal, meteora."		6. *De meteoris*	"Naturam meteorum."
"Magnes."	Fragment 8.	7. *De fossilibus*	"Magnetis directionem, coniunctionem et excitationem per geminos et diversos halitus vorticosos factam."
		8. *De corporibus vivis*	
"Stirpium et Animalium operationes."		9. *De stirpibus*	[Naturam] stirpium."
		10. *De animalibus*	"Motus animalium."
		11. *De bestia*	"[Naturam] bestiarum."
"Lux, lumen, colores."		12. *De homine*	"Mentem humanam [...]; [naturam] hominis."

Wassenaer, addressing Descartes, wrote indeed that

> since already many years, when nothing was yet brought to the public by you besides the *Discours de la méthode*, the *Météores*, and the *Dioptrique*, [Regius] taught, as is evident to many followers of his, the form and matter of natural things, the human mind, the laws of movement, the movements of animals, the forces of machines, the vortices of the heavens, the sun and fixed stars, the yearly and daily movement of planets, tides, the comets, the excitation of the magnet by vortical exhalations; the nature of meteors, minerals, plants, beasts, man, and many other physiological and medical things, both theoretical and practical [...], not read in any author.[95]

This is a list of topics basically matching the contents of Regius's *Fundamenta physices* and *Fundamenta medica* (1647), and, even if these topics could have been taught by Regius before their appearance, the presence of a theory of magnetism based on a vortex theory suggests that Wassenaer was probably also relying on Regius's *Fundamenta physices* (in turn influenced by Descartes's *Principia philosophiae*), or on lectures taking place after 1644. In fact, if we compare Wassenaer's list with other lists of topics taught by Regius, and ascribed by him to his teachings of the late

---

95 "Iam ante multos annos, cum a te nondum quicquam praeter Methodum, Meteora, et Dioptricam, in publicam lucem prodiisset, docuit, ut plurimis eius auditoribus constat, formam et materiam rerum naturalium in extensione motu quiete situ figura et magnitudine partium consistentem; mentem humanam; leges motus; motus animalium; vires machinarum; coelorum vortices; solem; stellas fixas; planetarum annuum et diurnum motum; aestum maris; cometas; magnetis directionem, coniunctionem et excitationem per geminos et diversos halitus vorticosos factam; naturam meteorum, mineralium, stirpium, bestiarum, hominis, aliaque multam physiologica et medica, tum theoretica tum practica dicta, in nullis authoribus lecta," HENRICUS REGIUS, *Brevis explicatio mentis humanae*, Utrecht, Ex officina Theodori Ackersdicii, 1648, p. 48.

1630s, we get a more essential picture of the possible contents of his *dictata*, and a confirmation that the list provided by Wassenaer probably traced to later years (i.e. after 1644). Such lists are proposed in Regius's letter to the reader given — with a notable variant — in his *Praxis medica* (1657)[96] and *Medicina et Praxis medica* (1668).[97] According to the 1657 version,

> Descartes himself, [having] seen my *Cogitata physica*, by which I had even then described by true, clear, intelligible, always observable, and unique principles the magnet, tides, and all the remaining universality of things, publicly testified in his *Epistola ad Patrem Dinet* that "as [I, Regius] saw his *Dioptrique* and *Météores*," at the time, around the year 1637, when only [these] were published together with the *Discours de la méthode*, "[I] was [of] such a sagacity, that within a few months [I] thence prepared a complete physiology."[98]

In the 1668, in turn, a reference to the explanation of man (i.e. physiology) is added:

> Descartes himself, [having] seen my *Cogitata physica*, by which I had even then described by true, clear, intelligible, always observable, and unique principles man, the magnet, tides, and all the remaining universality of things, publicly testified […].[99]

In other words, according to the 1657 version Regius's *Cogitata physica* concerned only natural philosophy, without a physiological or medically-oriented part. In the 1668 version, in turn, there is a clear reference to a theory of man.

In the light of all this, we can advance some hypotheses. First, that Descartes's judgment given in his *Epistola ad Dinet* concerned physiology rather than natural philosophy, i.e. it was decidedly medically-oriented and was based only on his *Essais de Médecine* or notes on Trincavelli sent by Regius to Descartes in August 1638.[100] These, in fact, might have contained an essential but at the same time complete theory of man, regardless of the fact that in May 1639 Regius was still finishing his "short

---

96 Bound at the end of the book and dated 20/30 November 1656.
97 Bound at the beginning of the book and dated 20/30 January 1668.
98 "[…] ipse Cartesius, visis meis Physicis cogitatis, quibus magnetem, aestum maris, totamque reliquam rerum universitatem, per principia vera, clara, intelligibilia, ubivis observabilia, et unica, iam tum discripseram, publice in Epistola ad P. Dinetum testatus fuerit *me visa sua Dioptrica et Meteorologia*, quo tempore illae, circa annum 1637 solae, cum Dissertatione de methodo, in lucem primum prodierant, *ea fuisse sagacitate, ut intra paucos menses integram physiologiam concinnarim*," HENRICUS REGIUS, *Praxis medica*, Utrecht, Typis Theodori ab Ackersdijck, et Gisberti a Zijl, 1657, *Lectori benevolo*, p. 2 (unnumbered).
99 "[…] ipse Cartesius, visis meis Physicis cogitatis, quibus hominem, magnetem, aestum maris, totamque reliquam rerum universitatem, per principia vera, clara, intelligibilia, ubivis observabilia, et unica, iam tum discripseram, publice in Epistola ad P. Dinetum testatus fuerit *me visa sua Dioptrica et Meteorologia*, quo tempore illae, circa annum 1637 solae, cum Dissertatione de methodo, in lucem primum prodierant, *ea fuisse sagacitate, ut intra paucos menses integram physiologiam concinnarim*," HENRICUS REGIUS, *Medicina et praxis medica, medicationum exemplis demonstrata*, Utrecht, Ex officina Theodori ab Ackersdijck, 1668, *Lectori benevolo*, p. 2 (unnumbered).
100 See *supra*, n. 7.

propositions [...] touching physiology,"¹⁰¹ and that in 1657 he omitted the reference to man in his list of topics: either because he was referring to later writings concerning more natural philosophy than physiology, or because he just wanted to emphasize his having developed as early as 1638 a theory of magnetism and tides, usually assumed as samples, by Regius, of his capacity of getting rid of traditional explanations based on substantial forms and occult qualities.¹⁰² This might have been possible: indeed, in 1639 Regius had already developed a theory of magnetism.¹⁰³ Moreover, even if his theory of tides was clearly inspired by Descartes, who expounded it for the first time in his *Le monde* (which Regius read only in 1641), Regius could have insights on Descartes's theory through Reneri, who assisted Descartes at Deventer from May 1632, while he was writing his treatise (preparation of which took place in 1630-1634 c.).¹⁰⁴

Second, we can hypothesize that Descartes's 1642 judgment was based on later writings by Regius (who, to his own advantage, did not correct Descartes's statement that he had completed his physiology already in 1638): either concerning natural philosophy only (in accordance with Regius's 1657 statement), or both natural philosophy and physiology (in accordance with the 1668 statement). Such later writings could be his *Compendium physicum*, *Novae philosophiae prodromus*, *Physica fundamenta*, *Dictata physica*, or a further text submitted to him by Regius between August 1638 and May 1642 (when Descartes's *Epistola ad Dinet* appeared), labelled by Regius as *Cogitata physica* in 1657 and 1668.

Third, and more probably, we can suppose that in 1642 Descartes was referring to a text submitted to him by Regius in 1638 (viz. his *Essais de Médecine*) and that in 1657 and 1668 Regius, with the aim of vindicating his own originality, claimed that Descartes based his judgment on a text including also a theory of tides — which, however, was probably discussed in a later text by Regius: in fact, is unlikely that Regius inserted such a theory in a short medical commentary like the one he sent to Descartes in August 1638.

Nonetheless, Regius most probably developed the physiological ideas he expounded in his later texts, such as his *Physica fundamenta*, as early as in 1638, in particular, in the case of his treatment of plants. Such a topic was notably absent from Descartes's *Principia philosophiae* — and from his other printed texts, being a discussion of plants and animals foreseen as the fifth section of his *Principia*, while a sixth was to be devoted to man, which however were never completed.¹⁰⁵ In turn,

---

101 See *supra*, n. 9.
102 See *supra*, nn. 65 and 66.
103 See *supra*, n. 71.
104 MATTHIJS VAN OTEGEM, *A Bibliography of the Works of Descartes (1637-1704)*, Utrecht, Zeno: The Leiden-Utrecht Research Institute of Philosophy, 2002, p. 538-540; BUNING, *Henricus Reneri*, p. 47-49 and 143-144. In any case, cogent evidence of an explanation, by Regius, of tides emerged only in late 1641: see *supra*, n. 70.
105 For a reconstruction of Descartes's botanical study, see FABRIZIO BALDASSARRI, "The Mechanical Life of Plants: Descartes on Botany," *British Journal for the History of Science*, 52/1 (2019), p. 41-63; for thorough discussion of these collaborations, see FABRIZIO BALDASSARRI, "Descartes and the Dutch: Botanical Experimentation in the Early Modern Period," *Perspectives on Science*, 28/6 (2020), p. 657-683.

it was probably part of Regius's private teaching, which he gave at Utrecht in 1638, before his assuming his post at the University, which included the teaching of botany (which from April 1639 could take place also in the Utrecht *hortus*).[106] Indeed, we do find an explanation of the powers of plants consistent with Regius's later positions in two theses of a *Disputatio physica continens theses aliquot illustriores* taking place at Utrecht on 17/27 March 1638, presided over by Reneri and in which the student Antonius Mudenus (Anthony van Muyden, mentioned in section 2) figured as *respondens*. In fact, the disputation is dedicated — besides Reneri and the professor of medicine Gulielmus Stratenus (Wilhelm van der Straten, 1593-1681) — to Regius himself, who therefore was most probably a private teacher of Mudenus, and taking part in its preparation.[107] According to these two theses,

---

106 BOS 21; BALDASSARRI, "Descartes and the Dutch," p. 672. According to the *Narratio historica* and to Schoock, Regius was attacked as being ignorant in botanics in some corollaries of a now lost disputation *De scorbuto* presided over by Stratenus on 22 December 1641 (Julian calendar, apparently): "13. Cochlearia non est Britannica, nec Telephium veterum. 14. Flos Armenius non est Saponaria. 15. Helleboraster non est Helleborus verus niger. 16. Helleborus ferulaceus non est Doronicum Americanum. 17. Filipendula ita dicta est, quod radices quasi filis pendere videantur, non quod flores. 18. Solanum Hortense non est Amara dulcis: nisi plantarum nomina ignorantibus liceat aliena nomina ignotis plantis indere," VOETIUS *et al., Testimonium*, p. 24-25; cf. SCHOOCK, *Admiranda methodus*, Praefatio, p. 53 (unnumbered), and 9, 37-38, and 43. In his *Epistola ad Voetium*, Descartes was to defend Regius's characterization of *Helleboraster* as 'Helleborus verus niger' as having been drawn from the *Stirpium historiae pemptades sex* (1583) by Rembert Dodoens (1517-1585), where *Helleboraster* is identified with the *Veratrum nigrum*, and the *Helleborum* with the *Veratrum album*: AT VIII-2 15-16; BO 1504-1506; cf. REMBERT DODOENS, *Stirpium historiae pemptades sex, sive libri XXX*, Antwerp, Ex officina Christophori Plantini, 1583, p. 261 and 379-382. Regius seems nonetheless to have corrected his classification of plants, as in his *Hortus academicus Ultraiectinus* (1650) he identifies the *Helleboraster* with the *Elleborus niger spurius* (rather than with 'verus'): "Elleborus niger spurius alter s. Elleboraster," HENRICUS REGIUS, *Hortus academicus Ultraiectinus*, Utrecht, Typis Theodori ab Ackersdijck, et Gisberti a Zijl, 1650, p. 6 (unnumbered) — a more blunt differentiation between *Helleborus albus* and *Helleborus niger* is in any case kept by Regius across his *Fundamenta medica* (1647). Moreover, in his *Catalogus* Regius identifies the *Dulcamara* with the *Solanum lignosum* white flowers, and not with the *Solanum hortense*: "Dulcamara s. Solanum lignosum fl. alb. [...] Solanum hortens. fl. alb.," REGIUS, *Hortus*, p. 6 and 14 (unnumbered). Such a differentiation by Regius matches the one provided in DODOENS, *Stirpium historiae pemptades sex*, p. 397-398 and 450-451. The criticisms contained in the other corollaries do not match the characterization of plants given in the *Catalogus*.

107 As discussed in BUNING, *Henricus Reneri*, p. 163-164, noting how this disputation has a more marked Cartesian character than Reneri's other disputations. See also BALDASSARRI, "Descartes and the Dutch," p. 668-669. Regius is listed among Mudenus's "[s]tudiorum suorum promotoribus ac fautoribus summis," HENRICUS RENERI (*praeses*) and ANTONIUS MUDENUS (*respondens*), *Disputatio physica continens theses aliquot illustriores*, Utrecht, Ex officina Aegidii Roman, 1638, dedicatees's page. Mudenus, from Utrecht, later enrolled at Leiden as a student of medicine (21 October 1639), while in 1640 he acted as *respondens*, at Utrecht, in four disputations *De febribus* presided over by Stratenus. He eventually graduated in medicine at Utrecht with a disputation *De phtisi* (22 December 1640) and a disputation *De peste et febribus pestilentibus* (February 1641). He was certainly a friend of Schuyl, who enrolled at Leiden as a student of philosophy on the same day as him. See the database geni.com, entry "Anthony van Muyden," https://www.geni.com/people/Anthony-van-Muyden/6000000021002536887 (accessed on 24 December 2021); GULIELMUS STRATENUS, *Disputationum medicarum prima[-septima] de febribus*, Utrecht, Ex officina

I. In plants, besides matter and its various accidental dispositions, and nutritive juice, it is not necessary to pose any substantial form, which is the principle of the operations of the plant. [...] VII. Plants have no faculty attracting the aliment, even less an appetite, by which [they] are attracted to this or to that aliment.[108]

Starting from thesis 7: in his *Physiologia, De actionibus naturalibus, Pars prior*, Regius was to provide a criticism of the idea that any attractive force (including a magnetic one) is at work in the human body,[109] even if Descartes suggested to him to drop the explanation of magnetism, which Regius was certainly providing in his private lectures, and which was discussed during Schuyl's inaugural disputation of 1639. In turn, the rationale of thesis 1 was to later recur in Regius's *Physiologia*, the text of which also saw the intervention of Descartes. Regius, following Descartes's commentary on a first version of the text he to proposed him (which Descartes deemed linguistically inappropriate), claimed that (1) one can attribute to animals and plants a vegetative and a sensitive soul — intended as a first principle of their operations. In turn, (2) one cannot legitimately attribute a vegetative or sensitive *soul* to man, given the fact that the first principle of operations, in man, is the rational only: more properly, man has a vegetative *force* (*vis vegetativa*) which is nothing but a certain disposition of the parts of the body "by which the dissipation of bodily substance and heat is prevented by means of a juice prepared in the heart and thrust into the parts [of the body]," while the sensitive force (*vis sensitiva*), similarly, is a conformation of the parts of the body enabling sense reception and movement. Together, the two *vires* constitute the *temperies* of the human body, "by which all their operations can be performed, as in a clock and in other automata many admirable operations are accomplished by the conformation of parts only: so that there is no need to feign any substantial and occult form [...] and [...] multiply entities beyond necessity."[110]

Aegidii Roman, 1640, reprinted as *Causae, signa et medela febrium, comprehensa et proposita septem disputationibus*, Utrecht, Ex officina Aegidii Roman, 1641 (1640 on the frontispiece): Mudenus acted as *respondens* in disputations 1-3 and 6; ANTONIUS MUDENUS, *Disputatio inauguralis medica prima de phthisi*, Utrecht, Ex officina Aegidii Roman, 1640; *Album studiosorum Academiae Lugduno Batavae MDLXXV-MDCCCLXXV*, ed. by Willem Nicolaas du Rieu, The Hague, Apud Martinum Nijhoff, 1875, p. 309; *Album promotorum, qui inde ab anno 16360 usque annum 1815um in Academia Rheno-Trajectina gradum doctoratus adepti sunt*, ed. by Frans Ketner, Utrecht, Broekhoff, 1936, p. 2; ANTOON KERKHOFF, *IJsbrand van Diemerbroeck: verhandeling over de pest: ingeleid, vertaald en van aantekeningen voorzien*, Enschede, University of Twente, 2013, p. 36, n. 37.

108 "I. In plantis praeter materiam et eius varias dispositiones accidentarias, et succum alimentarium nullam formam substantialem ponere est necesse, quae sit principium operationum plantae. [...] VII. Plantae nullam habent facultatem alimenti attractricem, multo minus appetitum, quo in hoc potius quam illud alimentum ferantur," RENERI, *Disputatio*, theses 1 and 7.

109 See *supra*, n. 73.

110 "16. Vis autem vegetativa in homine nihil aliud est, quam certa partium corporis constitutio, qua substantiae corporeae calorisque perpetuam dissipationem per succum a corde praeparatum, et in partes impulsum, conservamus. 17. Vis autem sensitiva est partium humani corporis in spiritus, nervos et alia sensoria: item fibras, musculos, et artus talis conformatio, qua homo ab obiectis, tum internis, tum externis, variis motibus citra cogitationem, affici, totoque corpore se de loco in locum movere potest. 18. Hae duae itaque (quae natura corporis appellari possunt) nihil aliud sunt, quam corporis humani apte conformati apta temperies: quandoquidem omnes illarum operationes ab

If we compare the 1638 disputation with Regius's final text, we do find the recurrence of the same concepts: the idea of a principle of operations in the body which is nothing but the disposition of the parts of matter, the centrality of the alimentary juice, the rejection of substantial forms on the basis of a principle of economy, and the negation of attraction. In other words, Regius developed a theory of man out of a theory of plants, and started to do so as early as in 1638-1639, when he was teaching a theory of plants and had already developed a theory of magnetism. This move from plants to animals can be noted also in his *Fundamenta physices*, where Regius devoted chapter 9 to plants, which is preceded by a chapter on living bodies as such (chapter 8), and followed by chapters on animals (10-11), and man (12)), thereby fulfilling the same plan expounded by Descartes in his *Principia philosophiae*. A fulfillment made possible not only by Regius's well-known longstanding focus on the physiology of animals and man, but also on plants, which was at the center of his teaching well before the appearance of his *Fundamenta physices*.

---

hac ita fieri queunt, ut in horologio et aliis automatis plurimae actiones admirandae a sola partium conformatione peraguntur: ita ut non opus sit aliquam substantialem incognitamque formam hic vel alibi in similibus fingere, entiaque contra verissimum philosophiae dictatum, multiplicare absque necessitate," REGIUS, *Physiologia*, p. 15-16; cf. Descartes to Regius, early May 1641, in BOS 63-65; AT 369-372; BL 1456-1459; CSMK 181-182. See also FABRIZIO BALDASSARRI, "Failures of Mechanization: Vegetative Powers and the Early Cartesians, Regius, La Forge, and Schuyl," in *Vegetative Powers: The Roots of Life in Ancient, Medieval, and Early Modern Natural Philosophy*, ed. by Fabrizio Baldassarri and Andreas Blank, Cham, Springer, 2021, p. 255-275.

DANIEL SAMUEL

A British Response to *The Passions of the Soul*

▼ ABSTRACT Numerous vernacular treatises on the passions were published in England in the first half of the seventeenth century. A standard definition of the passions appeared in many of these works which situated emotions within the Aristotelian and Galenic traditions. In section one, I describe this traditional account of emotion by looking at treatises on the passions and medical sources such as regimens. In section two, I examine how Descartes' treatise on the passions challenged this mainstream view. In section three, I chart how Descartes' reformulation of the passions influenced three prominent English intellectuals: Henry More, Thomas Willis and Walter Charleton. This chapter highlights the important role of medicine in the development of theories of emotion over the course of the seventeenth century.

▼ KEYWORDS Passions, England, Psychology, Physiology, Nerves

The Arabic to Latin translation movement of the eleventh to thirteenth centuries played an important role in establishing the passions of the soul as part of the Western medical tradition. Listed as one of the 'six non-naturals' alongside air, diet, exercise, sleep, and bodily evacuation, the passions were seen as one of the factors that could influence bodily health in either beneficial or detrimental ways.[1] Throughout the medieval and early modern period the passions were also as topic of study across a range of academic disciplines including rhetoric, moral philosophy and natural

---

1 Luis García-Ballester, "On the Origin of the 'Six Non-Natural Things' in Galen", in *Galen and Galenism*, ed. by Jon Arrizabalaga et al., Aldershot, Ashgate, 2002, p. 105-115.

Daniel Samuel • The Warburg Institute, University of London, UK. Contact: <daniel.samuel@postgrad.sas.ac.uk>

philosophy.² At the start of the seventeenth century, the vernacular treatise on the passions emerged as popular textual genre both in France and England.³ These works, often authored by individuals with a theological background, tended to examine the moral dimension of the passions. One of the first treatises to appear in English was *The Passions of the Minde* (1601) authored by the Jesuit priest Thomas Wright, while in France the *Traitte des Passions de L'ame* (1614) was composed by the bishop Jean-Pierre Camus.⁴

René Descartes' *The Passions of the Soul* first appeared in Paris and Amsterdam in 1649 with the title *Traité des Passions de l'âme*, and it was translated into English and printed in London the following year. In one of the prefatory letters preceding the main body of the work, Descartes stated his "designe was not to lay open the passions like an oratour, nor yet a morall philosopher, but onely as a physician," and also remarked how the chosen title "may invite more people to read it."⁵ These comments suggest that Descartes was aware of the popular demand for treatises on the passions, and that he may have wanted to use the genre to promote his new ideas.

In this chapter, I will first set out the traditional psychological and physiological account of the passions by examining some of the treatises on the passions as well as various medical texts. I will then show how Descartes' intervention challenged some of the long-held ideas about them. Finally, I will analyse how Descartes' views influenced the writings of some of England's leading philosophers and physicians in the decades immediately following the publication of *The Passions of the Soul*.

1. The Traditional Psychology and Physiology of the Passions

In the first half of the seventeenth century the printing presses of London witnessed a boom in the publication of vernacular treatises on the passions. Several of these books were original works by British authors, however many were translations from recently composed French texts suggesting a ready audience for this type of literature.⁶ Near

---

2   On the passions in moral philosophy see SUSAN JAMES, "Reason, the passions and the good life", in *The Cambridge History of Seventeenth Century Philosophy*, ed. by Daniel Garber and Michael Ayers, Cambridge, Cambridge University Press, 1998, p. 1358-1396; JILL KRAYE, "Conceptions of Moral Philosophy" also in *The Cambridge History of Seventeenth Century Philosophy*, Cambridge, Cambridge University Press, p. 1279-1316. On the passions in rhetoric see RITA COPELAND, "Pathos and Pastoralism: Aristotle's Rhetoric in Medieval England", *Speculum*, vol. 89, no. 1 (2014), p. 96-127.
3   NOGA ARIKHA, *Passions and Tempers: A History of the Humours*, New York, HarperCollins, 2007, p. 217-220.
4   ANTHONY LEVI, *French Moralists: The Theory of the Passions, 1585-1649*, Oxford, Oxford University Press, 1964, p. 127.
5   From RENÉ DESCARTES, *The Passions of the Soule*, London, printed for A. C., sold by J. Martin and J. Ridley, 1650.
6   Examples of original English treatises include THOMAS WRIGHT, *The Passions of the Minde*, 1601; THOMAS COOPER, *The Mysterie of the Holy Government of our Affections*, 1620; WILLIAM FENNER, *A Treatise on the Affections*, 1640. English translations from the French include NICHOLAS COEFFETEAU, *A Table of Humane Passions*, 1621; NICOLAS CAUSSIN, *The Command of Reason over*

the beginning of a number of these treatises several authors attempted to provide a brief definition of a passion. Many of them were strikingly similar as can be seen here:

> A passion, is a motion of the sensitive appetite, stirred up by the apprehension, either of good or evil in the imagination, which worketh some outward change in the body.[7]

> Passion then is nothing else, but a motion of the sensitive appetite, caused by the imagination of an appearing or veritable good or evil, which changeth the body against the laws of nature.[8]

> That which is called passion, say they, is no other thing, but a motion of the sensitive appetite, caused by the apprehension or imagination of good or evill, the which is followed with a change or alteration in the body, contrary to the lawes of nature.[9]

An immediate conclusion one can draw from these remarks is that passions were generally held to be both psychological and physiological, that is, they were present in both the soul and the body.

The idea that passions were motions of the sensitive appetite, the first part of the standard definition, was grounded in the Aristotelian-based faculty psychology that was still taught in universities throughout Europe at the beginning of the seventeenth century.[10] According to this model, there were three types of soul, each consisting of a collection of powers, or faculties. Plants possessed a vegetative soul which gave them the powers of nutrition, growth and reproduction. Animals had a sensitive soul which contained the aforementioned powers but also imbued them with the powers of sensation and locomotion. Humans alone had a rational soul which gifted them with the additional faculties of the intellect and will. Passions were produced by the appetitive faculty of the sensitive soul and were generally subcategorised as either concupiscible or irascible.[11] An influential taxonomy of the passions first proposed by Thomas Aquinas was repeatedly referenced in many of the treatises on the passions. According to the scheme set out by Aquinas there were the six concupiscible passions of love, hatred, joy, sorrow, desire and aversion, and the five irascible passions of hope, despair, boldness, fear and anger. This elevenfold classification was presented on the titlepage of the English translation of Jean-Francois Senault's *The Use of Passions* (1649),

---

the Passions, 1638; MARIN CUREAU DE LA CHAMBRE, *The Characters of the Passions*, 1650.
7 JOHN WEEMSE, *The Portraiture of the Image of God in Man*, London, 1636, p. 139.
8 JEAN-FRANCOIS SENAULT, *The Use of Passions*, London, 1649, p. 17.
9 COEFFETEAU, *A Table of Humane Passions*, p. 2.
10 KATHARINE PARK, "The Organic Soul" in *The Cambridge History of Renaissance Philosophy*, ed. by Charles B. Schmitt et al., Cambridge, Cambridge University Press, 1988, p. 464-485.
11 On the tradition of passions as movements of the will see JOHN DRUMMOND, "John Duns Scotus on the Passions of the Will", in *Emotion and Cognitive Life Medieval and Early Modern Philosophy*, Oxford, Oxford University Press, 2012, p. 53-74; SIMO KNUUTTILA, "Sixteenth-Century Discussions of the Passions of the Will", also in *Emotion and Cognitive Life Medieval and Early Modern Philosophy*, p. 116-132. One distinction between the passions of the sensitive appetite and those of the rational appetite (the will) were that the latter did not directly involve bodily change.

which pictured reason as an enthroned queen attempting to manage the passions while receiving assistance from divine grace. Another faculty of the sensitive soul that played an important role in the formation of the passions was the imagination, which was generally thought to be housed in the middle ventricle of the brain.[12] Before a passion arose in the soul, the imagination had to judge whether any object presented to it was either beneficial or harmful. If what was presented was deemed to be good then the appetite would prepare to embrace it, whereas if it was judged to be evil then the appetite would get ready to avoid it.

As treatises on the passions were primarily concerned with issues of morality they tended to focus upon the psychological dimension of the passions. Some however, such as Thomas Wright's *The Passions of the Minde*, also attempted to address their physiological component. After acknowledging passions as motions of the sensitive appetite, in accordance with tradition, Wright asked whether this faculty of the soul was allotted to a specific part of the body and concluded "I answer, that the very seat of all passions, is the heart".[13] In his treatise *A Table of Humane Passions* (1621), the French bishop Nicolas Coeffeteau similarly located passions in the heart stating "in motions of joy and desire, the heart melts with gladness. In those of sorrow and trouble, it shrinks up and freezeth with grief".[14] The association of the passions with the heart did not just belong to the speculation of priests, it was also confirmed by centuries of teaching within the medical tradition.

Medieval and Renaissance medical theories of the passions were based upon principles derived from Galenic physiology such as the innate heat, humours and spirits.[15] A popular medieval account of the spirits held there to be three types of this subtle substance flowing through the body. According to this system, natural spirits were produced in the liver and flowed through the veins, vital spirits were produced in the heart and flowed through the arteries, and animal spirits were produced in the brain and travelled through the nerves. During the Renaissance the nature of the spirits was disputed with some physicians rejecting one or more of the different varieties.[16] Nevertheless, medical accounts of the passions were always associated with this bodily substance. Many Latin manuscripts that discussed the passions in a medical context were translations of earlier Arabic works, and many of them would go on to be printed over the course of the sixteenth century. One such example was the *Pantegni* by Constantine the African, which was first composed in the eleventh

---

12   RUTH HARVEY, *The Inward Wits: Psychological Theory in the Middle Ages and the Renaissance*, London, Warburg Institute, 1975, p. 43-44.
13   THOMAS WRIGHT, *The Passions of the Minde in General*, 1630, p. 32-33.
14   COEFFETEAU, *A Table of Humane Passions*, p. 17.
15   For medical spirits see JAMES J. BONO, "Medical spirits and the medieval language of life", *Traditio*, vol. 40, 1984, p. 91-130. For innate heat see ELISABETH MOREAU, "Innate Heat", in *Encyclopedia of Renaissance Philosophy*, ed. by Marco Sgarbi, Cham, Springer. 2015, https://doi.org/10.1007/978-973-319-02848-4_399-391.
16   See FABRIZIO BIGOTTI, *Physiology of the Soul*, Turnhout, Brepols, 2019, p. 89-91; HIRO HIRAI, "Spirit in Renaissance Medicine" in *Encyclopedia of Renaissance Philosophy*, ed. by Marco Sgarbi, Cham, Springer. 2018, https://doi.org/10.1007/978-973-319-02848-4_1107-1101.

century and consisted of translated parts of a medical encyclopaedia by 'Alī ibn al-'Abbās al-Maǧūsī.[17] In this work, the passions were primarily seen as movements of the vital spirits and innate heat either away from, or back towards, the heart.[18] In particular, joy and anger were associated with movement of the spirits and heat away from the heart. The motion was slow in joy and quick in anger. Conversely, distress and fear were linked to movements back towards the heart. This time the motion was slow in distress and quick in fear. This fourfold scheme became a popular way of medically classifying the passions and the physiological changes they produced. Similar classifications appeared in both Ibn Hunayn's *Isagoge ad Artem Galeni* and Avicenna's *De Viribus Cordis*, both of which were highly influential in European medical education well into the sixteenth century.[19] The fourfold classification of the passions also appeared in a branching diagram in Johannes Wecker's *Medicinae Utriusque Syntaxes* (1576).[20] In the diagram, anger and joy were associated with the movement of blood and spirits to the exterior of the body, whereas fear and sorrow had them to move to the body's interior. The same scheme also appeared in a sixteenth century English medical treatise authored by the Cambridge educated physician Christopher Langton. In a section describing their effects upon the body, he states how the passions:

> make great alteration in the body, which amongst all others fear, joy, anger and sorrow declare evidently. Fear by drawing the spirit and blood into the inner parts leaves the outer pale for cold. Anger sets the body on fire with moving of the blood to the outer parts [...] Sorrow is an affection in which the heart as though it were smitten, is drawn together and doth tremble and quake [...] Joy is a sudden motion in which the heart rejoicing dilates himself and suddenly sends forth all his natural heat and spirits.[21]

As Langton's description makes clear, the passions were known to significantly affect bodily physiology and doctors understood that if they weren't properly managed, they had the potential to cause various diseases. The idea that uncontrolled passions could lead to physical illness was not a notion reserved for university trained physicians alone. Regimens were a widely read textual genre that offered advice on how individuals could manage the six non-naturals to promote their physical health, and

---

17 On the *Pantegni* and other aspects of the Arabic to Latin translation movement see DANIELLE JACQUART and CHARLES BURNETT, eds, *Constantine the African and 'Alī Ibn al-'Abbās al-Maǧūsī: The Pantegni and related Texts*, Leiden, Brill, 2004.
18 SIMO KNUUTTILA, *Emotions in Ancient and Medieval Philosophy*, Oxford, Oxford University Press, 2004, p. 212-215.
19 A translation of Ibn Hunayn's *Isagoge* can be found in *A Source Book in Medieval Science*, ed. by Edward Grant, Cambridge MA, Harvard University Press, 1974, p. 705-715 (p. 708). For the Isagoge in the medical teaching see JON ARRIZABALAGA, *The Articella in the Early Press c. 1476-1534*, Cambridge, Cambridge Wellcome Institute for the History of Medicine, 1998. On Avicenna's De Viribus Cordis see KRISTIN ELIZABETH PETERSON, *Translatio libri Avicennae De Viribus Cordis et medicinis cordialibus Arnaldi de Villanova*, Harvard PhD dissertation, 1993, p. 91.
20 JOHANNES WECKER, *Medicinae Utriusque Syntaxes*, Basle, 1576, p. 181.
21 CHRISTOPHER LANGTON, *A Very Brefe Treatise Ordrely Declaring the Principal Partes of Physick*, London, 1547. I have adapted the quotation into modern English.

discussions on the passions would commonly feature in these works.[22] Thomas Elyot's *The Castle of Health* (1534) was one of the first printed English vernacular regimens and it appeared in multiple editions over the course of the sixteenth and seventeenth centuries.[23] Surveying the bodily effects of anger Elyot noted how it could lead to fevers, trembling palsies and indigestion.[24] In a regimen entitled *Klinikē, or A Diet for the Diseased* (1633) by James Hart, the Northampton based physician noted how passions could affect the body's humoral constitution. He wrote "passions excite and stirre up some particular humour: as joy stirreth up the blood, and anger choler; so doth feare and greife stirre and move melancholy".[25] Hart included irrecoverable consumption, apoplexies and gout as just some of the illnesses brought about by an excess of passion.[26] In a section on the physical effects of joy, Hart, in line with tradition, described how it caused the blood and spirits to fly away from the heart and towards the outer parts of the body. He further noted how in rare cases joy could leave the heart so destitute that a person could die from an excess of this passion.[27]

In England, in the first half of the seventeenth century, it was possible to find a standard definition of the passions in numerous treatises on the passions. This definition situated the passions within the context of a faculty psychology derived from Aristotle and a medical theory based on Galenic principles.[28] From a psychological viewpoint they were understood to be motions of the sensitive appetite caused by the apprehension of good or evil in the imagination and they could be subdivided into the concupiscible or irascible types. From a physiological viewpoint the passions were primarily associated with motions of the innate heat, blood and spirits away from, or back towards, the heart. It was against this background that Descartes put forward his own views on the topic.

2. Descartes' Theory of the Passions

Descartes began his treatise on the passions by attempting to distinguish between the functions of the soul and those of the body. By limiting the functions of the

---

22 For an introduction to regimens in the early modern period see SANDRA CAVALLO, "Conserving Health: the Non-Naturals in early modern culture and society", in *Conserving Health in Early Modern Culture*, ed. by Sandra Cavallo and Tessa Storey, Manchester, Manchester University Press, 2017, p. 1-20.
23 PAUL SLACK, "Mirrors of health and treasures of poor men: the uses of the vernacular medical literature of Tudor England", in *Health, Medicine, and Mortality in the sixteenth century*, ed. by Charles Webster, Cambridge, Cambridge University Press, 1979, p. 250.
24 THOMAS ELYOT, *The Castle of Health*, London, 1610, p. 96.
25 JAMES HART, *A Diet for the Diseased*, London, 1633, p. 394.
26 *Ibid.*, p. 391, 393.
27 *Ibid.*, p. 400.
28 The precise nature of the passions was debated in both the late scholastic and humanist traditions. See PETER KING, 'Late Scholastic Theories of the Passions: Controversies in the Thomist Tradition', in *Emotions and Choice from Boethius to Descartes*, ed. Henrik Lagerlund and Mikko Yrjonsuuri, Dordrecht, Kluwer Academic Publishers, 2002, p. 229-258; LORENZO CASINI, *Cognitive and Moral Psychology in Renaissance Psychology: A Study of Juan Luis Vives' De anima et vita*, Uppsala, Universitetstryckeriet Uppsala, 2006, p. 131-160.

soul to thought alone, he challenged centuries of tradition that held the soul to be the principle that gave the body both life and form. In rejecting the standard vital and sensitive powers of the soul, including the sensitive appetite, he also dismissed the traditional psychological home of the passions. Thus, in the twenty-seventh article of the treatise he offered an alternative definition of the passions stating them to be:

> perceptions, or sensations, or emotions of the soul that we refer particularly to the soul itself, and that are caused, sustained and fortified by some movement of the spirits.[29]

For Descartes, the immediate cause of the passions was no longer the apprehension of a particular good or evil in the soul, but rather, as he goes on to state, "nothing other than the vibration imparted by the animal spirits to the little gland in the middle of the brain".[30] Descartes further rejected the apportioning of the passions into their concupiscible or irascible types and proposed a new classification instead. He claimed that there were six fundamental passions; wonder, love, hatred, desire, joy and sadness, and suggested that all the others were either compounds of or variants of them.[31]

Descartes' new taxonomy was intricately bound up with his new physiology of the passions. Departing from the medical orthodoxy of the period, Descartes rejected the idea that the heart was the seat of the passions.[32] Rather he saw the cavities of the brain, and the animal spirits contained therein, to be the key location for their production.[33] This relocation of the seat of the passions is most clearly evident when he discussed wonder, which he claimed to be the first of all the passions.[34] For Descartes, wonder arose when an object took an individual by surprise and was judged to be new. Importantly, this passion appeared before an object was deemed to be beneficial or harmful for the individual involved, and since wonder was not focused on whether an object was good or bad, Descartes stated "it has no relationship with the heart or the blood, on which all the good of the body depends, but only with the brain".[35]

In contrast to wonder, Descartes reported how the passions of desire, love, hatred, joy, and sadness, and those that derived from them, could significantly affect the heart, blood and other bodily viscera. At an early point in the treatise Descartes suggested that the passions had traditionally been associated with the heart because a 'little nerve that descends to it from the brain' caused people to 'feel' alterations in the organ.[36] When discussing the physiological effects of fear he described how this particular passion caused spirits in the brain to flow into 'the nerves that contract

---

29 RENÉ DESCARTES, *The Passions of the Soul*, translated by Michael Moriarty, Oxford, Oxford University Press, 2015, p. 206.
30 *The Passions of the Soul*, p. 219.
31 Ibid., p. 223.
32 Ibid., p. 209.
33 Ibid., p. 211.
34 Ibid., p. 220.
35 Ibid., p. 224.
36 Ibid., p. 209.

or expand the orifices of the heart'.³⁷ And in a later passage documenting how love moves the blood and spirits in the body he reported how 'the brain sends animal spirits, through the nerves of the sixth pair, towards the muscles of the intestine and stomach'.³⁸ Crucially, for Descartes, the physiological changes brought about by the passions in the various bodily organs fed back to the brain to both sustain and fortify them. Love, for example, condensed the blood which caused large and agitated spirits to enter back into the brain to reinforce this passion.³⁹

Descartes had observed the nerves of the sixth pair and "the little nerve of the heart" during his own animal dissections, and their inclusion in his explanation of the passions marked a significant departure from the standard medical explanation of his day.⁴⁰ For Descartes, passions originated as movements of the animal spirits in the brain that then travelled through the nerves to the various muscles and organs of the body where they could go on to initiate a spectrum of physiological changes. These changes could in turn affect the size and motion of the animal spirits in the brain which fortified and sustained the experience of the passions. This cranio-centric physiology of the passions, which stood in contrast to the traditional cardio-centric medical account, would prove to be influential in the second half of the seventeenth century.

3. Three British Responses to *The Passions of the Soul*

The philosopher and theologian Henry More was born in the English town of Grantham in 1614. After studying at the local grammar school and Eton College, he went up to Christ's college, Cambridge where he was made a fellow in 1641. More first read Descartes' *Principia Philosophiae* in 1646 and was immediately captivated by many of the concepts that were contained in it.⁴¹ Two years later More initiated a brief correspondence with Descartes that abruptly ended following the latter's death in 1650. Over the next decade More produced a range of philosophical works in which he presented a host of original ideas alongside those he had gathered from ancient and modern authors.

---

37   *Ibid.*, p. 210.
38   *Ibid.*, p. 236.
39   *Ibid.*
40   ANNIE BITBOL-HESPÉRIÈS, "De toute la nature de l'homme: de *L'Homme à La Description du corps humain*, la physiologie des *Passions de l'âme* et ses antécédents médicaux", in *Les Passions de L'âme et leur Réception Philosophique*, ed. by Giulia Belgioioso and Vincent Carraud, Turnhout, Brepols, 2020, p. 67-100, esp. p. 88-89.
41   JOHN HENRY, "Henry More", *The Stanford Encyclopedia of Philosophy* (Winter 2020 edition), ed. by Edward N. Zalta, URL = https://plato.stanford.edu/archives/win2020/entries/henry-more/. For the influence of Descartes on More see ALAN GABBEY, "*Philosophia Cartesiana Triumphata*: Henry More (1646-1671)", in *Problems of Cartesianism*, ed. by Thomas M. Lennon *et al.*, Canada, McGill-Queen's University Press, 1982, p. 171-250. For More's place in the reception of Cartesianism in Britain see SARAH HUTTON, "Cartesianism in Britain", in *The Oxford Handbook of Descartes and Cartesianism*, ed. by Steven Nadler, Tad M. Schamltz, Delphine Antoine-Mahut, Oxford, Oxford University Press, 2019, p. 496-513.

In *The Immortality of the Soul* (1659), More made repeated references to the writings of Descartes. In a chapter discussing the role of the pineal gland in the perception of external objects, More specifically referred the reader to the thirty-fifth article of the *Passions of the Soul* before going on to refute Descartes' explanation.[42] Other references in this work to the soul's 'aereal vehicle' and 'plastick faculty' suggest further differences between More's view of the soul and that of his erstwhile correspondent.[43]

In 1667 More published, in Latin, a work of moral philosophy entitled *Enchiridion Ethicum*, which was translated into English and printed posthumously as *An Account of Virtue* (1690). Since antiquity, the passions had regularly featured in writings on morality, and the ancient debate as to whether a virtuous life consisted in moderating the passions or extirpating them altogether continued into the Renaissance and beyond.[44] More's manual of ethics featured an extended analysis of the passions and in a chapter attempting to lay out the different types he stated "no man has, in my opinion, more accurately summed up, or distinctly defined the several kinds of species of passions, than the renowned philosopher Des Cartes; I will tread, for the most part, in his footsteps."[45] Going on to give a general definition of the passions that closely resembled Descartes', he wrote:

> Passion then is a vehement sensation of the soul, which refers especially to the soul itself, and is accompanied with an unwonted motion of the spirits.[46]

After providing his definition, More offered an explanation of each of its parts and again heavily borrowed from Descartes' treatise to do this. However, he made it clear that passions accompany the motion of spirits rather than result from them, further explaining how "the soul moves the spirits, and not the spirits the soul" when external objects "agitate the sense or imagination".[47]

More's selective use of Descartes is present once again when he goes on to offer his classification of the passions. More initially appeared to agree with Descartes' taxonomy stating "Des Cartes brings all the passions of the soul under six principal and primitive kinds; Namely, admiration, love, hatred, cupidity, joy and grief."[48] Like Descartes he placed admiration (synonymous with Descartes' wonder) at the head of the list and labelled it "the very first passion".[49] More's account of wonder echoed that of Descartes and he explained how this passion appeared when a "new object, or an old one under new circumstances" captured the beholder's attention. Agreeing with Descartes once more, he reported how wonder arose before an object

---

42 Henry More, *The Immortality of the Soul*, Cambridge, 1659, p. 163.
43 For More's view of the soul see John Henry, "A Cambridge Platonist's Materialism: Henry More and the Concept of Soul", in *Journal of the Warburg and Courtauld Institutes*, vol. 49, 1986, p. 172-195.
44 Jill Kraye, "Moral Philosophy", in *The Cambridge History of Renaissance Philosophy*, ed. by Charles B. Schmitt et al., Cambridge, Cambridge University Press, 1988, p. 339-342, 364-367.
45 Henry More, *An Account of Virtue*, London, 1690, p. 43.
46 More, *An Account of Virtue*, p. 43.
47 Ibid., p. 43-44.
48 Ibid., p. 44.
49 Ibid.

was understood to be 'grateful or ungrateful' to the individual concerned and further explained how love was kindled when an object was judged to be good while hatred originated when an object was deemed to be evil. At this point More departed from Descartes' classification, explaining how cupidity, joy and grief derived from love and hatred. Thus, More offered a list of three primitive passions; wonder, love and hatred. Seeing a correspondence between the fundamental nature of love and hatred in his own list and the scholastic categorisation of the passions as concupiscible and irascible, he stated, in a somewhat reconciliatory tone, that the old way of dividing the passions "deserves not to be so contemptuously exploded, if but interpreted aright."[50]

As we have seen, More's definition and classification of the passions were deeply influenced by Descartes. So too was his account of their bodily seat, and like his French counterpart, he placed wonder in the brain. However when he wrote about love and hatred he noted how they were 'properly seated' and had 'their proper residence' in the heart, going against the titular declaration of article thirty-three of Descartes' treatise which clearly stated how the seat of the passions was not the heart.[51] Any pronouncements by More about the physiology of the passions were tempered however when he reminded his reader that the work at hand was one of moral, not natural philosophy.[52] He also stated his intention to "willingly and knowingly" pass by the remote and abstruse natural causes of the passions and the question of whether they were associated with "the brain, or to certain motions of the blood or spirits [...] to the nerves of the bowels and stomach, or to the spleen and liver, or finally, to the heart itself".[53] A contemporary of Henry More who did attempt to give a detailed natural philosophical account of the passions was the physician Thomas Willis.

Thomas Willis was born in the county of Wiltshire in 1621 and went on to study at the University of Oxford just before the outbreak of the English civil war. After a period of service on the side of the royalists, Willis gained his medical degree and returned to Oxford to set up his practice. At Oxford he became acquainted with some of the newly emerging groups dedicated to carrying out scientific experiments and came to know many of the pioneers of the period including Robert Hooke and Robert Boyle. In 1660, Willis was appointed Sedleian Professor of Natural Philosophy at the university, and in 1664 he published his ground-breaking *Cerebri Anatome: Cui Accessit Nervorum Desciptio et Usus* which pictured and described the brain and nervous system in unprecedented detail.

One of the major innovations contained in this work was a reclassification of the cranial nerves. Medical tradition had generally held there to be seven pairs of nerves that emerged from the brain.[54] Not only was this view of Galen, the most authoritative of the ancient authors, it was also confirmed in the writings of modern anatomists

---

50 *Ibid.*, p. 45.
51 *Ibid.*, p. 45-46.
52 *Ibid.*, p. 54.
53 *Ibid.*, p. 53.
54 JMS PEARCE, "Naming the Cranial Nerves: A Historical Note", in *ACNR*, vol. 16, no. 5, 2017, p. 12-13.

such as Andreas Vesalius. Based upon his own dissections, Willis instead proposed there to be nine pairs of cranial nerves and he described the structure and functions of each in the *Cerebri Anatome*. What Descartes referred to as the nerves of the sixth pair in *The Passions of the Soul*, Willis reclassified as the nerves of the eighth pair. These nerves were alternatively known as the wandering pair due to the branching and meandering course they took from the brain to the various organs of the body. Willis, like Descartes, saw the movement of animal spirits through these nerves as one of the key routes enabling the transmission of the passions from the brain to the other parts of the body. In a discussion on the actions and uses of the nerves of the eighth pair, Willis identified a shoot of this nerve that fed into the structures responsible for speech and suggested that it was through this branch that "in every violent passion, as of anger, fear, joy and the like…the tongue sends forth a voice."[55] Further detailing the branches of the wandering nerve that innervated the heart, he wrote of their involvement in the "irregular motion, stirred up in the praecordia, by the force of the passions."[56] The references to the passions in *Cerebri Anatome* are scattered and brief, however in later work exploring the nature of the soul, Willis provided a detailed account of the topic.

In *De Anima brutorum* (1672) later translated into English as *Two Discourses Concerning the Soul of Brutes* (1683), Willis discussed both the psychology and physiology of the passions. His version of the soul differed from both the traditional scholastic account as well as the one proposed by Descartes. Instead, Willis' view of the soul was much closer to the one put forward by the French philosopher and priest Pierre Gassendi (1592-1655) whose influence he acknowledged in the work's dedicatory epistle.[57] For Willis, each human being had two distinct souls. The superior rational soul was immaterial and immortal while the inferior animal soul (which gave the work its title) was corporeal, extended and mortal. The animal soul was itself understood to consist of two parts, the vital soul which imbued the body with life and the sensitive soul which gave it the power of sensation. Willis seated the fiery particles of the vital soul in the blood circulating through the heart, arteries, and veins. Meanwhile the lucid particles of the sensitive soul were identified with the animal spirits housed within the brain and nerves.[58]

Willis dedicated two chapters of *De Anima brutorum* to the passions. The first explored the passions in general while the second studied particular passions in greater detail. Willis' initial explanation regarding the causes of the passions resembled the traditional scholastic answer and he described how they arose in the sensitive soul after an object in the sense and imagination was seen to be good or evil.[59] Beneath

---

55 Many of Thomas Willis' works were collected and published in English translation in the volume *The Remaining Works of that Famous and Renowned Physician Dr Thomas Willis*, London, 1681. The quotations are taken from the section of the work entitled *The Description and Use of the Nerves*, p. 149-150.
56 THOMAS WILLIS, *The Description and Use of the Nerves*, p. 153.
57 THOMAS WILLIS, *Two Discourses Concerning the Soul of Brutes*, London, 1683.
58 *Ibid.*, p. 22.
59 *Ibid.*, p. 45.

the familiar language of the schoolmen however, Willis' idea of the sensitive soul as a corporeal entity made of particles belied a significant break with tradition. When Willis went on to describe the particular passions, he did so according to the familiar eleven-fold taxonomy, despite calling this classification both incongruous and insufficient.[60] Willis instead preferred to see pleasure and grief as the two principal passions due to their opposite effects in the corporeal soul.[61] He explained how in pleasure, the sensitive soul dilated causing the animal spirits to spread through the nerves which in turn made the hands, face and eyes "shine, and as it were leap forth". Furthermore, under the influence of the brain and "delivered by means of the nerves", pleasure induced the heart to thrust blood more rapidly around the body. In an opposing fashion, grief contracted the soul which slowed the movement of the spirits, leading the limbs to grow feeble and the heart to contract "by reason of the nerves carrying the same affection from the brain".[62]

In the opening pages of *De Anima brutorum*, Willis referred to René Descartes as 'the most illustrious Cartesius'.[63] However, he did not accept Descartes' vision of the soul, nor did he adopt to his definition and taxonomy of the passions. But like Descartes, Willis primarily associated the passions with movements of the animal spirits within the brain. Both men also described the crucial role played by the nerves, especially the nerves of the eighth pair (or the sixth pair for Descartes) in the transmission of the passions to the various parts of the body. The account of the passions provided by Descartes and Willis would both prove to be highly influential upon another English physician.

Walter Charleton was born in Somerset in 1619, obtained his medical degree from Oxford in 1643, and was appointed physician to King Charles I soon after. Following the king's demise, he moved to London where he set up a medical practice and joined the city's College of Physicians.[64] Charleton's publishing career consisted of translations of works by European authors such as Jan Baptist van Helmont and Pierre Gassendi as well as a number of original titles on a variety of topics ranging from physiology to natural theology.

A Natural History of the Passions was published in London in 1674, twenty-five years after the first appearance of Descartes' treatise on the same topic. In the prefatory epistle to the reader Charleton declared his intention in writing the work, and imitating Descartes' own prefatory remark he stated, "my design was to write of this argument, neither as an orator, nor as a moral philosopher, but only as a natural one conversant in pathology".[65] He later acknowledged that much of what he had to say on the topic was gleaned from the recent writings of other authors, disclosing that his description of the passions had interwoven threads taken from "those three

---

60 Ibid., p. 49.
61 Ibid., p. 48-49.
62 Ibid., p. 48.
63 Ibid., p. 3.
64 For the life and work of Charleton see EMILY BOOTH, *'A Subtle and Mysterious Machine': The Medical World of Walter Charleton (1619-1707)*, Dordrecht, Springer, 2005.
65 WALTER CHARLETON, *A Natural History of the Passions*, London, 1701. Prefatory epistle.

excellent men", Gassendi, Descartes and Thomas Hobbes.[66] He further admitted that a large segment of the work was indebted to Thomas Willis' *De Anima brutorum*, and he proceeded to invite the reader to seek out "that useful book".[67] Charleton's account of the soul closely followed that of Willis, and like his fellow physician he thought every human possessed two distinct and co-existent souls, one rational and the other sensitive. Despite claiming an inability to conceive of something immaterial residing in something material, Charleton seated the rational soul in the middle part of the brain that housed the imagination.[68] Dismissing Descartes assertion that it was the pineal gland that housed the rational soul, Charleton stated "had this excellent man, Monsieur des Cartes been but half as conversant in anatomy, as he seems to have been in geometry, doubtless he would never have lodged so noble a guest as the rational soul, in so incommodious a closet of the brain, as the glandula pinealis".[69] Charleton, like Willis, saw the sensitive soul as a subtle corporeal substance partitioned into a fiery part that was chiefly linked to the blood, and a lucid part associated with the animal spirits.[70]

In a chapter dedicated to discussing the passions in general, Charleton laid out the orderly sequence of bodily events that took place when any passion was aroused in the soul. He first noted how a passion initially arose when the imagination conceived an object to be embraced as good or avoided as evil. This event stirred the animal spirits residing in the brain to form an appetite therein. This appetite was then transmitted to the heart, which accordingly contracted or dilated, moving the blood in an irregular motion. Explaining how the information was transmitted between the brain and heart he reported how it is through the nerves "betwixt those sources of life and sense" that "such a quick transmission of spirits first from the brain into the precordia, and thence back again" occurred. As well as reaching the heart, the appetite formed in the brain also travelled through the nerves to affect the body's solid parts. Summarising the sequence, Charleton concluded that every passion successively excited "the phantasy, spirits, blood and solid parts".[71] So, like Descartes and Willis, he saw the nerves deriving from the brain as playing a crucial role in the transmission of the passions to the rest of the body.

Charleton's comments on the general physiology of the passions resembled those of Willis, however he chose to adopt the classification first set out by Descartes when he went on to detail them one by one. Providing a genealogy of the passions, he claimed "there are only six that seem to be simple and principal, namely admiration, love, hatred, desire, joy and grief".[72] Charleton's psychological and physiological account of admiration also followed that of Descartes. From a psychological perspective he first explained how admiration came about when a new or strange object appeared

---

66 Ibid.
67 Ibid.
68 Ibid., p. 61.
69 Ibid., prefatory epistle.
70 Ibid.
71 Ibid., p. 71.
72 Ibid., p. 164.

in the soul. From a physiological viewpoint he reported how neither the heart nor blood were altered in this passion as the object under consideration was seen to be new, but not yet as good or evil.[73] By contrast, when love appeared in the soul after an object was deemed beneficial he noted how the "animal spirits are like lightning dispatched from the brain by the nerves instantly into the heart", which in turn pulsed with more force to make "the circulation of the blood more nimble".[74] Charleton also explained how hatred caused the soul to withdraw from an object judged to be evil. Moreover this passion caused the animal spirits to retract inwards towards the brain which in turn led to a "destitution in the heart" and a weakening of the pulse.[75] When describing the possible health hazards of anger, Charleton wrote "it is not then without reason physicians advise men to decline this passion, as a powerful enemy to health [...] it inflames first the spirits, then the blood, and when violent it puts us into fevers and other acute distempers".[76] He further noted how anger could fire people into madness, apoplexies, epilepsies, convulsions, palsies, and gout, adding that the books of physicians are full of such cases.[77]

4. Conclusion

The passions of the soul were a well-established topic in medicine and natural philosophy when Descartes wrote his treatise on the topic. Vernacular treatises on the passions published in England during the first half of the seventeenth century suggest the presence of a dominant theory of emotion in this period. From a psychological viewpoint, passions were seen as motions of the sensitive appetite brought about by the apprehension of a particular good or evil. This perspective placed the passions within the context of the Aristotelian derived faculty psychology that continued to be taught in the universities well into the seventeenth century. From a physiological viewpoint, passions were considered in a largely Galenic context and were primarily associated with the movement of blood, heat and spirts towards and away from the heart. As one of the six non-naturals they had long been recognised as a factor that could have either beneficial or detrimental effects for the health of the body.

Going against the mainstream tradition of his time, Descartes offered a radically new interpretation of the emotions when he wrote his treatise 'as a physician'. Descartes denied the existence of a sensitive appetite within the soul and thereby deprived the passions of their traditional psychological location. Instead, he argued that the passions arose in the soul as a result of the movement of the animal spirits as they struck the pineal gland in the middle of the brain. Nevertheless, each passion involved a judgement regarding the object under consideration with Descartes

---

73 *Ibid.*, p. 89-90.
74 *Ibid.*, p. 107.
75 *Ibid.*, p. 111.
76 *Ibid.*, p. 113.
77 *Ibid.*, p. 114.

organising his new classification of the emotions accordingly. Wonder, the first of the passions, arose when something was judged to be new or rare. The other fundamental passions: desire, love, hatred, joy and sadness occurred after an object was deemed to be beneficial or harmful for the individual. While Descartes situated wonder in the brain, the other fundamental passions involved movements of the heart and blood and it was the nervous system that provided the means of communication between the two. Descartes' introduction of the nerves of the sixth pair into physiological accounts of emotion was a major medical innovation likely to have been inspired by his own anatomical studies.

Descartes' treatise on the passions had a significant influence upon establishment thinkers in England in the decades immediately after its initial publication. Henry More, a professor of divinity at the University of Cambridge, adopted and modified Descartes' definition of the passions in a treatise on ethics. Thomas Willis, physician and professor of natural philosophy at the University of Oxford, directly referenced Descartes' work in his ground-breaking neuroanatomical publications. Although he ultimately rejected Descartes' vision of the soul, like Descartes he saw the brain and nervous system as being central to a physiological account of emotion. Willis, following on from his own neuroanatomical dissections, reclassified what Descartes termed the nerves of the sixth pair as the nerves of the eighth pair, and like his French counterpart he saw this structure as a crucial component for the transmission of emotions throughout the body. Walter Charleton, a physician to the king and prominent member of the early Royal Society, referred to the works of Descartes and Willis when he composed his own treatise on the passions. His work reinforced the importance of the nerves 'betwixt those sources of life and sense' (the heart and the brain) and contributed to this structure being central to any future medical account of emotion. The passions remained an important medical topic throughout the eighteenth century, and their physiological association with the nervous system, rather than the heart, was consolidated during this period.[78] In its attempt to reformulate the physiological basis of emotion René Descartes' *The Passions of the Soul* marks an important moment, not only for the philosophical tradition, but also for the history of medicine.

---

78 See MICHAEL STOLBERG, "Emotions and the Body in Early Modern Medicine", *Emotion Review*, vol. 11, no. 2, 2019, p. 113-122.

MIHNEA DOBRE

Jacques Rohault on Medicine*

▼ ABSTRACT This chapter is an introduction to Jacques Rohault's medicine. It offers a reconstruction of the circumstances in which Rohault developed his views about physiology and the functions of the human body. Printed as the fourth section of his celebrated *Traité de physique* (1671), Rohault's medicine seems to have been long in the making. It is grounded on recent early modern anatomical discoveries, including the practice of dissection, but more importantly, on the theory of the circulation of the blood. Rohault adds a Cartesian reading in terms of mechanical explanations of bodily processes, which are all reducible to the motion of small particles of matter.

▼ KEYWORDS Cartesian, Medicine, Rohault, Anatomy, Dissections

1. Introduction

On 28 July 1657, Cyrano de Bergerac died. His *Histoire comique contenant les états et empires de la Lune* was published soon after.[1] The editor, Henry Le Bret (Lebret), mourned the loss of the famous Frenchman after a long illness.[2] While the nature of

---

* This work was supported by a grant of Ministry of Research and Innovation, CNCS-UEFISCDI, project number PN-III-P1-1.1-TE-2019-0841, within PNCDI III. I would like to thank Ovidiu Babeș, Ioana Bujor, Trevor McClaughlin, John Schuster, and Grigore Vida for their valuable comments and suggestions on the prior draft.

1 For details about Cyrano's life and works, see MADELEINE ALCOVER, *Cyrano relu et corrigè: Lettres, Estats du soleil, Fragment de physique*, Genève, Droz, 1990.

2 See the unpaginated preface to SAVINIEN DE CYRANO DE BERGERAC, *Histoire comique contenant les états et empires de la Lune*, Paris, Charles de Sercy, 1657. For a study on Le Bret, see MADELEINE ALCOVER, "Le Bret, Cuigy, Casteljaloux, Bignon, Royer de Prade et Regnault des Boisclairs: du

Mihnea Dobre • ICUB-Humanities, University of Bucharest, Romania. Contact: <mihnea.dobre@unibuc.ro>

Descartes and Medicine: Problems, Responses and Survival of a Cartesian Discipline,
ed. by Fabrizio Baldassarri, Turnhout, 2023 (DESCARTES, 6), p. 361-376
© BREPOLS PUBLISHERS   10.1484/M.DESCARTES-EB.5.132898

Cyrano's disease is not known with certainty, a brief note in Le Bret's introduction to the *Histoire comique* indicates that at least one of Cyrano's friends identified it correctly:

> Monsieur Roho, [...] cet illustre Mathematicien qui a tant fait de belles espreuves Phisiques [...], eut tant d'amitiè pour Monsieur de Bergerac, [...] qu'il fut le premier qui descouvrit la veritable cause de sa maladie, & qui rechercha soigneusement, avec tous ses amis, les moyens de l'en delivrer.[3]

The remark is quite curious, because Rohault was not a physician, but a physicist, and his 'beautiful physical proofs' were not published at that time. Most of Rohault's works appeared later in life, only one year before his death in 1672.[4] So, what are Rohault's views about medicine?

The *Traité de physique* and the *Entretiens sur la philosophie* were published in 1671. Of interest for the current chapter is the *Traité de physique*, which is a systematic textbook on natural philosophy, dealing with the general notions of physics (part I), cosmology (part II), the earthly and meteorological phenomena (part III), and the living bodies (part IV).[5] Part IV, on living bodies, covers topics related to anatomy, physiology, and pathology. The section dedicated to pathology is brief and it reproduces a lecture delivered by Rohault in one of the meetings hosted by Habert de Montmor in the early 1660s. The lecture was published anonymously in 1664 as part of Descartes' *Le Monde ou Traité de la Lumiere*, and it concerns the problem of fevers.[6] This chapter aims to provide an introduction to Rohault's medicine, from the early episode revealed by Le Bret, the conference presented at Montmor, up to the publication of the *Traité*.

---

nouveau sur quelques bons amis de Cyrano et sur l'édition posthume des *États et Empires de la Lune* (1657)", *Les Dossiers du Grihl*, 2009 http://journals.openedition.org/dossiersgrihl/3414 [accessed 16 June 2021].

3 "Monsieur Roho [Rohault] [...] this illustrious mathematician who carried out so many beautiful physical proofs [...] had so great a friendship for Monsieur de Bergerac [...] that he was the first to discover the true cause of his illness, and carefully sought, with all his friends, [to find] the ways to relieve him". Le Bret's preface is not paginated, see CYRANO DE BERGERAC, *Histoire comique*.

4 For an account of Rohault's life and works, see TREVOR MCCLAUGHLIN, "Jacques Rohault and the Natural Sciences" (unpublished PhD. Dissertation), University of Cambridge, 1972; PIERRE CLAIR, *Jacques Rohault (1618-1672). Bio-Bibliographie*, Paris, Centre National de la Recherche Scientifique, 1978; SIMONE MAZAURIC, "Préface", in JACQUES ROHAULT, *Traité de physique*, Paris, Comite des Travaux Historiques et Scientifiques, 2014, p. VII-XXXVI; MIHNEA DOBRE, *Descartes and Early French Cartesianism: Between Metaphysics and Physics*, Bucharest, Zeta Books, 2017; MIHNEA DOBRE, "Rohault, Jacques", in *Encyclopedia of Early Modern Philosophy and the Sciences*, ed. by Dana Jalobeanu and Charles T. Wolfe, Cham, Springer International Publishing, 2019, p. 1-6, Doi: 10.1007/978-973-319-20791-9_155-151.

5 An overview of Rohault's natural philosophy, with a discussion of the two books, is in MIHNEA DOBRE, "Jacques Rohault and Cartesian Experimentalism", in *Oxford Handbook of Descartes and Cartesianism*, ed. by Steven Nadler, Tad M. Schmaltz and Delphine Antoine-Mahut, Oxford, Oxford University Press, 2019, p. 388-401.

6 See RENÉ DESCARTES, *Le monde ou Traité de la Lumiere*, Paris, Theodore Girard, 1664.

2. The context: Rohault in Paris

Time and again, Rohault is praised in the literature for his assiduous work in the dissemination of Descartes' philosophy.[7] By the time of the publication of his *Traité de physique*, Rohault was already famous in the Parisian circles, where he passed not only as the son-in-law of Claude Clerselier, the literary executor of Descartes' unpublished works, but also as a populariser of Cartesian natural philosophy. Since the end of the 1650s, he offered public lectures on a variety of topics, including experiments with magnets, the explanation of vision, and pneumatic trials. He was part of the savant community interested in all sorts of natural phenomena, as best illustrated by the study of glass drops.[8] Based on the correspondence and reports of other scholars traveling to Paris and attending the various conferences of the early 1660s, Rohault's conferences were quite popular.[9] He also lectured at his own house — the famous 'Mercredies' (Wednesday) conferences — and details about these talks are available not only from indirect reports, but also from the notes taken by an unnamed lawyer (a certain 'F.') and the unofficial manuscript printed recently, *Physique nouvelle (1667)*.[10] In brief, the available sources are scarce, yet some image of Rohault's interest in medicine can be derived from them, especially when placed in the proper context.

The Parisian intellectual life was blooming in the 1660s.[11] Public conferences on assorted topics, open anatomical lectures, experiments performed in front of various audiences, all contributed to a very dynamic cultural scene. The emergence of state

---

7 See CLAIR, *Jacques Rohault*; TREVOR MCCLAUGHLIN, "Was There an Empirical Movement in Mid-Seventeenth Century France? Experiments in Jacques Rohault's *Traité de Physique*", *Revue d'histoire des Sciences*, 49/4 (1996), p. 459-481; SOPHIE ROUX, "Was There a Cartesian Experimentalism in 1660s France?", in *Cartesian Empiricisms*, ed. by Mihnea Dobre and Tammy Nyden, Dordrecht, Springer, 2013, p. 47-88; MIHNEA DOBRE, "Rohault's Cartesian Physics", in *Cartesian Empiricisms*, p. 203-226.
8 The tear-shaped glass object has stirred the interest of natural philosophy in mid-seventeenth century. See, for example, MIHNEA DOBRE, "On Glass-Drops: A Case Study of the Interplay Between Experimentation and Explanation in Seventeenth-Century Natural Philosophy", *Journal of Early Modern Studies*, 2 (2013), p. 105-124.
9 These sources are discussed in CLAIR, *Jacques Rohault*; ROUX, "Was There a Cartesian Experimentalism"; DOBRE, "Rohault's Cartesian Physics".
10 For the Wednesday conferences, see CLAIR, *Jacques Rohault*. The two manuscripts were not authored by Rohault; see JACQUES ROHAULT, "Conférences sur la physique, faites en 1660-1661, par Jacques Rohault, et recueillies par un de ses auditeurs qui, dit-il, y a ajouté du sien", Paris, Manuscript in the archives of the Bibliothèque Sainte-Geneviève, 1660, MS 2225; JACQUES ROHAULT, *Physique nouvelle (1667)*, Paris-Milan, Séha-Archè, 2009.
11 It is not the place in this paper to explore the context in depth. For the topic under discussion, see for example HARCOURT BROWN, *Scientific Organizations in Seventeenth Century France (1620-1680)*, Baltimore: The Williams and Wilkins Company, 1934; ROGER HAHN, *The Anatomy of a Scientific Institution: The Paris Academy of Sciences, 1666-1803*, Berkeley, University of California Press, 1971; TREVOR MCCLAUGHLIN, "Sur les rapports entre la Compagnie de Thévenot et l'Académie royale des Sciences", *Revue d'histoire des sciences*, 28.3 (1975), p. 235-242; LAURENCE W. B. BROCKLISS, *French Higher Education in the Seventeenth and Eighteenth Centuries: A Cultural History*, Oxford and New York, Clarendon Press-Oxford University Press, 1987; ROUX, "Was There a Cartesian

sponsored academies and the appearance of the first scientific journal were the effects of such vibrant community.[12] Rohault joined the Parisian intellectual life in the 1640s. He received a degree in mathematics, and early notarial documents refer to him as a 'mathematics professor' living in Paris.[13] He was not teaching at the university, so he must have offered lessons in private. Unfortunately, Rohault's activities in the 1640s and most of the 1650s are difficult to assess. In any case, by the end of the 1650s, he was already giving public lectures at his own house and in other Parisian assemblies. Most of the contemporary reports describe the experimental component of his conferences.[14] He was not the only one to do so, as a tradition of public lectures at the *Jardin des Plantes* was well established. Lectures in medicine and chymistry were usually accompanied by experiments and practical demonstrations.[15] As documented below, Rohault must have been watching dissections and vivisections. But what was his interest in the study of medicine? And what was the intended readership of his *Traité*?

Before attempting an answer to these questions, let us recapitulate the sources in chronological order. In 1657, Le Bret refers to Rohault as the first of Cyrano's friends to detect his illness, which might suggest some interest (or even training) in medicine. A few years later, in 1664, Rohault delivers a lecture on fevers in the conferences hosted by Montmor. The lecture is printed together with Descartes' *Traité de la Lumiere*, the first part of *Le Monde*. Two manuscript sources — with dates ranging from 1660 to 1669, but not authored by Rohault — contain no trace of medicine. It is only in 1671, when Rohault published his *Traité de physique*, that his views on medicine were presented

---

Experimentalism"; ANITA GUERRINI, *The Courtiers' Anatomists. Animals and Humans in Louis XIV's Paris*, Chicago, The University of Chicago Press, 2015; PETER SAHLINS, *1668: The Year of the Animal in France*, New York, Zone Books, 2017.

12   See HAHN, *The Anatomy of a Scientific Institution*; MIHNEA DOBRE, "The Scientific Journals of the Seventeenth-Century: Cartesianism in *Journal des Sçavans* and *Philosophical Transactions*, 1665-1670", in *Branching off: The Early Moderns in Quest of the Unity of Knowledge*, ed. by Vlad Alexandrescu, Bucharest, Zeta Books, 2009, p. 333-358.
13   Details about Rohault's early life are based on CLAIR, *Jacques Rohault*.
14   See for example CHRISTIAAN HUYGENS, *Oeuvres Complètes. Tome XXII. Supplément à La Correspondance. Varia. Biographie. Catalogue de Vente*, Oeuvres Complètes, XXII, La Haye, Martinus Nijhof, 1950, p. XXII; HENRY OLDENBURG, *The Correspondence of Henry Oldenburg*, 13 vols, Madison London, University of Wisconsin Press Mansel, Taylor & Francis, 1965. These reports are discussed in McCLAUGHLIN, "Rohault and the Natural Sciences"; TREVOR MCCLAUGHLIN, "Descartes, Experiments, and a First Generation Cartesian, Jacques Rohault", in *Descartes' Natural Philosophy*, ed. by Stephen Gaukroger, John Schuster, and John Sutton, New York-London, Routledge, 2000, p. 330-346; ROUX, "Was There a Cartesian Experimentalism"; DOBRE, "Rohault's Cartesian Physics".
15   For the experimental tradition developed at the *Jardin des Plantes / Le Jardin du Roi*, see JOSEPH SCHILLER, "Les laboratoires d'anatomie et de botanique à l'Académie des Sciences au XVIIe siècle", *Revue d'histoire des sciences et de leurs applications*, 17.2 (1964), p. 97-114; BRUCE MORAN, "A Survey of Chemical Medicine in the seventeenth century: Spanning Court, Classroom, and Cultures", *Pharmacy in History*, 38/3 (1996), p. 121-133; ANTONIO CLERICUZIO, "Teaching Chemistry and Chemical Textbooks in France. From Beguin to Lemery", *Science & Education*, 15/2-4 (2006), p. 335-355; ANTONIO CLERICUZIO, "'Sooty Empiricks' and Natural Philosophers: The Status of Chemistry in the Seventeenth Century", *Science in Context*, 23/3 (2010), p. 329-350. For an overview of medicine in this period, see HAROLD J. COOK, "Medicine", in *The Cambridge History of Science. III. Early Modern Science*, ed. by Katharine Park and Lorraine Daston, Cambridge, Cambridge University Press, 2006, p. 407-434.

to the public. There are several possible reasons to explain this development. For example, the early episode related to Cyrano's illness might have very well triggered a life-long interest in medical topics. However, there is no evidence available to speculate on this subject. Alternatively, Rohault might have been trying to offer a wide-raging textbook, and he decided to complement the manuscript on natural philosophy with a short 'treatise' on medicine. Or he was — for various reasons — attracted by the contemporary debates and developments in medicine, in general, and anatomy, in particular. Regardless of the possible reasons involved, the publication of his discourse on fevers is, indeed, very peculiar and this deserves our attention.

Just like in 1657, at the beginning of 1664, Rohault lacked any publication. Despite this, in a letter of 1 March 1664, Dom Robert Desgabets confessed to Claude Clerselier that while he was reading Descartes' *Le Monde*, he recognised 'l'esprit' of Cordemoy and Rohault in the two anonymous discourses.[16] Desgabets correctly identifies the two authors, so he must have been familiar with their public lectures. Previously, in Clerselier's preface to the second volume of Descartes' correspondence (1659), Rohault was praised for his Wednesday conferences.[17] His experimental skills were admired by Florin Périer in the preface to Pascal's *Traitez de l'équilibre des liqueurs, et de la pesenteur de la masse de l'air*, published at the end of the 1663.[18] This brief overview of Rohault's early activities is only meant to establish that he was a mathematics professor in Paris and his initial fame was connected to the pneumatic experiments in Pascal's tradition.[19] He performed most of the classic experiments with pumps, syringes, water vessels, and he designed his own instruments (i.e., the *chambre de Rohault*). He was not only engaged in a variety of experiments, but he routinely performed them in front of an audience.[20] These were meant either to entertain or to educate the public.[21] The

---

16 See SIEGRID AGOSTINI, "Cordemoy: Is He a Cartesian Outsider? Desgabets's Interpretation of Cordemoy's Atomism", *Society and Politics*, 12/1 (2018), p. 101-126, esp. p. 103.
17 The reference follows the standard notation to indicate the French and English editions, respectively: RENÉ DESCARTES, *Œuvres de Descartes*, eds Charles Adam and Paul Tannery, 11 vols, Paris, Vrin, 1974-1986; RENÉ DESCARTES, *The Philosophical Writings*, trans. by John Cottingham and others, 3 vols, Cambridge, Cambridge University Press, 1984-1991. Hereafter AT and CSM respectively: AT V 630: "l'Assemblée qui se tient tous les Mercredis chez Monsieur Rohault, tres-Sçavant Mathématicien, & fort experimente dans les Mechaniques, & celuy de ma connoissance qui est le plus versé dans cette Philosophie [new philosophy]"; RENÉ DESCARTES, *Lettres de M. Descartes*, 3 vols, Paris, Charles Angot, 1659, vol. 2.
18 Pages of the preface are not numbered. Rohault's name is spelled "Rho"; see BLAISE PASCAL, *Traitez de l'équilibre des liqueurs, et de la pesenteur de la masse de l'air*, Paris, Guillaume Desprez, 1663.
19 A similar point was made in PAUL MOUY, *Le développement de la physique cartésienne: 1646-1712*, Paris, Vrin, 1934.
20 On Rohault's conferences and his experimental approach, see McCLAUGHLIN, "Was There an Empirical Movement"; McCLAUGHLIN, "Descartes, Experiments"; ROUX, "Was There a Cartesian Experimentalism"; DOBRE, "Rohault's Cartesian Physics"; MIHNEA DOBRE, "Cartesianism and Experimental Philosophy", in *Encyclopedia of Early Modern Philosophy and the Sciences*, p. 1-10 <https://doi.org/10.1007/978-973-319-20791-9_52-51>.
21 See for example the experiment with magnets performed on 3 July 1667 in front of a small audience — D'Alibert, Clerselier, and Father Blanchard of St Génevéve — as documented in ADRIEN BAILLET, *La Vie de Monsieur Descartes*, 2 vols, Paris, Daniel Horthemels, 1691, vol. 2,

available reports about his conferences reveal a rather steady interest in some standard experiments, from the early 1660s up to the publication of the *Traité*.

The success of Rohault's approach was extended even beyond his lifetime, with a Latin translation of his treatise, which was reprinted numerous times across Europe. The posthumous use of Rohault's treatise as a textbook in universities was facilitated not only by the Latin versions of the text, but also by commentaries made by Antoine Le Grand and Samuel Clarke.[22] The latter's annotations are particularly relevant for the historians of philosophy and science. However, for the topic of the current chapter, I should only remark the absence of notes in the fourth part of the treatise. The abundance of (changing) annotations in the first part of the treatise has attracted most of the scholarly attention, and consequently obscured the last part of Rohault's *Traité*, which is yet another reason to explore his views on medicine and the anatomy of the body.

3. Medicine in Rohault's *Traité*

But what is discussed in Rohault's section 'Of the Animated or Living Body', the fourth part of the *Traité de physique*?[23] As the title suggests, the central issue is the study of the animated body. Rohault explains from the very beginning that such a task would be too broad due to the 'infinite Number of Species' and announces he will limit his discourse only to the human body.[24] Nevertheless, the same should hold true for

---

p. 442. On the public gathered for Rohault's conferences, see also ROUX, "Was There a Cartesian Experimentalism", p. 74.

22 For the reception of Rohault's physics, see GEORGE SARTON, "Second Preface to Volume 38: The Study of Early Scientific Textbooks", *Isis*, 38.3-4 (1948), 137-148; MICHAEL HOSKIN, "'Mining All Within': Clarke's Notes to Rohault's *Traité de Physique*", *The Thomist*, 24 (1961), 353-363; GEERT VANPAEMEL, "Rohault's *Traité de Physique* and the Teaching of the Cartesian Physics", *Janus: Revue Internationale de l'Histoire des Sciences, de La Médecine et La Technique*, 71 (1984), 31-40; VOLKMAR SCHÜLLER, "Samuel Clarke's Annotations in Jacques Rohault's *Traité de Physique*, and How They Contributed to Popularising Newton's Physics", in *Between Leibniz, Newton, and Kant: Philosophy and Science in the 18th Century*, ed. by Wolfgang Lefèvre, Dordrecht, Springer, 2001, p. 95-110; GEERT VANPAEMEL, "The Louvain Printers and the Establishment of the Cartesian Curriculum", *Studium: Tijdschrift Voor Wetenschaps- En Universiteits-Geschiedenis | Revue d'Histoire des Sciences et des Universités*, 4.4 (2011), 241-254; MIHNEA DOBRE, "Mixing Cartesianism and Newtonianism: The Reception of Cartesian Physics in England", in *Scientific Cosmopolitanism and Local Cultures: Religions, Ideologies, Societies, Proceedings of 5th International Conference of the European Society for the History of Science*, ed. by Gianna Katsiampoura, Athens, National Hellenic Research Foundation/Institute of Historical Research, 2014, p. 126-131.

23 In what follows, I refer to the *Traité de physique* by indicating the part of the book (PI to PIV), followed by the chapter number, and then the number of the article (e.g., PIV.1.1. refers to Article 1, Chapter 1 of the fourth part of the book). The English quotations are from the early modern translation made by John Clarke, Samuel's brother. See JACQUES ROHAULT, *System of Natural Philosophy, Illustrated with Dr Samuel Clarke's Notes, Taken Mostly Out of Sir Isaac Newton's Philosophy*, 2 vols, New York-London, Garland Publishing, 1987; JACQUES ROHAULT, *Traité de physique*, Paris, Comite des Travaux Historiques et Scientifiques, 2014.

24 PIV.1.1. in ROHAULT, *System of Natural Philosophy*, vol. 2, p. 248.

'the greatest Part of *Beasts*'.²⁵ It follows that Rohault is interested in the structure and properties of the body. Just like in the case of other natural philosophical problems, Rohault argues that knowledge on this topic comes from both senses and reason.²⁶ This claim is indicative of the method proposed by Rohault; one should begin from the senses: 'for it is certain, that *that which falls under the Notice of our Senses, is a Sort of Rule or Foundation for our Judgement in what does not fall under the Notice of our Senses*'.²⁷ His methodological claim is further detailed in Article 3, where he makes a distinction between 'external' and 'internal' 'Parts' ('choses' in French) of the body.²⁸ The external ones are easily known, because they are common and visible (e.g., arms, the head etc.). Knowledge of the internal parts is not so easy, because it depends on 'some foregoing Preparation; such as those which are discovered by the Dissection of a dead Body'.²⁹ In the fourth section of the *Traité*, Rohault will mention dissection frequently, which is not surprising given the prominence of this method in the early modern period.³⁰ However, the heavy emphasis on observation and practice is worth stressing out, as they are not usually associated with Cartesianism.³¹

A constant opponent in Rohault's *Traité* is the scholastic tradition; but here he warns the reader about those who 'vitiate and corrupt the Judgement of a great many who make a Science of *Words* rather than of *Things*'.³² In order to avoid jargon, one should direct the attention to the study of things (i.e., parts of the body), as they appear to the senses and not as they are presented in one theory or another.³³ A curious choice of terms appears in the title of Article 5, which is about the usefulness of 'this Treatise'.³⁴ Is he referring to the entire *Traité* — so, the two volumes, which include

---

25 ROHAULT, *System of Natural Philosophy*, vol. 2, p. 249.
26 See PIV.1.2. in ROHAULT, *System of Natural Philosophy*.
27 ROHAULT, *System of Natural Philosophy*, vol. 2, p. 249.
28 For the French text, see ROHAULT, *Traité de physique*, vol. 2, p. 314.
29 ROHAULT, *System of Natural Philosophy*, vol. 2, p. 249.
30 Even Descartes, in the *Discourse*, had encouraged the reader to observe a dissection of the heart: "so there may be less difficulty in understanding what I shall say, I should like anyone unversed in anatomy to make the trouble, before reading this, to have the heart of some large animal with lungs dissected before him (for such a heart is in all respects sufficiently like that of a man)" (DESCARTES, *Discours de la Méthode*, IV, AT VI 47; CSM I 134). For Descartes' views on medicine, see DENNIS DES CHENE, *Physiologia. Natural Philosophy in Late Aristotelian and Cartesian Thought*, Ithaca-London, Cornell University Press, 1996; DENNIS DES CHENE, *Sprits and Clocks. Machine and Organism in Descartes*, Ithaca-London, Cornell University Press, 2000; ANNIE BITBOL-HESPÉRIES, "Cartesian Physiology", in *Descartes' Natural Philosophy*, ed. by Stephen Gaukroger, John Andrew Schuster, and John Sutton, London-New York, Routledge, 2000, p. 349-382; VINCENT AUCANTE, *La philosophie médicale de Descartes*, Paris, Presses Universitaires de France, 2006; DELPHINE ANTOINE-MAHUT and STEPHEN GAUKROGER, eds, *Descartes' Treatise on Man and Its Reception*, Dordrecht, Springer, 2016. The sources are in the *Discourse* (Part 5), the *Passions* (Part I, art. 7-16), and *L'Homme*.
31 For some recent scholarship on Cartesianism, which broadens the perspective by taking a fresh examination of the relation between metaphysics and physics, see MIHNEA DOBRE and TAMMY NYDEN, "Introduction", in *Cartesian Empiricisms*, p. 1-21; DELPHINE ANTOINE-MAHUT and SOPHIE ROUX, eds, *Physics and Metaphysics in Descartes and in His Reception*, London, Routledge, 2018.
32 ROHAULT, *System of Natural Philosophy*, vol. 2, p. 249.
33 See PIV.1.4. in ROHAULT, *System of Natural Philosophy*.
34 ROHAULT, *System of Natural Philosophy*, vol. 2, p. 250.

all the four sections presented above — or to the last part, on the living bodies? The term will repeat several times, sometimes signifying the entire book, while, in other cases, Rohault seems to refer to the section on living bodies.[35]

This might be due to a later development of the topic, conceived at first as a separate treatise and only later joined to the other sections on which he lectured for more than a decade. In any case, the methodological goal presented in the first chapter is worth stressing: one should pay closer attention to the senses and to all observations made during dissections. Article 5 elaborates further on the intended readership:

> the Description which I shall give of some of them [the internal parts], is not so much to inform those who have never seen them; as to bring them again into the Minds of those who have before observed them in a dead Body, or at least, have considered them in the Bodies of some Animals, whose internal Parts are like those of a Man.[36]

It follows that Rohault is addressing a narrow audience, readers already familiar with dissections (especially on human bodies). From this perspective, Rohault's text seems to be aimed at slightly more advanced readers. However, in the 26 chapters composing Rohault's section on the 'Animated or Living Body', the reader is repeatedly informed that the topic is only partially addressed.[37] Yet, Rohault carefully introduces the reader to the subject matter, and in Chapter 2, he provides 'A General Description of the larger Parts contained in an humane Body'.[38]

The text builds as a brief anatomical treatise, which introduces the physiological section (from Chapter 12 onwards). In this context, each article in Chapter 2 discusses one part of the human body: the brain, the skull, the trunk of the body (the belly, the lungs, the heart) and the diaphragm, the liver, the gall-bag, the spleen etc. A biographical note inserted in Chapter 1, Article 6, indicates Rohault's familiarity with medical observations:

> about twenty Years ago, I saw a dead Body, in which these Parts had a quite contrary Situation; the Liver was on the left Side, and the Spleen on the right; which is so rare a Thing, that it has never been observed before.[39]

Unfortunately, details about the case of transposition of the liver and spleen are not provided by Rohault.[40] The timeframe would suggest an observation made around

---

35 The reference to the entire book can be found in PIV.18.1. and PIV.25.2., and the suggestion that the word "treatise" refers only to the fourth part of the book is at PIV.1.6. in ROHAULT, *System of Natural Philosophy*.
36 ROHAULT, *System of Natural Philosophy*, vol. 2, p. 250.
37 See for example PIV.1.6. in ROHAULT, *System of Natural Philosophy*, vol. 2, p. 250: "But because I do not undertake to write a compleat Treatise upon this Subject, but only to consider it with some particular Views, [...] therefore I shall forbear speaking of them in this Treatise"
38 ROHAULT, *System of Natural Philosophy*, vol. 2, p. 250.
39 ROHAULT, *System of Natural Philosophy*, vol. 2, p. 251.
40 Quite interestingly, Molière includes a case of transposition of the organs in one of his plays: *Le Médecin malgré lui* (*A Doctor in Spite of Himself*). The play was staged for the first time in August 1666. See ERIKA FISCHER-LICHTE, *History of European Drama and Theatre*, London, Routledge, 2002; DAVID BRADBY and ANDREW CALDER, eds *The Cambridge Companion to Molière*, Cambridge,

1651, so a few years before any of the episodes mentioned so far in the chapter. No other clues are provided, and the case is recalled here as a mere curiosity. The chapter concludes with a defence of the methodology adopted:

> by having gained a general Knowledge of the Order and Disposition of all these Parts, we may form to our selves at first a general Idea of the whole Machine of a human Body, which is the Object of our Inquiry. I come now to those Things which require more Application, and a more exact Description.[41]

This helps us to infer something about Rohault's pedagogy. He preserves the same order as in other parts of the treatise: first, definitions and general topics, then — by moving from general to particular — the relevant cases and phenomena.[42] Rohault puts some emphasis on the curiosities, which are always a reason to defend the utility of his studies.

Anatomy is discussed in the next nine chapters. First, the anatomy of the brain (Chapter 3). Rohault uses the latest observations made by Steno, especially those of the nervous system.[43] He even adds an illustration — inspired by Steno's work — depicting the structure of muscles, and he seems to be accustomed to the practice of dissection. Since Steno performed countless dissections in front of a public, during his sojourn in Paris, it is not implausible to think that Rohault was in the audience. In any case, Rohault's constant references to dissections indicate his familiarity with this practice.

When discussing the heart (Chapter 4), Rohault refers in passing to 'a curious Anatomist, (who thought of boyling a Heart, in order to the better and more easily finding out the Disposition of its Parts) observed that the Fibres of its Flesh are disposed two different Ways'.[44] In the next chapter, Rohault praises William

---

Cambridge University Press, 2006. For the relation between Molière and Rohault, see GÉRARD MILHAUD, "Rohault et Molière", *Europe*, 50.523-524 (1972), 37-49; TREVOR MCCLAUGHLIN, "Quelques mots sur Rohault et Molière", *Europe*, 54.569 (1976), 178-183.

41 ROHAULT, *System of Natural Philosophy*, vol. 2, p. 252.
42 For an analysis of Rohault's method in the *Traité*, see DOBRE, "Rohault's Cartesian Physics".
43 See PIV.3.6. The reference is not very precise, and this can be either from the 1664 edition of Steno's anatomical works — *De Musculis et Glandulis*; see Fig. 6.1. in TROELS KARDEL, "Steno's Myology: The Right Theory at the Wrong Time", in *Steno and the Philosophers*, ed. by Raphaële Andrault and Mogens Lærke, Leiden, Brill, 2018, p. 143 — or from the *Myology* of 1667 (see Figs 6.2. and 6.3.). For more details about Steno, see DOMENICO BERTOLONI MELI, "The Collaboration between Anatomists and Mathematicians in the Mid-Seventeenth Century with a Study of Images as Experiments and Galileo's Role in Steno's *Myology*", *Early Science and Medicine*, 13.6 (2008), 665-709; RAPHAËLE ANDRAULT, "Anatomy, Mechanism and Anthropology: Nicolas Steno's Reading of *L'Homme*", in *Descartes' Treatise on Man and Its Reception*, p. 175-192; TROELS KARDEL and PAUL MAQUET, eds, *Nicolaus Steno. Biography and Original Papers of a 17th Century Scientist*, 2nd ed, Dordrecht, Springer, 2018. Steno's works that are relevant for this discussion are NICOLAUS STENO, *De Musculis et Glandulis observationum specimen*, Copenhagen, Matthiae Godicchenii, 1664; NICOLAUS STENO, *Discours de Monsieur Stenon, sur l'anatomie du cerveau a messieurs de l'Assemblée, qui se fait chez Monsieur Thevenot*, Paris, Robert de Ninville, 1669; NICOLAUS STENO, *Myologiæ Specimen: seu Musculi descriptio Geometrica*, Amsterdam, Johan Janssonium, 1669.
44 ROHAULT, *System of Natural Philosophy*, vol. 2, p. 254. The unnamed anatomist might be Steno, who recalls in a letter of 1677 to Leibniz, that in his youth, he performed such an experiment. The relevant passage is translated in KARDEL and MAQUET, *Nicolaus Steno*, p. 104. Interestingly, the experiment was meant to confirm Descartes' system ("as far as these were concerned, I considered

Harvey for the discovery of the valves of the veins.[45] His account of the lacteal and lymphatic veins is almost entirely grounded on discoveries made by Gasparo Aselli and Jean Pecquet. Pecquet's anatomical observations from the 1650s and 1660s have stirred some strong reactions from the Medical Faculty in Paris, especially from Jean Riolan.[46] Controversy aside, the manner in which Rohault presents Pecquet's work as complementing Aselli's discoveries, suggests once more his familiarity with medical practice:

> A Physician of my Acquaintance (Mr *Pecquet*) ['Un Medecin de nos amis (nommé M. Pecquet)'] has added to this Discovery another kind of *Receptacle* which is fixed to the Vertebræ a little above the Kidneys, which he has often shown me ['qu'il nous a fait voir plusieurs fois'] full of a Juice like that the lacteal Veins are filled with.[47]

At other times, Rohault adds a general reference to the received knowledge — ancients and moderns alike — 'Of the Tongue and saliva Ducts'. Despite his opening remark that he expects the reader to be familiar with dissections, his chapters on the parts of the body — including Chapters 8-11 (on lungs, liver, spleen, kidneys and the bladder) — are rather introductory. He complements the description of these parts with scattered references to empirical practices: 'We do not find any sensible Vessels in cutting the Liver' or 'I saw a Dog once whose Spleen has been taken out six Months; the Wound necessary for this Operation, having been sew'd up, healed by Degrees, and the Dog recovered his Strength again in Proportion.'[48]

If Rohault's readers were not yet convinced by the advantages of anatomical observations, the section on physiology — which starts with Chapter 12 — is meant to provide an additional argument based on the modern explanation of the circulation of the blood. He explains that in order to know the motion of the blood, one should depart from the sole use of reason and use experience instead. He elucidates this remark:

---

the system of Mr Descartes as infallible"). The fragment is also discussed in EVAN R. RAGLAND, "Mechanism, the Senses, and Reason: Franciscus Sylvius and Leiden Debates Over Anatomical Knowledge After Harvey and Descartes", in *Early Modern Medicine and Natural Philosophy*, ed. by Peter Distelzweig, Benjamin Goldberg, and Evan R. Ragland, Dordrecht, Springer, 2016, p. 173-205 (p. 199-200).

45 See especially PIV.5.10. in ROHAULT, *System of Natural Philosophy*, vol. 2, p. 257.
46 The episode is discussed in GUERRINI, *The Courtiers' Anatomists*.
47 See ROHAULT, *System of Natural Philosophy*, vol. 2, p. 258; for the French, see ROHAULT, *Traité de physique*, vol. 2, p. 329. The reference to Pecquet suggests that Rohault was somehow acquainted with him, even if this was done through his public anatomical lessons. However, the English is a bit confusing: "shown me", suggests a stronger connection than the one alluded by the French original ("nous a fait voir"). In any case, the text indicates that Rohault's observations were repeated several times, from which we can conclude that he was a constant presence in the audience. For Pecquet's works, see JEAN PECQUET, *Experimenta nova anatomica [...]. Eiusdem Dissertatio anatomica de circulatione sanguinis, et chyli motu*, Paris, Sebastianum Cramoisy et Gabrielem Cramoisy, 1651 (2nd ed. in 1654). A detailed analysis of his contribution in the context discussed in this chapter is in MELI, "The Collaboration".
48 See PIV.9.1. and PIV.10.2. in ROHAULT, *System of Natural Philosophy*, vol. 2, p. 260-261.

since we do not submit so blindly to *Authority* in such Matters as these, we find that this Opinion [of the Ancients] is only mere Imagination without any Ground, and that it ought to be utterly rejected: [...] where we find by Experience [...]. I shall content my self with endeavouring to establish another Conjecture, the Reason for which appear to me so plausible.[49]

It is experience that helps one to correct the received view, as the reader is quickly reminded ('as we find by Experience').[50] The new theory is described in the next few articles, and Rohault concludes with the praise of Harvey for making this discovery of the circulation of the blood.[51] Once established 'that the Circulation of the Blood is a necessary Consequence of the Disposition of the Vessels, which contain it', Rohault provides two additional arguments in its favour.[52] First, vivisection ('If the Breast of a live Animal be cut open'), and second, the experiment showing the motion of the blood in the veins, from the extremities to the middle.[53] Contradicting the ancients is not a goal in itself. Rohault is rather keen to present the superiority of the new explanation. He defends an account based on the material structure of the human body: organs, vessels, and blood form a mechanism, which is subject to the laws of mechanics. Once more, experience should suffice in grasping what the pulse is, but when it comes to more difficult topics, such as the 'Fabrick' of the heart, direct anatomical observation is needed.[54]

Chapter 14 is about 'What Time the Blood circulates in'. Rohault offers a calculation based on his own pulse — the result is that 'the whole Blood circulates three times in an Hour' — but this is provided only as an example, because the result would depend on each person's pulse.[55]

With the theory of the circulation of the blood in place, Rohault moves to discuss some of the main effects derived from it. He explains natural heat (Chapter 15) and nourishment and growth (Chapter 16). There is always change in the organism of the human body. When the change is due to an increase of quantity of bodily parts, it is called growth and it takes place by nutrition. Explanations in terms of the occult faculties or properties of the body are contrary to reason.[56] Instead, he offers an explanation in terms of the motion and structure of matter:

> And thus *Nutrition* is made, when that which wastes at one Extremity of the Fibres of the Flesh, is repaired by an equal Quantity of Matter joining or uniting itself to

---

49 See P.IV.12.3. in ROHAULT, *System of Natural Philosophy*, vol. 2, p. 263.
50 See P.IV.12.5. in ROHAULT, *System of Natural Philosophy*, vol. 2, p. 263.
51 See P.IV.12.8. in ROHAULT, *System of Natural Philosophy*, vol. 2, p. 264.
52 See P.IV.12.9. in ROHAULT, *System of Natural Philosophy*, vol. 2, p. 264-265.
53 See P.IV.12.12. and P.IV.12.13. in ROHAULT, *System of Natural Philosophy*, vol. 2, p. 266.
54 He refers to the pulse in P.IV.13.1. and to vivisection as a method to examine the structure of the heart in P.IV.13.4., ROHAULT, *System of Natural Philosophy*, vol. 2, p. 267.
55 See ROHAULT, *System of Natural Philosophy*, vol. 2, p. 268.
56 Curiously, the English translation skips Article 3 of the French (but not entirely, because the title is kept — the title of Article 4 is missing, though). The omission is due to John Clarke (the article is in all Latin editions of Samuel Clarke) and it was not corrected in the subsequent English reprints (1728-1729 and 1735). See P.IV.16.3. in English, P.IV.16.4. in French, and P.IV.16.4. in English, P.IV.16.5. in French, respectively.

the other Extremity, and impelling or driving the Fibres before it; And *Growth* is performed, when more new Matter is added than is wasted away of the old.[57]

When matter is sufficiently small and swift — as the one described in Chapter 17 — it is called 'Animal Spirits'. The term designates matter imperceptible to the senses, 'which is like very fine and much agitated Air'.[58] The analogies with liquids and air are meant to express not only the materiality of the smallest parts of the body, but also to assure the reader that similar rules govern the changes in both visible and invisible interactions of matter. The mechanism proposed here relies on the motion of all particles (the grosser part of blood, but especially the swift motion of animal spirits), which extends throughout the entire body: from the brain into the smallest muscles.[59] Thus, mechanism of the body is regulated by the motion of animal spirits, just like the motion of all bodies in the world can be reduced to the interaction between the smallest particles of matter.[60] A direct consequence derived from this approach is the transfer of the causal explanation from the visible parts to the invisible ones. Animal spirits have sufficient explanatory power, because they allow new hypotheses to be established, as in Chapter 19, 'Of Walking and Sleeping', Article 2 ('What being awake consists in').[61] Rohault's conjecture is coherent with the Cartesian theory of matter, in the sense that one should only imagine possible configurations of matter as causes for perceptible effects. In this context, the matter will be described in terms of nerves, muscles, and animal spirits travelling swiftly between the brain and the extremities of the human body. The explanation extends not only to sleeping and walking, as in the title of the chapter, but also to dreams. Animal spirits are useful, once more, to account for change, and depending on how agitated or how many they are in the parts of one's brain, they will produce different types of dreams.

A remark is in place: so far in his discourse on living bodies, Rohault praised the advantages of direct empirical observation of the parts of the human body, and the need to frame theoretical explanations on sense experience. In some cases, where observation proves impossible — either due to the limitations of the instruments (microscopes) or due to the ontological status of the explanans — such as in the case of the 'animal spirits', the use of hypotheses is the only way to assess the visible phenomena.

Of course, experiment and observation will continue to play an important part in the process. This is recognisable in Chapter 20, 'Of the Concoction of Meat', where Rohault describes an experiment performed 'oftentimes', and details some of the trials of the modern chymists.[62] From the pedagogical point of view, Rohault's sole goal in these chapters seems to be to offer an alternative to the explanation of the ancients.[63] In Chapter 21, 'Of the Motion of the Chyle', this is made abundantly

---

57 ROHAULT, *System of Natural Philosophy*, vol. 2, p. 271.
58 ROHAULT, *System of Natural Philosophy*, vol. 2, p. 271; ROHAULT, *Traité de physique*, vol. 2, p. 349.
59 PIV.17.5. in ROHAULT, *System of Natural Philosophy*, vol. 2, p. 272-273.
60 No atoms can exist, as matter can always be divided.
61 See ROHAULT, *System of Natural Philosophy*, vol. 2, p. 275-276.
62 See PIV.20.4-5. in ROHAULT, *System of Natural Philosophy*, vol. 2, p. 279.
63 See for example articles PIV.20.2. and PIV.21.2. in ROHAULT, *System of Natural Philosophy*.

clear by contemporary experiments — anatomical observations — performed by Pecquet and Gayant. Both are mentioned because of the methods employed to make the course of the chyle visible to the people in the audience. But observation is just the initial step in providing an explanation, and Rohault adds his hypothesis:

> Nor it is all necessary, in Order to explain how *the Chyle comes out of the Intestines*, to ascribe Power of sucking to the lacteal Veins as the Ancients did to the mesentery Veins. It is sufficient to imagine, what is agreeable to reason and Experience; that every Thing which is in the Intestines is in a continual Fermentation or Agitation, which makes all the Parts to have a Tendency to dilate themselves every Way.[64]

This is a good example for the application of Rohault's method in natural philosophy: the conjecture expresses a possible cause for an observed phenomenon. The cause must not be contradicted either by reason (i.e., theory) or by experience (i.e., observations, experiments); and it must cohere with both. Further confirmation and testing are needed, but as far as no contradiction is involved, the hypothesis can pass as accepted. This is explicitly stated in Chapter 23 ('Of the Excrements'), where Rohault explains that 'since Philosophy begun to be improved with greater Diligence than formerly, and Nature has been more exactly enquired into', new hypotheses have been made.[65] While plausibility is a necessary condition for a hypothesis, it is not sufficient, and more research is needed: 'because I have not yet met with any Experiment to confirm this Conjecture, I shall determine nothing further about it'.[66]

The final two chapters — 'Of Sickness and Health' (Chapter 25) and 'Of a Fever' (Chapter 26) — are built on his prior lecture delivered at Montmor. Health is defined as 'a particular Disposition of the Body whereby it is enabled readily to perform all the Duties belonging to it'.[67] By way of contrast, sickness is described as 'a particular Disposition of the Parts of the body, which renders them incapable of duly performing their respective Functions'.[68] It follows that a 'distemper' is caused by a malfunction of the body. But since the list of diseases is long, Rohault announces he will focus on one of the most common, yet 'surprising' for 'all Philosophers'.[69]

The disease highlighted in Rohault's textbook is fever, which in the 1664 text was defined in the following manner: 'une suite de quelque déreglement qui arrive dans le corps de l'animal'.[70] His purpose is now 'to explain all the surprizing Phænomena or *Symptoms of a Fever*. For we need only to imagine [...] it resembles green Wood'.[71] The appeal to imagination — 'en supposant seulement' in French — is coherent with his

---

64 PIV.21.9. in ROHAULT, *System of Natural Philosophy*, vol. 2, p. 282. The English uses the expression "sufficient to imagine" for the French "suffit de concevoir"; ROHAULT, *Traité de physique*, vol. 2, p. 366.
65 ROHAULT, *System of Natural Philosophy*, vol. 2, p. 285.
66 ROHAULT, *System of Natural Philosophy*, vol. 2, p. 286.
67 See PIV.25.1. in ROHAULT, *System of Natural Philosophy*, vol. 2, p. 287.
68 ROHAULT, *System of Natural Philosophy*, vol. 2, p. 287.
69 ROHAULT, *System of Natural Philosophy*, vol. 2, p. 288.
70 JACQUES ROHAULT, "Discours de la fiévre", in *Le Monde*, by René Descartes, 1664, p. 6.
71 ROHAULT, *System of Natural Philosophy*, vol. 2, p. 288.

prior methodological discussion.⁷² The use of the green wood analogy — frequently mentioned in the chapter — seems to be preserved from the early text, where it was employed to illustrate the quality of the blood.⁷³ According to Rohault's hypothesis, animal spirits are responsible for the visible effects, including different types of fevers.⁷⁴ The reader is made aware that differences between the four types of fevers are not due to occult qualities, but are the effect of mechanical interactions. The number of animal spirits in one part of the body or their speed through the arteries and veins are all that Rohault needs in order to defend his hypothesis.⁷⁵ In the early version, he expressed this in a much stronger manner: the visible is explained by the invisible, but in order to understand the relation, one needs to ground it on the law of circulation ('par la loy de la circulation').⁷⁶ Without the circulation of the blood, the entire explanation would collapse and this is true for the argument developed in the *Traité*, too.

The section on living bodies relies on the circulation of the blood, which allows Rohault to formulate his mechanistic explanation. But, as confident as he is on the soundness of his theory, Rohault takes a cautious attitude in the final article of his treatise. He states that the study of human body is a difficult topic, and one needs to 'get more Knowledge, from the Experiments which so many learned Gentlemen of the famous Academy are continually making with so good Success'.⁷⁷ Rejecting the received knowledge and praising the results of the new philosophy and science, Rohault concludes:

> That by following the Light and pursuing the Discoveries of these great Genius's and first Masters of Science we may with more Assurance speak concerning so nice and important a Subject; of which what we do already know, as little as it is, plainly show us, that whole Schools have been deceived for many Ages, in establishing their Maxims and Decrees, the very Foundation of which is false. Wherefore, when these gentlemen shall be pleased to communicate to the Publick, what they have by their Labour and Care discovered; I hope they will permit me to make Use of their Discoveries, and to look upon them as belonging to me, in the Use and Application which I expect one Day to make of them; not by censuring what they intended for Instruction, but that I may correct my self, if it does not appear to agree with the Principles which I have laid down, or else that I may be the more strongly confirmed in the Truth of them.⁷⁸

This final remark is very different from the bashing of anti-medicine people ('ces enemies de la Medecine'), which he denounced at the end of the 1664 text.⁷⁹ One

---

72   See ROHAULT, *Traité de physique*, vol. 2, p. 375-376.
73   For the 1664 text, see ROHAULT, "Discours de la fiévre", p. 14, 17, 24. For the 1671 publication, see Articles 1, 6, 15.
74   See PIV.26.14. and ROHAULT, "Discours de la fiévre", p. 22-23.
75   See PIV.26.2-14; ROHAULT, "Discours de la fiévre", p. 17-24.
76   ROHAULT, "Discours de la fiévre", p. 17.
77   ROHAULT, *System of Natural Philosophy*, vol. 2, p. 292; ROHAULT, *Traité de physique*, vol. 2, p. 381.
78   ROHAULT, *System of Natural Philosophy*, vol. 2, p. 292; ROHAULT, *Traité de physique*, vol. 2, p. 381-382.
79   ROHAULT, "Discours de la fiévre", p. 28.

question is who was Rohault's intended reader in this final remark? Was Rohault trying to find a place for himself in one of the recent Parisian academies, and for this reason, he was praising the activities of the academies? Or was he trying to secure his right to use and debate about some of the recent topics of discussion in the Royal Academy?

4. Conclusions

The detailed analysis of Rohault's fourth part of the *Traité*, 'Of the Animated or Living Bodies', offers us an image of his medical views. While Descartes' name is never mentioned in Rohault's text, the Cartesian link is beyond any doubt. The explanation is built in a similar manner: the human body functions due to the motion of particles, most of them invisible. Details about the structure of the body are learned from experience, especially from dissection. Yet, there is a gap between the minute bodily parts that can be observed either with the naked eye or through the microscope, and the never-ending divisibility of matter. The animal spirits responsible for causal action in human bodies escape observation and they can only be presented as hypotheses. Rohault is aware of the general problem of using hypotheses, as attested in the first part of the *Traité*:

> If that which we fix upon, to explain the particular Nature of any Thing, do not account clearly and plainly for every Property of that Thing, or if it be evidently contradicted by any one Experiment; then we are to look upon our Conjecture as false; but if it perfectly agrees with all the Properties of the Thing, then we may esteem it well grounded, and it may pass for very probable.[80]

Several hypotheses can explain the same effect, and they need to be confirmed by experience. One such example was mentioned above in the discussion of Chapter 23, where the explanation of the ancients was considered plausible, yet not confirmed by experience. Lacking contradiction is not sufficient, and more investigations are needed. From the methodological point of view, this was expressed in the first part of the treatise: 'in order to find out what the Nature of any Thing is, we are to search for some one Particular in it, that will account for all the Effects which Experience shows us it is capable of producing.'[81] This is the framework in which Rohault's discussion of the opposition between the ancients and the moderns should be placed. The moderns — Harvey, Steno, Pecquet, Aselli, Gayant — were fervent explorers of the anatomy of the human body. They discovered new wonderful effects, often presented in public lessons. Rohault praised Pecquet and Gayant for their methods revealed during dissections to the attendees, which turned invisible processes — such as the motion of the chyle — into visible motions. Naturally, the effects freshly observed require explanation, and if it is not to be found in traditional theories, then new hypotheses should be framed. Defending the explanatory power of the hypotheses, Rohault allows them to pass as highly probable:

---

80 PI.3.2. in ROHAULT, *System of Natural Philosophy*, vol. 1, p. 13-14.
81 See PI.3.1. in ROHAULT, *System of Natural Philosophy*, vol. 1, p. 13.

> Thus we must content our selves for the most part, to find out how Things may be; without pretending to come to a certain Knowledge and Determination of what they really are; for there may possibly be different Causes capable of producing the same Effect, which we have no Means of explaining.[82]

It follows that at least from the methodological point of view, Rohault's medicine builds upon the foundation of knowledge established in the first part of the *Traité*. What the fourth part of the book brings more to the surface is the empirical component of Rohault's philosophy. He constantly refers to the practice of dissection, and some of these references suggest his familiarity with it. But this is not surprising for Paris in the 1660s, when Pecquet, Steno, Gayant and many others presented publicly their anatomical discoveries. Unfortunately, we do not know the relation between Rohault and these figures, but the text of the *Traité* shows striking similarities with Pecquet's interest in anatomy and physico-mathematical science.[83] After all, Rohault's early fame emerged from his various trials of the Torricellian experiment and, given the prominence of this experiment in Pecquet's *Experimenta*, it would be worth exploring further the connection between the pneumatic experiments and Cartesian medicine. Such reading would also invite fresh evaluations of Rohault's 'Cartesianism', which seems to emerge from a general mechanistic framework and not from a physics grounded on metaphysics. However, unlike Pecquet, Steno, Gayant, Jean-Baptiste Denis, François Bayle and many other medically-trained thinkers of the period, Rohault was not contributing to the improvement of the medical experiments. He was taking part to (probably numerous) discussions about physiology, but he was not trying to improve the practice as he did in his early life with the pneumatic experiments. For this reason, at the end of the 1660s, what Rohault could do was simply to explain the visible effects and he did this by following the explanations of the leading anatomists of the time. Yet, as indicated several times in the text, Rohault aimed to address to a reader already familiar with the practice of dissection and the anatomy of the human body. It remains an open question what was the purpose of this treatise — including here the ambiguity of the term 'treatise', allowed by Rohault — but one should not neglect the possibility that the fourth part of the book was written in order to gain the admission in the Academy. Seeking for social advantages was one of Clerselier's constant goals, and it is not implausible to imagine Rohault playing the same game. But exploring that larger social context would take us further than the space of the current chapter.

---

82 PI.3.3. in ROHAULT, *System of Natural Philosophy*, vol. 1, p. 14.
83 See for example Pecquet's section on "Experimenta physico-mathematica de vacuo" in PECQUET, *Experimenta nova anatomica*.

ELENA RAPETTI

On Cartesian Embryology

A Debate on Monsters at the Bourdelot Academy

▼ ABSTRACT This essay aims to contribute to the discussion concerning the relationship between theories of imagination in mechanist embryology and theories of imagination in Late Aristotelian embryology, by examining a *Conversation* about a monstrous birth that took place in the late 1660s at the Bourdelot Academy. This *Conversation*, in which the participants debate the *Discours touchant les forces de l'imagination* by the Protestant physician Pierre de Galatheau, represents a little-known episode in the reception of Descartes' *L'Homme* and of La Forge's *Remarques*, confirming that embryology is the most difficult chapter of Cartesian medicine.

▼ KEYWORDS Embryology, Descartes, Imagination, Monsters, Bourdelot Academy

Recently some scholars have paid attention to the mechanistic embryology outlined by Descartes in *L'Homme* and its development in the *Remarques* of the Cartesian physician Louis de La Forge.[1] In his article, "Imagination and the Problem of Heredity in Mechanist Embryology," Justin Smith claims that "in spite of the intense effort on the part of the mechanist physiologists to eradicate Aristotelian formative virtues from their account of sexual generation, in seeking to explain heredity in terms of congenital acquisition alone, something very much like the Aristotelian notion of a formative virtue persists under a new guise."[2] According to Smith, within mechanistic embryology, imagination would fill the vacuum left by the abandonment of the

---

1 RENÉ DESCARTES, *L'Homme et un Traitté de la formation du foetus… Avec les Remarques de Louis de La Forge*, Paris, Charles Angot, 1664.
2 JUSTIN E. H. SMITH, "Imagination and the Problem of Heredity in Mechanist Embryology," in *The Problem of Animal Generation in Early Modern Philosophy*, ed. by Justin E. H. Smith, New York, Cambridge University Press, 2006, p. 81.

Elena Rapetti • Università Cattolica del Sacro Cuore, Milano, Italy. Contact: <elena.rapetti@unicatt.it>

formative faculty, performing the same functions performed by this latter, but without any notion of an immaterial force or a teleology.

Starting from Smith's conclusions, Andreas Blank points out that "the relationship between theories of imagination in mechanist embryology and theories of imagination in Late Aristotelian embryology is more complex than suggested by Smith:" on the one hand "some elements of mechanist theories of the role of imagination in animal generation were anticipated in the Late Aristotelian tradition," on the other hand "the Late Aristotelian tradition was also considerably more sophisticated than Cartesian embryology."[3]

Examining the Cartesian explanation of the maternal imagination's role in the formation of birthmarks and monstrous births, Rebecca Wilkin agrees with Smith about the difficulty of explaining the resemblance between the parents and their offspring in mechanistic terms, but she remarks that it is only with Malebranche that maternal imagination assumes the role that belonged to the formative faculty. "Neither Descartes nor La Forge turned to the imagination of the pregnant woman as a palliative to the teleological principles at work in Aristotle's accounts of generation. Nor did they reserve a positive role for the maternal imagination in the formation of the fetus."[4] Rather, maternal imagination intervenes only in cases such as that of birthmarks, which are deformations or monstrosities in miniature.

This essay aims to contribute to this discussion by examining a *Conversation* about a monstrous birth that took place at the Bourdelot Academy, which was considered — among the Parisian scientific circles of the mid-seventeenth century — a haven for Cartesians.[5] At the Bourdelot Academy one could meet the leading exponents of that party, such as René Fédé, Jacques Rohault, or Géraud de Cordemoy, not to mention Bourdelot himself, who did not hide his sympathies for Descartes. Other regulars included Adrien Auzout, Pierre Petit, Gilles Personne de Roberval, some Jesuit such as Ignace-Gaston Pardies, some physicians such as Claude Perrault, Jean-Baptiste Denis, Louis Gayant, and other promising anatomists such as Nicholas Steno and Reigner De Graaf. The discussions held in the Bourdelot cabinet were collected by its secretary, Le Gallois, and were published in two editions of *Conversations Academiques tirées de l'Academie de Monsieur l'Abbé Bourdelot*: the first in 1672 and the second, in two parts, in 1674.[6]

---

3 ANDREAS BLANK, "Material souls and imagination in Late Aristotelian embryology," *Annals of Science*, 67/2 (2010), p. 187-204, esp. p. 187 and 190.

4 REBECCA M. WILKIN, "Essaying the Mechanical Hypothesis: Descartes, La Forge and Malebranche on the Formation of Birthmarks," *Early Science and Medicine*, 13/6 (2008), p. 538-539. On this aspect, see Lynda Gaudemard in this volume.

5 On Pierre-Michon Bourdelot (1610-1685), see JEAN LEMOINE AND ANDRÉ LICHTENBERGER, *Trois familiers du Grand Condé: l'abbé Bourdelot, le P. Talon, le P. Tixier*, Paris, Champion, 1908; RENÉ-JEAN DENICHOU, *Un médecin du grand siècle: l'abbé Bourdelot*, Paris, Louis Arnette, 1928. On his *cabinet*, see RENÉ PINTARD, *Le libertinage érudit dans la première moitié du XVIIe siècle*, Paris, Boivin, 1943, and ALAN GABBEY, "The Bourdelot Academy and the Mechanical Philosophy," *Seventeenth Century French Studies*, 6 (1984), p. 92-103.

6 FRANÇOIS LE GALLOIS, *Conversations de l'académie de M. l'abbé Bourdelot*, Paris, T. Moette, 1672, re-edited in 1673 and 1675; ID., *Conversations académiques tirées de l'académie de monsieur l'abbé Bourdelot*, Paris, C. Barbin, 1674.

The *Conversation* I'm focusing on dates back to the late 1660s and represents a little-known episode in the reception of Descartes' *L'Homme*, since proponents and detractors of the new Cartesian embryology confront each other starting from some pages of Descartes' *L'Homme* and of La Forge's *Remarques*.[7] As it will be shown, this debate confirms the many difficulties involved in a mechanical explanation of the plastic role of the maternal imagination in the fetus. It is no coincidence that, after La Forge's attempt to explain the formation of birthmarks in detail, no Cartesian will take up his account. Moreover, it corroborates Rebecca Wilkin's thesis that the formation of birthmarks, and more generally of monstrosities, was considered a test to demonstrate the heuristic capacity of mechanism. Finally, it shows that the field of medicine in France at the end of the 1660s was an empire divided between those who adhere to the new mechanical embryology despite its many obscurities, and those who consider it insufficient and prefer to follow the 'old path', while trying to renew it.

1. The Background of the Conversation: Pierre de Galatheau and his Discourse on the Power of Imagination

The gathering at Bourdelot's cabinet examines a *Discours prononcé dans une tres-celebre Academie sur le sujet d'un monstre produit par une femme*. The very famous academy mentioned in the title of the *Conversation* is the one created in 1664 by Henry-François Salomon de Virelade in Bordeaux. Inspired by the newborn *Académie des sciences* in Paris, this provincial academy aimed to conduct experiments on animal anatomy and research on plants, and organized conferences on various physical subjects.[8] In this assembly, the Protestant physician Pierre de Galatheau had given a *Discours touchant les forces de l'imagination. Sur le sujet d'un fœtus humain, changé en celuy d'un singe, par la seule force de l'imagination*, published in 1669.[9] This issue had been brought to the attention of the Bourdelot Academy by Claude Perrault, who had met Galatheau

---

7 On the edition and the reception of this text, see Franco A. Meschini, *Neurofisiologia cartesiana*, Florence, L. S. Olschki, 1998; Delphine Antoine-Mahut and Stephen Gaukroger, eds, *Descartes' Treatise on Man and Its Reception*, Cham, Springer, 2016.
8 This academy, which included scientists and physicians, did not survive the death of its founder, Salomon de Virelade, member of the *Académie française* since 1644, who died in 1670. See Paul Courteault, *Une académie des sciences à Bordeaux au XVIIe siècle*, Paris, A. Picard et fils, 1913.
9 Pierre de Galatheau, *Discours prononcé dans l'Assemblée de M^r le President Salomon. Touchant les forces de l'imagination. Sur le sujet d'un fœtus humain, changé en celuy d'un singe, par la seule force de l'imagination*, Bordeaux, G. de la Court, 1669. This discourse aroused a lively controversy: a Catholic physician wrote the *Censure du discours prononcé sur le changement d'un foetus humain en singe*, S.l. n.d., to which Galatheau replied with the *Censure de la Censure*, Bordeaux, Pierre Abégou, 1670. The censor's last reply is the *Apologie du censeur du discours prononcé dans l'Académie de Bordeaux*. Besides the *Discours*, Galatheau authored two dissertations: the *Dissertation sur la digestion de l'estomach touchant l'humeur acide*, Paris, Muguet, 1675, and the *Dissertation touchant l'empire de l'homme sur les autres animaux, et sur toutes les créatures sublunaires*, Paris, Barbin, 1676, in which he criticises Guillaume Lamy for taking into account only the efficient causes in order to explain physiological processes, denying the final causes. The Epicurean physician replied in

during his voyage to Bordeaux. The Bordelais physician had given a copy of his speech to Perrault and had shown him the monkey-looking fetus.[10]

The topic of this discourse, divided into four points, is the metamorphosis of a human fetus into an ape through the power of imagination. Galatheau begins his *Discours* presenting the circumstances of this extraordinary case: a tailor's wife, three months pregnant, goes to an acrobat's show where the main attraction is a monkey. When she returns home, she tries in vain for three days to get the image of this animal out of her mind. Three months later she aborts a dead fetus. Then, Galatheau describes the aborted fetus: the skin is the only human feature. Otherwise, it has a quadrupedal posture, its arms and legs are the same length, it has no kneecap and its hands have only four fingers, no thumbs. The fetus has an outgrowth running from the shoulders down to the loins, reminiscent of the monkey's jacket.[11]

In the second point, Galatheau addresses the metaphysical issue of the soul of the fetus and he gives 'two invincible reasons' to show that it had only one soul, namely the rational one. The first reason is taken from the traditional Aristotelian doctrine, commonly accepted by the physicians at the time: the movements of the fetus in the mother's womb, before metamorphosis took place, prove the presence of the soul. Since there is no succession of souls, i.e. it is inconceivable that the soul of a human embryo was succeeded by that of an animal embryo, then the fetus possessed only the rational soul. Moreover, the imagination may alter the appearance of the fetus, but it does not affect the soul. The second reason is the fetal skin, which is identical to human skin. The skin is one of the specific differences to identify the various animal species, it is the sense organ for touch, and the basis of all the animal faculties. Since the fetal skin is human, therefore its soul will also be human.

The most interesting point is the third one. Galatheau presents five possible causes for this monstrous birth: a supernatural one, namely God and his punishment; the astral influence; the excess or the defect of seminal matter; the mixing of semen of different animal species, and imagination. Having discarded the first two 'metaphysical' causes and the next two physical ones — because the metamorphosis took place after the third month of gestation, and therefore when the fetus was already formed — Galatheau considers the last cause to be the most plausible.

This list provided by the physician is in line with the classic teratological explanations that could be found in *De Monstrorum caussis, natura, et differentiis* by Fortunio Liceti,[12] expressly quoted by Galatheau. For the first time, Liceti had classified monstrosities according to morphological criteria and he had distinguished different causes in the generation of monsters: supernatural — i.e. the divine chastisement — sensual — i.e.

---

the *Réponse aux raisons par lesquelles le sieur Galatheau prétend établir l'empire de l'homme sur tout l'univers*, Paris, Roulland, 1678. On this debate, see ALAN CHARLES KORS, *Epicureans and Atheists in France (1650-1729)*, Cambridge, Cambridge University Press, 2016, p. 132-138.

10 According to Perrault's account, Galatheau gave him his discourse on 3 October 1669 and showed him the monkey-looking fetus on the 23rd of the same month. See CLAUDE PERRAULT, *Voyage à Bordeaux* (1669), ed. by Paul Bonnefon, Paris, Librairie Renouard, 1909, p. 193 and 209.

11 GALATHEAU, *Discours*, p. 4. The insistence on the number three suggests a somewhat fictional account.

12 FORTUNIO LICETI, *De Monstrorum caussis, natura et differentiis*, Patavii, Crivellarium, 1616.

derived from the maternal imagination — physical — i.e. dependent on a defect in the development of the fetal parts. Among the physical causes, Liceti listed the narrowness of the uterus and the membranes enclosing the fetus, the abnormalities in placental function, and adhesions of the amnion to the embryo. Before Liceti, Ambroise Paré (*Des monstres et prodiges*, 1573) had argued that these monstrous generations could be caused by an excessive amount of seminal matter, by a defect in the semen, or by the narrowness of the uterus, but Liceti was the first to foresee in a systematic way the possibility that the cause of malformations could be attributed to fetal diseases.[13]

However, Galatheau attributes this extravagant production to 'the tyranny of imagination'.[14]

The role of the maternal imagination in generation had been recognized since Antiquity and then again in the Renaissance, in particular to explain the resemblance of offspring to their parents. The maternal imagination imprints a certain shape on the child at the moment of conception and could therefore also be used to account for a number of irregularities (from Hippocrates onwards, medical literature recorded cases of women who gave birth to children who were colored, or covered in hair, depending on the images they had seen), and even monstrosities.[15]

Galatheau mentions a long list of medieval and early modern philosophers and physicians who have dealt with the power of imagination: Thomas Aquinas, Thomas Feyens, Daniel Sennert, Campanella, Joan Baptista Van Helmont, Johannes Sambucus, and Jean Fernel. In his opinion, however, these authors gave a large number of examples, but they did not fully explain how this faculty can produce its extraordinary effects in such a powerful way.[16]

Having rejected the thesis of a long-distance action of the imagination — which he attributes to Avicenna, Averroes and the Platonists — as a paradox against philosophy and religion, Galatheau proposes instead a general hypothesis. Echoing Van Helmont's view that imagination works through a kind of sympathetic emanation, Galatheau links the action of the imagination to the sympathy and antipathy that exist between all beings in the universe: solid bodies emit spirits and, in this way, gold attracts mercury, the magnet attracts iron, and the contagious vapor of the plague penetrates

---

13 On this topic, see ALAN W. BATES, *Emblematic Monsters: Unnatural Conceptions and Deformed Births in Early Modern Europe*, Amsterdam-New York, Rodopi, 2005; RÉGIS BERTRAND and ANNE CAROLE, eds, *Le "monstre" humain: imaginaire et société*, Aix-en-Provence, Publications de l'Université de Provence, 2005; ANNE BITBOL-HESPÉRIÈS, "Monsters, Nature, and Generation from the Renaissance to the Early Modern Period," in *The Problem of Animal Generation in Early Modern Philosophy*, p. 47-62.
14 Galatheau, like Thomas Fienus, uses the terms *phantasie* and *imagination* as synonyms. On these notions throughout the centuries, see MARTA FATTORI and MASSIMO BIANCHI, eds, *Phantasia-Imaginatio. V Colloquio Internazionale del Lessico Intellettuale Europeo*, Rome, Edizioni dell'Ateneo, 1988.
15 There is a very extensive literature on this subject. I restrict my self to a few studies: JACQUES ROGER, *Les sciences de la vie dans la pensée française du XVIIIème siècle*, Paris, A. Colin, 1963; MASSIMO ANGELINI, "Il potere plastico dell'immaginazione nelle gestanti tra XVI e XVIII secolo: la fortuna di un'idea," *Intersezioni*, 14 (1994), p. 53-69; CLAUDIA PANCINO, "La croyance aux envies maternelles entre culture savante et culture populaire," *Ethnologie française*, 27 (1997), p. 154-162.
16 GALATHEAU, *Discours*, p. 8.

into the ventricles of the heart, corrupting its substance. As in the case of vapors that propagate disease, so in the case of the imagination, some spirit or vapor in which the image is imprinted may propagate and produce a similar image elsewhere. These spirits flow out of the seat of the imagination, namely from the anterior part of the brain, and — according to the image impressed upon them, to the manner in which they are impelled, and to the arrangement of their parts — they can determine a matter so that 'like produces like'.[17]

For Galatheau this could be the general explanation of the power of imagination, but how to explain the particular case of this monstrous birth? In this context Galatheau relates the doctrine of *Messieurs les Cartésiens*, adapting it to the case of the image of the monkey.

1.1. Descartes and La Forge on Birthmarks

Descartes had dealt with the topic of the maternal imagination's ability to form birthmarks on the fetus in several writings and he had given two slightly different accounts of it, in an attempt to overcome wonder and provide a more satisfactory explanation than the traditional ones. In *La Dioptrique*, Descartes treated this issue as an optical problem and provided a mechanical explanation: birthmarks derive from the images of objects, which are transported from the mother's retina to her pineal gland — the seat of common sense — and from there through the pregnant woman's arteries to some limb of her child, on which they are imprinted.[18] Descartes suggested in this text that the pineal gland might play an important role in this process. In a letter to Mersenne, dated 30 July 1640, he addressed the case of birthmarks resulting from the mother's craving for a fruit, for example for strawberries or cherries. Descartes assumed the existence of a connection between mother and child: "the same disposition which was in the brain of the mother and caused her craving, is also found in that of the child [...] For generally every limb of the child corresponds to every limb of the mother, as can be proved by mechanical reason."[19] In a way, the fetus mirrors the mother. So the image of the fruit desired by the pregnant mother can pass from the maternal brain, where the image is formed, to the fetal brain, and from there to the infant's skin, where this image is imprinted. Although he spoke again in the *Passions de l'âme* of a connection between the mother's movements and those of

---

17   Galatheau recalls the sixteenth-seventeenth century theme of the *vis sympathetica*, to which the power of the maternal imagination was equated. In this context, he mentions Descartes' explanation of magnet. GALATHEAU, *Discours*, p. 10. On Van Helmont, see WALTER PAGEL, *Joan Baptista Van Helmont. Reformer of science and medicine*, Cambridge, Cambridge University Press, 1982; GUIDO GIGLIONI, *Immaginazione e malattia. Saggio su Jan Baptiste Van Helmont*, Milano, Franco Angeli, 2000.

18   See DESCARTES, *La Dioptrique*, AT VI 129, 22-28; BOp I 186. On birthmarks, besides Wilkin's essay, see LYNDA GAUDEMARD, "Les 'marques d'envie': métaphysique et embryologie chez Descartes," *Early Science and Medicine*, 17 (2012), p. 309-338; RENÉ DESCARTES, *Écrits physiologiques et médicaux*, ed. by Vincent Aucante, Paris, PUF, 2000; FABRIZIO BALDASSARRI, *Il metodo al tavolo anatomico. Descartes e la medicina*, Rome, Aracne editrice, 2021, p. 203-204.

19   Descartes to Mersenne, 30 July 1640, AT III 120-121; B 1228.

the child in her womb, he did not detail either the exact nature or the functioning of this maternal/fetal sympathy.[20] In *L'Homme* Descartes repeated that the traces of the ideas "travel through the arteries towards the heart, and thus ray out in all the blood," and he suggested that "they can sometimes be determined by some of the mother's actions, and be imprinted on the members of the child who is forming in her womb."[21]

Even if Descartes thought he could clarify the way the mother's ideas, traced in her pineal gland, can reach the fetal brain thanks to the maternal and fetal bloodstream, and finally be imprinted on the child's skin, many issues remained unsolved for Descartes' successors: how exactly do this shared disposition between the pregnant woman and the fetus, and this arterial impression work?

Commenting on the passage from *L'Homme* quoted above, Louis La Forge — in one of his longest *Remarques* — admitted the obscurity of the Cartesian account of birthmarks, but he took up the challenge of shedding light on this matter, since for him the credibility of Cartesian physics depended on its ability to explain all phenomena, including this one, in a mechanical manner.[22]

La Forge argued that birthmarks result from the mother's violent desire and imagination and made three observations. First, because the mother is not aware of the effect she produces, the formation of birthmarks is an involuntary process, namely a bodily process, not pertaining to the mind, but depending on a corporeal disposition. Second, the animal spirits do not always flow out of the same pores of the brain, nor in the same way. The formation of birthmarks depends on the speed with which the spirits whizz through the pores of the pineal gland and drag the other spirits contained in the arteries along in their wake. Thus, the traces of ideas that are on the maternal gland travel through the arteries towards the heart, and from there they ray out in all the blood. La Forge maintained that the power of maternal imagination depends on the inclination the spirits have to rush towards the image formed on the pineal gland, which directs their course, and the more intense the image is, the more it attracts the spirits by altering them.

Third, following Descartes, La Forge emphasized the great communication and sympathy existing between mother and child. Using a musical metaphor, he compared them to two strings of two lutes set to the same pitch.[23] When the mother is caught up in a strong imagination or a violent passion, an opening is formed on the surface of her brain ventricles and the figure is traced on her gland. The spirits flow out of this opening on the brain, and the spirits of the other arteries follow the same path,

---

20 *Passions de l'âme*, art. 136, AT XI 429, 7-14; BO 2454. On Descartes' reappraisal of the theme of sympathy, see DESCARTES, *Écrits physiologiques et médicaux*, Appendice 4, p. 227-237.
21 *L'Homme*, AT XI 177, 14-19; CSM I 106; BOp 460-462. Descartes uses the notion of 'rayonnement' to explain the formation of images in perception. See also *Passions de l'âme*, art. 34, AT XI 354, 8-13: "The soul has its principal seat in the small gland located in the middle of the brain. From there it radiates through the rest of the body by means of the animal spirits, the nerves, and even the blood, which can take on the impressions of the spirits and carry them through the arteries to all the limbs" (CSM I 341; BO 2364).
22 LA FORGE, *Remarques*, p. 335.
23 LA FORGE, *Remarques*, p. 338.

imitating them. In this way, the idea traced on the mother's gland is communicated through the maternal bloodstream to the fetal arteries and from there to the fetal gland.

Then, La Forge explained how the idea imprinted on the infant's gland can mark one of his limbs. Since the mother and the child are two similar machines, there is a correspondence between their animal spirits and between the fibers in the fabric of their brains. Therefore, the infant's spirits follow the same course of the maternal ones but in reverse: they enter the fetal gland where the mother's spirits had come out. Accordingly, the image imprinted on the child's gland is inside out compared to the maternal one: where there was a bump in the mother's brain there is a depression in the fetal brain, while where there was a depression in the mother's brain there is now a bump.

From the child's gland, the spirits circle back to the maternal brain, where they are pulled along by the spirits rushing through the opening in her brain. By means of this pulling action the birthmark is formed in the place of the child's skin where the animal spirits end up.

La Forge claimed that "since this bump corresponds [*conforme*] to the idea that is on the gland of the infant, and that this idea corresponds to that which is on the gland of the mother, the depression that is on the skin of the infant must have some relation to the perception of the mother, and resemble the idea that is then formed on her gland and in her brain."[24]

1.2. *Galatheau's* pars destruens

In his *Discours* Galatheau examines La Forge's mechanical account of birthmarks and points out the many difficulties involved in it.

First, speaking in Aristotelian terms, he observes that the Cartesian explanation omits the final cause: what is the purpose of this transmission of images from the mother's gland to the child, given that it produces birthmarks and deformities? Galatheau raises a problem of theodicy: assuming the Cartesian perspective, God could be accused of having omitted something in the economy of his work. Even provided that animals are merely machines, one could reproach God for having done something wrong, since this transfer of images causes marks and deformities, just as one would reproach the craftsman who builds a machine producing unruly movements.

Second, the Cartesian explanation also lacks the efficient cause: "I do not believe" —Galatheau writes — "that we find it only in that inclination, which the spirits of the arteries have to follow those which come out through the holes (*trous*) of the gland (as Monsieur la Forge says)."[25]

Galatheau discusses La Forge's notion of '*inclination*', which he considers too vague and inadequate to explain the formation of birthmarks. Rather, following Descartes and La Forge in the field of optics, he assumes that the image traced on the mother's gland should ray out into the bloodstream only by means of true reflection which must take place in a straight line. But, from the anatomical point of view, the spirits which

---

24 La Forge, *Remarques*, p. 343.
25 Galatheau, *Discours*, p. 12.

came out of the mother's brain cannot keep a straight line in their long and tortuous route through the circulatory system towards the child's gland. Following the path of maternal blood towards the heart of the fetus, Galatheau emphasizes all the detours and changes it has to undertake. In order to reach the embryo's heart, the blood should pass by anastomosis from the vena cava to the venous artery and from the arterial vein to the aorta, but in the first months of gestation the embryo's heart is not yet fully formed and is not endowed with cavities to receive blood. The difficulty is no less in subsequent months because, mentioning Descartes, Galatheau observes that the blood in the heart rarefies and then condenses again, taking on a new form. The blood of the fetus is therefore different from that of the mother, besides the fact that the mother's heart and the fetus's one are not synchronized.[26] Thus, according to the principles of motion outlined by Descartes, the image transmitted from the mother's brain to the fetus should pass through three contrary determinations on its path and consequently it is impossible for it to reach its destination without being irreparably altered.[27]

The physician not only points out the intricacy of the Cartesian account, but he also highlights some anatomical errors made by La Forge. In particular, following the views of Aristotle, Galen, Fabricius ab Aquapendente and other physicians, La Forge claimed that spirits travel through the vessels of the matrix and reach the umbilical ones. On the contrary, siding with those who, like Julius Caesar Arantius, Adrianus Spigelius and William Harvey, rejected any direct communication between the placenta and the uterus, Galatheau denies that the umbilical vessels are conjoined by anastomosis to those of the uterus.[28]

Following Descartes' account in *L'Homme*, Galatheau mentions three causes for the formation of an image on the surface of the pineal gland: the external object, which produces the indentation on the fabric of the brain, the power of the soul, and the course of the spirits,[29] to which La Forge added a fourth cause: the traces of images. "But there is nothing of the sort to form the image" — remarks Galatheau.[30] In the fetal gland there is a bump, not an indentation; there is no external object; and one cannot speak of the power of the soul, not only because this process — according to the Cartesians themselves — happens involuntarily, but because it would be a very easy way to produce monsters and all sorts of deformities. Moreover, in the fetus the spirits should produce an opposite effect since they pass from the fabric of the brain

---

26 Descartes acknowledged that the mother's heartbeat does not govern the child's heartbeat, but nevertheless he thought that it is responsible for the formation of the fetus' limbs and therefore also for malformations in case of maternal disturbed imagination. See *Excerpta anatomica*, 52, in AUCANTE, p. 87.
27 GALATHEAU, *Discours*, p. 14. The physician bases his criticism on a forced interpretation of *Principles of philosophy*, II, § 44: *The opposite of motion is not some other motion but a state of rest; and the opposite of the determination of a motion in a given direction is its determination in the opposite direction* (CSM I 244; AT VIII 67; BOp 1814-1816).
28 GALATHEAU, *Discours*, p. 13. On this topic, see FOSTER DE WITT, "An Historical Study on Theories of the Placenta to 1900," *Journal of the History of Medicine and Allied Sciences*, 14/3 (1959), p. 360-374.
29 See *L'Homme*, AT XI 180, 1-6; 185, 7-9; BOp 466 and 478.
30 GALATHEAU, *Discours*, p. 15.

to the gland and not vice versa. Finally, there cannot be any traces of the images in the embryo since it is devoid of knowledge.

Lastly, Galatheau criticizes the musical analogy employed by La Forge to clarify the sympathy between mother and child: since the image traced in the child's gland is inside out compared to the maternal one, the fibers in the fabric of the maternal brain, which are like the strings of this machine, are loose, while those of the fetal brain are tense, and therefore the fabric of maternal and fetal brains cannot be considered as two machines tuned on the same note.

1.3. Galatheau's Account of the Role of Maternal Imagination on the Fetus

Having completed his critique, Galatheau sets out his own explanation, which he wants to conform to "the famous Doctors of the Ancient Philosophy," namely Aristotle, Hippocrates and Galen.[31]

Relying on Hippocrates, Galatheau states that the seed comes from all the parts of the parents's body and each of these parts imprints its own idea on it, and — agreeing with Galen — he maintains that the seed is endowed with an active agent: the formative power. This power is responsible for the organic development of the fetus in accordance with those models, by means of the spirits that are like the burins with which the painter (i.e. the formative power) engraves his painting.

Following the thesis developed by Thomas Fienus in *De viribus imaginationis*,[32] Galatheau regards the imagination as the 'director' of the formative power, which is in a relationship of dependence and subordination to the imagination. Thus, when the maternal imagination is shaken by some violent passion, the spirits abandon the formative power to follow the motions of this passion. Since the formative power can no longer find its model-ideas, it turns to imagination, which exercises its power, or rather its tyranny, on the formative faculty, by seducing it and providing it with completely different ideas from those it had before.[33] The formative power then becomes like a painter using brushes dipped in colors quite different from those it had previously used.[34]

---

31 GALATHEAU, *Discours*, p. 15.
32 On Thomas Feyens or Fienus, professor of medicine at the University of Louvain, see: LELLAND J. RATHER, "Thomas Fienus' (1567-1631) Dialectical Investigation of the Imagination as Cause and Cure of Bodily Disease," *Bulletin of the History of Medicine*, 41 (1967), p. 349-367; HIRO HIRAI, "Imagination, Maternal Desire and Embryology in Thomas Fienus," in *Professors, Physicians and Practices in the History of Medicine*, ed. by Gideon Manning and Cynthia Klestinec, Cham, Springer, 2017, p. 211-225.
33 GALATHEAU, *Discours*, p. 15. Fienus mentioned the metamorphosis of the fetus into a monkey by the power of the imagination as a case in which "phantasiae vires maxime elucescere." THOMAS FIENUS, *De viribus imaginationis*, Lovanii, In Officina Typographica Gerardi Rivii, 1608, p. 192. He stated that imagination can direct formative power through species in the way of a model (*exemplariter*), but he thought that species are communicated to the heart through the nerves, where they are imprinted in the blood, and then pass to the fetus through the maternal arteries and the umbilical artery. Ibi, p. 161.
34 A similar metaphor is found in Kircher: imagination acts like a painter, the *spiritus corporeus* is its paintbrush, the *species fantasticae* are the colors and the child's body is the canvas. See ATHANASIUS KIRCHER, *Ars magna lucis et umbrae*, Rome, Scheus, 1646, p. 806.

Echoing Plato's philosophical style, Galatheau clarifies his theory by introducing two metaphors. The formative faculty and the imagination are like two architects working successively on the construction of the king's citadel: the former lays the foundations, while the latter changes the shape of the building. And again: imagination is like the writing master who takes the hand of his pupil (the formative power), making him draw new characters from those he had already traced.

Unlike Fienus, Galatheau maintains that there is sympathy between the imagination and the formative power and therefore he borrows La Forge's musical metaphor to apply it to these two powers: "this comparison proves quite well that the fancy cannot be struck unless there is a reaction (*contre-coup*) in the formative faculty."[35]

Galatheau ends his argument by listing the four causes that come into play in this monstrous birth: the remote efficient cause — the formal one — is the imagination, which acts on the appetitive power, that drives and moves the spirits. The proximate efficient and instrumental cause are the spirits, which act on the fetus as the material cause, changing its shape according to the image of the monkey, namely to the exemplary/final cause. Here Galatheau draws partly from Fienus and partly from Daniel Sennert. For Fienus emotions do not mark the fetus *per se et effective*, but are only the instrumental cause (*causam adiuvantem*) and, especially, the *causa sine qua non*, insofar as they reinforce the fantastic species, applying them to the true efficient cause which is the formative power. As for the imagination, it can only accidentally, i.e. indirectly, be the efficient cause of changes in the fetus. In turn, Sennert considered imagination as the remote cause of modifications in the body, while spirits and humors are the proximate cause.[36]

2. At the Bourdelot Academy: the Defence of Mechanism

Although Galatheau seems to raise at some points some specious criticisms against Descartes and La Forge, he had stuck the knife in the Cartesian mechanical explanation showing its defects and, in order to solve the issue of the monstrous metamorphosis, he had chosen to remain rooted in the Aristotelian-Galenic idea of the finalism of physiological processes and in the traditional thesis of the role played by an extra-mechanical principle, the formative power, seduced and corrupted by maternal imagination.

In Paris, Perrault-Nicandre reports Galatheau-Cleon's *Discours* to the gathering and the resulting debate shows that participants side with Cartesian mechanism and their arguments closely follow those that could be found both in Descartes' writings

---

35 GALATHEAU, *Discours*, p. 21. Contrary to Galatheau, Fienus denied any sympathy between the imagination and the formative power, while he admitted it between the brain, the seat of the imagination, and the heart, the seat of the emotions: "Propter sympathiam cerebri et cordis; appetitus et potentiarum cordis, communicantur cordi, et sanguini et spiritibus imprimuntur. Eodem momento insurgens motiua cordis agitat spiritus et humores, et impellit in varia partes, maxime uterum et foetum: illi ita impulsi secum deferunt species, quas in corde hauserunt" (FIENUS, *De viribus imaginationis*, p. 162).
36 DANIEL SENNERT, *Opera*, Lugduni, Huguetan et Ravaud, 1650, III, p. 787.

and in those of Cartesians such as Rohault or Cordemoy, as well as La Forge.[37] Only the Aristotelian Pancrace clumsily tries to support Galatheau's thesis by invoking the necessity of the substantial forms.[38]

2.1. Physiology Does not Need Neither Teleology nor Metaphysics

Concerning Galatheau's first objection (the absence of the final cause), both Perrault-Nicandre and Oronte deplore Galatheau's attitude, which they describe as "too moral for a physicist" (*trop moral pour un Physicien*).[39] In natural processes — says Perrault — one must consider only matter and motion, without seeking the purposes that only God — *supréme Ouvrier* — knows. For Oronte, a physicist should know better than anyone that in the world there are portions of matter, endowed with particular figures, whose movements are determined by ineluctable rules established by God, without needing to admit substantial forms or moving intelligences that lead material beings to particular ends. This tirade against finalism — admitted in a general way (the glory of God), but unknowable to men in its concrete determination since any attempt to grasp particular goals is nothing but "imaginations de quelques Contemplatifs" — ends with the distinction between the natural world and the divine world. The latter is the realm of grace, which must be left to theologians, while the former is a machine, which moves inertially after having acquired its first movement, without its individual parts being able to know the purpose for which they are moved: "God alone knows this, and that is enough."[40] In this regard, it is significant that the gathering does not even mention the issue of the soul of the fetus, although Galatheau had devoted the first part of his *Discours* to it. Metaphysics, like theology, should be excluded from physical inquiries.

Like the world, the human body is a machine: Periandre-Bourdelot draws an analogy to answer Galatheau's objection regarding the lack of efficient cause: just as in a well-designed machine the motion of the first wheel is communicated instantly to the other wheels, up to the furthest of all, so the spirits, which are very subtle and very mobile, whizz from one end of the body to the other without losing anything of what they carry. For this reason, Galatheau's opinion that the communication of images should take place by means of a direct reflection in a straight line is very useless.

---

37 Before getting into the heart of the conversation, it should be mentioned that the identity of the attendees in Bourdelot's *Conversations* is hidden behind fictitious names (Nicandre, Cleon, Oronte, Eusebe, Ergaste, etc.), perhaps taken from Molière's comedies. Only Bourdelot's fictitious name — Periandre — is known. So it is uneasy to precisely discover which of the *savants* above mentioned hides behind each mask. For this reason, I shall limit myself to distinguish the main positions taken by the participants in this discussion, mentioning only the names of those learned men whose presence I am certain of.
38 Le Gallois, *Conversations*, 1674, p. 151. The *portrait* of Pancrace in the *Conversations* follows the stereotype of the pedantic Aristotelian: he often speaks in Latin, his style is grandiloquent, but he is the laughingstock of the assembly. More than a real person, he seems to be a fictional character, imitating the Pancrace of Molière's *Mariage forcé*.
39 Le Gallois, *Conversations*, 1674, p. 148.
40 Le Gallois, *Conversations*, 1674, p. 150.

2.2. Against Occult Faculties: Beings should not be Multiplied without Necessity[41]

As for Galatheau's appeal to the traditional formative power and its subordination to imagination in his explanation of the fetus's metamorphosis, the gathering sides with Descartes in stressing the futility of faculties.

For Bourdelot-Periandre the metaphors put forward by Galatheau are only *belles imaginations*, a rhetorical exercise rather than a sound demonstration, and Galatheau's alleged faculties are unnecessary: bodies in motion can produce different impressions, according to the nature of their movement, their figures and the disposition of the subjects they affect, and they can account for the formation of the fetus. Quoting the Cartesian example of wax, Bourdelot asserts that ideas act by themselves, imprinting in the brain some traces which move the spirits and determine them to move the muscles in a certain manner. In the same way, the embryo is a soft wax on which spirits trace the ideas received from objects as easily as the hand can imprint the image of the seal on wax.[42]

Oronte goes a step further than Bourdelot: not only are these faculties superfluous, but they are also useless terms. Actually, the words 'imaginative power' and 'formative power' refer to two impressions: the one in the mother's brain by means of the object and the one in the embryo. These impressions are only moved spirits that move other ones. So, these effects are produced only by the motion of spirits without resorting to finalistic explanations. Besides, Galatheau's account differs from the Cartesian one only in words, but not in substance: although he uses the word 'formative power', in fact the maternal image is transported to the infant by the spirits. Therefore, his criticism is based on prejudice: Descartes simply does not use the Aristotelian terms, which, however, are useless.[43]

In this context, Oronte comes out with the famous metaphor of the clock, used by Descartes in *L'Homme*.[44] In a sort of scale of different minds (*esprits*), the zero level is represented by those who have never seen a clock, those *foibles esprits* who invoke prodigies and miracles as an explanation. The more skillful minds simply

---

41   LE GALLOIS, *Conversations*, 1674, p. 169: "Il n'est pas besoin de faire avec beaucoup d'appareil ce que l'on peut faire à peu de frais, suivant la maxime de l'Echole."
42   See LE GALLOIS, *Conversations*, 1674, p. 168. In his *Rules for the Direction of the Mind*, Descartes described sensation as the imprinting of a seal on wax: "Sense-perception occurs in the same way in which wax takes on an impression from a seal. It should not be thought that I have a mere analogy in mind here: we must think of the external shape of the sentient body as being really changed by the object in exactly the same way as the shape of the surface of the wax is altered by the seal" (AT X 412; BOp 749; CSM I 40).
43   See LE GALLOIS, *Conversations*, 1674, p. 171-172. A similar invective against the *science des mots* and the *verbiage* can be found in JACQUES ROHAULT, *Traité de physique*, Paris, Chez la Veuve de Charles Savreux, 1671, T. II, p. 315.
44   The clock analogy is used by Descartes (to Regius, june 1642, AT III 566; *Passions de l'âme*, AT XI 331; *L'Homme*, AT XI 202) and by the Cartesians: LA FORGE, *Remarques*, p. 173 and p. 215-216; GÉRAUD DE CORDEMOY, *Le discernement du corps et de l'ame en six discours*, Paris, Lambert, 1666, p. 59-60; JACQUES ROHAULT, *Entretiens sur la philosophie*, Paris, Le Petit, 1671, p. 152-154.

say that the cause is unknown, without resorting to supernatural. Finally, the most gifted ones assert that the movement of the clock hand is probably caused simply by wheels hidden behind the clock face and moved by a mechanism which makes the clock hand go round in 24 hours. Galatheau behaves like someone who explains the movement of the clock hand by a mysterious 'rotating virtue' (*faculté tournante*), rather than by the movements of the wheels. Hence, Galatheau's science is nothing more than a vain science based on empty words and made to bring confusion.

2.3. Anatomical Doubts

While the participants largely agree that maternal imagination can affect the fetus through a mechanical process, the two main anatomical criticisms raised by Galatheau arouse a lively discussion first of all about the fetus's pineal gland: Oronte notes that the fetus, at that stage of its development, is not yet endowed with a pineal gland and, if it had one, it would be so small that it could not be affected by the movement of maternal spirits. For Nicandre-Perrault, on the contrary, the pineal gland is one of the first parts being developed in the fetus, whose softness makes it particularly apt to receive impressions.[45] Therefore, when the maternal spirits affect the child's pineal gland with some image, his spirits — which have the same nature as the maternal ones — transport it and mark it on the limb designated by the maternal imagination.

Admitted that spirits are the vehicle through which the maternal image is transported to the infant, the audience is divided on the way this transfer occurs. Periandre-Bourdelot claims that this communication takes place through the arteries connecting the uterus with the placenta, while Oronte — who sides with Galatheau on this point — reports having separated the placenta from the matrix in a pregnant dog without any blood coming out, which would show the opposite. Periandre replies that, despite this separation, the fetus feeds on menstrual blood and therefore, a fortiori, spirits — which are much finer than blood — can easily pass through the placenta. Nicandre-Perrault suggests that there may be perspiration between the uterus and the placenta, and between the placenta and the fetus. The debate ends with Nicandre's open question: "who knows how it happens?"[46]

2.4. On Birthmarks

In the last part of the *Conversation* Nicandre-Perrault raises the issue of birthmarks and asks the assembly how could it occur that when the mother touches a part of

---

45 La Forge had also argued that the smallness of the gland made it more manoeuvrable and therefore more susceptible to the power of imagination. See LOUIS DE LA FORGE, *Traitté de l'esprit de l'homme, de ses facultez et fonctions, et de son union avec le corps, suivant les principes de René Descartes*, Paris, Bobin et Le Gras, 1666, p. 303.
46 LE GALLOIS, *Conversations*, 1674, p. 161.

her body while her mind is affected by the idea of a fruit (a cherry or a blackberry, for example), this idea marks the corresponding part of the child's body?[47]

The most articulate answer comes from Bourdelot-Periandre, who suggests that spirits have particular features and figures that make them more suitable to one part of the body than to another. Similarly, in every part of the body there are some pores endowed with particular shapes that can receive only one kind of spirits. Hence the mother's spirits, moved by the idea of the desired object, can only reach the part of her body whose pores are proportioned to their shape. Given the connection between mother and child, the same happens in the fetus: the fetal gland, altered by the mother's idea, sends the suitable spirits for imprinting the maternal image on the part of the child's body corresponding to that touched by the mother.[48] Bourdelot's explanation relies on the fact that spirits have different shapes proportioned to different pores: the variety of spirits and pores, combined with the sympathetic mother/child relationship, would explain why touching a certain part of her body, the mother marks the corresponding part of the infant's body.

Unpersuaded by this argument, Eusebe reports a particular case in which it is impossible to simply attribute the birthmark to the shape of spirits: a pregnant woman, while seeing a rotting corpse, realized that someone has stepped on her dress and suddenly touched her back. She gave birth to a baby marked by a corpse on his back. For Eusebe, chance (*l'hazard*) or maternal will can explain this case better than the spirits moved by the idea of the corpse, since an external cause (the man stepping on the woman's dress) intervened to make the woman touch a certain part of the body rather than another.

Here, too, uncertainty reigns: both opinions are probable, or perhaps even false, and at the end of the conversation Periandre says: "Everyone is free to think what he wants."

3. Conclusion

Despite the wide consensus on the power of imagination in the formation of monsters and birthmarks, this discussion shows that the explanation given by La Forge in his *Remarques* was not entirely convincing nor satisfactory. Throughout the *Conversation*, La Forge's name appears only once. The machine and the clock metaphors, employed by Bourdelot and Oronte, seem to serve mainly a polemical purpose — to stress the need to explain these phenomena in mechanical terms without resorting to the traditional occult qualities and to extra-mechanical causes — but none of the participants can really detail the mechanism and functioning of these 'machines'. Their agreement seems to consist above all in the firm rejection of the traditional view exposed by Galatheau, which however Oronte try to reconcile with the Cartesian

---

47 This topic was discussed by Descartes in his letter to Mersenne of 30 July 1640 and, more in detail, by LA FORGE, *Remarques*, p. 342-344.
48 LE GALLOIS, *Conversations*, 1674, p. 187.

one, reducing differences to simple terminological issues. Uncertainty remains, especially in the anatomical field, and the doubts about the way in which the image traced in the mother's brain can reach the child and change its features or mark its skin are not dispelled: the *voie artérielle* traced by Descartes remains mysterious, despite all attempt to clarify it.

In this regard, it is telling that in *La mécanique des animaux* (1680) Perrault will find it easier to explain the case of monsters, such as two-headed babies, through the different development of certain embryonic parts as a result of the motion of humors agitated by imagination, than to argue that imagination, or some formative power, can form some additional limb of the fetus by carrying the blood toward a certain part of the fetus rather than another.[49] By preferring the preformist hypothesis to the epigenetic one, Perrault seems to confirm that embryology is the most difficult chapter of Cartesian medicine.

---

49 CLAUDE PERRAULT, *Œuvres diverses de physique et de mechanique*, v. I, Leiden, Van der Aa, 1721, p. 490-491. On Perrault, see ANTOINE PICON, *Claude Perrault, ou la curiosité d'un classique*, Paris, Picard, 2000²; ANITA GUERRINI, *The Courtiers' Anatomists. Animals and Humans in Louis XVI's Paris*, Chicago and London, The University of Chicago Press, 2015.

NABEEL HAMID

The Cartesian Physiology of Johann Jakob Waldschmidt*

▼ ABSTRACT This chapter examines Descartes's impact on medical faculties in the German Reformed context, focusing on the case of the Marburg physician Johann Jakob Waldschmidt (1644-1689). It first surveys the wider backdrop of Descartes-reception in German universities, and highlights its generally conciliatory character. Waldschmidt appears as a counterpoint to this tendency. The essay then situates Waldschmidt's work in the context of confessional politics at the University of Marburg, and specifically of the heightened controversy in Hesse around the teaching of Descartes in the last years of Waldschmidt's life. The second half of the essay details Waldschmidt's ambitious program for reforming medicine along Cartesian lines, in physiology, pathology, and therapy, and evaluates its merits and limits.

▼ KEYWORDS German Cartesianism, Medical Cartesianism, Iatro-mechanism, Radical Pietism

1. Descartes Among the German Physicians

The medical faculties of Central Europe were among the more fertile grounds for the reception of Descartes's natural philosophy. The corpuscular theory of matter and its attendant theory of motion offered physicians a promising new framework for the study of physiology and anatomy. By the end of the seventeenth century, Cartesian ideas had been absorbed in medical teaching and research at Duisburg, Louvain, Leiden, Bern, Marburg, Frankfurt (Oder), and Halle. This circumstance would

---

* I would like to thank Gary Hatfield and Devin Curry for comments on an earlier draft of the paper.

Nabeel Hamid • Department of Philosophy, Concordia University, Montreal, Canada. Contact: <nabeel.hamid@concordia.ca>

have pleased Descartes, whose lifelong ambition to contribute to the advancement of medicine is well attested.[1]

The German medical reception of Descartes, however, was not so much a revolution as an assimilation to a burgeoning spirit of reform. Sixteenth-century developments in medicine and allied disciplines, from Vesalius's anatomy to Paracelsian chemistry, had made steady inroads in German medical faculties by Descartes's time. Separate chairs in anatomy had become increasingly common. New subfields emerged. In 1609 Marburg appointed Johannes Hartmann (1568-1631) to a new chair of *chymiatrie* within its medical faculty. In Wittenberg, Daniel Sennert (1572-1637) attempted to reconcile explanations of manifest qualities in terms of the chemical *tria prima* (mercury, sulphur, and salt) with the Aristotelian doctrine of elements in his *De chymicorum cum Aristotelicis et Galenicis consensu ac dissensu* (1619). Sennert's student, Werner Rolfinck (1599-1673), professor at Jena from 1629, embraced William Harvey's new theory of the circulation of blood while also retaining his teacher's chemical ontology. In brief, by the mid-seventeenth century the synthesis of Aristotelian natural philosophy and Galenic medicine, as received both in the medical texts of Avicenna and Rhazes and in the humanistic turn toward the ancient sources, had been gradually eroded.

Descartes's mechanical hypothesis concerning the human body thus appeared in an intellectual climate receptive to innovation, in which it had to jostle for influence among rival theories.[2] Unsurprisingly, its impact varied in force and in content from one site to another. It was also invariably colored by theological disputes in the still-tense confessional landscape of German academia in the aftermath of the Thirty Years' War. In this milieu, Reformed institutions in the Rhineland, with their geographical proximity to the Netherlands, played a key role in the transmission of Cartesian ideas.[3] In particular, an incongruous alliance between Cartesianism and a certain strain of Dutch Calvinism, Cocceianism, led the way in habilitating Descartes in Germany.

The preeminent locus of Descartes-reception was the newly-founded university in Duisburg, and its key representative the Dutch-trained philosopher and Cocceian theologian Johann Clauberg (1622-1665).[4] Clauberg's commentaries on Descartes

---

1 *Discourse on Method*, VI, AT VI 62; Descartes to Chanut, 15 June 1646, AT IV 441; Descartes to Cavendish, October 1645, AT IV 329.
2 The idea for medical purposes of the human body as a machine, or "iatromechanism", is not original with Descartes. Earlier in the seventeenth century, the Padua professor of anatomy Santorio Santori (1561-1636) had developed an account of bodily functions as analogous to the operations of a clockwork, together with a geometrical theory of matter, and a theory of health and disease in quantitative terms. Santorio does not appear to have had much of an impact in German universities, however, even among Padua-trained physicians such as Rolfinck. See FABRIZIO BIGOTTI, *Physiology of the Soul: Mind, Body and Matter in the Galenic Tradition of the Late Renaissance* (1550-1630), Turnhout, Brepols, 2019, p. 225-268, for Santorio's contributions to anatomy and physiology.
3 See HEINZ SCHNEPPEN. *Niederländische Universitäten und deutsches Geistesleben*, Münster, Aschendorff, 1960, p. 85-92.
4 See FRANCESCO TREVISANI, *Descartes in Deutschland. Die Rezeption des Cartesianismus in den Hochschulen Nordwestdeutschlands*, trans. by Eckehart Stöve and Klaus Sczibilanski, Vienna, LIT Verlag, 2011, p. 21-38, and NABEEL HAMID, "Domesticating Descartes, Renovating Scholasticism:

played a central role in introducing subsequent generations of German academics to Cartesianism. They also set the tone for the broadly eclectic approach to the new philosophy characteristic of German Cartesianism. Despite his vigorous advocacy of Descartes, Clauberg presented his work not as a replacement for the existing curriculum, as Descartes had hoped the *Principia philosophiae* would be, but as an emendation. In logic and metaphysics, his intent was openly conciliatory. In both areas, Clauberg introduced significant adjustments to later scholastic orthodoxy by means of Cartesian resources which, in the process, led to equally significant divergences from Descartes.[5] It was perhaps in his physics that Clauberg came nearest to fulfilling Descartes's ambition of supplanting Aristotelian natural philosophy. Yet, even here, tensions remained, for example between Clauberg's acceptance of genuine secondary efficient causation and the passivity of Cartesian bodies; in his notion of impenetrability; and in his employment of a scholastic distinction between *materia prima* and *materia secunda* to interpret Cartesian *res extensa*, such that the former should be the universal passive principle that God arranges in certain ways to produce secondary matter, or individual corporeal substances.[6]

As rector and doctor of theology, Clauberg's influence in setting the early intellectual spirit of Duisburg extended beyond the arts curriculum. He saw physics as the "root and foundation" of law and medicine and, echoing Descartes, identified the deficient theoretical basis supplied by scholastic physics as a key impediment to the reform of medicine.[7] To remedy the situation, he endorsed Descartes's vision of a practical physics suited to medical physiology. Clauberg sketches the outlines of a new physiology in the third part of his *Physica*, the *Theoria corporum viventium* (1664). He begins with an embrace of Descartes's sharp distinction between mental and corporeal substances, and an account of the latter that explains the operations of bodies in terms of local motions rather than formal powers. The Cartesian theory of matter and its laws supply the basis for a representation of the organic body — plant, animal, or human — as a clockwork, whose parts are disposed to perform their functions strictly by means of corpuscular motions. The suitability of organic parts for particular operations, meanwhile, derives from the divine origins of

---

Johann Clauberg and the German Reception of Cartesianism", in *History of Universities*, 30/2 (2020), p. 57-84, for the context of Descartes's reception in Duisburg.

5 See TREVISANI, *Descartes in Deutschland*, p. 63-83, for some of Clauberg's departures from Descartes in logic and ontology. See MASSIMILIANO SAVINI, *Methodus cartesiana et ontologie*, Paris, Vrin, 2011, for a careful study of Clauberg's debts to and departures from both scholasticism and Cartesianism.

6 CLAUBERG, Disp. phys. IV. 14-17; XXII. 8-9. References to Johann Clauberg are from *Johannis Claubergii Opera Omnia Philosophica*, ed. by Johann Schalbruch, Amsterdam, J. Blaeu, 1691. Cartesian themes certainly predominate in natural philosophy disputations at Duisburg between 1656-1661, as TREVISANI, *Descartes in Deutschland*, p. 78, notes. Yet Trevisani agrees with the long-held view, introduced by JOSEF BOHATEC, *Die cartesianische Scholastik in der Philosophie und reformierten Dogmatik des 17. Jahrhunderts*, Leipzig, Deischert, 1912, of treating Clauberg as a 'scholastic Cartesian'. See FRÉDERIC DE BUZON, "La nature des corps chez Descartes et Clauberg. Physique, mathématique et ontologie", in *Chemins du cartésianisme*, ed. by Antonella del Prete and Raffaele Carbone, Paris, Classique Garnier, p. 85-108, for some of the tensions in Clauberg's physics.

7 CLAUBERG, Disp. phys. I. 11; Th. corp. viv. Praefatio.

living machines. In step with Descartes's fable in *Le monde*, Clauberg frames animal bodies as divinely-crafted automata. The difference between healthy and diseased, and ultimately living and dead, bodies is simply that in the latter but not the former the parts of the clockwork have broken down or stopped functioning altogether.[8] The whole human being, meanwhile, is defined as "a thing composed from a finite mind and an organic body", the two substances conjoined by a special, divinely instituted relation.[9]

Clauberg not only laid the theoretical foundation of mechanical physiology at Duisburg but was also instrumental in recruiting professors of medicine committed to the new program, and forcing out those who were not. In his magisterial study of Duisburg Cartesianism, Francesco Trevisani has provided a detailed account of the symbiotic development of Cartesian natural philosophy and medicine in the careers of Tobias Andreae (1633-1685) and Friedrich Gottfried Barbeck (1644-1703). Trevisani's work also makes clear that in the Duisburg school Descartes's hydraulic machine was never entirely rid of non-mechanical principles. In particular, the chemical theory of ferments as propounded by the Leiden professor Franz de la Boë, or Sylvius (1614-1672), exerted a strong influence in Duisburg, as in many other universities. Unlike Descartes's account of the production of chyle, blood, and animal spirits by means of filtration, rarefaction, and the action of "a fire without light" in the heart, Sylvius's theory of fermentation grew out of the chemical tradition of Paracelsus and van Helmont. It explained basic metabolic processes by means of opposed acids and alkalis characterized by irreducible qualitative powers. Indeed, while applauding Descartes's mechanistic physiology, Sylvius also proved to be a trenchant critic of his medical theories on both methodological and substantive grounds. Following Sylvius, many professed Cartesians freely rejected Descartes's specific mechanistic speculations concerning, for instance, respiration or glandular secretion in favor of the actions of tinctures couched in terms of qualities of chemical elements.[10] As Trevisani observes in the case of Andreae, "only the [theory of] blood circulation obeys mechanical, or better thermodynamic, criteria". The rest depends on biochemical processes operating through ferments, and a kind of "*architectus* [that is] nothing other than a a manifestation of the *anima mundi*".[11]

A still more diluted appeal to Descartes appears in the later seventeenth and early eighteenth centuries in the influential work of the Halle professor Friedrich Hoffmann (1660-1742). Hoffmann has sometimes been seen as an important proponent of Cartesian iatromechanism, especially when contrasted with his equally influential

---

8   CLAUBERG, Th. corp. viv. XXII. 507-510.
9   CLAUBERG, Th. corp. viv. XXIV. 582-594: '*Res composita ex mente finita & corpore organico*'. See TREVISANI, *Descartes in Deutschland*, p. 83-99, for an outline of Clauberg's transition from physics to medicine along Cartesian lines.
10 For some of Sylvius's criticisms of Descartes, see EVAN R. RAGLAND, "Mechanism, the Senses, and Reason: Franciscus Sylvius and Leiden Debates Over Anatomical Knowledge After Harvey and Descartes", in *Early Modern Medicine and Natural Philosophy*, ed. by Peter Distelzweig, Benjamin Goldberg, and Evan R. Ragland, Dordrecht, Springer, 2016, p. 173-205, esp. p. 191-200.
11 TREVISANI, *Descartes in Deutschland*, p. 124.

vitalist colleague, Georg Ernst Stahl (1659-1734).[12] As de Ceglia has argued, however, despite his sincere admiration for Descartes's mechanical vision, Hoffmann remained rooted in the chemical approach of his teacher at Jena, Georg Wolfgang Wedel (1645-1721), and, especially after his encounter with Robert Boyle, broke sharply with Cartesian speculation in favor of the "experimental philosophy". Hoffmann's mature physiology, de Ceglia observes, is thoroughly eclectic. He accepts both Descartes's three-element account of matter and the five-element ontology (water and earth, plus salt, sulphur, and mercury) of seventeenth-century iatrochemistry; he attributes the origin of nervous fluid to an active ether; and he identifies animal spirits with the sensitive soul, ascribing to them the power of moving themselves by choice.[13] What remains of Descartes is the mere image of the hydraulic body-machine.

An initial survey of the German medical reception of Descartes could thus leave one with the impression that Cartesian natural philosophy was largely a seductive idea for medical science, for the details of which it was deemed not truly serviceable. It was a philosopher and theologian, Clauberg, who advocated for the reform of medical theory by founding it on Cartesian physics. The *medici and physici*, however, appear never to have abandoned the anatomical and chemical traditions in which they had been trained, and only took from the new physics what would not disturb established modes of explanation. The object of this essay is to challenge this impression by directing attention to a lesser-studied exponent of German medical Cartesianism who, at least in the theoretical parts of medicine, defies the dominant pattern. At Marburg, Johann Jakob Waldschmidt made perhaps the most thorough use of Cartesian physics in medical physiology. His case is also a microcosm of the complex intersections of religious, academic, and political forces at play in the Protestant German reception of Descartes.

2. Waldschmidt and Marburg

Born in Rodheim vor der Höhe, Johann Jakob Waldschmidt (1644-1689) studied medicine in Prague and Vienna before returning to Hesse to earn his degree in Giessen. Already in the 1660s, he had absorbed the leading themes of Descartes's natural philosophy, likely from his reading of Cartesianizing medical and physical writers including Florent Schuyl (1619-1669), Jacques Rohault (1618-1672), and the Duisburg trained Theodor Craanen (1633-1688).[14] He arrived in 1674 at the University of Marburg as professor of medicine, to which he added in 1682 a chair in physics. In keeping with a common practice at the Hessian court, he also served as personal

---

12 For a detailed study of Hoffmann's iatromechanism, see INGO WILHELM MÜLLER, *Iatromechanische Theorie und ärtzliche Praxis im Vergleich zur galenistichen Medizin*, Stuttgart, Franz Steiner, 1991.
13 FRIEDRICH HOFFMANN, *Fundamenta medicinae*, Halle, Hübner, 1695, I. 3. 11-13; I. 5. 44-47; I. 6. 3. See FRANCESCO PAOLO DE CEGLIA, "Matter is Not Enough: Georg Ernst Stahl, Friedrich Hoffmann and the Issue of Animism", *HOPOS: Journal of the History of Philosophy of Science*, 11 (2021), p. 502-527.
14 FRANCESCO TREVISANI, "J. J. Waldschmidt: Medicus Cartesianus", *Nouvelles de la Republique des Lettres*, 2 (1981), p. 143-164, esp. p. 144.

physician and councilor to the Landgrave of Hesse-Kassel, alongside his friend and collaborator, Johann Doläus (1651-1707). With powerful patrons, he was able to teach and write in relative freedom. Nevertheless, toward the end of his life his enthusiasm for Cartesianism in philosophy and medicine and for Cocceianism in Reformed theology got him embroiled in controversies, from which he was extricated by his untimely death from dysentery.

Waldschmidt's brief career mirrors the turbulent history and confessional politics of the University of Marburg in the seventeenth century. Founded as a Protestant institution in 1527, the university's religious affiliation fluctuated between the Lutheran and the Reformed (Calvinist) over the next century. Around 1600, however, it had become established as a center of Reformed learning. Although technically pluralistic, inasmuch as it also housed Lutheran professors, Marburg attracted a disproportionate number of students from Calvinist communities across Central Europe.[15] Its confessional identity became official in 1605 with the conversion of the Landgrave of Hesse-Kassel, Moritz the Learned, who had inherited the territories of Hesse-Marburg the previous year. Henceforth, the university assumed an important role in the program of furthering the Reformation along Genevan lines. Lutheran professors who refused to embrace Moritz's creed left and founded in 1607 the University of Giessen under the patronage of the Lutheran Landgrave of neighboring Hesse-Darmstadt. With the intellectual resources of the university now at his disposal, Moritz undertook an ambitious program of educational reform at all levels of Hessian society.[16] In 1615, he also personally dispatched his court chaplain and, from 1619, professor of theology, Johannes Crocius (1590-1659), to Brandenburg to minister to its newly converted Elector, Johann Sigismund. In medicine, meanwhile, Moritz's fascination with alchemy and hermeticism decisively remade the faculty. In 1609, Johannes Hartmann was appointed to the first dedicated chair of medical chemistry in Europe, who, in accordance with his patron's vision, advanced a vigorously Paracelsian and anti-Galenic agenda.[17]

This *Blütezeit* ended abruptly soon after the outbreak of the Thirty Years' War. In 1624, the armies of Ludwig V, Lutheran Landgrave of Hesse-Darmstadt and an imperial ally, conquered Marburg. The Reformed professoriate of the university was disbanded and replaced by professors from Giessen. The remainder of the war years were a time of decay, culminating in the disastrous Hessian War of 1645-1648. In the post-war reconstruction, Marburg gradually acquired a more ecumenical and

---

15 HEINRICH HERMELINK and SIEGFRIED AUGUST KAEHLER, *Die Universität Marburg von 1527-1927*, Marburg, Elwert, 1927, p. 216.
16 ARND FRIEDRICH, *Die Gelehrtenschulen in Marburg, Kassel und Korbach zwischen Melanchthonianismus und Ramismus in der zweiten Hälfte des 16. Jahrhunderts*, Darmstadt und Marburg, Hessischen Historischen Kommission, 1983, p. 117-128.
17 HERMELINK and KAEHLER, *Marburg*, p. 218; For a detailed account of the 'Second Reformation' in Hesse-Kassel, see GERHARD MENK, "Die 'Zweite Reformation' in Hessen-Kassel. Landgraf Moritz und die Einführung der Verbesserungspunkte", in *Die reformierte Konfessionalisierung in Deutschland — Das Problem der 'Zweiten Reformation'*, ed. by Heinz Schilling, Gütersloh, Gerd Mohn, 1986, p. 154-183.

less radical, though still Reformed identity. A new set of statutes promulgated in 1653 exhorted faculty to avoid impassioned polemics and instead to present their views "restrainedly and reverently". While the Republic of Letters was to be granted its freedom to philosophize, it was also to be kept in check in order to prevent it from descending into the bitter conflicts of the previous decades.[18] It was in all likelihood for the sake of warding off threats to academic peace that the statutes also included a proscription on the teaching of Cartesianism. The official reasons for the ban were its method of doubt, which could lead students to atheism, and its incompatibility with Aristotle.[19]

Despite the official ban, Cartesian ideas gradually made their way to Marburg. As was the case in Duisburg, the transmission of Cartesianism here occurred as part of an unusual alliance it had forged with the Leiden theologian Johannes Cocceius's federalist (or covenantal) version of Reformed theology. As Willem van Asselt explains, the distinctive feature of Cocceius's theology is its character as Biblical exegesis as opposed to metaphysical speculation. For Cocceius, the object of theology is not so much doctrinal questions concerning the nature of the divinity but rather practical ones concerning piety and the attainment of the love of God. The means to this end is a hermeneutical approach to Scripture as an account of God's covenant with humanity in history, "an attempt to move theological theorizing from the realm of eternity to the plane of history and human experience".[20] Theologians and philosophers in the Cocceian-Cartesian network certainly claimed doctrinal affinities between the two systems, in particular their namesakes' shared belief that philosophy and theology had separate aims — the former aimed at knowledge of nature, the latter at devotion — and thus required separate foundations. There is certainly a suggestive parallel between Cocceius's emphasis on piety and Descartes's oft-repeated scepticism about the value of scholastic theology. As Descartes remarked to Franz Burman: "Why do we need to spend all this effort on theology, when we see that simple country folk have just as much chance as we have of getting to heaven?"[21] Nevertheless, the alliance is probably better explained by external factors, above all by its advocates' common enmity toward orthodox Calvinism and its alliance with scholastic Aristotelianism.[22]

---

18 HERMELINK and KAEHLER, *Marburg*, p. 285-287.
19 HERMELINK and KAEHLER, *Marburg*, p. 296.
20 WILLEM J. VAN ASSELT, *The Federal Theology of Johannes Cocceius (1603-1669)*, Leiden, Brill, 2001, p. 1-2. For Cocceius's influence on the German Reformed community in the Rhineland and its association with Cartesianism, see VAN ASSELT, *Federal Theology*, p. 73-86, and SCHNEPPEN, *Niederländische Universitäten*, p. 85-92, Cocceius expressed his views on Descartes in several texts, which van Asselt reviews. The Cocceianism of Duisburg's theologians is well-attested: e.g. TREVISANI, *Descartes in Deutschland*, p. 31. See THEO VERBEEK, *Descartes and the Dutch*, Carbondale, IL, Southern Illinois University Press, 1992, for a study of Descartes's reception, with especial reference to concerns of Reformed theology, in Dutch universities to which German Reformed academies looked for guidance.
21 Conversation with Burman, AT V 176; see also, Descartes to Mesland, AT IV 119.
22 SCHNEPPEN, *Niederländische Universitäten*, p. 89; VAN ASSELT, *Federal Theology*, p. 81-86.

The Cocceian-Cartesian network supplied Marburg's theological faculty in the early 1670s with Reinhold Pauli (1638-1682) and Samuel Andreae (1640-1699), a cousin of Tobias Andreae. Pauli earned his doctorate from Heidelberg, having previously studied under Clauberg in Duisburg as well as in Groningen, Leiden, and Utrecht. Andreae took his doctorate from Basel, having also studied in the leading Reformed universities of Heidelberg and Groningen. Once in Marburg, they directed their energies neither to upholding the prohibition on Cartesianism nor at their orthodox Calvinist opponents, but rather at a Socinian revival in their shared hometown of Danzig. Cartesian natural philosophy, meanwhile, had already made its way to Marburg by the early 1660s, and was being taught by Johannes Magirus (1615-1697), who had studied in Leiden and was once personal physician to Johann Sigismund's daughter, Maria Eleonora of Brandenburg.[23] Descartes would not fall under serious scrutiny until 1687, with the arrival of the Huguenot theologian Thomas Gautier (1638-1709) following the revocation of the Edict of Nantes. Gauthier's initial antagonist in the ensuing *Cartesianismusstreit* was his fellow Huguenot refugee, Dénis Papin (1647-1713), a mathematician and experimentalist who had collaborated with Christiaan Huygens and Robert Boyle. But the polemics quickly drew in Waldschmidt, whose position in the Hessian court further inflamed the controversy.[24]

After a cautious start, Waldschmidt had begun to teach and write with open reference to Descartes and to the by-now well-established Dutch Cartesian network. A series of disputations in the late 1670s and 1680s with Waldschmidt as *praeses* defend Cartesian theses concerning the etiology of various diseases. Chilblains (*De pernionibus*, 1687), for example, are caused by the expansion of tissue near the surface of the skin due to the stagnation of bodily fluids as a result of exposure to cold.[25] Seizures (*De stupendo affecti catalepsi*, 1678) are not, *per* the received view, caused by congelation of the animal spirits but rather by the blockage of one side of the organ of common sense, namely the pineal gland.[26] Two disputations from 1687, "*Medicus cartesianus*" and "*Chirurgus cartesianus*", lay out programmatic arguments for medical reform.

Waldschmidt's direct involvement in the Hessian controversy over Cartesianism, however, took the form of a pamphlet he authored anonymously, *Copia eines Schreibens an eine Hohe Stands-Person in Teutschland von der cartesianischen Philosophi und coccejanischen Theologi* (1687). The *Copia* was perceived as targeting the orthodox Reformed court chaplains, to whose defense rose their junior colleague Caspar Baum. The *Copia*, the response (*Gegenschall*), and a counter-response (*Nachbericht... auf der Gegenschall*) were all published anonymously but the authorship of Waldschmidt

---

23 See SABINE SCHLEGELMILCH, "The Scientific Revolution in Marburg", in *Early Modern Disputations and Dissertations in an Interdisciplinary European Context*, ed. by Meelis Friedenthal, Hanspeter Marti and Robert Seidel, Leiden, Brill, 2020, p. 288-311, esp. p. 295-296.
24 HERMELINK and KAEHLER, *Marburg*, p. 308-313.
25 Disp. VI. 7-8. I cite Waldschmidt's texts from *Opera medico-practica... omnia ad mentem Cartesii*, Frankfurt-am-Main, Friedrich Knoch, 1695, using the following abbreviations: [IMR] for the *Institutiones medicinae rationalis*; [Disp.] for the *Disputationes medicae varii argumenti*.
26 Disp. XV. 12; XV. 17-18.

and Baum was soon exposed.[27] In his polemics, Waldschmidt makes a full-throated defense of Descartes against the charges of atheism, defending his sceptical method as *"investigatio veritas"* and *"pia dubitatio"*, attacking scholastic theology, and accusing his opponents of not having read Descartes's texts. He has less to say about Cocceianism, conceding that his knowledge of its theological details is imperfect. Yet, he likens Cocceius to the figure of Paul, and affirms that Cocceians and Cartesians are "good friends" in virtue of having common enemies of truth, the orthodox Calvinism represented by Gisbert Voet and its adherence, enshrined in the Marburg statutes of 1653, to Aristotelianism. The *Copia* lays bare Waldschmidt's sympathies with an anti-clerical current in late seventeenth-century German Protestantism, in whose service he recruits Descartes and Cocceius as philosophical and theological patrons.

Waldschmidt's career reflects a common pattern of German Cartesianism's entanglement in theological controversies. From his first reception in Duisburg, Descartes became caught up in internal disputes in Germany's Protestant communities. These disputes, however, ended up serving as vital conduits for the dissemination of Descartes's philosophy, especially his physics, in the universities. Duisburg's theologians had much to do with cultivating an alliance between Descartes and one divergent form of Reformed Protestantism, that of Cocceius, which ensured the survival of Cartesianism in the face of orthodox opposition. As the century wore on, growing polarization would lead to Cartesianism becoming linked to increasingly radical movements in German Protestantism, once labeled "Separatism" and more recently "Radical Pietism".[28] Waldschmidt appears as a zealous participant in these currents, his advocacy of Cartesian physiology in his medical vocation conjoined in his mind with his convictions concerning the proper means to salvation. With this context in view, we can turn to his program of medical reform.

3. Waldschmidt's Physiology

Waldschmidt presents his system of medicine in two texts: *Fundamenta medicinae* (1685), and *Institutiones medicinae rationalis* (1688). Both are based on materials drawn from his dissertations and disputations, and are similar in content. The latter is included in his *Opera medico-practica... Omnia ad mentem Cartesii* (1695; subsequent editions in 1707, 1717, 1736), together with a large collection of case

---

27 FRIEDRICH WILHELM STRIEDER, *Grundlage zu einer hessischen Gelehrten und Schriftsteller Geschichte*, vol. 1, Göttingen, Barmeier, 1781, p. 290-294; HERMELINK and KAEHLER, *Marburg*, p. 304-313.

28 For the Separatist movement in Hesse during Waldschmidt's time, see Norbert Fehringer, "Philadelphia und Babel: der hessische Pietist Heinrich Horche und das Ideal des wahren Christentums", Doctoral thesis, University of Marburg, 1971. Horch (1652-1729) was the respondent in a disputation under Waldschmidt (*De venenis pestilentialis*, 1675). See FRANCESCO TREVISANI, "Studi sul cartesianesimo tedesco: Johann Jacob Waldschmidt", *Annali dell'Istituto storico italo-germanico in Trento*, 17 (1991), p. 187-223, for an examination of Waldschmidt's place at the intersection of Cartesianism and German Pietism. See also, HANS SCHNEIDER, "Der radikale Pietismus im 17. Jahrhundert", in *Geschichte des Pietismus* Bd. 1, ed. by Martin Brecht, Göttingen, Vandenhoeck & Ruprecht, 1993, p. 391-439.

studies, practical advisories (*monita*) to medical students, disputations, scholarly correspondence with Johann Doläus, an essay in German on the therapeutic benefits of tea and, intriguingly, inserted among his letters to Doläus, a copy of the vehemently anti-scholastic pamphlet, published anonymously by a medical doctor under the initials H. O. M. D, titled *Vernünfftige Gedancken über die aristotelische und cartesianische Philosophie*.[29]

Waldschmidt's *Institutiones* is structured in the manner of a traditional medical textbook. A chapter on the object and end of medicine is followed by separate parts on physiology, pathology, semiotics (diagnostics and prognostics), hygiene, and therapy. Medicine is conceived as the "*ars* sive *scientia*" of the complete human body. It is an art insofar as it includes the work of the surgeon and of the pharmacist; it is a science inasmuch as the causes of disease are explicated through philosophical principles. Medicine has as its object "both of contemplation and of application, the state of the living human being or the living human body".[30] Waldschmidt calls for reform in both the theoretical and practical aspects of medicine. It is in the former, however, that his innovations appear most distinct.

Surveying the history of the discipline, Waldschmidt identifies six medical sects: the "empiric" (the ancient Egyptians); the "dogmatic or rational" (Hippocrates and Galen); the "methodical" (which he associates with the Paduan physician Ercole Sassonia (1551-1607)); the "Spagyrical, chemical, hermetical, Paracelsist" in which he also includes van Helmont and Sylvius; a mixed "dogmatico-hermetical" school; and finally, the new "dogmatico-mechanical" sect of Descartes and Gassendi. Waldschmidt aligns with the last camp, emphasizing its importance for advancing medicine as a science, that is, as an inquiry into causes. Indeed, Descartes is referred henceforth simply as *Philosophus*. Accordingly, "*Oeconomia animalis*", the label for medical physiology popularized by Dutch Cartesian doctors, "is to be explained by motion and figure, and we should admit nothing that we cannot perceive clearly and distinctly through the force of mechanical principles".[31] Waldschmidt further defends a view of the human body as a clockwork or automaton against its detractors, who object that it makes it impossible to account for life and for the nourishment and growth of the body. To that end, he turns to Descartes's metaphysics of substance. For Waldschmidt, the human being should be understood as composed of two distinct substances, a *substantia cogitans* and a *substantia extensa*, each of which contributes separately to life and health. "The life and activity of the former consists in *thinking*;

---

29 To my knowledge, neither the identity of the text's author nor its precise publication date have yet been established. The Herzog August Bibliothek in Wolffenbüttel proposes a publication year around 1650. HANSPETER MARTI, "Aristoteles und Descartes", in *Reformierte Orthodoxie und Aufklärung*, ed. by Hanspeter Marti and Karin Marti-Weissenbach, Cologne, Böhlau, 2012, p. 147-164, suggests that it was published around 1700. The pamphlet's inclusion in Waldschmidt's posthumously published *Opera omnia* raises but does not settle the question of his authorship.

30 IMR I. 1. 5-7: "*Objectum* tum contemplationis tum applicationis, est statua humana vivens sive corpus humanum vivens".

31 IMR I. 1. 3: "Quod Oeconomiam animalem per motus & figuram interpretemur, nihilque admittamus, quod non clare & distincte vi principiorum mechanicorum percipere possimus".

that of the latter in *extension* modified in a certain way".[32] That is, each substance has its own conditions that conduce to life: thought in the former, and certain patterns of motion in *res extensa* that make some bodies but not others count as living. The whole human being results from the two substances being "conjoined under fixed laws by God", such that "certain corporeal motions, especially in the pineal gland of the brain, are followed by certain thoughts in the mind", and vice versa. Human life consists in the mutual commerce of the two substances, death in its cessation.[33] For Waldschmidt, it is crucial not to confuse the states attributed to each kind of substance and, from the standpoint of physiology, to regard the body strictly as a "*Machina hydraulico-pneumatica*". The practical end of medicine, or healing, can then be framed as the restoration of the fragile structure of the machine when it is damaged.[34]

Waldschmidt rests his physiology on a new theory of elements borrowed from Descartes (at *Principia philosophiae* III.52). He supposes that God divided *substantia extensa* into three kinds of corpuscles— *prima, secunda,* and *tertia*. To the first kind belong corpuscles of indefinite motion, figure, and magnitude moving at high speed, which can fill up any space whatsoever, and which compose lucid bodies. The second kind of corpuscle is of determinate figure and magnitude and composes pellucid bodies, or those that can transmit light. The third kind of corpuscle is the least apt for motion, of an angular shape, opaque, and the dominant component of terrestrial bodies. The metabolically significant phenomena of fermentation and effervescence are principally explained in terms of the arrangements of corpuscles of the third kind. Besides these three, there are no other basic divisions in matter: "the world of bodies is exhausted by *lucid, pellucid, and opaque,* or *light emitting, light transmitting, and light reflecting* bodies".[35] All other corporeal properties should be reducible to differences in the proportions and arrangement of the three kinds of corpuscle of which they are composed. Waldschmidt dismisses competing theories of matter. The four Aristotelian elements are better treated as mixed bodies resulting from Descartes's three elements. The same goes for the various chemical taxonomies in the Paracelsian tradition. Least of all should we accept van Helmont's privileging of water as the single element into which all others resolve.[36]

Waldschmidt is happy to retain certain chemical notions employed by iatrochemists, in particular the division of salts into acids and alkali. In the chemical tradition, the acid/alkali division underlies various "composite natures", including the secretions

---

32 IMR I. 1. 8: "Illius vita & esse actuosam consistit in *cogitatione*; hujus vero in *extensione* certo modo modificata".

33 IMR I. 1. 8: "Tandem cum duae haec substantiae certis sub legibus a Deo sint conjunctae, & certos motus corporis & praesertim cerebri ejusque glandulae pinealis sequi debeant certae cogitationes mentis, & vicissim certas cogitationes mentis certi motus corporis, hominis sive totius compositi vita in mutuo hoc commercio ponitur, mors vero in cessatione totali".

34 IMR I. 1. 9-10: "*Finis* Medicinae est *mederi*, & fragilis hujus machinae fabricam quantum in artis est potestae sartam tectamque servare, aut fractam & labefactatam resarcire & in integram restituere".

35 IMR I. 2. 2: "Quandoquidem totum hoc universum corporibus *lucidis, pellucidis & opacis,* sive *lucem emittentibus, lucem transmittentibus, & lucem remittentibus,* exhaustitur".

36 IMR I. 2. 3-5. Waldschmidt's characterization of van Helmont is clearly uncharitable, but we need not examine the details here.

of organs that account for metabolic processes and whose deviations from normal function are associated with disease. But Waldschmidt insists that the concepts of acid and alkali are merely descriptively useful, and that their causal roles in health and disease must be traced to the fundamental properties of matter. He does not shy away from speculation concerning the details of the latter. Acids, he supposes, are "rigid bodies, oblong in figure, resembling gladioli". Alkali, by contrast, are "rigid bodies more or less tapering in shape but more porous".[37] What grounds the strong correlations between phenomena described as effervescence or fermentation and the processes attributed to the activity of acids and alkalis, for Waldschmidt, are differences in shape, porosity, and the relative speeds of interacting corpuscles and the characteristics of the organ tissue from which they are secreted and into which they are taken up. Only under this theoretical axiom of the dogmatico-mechanical school does Waldschmidt admit operational definitions of concepts whose utility in diagnosis and treatment is well-established, such as the divisions of salts into relatively more fixed or volatile, manifest or occult, acrid or corrosive.[38]

The reductionist approach extends to the theory of bodily fluids and their roles in the functions of nutrition and growth as well as sensation and movement. Waldschmidt's physiology thus elaborates Descartes's project of mechanizing both the vegetative and the sensitive souls of the Galeno-Aristotelian tradition.[39] Chapters 3 and 4 (*De chylo et sanguine; De spiritibus*) describe the process of bodily nourishment: the mastication of food by the teeth, the effect of saliva to ease its propulsion down the gullet, its refinement into chyle once it comes into contact with acidic matter in the stomach, the concoction of chyle into blood and lymph in the liver, the still further rarefaction of blood by the heat of heart to produce spirits whose separation from the blood in the mid-brain yields the animal spirits, which then mediate sensory and motor functions. "All this work is merely mechanical", he declares.[40] The key principles underwriting these metabolic processes include, first, the differential porosities of the matter composing organs, glands, and vessels, resulting in the filtration of corpuscles of differing sizes, shapes, and speeds; and second, the action of heat, notably in the heart, that accelerates the filtration process by rarefying blood to produce what the medical tradition calls "vital spirits". Rarefaction is conceived in the manner of Descartes, not as the action of a separate ethereal substance displacing matter, but of finer, faster moving corpuscles of the same type flowing in to occupy interstitial spaces in the structure of a solid body.[41] The liquid that flows out of the pulmonary artery to the lungs and then to the rest of the body contains vital spirits, which are nothing but the subtler parts of the blood. The separation of these spirits occurs in

---

37 IMR I. 2. 7: "Describitur autem sal *acidum* quod sit corpus rigidum, figurae oblongae, gladiorum instar... Sal *alkali* autem est corpus rigidum plus minus acuminatum, sed magis porosum".
38 IMR I. 2. 8.
39 See GARY HATFIELD, "Mechanizing the Sensitive Soul," in *Matter and Form in Early Modern Science and Philosophy*, ed. by Gideon Manning, Leiden, Brill, 2012, p. 151-186.
40 IMR I. 3. 2: "Totum autem hoc negotium mere mechanicum est". Waldschmidt's description parallels Descartes's in *Traité de l'homme*, AT XI. 121-122.
41 IMR I. 3. 12-13; cf. DESCARTES, *Principia philosophiae* II, art. 6, AT VIII-1 43.

the brain, as Waldschmidt explains citing Descartes's *Les passions de l'âme*, I, article 10. When the arterial fluid hits upon the brain surface, its subtlest and fastest moving particles enter the brain cavities, and are then called animal spirits, though they are not different in nature from blood, lymph, chyle or any other material body.[42] These finest of the bodily fluids flow into tubes leading to the external sense organs, whence by means of their motions they relay information about the external world to the internal senses of memory, imagination, and the common sense.

Following Descartes, Waldschmidt casts the functions of the sensitive soul in mechanistic terms. The *sensorium commune*, which receives motions from all the external organs, is identified with the pineal gland; *phantasia* is a "certain radiation of the animal spirits... upon the pineal gland"; and memory consists in impressed brain traces, which, when flush with animal spirits, give the mind occasion to recall past thoughts.[43] The immaterial mind enters the picture at the pineal gland to interpret the patterns formed by the course of the animal spirits and to redirect them according to its appetites. Nourishment, for example, occurs because violent agitations caused by food scraps tumbling about in an otherwise empty stomach are conveyed through the nerve fibers to the pineal gland, where they give occasion to the mind to conceive the idea of hunger.[44]

Waldschmidt adopts a simple occasionalist model to account for mind-body interaction at the pineal gland. He divides the process into three stages: reception, perception, and judgment. Receptivity is attributed solely to the body, and consists in nothing other than the motion of bodily fluids arising from impingements upon the external sensory organs. These motions occasion in the mind perceptions of the state of the body, which are then followed by judgments of benefit or harm.[45] Waldschmidt shows no interest, however, in exploring the conceptual problems arising from occasionalism about mind-body interaction, or concerning causation in general in the Cartesian framework. Given his broad familiarity with contemporary Cartesian occasionalists who dealt with these issues — Géraud Cordemoy, Jacques Rohault, and Pierre-Sylvain Régis, for instance, are regularly cited in his work — we

---

42 IMR I. 4. 5.
43 IMR I. 4. 14: "*Sensorium commune* quod omnium sensuum externorum motus recipit, est *glandula pinealis*... *Phantasia* est certa spirituum animalium radiatio, sive certa illorum cursus forma, super glandulam pinealem... *Memoria* consistit in vestigiis cerebro impressis, unde si spiritus animales in eadem incidunt, eandem suscipiunt cursus formam, cujus occasione menti priores occurrunt cogitationes".
44 IMR I. 3. 1: "Cibi reliquiae, vacuo in ventriculo hinc inde oberrantes, mora & agitatione acriores factae, superius ventriculi orificium ex fibrillis nerveis contextum vellicant, ex cujus motus occasione, mediantibus nervis ad sensorium commune... delati, mens ideam *famis* concipit, atque de cibo sumendo cogitat, qui cogitationis modus *appetitus* nomine venit".
45 IMR I. 4. 8: "*Receptio* nil nisi motus est, attributum solius corporis, quia tamen in nobis praeter corpus alia quoque est substantia cogitans, occasione motuum certas habens cogitationes & percipere & judicare nunquam in corpus, sed in mentem cadunt, sensus in homine ad totum spectant compositum, eumque in finem illi dati sunt, ut horum opesciat, quae sibi sint commoda vel incommoda, utilia vel noxia". Waldschmidt's discussion corresponds to Descartes's three-stage model in *Sixth Replies*, AT VII 436-437.

may surmise that he simply deemed the metaphysical questions as not directly relevant to his audience of medical students. His approach resembles that of other Cartesian doctors such as Craanen, as well as physicists such as Rohault and Régis, who adopt occasionalism as a working hypothesis for mind-body interaction while continuing to treat bodies as real causes of effects in other bodies. Waldschmidt's energies are directed toward deploying Cartesian natural philosophy in medicine rather than examining its metaphysical foundations.[46]

Accordingly, Waldschmidt's medical etiology assumes that bodies possess powers to produce determinate effects in other bodies. Here again, his approach displays a renovation of existing medical concepts guided by the new natural philosophy. In Book II (*Pathologica*) of the *Institutiones*, he classifies the efficient causes of disease under the traditional rubric, namely the six *non naturales*; the condition of *plethora*, or an overabundance of blood; *cacochymia*, a broad class of ill-humours; poison; and the peregrinous aether. The category of *non naturales* comprises external factors known to play a role in health and disease: air, food and drink, sleep and waking, exercise and rest, the *excreta* and *retenta*, and the *pathemata*, or accidents of the soul, which roughly correspond to the modern category of emotions. Waldschmidt notes the peculiarity of the label "*non naturales*", inasmuch as none of the items in the list relate to bodies other than as natural or physical things.[47] Yet, he retains the terminology, and subsequent chapters summarize received wisdom concerning the relevance of diet, sleep, and physical activity for disease.

This outwardly standard presentation of pathology departs importantly with respect to the sixth category of the *non naturales*, the accidents or passions of the soul. Galenic doctors had placed these among the non-naturals inasmuch as they were conceptualized as occurrences external to the person, or not determined by the natural composition of the body. The *pathemata* were first imprinted on the soul and then on the body, where they gave rise to characteristic physiological effects described as, for instance, the boiling of blood, or excess production of bile.[48] By contrast, Waldschmidt adopts Descartes's definition of the *passionibus animi* (from the Latin translation of *Les passions de l'âme*, I.27) as, "those perceptions, sensations, or agitations of the soul, which are particularly referred to it, and which are produced, conserved, and strengthened by some movement of the animal spirits".[49] For Waldschmidt, Descartes's definition implies that the production of passional states involves other fluids as remote causes, before the animal spirits forming at the pineal gland occasion

---

46 In this regard, we may note his contrast with Clauberg. While Clauberg is an equally enthusiastic advocate of Cartesian physiology in medicine, his primary vocation is that of a metaphysician and theologian, and his natural philosophy culminates in a lengthy treatise on the mind-body problem, *Corporis et animae in homine conjunctio* (1664).
47 IMR II. 4. 2-3.
48 For an account of the theory of the *pathemata* in Galen, Avicenna, and their reconcilers, see NAAMA COHEN-HANEGBI, "A Moving Soul: Emotions in Late Medieval Medicine," *Osiris*, 31 (2016), p. 1-21.
49 IMR II. 10. 1: "*Perceptionem, sensationes aut commotiones animae, quae ad eam speciatim referuntur, quaeque producuntur, conservantur & corroborantur per aliquem motum spirituum animalium*". Note: Waldschmidt interpolates '*animalium*' here in quoting the Latin text of the *Passiones animae*.

sensations in the soul. For in the natural state of the body, blood, lymph, and spirits press upon one another, and it follows that, in a passional episode, the state of the whole body is implicated, and can thus be altered and disturbed, especially if the bodily changes are indulged by dwelling upon them.[50] An episode of sadness or grief (*tristitia & moerere*), for instance, is characterized by blood flowing sparingly from the heart, a slow pulse, feeble respiration, and chylification growing weak. These physiological phenomena, however, are not simply accompaniments or effects of external factors directly impacting the soul, but rather remote efficient causes of the production or maintenance of a state of sadness. Weaker blood flow and changes in digestion modify the patterns of animal spirits flowing on the surface of the pineal gland, which gives rise to or sustains melancholic sensations.[51] The internal activity of the soul, in turn, can play a role in determining the strength, duration, or cessation of the bodily syndromes involved in passional episodes. In this way, the dual sources of life and activity, mind and body, play distinct causal roles in the state of the whole human being.

The foregoing is a sketch of how Waldschmidt systematically implements the Cartesian idea of the human body as a hydraulic machine in his physiology and pathology. A key feature of his program is the dissolution of the relatively clear boundaries between the core physiological and pathological categories of the Galenic and the more recent chemical traditions: elements, complexions, humours, and the chemical principles of van Helmont or Sylvius. The hydraulic machine and all its parts are composed of a uniform kind of matter in terms of which the explanatory roles previously attributed to humours and complexions, acids and alkalis, must be recast as at best operationally useful notions. He conceives physiological facts as fully reducible to the relative speeds of fluid particles, their densities and porosities, and their differential uptake in various organs. The body-machine is stripped of faculties and powers as well as chemical ferments, and joined only to an immaterial soul that governs it in light of its ends, among which the preservation of health and the prolongation of life are the main concern of the *medicus*. In brief, Waldschmidt the physicist and physiologist seeks a broad overhaul of medical theory along Cartesian lines. We may further ask: what lessons does Waldschmidt the medical practitioner learn from Descartes?

4. *Medicus Cartesianus*?

As was common in many universities, Waldschmidt taught both medicine and natural philosophy. He viewed physics as necessary preparation for the work of a medical doctor. We have seen some respects in which he brought Cartesian natural philosophy to bear on medical physiology and pathology. His ambition to extend this agenda to the applied parts of medicine is exemplified in a pair of disputations

---

50 IMR II. 10. 2.
51 IMR II. 10. 3.

from 1687, *Medicus cartesianus* and *Chirurgus cartesianus*. These two programmatic documents set out a case for urgently needed reform in regimens for the diagnosis (*Semiotics*), conservation (*Hygiene*) and restoration (*Therapy*) of health. Social and technological constraints, however, meant that Waldschmidt's medical practice largely remained in step with established procedures.

Medicus cartesianus, as scholars have noted, is a largely polemical exercise aimed at defending a corpuscular theory of disease and, further, at promoting *libertas philosophandi* in medicine.[52] Waldschmidt rails against the errors that have been introduced in medicine due to faulty physical theory. His principal target is the Galenic model of explaining disease in terms of humoural imbalances and of recommending treatment based on opposed qualities of hot/cold and dry/moist. Waldschmidt advocates instead for the greater explanatory power of the mechanical framework and, as a consequence of better causal understanding of disease, its potential for improved treatment. The disputation concludes with a list of specific errors "resulting from the ignorance of animal economy and the mechanical philosophy", such as that melancholy is due to an enlarged spleen; prescribing cold foods for treatment of fevers; or that kidney stones are cured by diuretics.[53] *Chirurgus cartesianus*, defended by Waldschmidt's son Wilhelm Hulderich, is likewise rich in polemic, demanding that surgeons become informed about the Cartesian theory of blood circulation, and concluding with the promise of the iatromechanical framework for surgical intervention. What neither disputation offers is much in the way of detail concerning alternate prescriptions and practices.

In fact, attention to the remaining parts of Waldschmidt's *Institutiones* reveals a large gap between the promise of Cartesian physiology and the contemporary realities of medicine. Despite his rigorously mechanistic approach to the former, diagnosis and prognosis rest on a congeries of earlier practices. Qualitative examinations of urine, feces, and pulse remain the principal tools for interpreting the state of the body, for which traditional authorities provide hermeneutical guidance. Waldschmidt's catalogue of prognostic signs likewise draws overwhelmingly on the Hippocratic corpus.[54] Medical astrology also features among his prognostic tools. A sudden change in the course of disease (*crisis*), for instance, is interpreted by means of factors such as the influx of the moon and its conjunction or opposition with other planets.[55] Waldschmidt's recommended treatments similarly draw on standard *materia medica*. His disputations confirm this character of his work. One on kidney stones criticizes the standard prescription of diuretics based on the theory, which he rejects, that stones are caused by the coagulation of urine in the kidneys. His alternate treatments, however, are aimed at pain management during the passing of stones for which he prescribes an analgesic made from various herbs, honey, and scorpion flesh.[56] Among

---

52 Trevisani, *Medicus cartesianus*, p. 140; Schlegelmilch, *Revolution in Marburg*, p. 303-304.
53 *Medicus cartesianus*, Thes. XIII: "Sed ne partium studio laborare videar, catalogum hunc errorum intuere, hactenus ex ignoratia oeconomiae animalis & Philosophiae mechanicae commissorum".
54 IMR III. 2-6.
55 IMR III. 9. 9.
56 Disp. XXVI. 21.

his disputations is one devoted entirely to the preparation and use of *theriaca coelesti*.⁵⁷ In brief, the impact of Descartes on Waldschmidt's medicine is inevitably limited to the mechanical framework for its account of physiology and anatomy, to theory rather than to praxis. Technological constraints and the need to meet the historically conditioned expectations of patients and practitioners beyond the academic setting meant that little changed on the ground. One innovation in hygiene that Waldschmidt does trumpet — the benefits of tea and tobacco for keeping the blood, lymph, and spirits nimble and agile — has only the barest connection to Cartesian physiology.⁵⁸

Waldschmidt's career encapsulates the various cultural currents among which Cartesianism flows in Protestant Germany. Descartes appears among the neoteric *medici* not only as a natural philosopher but also as an ally in heterodox movements within the German Reformed community. These grew particularly radical toward the end of the century, and it is difficult not to suspect that Waldschmidt's religious sympathies, and the circumstances in Hesse in the 1680s, contributed to his further entrenchment in the Cartesian camp. His programmatic disputations as well as his correspondence with Johann Doläus display a feverish optimism, echoing the millenarian universal reform movements of the early seventeenth century. His physiology conveys a thoroughgoing embrace of Descartes's mechanical model of the human body. More than most other Cartesian medical doctors of the century, Waldschmidt strives to rid physiology and anatomy of humours and chemical elements as part of a broad attack on the scholastic establishment and its perceived alliance with Reformed orthodoxy. Yet, for him as for his fellow doctors, the promise of medical Cartesianism meets its limits in the face of the exigencies of medical practice. As *medicus*, Waldschmidt moves with the times.

---

57 Disp. XI.
58 Waldschmidt devotes an essay to the health benefits of tea, specifically for soldiers on the battlefield: "*Gründlicher Bericht, wie ein jeder dem seine Gesundheit lieb ist das Thee nicht allein zu hause gebrauchen sondern wie auch ein Soldat sich im Felde darmit praeserviren könne. Auch ob und was für Medicamenta bey dem Thee-Wasser nöthig seyen*". Cornelis Bontekoe is Waldschmidt's likely inspiration for this opinion.

STEFANO GULIZIA

Cartesianism between Northern Europe, Germany, and the Medici Court

*Charting a New Map**

▼ ABSTRACT This essay is dedicated to the cultural infrastructure of Cartesianism, and to the archival practices that accompanied its dissemination, within disciplines such as medicine, biology, and much beyond. It also represents a first attempt to draw a more inclusive map of the European reception of Descartes, by focusing on some neglected evidence that documents the spread of key textbooks, and especially the conversation they spurred. The analysis proceeds by triangulating book trading and academic practices together with courtly culture. After a review of the center-periphery in Cartesian intellectual history, subsequent sections try to answer these questions: what was the relation between the Low Countries and Medici Florence in the 1660s and 70s? How open-ended was Cartesianism, outside of that milieu? Did competition with the Galenic and scholastic legacy made Cartesian medicine more prone to accommodation? The conclusion recaps avenues for new research.

▼ KEYWORDS Medici court, Cartesianism, Lorenzo Panciatichi, Academy of the Cimento, Van Hogelande, Swammerdam

1. Introduction

Since the 1640s, Cartesian thinkers promoted an agenda that was rightly perceived to be alternative to the 'traditionalist' or Aristotelian view, which by then enjoyed a

---

* Support for this research came from the project 'TacitRoots', PI Giulia Giannini, funded by the European Research Council (ERC) under the European Union's Horizon 2020 Research and Innovation Programme (GA n. 818098). The author would also like to thank Gideon Manning, Ovanes Akopyan, and Kristin Raffa for their help and feedback.

Stefano Gulizia • Department of History, University of Milan, Italy. <stefano.gulizia@unimi.it>

Descartes and Medicine: Problems, Responses and Survival of a Cartesian Discipline, ed. by Fabrizio Baldassarri, Turnhout, 2023 (*DESCARTES*, 9), p. 411-436
© BREPOLS PUBLISHERS   10.1484/M.DESCARTES-EB.5.132901

curricular dominance. Cartesianism spearheaded a greater complexity not only in the philosophical debates, but throughout the compass of early modern intellectual life. In addition, another cultural force that reshaped the impact of these *novatores* was pedagogical efficiency. A growing trend in recent scholarship emphasizes that the academic milieu was an environment less conducive to open polemic or discord than to adjustment, transformation, and accommodation.[1] And although this rarely makes its way as a full comparison within our literature, it seems that an increasing number of Cartesian specialists would subscribe to Howard Hotson's main claims on the dissemination of Ramism, namely, that it was pivoted on teaching practices, and that the dynamic role played by marginal locales and frontiers, operating from the borders of fluctuating political powers, was vital. In fact, it was strong enough to configure a geographical, center-periphery model turned on its own head.[2]

It is quite stimulating to reflect about Cartesian medicine like a pragmatic system. Did competition with the Galenic and scholastic heritages provoke a more refined systematization able to withstand academic pressure, or a hybrid mix?[3] This essay fully supports such a perspective, in which natural philosophy is seen through the lenses of the history of universities, and 'new philosophies' co-exist with the older tool-box, humanist or antiquarian, instead of supplanting it.[4] Yet, it acknowledges two potential risks that one needs to overcome in dealing with this topic. The first of these is easier to approach. The way in which historians of philosophy have told us the story of Descartes and his readers followed a conceptualized divide between friends and rivals, exactly as one would have expected. This split is often quite real and dramatic; one only needs to read a blunt reply by the Leuven professor Erycius

---

[1] See NABEEL HAMID, "Domesticating Descartes, Renovating Scholasticism: Johann Clauberg and the German Reception of Cartesianism", *History of Universities* 30 (2020), p. 57-84, and ANDREA SANGIACOMO, "Modelling the history of early modern natural philosophy: the fate of the art-nature distinction in the Dutch universities", *British Journal for the History of Philosophy* 27/1 (2018), p. 46-74.

[2] HOWARD HOTSON, *Commonplace Learning. Ramism and its German Ramifications, 1543-1630*, Oxford, Oxford University Press, 2007, p. 25-37.

[3] As NUNO CASTEL-BRANCO, "Dissecting with Numbers: Mathematics in Nicolaus Steno's Early Anatomical Writings, 1661-1664", *Substantia* 5/1 (2021), p. 29-42, at p. 37, correctly reminds us, since Galen and Erasistratus, there has been in anatomy a habit of using mechanical analogies, which had nothing to do with the Cartesian body-to-machine comparison; this tradition created new trends, more or less syncretic, in various academic contexts, both Protestant and Catholic.

[4] STEFANO GULIZIA, "Ethics and Disciplines at Helmstedt: Aristotelian Debates in the Scholarly Career of Nicolaus Andreae Granius (1607-1617)", *History of Universities* 34/2 (2021), p. 38-64, and STEFANO GULIZIA, "Francesco Patrizi da Cherso and the anti-Aristotelian tradition: interpreting the *Discussiones Peripateticae* (1581)", *Intellectual History Review* 29/4 (2019), p. 561-573. The philological or praxeological argument developed in the last cited articles, concerning the co-existence of new philosophy and erudite tools, is quite different from studies like the classic demonstration of ROGER ARIEW, *Descartes and the Last Scholastics*, Ithaca, Cornell University Press, 1999, that Descartes was heavily indebted to a previous tradition; on the convoluted history of reading and experimenting, see also RENÉE RAPHAEL, "Literary Technology and Its Replication: Teaching the Torricellian Void and the Air-Pump at the Collegio Romano", in *Teaching Philosophy in Early Modern Europe*, ed. by S. Berger and D. Garber, Dordrecht, Springer, 2021, p. 241-263.

Puteanus (1574-1646) to the Dutch statesman Constantijn Huygens (1596-1687) on June 25, 1638: "I do not admire Descartes".[5] Compared to how these fissures are imagined to shape history, however, it must be admitted that they do not adhere to what the historical actors sought to achieve, and quite often they are an outcome of contingency.[6] A suitable solution, I would suggest, is to redirect some of the energy that is currently attached to the description of philosophical discrepancies towards the study of the material dynamic and social infrastructure of Cartesian disputes.[7] The second risk is perhaps more difficult and has to do with regional distribution.

2. A Geographical Bias

To put it in the simplest of available terms, our perception of Descartes' 'novelty' is geographically biased in favor of France and the Netherlands.[8] There are of course salutary counter-claims and deepening horizons. Even the British context — at first Baconian, despite significant internal differences, and then Newtonian, almost *de rigueur* — has been persuasively shown to be far from impermeable to Cartesian influence.[9] By design, however, or by necessity, narratives of Cartesian modernity remain primarily French or Dutch. Thus, the challenge here would be to produce a geographical enlargement without denying the role of the Low Countries as a true laboratory for new ideas.[10] In what follows, I track some neglected evidence from

---

5   *Briefwisseling van Constantijn Huygens*, ed. by J. A. Worp, The Hague, Nijhoff, 1911, vol. 2, p. 442.
6   For events falling outside the explanatory frame, see STEPHEN GAUKROGER, "Overview: Contingency in Nature", in *Contingency and Natural Order in Early Modern Science*, ed. by P. D. Omodeo and R. Garau, Dordrecht, Springer, 2019, p. 1-7.
7   I certainly agree with PAOLO ROSSINI, "The Networked Origins of Cartesian Philosophy and Science", *HOPOS* 12/1 (2022), p. 97-120, that we currently need more research on Cartesian negotiations as a mechanism of intellectual dissemination, even if it comes at the expense of traditional HPS papers on the divergence of theoretical methods; yet, I remain skeptical that a purely quantitative approach is the answer. Rossini's article actually contains a valuable discussion of why databases like ePistolarium and EMLO are unreliable, in so far as they underrepresent women and do little to mitigate the exclusion of areas such as Germany and Italy from proper consideration, which I am attempting to address in this essay.
8   See especially THEO VERBEEK, *Descartes and the Dutch: Early Reactions to Cartesian Philosophy, 1637-1650*, Carbondale, Southern Illinois University Press, 1992; ROGER ARIEW, *Descartes and the First Cartesians*, Oxford, Oxford University Press, 2014; TAD M. SCHMALTZ, *Early Modern Cartesianisms: Dutch and French Constructions*, Oxford, Oxford University Press, 2017; and ALBERT GOOTJES, "The First Orchestrated Attack on Spinoza: Johannes Melchioris and the Cartesian Network in Utrecht", *Journal of the History of Ideas* 79/1 (2018), p. 23-43.
9   GIOVANNI GELLERA, "The Reception of Descartes in the Seventeenth-Century Scottish Universities: Metaphysics and Natural Philosophy (1650-1680)", *The Journal of Scottish Philosophy* 13 (2015), p. 179-201.
10 Consider, briefly, one of the best volumes in the field: TAD M. SCHMALTZ, ed., *Receptions of Descartes: Cartesianism and anti-Cartesianism in early modern Europe*, London, Routledge, 2005. Its basic outline is French-Dutch, with the addition of Sarah Hutton's work on Princess Elisabeth and Anne Conway; the end is taken by explorations of England and Italy, which features primarily because of Naples as a coalescing 'Cartesian school' and for the Roman Inquisition.

Germany and Italy but not because I hope to reorient the debate. That would require several books. Rather, I aim to focus on a few points in this blurred map, trusting that a 'cosmopolitan' history of Cartesianism can only be achieved by investigating across different regions, languages, and backgrounds.[11] Besides, as we will see, the German and Italian cases present specific features that enable a valuable historical reappraisal. Specifically, while scholars concentrated on Naples and the South as the 'natural' area of Cartesian penetration,[12] the evidence from Medici Tuscany is a phenomenon robust enough to deserve investigation, as well as counterintuitive.

Although for now what can be achieved in a single piece of writing is only a sketch, I genuinely believe that the study of how Descartes' ideas were discussed in Europe would greatly benefit from a comparative, global approach that extends to all the territory north of Rome, and south-east of the only small region that has occupied scholars so far.[13] Just like historian Charles H. Parker sought to reveal the inherent tensions between accommodation and orthodoxy by comparing both Calvinist and Christian missionary enterprises,[14] Cartesian studies could profitably analyze how local academic and courtly cultures faced, solved, or shared similar problems, and uncover if the results promoted the adoption of syncretistic or antagonistic approaches. It is possible that the tendency to integrate would prove superior to all the polemics.

To highlight my goals, I must return to Italy a little while longer. The country is an interesting case because the heritage of Galilean teaching — and the deep nostalgia it is associated with, from the 1640s onwards, with the scientist still alive and going blind — is inextricably related to the formation of the earliest scientific academies. Some of these academies looked to Descartes as well for a theoretical foundation. It is not for shortage of evidence if scholars had done comparatively less with these facts, but for sheer reluctance to look away from Galileo's shadow, and the original neglect of his close followers for the Cartesian textbooks that Mersenne brought to Italy.[15] In such a scenario, it is easy to be seduced by labeling. Susana Gómez López

---

11 For two good models of such a polycentric outlook, see NICCOLÒ GUICCIARDINI, *Reading the Principia: The Debate on Newton's Mathematical Methods for Natural Philosophy from 1687 to 1736*, Cambridge, Cambridge University Press, 1999, MOGENS LAERKE, *Les Lumières de Leibniz: controverses avec Huet, Bayle, Regis et More*, Paris, Garnier, 2015, p. 11-46.

12 For a sample of a literature that is as rigorous and well-developed, as it is intensely local, see GIULIA BELGIOIOSO, *Cultura a Napoli e Cartesianesimo*, Lecce, Congedo, 1992; MAURIZIO TORRINI, "Cartesio e l'Italia: un tentativo di bilancio", *Giornale critico della filosofia italiana* 80 (2001), p. 214-230; GIULIA BELGIOIOSO, "Images of Descartes in Italy", in *Receptions of Descartes*, p. 157-180; and RAFFAELE CARBONE, "The Critical Reception of Cartesian Physiology in Tommaso Cornelio's *Progymnasmata Physica*", in *Descartes' Treatise on Man and its Reception*, ed. by D. Antoine-Mahut and S. Gaukroger, Dordrecht, Springer, 2016, p. 91-101.

13 I refer, of course, to the Paris-Amsterdam axis, which is almost, willingly or not, the teleological end of modern reconstructions of the "Republic of Letters".

14 See CHARLES H. PARKER, "Converting souls across cultural borders: Dutch Calvinism and early modern missionary enterprises", *Journal of Global History* 8 (2013), p. 50-71, and CHARLES H. PARKER, *Global Calvinism: Conversion and Commerce in the Dutch Empire, 1600-1800*, New Haven and London, Yale University Press, 2022.

15 The topic is well-known, but see at least RIVKA FELDHAY, "On Wonderful Machines: The Transmission of Mechanical Knowledge by Jesuits", *Science and Education* 15 (2006), p. 151-172.

advanced an argument, according to which one might draw distinctions among the various schools operating in the field of post-Galilean epistemology on the basis of "deductive" reasoning.[16] This thesis only works if we accept a *de facto* leadership in the experimental field by the Southern-born physiologist Giovanni Alfonso Borelli (1608-1679), whose work was associated with the Academy of the Cimento but who after the disbandment of that network continued to work alone, originating harsh and vitriolic priority disputes over to whom belonged the legacy of the same group.

If, by contrast, as Maurizio Torrini reasonably observed,[17] Borelli is recognized as a school of his own and therefore removed from the equation, what begins to emerge is a picture where London, Bologna, and Florence are engaged as counterparts in a pursuit that is 'inductive' in the cosmopolitan and de-centralized parlance in which Cartesianism has been absorbed in the Holy Roman Empire. It is true, this sense of the term is theoretically weak. In large part, such a 'Cartesian' denominator is little more than a preference for non-reductive mechanicism.[18] But even like this, like a brand favored by *novatores*, it demarcates a crucial and underappreciated history. In what ways, we may then ask, was Descartes discussed in Pisa or in the state of Brandenburg, as opposed as in Utrecht? Do these locales echo the main guidelines deriving from Paris and Amsterdam? Do they represent the fuzzy outskirts of what remains an organic, integral map? Are these debates hopelessly provincial or not?

3. 'Central' vs. 'Peripheral' in the Cartesian Reception

To progress in our exploration, we must now turn to the surprising archive of some sophisticated, metropolitan émigrés, who are epitomized by the diverse interests of the Roman aristocrat Lorenzo Magalotti (1637-1712) and who in a form or another established themselves in the service of Medici power and acted as a clearinghouse for information of all sorts, including book trading in the 1660s.[19] Before we can do so, however, we need to discuss how scholars have used the center-periphery trope as a serious explanatory model and not simply as a metaphor. In some respects, it would seem that two variants are prevailing. Historians talk of a dialectics between center and periphery to describe a shift in the research questions of a field. A great example of this use is seen in the way Leibniz started studying the Latin edition of Descartes' *Géométrie* as early as 1673, judging that in its reliance on construction

---

16 SUSANA GÓMEZ LÓPEZ, *Le passioni degli atomi. Montanari e Rossetti: una polemica tra galileiani*, Florence, Olschki, 1997.
17 MAURIZIO TORRINI, "Descartes e il cartesianesimo nelle corrispondenze italiane al tempo della rivoluzione scientifica", *Rivista di filosofia neo-scolastica* 93/4 (2001), p. 550-570.
18 DENNIS DES CHENE, "Mechanisms of life in the seventeenth century: Borelli, Perrault, Régis", *Studies in History and Philosophy of Biological and Biomedical Sciences*, 36 (2005), p. 245-260.
19 On these individuals as a cultural type, see DANIEL STOLZENBERG, "A Spanner and His Works: Books, Letters, and Scholarly Communication Networks in Early Modern Europe", in *For the Sake of Learning: Essays in Honor of Anthony Grafton*, ed. by A. Blair and A.-S. Goeing, Leiden, Brill, 2016, vol. 1, p. 157-172.

problems the textbook's priorities had lost their impact and "became peripheral in the mathematical practice".[20] Another, more common use of the center-periphery model is used, implicitly or explicitly, to identify a geographical area that depends on another (or exploits it) for a variety of commercial and intellectual reasons.

The decline of the Venetian printing press, for example, in relation to its Northern European competitors, first because of Amsterdam's powerful rise and later, by or around 1700, vis-à-vis London's renewed centrality, is a well-established feature of our historiographies.[21] In Maurizio Torrini's eloquent yet subjective reconstruction, the "Galilean school" in Italy represented Europe's scientific vanguard as long as it strictly followed the master's protocols. In this view, Torricelli was the last scientist to just zero on his given discipline and, like Galileo himself had done before, never abandon active natural research on outside landscapes and phenomena in favor of the kind of erudite or bookish explorations that one could indulge in a library.[22]

Torrini's explanation has merits, but is perhaps authoritative beyond its scopes for the simple reason that it is entrenched in, and symbolic of, a national traditional of the history of science. It is debatable that by the time Vincenzo Viviani (1622-1703) and others managed to assemble a remarkable array of printed editions, these very efforts would signal their irreversible intellectual decline. More importantly for our goals, the main idea is that Descartes' presence is mediated by a new 'encyclopedic' orientation among the Galilean successors and symptomatic of a sense of exclusion or delay compared to the Transalpine market. Peripheral here is synonymous with frustration (in ranking) and isolation (in spatial terms).[23] A recent, alternative view has been proposed by Andrea Sangiacomo and his team of researchers, who attend to the evolution of early modern natural philosophy and conceive a neat succession of three layers:[24] the activities of a core or 'primary' group of authors, then a buffer zone next to it, and finally a 'periphery' that is secluded but, unlike in the derivative perspective of Torrini, still contributes to the main debate. While the results of this project are still ongoing, its advantages concern the possibility to adopt systematic formalizations of trends and also the effective translation to academic practices of what in the past used to conceptualized only in the shape of geopolitical maps and territorial arrangements. All of this is quite useful to study a global Cartesianism.

My underlying methodological intuition, moreover, is that one should switch away from theoreticians to some extent and consider a range of historical actors that

---

20 DAVIDE CRIPPA, "One String Attached: Geometrical Exactness in Leibniz's Parisian Manuscripts", in *Leibniz and the Structure of Sciences*, ed. by Vincenzo De Risi, Dordrecht, Springer, 2019, p. 203-252 (citation at p. 209).
21 See ASA BRIGGS and PETER BURKE, *A Social History of the Media: From Gutenberg to the Internet*, New York, Wiley, 2002.
22 MAURIZIO TORRINI, "La biblioteca di Galileo e dei galileiani", *Intersezioni* 21/3 (2001), p. 545-558.
23 On the question of social capital and the political outcome of having people cut off or less connected, see RONALD S. BURT, *Brokerage and Closure: An Introduction to Social Capital*, Oxford, Oxford University Press, 2005.
24 ANDREA SANGIACOMO, RALUCA TANASESCU, SILVIA DONKER, and HUGO HOGENBIRK, "Mapping the evolution of early modern natural philosophy: corpus collection and authority acknowledgment", *Annals of Science* 78/1 (2021), p. 1-39.

includes projectors, book agents, translators, merchants, diplomats, and artisans. It is the combination of these social forces and variable contingencies that can better represent Cartesian communities in Europe as specific clusters in the disciplines of knowledge. And as far as universities are concerned, it seems also wiser to imagine that not every early modern professor was engaged in groundbreaking research or embroiled in sectarian divisions. Many of them waited for the end of the semester, then as now, and adapted Descartes to supplement already existing reading lists[25] — much like for Ramus in previous generations, despite protestations of doctrinal purism made by some Aristotelians in a public statement, but seldom, and I add, significantly so, in private teaching and in note-taking. Some characterizations that we have might be too militant.[26] The reality suggests a vast canvas of blending.

In the case of France, for example, the hybridization of French Cartesian authority with some of its direct competitors ensured a longer institutional survival and also stabilized the selling of printed editions.[27] Similarly, in Italy's case, a pattern based on crossbreeding is widespread. In his Pisan courses, Claude Bérigard (1578-1663) incorporated mechanical principles taken by both Descartes and Gassendi not out of intellectual laziness, compromise, or for a lack of imagination.[28] It is therefore understandable that one of the very few philosophical books, that is, not related to mathematics or military applications, which belonged to the library of Evangelista Torricelli (1608-1647), was indeed Bérigard's 1643 *Circulus Pisanus*.[29] It is plain to see, given the scarcity of copies and translations at this juncture, and also given the scientist's propensity to disengage from astronomy or theory altogether, and to see himself as a *totus geometra*, that Torricelli must have known what he knew about Descartes primarily from this very eclectic source originating in the Galilean city of Pisa.

Everything, thus far, suggested to also look beyond these academic discourses. The astonishing demand for Cartesian production and the dialectics between tradition and innovation that it spurred were surely not limited to early modern universities. Cartesian authority unfolded as a variable within the learned marketplace of print. The logistical trouble of supplying and prohibitive cost placed textbooks beyond the reach of most European pockets.[30] And it was also a variant of courtly culture, able

---

25 Others still left unfinished business because of confessional strife or the outbreak of epidemics.
26 I am thinking, specifically, of ERIC JORINK, "*Modus politicus vivendi*: Nicolaus Steno and the Dutch (Swammerdam, Spinoza and other friends), 1660-1664", in *Steno and the Philosophers*, ed. by R. Andrault and M. Laerke, Leiden, Brill, 2018, p. 12-44, not because I necessarily disagree with it, but as a representative of this trend.
27 SANGIACOMO, TANASESCU, DONKER, and HOGENBIRK, "Mapping the evolution of early modern natural philosophy", p. 30.
28 RENÉE RAPHAEL, "Eclecticism as a Vibrant Philosophical Program: Claude Bérigard and Mauro Mancini on the University of Pisa", *History of Universities* 29/1 (2016), p. 1-28.
29 See TORRINI, "La biblioteca di Galileo", p. 548.
30 This point has been made very clearly by MARTHA BALDWIN, "Pious Ambition: Natural Philosophy and the Jesuit Quest for the Patronage of Printed Books in the Seventeenth Century", in *Jesuit Science and the Republic of Letters*, ed. by M. Feingold, Cambridge, MIT Press, 2003, p. 285-329, who stresses how Jesuit authors always targeted a double audience: one inside the Society of Jesus, and including those enrolled in their classrooms, and on the outside, the European intelligentsia.

to illuminate patronage strategies and deeply intertwined with the organization of the first scientific academies. As Marco Cavarzere recently noted, the boundaries between countries were porous, even when facing confessional opposition. It was one of the prerogatives of the European intelligentsia to rely on a web of contacts, which could orchestrate book requests and especially transcend, when necessary, the local and national scales. In this respect, what happened to Descartes is similar to Hugo Grotius or to the dissemination of the German jurist Hermann Conring.[31]

To take only one example, it was through the services of Antonio Magliabechi (1633-1714) that the preceptor of the Grand Duke's son, Bernardo Benvenuti, prior of the Benedictine monastery of Santa Felicita in Florence, obtained his copy of Descartes' *De homine*, among other titles of Calvinist origin.[32] As a channel, it was well-established, ranging from the foundation of the Academy of the Lincei to the Academy of the Crusca, and one that managed to operate without major upheavals or suspicions of heterodoxy, regardless of its dangerous ideological spectrum.[33]

Cartesian authors of books, even those who dedicated themselves to more abstract and theoretical scientific matters, customarily interacted with the market in print and occasionally claimed that a particular topic should be of interest to the learned nobility. As a specimen or exposition of early Enlightenment culture, the Cartesian reception was never distant from the wishes of Athanasius Kircher, who in addition to catering to his patrons with individual, neatly-packed presentation copies, had frequently claimed in his career to have designed works for prominent readers, as when he wrote an astronomical treatise at the urging of Ferdinand III, who wished to receive better instructions about the "perplexing novelties of the skies".[34]

4. Piecemeal Science

As a result of previous considerations, and to bridge across the caveats identified in this essay, the targeted historical evidence is provided by individuals who could be a natural link between court, academia, and book trading. A great embodiment of this type is the singular figure of the merchant, diplomat, and intelligencer Cosimo

---

[31] MARCO CAVARZERE, "An Interrupted Dialogue? Italy and the Protestant Book Market in the Early Seventeenth Century", in *Fruits of Migration: Heterodox Italian Migrants and Central European Culture, 1550-1620*, ed. by C, Zwierlein and V. Lavenia, Leiden, Brill, 2018, p. 27-44.

[32] A. MIRTO, "Lettere di Antonio Magliabechi a Bernardo Benvenuti", *Studi secenteschi* 39 (1998), p. 205-242.

[33] See A. MIRTO, "Antonio Magliabechi e Carlo Dati: lettere", *Studi secenteschi* 42 (2001), p. 381-433; SABINA BREVAGLIERI, "Science, Books and Censorship in the Academy of the Lincei: Johannes Faber as Cultural Mediator", in *Conflicting Duties: Science, Medicine and Religion in Rome (1550-1750)*, ed. by M. P. Donato and J. Kraye, London-Turin, The Warburg Institute-Nino Aragno Editore, 2009, p. 109-133; and INGEBORG VAN VUGT, "Geografia e storia di una rete epistolare: Contatti e mediazioni nell'epistolario di Magliabechi", in *Antonio Magliabechi nell'Europa dei saperi*, ed. by J. Boutier, M. P. Paoli, and C. Viola, Pisa, Edizioni della Normale, 2017, p. 257-290.

[34] I paraphrase from the prefatory letter of ATHANASIUS KIRCHER, *Itinerarium exstaticum*, Rome, 1656.

Brunetti (d. 1677). Relatively better known as the first Italian translator of Pascal's *Lettres provinciales*, which appeared posthumously in 1684,[35] and for his work as clergyman and secretary to Jan III Sobieski, who granted him the Polish nobility,[36] Brunetti traveled to the Antilles and achieved a remarkable career by maximizing a genuine sense of being 'at ease' in the most diverse places — Florence, London, and Warsaw, but also Paris, Denmark and much beyond — from which he sent detailed dispatches. He cultivated a close friendship with Leopoldo de' Medici (1617-1675).

Brunetti moved also inside the circle of the Neapolitan painter and satirist Salvator Rosa, which was characterized by absorbing interests in natural philosophy and in the works of *novatores*.[37] Unsurprisingly, for a man of these credentials, Brunetti was acquainted with Cartesian debates as well, of which he is giving a profile that is all the more interesting because it is not the result of an internalist development, but rather the product of disengaged, external observations. *Disengaged*, however, in the limited accentuation of 'globalism' befitting a wandering scholar, does not at all mean that Brunetti's reports were built around a *disembodied* rationalism.[38] He was still the member of a pro-French, international party and, possibly, even a paid spy. Presumably, this is what worked out so spectacularly in the early 1670s during his advancement in Poland's court. At the same time, Brunetti remained a loyal and trusted advisor to the Medici regime and was a recognizably Tuscan figure.[39]

On June 14, 1660, Brunetti penned a letter to Leopoldo, which touches upon optics and mechanics, as well as astronomy,[40] with some noticeable emphasis placed on Christiaan Huygens' pathbreaking contribution to the disputes on Saturn's rings.[41]

---

35 In addition to the extremely brief mention in the collection of the seventeenth-century botanist Giovanni Targioni Tozzetti, *Notizie degli aggrandimenti delle scienze fisiche accaduti in Toscana*, Florence, 1780, t. III, p. 116-117, where Brunetti has a slot among other voyagers, see also Uberto Limentani, "Per la biografia di Cosimo Brunetti", *Studi secenteschi* 19 (1978), p. 109-127, and A. M. Crinò, "Una relazione inedita di Cosimo Brunetti sulle Antille", *Universo* 45 (1965), p. 692-700.

36 For the Polish period, see the 1881 edition in Cracow of the *Acta Ioannis Sobieski*, vol. I:2, p. 1413, and Karolina Targosz, "Cosimo Brunetti: voyageur érudit, secretaire du roi Jean III Sobieski", *Organon* 14 (1978), p. 119-127.

37 C. Volpi, "Filosofo nel dipingere: Salvator Rosa tra Roma e Firenze (1639-1659)", in *Salvator Rosa tra mito e magia*, Naples, Electa, 2008, p. 28-46, and Eva Struhal, "Natural Painting and the New Science in Seventeenth-Century Florence: Lorenzo Lippi's *pura imitazione del vero*", *Nuncius* 32/3 (2017), p. 683-708.

38 Denis Cosgrove, "Globalism and Tolerance in Early Modern Geography", *Annals of the Association of American Geographers* 93 (2003), p. 852-870, recalls the high-profile and Habermasian origin of a debate in which the construction of Cartesian cosmopolitanism bears fruits on the larger theme of European toleration.

39 The closest comparison is the activity of another 'projector' active in Central Europe on whom see Ilario Tancon, *Lo scienziato Tito Livio Burattini (1617-1681) al servizio dei re di Polonia*, Trento, Università degli Studi di Trento, 2005; for more on Brunetti's brokering, see Giulia Giannini, "An Indirect Convergence between the Accademia del Cimento and the Montmor Academy: the Saturn dispute", in *The Institutionalization of Science in Early Modern Europe*, ed. by G. Giannini and Mordechai Feingold, Leiden, Brill, 2020, p. 83-108, at p. 100.

40 Now housed in Florence, Biblioteca Nazionale Centrale, MS Gal. 276, cc. 30^r-31^r.

41 See, above all, the seminal work of Albert Van Helden, "The Accademia del Cimento and Saturn's Ring", *Physis*, XV (1973), p. 237-259.

Brunetti also informs Leopoldo about Hevelius in Gdańsk and excuses himself for not entering too deeply into current controversies on Descartes in the Netherlands because, he says, "other, more qualified informers will".[42] There is no space here to unpack in full the stimulating clues and suggestions that this document preserves.

Two aspects, though, stand out. One is that the conversation on Dutch Cartesians is obviously presented as ongoing and, to that extent, taken for granted as a topic. There is nothing surprising about it, not even Brunetti's convenient deferring to a better authority in the field. This attitude further reveals the great extent to which scholarly discussions relied on free-flowing, unrecorded exchange; sometimes, the conviviality degenerated because of passion and alcoholic haze, or both.[43] In any event, orality punctuated, grounded, and arguably overwhelmed the commerce of books. This is even more pressing in the case of field notes that did not conform to pre-formed questionnaires or lines of inquiry (like the "General Heads" published by Robert Boyle in the *Philosophical Transactions* of 1666),[44] but unfolded much more freely, either because produced by a traveling virtuoso and out of curiosity, or simply because part of the general flow of news. Orality is a neglected aspect of the early modern Cartesian debates, just as it is of the Medici scientific networks that connected Florence with the Northern axis of Paris and Amsterdam, and beyond.[45]

The other aspect of Brunetti's report that is worth pursuing, briefly, has to do with its filing. Like many others, this letter was copied by a secretary at court. This was done for the benefit of other users[46] and had the side-effect of showing how travel information was incorporated into Leopoldo's archive, the modern re-organization of the so-called 'Galilean' manuscripts in Florence notwithstanding. Obviously, like every student of the early modern laboratory is familiar with, data-replication and the methodization of knowledge claims were routine activities in the early modern period. But travel reports were also part of standardization strategies.[47] One could

---

42 MS Gal. 276, c. 30^v: "[...] n'è ragguagliata da altri più esattamente e più dottamente".
43 Massimo Bucciantini, "Teologia e nuova filosofia. Galileo, Federico Cesi, Giovambattista Agucchi e la discussione sulla fluidità e corruttibilità del cielo", in *Sciences et Religions de Copernic à Galilée (1540-1610)*, ed. by C. Brice and A. Romano, Rome, École française de Rome, 1999, p. 411-442, recalls a heated debate at dinner time, in Rome around the time of Galileo's affair, with Giulio Cesare Lagalla defending a cosmological viewpoint and the passionate discussion degenerating into an altercation.
44 Daniel Carey, "Inquiries, Heads, and Directions: Orienting Early Modern Travel", in *Travel Narratives, the New Science, and Literary Discourse, 1569-1750*, ed. by J. A. Hayden, London, Routledge, 2012, p. 25-51.
45 For the importance of orality, see Mordechai Feingold, "Confabulatory Life", in *Duncan Liddel (1561-1613), Networks of Polymathy and the Northern European Renaissance*, ed. by P. D. Omodeo and K. Friedrich, Leiden, Brill, 2016, p. 22-34, and Joad Raymond and Noah Moxham, eds, *News Networks in Early Modern Europe*, Leiden, Brill, 2016. As a token of a larger strategy, Van Vugt, "Geografia e storia di una rete epistolare", p. 287, reminds of Leopoldo's specific recommendation to Heinsius, which allowed Magalotti and Panciatichi, in 1667, to tour Holland and promote the Cimento group.
46 Occasionally, as in MS Gal. 276, c. 46^v, Magalotti drafts a review on the back of the letter.
47 Marianne Klemun and Ulrike Spring, eds, *Expeditions as Experiments: Practising Observation and Documentation*, New York, Palgrave Macmillan, 2016, p. 1-25.

even build on Hans-Jörg Rheinberger's idea of scientific 'cooperation' refracted in various locales to better appreciated what Brunetti brought to Leopoldo and what the other correspondence from the same period has the benefit of documenting.

As it turns out, Brunetti's prudent or laconic postponement to other informers did not sit well with Leopoldo's burning curiosity. We do not possess, in this and many cases, the Prince's side of the epistolary exchange. Yet, from what Brunetti relays in his next letter written on September 9, 1660, this time in Paris, it is quite obvious that Leopoldo must have pressed Brunetti to bring out more specific information on Cartesian debates. The letter is unusually rich, and it also contains a mechanical drawing (Fig. 1), along with a variety of experimental topics.[48] Without following a strict order, the section concerning Descartes is clearly identifiable. It is divided in two parts. In the first of these, Brunetti freely extols the inventiveness of Johannes Clauberg (1622-1665), identifying him with historical precision as a partisan of the French theoretician[49] as well as a very prolific author on his own. At this juncture, given his exposition, Brunetti appears to have read in print the "Exoterica" or Pars Prior of the *Defensio Cartesiana* published in 1652. However, he records advance praise for the second installment of that project because it will be "speculative" in a most "curious" way.[50] The second part of the Cartesian report moves away from Clauberg and gives Leopoldo details about several books that have gained scholarly approval. Once again, these are works about, rather than by, Descartes himself: an adaptation in a different linguistic domain or the continuation of his successors.

One by one, Brunetti lists the 1659 Latin translation of Descartes' *Geometry* made by the Dutch mathematician Frans van Schooten,[51] which he knew from an edition with Florimond de Beaune's own notes in appendix (although it is not evident from the context if he saw these as printed separately). Then he mentions the *Consensus veritatis in Scriptura divina* by the Dutch theologian Christoph Wittich and finally the *Specimina philosophiae Cartesianae* by Daniel Lipstorp, which was written by a Lutheran author educated between Lübeck and Rostock, even if the book itself was printed in Leiden in 1653.[52] In a fascinating closing remark, Brunetti says that he would gladly send all these editions to Florence from Paris, where he was at that time, were it not for the fact that the titles belonged to the Dutch market, and from such a direct channel it would be easier for a shipment to reach the Medici court.[53]

This context leaves no doubt that Leopoldo wanted — and by the turn of one year or two would have likely obtained — these Cartesian books in their entirety. On the

---

48 I am preparing a translation and close reading of this text elsewhere.
49 Florence, Biblioteca Nazionale Centrale, MS Gal. 276, c. 62^r: "[Q]uesto Claubergio si mostra molto parziale di monsieur d'Escartes".
50 MS Gal. 276, c. 62^r: "conterrà materie del tutto speculative, sarà la più curiosa".
51 DAVID RABOUIN, "*Ingenium, Phantasia* and Mathematics in Descartes's *Regulae ad directionem ingenii*", in *Descartes and the* Ingenium: *The Embodied Soul in Cartesianism*, ed. by R. Garrod and A. Marr, Leiden, Brill, 2021, p. 64-90.
52 For this context, see at least RIENK VERMIJ, *The Calvinist Copernicans. The reception of the new astronomy in the Dutch Republic*, Amsterdam, Edita KNAW, 2002.
53 MS Gal. 276, c. 62^r: "i quali libri io li haverei mandati a V. A. S. se, essendo stati stampati in Ollanda, io non sapessi che è molto più facile il farli venire per quella via".

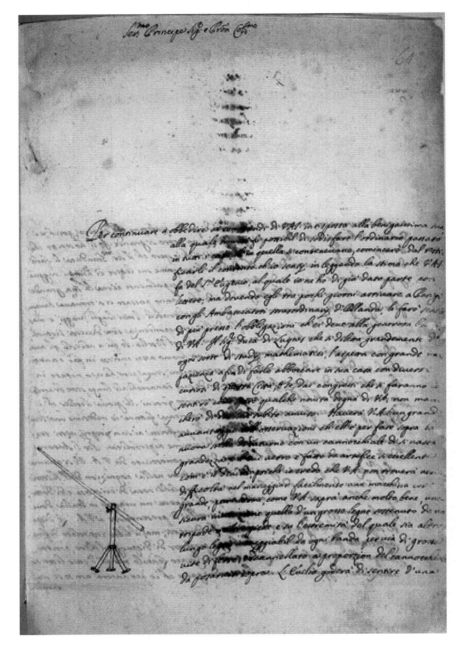

Figure 1. Copy of Cosimo Brunetti's letter to Leopoldo de' Medici of September 9, 1660, with the illustration of a telescopic instrument used by Hevelius; Florence, Biblioteca Nazionale Centrale, MS Gal. 276, c. 61r.

one hand, not everything in Brunetti's dispatch is 'newsworthy' in a modern sense. The majority of the books he cites are from the previous decade, with the exception of Wittich's *Consensus*, which in 1660 was fresh off the presses in Nijmegen. On the other hand, there is passion and philological rigor in his letter. Brunetti's notes on Lipstorp, for example, correctly convey that the author's intention was to defend Cartesian philosophy to provide a natural basis for the Copernican system.[54]

5. Panciatichi's Report to Leopoldo

In the summer of 1671 at the age of 36, the travelling scholar Lorenzo Panciatichi addressed to Leopoldo de' Medici, a newly made cardinal, a three-page report from Amsterdam.[55] This dispatch touched on issues of trade, politics, and the ambitious editorial plans of the Blaeu printing firm. The presence of a Medici intelligencer in the Netherlands highlights the marketing reality that Dutch publishers competed for streams of foreign income,[56] but it also validates, from the point of view of distribution, that by then, and certainly by the mid-1660s, every ambitious author and collector in Florence or Rome knew that the best place to publish books was Amsterdam.[57] Panciatichi's scholarly news contained, as well, impressions of a visit to the renowned cabinet of curiosities of the city physician Jan Swammerdam (1637-1680). Swammerdam, Panciatichi writes, had just compiled a natural history of the insects, "whose imaginative scope was pivoted on his new observations".[58]

The reference here is to the 1669 *Historia insectorum generalis, ofte, Algemeene verhandeling van de bloedeloose dierkens*, which was particularly remarkable for imposing lexical standards to vernacular entomology and for how painstakingly it

---

54 PIETRO DANIEL OMODEO, "Lodewijk de Bils' and Tobias Andreae's Cartesian Bodies: Embalmment Experiments, Medical Controversies and Mechanical Philosophy", *Early Science and Medicine* 22 (2017), p. 301-332: p. 319.
55 Florence, Biblioteca Nazionale Centrale, MS Gal. 279, cc. 80^r-81^r.
56 On the relations with the Medici world, see ALFONSO MIRTO and HENK TH. VAN VEEN, eds, *Pieter Blaeu: Lettere ai fiorentini, Antonio Magliabechi, Leopoldo e Cosimo III de' Medici, e altri, 1660-1705*, Amsterdam, APA-Holland University Press, 1993; on Amsterdam's prominence, see JONATHAN ISRAEL, *Dutch Primacy in World Trade, 1585-1740*, Oxford, Clarendon Press, 1989, and ANDREW PETTEGREE and ARTHUR DER WEDUWEN, *The Bookshop of the World: Making and Trading Books in the Dutch Golden Age*, New Haven and London, Yale University Press, 2019.
57 An illustration of this point is the lavish edition of ATHANASIUS KIRCHER, *Mundus subterraneus*, 1665, or the remunerative contract that granted the printer Janssonius exclusive rights for selling Kircher's future and past works. On *Mundus*, see LUCA CIANCIO, "Immoderatus fervor ad intra coërcendus: Reactions to Athanasius Kircher's Central Fire in Jesuit Science", *Nuncius* 33 (2018), p. 464-504; for Kircher's careful cultivation of protestants in the North, see JOHN FLETCHER, "Athanasius Kircher and his correspondence", in *Athanasius Kircher und seine Beziehungen zum gelehrten Europa seiner Zeit*, ed. by J. Fletcher, Wiesbaden, Harrassowitz, 1988, p. 146.
58 MS Gal. 279, c. 80^r: "[…] ha compilato un'istoria naturale degli insetti speculate sul fondamento delle sue nuove osservationi".

depicted the development from larvae into adults.⁵⁹ Significantly, Panciatichi did not praise Swammerdam's *Historia* for its high skills in dissecting, nor for the conjectures enabled by technical improvements in lens-grinding or microscopy;⁶⁰ rather, this title was stunning because of its advanced displays of epistemology.⁶¹ That is, the world of insects obeyed predictable shapes⁶² and was law-bound.

While Panciatichi did not mention Descartes, Swammerdam himself, as we shall see, was a rationalist and uniformly fits logically within the Cartesian tenets for the study of medicine and natural philosophy, including vortexes, light, or motion — in short, his definition of nature's living functions, from seeds to organisms, as a manifestation of *res extensa*.⁶³ Having said that, we should be cautious. First of all, because the evidence is limited — although it could be that a form or another of the Cartesian reception in the Netherlands was so pervasive that it hardly needed to be spelled out —⁶⁴ it stayed hidden in plain sight, like E. A. Poe's story of *The Purloined*

---

59 Brian W. Ogilvie, "Order of Insects: Insect Species and Metamorphosis between Renaissance and Enlightenment", in *The Life Sciences in Early Modern Philosophy*, ed. by O. Nachtomy and J. E. H. Smith, Oxford, Oxford University Press, 2014, p. 222-245. Swammerdam's attention to the developmental stages in the life of insects would be matched by another Dutch master of the 'visible proof', Antoni van Leeuwenhoek (1632-1723); Sietske Fransen, "Antoni van Leeuwenhoek, His Images and Draughtsmen", *Perspectives on Science* 27 (2019), p. 485-544: p. 515, noted how drawings of insects, by design, stand out in their subtlety.

60 Of course, these developments ran in parallel, and with obvious pride on Swammerdam's part; see Marvin Bolt, Tiemen Cocquyt, and Michael Korey, "Johannes Hudde and His Flameworked Microscope Lenses", *Journal of Glass Studies* 60 (2018), p. 207-222.

61 In particular, Swammerdam's efforts to reduce diversity into four distinct classes or modes, and to systematically relate insect transformation (out of 'imperfection') to classification.

62 The literature on this point fundamentally agrees that Swammerdam believed in a homogeneous nexus of rule, but with different nuances: Domenico Bertoloni Meli, "The representation of insects in the seventeenth century", *Annals of Science* 67 (2010), p. 405-429, follows a comparative template, Eric Jorink, "Between emblematics and the 'argument from design': The representation of insects in the Dutch republic", in *Early Modern Zoology: The Construction of Animals in Science, Literature, and the Visual Arts*, ed. by K. A. E. Enenkel and P. J. Smith, Leiden, Brill, 2007, p. 147-175: p. 160-162, insists that, in its staunch refusal of symbolism, Swammerdam's *Historia* is *both* radical *and* Cartesian, whereas Charlotte Sleigh, "Jan Swammerdam's Frogs", *Notes and Records of the Royal Society of London* 66 (2012), p. 373-392, thinks that Jorink himself goes too far in his desire to counter the received wisdom about the Dutch microscopist being an isolated or erratic mystic.

63 While Descartes maintained an obvious loyalty to the foundation of his physics, scholars have noted a shift, in the passage from the *Discourse* to the *Principia philosophiae*, characterized by increased demands on experiments and observations to buttress an argument. See Daniel Garber, *Descartes Embodied: Reading Cartesian philosophy through Cartesian science*, Cambridge, Cambridge University Press, 2001. Vincent Aucante, *La philosophie médicale de Descartes*, Paris, PUF, 2006, p. 314-322, argues that Descartes's medical views were progressively adjusted to fit the empirical data, including anatomical finding. On this, see also Fabrizio Baldassarri, *Il metodo al tavolo anatomico. Descartes e la medicina*, Roma, Aracne, 2021. On the unity of *res extensa*, see Dennis Des Chene, *Spirits & Clocks: Machine and Organism in Descartes*, Ithaca, Cornell University Press, 2001, and Jed Buchwald, "Descartes' experimental journey past the prism and through the invisible world to the rainbow", *Annals of Science* 65/1 (2008), p. 1-46.

64 See Verbeek, *Descartes and the Dutch*, and Andrea Strazzoni, *Dutch Cartesianism and the Birth of Philosophy of Science: From Regius to 's Gravesande*, Berlin, De Gruyter, 2019.

Letter. On the one hand, we are now accustomed to the fact that mechanization, as a paradigm, affected domains previously conceived as peripheral like meteorology, chemistry, and anatomy itself.⁶⁵ In this sense, as Swammerdam reflected intensely on the cognitive or embodied aspects of his micrography, he was walking on a well-trodden path in Cartesian environments. On the other hand, as Saskia Klerk aptly noted, Swammerdam's classifying bent tied him to late-Renaissance encyclopedists in the vein of Gessner and Aldrovandi.⁶⁶ As a result of this ambivalence, it could be that we can only hope to describe Swammerdam's method, at best, like a mirror of the scientific and experimental tradition at Leiden, which itself was deeply shaped by Cartesian empiricism.⁶⁷ In the end, it all depends on how much of Descartes we presume was left unsaid. That is especially true of intelligence like Panciatichi's, in which a great amount of oral discussion was excised for the readers. Leopoldo only saw an abbreviated version of a *compte rendu* that advocated a recent monograph as a masterful work of induction, Cartesian or not, and a worthy representative of trends in "new philosophy" that resonated well with ongoing research in Tuscany.

The modern reader might be tempted to dismiss Panciatichi's short entries as a typical exercise, the travel notes of an eclectic bibliophile. But it is revealing that the Florentine patrician's enthusiasm for Swammerdam neatly aligned with the approbation that the Royal Society published in the 1670 issue of *Philosophical Transactions*. The reviewer emphatically made the point that the transformations observed in the animal kingdom, no matter how small, followed an evolutionary pattern and that as an implicit corollary, building a *historia* was not, at least not primarily, a work of mere accumulation as in the Aristotelian system.⁶⁸ In addition, the *Transactions'* account astutely engaged in three insinuations that ultimately enhanced the British protocols for natural science. First, it recognized a crucial role played by the caterpillar's case, demonstrated before Cosimo III de' Medici, within Swammerdam's design.⁶⁹ It also assured the journal's readers that both Thévenot and Magalotti lent credibility to some

---

65 Daniel Garber and Sophie Roux, eds, *The Mechanization of Natural Philosophy*, Dordrecht, Springer, 2013, esp. p. 217-301. The historiographical process of reclaiming Cartesian territories is still under way: Fabrizio Baldassarri, "The mechanical life of plants: Descartes on botany", *British Journal for the History of Science* 52/1 (2019), p. 41-63, extends the mechanistic framework to the plants, although he carefully refuses to call Descartes a botanical virtuoso because of his disdain for taxonomies.

66 Saskia Klerk, "Natural history in the physician's study: Jan Swammerdam (1637-1680), Steven Blankaart (1650-1705), and the 'paperwork' of observing insects", *British Journal for the History of Science* 53 (2020), p. 497-525: p. 509. Klerk further stresses Swammerdam's independence from the kind of common-placing and reshuffling that physicians did on paper, for which see Michael Stolberg, "Medical note-taking in the sixteenth and seventeenth centuries", in *Forgetting Machines*, ed. by A. Cevolini, Leiden, Brill, 2016, p. 143-264.

67 Tammy Nyden, "De Volder's Cartesian Physics and Experimental Pedagogy", in *Cartesian Empiricisms*, ed. by Mihnea Dobre and T. Nyden, Dordrecht, Springer, 2013, p. 227-249.

68 The review appeared on 10 October 1670, in Volume 5, Issue 64 of *Philosophical Transactions*, p. 2078-2080. One of the main claims of Klerk, "Natural history", p. 501, is that Swammerdam integrated individual dissections into histories, and privileged collation.

69 Jorink, "Between emblematics", p. 161, stresses the importance of this episode.

experiments by being there in person.⁷⁰ And finally, it declared that Malpighi's Latin dissertation *De Bombyce*, published in the summer of the same year and explicitly dedicated to the Society as a mutual token of goodwill, was confirmed and vindicated by the young Dutch experimenter.⁷¹

Reading through scientific book reviews of the time, moreover, suggests how rare it was for two theoreticians to agree on the nature of experimental reports. In other words, the problem of what form of paperwork was correct for the development of natural history was not something felt only by the Baconian community, although we rely, at first intuitively and, by accrual, almost exclusively, on the organizational layout that emerged in this field of research over the last two decades.⁷² It is fairly obvious from his choice of words and the leading edge of the term *speculata* that Panciatichi preferred matters of fact to cede the ground to hypotheses. Perhaps he expected that his report on Swammerdam would circulate beyond Leopoldo's circle and be evaluated by leading academicians of the Cimento's recently disbanded net, such as Viviani or Borelli. If, however, the Royal Society openly credited Magalotti as a trusted witness, how well would Panciatichi measure up? Did he have enough credentials to assess *Historia insectorum*? Panciatichi's heterogeneous interests were exuberant and potentially digressive, if not heterodox: a reason why he was under serious scrutiny by Roman authorities. Like Carlo Roberto Dati (1619-1676), he simultaneously held multiple academic affiliations and was a true erudite. In a

---

70 As the text puts it, "Two very Intelligent and Cautious persons", p. 2079. Apparently, the action of assent performed by Thévenot and Magalotti recalls the threefold technology, material, literary and social, of the 'virtual witness' in the classic thesis of Steven Shapin and Simon Schaffer, *Leviathan and the Air-Pump*, Princeton, Princeton University Press, 1985; moreover, this might seem odd given how Magalotti cared for rhetoric, and loathed to get his hands soiled. In reality, the social conventions at play ought to have been far less important for Swammerdam, who operated through several retrials, than when different experimenters reproduced a laboratory experience. JUTTA SCHICKORE, "Trying Again and Again: Multiple Repetitions in Early Modern Reports of Experiments on Snake Bites", *Early Science and Medicine* 15 (2010), p. 567-617: p. 571, insists that repetition and replication should be kept apart, also as a way to question Karl Popper's theory of falsification; CHRISTIAN LICOPPE, "The crystallization of a new narrative form in experimental reports (1660-1690)", *Science in Context* 7 (1994), p. 205-244, is attentive to the redistribution of authority among scholars, while MARIO BIAGIOLI, "Witnessing Astronomy: Kepler on the Uses and Misuses of Testimony", in *Nature Engaged: Science in Practice from the Renaissance to the Present*, ed. by M. Biagioli and J, Rifkin, New York, Palgrave Macmillan, 2012, p. 103-123, has more recently suggested that artisans were also brought in to do a significant amount of witnessing.

71 MATTHEW COBB, "Malpighi, Swammerdam, and the Colourful Silkworm: Replication and Visual Representation in Early Modern Science", *Annals of Science* 59 (2002), p. 111-147: p. 118, who cites the Royal Society review in connection with the epistolary exchange of Swammerdam and Malpighi, mentions the monographic nature of *De Bombyce* as a key innovation; see also DOMENICO BERTOLONI MELI, *Mechanism, Experiment, Disease: Marcello Malpighi and Seventeenth-Century Anatomy*, Baltimore, Johns Hopkins University Press, 2011, p. 271-307.

72 Regardless of personal preferences, it is clear that these studies are defined, and consequently also limited, by English case studies; among my favorites are RICHARD YEO, *Notebooks, English Virtuosi and Early Modern Science*, Chicago, University of Chicago Press, 2014, and ELIZABETH YALE, *Sociable Knowledge: Natural History and the Nation in Early Modern Britain*, Philadelphia, University of Pennsylvania Press, 2016.

darker development, a depression drove Panciatichi to commit suicide in 1676. It is intriguing to draw parallels between this psychological introspection and the fading career of a specific intellectual type, the virtuoso or gentlemanly amateur, who, in Roger Chartier's opinion, expressed an elitist scorn for print and lived with his peers in the shadow of public service and in the voluntary avoidance of courtly sociability.[73] As it is well known, anonymity and the self-effacement of authorship are integral to the burgeoning genre of encyclopedias. Put differently, deficiency and overload of information are equally symptomatic of the age of dictionaries.[74]

In point of fact, Panciatichi's most important contribution, like Dati's, consisted in his robust collaboration to the third edition of the *Vocabolario della Crusca* (1691), which of all the various editions of this enterprise was the most inclusive of post-Galilean epistemology and science more generally. This puts the Amsterdam report of 1671 in context. On the one hand, repeated foreign missions were a standard in Europe for collecting and validating information.[75] Yet, it is impossible to believe that, even if he could not read the original Dutch, Panciatichi with his engagement in the creation of a vernacular epistemic language would be unmoved by *Historia*, on the other. As a result, reporting to Leopoldo, Panciatichi conveyed the prowess of Swammerdam's experimental activities with some trepidation. The autograph's handwriting remained nervous throughout.[76] Despite the letter's brevity, it is made clear that Tacitism would soon gain fresh titles in print or that the Dutch intended to champion Paolo Sarpi, despite the controversy that the intrepid priest invited.[77]

We must assume that Panciatichi was well aware of Leopoldo's interests and that both men saluted these editorial facts with pride and favor. After all, this journey to the Netherlands was not isolated and the Medicis would try, unsuccessfully, to purchase Swammerdam's cabinet in the mid-1670s.[78] Without this background of

---

73 ROGER CHARTIER, *The Order of Books*, Stanford, Stanford University Press, 1994, p. 38-39.
74 MARTIN MULSOW, "Practices of Unmasking: Polyhistors, Correspondence, and the Birth of Dictionaries of Pseudonymity in Seventeenth-Century Germany", *Journal of the History of Ideas* 67 (2006), p. 219-250.
75 See NICHOLAS DEW, "Reading travels in the culture of curiosity: Thévenot's collection of voyages", *Journal of Early Modern History* 10 (2006), p. 39-59, and Rina Knoeff, "The Visitor's View: Early Modern Tourism and the Polyvalence of Anatomical Exhibits", in *Centers and Cycles of Accumulation in and around the Netherlands during the Early Modern Period*, ed. by L. Roberts, Münster, LIT Verlag, 2011, p. 155-175.
76 The situation is far from unusual, within the Cimento's network, and enhanced by the fact that the real 'keeper' of their epistemic projects was Vincenzo Viviani, not Magalotti; and while Viviani, for sure, had an idiosyncratic and distinctly cursive handwriting, we must assume that some of the recorded hesitancy also had to do with the crossing between disciplines in this academy; see W. E. KNOWLES MIDDLETON, "When Did Charles II Call the Fellows of the Royal Society?", *Notes and Records* 32/1 (1977), p. 13-16, and STEFANO GATTEI, "Galileo's legacy: a critical edition and translation of the manuscript of Vincenzo Viviani's *Grati Animi Monumenta*", *British Journal for the History of Sciece* 50 (2017), p. 181-228.
77 ANDREEA BADEA, "Chi deve confutare Sarpi? Scrivere storia nella Roma del Seicento", *Cristianesimo nella storia* 37 (2016), p. 467-494.
78 The episode is relatively well-known; see especially the literature cited on note 8 and GERRIT A. LINDEBOOM, *The Letters of Jan Swammerdam to Melchisedec Thévenot*, Amsterdam, Swets & Zeitlinger, 1975, p. 72-73. DÁNIEL MARGÓCSY, *Commercial Visions: Science, Trade, and Visual Culure in the Dutch*

cultural interlacement, why should this traveler, respected or experienced enough to have conversed with Robert Boyle (1627-1691) and Isaac Vossius (1618-1689), linger on commercial details that extend beyond the international book trade? The last part of Panciatichi's letter expressed concerns for a ban placed on the export of French wines and a more comprehensive fracture in the flowing of economic life.[79]

As the writer feared, this embargo seemed unwise and unreasonable. And given his patron's lofty standards of trading and communication, Panciatichi's assessment of this sudden hiatus in the circulation of wares, partially mitigated by the conviction that the current stalemate would eventually spur new trading adjustments, is quite illuminating on the multiconfessional European circuit that linked these actors. It is true that Swammerdam declined the Medici's offer to move to Italy. Still, this did not prevent Dutch and Tuscan parties to commerce with each other, intensely as well as intentionally.[80] We are far beyond the image of the post-Galilean science as sadly and inevitably declining into years of provincial frustration and inertia.

6. A Final Case Study: Van Hogelande's *Cogitationes* in Germany

It is indeed over a large geographic range that one must see familiar constructions such as "Cartesian mechanism" or "beast-machine analogy". They acted as nodes or multipliers in the networks that connected Protestant and Catholic Europe. Consider Cornelis Van Hogelande's *Cogitationes*, first published in Amsterdam in 1646 (Fig. 2) and then reprinted by Johannes van Gelder in Leiden thirty years later.[81] The book was deeply and decidedly Cartesian. Its ostensible goal was to offer a definitive, scathing rejection of natural teleology, which had provided the scaffolding for so much of

---

Golden Age, Chicago, University of Chicago Press, 2014, p. 118-120, continues a tradition of studies for which wealthy bourgeois of Dutch cities preferred to be seen as a *mercator sapiens*, rather than courtiers; ascribing Swammerdam to these figures, Margócsy stresses that he did not conform to a specific patron, but reached out to all potential buyers in Europe by using sale catalogues and newspaper advertisements.

79 MS Gal. 279, c. 81^r: "[...] questo totale interrompemento di commercio pregiudiciale".
80 Using the case of the relatively more lenient system of ecclesiastical censorship that prevailed in mid-seventeenth-century Italy, DANIEL STOLZENBERG, "The Holy Office in the Republic of Letters: Roman Censorship, Dutch Atlases, and the European Information Order, circa 1660", *Isis* 110 (2019), p. 1-23, makes the point that the shaping force of these normative ideals of reading offered both obstacles and opportunities, which the historical actors were savvy to exploit. For censors as mediators, see MARCO CAVARZERE, *La prassi della censura nell'Italia del Seicento tra repressione e mediazione*, Rome, Edizioni di Storia e Letteratura, 2011.
81 The printer van Gelder operated under the sign of Minerva, which functioned as a classicizing trademark for the book business that retained a special relation to Leiden university; see LEA HAGEDORN, "Minerva in the Printshop: Publisher's Advertising in Frontispieces and the Media Presence of Early Modern Printer-Publishers", in *Gateways to the Book: Frontispieces and Title Pages in Early Modern Europe*, ed. by G. Bertram, N. Büttner, and C. Zittel, Leiden, Brill, p. 92-123.

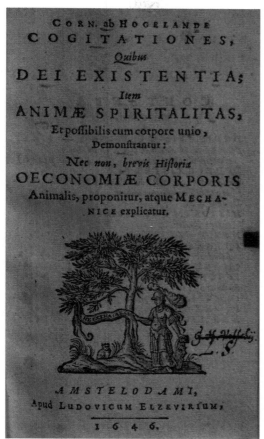

Figure 2. Front page of CORNELIS VAN HOGELANDE, *Cogitationes quibus Dei existentia [...] explicantur*, Amsterdam, Elzevir, 1646; copy marked as Phil 1632 at the Staats- und Stadtbibliothek in Augsburg.

early modern Aristotelian learning.[82] At the same time, its interesting concentration on the 'animal' and its coordination of functions,[83] as in the case of the craft of the

---

82 The second edition of CORNELIS VAN HOGELANDE, *Cogitationes, quibus Dei existential [...] brevis historia oeconomiae corporis animalis, proponitur, atque mechanice explicatur*, Leiden, Van Gelder, 1676, p. 202, is peremptory about this: "Philosophia vulgaris est inutilis in Medicina". In the 1646 edition, there is a well-known passage that equates animals and machines, at p. 276-277: "Omnes autem naturales, id est, a corporibus procedentes actiones, et quascunque in natura vel naturalibus videmus alterationes et motus, mechanice, id est, secundum praedictas aut similes leges". See GIDEON MANNING, "Descartes' Healthy Machines and the Human Exception", in *The Mechanization of Natural Philosophy*, p. 238, and EVAN R. RAGLAND, "Mechanism, the Senses, and Reason: Franciscus Sylvius and Leiden Debates Over Anatomical Knowledge After Harvey and Descartes", in *Early Modern Medicine and Natural Philosophy*, ed. by P. Distelzweig, B. Goldberg, and E. R. Ragland, Dordrecht, Springer, 2016, p. 173-205, p. 186.

83 JUSTIN E. H. SMITH, *Divine Machines: Leibniz and the Sciences of Life*, Princeton, Princeton University Press, 2011, p. 62: "[...] animal economy is a sort of limit case of micro-economics, looking into the internal economy of what in today's economic science would be taken as the basic unit of analysis:

muscles,⁸⁴ is designed to both reveal and foreground the astounding autonomy of nature's skillful physiology and its mechanical laws.

A trusted friend of Descartes, Van Hogelande has once lodged in the same house in Leiden and consulted with him on medical cases. Although he would be eclipsed in time by Regius's formidable career, Van Hogelande represents an early attempt to set a new course for Cartesian medicine in the Netherlands.⁸⁵ When related in this way to Descartes and his inner circle, *Cogitationes* had the advantages of explicitly championing certain philosophical sympathies but also the discomforts of political branding. Such a marked contrast was not lost on Descartes himself. On the basis of his intimate correspondence with Elisabeth of Bohemia (1618-1680) already in March of 1647, one notices in Descartes the perplexity of having Van Hogelande on his side, yet professing principles he viewed as alien.⁸⁶ Usually, historians attribute the alienation to a protracted discussion of Harvey's theory of circulation; however, the textbook contains other elements that may have prompted similar feelings. For example, it hosts a discussion of the trancelike behavior of cataleptic limbs, which is puzzling in light of the Cartesian dualism between "extended" and "thinking" as two incompatible classes of substance and which inspires the author a strange and parenthetical comparison of the suffering body with a self-moving automaton.⁸⁷

The ramifications of Descartes' disconcertment with Van Hogelande go beyond the scope of this contribution. As Evan Ragland remarked in a mid-1640s debate that opposed Cartesians and followers of Harvey, Van Hogelande defended more than a single position.⁸⁸ In part, this is problematic for purely theoretical reasons. In part,

---

the individual active body".

84 In general, anatomy in *Cogitationes* serves as a way to offer conspicuous examples of astuteness, often in conjunction with the adjective 'miranda' or 'mirandum' (including in the dedicatory letter to Descartes); Van Hogelande's use of the term *fabrica*, to signify construction or workmanship in the bodily domain, is strongly Vesalian, although the background of discussion is not. Compared to the German tradition of anatomical practice as self-knowledge, conceived as a means of obtaining access to the providential design, for which see VIVIAN NUTTON, "Wittenberg Anatomy", in *Medicine and the Reformation*, ed. by O. P. Grell and A. Cunningham, London, Routledge, 1993, p. 11-32, Van Hogelande was conveying the idea that organic parts of the body could not violate their laws.

85 SCHMALTZ, *Early Modern Cartesianisms*, p. 256. For reason of space, I am condensing here a very complex situation, suffice to think of corpuscular reductionism or the example of 'circumpulsion' and pneumatics as Cartesian arguments; see ANDREA STRAZZONI, *Burchard de Volder and the Age of the Scientific Revolution*, Dordrecht, Springer, 2019, p. 233 and 399.

86 Descartes to Elisabeth, March 1647, AT IV 627; see SABRINA EBBERSMEYER, "An Inventory of the Extant Correspondence of Elisabeth of Bohemia, Princess Palatine (1618-1680)", *Journal of the History of Philosophy* 58 (2020), p. 325-398, and DENIS KAMBOUCHNER, "What is Elisabeth's Cartesianism?", in *Elisabeth of Bohemia (1618-1680): A Philosopher in Her Historical Context*, ed. by S. Ebbersmeyer and S. Hutton, Dordrecht, Springer, 2021, p. 205-214.

87 VAN HOGELANDE, *Cogitationes* (ed. 1676), p. 220: "Si stantem propuleris passus aliquot, machinae instar automaticae, progredientem miraberis. Motum partium aliquantod quidem difficiliorem subinde in Catalepticorum historiis annotant Medici, sed eum per accidens huic morbo adesse postea ostendam". For the fascination with automata, see MATTIA MANTOVANI, "Descartes' Man Under Construction: The Circulatory Statue of Salomon Reisel, 1680", *Early Science and Medicine* 25 (2020), p. 101-134.

88 RAGLAND, "Mechanism, the Senses, and Reason", p. 185.

it is due to peer pressure. If *Cogitationes* were in conformity with the opinion that experience serves to demonstrate the truth of hypotheses, one could argue that the stunning anatomic displays of the animal economy are consciously emphasized to provide a feasible entry into the underlying Cartesian 'clockwork'.[89] In this respect, Van Hogelande's view is ultimately grounded in an enduring dilemma of the Dutch intellectual landscape, namely, how to properly balance theories and experiments.

In Ragland's account of Van Hogelande's approach to Cartesian physiology, a very significant role is played by an experiment on the fermentation of blood, which was performed on the heart of a large eel.[90] Apart from arguing about heat and motion, Van Hogelande affirms that he repeated the experiment with success, but deflects almost immediately any impression of haste in disseminating these observational results by blaming the printer's hurry.[91] In itself, a lament against the schedule of a publisher is a traditional gesture by authors wishing not to appear careless, as well as an important building block in the ethical construction of *politesse* in a scholarly exchange.[92] From the context, however, it seems logical to conclude that a primary concern for Van Hogelande's *Cogitationes* was to assuage those who distrusted the rationality of deduction.[93] And while induction *a posteriori* is explicitly devalued in the text,[94] it is equally reasonable to assume that, at this juncture, the experiments were prized for the capacity to offer analogies and adjustments within a theory.

According to Jed Buchwald, Cartesian experimental procedures are geared toward the isolation of dependencies.[95] Experiments, in other words, have a modelling role that is vital, in that they help us to identify how a path is branching, provided that one already knows those paths beforehand. They enable further progress, but they are not as foundational as in the active methodology advocated by William Harvey in which autopsy is the real broker of meaning and the essential, sobering contrast to the agitations and phantoms of the mind.[96] But despite these

---

89 The opinion that the Cartesian move was to deduce all empirical evidence in a confident manner is vindicated especially by the citations gathered by STRAZZONI, *Burchard de Volder*, p. 247.
90 RAGLAND, "Mechanism, the Senses, and Reason", p. 189-190; with references to VAN HOGELANDE, *Cogitationes* (1646), p. 147-149.
91 VAN HOGELANDE, *Cogitationes* (1646), p. 147: "atque hoc experimentum eisdem particulis simili etiam successu iteravi; dum typographus festinat".
92 RAPHAËLE GARROD, "La Politesse de *L'Esprit*: Cartesian Pedagogy and the Ethics of Scholarly Exchanges", in *Descartes and the* Ingenium, p. 184-203.
93 VAN HOGELANDE, *Cogitationes* (1646), p. 149: "in gratiam tamen omni ratiocinationi diffidentium, silique experientiae credentium".
94 VAN HOGELANDE, *Cogitationes* (1646), p. 149: "ne quis existimet, me praecedentes rationes a posteriori (scilicet praedicto experimento prius facto) collegisse".
95 BUCHWALD, "Descartes' experimental journey", p. 5.
96 The key statement in Harvey comes as an incidental remark during an exposition, and with admirable clarity: WILLIAM HARVEY, *Exercitatio anatomica de cordis et sanguinis motu*, London, Roger Daniels, 1661, p. 187: "per sensum et experientiam, confirmatam reddere, anatomico more, tanquam majori authoritate, volui". In his classic study, ANDREW WEAR, "William Harvey and the 'Way of the Anatomists'", *History of Science* 21 (1983), p. 223-249: p. 238, suggests that with the idea that the mind's imagination produces a 'confused universal' Harvey arrives almost at a Cartesian inversion. For experience like a tutor, or the result of long training, see also BENJAMIN GOLDBERG,

jarring resonances, many physicians in Holland and abroad passionately objected to Cartesianism not because they could not accept its micro-level mechanical obstinacies, but because they could not adapt to the link between metaphysics and medicine that Descartes continued to claim.[97] This is why historians should be wary of whiggish narratives that equate the growth of Cartesian medicine with the liquidation of encyclopedic curiosities and with a progressive compromise with the experimental practice of the *novatores*. At best, we can claim that *to some extent* traditions in anatomy and chymistry became more autoptic and reliant on sensory intuition. And conversely, Cartesians were happy *to some extent* to subordinate experience to reasoning and satisfied to be portrayed as theoreticians who did so. Yet such a tension cannot be resolved. Rather than a clear bifurcation, this was always a promiscuous terrain.

It could be further argued that the explanation for this uncertainty lies in national categories. When Cartesian medicine as a system reached its maturity, it reflected the eclectic, pragmatic, and 'open-ended' features of the Dutch golden age.[98] Or we may alternatively want to posit a sort of trading zone for exactly the same purpose between Cartesians and their academic predecessors. Although, despite our current fondness for these economic metaphors, the heated debates that unfolded between the so-called Utrecht crisis in 1641 and Johannes Clauberg's apologetic writings in the late 1650s were articulated along the lines of corollaries and Latin disputations. That is, they followed hermeneutical traits and scientific genres strongly associated with the Scholastic philosophy.[99] Yet, when studying Cartesian reception, a purely national frame is difficult to sustain. Was Dutch identity important to a Revius or a Clauberg?[100] If we take the "Dutch" scholarly persona to be influenced by ideals of tolerance, very few documents would qualify. Among them in our evidence, there is a letter cited by Verbeek, in which the stadtholder William II (1626-1650) pleaded moderation.[101] Pluralism and willingness to compromise emerge in a most valuable way once we view these Cartesian discussions from an international perspective.

The peculiar, unexpected size of Van Hogelande's *Cogitationes*, a duodecimo book, accompanied its reception in German universities and facilitated some mechanism

---

"William Harvey on Anatomy and Experience", *Perspectives on Science* 24 (2016), p. 305-323, and for Harvey as the ideal type of the natural investigator, see ROSE-MARY SARGENT, *The Diffident Naturalist: Robert Boyle and the Philosophy of Experiment*, Chicago, University of Chicago Press, 1995, p. 83. On the relationship between Descartes and Harvey, see Goldberg in this volume.

97 See especially THEO VERBEEK, ed., *Johannes Clauberg (1622-1665) and Cartesian Philosophy in the Seventeenth Century*, Dordrecht, Springer, 1999.

98 For a summary and a thoughtful critique of this historiographical trend, see HOWARD HOTSON, *The Reformation of Common Learning: Post-Ramist Method and the Reception of the New Philosophy, 1618-c. 1670*, Oxford, Oxford University Press, 2020, p. 192-199.

99 HAMID, "Domesticating Descartes".

100 See HOTSON, *The Reformation of Common Learning*, p. 193, and AZA GOUDRIAAN, ed., *Jacobus Revius: A Theological Examination of Cartesian Philosophy. Early Criticisms (1647)*, Leiden, Brill, 2002.

101 VERBEEK, *Descartes and the Dutch*, p. 121.

of collecting, which we are still, partially, in a position to evaluate.¹⁰² Of a half dozen copies extant or traceable in the German library system, two are of special interest. In one case, Cornelius Van Hogelande is bound with a Dutch Reformed theologian, Jacobus Revius (1586-1658), whose *Methodi cartesianae consideratio theologica* of 1648 is the third and conclusive title in a print miscellany of the Herzog August Bibliothek in Wolfenbüttel, marked as A: 1229.5 Theol. Another case is also a HAB *Sammelband* within the "Theologica" section marked as A: 1248.3 and bringing together Van Hogelande's *Cogitationes* with the 1645 edition from Hardwijk of the *Rescriptio Scholastica* by the English Puritan controversialist William Ames (1576-1633).¹⁰³ Although these books are not part of the Helmstedt collection, it is obvious that the Scholastic and theological background of the university exerted a profound influence on the way both Cartesian and anti-Cartesian discourses were re-shaped.

And while a form of Aristotelian accommodation was already present in the Dutch debates around Descartes,¹⁰⁴ it is fair to observe by judging on the printed evidence that in Northern Germany discussions on anatomy or experimental practices were not limited to the medical faculties and were filtered through the lenses of theology and church history. As a consequence, a series of categories are turned inside-out. And it becomes even more problematic to uphold a rigid distinction of Cartesian or anti-Cartesian figureheads at odds and fighting with each other; as early as in the 1640s and 50s, German readers saw things differently. They did not approach this field like intellectual historians, but rather as antiquarians and eclectics. In fact, the main ground for the blending of traditions of *novatores* that we tend to perceive as antithetical or differentiated was not the philosophical curriculum, but the history of reading and the tools developed within that frame such as book-binding, note-taking, and so on. As Hotson suggestively observed,¹⁰⁵ the young Leibniz in 1669 was a keen observer of this German intellectual tendency when he wrote that "such great men

---

102 A comprehensive history of the *receptio Cartesiana* in Germany still awaits to be written, apart from recent exceptions, such as HAMID, "Domesticating Descartes", and OMODEO, "Lodewijk de Bils", and considering that the best book in the field, FRANCESCO TREVISANI, *Descartes in Germania: La ricezione del cartesianesimo nella Facoltà filosofica e medica di Duisburg (1652-1703)*, Milan, Franco Angeli, 1992, remains a masterful case study of one specific locale.

103 To these two composite volumes, one should add the *Sammelband* marked as A: 576.13, in the "Quodlibetalis" section of the HAB, which binds together Revius' *Libertas Christiana* (1647) with his *Statera Philosophiae Cartesianae* (1650), both in duodecimo. There is also a letter by Johann Valentin Andreae (1586-1654), preserved in the MS Guelf. 65.1 Extrav., c. 100ʳ and dated to August 1643, in which he leaves a marginal note concerning Revius and Jacobus Trigland's Dissertatio theologica de civili et ecclesiastici potestate (Amsterdam, Jansonius, 1642). See FRANCESCO CERRATO, "Tra Rinascimento e modernità: le dialettiche nel dibattito filosofico olandese del primo Seicento", in *Dialettica: Tradizioni, problemi, sviluppi*, ed. by Alberto Burgio, Macerata, Quodlibet, 2007, p. 1-20, and JEROEN M. M. VAN DE VEN, *Printing Spinoza: A Descriptive Bibliography of the Works Published in the Seventeenth Century*, Leiden, Brill, 2022, p. 21.

104 ANDREA STRAZZONI, "La filosofia aristotelico-cartesiana di Johannes de Raey", *Giornale critico della filosofia italiana* 7 (2011), p. 107-132.

105 HOTSON, *The Reformation of Common Learning*, p. 192.

as Bacon, Gassendi, Hobbes, Digby, and Cornelis van Hogelande… are commonly jumbled together with the Cartesians (i.e. *Cartesianis confundit*)".[106]

Viewed from an international perspective, Descartes' qualified approval of some of his mutual Dutch friends and, by implication, the distancing among themselves of Cartesian followers, reveal a much more complex story. "Inductive" and "deductive" categories are used promiscuously, and what is conspicuously absent is the specific signification that many contemporary scholars attribute to the term 'experimental philosophy' at this stage.[107] In Swammerdam's example, when he extols the value of experiments, he continues to operate within Cartesian tenets but at a time when Descartes had demonstrably poor credentials as an anatomist, despite his own self-regard. Therefore, Swammerdam's embrace of induction is only really Cartesian in the hybrid, international sense that culminated in Leibniz's letter to Thomasius.[108]

7. Concluding Remarks

It is easy for historians to forget that the living mechanism of scientific academies and courtly culture was grounded on oral exchanges and cemented by a system of international reviews of recent publications. Since for many academies, including the Royal Society itself, 'publishing' was a relatively low priority in this period, one could further observe that the impact of reading suggestions, coming from abroad, was more important than some of their own signature product.[109] From this angle, this essay has focalized on some unglamorous archival evidence to shed more light on the "interactive awareness" between research facilities, located at great distance from one another.[110] It is clear that the self-serving purpose of patronage

---

106 Leibniz to Thomasius, 20/30 April 1669; AA II-1, p. 24-25. The letter is well-known to students of Leibniz, and generally inscribed in the philosopher's neo-Aristotelian efforts, in this period, to harmonize theory of motion with God as the prime mover. For obvious reasons, I find Hotson's point important and well-taken, but I find that the letter is better seen from another standpoint. To simplify, a main contention in Hotson's book is that the United Provinces offered less substantial pluralism compared to the Protestant states, at the peak of their confessional struggles and despite their pessimistic eschatology. Leibniz, however, criticizes Descartes for arbitrarily introducing 'speculative' ideas, which are unrelated to the model endorsed ("[…] ab illa severitate prorsus remisit, et ad Hypotheses quasdam miras ex abrupto delapsus est"); thus, the associative merging of schools, inspired by the eclectic and 'federal' theology of the Cartesian Johannes Cocceius (1603-1669) remains compelling, but Leibniz actually sees Hobbes as the most rigorous among the modern, admirable masters that he 'jumbles' around the name of Descartes.
107 For a critique of anachronism, see MORDECHAI FEINGOLD, "Experimental Philosophy: Invention and Rebirth of a Seventeenth-Century Concept", *Early Science and Medicine* 21/1 (2016), p. 1-28.
108 KLERK, "Natural history", p. 509-511.
109 NOAH MOXHAM, "Fit for print: Developing an institutional model of scientific periodical publishing in England, 1665-c. 1714", *Notes and Records of the Royal Society* 69 (2015), p. 241-260.
110 This idea was introduced by MORDECHAI FEINGOLD, "The Accademia del Cimento and the Royal Society", in *The Accademia del Cimento and its European Context*, ed. by M. Beretta, A. Clericuzio, and L. M. Principe, Sagamore Beach, Watson Publishing International, 2009, p. 229-242: p. 236.

strategies is insufficient to account for this documentation. And once we place Cartesianism within the world of scholarly news and endorsements — that is to say, inside the high mobility of savants and the logistics of book trading which they orchestrated — even the most physically (and conceptually) humble clues become significant.

We obtain something similar to the "buffer zone" hypothesized in a recent article, a periphery of Cartesian debates, as it were, working as a supplement.[111] The desire to read Cartesian textbooks or to accommodate their content through a personal or public library collection runs in parallel with the way letters and reviews provided skeletal guidelines for experimental replication. In both cases, we are dealing with a type of blueprint on how to 'get things right' when attempting to record or re-run an experience in the laboratory. As a result, enlarging a Cartesian map beyond the Low Countries allows us to gain a better understanding of the relationship between contingency and decisiveness in the history of experimental science.[112]

In the case of reports such as Brunetti's and Panciatichi's, we saw how carefully the Medici rulers tried to project and sell their cultural output in Northern Europe and in the Netherlands. The flow was not one-way. And the emerging picture is hardly that of a culturally dominant region versus one that is lagging behind; studying the dissemination of Cartesian debates in a global, pan-European fashion substantially mitigates the impression of backwardness in the post-Galilean epistemology.

In essence, the globalization of science within the territorial limits of the 1660s and 1670s required serious administrative efforts. The importance of management is in fact stressed in the charters of the early scientific academies or is highlighted in the cases of those that chose not to formalize a statutory language. Thus in Florence as in London, or at the Dublin Philosophical Society after 1683,[113] we find offices like Leopoldo's chancellery, where secretaries copied letters and extracted summaries, lists, and bullet points. It was in these emerging archival practices that news about Swammerdam's newly 'discovered' territories in the life-cycle of the insects drew a renewed attention, from the smallest imaginable domains, about the confirmatory power of experiments. Both processes — the actual dissection and sifting through news — were "preparatory" and based on collation and replication of data. Indeed, agents, informants, projectors, learned librarians,[114] and book reviewers were not unlike Jesuits, in that they struggled

---

111 SANGIACOMO, TANASESCU, DONKER, and HOGENBIRK, "Mapping the evolution of early modern natural philosophy", p. 9-11.
112 See SCHICKORE, "Trying Again and Again", and Elaine Leong and ALISHA RANKIN, "Testing Drugs and Trying Cures: Experiment and Medicine in Medieval and Early Modern Europe", *Bulletin of the History of Medicine* 91 (2017), p. 157-182.
113 CONSTANCE HARDESTY, "Mirror, Model, Muse: Institutional Memory and Identity in the Dublin, Oxford and Royal Societies", in *Memory and Identity in the Learned World: Community Formation in the Early Modern World of Learning and Science*, ed. by K. Scholten, D. van Miert, and K. A. E. Enenkel, Leiden, Brill, 2022, p. 199-234.
114 See, for the important example of Lucas Holstenius, PETER RIETBERGEN, *Power and Religion in Baroque Rome: Barberini Cultural Policies*, Leiden, Brill, 2006, p. 256-295.

constantly with issues like social obedience, compliance, and control, especially if Fathers were far away in Japan or India.[115] The scholarly management was based on a trial-and-error approach for developing technologies, not on a celebration of wealth and power in a given cultural setting, and was too tentative and inherently unstable to be, at first, politically shrewd.[116]

---

115 MARKUS FRIEDRICH, "Government in India and Japan is different from government in Europe: Asian Jesuits on Infrastructure, Administrative Space, and the Possibilities for a Global Management of Power", *Journal of Jesuit Studies* 4 (2017), p. 1-27.
116 The archival fragility of the investigations at the Medici court is rarely considered, and the impression of them being costly and entertaining, *pace* PAULA FINDLEN, "Controlling the Experiment: Rhetoric, Court Patronage, and the Experimental Method of Francesco Redi", *History of Science* 31/1 (1993), p. 35-64, can only derive by our exclusive reliance on printed materials, which actually belong to a different genre, like the *Saggi di naturali esperienze* and Thomas Sprat's *History of the Royal Society*, both published in 1667, in Florence and London, and the only propagandist works in the corporate life of their supporting institutions.

MARIA CONFORTI

"Se fusse meno cartesiano lo stimarei molto"

Anti-Cartesian Motifs in Italian Medicine

▼ ABSTRACT   In this chapter, I deal with some anti-Cartesian motifs in Southern Italy, Pisa, and Bologna, especially connected to Cartesian medicine. Still, several nuances reveal a blurred picture, in which Descartes was early criticized, but later appreciated, for his systematic program. However, several problems persist, as highlighted in this chapter, as Italian scholars and physicians faced the same problems of Descartes' philosophy, namely, the difficulties in dealing with life or in the foundation of iatromechanism. Somehow confronting with, or moving from Cartesian mechanization, the explanation of how bodies function gained momentum in seventeenth-century Italian medicine (and natural philosophy), while diverse traditions mitigate this mechanical strand, as scholars tended to combine the latter with Epicureanism, in order to fill its gaps. A thriving picture thus surfaces, revealing the vitality and the importance, together with the limitations, of Cartesianism in early modern Italy studies.

▼ KEYWORDS   Cartesianism, Cornelio, Galilei, Borelli, Malpighi, Iatromechanism, Epicureanism

Writing to Marcello Malpighi in March 1664, Giovanni Alfonso Borelli (1608-1679), never tired of discussing new books and opinions, mentioned a recent work, the *Progymnasmata physica*, by the Neapolitan physician and mathematician Tommaso Cornelio (1614-1684). Despite the fact that one Epistle in the book was dedicated to Borelli himself, his judgement on Cornelio's work was somewhat

Maria Conforti • Sapienza University of Rome. Contact: <maria.conforti@uniroma1.it>

harsh.¹ It hinted at his being a follower of Descartes — something that Borelli disapproved of — and at the acceptance of friends' whims and defects: "I am glad that you have seen the book by Corneli, and that you found in it things to like; and really, if Sig. Corneli was less uncompromising, and less Cartesian, I would appreciate him much; however, in friends one must look for what is good, and accept imperfection".²

As shown by several scholars, Descartes' reception in Italy was extremely nuanced, and went from a clear acceptance to a somewhat reluctant inclusion in a pantheon of 'modern' thinkers and natural philosophers.³ In what follows, I am going to explore some anti-Cartesian motifs, or opinions, in Italian medicine in the late seventeenth century. My geography is a limited one, including the Southern part of the Peninsula, with Naples and Messina — but also Pisa, and Bologna, albeit only indirectly. This choice consciously excludes important figures, like Nicolas Steno or — on the technical and anatomical side — Carlo Fracassati, as well as a number of other authors who also dealt with Descartes and its medical philosophy — accepting it, rejecting it or finding a compromise between these two extremes. I also have a short chronology, approximately from the 1640s to the 1680s: only four decades in the long history of Italian medicine. In fact, my focus will be on a much more limited number of years. I will first briefly deal with the Kingdom of Naples, and Cornelio's acceptance of Descartes; I will then go back to Pisa and Messina, to Borelli and Malpighi, using their correspondences to highlight some of the ways Descartes was used, interpreted, and rejected.

1. Descartes in Naples: Tommaso Cornelio

The lawyer and staunch champion of the 'moderns' Francesco D'Andrea (1625-1698), writing his memories at the end of the seventeenth century, stated that Naples was indebted to Tommaso Cornelio for the introduction in the Kingdom, at the end

---

1 Borelli was the dedicatee of the fictional ("fabulosa") epistle from Marco Aurelio Severino to Timaeus Locrensis, dealing with the plague and the state of scientific culture in Naples at the time, as well as with astrology and specific aspects of the ancient&moderns controversy: TOMMASO CORNELIO, *Progymnasmata physica*, Venetiis, Haered. Fr. Babae, 1663, p. 149-190. It may be possible that Borelli did not entirely appreciate the style and genre of the part of the book Cornelio had chosen to dedicate to him.
2 GIOVANNI ALFONSO BORELLI to Marcello Malpighi, Pisa, 21 March 1664, in HOWARD B ADELMANN, ed., *The correspondence of Marcello Malpighi*, Ithaca Cornell University Press, 1975, vol. I, letter 197, p. 204: "Piacemi che VS abbia veduto il libro del Dr Corneli, e che vi abbi trovato cose di suo gusto, e veramente se il Sig. Corneli fosse meno risoluto, e meno Cartesiano io lo stimarei molto, tutta via degli amici bisogna goder il buono, e compatir l'imperfezione." [Translation is mine.]
3 The bibliography on Descartes' reception in Italy is too large to be easily summarized; for Naples, *Dalla scienza mirabile alla scienza nuova. Napoli e Cartesio, Catalogo della mostra bibliografica e iconografica*, Napoli, Istituto Italiano per gli Studi Filosofici, 1997; ETTORE LOJACONO, *Immagini di René Descartes nella cultura napoletana dal 1644 al 1755*, Lecce, Conte editore, 2003.

of the 1640s, of the philosophy and medicine of Descartes.⁴ Works by the French philosopher had allegedly been brought and introduced by Cornelio to the backward Italian South after a journey to the Center-North of the peninsula, together with those by other modern authors. This enabled a revolutionary innovation in natural philosophy, allowing to overcome the stale intellectual habits of Scholasticism and Aristotelianism. In many ways, as it has been repeatedly and concincingly shown, this was a retrospective reconstruction, meant as a vindication of D'Andrea's and his friends' role in the development of the civic and cultural life in the city.⁵ The 1640s had witnessed political unrest and revolts in Spanish dominions, in Cataluña as in Naples: the revolution in philosophical methods and science was meant as a necessary complement to the political change required by the middling, professional class ("ceto civile"), which also included many physicians and medical men.⁶

To nuance and better situate this reconstruction, it is to be mentioned that D'Andrea, while extolling Cornelio's and his own role in changing (bad) intellectual attitudes in the Kingdom of Naples, had just remembered in his autobiographical text a champion of innovative thought of a totally different kind, Tommaso Campanella. As he writes, after the 1647 anti-Spanish revolt he took refuge in Chieti for some months in a convent of the Padri delle Scuole Pie. He had found there, and read with great interest, works by Cicero and a "manuscript volume of the *questioni* by father Campanella".⁷ He liked the latter so much that he asked permission to bring it to Naples with him when he came back in the city in September 1648. This glimpse of D'Andrea's reading habits and tastes is meaningful: to a certain extent, late-Renaissance naturalism never declined in the Kingdom, providing a convenient if unlikely (in our terms) frame for later or more up-to-date authors.

D'Andrea was not alone in maintaining this attitude: in one of the inventories of the library of the learned surgeon, Marco Aurelio Severino (1580-1656), an entry reads "physica Renati Cartesij".⁸ The inventories arguably date from the end of the 1640s (Severino died during the plague of 1656), so this is yet another witness to the presence of Descartes' works in the city in about the same period as Cornelio's return. In fact, Severino was one of Cornelio's *maestri*, and the presence of this work implies a circulation of news on Descartes in the circle of *novatores* both belonged to. Maybe it was Cornelio himself who gave it to Severino. The surgeon, who corresponded with

---

4 FRANCESCO D'ANDREA, *Avvertimenti ai nipoti*, ed. by Imma Ascione, Naples, Jovene, 1990, ch. 19, p. 203. On D'Andrea, BIAGIO DE GIOVANNI, *Filosofia e diritto in Francesco D'Andrea. Contributo alla storia del previchismo*, Milano, Giuffrè, 1958; ANTONIO BORRELLI, *D'Andrea atomista. L'"Apologia" e altri inediti nella polemica filosofica della Napoli di fine Seicento*, Naples, Liguori, 1995.
5 On the general evolution of philosophical culture in Naples, NICOLA BADALONI, *Introduzione a G. B. Vico*, Milano, Feltrinelli, 1961; BIAGIO DE GIOVANNI, *La vita intellettuale a Napoli fra la metà del '600 e la restaurazione del Regno*, in Storia di Napoli, vol. VI, p. I, Napoli, Società editrice Storia di Napoli, 1970, p. 403-534.
6 ROSARIO VILLARI, *Un sogno di libertà: Napoli nel declino di un impero, 1585-1648*, Milano, Mondadori, 2012.
7 D'ANDREA, *Avvertimenti*, p. 202: "un volume manoscritto delle questioni del padre Campanella", arguably the *Quaestiones physiologicae* added to the *Philosophia realis* in the Paris 1637 edition.
8 Biblioteca Lancisiana, Roma, Ms. 28 LXXIV.2.6/3, fol. 26ʳ.

scholars throughout Europe and was interested in natural philosophy, had in turn been a loyal follower of Campanella. However, he was also well acquainted with the work of William Harvey, at a time when the latter's controversy on circulation with Descartes was well known. So, it may well be that the book was *his* book, after all.[9]

Obviously, this does by no means imply that readings of Descartes were accurate or influential. While his name resurfaced repeatedly together with those of many other champions of modern thought, often a kind that we would not immediately associate with him — from Galilei to Gassendi, to Digby, to Harvey — an in-depth discussion of his method and theories seemingly lacked in Naples at the time.

The niceties of the Neapolitan philosophical debates may not seem of primary interest for Descartes' scholarship, or for the history of the reception of Descartes' medical philosophy. However, as Ettore Lojacono has shown, they shed light on the development of the philosophical and scientific world in Italy at large, also in view of the impact of Descartes' works on Giambattista Vico's philosophy and theory of history.[10] They are also extremely meaningful, albeit often in an indirect way, to clarify the reception of Descartes' system in medicine and what we would now call physiology. Giovanni Alfonso Borelli's and Marcello Malpighi's position on Descartes' science in the 1660s, which is at the center of my contribution today, is one of such cases.

How much Cartesian was Naples from the 1640s to the 1660s? As shown by many modern interpreters, and as already hinted to, not much. Things, however, changed at the end of the century.[11] In the 1690s the 'Cartesian turn' became real and effective, with methodologically minded commentaries and analyses of Descartes' works and philosophy. However, even in that period, Cartesianism was moderated if not corrected by the very diversity of the intellectual landscape in the city. Indeed, it would be very interesting, and likely to yield unexpected results, to endeavor to precisely map other intellectual influences, prominently the one of another French natural philosopher, Pierre Gassendi. His influence in Naples and in Italy at large, while by no means unnoticed by historiography, has received less attention than it would have deserved, and would likely help in explaining some of the interest of Neapolitan intellectuals and medical men in atomism and corpuscularianism, as well as many objections against Descartes' 'system', as his philosophy was generally perceived to be.

Who were the Cartesian physicians in Naples? Cornelio certainly was one, and, as shown by the quotation by Borelli, well known as such. This interpretation has been supported, with the necessary caution, by recent studies.[12] Apart from Borelli's opinion,

---

9 On Severino, ORESTE TRABUCCO, in *Dizionario Biografico degli Italiani*, vol. 92, Roma, Istituto dell'Enciclopedia Italiana, 2018, ad vocem.
10 ETTORE LOJACONO, *Immagini di René Descartes nella cultura napoletana dal 1644 al 1755*, Lecce, Conte editore, 2003.
11 See *infra*, note #41#.
12 RAFFAELE CARBONE, "The Critical Reception of Cartesian Physiology in Tommaso Cornelio's *Progymnasmata Physica*", in *Descartes'* Treatise on Man *and its Reception*, ed. by D. Antoine-Mahut and S. Gaukroger, Cham, Springer, 2016, p. 91-101. On Cornelio, MAURIZIO TORRINI, *Tommaso Cornelio e la ricostruzione della scienza*, Napoli, Guida, 1977; on his medicine, ROSARIO MOSCHEO,

among other non-Neapolitan witnesses to Cornelio's Cartesianism, or Cartesian reputation, are the English anatomists, and possibly spies, John Finch and Thomas Baines, who were in Naples on behalf of Leopoldo de' Medici. In November 1663, they wrote to from Naples, offering a lengthy report on their journey, detailing chemical and volcanic experiences, and the learned men they had met. "In Naples we have had very special news of Signor Tomaso Cornelio, a mathematician and physician of great renown and a friend of Signor Michel Angelo Ricci. He has written a book entitled *Progymnasmata Physica*: it is printed in Venice and a part of it is dedicated to Signor Alfonso Borelli. He is a Cartesian and a great defender of new things, hence he is hated in Naples by those who swear allegiance to their masters."[13] In fact, Tommaso Cornelio's main work, the *Progymnasmata physica* (1663), was being published in Venice during Finch and Baines' stay in the city.

Cornelio's reputation for Cartesianism was also remembered in the *Philosophical Transactions*, where a perceptive account of his book was published in 1666. Cornelio was judged to be "a friend to the Cartesian philosophy"; however, the author of the account also underlined a number of non-Cartesian features of the book. First of all, Cornelio recommends "the Use of Chymistry ...and the study of Mechanicall Principles"[14] (in this order). Cornelio's medical interest in chymistry, apparent in many passages in the *Progymnasmata*, is also mentioned in a letter by Michelangelo Ricci — who was arguably the person who introduced him to the Cartesian philosophy in the 1640s[15]. Generally speaking, the author of the account writes, he "approves of the Cartesian [principles], esteeming, that none ever looked so like truth, as those; though he thinks them defective in this, that, how well soever they shew the production of things out of Matter variously modified, yet they seem not to have sufficiently accounted for the efficient power thereof."[16] The account further underlines the non-Cartesian character of Cornelio's *progymnasma* on life itself, *De vita*: "this latter proceeds not from the heat of the Bloud (as Des Cartes would have it) but the moist steams and expirations of the Heart."[17] The account in the *Philosophical Transactions* was possibly written by John Dodington (1628-1673), who was the English resident in Venice and acted as a middleman between Cornelio (and other Italian scholars) and

---

Francesco Trevisani, "Between Ancients and Moderns: Tommaso Cornelio's medical teaching abd an unpublished comment by him on the Galenic Ars Parva", *Nouvelles de la République des Lettres*, 2 (1983), p. 59-73.

13 "A Napoli habbiamo havuto particolarissima notitia del Sig.re Tomaso Cornelio, Matematico e Medico di grande grido, et amico del Sig.re Michel Angelo Ricci. Lui ha scritto un libro entitolato Progymnasmata Physica: l'è stampato a Venetia et una parte di esso dedicata al Sig.re Dottor Alfonso Borelli. Lui è Cartesiano et molto difensore delle cose nuove, onde viene a Napoli di esser odiato da quelli che giurorno fedeltà alli loro maestri" [translation is mine.] Biblioteca Nazionale di Firenze, Ms. Gal. 276, fols 224-225, November 24, 1663.

14 "Thomae Cornelii Consentini Progymnasmata Physica", *Philosophical Transactions*, 1-2 (1665-1666), p. 576-579.

15 Michelangelo Ricci a Leopoldo de' Medici, Di Roma li 2 aprile 1669, Biblioteca Nazionale Centrale di Firenze, Ms. Gal. 278, fol. 247^r.

16 "Thomae Cornelii Consentini Progymnasmata Physica", p. 577.

17 *Ibid.*, p. 579.

Henry Oldenburg.¹⁸ The latter always showed respect for, and interest in, Cornelio's work, asking reports on events of interest in the city of Naples.

However, how much a Cartesian can Cornelio be considered to be? As already mentioned, recent studies have underlined his 'critical' reception of the French philosopher. Indeed, some passages of his work rather limit the scope of mechanic laws as applied to living bodies:

> for all the functions and motions of inanimate bodies depend on the various modifications of matter, and take place entirely according to the laws of mechanics; yet who could persuade us that the living things are constructed like automatons [Gr.]; since most of their actions, especially those which pertain to the senses and the appetite, are not so bound by mechanical laws, that rather they seem to be in some way separated from the action of the body.¹⁹

Is this a Cartesian assertion? It may well be, since it points to a separation of mind and body and to the different impulses they provide for human action. However, here as in other instances in the *Progymnasmata* Cornelio rather speaks the semi-sceptical language of uncertainty and verisimilitude when moving from geometry, cosmology and astronomy to medicine and physiology. This attitude was widespread in Naples, and it was widely shared in the group of intellectuals gathering around Cornelio, the Accademia degli Investiganti.²⁰

Furthermore, the physicians Sebastiano Bartoli and Leonardo Di Capua, to mention only two of those who participated in it, believed in chymystry to the point that the hero of the former was Van Helmont, while the latter intensely admired Robert Boyle. As already mentioned, Cornelio was himself on the side of chymystry when giving medical advice. The final epistle in the *Progymnasmata* was addressed to Thomas Willis and Francis Glisson. Here Cornelio hinted at his own priority in a series of discoveries, but also at the closeness he felt with what was called *Anglicana schola*, the 'English school', whose main features, as he well knew, were an Harveian frame, joined with chymical philosophy and medicine.²¹

---

18 See TOMMASO CORNELIO to John Dodington, Naples, 9 January 1672, in *The correspondence of Henry Oldenburg*, Madison, The University of Wisconsin Press, ed. by A. Rupert Hall and Marie Boas, vol. 3, 1965, letter 1876a, p. 494-495: "Io mi confesso multo obbligato alla benignita di V. Illustrissima che si è degnata di leggere il mio libretto de Progimnasmi e darli quelle maggiori lodi che io haverei potuto sperare". On Dodington, see the biography by Alexandre J. Tessier in *The Correspondence of John Dodington*, http://emlo-portal.bodleian.ox.ac.uk/collections/?catalogue = john-dodington [accessed 9/2/2022].

19 "... fac enim omnes inanimorum Corporum functiones, motusque pendere a diversa materiae modificatione, et omnino iuxta leges mechanicae fieri, quis tamen nobis persuaserit ipsas etiam animantes instar automaton [gr.] fieri; cum pleraeque earum actiones maxime quae ad sensum appetitumque attinent, ita mechanicis legibus non sint obstrictae, ut potius ab actione corporis seiunctae quodammodo videantur." [my translation] CORNELIO, *Progymnasmata*, p. 37.

20 MAURIZIO TORRINI, "L'Accademia degli Investiganti. Napoli 1663-1670", *Quaderni storici*, 48 (1981), p. 845-883; ID, "La discussione sullo statuto delle scienze tra la fine del '600 e l'inizio del '700,'" in *Galileo e Napoli*, ed. by F. Lomonaco e M. Torrini, Guida, Napoli, 1987.

21 ROBERT G. FRANK, *Harvey and the Oxford physiologists: a study of scientific ideas*, Berkeley, University of California Press, 1980.

2. Pisa and Messina: Borelli and Malpighi

Let's now go back to Borelli's judgment of Cornelio's work. If we follow the thread of Borelli's and Malpighi's correspondence in the 1660s, we can easily see that a strong anti-Cartesian bent can be found in many instances, and on many different topics; however, the most virulent attacks come from Borelli. Malpighi, as typical of his character and of his scientific attitude, always remains extremely prudent — even if it must be underlined that in the majority of cases we lack his answers to his older and fiery friend. Borelli's strong opposition to Descartes' works and philosophy is apparent from the very first letters he sends to Malpighi. In one written at the beginning of 1660 he deals with an interesting aspect, the depiction of small details — in this instance, of anatomical details of the lungs, on which Malpighi was working at the time. Borelli is encouraging Malpighi to have drawn and publish illustrations of the particulars he has observed. He then advances the opinion that Descartes' text and illustrations in the *Dioptrique* and *Météores* (publ. 1637) were so suggestive that he has "affascinato" many gentlemen by means of his well-constructed images and explanations.[22] 'Affascinare' is an ambiguous term; it may be taken in the positive way, as we now currently do in Italian; it could be thus roughly translated with "capturing the imagination of". However, in this case it really seems more on the negative. In the first editions of the *Vocabolario* of the Accademia della Crusca, published more or less in the same years as Borelli's exchanges with Malpighi, the term is associated with witchcraft practices.[23]

In this case, Borelli is probably referring to the illustrations of particles in Descartes' texts; this sheds a light on his interest in the theories of matter, which is further clarified by his pointed interest for Gassendi and his version of corpuscularianism. In January 1663, writing from Pisa, Borelli requests Magliabechi, who is in Florence, to buy on his behalf a "corpo" (collection) of Gassendi's work, offered by the *libraio* Becalli. He shows great enthusiasm, asking the bibliophile to act rapidly ("non se le lasci scappare"); he also adds that he would gladly buy two exemplars, for his 'friends' in Pisa, who would likely benefit from reading it.[24] In a subsequent letter to

---

22 GIOVANNI ALFONSO BORELLI to Marcello Malpighi, Pisa, 4 January 1660 (1661), in ADELMANN, ed., *The correspondence*, vol. I, letter 29, p. 55: "Ne perche le cose sono assai piccole si dovranno stimare difficili a disegnarsi, e intagliarsi... una cosa simile fece il Cartesio nella sua filosofia, e meteora, il quale con quel suo bello, et artificioso modo di spiegarsi, e dichiararsi ha affascinato non pochi huomini da bene" [my translation].

23 A searchable version of the *Vocabolario* at http://www.lessicografia.it/Controller?q1 = affascinare&EdCrusca1 = 1&EdCrusca2 = 1&EdCrusca3 = 1&submit2 = Visualizza+elenco+forme&-SettImpostazioni = LancioRicerca&maxresults = 50&TipoOrdinamento = 1&TipoRicerca = 0&EF = 1&EvidenziaKeyword = 1&EvidenzSfondoContesto = 1&EvidenzSfondoMicroContesto = 1&IgnoraAccenti = 1 (accessed September 3, 2022). See also *infra* #note 29#, where 'affascinare' is used again by Borelli speaking of Descartes in a disparaging way.

24 GIOVANNI ALFONSO BORELLI to Antonio Magliabechi, Pisa 25 gennaio 1663, in MODESTINO DEL GAIZO, *Alcune lettere di Giovanni Alfonso Borrelli: dirette una al Malpighi e le altre al Magliabechi*, Napoli, tip. della R. Accademia delle Scienze, 1886, p. 34. See also PAOLO GALLUZZI, "Lettere di Giovanni Alfonso Borelli ad Antonio Magliabechi," *Physis*, 12/3 (1970), p. 267-298.

Magliabechi, written in November of the same year, he specifies that he is looking for Gassendi's work for another friend, this time in Sicily; the man is extremely erudite, "molto virtuoso". Borelli also rebutts Padre [Bruno] Tozzi's critiques of Gassendi.[25] In 1661, however, he had asked Magliabechi for Descartes' epistles, among other books; for all his dismissive remarks, he seemingly did not refrain from keeping himself informed of what he had written.

It is thus unsurprising that, like many others in the *République des Lettres*, he became aware of the posthumous publication of Descartes' *De Homine* in 1662. In March 1663, he wrote to Malpighi, harshly addressing in a couple of lines at least three of his adversaries — the English anatomists, Finch and Baines, who were about to meet and admire Cornelio the Cartesian in Naples; and the French philosopher himself. Borelli attributed Finch and Baines' errors and misdeeds to a hatred towards the Italians, and to their adhesion to Cartesianism and its novelties, "novità spiritate". He then adds, as in an aside, that he has heard about *De Homine*, but that he does not even want to read it, nor even to see it, because it seems to him downright "nauseous".[26] Once again, 'spiritate' is a meaningful word to apply to Cartesian ideas and theories — being usually referred to persons who are possessed by Daemons, or, in a less literal sense, to people or things which are enraged, or full of fury. Borelli's letters are among the most likeable and witty written in Italy at the time, and there is no doubt that by using a language normally applied to those bewitched or possessed he is underlining that Cartesianism is a presence to be reckoned with, and a rather strong one for that.

While it is certain that Malpighi, who was now occupied with the structure of the brain and the nerves, shared at least some of Borelli's perplexities on the theories exposed in *De Homine*, his attitude was not necessarily the same as the one of his mentor and friend. Borelli, however, used this sensitive topic in order to foster his own, decidedly anti-Cartesian, point of view. Clarifying the anatomy and use of the nerves also helped posing crucial questions, such as their role in enabling the muscular and motory functions, an issue Borelli had had a keen interest in, as shown by his posthumous *De Motu animalium* (1681).[27] The latter work had taken years if not decades to be written, and Borelli considered it his *magnum opus*. A letter by Fracassati, in Pisa with Borelli, to Malpighi in Messina sheds light on this attitude and on the diversity of responses elicited by Malpighi's work. In March 1664, after reading a draft of the work that was to be published as *De cerebro*, Fracassati wrote that both he and Borelli enjoyed the reading, but Borelli characteristically rejoiced in what he perceived to be a

---

25 GIOVANNI ALFONSO BORELLI to Antonio Magliabechi, Pisa, 30 nov 1663, in DEL GAIZO, *Alcune lettere*, p. 37.

26 GIOVANNI ALFONSO BORELLI to Marcello Malpighi, Pisa, 30 march 1663, in ADELMANN, ed., *The correspondence*, vol. I, letter 75, p. 155: "Intorno a questi Sigri Anatomici Inglesi (Finch and Baines)... stroppiano le cose buone per mescolarle con l'anticaglie, e con le novità spiritate del Cartesio il che depende da scarsezza di giudizio aggiungavi ella certo livore, che hanno contro gl'Italiani ... Del Cartesio è uscito un nuovo libbro de Homine, ma questo mi riesce tanto nauseoso, che facilmente non mi curerò di vederlo" [my translation].

27 GIOVANNI ALFONSO BORELLI, *De Motu Animalium, opus posthumum*, Roma, ex typographia Angeli Bernabò, 1680-1681, pars secunda, prop. XVII and ff.

destruction of Descartes' theory of vision. Borelli once again remarked that Descartes was no novelty at all; in fact, besides calling him "foolhardy", he allegedly added that he "splendidly recooked stale food coming from the ancients".[28]

Slightly *spiritato* himself, Borelli did not leave things there, and kept insisting. Again in March 1664, he wrote to Malpighi, detailing the reaction already announced by Fracassati. He calls Descartes' theory a "presontuosa sentenza", a conceited opinion; he says he would have liked more from Malpighi on the point.[29] It can be gathered that Malpighi had entertained scruples regarding a direct and violent attack on the French philosopher. This impression is reinforced by a later message by Borelli, where once again he repeats that Descartes' fame is nothing to be afraid of; and that his reputation is at present failing.[30] In the *De cerebro*, Malpighi had explicitly addressed the question of Descartes' theory of the tripartite structure of the nerves, prudently calling it plausible ("plausibile"); nevertheless, he writes, it has proven impossible to observe the "filets" in the nerves that were crucial for Descartes' model. In general, Malpighi rather underlines that the whole mechanism of sensation as described by Descartes abounds in difficulties. A mild reaction, on the whole, similar to the one of many anatomists when confronted with hypothetic descriptions of fine structures. For Borelli, this was too weak a position to maintain, and one that did not serve him well.

We know that Malpighi and Borelli experienced some sort of rupture at the end of the 1660s; their correspondence stops and their research and human trajectories dramatically diverge.[31] Whatever the other reasons, the disagreement on the treatment of Descartes may have been an element in their dispute. After the years we have been dealing with, almost no other mention of Descartes is to be found in Malpighi's epistolary. There is a remarkable exception, though, in a letter by the German Jacob Barner (1641-1686), an iatrochemist who was teaching at Padua at the beginning of

---

28 CARLO FRACASSATI to Malpighi, Pisa, 30 march 1663, in ADELMANN, ed., *The correspondence*, vol. I, Pisa, 24 March 1664, letter 98, p. 205-206: "Ho vista la vostra lettera la quale e dal sig. Gio Alfonso è stimata molto bella ed anche da me particolarmente come nota il Sig. Borelli per esser cosa che con l'inventione ne porta getta à terra il Sistema della vista del Sig. des Cartes huomo apresso detto Sig. Borelli temerario et qui splendide recoquit vetera." [Translation is mine.]
29 GIOVANNI ALFONSO BORELLI to Marcello Malpighi, Pisa, 28 March 1664, in ADELMANN, ed., *The correspondence*, vol. I, letter 99, p. 207: "... particolarmente m'è piaciuto quella censura ch'ella fa alla presontuosa sentenza del Cartesio, la qual io avrei desiderato più copiosa, perche maggiormente spiccasse la stravaganza di quel cervello. Circa poi lo scrupolo di VS, che teme della grand'autorità del Cartesio, e che quasi non sia lecito nominarlo in vano, e mi par troppa scrupolosità. S'ha da dire il vero inculcandolo con ogni efficacia, e per carità di quegli, che si son lasciati affascinare da suoi modi astuti, et artifiziosi." [Translation is mine.]
30 GIOVANNI ALFONSO BORELLI to Marcello Malpighi, Pisa, 16 May 1664, in ADELMANN, ed., *The correspondence*, vol. I, letter 102, p. 212: "Intorno la sua epistola del nervo ottico devo dirgli, che il rispetto al Cartesio non lo deve trattenere da parlare con ogni libertà, perché non solo non è tanto accreditato quanto VS si figura, che per il contrario va continuamente scemando di credito, e di riputazione." [Translation is mine.]
31 CORRADO DOLLO, *Filosofia e medicina in Sicilia*, a cura di Giuseppe Bentivegna, Santo Burgio, Giancarlo Magnano San Lio, Soveria Mannelli, Rubbettino, 2004, p. 28; DOMENICO BERTOLONI MELI, "The Posthumous Dispute between Borelli and Malpighi", in *Marcello Malpighi, anatomist and physician*, ed. by D. Bertoloni Meli, Firenze, Olschki, 1997, p. 245-273.

the 1670s. He apparently had found no clear-cut difference between Malpighi's and Descartes' theory of the way the brain contributed to process sense impressions: Borelli would no doubt have appreciated the remark.[32] Unfortunately, Malpighi's answer to Barner is missing.

Barner, in fact, was not the only natural philosopher or physician who mentioned Descartes to Malpighi. One of the most mysterious, and interesting, figures in the Kingdom of Naples, the physician Giambattista Capucci (dates unknown — died in the 1680s), who had tried with no success to solve the dispute between Borelli and Malpighi, continued the conversation with Malpighi, on this and other points. We know very little about Capucci, a member of the Accademia degli Investiganti, except that into his old age he enjoyed a reputation for a deep and excellent knowledge.[33] Leaving Naples to retire in Crotone, in Calabria, he was in some ways lost — not for his contemporaries, however. It did not help that he published very little; we know that he was interested in iatrochemistry. His correspondence with Malpighi is a witness to the diversity and richness of his interests, as of his wide readings. Writing from Crotone to Malpighi in March 1670, Capucci sides with Jacob De Back (approx. 1598-1658), a follower of Harvey, against Descartes.[34] Capucci too, speaking of Descartes, chooses to describe him with a vocabulary where temerity and the lack of prudence is prominent: the French philosopher shows too great self-confidence, and he should have rather adopted the caution characterizing other modern authors, for instance Van Helmont. This association with a well-known iatrochemist, strange as it sounds for Descartes, reveals Capucci's preferences; nevertheless, he concludes, it is a good thing to be able to openly criticize ancient theories, as it is possible in times when the *libertas philosophandi* is widely accepted in the scholarly community. After a couple of months, Capucci once again goes back to Descartes, this time in comparison with a controversial atomist, Rossetti, and what he call his "sect".[35] Using Cartesian images, he writes that the French has "founded his philosophy within a *camera obscura*, with his eyes closed, so as to pay no attention to anything but his imaginations; and he wrote it, such as he thought it, without discussing it with the living, or with the dead,

---

32 JACOB BARNER to Marcello Malpighi, Padua, 6 February 1671, in ADELMANN, ed., *The correspondence*, vol. II, letter 244, p. 518-519: "Quae tua tunc sententia fuerit de gyris et anfractibus cerebri, non prope perceperam, in quantum illa a Cartesio recedat qui anfractibus illis quasi quibusdam loculis, diverso angulorum positu conformatis Ideas rerum per sensus receptarum in ultimam reminiscentiam usque contineri ingenuose satis excogitavit." [Translation is mine.]
33 BADALONI, *Introduzione a G. B. Vico*, p. 104, remembers the honourable mention of Capucci by another Investigante, Luc'Antonio Portio.
34 GIOVANNI BATTISTA CAPUCCI to Marcello Malpighi, Crotone, 26 March 1670, in ADELMANN, ed., *The correspondence*, vol. II, letter 219, p. 447: "arrischiato… troppa confidenza in se stesso… dottrine troppo animose… più cauto l'Helmontio… ma questa virtù o vizio che sia è tollerabile". See WILLIAM HARVEY, JACOBUS DE BACK, *Exercitatio anatomica de motu cordis & sanguinis… Accessit Dissertatio de corde doct. Jacobi de Back, vrbis Roterodami medici ordinarii* Roterodami, ex officinâ Arnoldi Leers, 1648. The book is also requested by Borelli to Magliabechi, in a letter from Pisa, 25 January 1663, in DEL GAIZO, *Alcune lettere*, p. 34-35.
35 SUSANA GÓMEZ LÓPEZ, *Le passioni degli atomi: Montanari e Rossetti: una polemica tra galileiani*, Firenze, Olschki, 1997.

and yet it has so gloriously succeeded in our century".³⁶ This was no compliment, on the whole; but still, it is a far cry from Borelli's tone and total disparagement.

Capucci's attitude is likely to reflect a widespread position among the Neapolitan group of the Investiganti, despite the (rather mild) Cartesianism of Cornelio. Leonardo Di Capua, the friend of Cornelio, was ridiculed for the endorsement of the Cartesian hypothesis on the rainbow.³⁷ However, as remarked by many of his opponents, Di Capua was no Cartesian at all: as already mentioned, he was rather on the side of chemical philosophy, and an enthusiast follower of Boyle. His judgment on Descartes can be compared with the one expressed by Capucci. In his *Parere sull'incertezza della medicina* (1681), while discussing the history of the difficult anatomical exploration of the structure of the brain, he writes that the great Descartes himself could not extricate himself from its intricacies; and that his *Homme* was in fact his own, and an ideal construction, not something to be taken as a real anatomical or physiological description of the body.³⁸ Di Capua too, as Capucci had done, sides with Harvey, not with Descartes, rhetorically expressing wonder at the latter's opinion that the heart is to be seen as the source of animal heat.³⁹ Nevertheless, these rather seem to him mistakes that can be condoned, also in view of the French philosopher's engagement against the Ancients. For Di Capua, as — to a certain extent — for Capucci, Descartes, while an important name in the arena of modern knowledge, is a man of the past decades. It is clear that in the 1680s, too much has happened in medicine and physiology to allow anyone to still see the French as a serious contender, in the age of Lower and Willis, Charleton and Malpighi, Fracassati and Boyle. A partially different situation, and thus a different chronology, would be apparent in wider discussions on matter and cosmology, where in Naples an effort is detectable to accommodate Descartes' corpuscularianism within Epicurean, if not openly atomistic, theories.⁴⁰ But despite the participation of many medically trained scholars in these controversies, this was not perceived to be an issue strictly pertaining to medicine, or anatomy, or physiology.

In many senses, Descartes was taken seriously by medics — his was believed to be a philosophical *system*. From this point of view, the tradition of Cartesianism at

---

36 GIOVANNI BATTISTA CAPUCCI to Marcello Malpighi, Crotone, 19 May 1670, in ADELMANN, ed., *The correspondence*, vol. II, letter 222, p. 459: "fondò la sua filosofia dentro una camera oscura, ad occhi chiusi, per non badar ad altro, ch'alle sue immaginazioni; e tale la scrisse, quale la pensò, senza discorrerla coi vivi, o coi morti, e pure è riuscita tanto gloriosa nel secol nostro." [Translation is mine.]

37 PAOLINO ORIGLIA, *Istoria dello Studio di Napoli... in cui si comprendono gli avvenimenti di esso piu notabili..., con buona parte della storia letteraria del Regno*, In Napoli, nella stamperia di Giovanni Di Simone, 1753, vol. 2, lib. v, p. 107.

38 LEONARDO DI CAPUA, *Parere... divisato in Otto Ragionamenti, ne' quali partitamente narrandosi l'origine, e 'l progresso della medicina, chiaramente l'incertezza della medesima si fa manifesta*, Napoli, Bulifon, 1681, Rag. III, p. 158: "E sì, e tanto egli è spinosa, ed intricata, che'l gran Renato delle Carte restandovici anche egli tutto inviluppato, e preso, ragionevolmente quell'huom, ch'egli compose per molti valent'huomini venne propriamente ideale, e suo huomo appellato".

39 *Ibid.*, Ragionamento IV, p. 299.

40 CARMEN DE CIAMPIS, "Metafisica dell'atomo e nuova antropologia negli scritti inediti di Francesco D'Andrea", *Atti dell' Accademia di Scienze Morali e Politiche*, vol. XCIV-1983, p. 235-256.

the beginning of the eighteenth century in Naples, as elsewhere in Italy, was alive and kicking: lively discussions on method, on the *passions de l'âme*, on matter, on cosmology, as well as a wealth of translations and interpretations took central stage. Suffice it to remember one of the first women-philosophers the Kingdom could boast of after Antiquity, Eleonora Barbapiccola (1700-1740), who in 1722 translated in Italian Descartes' *Principia philosophiae*.[41]

3. Conclusions

On the whole, in the second half of the seventeenth century in Italy Descartes was seemingly not appreciated as a medical authority by medics and other natural philosophers especially because he was believed to be too systematic, that is, too much given to theoretical constructions, and not enough keen to support hypotheses and conclusions with strict observational practices. I am not wishing to use distinctions between disciplinary fields that may seem clear-cut to us, but were by no means so clear-cut for many natural philosophers, and especially physicians, in the seventeenth Century. I am only to insisting on the point of the comparatively little interest physicians or anatomists seemed to have in the niceties of some debates (e.g. philosophical, theological, or metaphysical) when dealing with specific questions, such as those addressed by Malpighi in his research, or by chemical practitioners. The role of the latter in the development of the science of the living bodies in Italy, while not yet entirely clarified, has been primary.[42] It may be argued that for many medical practitioners at the time *anatomia subtilis* had two sides: one came from Malpighi's use of the microscope, and the second came from chymystry itself. The influence of Gassendi's in shaping this frame of mind cannot be underplayed, and deserves further attention.

However, as we have seen, in the last decades of the century Descartes was back — not an anatomical and medical one, but rather a methodological one. This does not mean that a moderate, and/or limited reception of Descartes had not taken place. The case of Cornelio is there to warn us that in many senses Italy can be compared to England as regards the reception of Descartes' philosophy, with a moderate and fragmented acceptance of Descartes' medicine, as in Charleton or even Willis.

---

41 On the Cartesian (re) turn in Naples, MAURIZIO TORRINI, "Il Cartesio di Giannone", in *Pietro Giannone e il suo tempo*, Napoli, Jovene, 1980, I, p. 417-430; MARIA T. MARCIALIS, "Il Cogito e la coscienza. Letture cartesiane nella Napoli settecentesca", *Rivista di Storia della Filosofia*, 51 (1996), p. 581-612; DAGMAR VON WILLE, Introduzione to NICOLA CIRILLO, *La filosofia di Cartesio. Philosophiae Cartesianae Synopsis. Lezioni inedite napoletane del 1704-1705*, Napoli, Bibliopolis, 2009; FABRIZIO LOMONACO, Introduzione to MICHELANGELO FARDELLA, *Lettere di un Cartesiano di fine Seicento*, ed. by Fabrizio Lomonaco, Canterano (RM), Aracne, 2019, p. 9-35; *Cartesio a Napoli. Le passioni dell'anima, Traduzione e lettere tra '600 e '700*, ed. by Fabrizio Lomonaco, Canterano (RM), Aracne, 2020.

42 ANTONIO CLERICUZIO, *Chemical Medicine and Paracelsianism in Italy (1550-1650)*, in *The Practice of Reform in Health, Medicine, and Science 1500-2000*, ed. by M. Pelling, S. Mandelbrote, Ashgate, Aldershot, 2005, p. 59-79.

In the Kingdom of Naples, including Borelli and thus to some extent Tuscany, what has been called Renaissance naturalism, that is, natural philosophy in the style of Telesio and Campanella, remained somewhat of a hindrance to a full comprehension and acceptance of mechanicism. Life — as in Cornelio's Progymnasma *de vita,* was difficult to reduce to mechanism, even for those who acknowledged Descartes' preeminence in method. The *Anglicana schola* seemingly provided a better, and more up-to-date, explanation on how living bodies functioned. Slightly later on, Boyle's chemical explanations provided an even better model, but still, there was a pointed effort at integrating chemical notions and mechanical philosophies, including the one by Descartes.[43]

The mention by Borelli of an Italian science of anatomy and physiology, two fields in which Italy was perceived to be excellent even before the later construction, in the nineteenth century, of its mythology, means that Borelli is pushing on Malpighi his own version of a 'new' medicine — or, as Cornelio has it, of a complete science of man. Cornelio himself, as already mentioned, had complained that the English had arrived more or less to the same results as he himself had — before them, obviously. The two, Borelli and Cornelio, despite their differences, belonged to a generation that had been used to systematic approaches and wide, sweeping pictures of the world. To a certain extent, and also keeping in mind the vicissitudes of Galilei and of the Galilaeans, a group to which both loosely belonged, it is not surprising that they should be interested in 'big pictures'. In this sense, for Borelli Descartes was a rival (or, for Cornelio, a fellow traveller), even if one belonging to the past — like Campanella, or Galilei. This is not true of the younger generation, the one of Malpighi; however, Borelli's disparagement of Descartes', or his fight against him, badly needed Malpighi's medical expertise and anatomical skill. Like Descartes — but unlike Cornelio — Borelli was no physician; he had received no formal education in the field, and he had never been a practicing professional. Borelli, like Descartes, loved to meddle in anatomical and medical studies and experiences; but they were used for his own ends. Maybe one important difference with Descartes was that he was able to establish a strong relationship (it could even be said: a parasitical one) with an exceptional anatomist, as Malpighi was.

I would also like to advance the hypothesis that the program of analysis of the organs of the senses Malpighi was pursuing in the 1660s, following the influence of Borelli's, might be — albeit vaguely — related to Campanella's theories, where senses played central stage.[44] While no mention of Campanella is made in the epistolary exchange between the two, his philosophy may still have made sense, or resonate, for the *novatores,* the Investiganti, in Naples. Was Borelli against metaphysics? as a Galilaean, that is — was he an enemy of Descartes because of Descartes' philosophical

---

43 Antonio Clericuzio, Maria Conforti, "Iatrochemistry and Iatromechanism in the Early Modern Era", in *Encyclopedia of Early Modern Philosophy and the Sciences,* ed. by D. Jalobeanu, Ch. T Wolfe, Cham, Springer, 2022, p. 883-895.

44 Germana Ernst, *Tommaso Campanella, Il libro e il corpo della natura,* Bari-Roma, Laterza, 2010 (I ed. 2002).

stance?[45] I do not believe this to be entirely true. I rather believe that Borelli was using Malpighi and working with him in order to develop and follow his own agenda. This was undoubtedly a mechanistic one, even if on some points he rather accepted (iatro)chemistry, as the *De Motu Animalium* abundantly show. However, and rather unsurprisingly, Borelli's mechanism was by no means the same as Descartes', even if both may be considered to have failed in their foundation of iatromechanism.

---

45 See e.g. Corrado Dollo, *Modelli scientifici e filosofici nella Sicilia spagnola*, Napoli, Guida, 1984, ch. VI, p. 182.

AARON SPINK

Embodied Difference and the Cartesian Soul

Pierre-Sylvain Régis and the Pineal Gland Problem

▼ ABSTRACT Perhaps one of Descartes' greatest blunders was being so specific in localizing the seat of the soul at the pineal gland. Of course, the pineal gland theory was quickly refuted, and Descartes' followers were, unsurprisingly, equally quick in abandoning the proposition. However, it was not merely a physical thesis, as Descartes presented several arguments that had connected metaphysical implications. In his influential Cartesian textbook, *Cours entier de philosophie*, Pierre-Sylvain Régis (1632-1707) was left with the difficult position of trying to salvage as much of the metaphysical argument while abandoning the questionable anatomical claims. On the metaphysical side, I claim that Descartes' arguments that depended on both the simplicity of the soul and some form of simplicity in the corporeal organ were natural implications of his larger systematic concerns. Because Régis was unable to find a suitable organ that fit Descartes' demands, he instead opted to select a larger portion of the brain: the *centrum semiovale*. My paper details the tensions created by such a move and Régis' strategies to defuse them. My main contention is that this move away from a particular type of simplicity in the physical organ increased the explanatory role the brain needed to play. In turn, this extra obligation lead Régis to move traditionally spiritual faculties, like reason and the will, entirely or in part, to the brain. With such a radical reduction in spiritual faculties, Régis located anything that might differentiate us as thinkers to the body, thus ruling out any type of intellectual egalitarianism one might expect to emerge from Descartes' dualism and reliance on clear and distinct perceptions.

▼ KEYWORDS René Descartes, Pierre-Sylvain Régis, Cartesianism, Faculties of the Soul, Mechanism, Cartesian Dualism

Aaron Spink • Department of Philosophy, Dartmouth College, USA. Contact: <aaronspink@gmail.com>

1. Equality Among Cartesian Minds

René Descartes' *Discourse on Method* opened with a *joke*: "Good sense is the best distributed thing in the world: for everyone thinks himself so well endowed with it that…[they] do not usually desire more of it than they possess".[1] But Descartes takes the premise of the joke, that everyone has the same amount of good sense, quite seriously and goes on to deny the implication: that some people must be mistaken about their own abilities. Yet, despite everyone having the same reasoning abilities, Descartes still finds a need to write a discourse on how to conduct one's reason well, which might seem a bit odd at first blush. Much of the *Discourse* can be understood as a means to remove this tension by uncovering all the youthful prejudices and bad habits that obfuscate or distort our natural ability to recognize truth. According to Descartes, once we remove all the barriers, leaving clear and distinct perceptions unbridled, we are all equally well equipped to perceive the truth of Cartesian philosophy. This radical equality among thinkers is deeply embedded in Descartes' metaphysics of the soul. Because our souls are simple beings, there is no room for differences in abilities, corruptions, or competing tendencies. And so, Descartes must conclude, as he does in Part I of the *Discourse*, "[reason] exists whole and complete in each of us".[2] A further reason for accepting equality in ability is the well-known epistemological implications of denying it: God must have given us all a minimum capacity to recognize truth from falsity, for if he had not, we might have cause to doubt his status as a non-deceiving God. All this would seem the pave the way for an enlightened philosophy of equality regardless of one's sex, gender, race, or any other physical characteristics; after all, we all have exactly the same type of soul, capable of clearly and distinctly perceiving the truth. As knowers, we have no brighter or dimmer natural lights. But in practice, Descartes is not nearly so idealistic and differentiates between thinkers; some are slow, others incapable of appreciating his philosophy, while yet others do not have the same strength of will to control their passions.[3]

If prejudices and bad habits alone are enough to adequately explain cognitive variability among humans, it remains to be explained how these habits are acquired, where they are located, and how they can distort the clarity and distinctness inherent in true ideas. There is little room to maneuver here, as there are at least two reasons to doubt whether these differences could be located in the soul. First, as we noted above, reason exists whole and complete in each of us and allowing any mental variation in the soul itself could create tension with this claim and might further require the soul to have parts, which we will see below is prohibited under Descartes' system. Second, and related to the first, we might worry that these differences being located in the soul

---

[1] RENÉ DESCARTES, *Discourse on Method*, I, AT VI 1-2; CSM I 111.
[2] *Discours de la Méthode*, I, AT VI 2; CSM I 112.
[3] Descartes' low regard of Fermat's ability to recognize even the most obvious of mathematical truths is infamous. But beyond the occasional insult (claiming that Pascal has too much vacuum in his head, for example) the *Passions of the Soul* also gives some evidence of how Descartes distinguished between thinkers (Descartes to Huygens, 8 December 1647, AT V 653; RENÉ DESCARTES, *Passions de l'âme*, AT XI 453-354; CSM 387-388).

might undermine arguments against skepticism. If these differences were in the soul, there would be no obvious reason why we should assume that we were not created with prejudices or defects from the start — in other words, Descartes' opening joke would have more truth to it than he would like. To avoid this consequence, the standard Cartesian response is to explain mental differences by locating them in the body.[4] Nicolas Malebranche, for example, explained his sexist assumptions about women's deficient mental capacities by resorting to the mechanical properties of their brain fibers.

> The delicacy of the brain fibers is one of the principal causes impeding our efforts to apply ourselves to discovering truths that are slightly hidden... This delicacy of the brain fibers is usually found in women... normally they are incapable of penetrating to truths that are slightly difficult to discover.[5]

Yet this was far from the universal response. Other Cartesians leaned more heavily on the equality between minds, minimizing the effect of bodily differences. François Poulain de la Barre, a Cartesian feminist, used this to great effect in arguing for the equality between the sexes in his treatise *A Physical and Moral Discourse concerning the Equality of Both Sexes*.

> It is easy to see that sexual differences apply only to the body. Since, strictly speaking, the body alone is involved in the reproduction of human beings and the mind merely gives its assent and does so in the same manner in everyone, it follows that the mind has no sex.[6]

For Poulain, perceived differences between the sexes are due to cultural and social causes. However, given the Cartesianism undergirding Poulain's theory, he cannot simply leave his argument here.[7] Due to the necessarily tight connection between the mind and body, Poulain also needs to defend against those, like Malebranche, who might accept equality in the mind while still arguing that the limitations of the body prevent a practical equality in our embodied state. An analogy could help here. While

---

4 Of course, this is not unique to Cartesianism. Elisabeth, in her correspondence with Descartes, makes an un-Cartesian reference to the "weakness of her sex" due to vapors infecting her body (Elisabeth to Descartes, 24 May 1645, AT IV 208).
5 NICOLAS MALEBRANCHE, *The Search After Truth*, trans. by Thomas Lennon and Paul Olscamp, Cambridge, Cambridge University Press, p. 130.
6 FRANÇOIS POULAIN DE LA BARRE, *The Equality of the Sexes*, trans. by Desmond M. Clarke, Manchester, Manchester University Press, 1990, p. 157.
7 There has been a great deal written on the compatibility of Cartesianism with feminism. See ERICA HARTH, 'Cartesian Women', in *Feminist Interpretations of René Descartes*, ed. by Susan Bordo, University Park, Pennsylvania, The Pennsylvania State University Press, 1999, p. 213-231; EILEEN O'NEILL, 'Women Cartesians, "Feminine Philosophy," and Historical Exclusion', in *Feminist Interpretations of René Descartes*, ed. by Susan Bordo, University Park, Pennsylvania, The Pennsylvania State University Press, 1999, p. 232-257; MARIE-FRÉDERIQUE PELLEGRIN, "Cartesianism and Feminism", in *The Oxford Handbook to Descartes and Cartesianism*, ed. by Steven Nadler, Tad Schmaltz and Delphine Antoine-Mahut, Oxford, Oxford University Press, 2019, p. 565-579; SIEP STUURMAN, "François Poulain de La Barre and the Origins of the Enlightenment", *Journal of the History of Ideas*, 58/4 (1997), p. 617-640.

we might have two ships with equally qualified captains, if one ship has poorly made controls and control surfaces, we can still justify special/discriminatory treatment of this malfunctioning ship despite the competency of the captain. Poulain often notes that no anatomical differences have been found between the sexes outside reproductive organs, thus we are all equally good captains in equally capable ships.[8] Oddly though, Poulain does tie mental ability to physical attributes occasionally. For example, he is more than happy to use physical descriptions of female anatomy to argue for not just equality but even female superiority in certain areas. Here we can see Poulain use a bit of speculative phrenology to argue just such a point.

> [Women] have a high, noble, and broad forehead, which is normally a sign of imagination and intelligence… That means that their brain is so disposed that it receives impressions from objects easily, including the weakest and lightest impressions that escape those with alternative dispositions.[9]

This tortured argument on superficial anatomy highlights some of argumentative strategies open to early Cartesians based on physical equality (or the lack thereof).

There are political and ethical implications around physical equality, too. Pierre-Sylvain Régis (1632-1707), one of the most prominent Cartesians of the seventeenth century,[10] blended Descartes' metaphysics and epistemology with Hobbes' ethics in a philosophical hodgepodge that was not entirely uncommon at the time.[11] On the one hand, despite Régis' perceived Cartesian orthodoxy, he does not rely on the mind's simplicity to ground equality.[12] Instead, in a Hobbesian fashion, Régis argues that despite our physical differences difference, we have a moral obligation to assume equality insofar as it leads us out of the state of nature and toward peace.[13] But it is unclear exactly how perfect an equality is necessary for this purpose. By book two

---

8 POULAIN DE LA BARRE, *The Equality of the Sexes*, p. 158.
9 Ibid., p. 179.
10 On Régis, see ROGER ARIEW, *Descartes and the First Cartesians*, Oxford, Oxford University Press, 2014; DESMOND M. CLARKE, "Pierre-Sylvain Régis: A Paradigm of Cartesian Methodology", *Archiv Für Geschichte Der Philosophie*, 62/3 (1980), p. 289-310; ANTONELLA DEL PRETE, 'Un Cartésianisme "Hérétique": Pierre-Sylvain Régis', *Corpus, Revue de Philosophie*, 61 (2011), p. 185-199; ANTONELLA DEL PRETE, 'The Prince of Cartesian Philosophers: Pierre-Sylvain Régis', in *The Oxford Handbook to Descartes*, p. 374-387; DENNIS DES CHENE, 'Cartesian Science: Régis and Rohault', in *A Companion to Early Modern Philosophy*, ed. by Steven Nadler, Malden, MA, Blackwell Publishing, 2002, p. 183-196; TAD M. SCHMALTZ, *Radical Cartesianism: The French Reception of Descartes*, Cambridge, Cambridge University Press, 2002.
11 Jacques Du Roure (fl. 1653-1683), who wrote one of the first Cartesian textbook also expounded on Hobbes ethics at some length, while Antoine Le Grand (1629-1699) adopted Samuel Pufendorf's moral philosophy into his own Cartesian textbook.
12 As will become clear in the second half of this paper, Régis was far from completely orthodox with regards to Descartes' theory of the mind/body union. Nevertheless, Régis is sometimes described by his peers as a slavish follower of Descartes; Pierre-Daniel Huet is perhaps the best propogandist on this front (for a particularly virulent example, see PIERRE-DANIEL HUET, *Nouveaux Mémoires Pour Servir à l'histoire Du Cartésianisme*, Paris, Ramond Mazieres, 1711).
13 PIERRE-SYLVAIN RÉGIS, *Cours entier de philosophie ou système general selon les principes de M. Descartes*, Amsterdam, Huguetan, 1691, vol. III, p. 418.

of his ethics, Régis had completely abandoned any claim to a broad ranging equality, instead insisting that reason dictates a natural moral inequality between the strong and the weak.

> We need to return to the idea of the state of nature and consider that, because it is a state of war between everyone, reason dictates that the strongest make themselves masters of the weakest, and consequently the mother be the master of the children.[14]

Strength is also the reason why a pregnant woman's child can be rightly claimed by a vanquishing army if she is a prisoner of war.[15] In fact, according to Régis, a woman's obligation to her children is dictated by nature because of her power relative to her children, but her relationship between her husband is one dictated by culture, religion, and the explicit contracts one consents to in marriage.[16] So here, and with Malebranche, we have the case of dedicated Cartesians who might very well admit that "the mind has no sex", all the while holding that the body certainly does have a sex and that is enough to ground significant levels of inequality. The odd question here then is, why? Under a Cartesian system, matter is just lifeless particles bouncing around the universe; so why would Régis not retreat to the soul for moral grounding and why aren't all Cartesians feminists? To answer this, I will be looking at the complicated history of Cartesians interacting with the rapidly changing anatomical theories of the period, which will give us two reasons motivating Régis's theory. First, following the demise of Descartes' theory of the pineal gland, Régis was forced to move many mental faculties from the spirit to the body, which in turn pressured a change in Descartes' demarcation principle between essential and inessential mental properties. And second, mostly flowing from my first point, this entailed that the famous rallying cry, "the mind has no sex" was made irrelevant in Régis' system.

2. Arguments for Simplicity: Excluding the Mind

Despite the various Cartesian analyses above, at least one boundary seems consistent; namely, that whatever inequality exists, clear and distinct perceptions cannot be substantially hampered by our bodies. I say "substantially" here because, as discussed above, Cartesians are unanimous that people will have varying degrees of strength in memory, imagination, effective will power, and control of passions, which can make arriving at clear and distinct perceptions more time consuming or rare for certain people. Yet, once perceived, every soul is equally unable to resist clear and distinct perceptions' compelling nature. In other words, the Cartesian claim seems to be

---

14 *Cours*, III, p. 466.
15 *Cours*, III, p. 467. While the majority of Régis's political/moral philosophy is taken directly from Hobbes without any significant modification, there is some reason to think they differ on familial relations: see RICHARD ALLEN CHAPMAN, 'Leviathan Writ Small: Thomas Hobbes on the Family', *The American Political Science Review*, 69/1 (1975), p. 76-90.
16 *Cours*, III, p. 480.

that while we all have the same epistemological capabilities potentially, we do not all have the same epistemological abilities actually.[17] I mentioned above that a possible explanation for this commitment is to stave off fear of a deceptive God dragging us into an absolute skepticism, but this is only one of the possible arguments. There are obvious empirical reasons for Cartesians to explain variation in bodily terms rather than spiritual terms. As the physical makeup of the brain was becoming more and more well known, natural philosophers were keen to ascribe functions to the newly described portions of the brain. It becomes a hallmark of early Cartesianism that certain mental faculties are composed of both the phenomenal experience, consistent across humans, as well as a quasi-reductive corporeal component, that can show variation. The result of this is that any difference between the sexes, or any two individuals for that matter, must be discovered in anatomical studies, not metaphysical ones. The problem for Cartesians is just how much of our mental lives and reasoning ability we can ascribe to the body. Let's call whatever it is that grounds our ability to individuate between people based on their mental abilities, and their associated moral implications, a *principle of difference*. In the following sections, I will detail Régis's search for just such a principle and the metaphysical problems associated with it. However, before addressing Régis directly, I need to discharge some obligations incurred in the introduction and flesh out exactly why we might assume such a principle of difference cannot be located in the soul itself for the Cartesians.

2.1. Descartes' Argument from Indivisibility

One of the most obvious answers to why a principle difference must be located in the body is the soul's lack of distinct parts. Under this reading, because the mind can have no parts, it is metaphysically impossible to contain two conflicting properties (i.e. a faculty of producing clear and distinct perceptions and one of obscuring them).[18] It will be helpful here to look over some of the standard Cartesian arguments to this effect.

Descartes' argument for the simplicity of the soul first occurs in the Sixth Meditation.[19] Considering himself only as a thinking thing, he argues that it is impossible to differentiate any real parts within himself. Unlike physical bodies, which can be cut and divided *ad infinitum*, the mind's lack of extension or discrete parts make a real division a conceptual non-starter. Crucially, the traditional divisions of

---

17 See AMÉLIE OKSENBERG RORTY, 'Descartes and Spinoza on Epistemological Egalitarianism', *History of Philosophy Quarterly*, 13.1 (1996), p. 35-53, esp. p. 35-36.
18 Régis, following his teacher Dom Robert Desgabets, believes this entails that the soul is essentially incorruptible, indefectible, and therefore immortal (SCHMALTZ, *Radical Cartesianism*, Cambridge, Cambridge University Press, 2002, p. 96, 189, 236.).
19 Descartes never actually uses the term "simple" to describe the soul. However, as we'll see, Descartes goes on to fill in his theory of the soul by ascribing to it a number of restrictive properties (i.e. it can have no parts, can only hold one thought at a time, non-spatial, etc.). These properties are expansive enough where it would be misleading to say the soul were "indivisible", so I have chosen the term "simple" as a way to encapsulate all the additional properties.

the mind's powers into faculties, which had been considered distinct parts in some strains of scholastic thought, are not *real* distinctions for Descartes.[20]

> As for the faculties of willing, of understanding, of sensory perception and so on, these cannot be termed parts of the mind, since it is one and the same mind that wills, and understands and has sensory perceptions.[21]

One plausible interpretation of this passage is that each faculty occupies the entirety of the mind. That is, when we have a sensation or an act of will, they occur sequentially and are instantiated entirely by the same mental substance. Thus, the distinction between faculties must be either a distinction of reason or modal distinction, rather than a real distinction, as they cannot exist independently at any given time.

To be sure, the intellect, as a faculty, exists wholly in the mind and can be thought of as separate from other faculties, say the will, insofar as it is the intellect that understands, whereas the will is the immediate cause of actions. But neither of these faculties can truly be separate, yet the same is not true for all the traditional faculties of the mind. Just a little later in Meditation Six, Descartes makes the surprising claim that we can indeed find a real distinction between our minds and the faculties of imagination and memory. He offers at least two arguments for grounding a distinction between essential and contingent faculties. The first relies again on separability.

> I find within myself certain faculties for certain special modes of thinking, namely imagination and sensory perception. Now I can clearly and distinctly understand myself as a whole without these faculties; but I cannot, conversely, understand these faculties without me, that is, without an intellectual substance to inhere in.[22]

The basic structure of the argument is that if we can potentially exist without a given faculty, it cannot be an essential part of our soul — I take this to be Descartes' generic strategy for proving any real distinction.[23]

The second argument relies on the properties of the objects of these "special" faculties. Certain faculties, like imagination have objects that are antithetical to a purely mental substance; namely, they refer to objects that are spatially extended. Although the logic for this claim is never fully spelled out, Descartes believes that there must be a physical component of cognition that is actually extended for an extended thing to be represented mentally. In other words, and perhaps most charitably, Descartes is claiming that something cannot represent anything unless it has something in common with it. In line with this, the faculties of imagination,

---

[20] See GALEN BARRY, 'Cartesian Modes and the Simplicity of Mind', *Pacific Philosophical Quarterly*, 96 (2015), p. 54-76., and STEPHEN VOSS, 'Simplicity and the Seat of the Soul', in *Essays on the Philosophy and Science of René Descartes*, ed. by Stephen Voss, Oxford Oxford University Press, 1993, p. 128-141.
[21] *Meditationes de prima philosophia*, AT VII 86; CSM II 59.
[22] *Meditationes de prima philosophia*, AT VII 78; CSM II, 54.
[23] While there might be some reason to think this is not the complete story (see ALICE SOWAAL, 'Cartesian Bodies', *Canadian Journal of Philosophy*, 34/2 (2004), p. 217-240, esp. p. 222-223, for example), I believe characterizing it in this way does not hurt my argument.

sensation, as well as memory, must have an extended component that, by definition, cannot be contained in our mental substance. However, this style of argument plays a secondary role at best, as Descartes is careful to qualify it as a merely "probable" argument indicating the existence of a physical organ of imagination and memory.[24]

2.2. Simplicity Extended: The Pineal Gland

Descartes' arguments for the soul's simplicity do not end in the spiritual realm. Instead, the metaphysical limitations on the soul required Descartes to reach to the corporeal to fully explain our experienced mental lives (i.e. uncontrollable thoughts, conflicting desires, mental obscurity, imagination, memory, etc.). But further, the soul's simplicity also places limitations on how it can interact with a body. This in turn puts a set of requirements on where it will be able to interact with the body, which leads to one of Descartes' most frequently caricatured theses: that the pineal gland is the seat of the soul.

The first published discussion of the pineal gland as the physical seat of the soul occurs in the *Dioptrique* in 1637 with the *Discourse on Method*. Here he only obliquely refers to a certain "gland H" that serves as location where subtle matter travelling through the optic nerves eventually terminates. At the time, this was enough for Descartes to claim gland H serves as the seat of the "common sense".[25] The full arguments for holding the pineal gland specifically as the seat of the soul are more robustly developed in his correspondence with Meyssonnier, Mersenne, and Villiers, although Jean Cousin, perhaps the first person to publicly defend Descartes' pineal gland thesis, appears to be an unnamed participant in the correspondence.[26] In these exchanges, Descartes lays out a series of conditions for the physical seat of the soul that mix anatomical considerations with metaphysical arguments. On the physical side, any seat of the soul must be mechanically connected to the parts of the body through arteries, nerves, and the flow of animal spirits. Because the influence exerted by the soul is directed only at that one location, the organ must also be able to move freely — as we will see, this is the only property of the pineal gland itself that is not analogically in the soul.[27]

On the metaphysical side of things, the gland must have the same sort of properties as the soul.[28] Descartes is explicit that the gland must share the soul's simplicity, "It

---

24 *Meditationes de prima philosophia*, AT VII 73-74; CSM II, 51. One obvious flaw in this argument is that while a physical component to imagination might be required, that does not entail that imagination is entirely physical. Later in Descartes' career he seems to backtrack on just this issue and claims that there is both physical and mental imagination.
25 While this is the first published instance of a reference to the pineal gland, Descartes had already been working on the concept in his posthumously published *Traité de l'Homme*.
26 See GERT-JAN LOKHORST and TIMO T. KAITARO, 'The Originality of Descartes' Theory about the Pineal Gland', *Journal of the History of the Neurosciences*, 10/1, (2001), p. 6-18. The lack of free movement is also why he rules out the pituitary gland as a candidate for the seat of the soul.
27 Descartes to Mersenne, 24 December 1640, AT III 263; CSMK 162.
28 Descartes never actual defends why there must be this parallel between the soul and the pineal gland. The demand that two completely dissimilar things have the same properties in some way is, to my mind, completely unwarranted and a point of tension with Régis, as we will see later on.

seems to me that the part of the body that is the most immediately joined with the soul must also be single and undivided into two parts".[29] Of course, the obvious objection is that any piece of extended matter can, by definition, be infinitely divided. A more natural reading would be that by "undivided" he means a homogenous whole or not separated by any intervening matter. However, both of these readings quickly run afoul of Descartes' austere metaphysics, where all extended substance is made of the same material, which means that the entire universe is a homogenous whole, in the sense that it is not separated by any intervening matter. We might modify this by claiming Descartes distinguishes one part from many by how it moves or the structure of its particles, while he never explicitly makes this argument, we can piece some of his reasoning together through what he rules out as the seat of the soul. In his letter to Mersenne, responding to Villiers, Descartes rules out the cerebellum being the seat of the soul because it contains the vermis, which itself is made up of two halves. Here Descartes seems to be either simply relying on anatomical divisions that were commonly discussed at the time or appealing to some kind of functional division.[30]

While the reasons for claiming the pineal gland is in fact undivided are less than thoroughly grounded, the requirement is part and parcel of Descartes broader argument against the soul being united to more than one organ. In the correspondence where he explicitly discusses the pineal gland (again to Meysonnier and to Mersenne), Descartes brings up his infamous "doubling argument". As perhaps the most apparently superficial reason for locating the pineal gland as the seat of the soul, Descartes' doubling argument relies on the pineal gland holding a unique position anatomically. Unlike the remainder of the body, where parts like arms, legs, eyes, lungs, brain hemispheres, etc., have mirrored versions of themselves, the pineal gland is singular. This now obviously false observation of the pineal gland played into a more philosophically significant argument. This secondary argument based on doubling explicitly occurs most clearly in his 1640 letter to Meysonnier.[31] Here Descartes notes that the doubling of things like optic nerves would indicate that there are actually two images being transmitted via the animal spirits. However, our phenomenal experience is only of one image; therefore, Descartes jumps to the rather hasty conclusion that those signals must be united at a single point somewhere.[32] The argument extends further than vision, as Descartes argues that since we only

---

29 Descartes to Mersenne, 30 July 1640, AT III, 123. For a more detailed description of this requirement, see Voss, p. 135-138. Lisa Shapiro, however, rejects Voss' contention that Descartes has an explicit requirement for simplicity (LISA SHAPIRO, 'Descartes' Pineal Gland Reconsidered,' *Midwest Studies in Philosophy*, 35 (2011), p. 259-286.)
30 While it might seem elicit to evoke anything like natural purpose, given Descartes' prohibition against teleology, I follow Alison Simmons' reading that certain teleological explanations were allowed by Descartes (ALISON SIMMONS, 'Sensible Ends: Latent Teleology in Descartes' Account of Sensation', *Journal of the History of Philosophy*, 39/1 (2001), p. 49-75).
31 A similar argument can also be seen in Descartes to Mersenne, 24 December 1640, AT III 265, and in the *Passions of the Soul*, AT XI 352-353; CSM I 340.
32 Perhaps the most glaring inconsistency here is that Descartes does not actually believe we are receiving one single bit of information. In his account of depth perception in the *Dioptrics* Descartes relies on each eye transmitting distinct information, such as the angle of the eye, when is then used

ever have one thought at a given time, the input from the body to the soul must, by necessity, be located at a single part of the brain.[33] The implications of this argument are twofold. First, if the soul were extended over multiple parts of the body it would necessitate receiving multiple distinct impressions at the same time. Second, if the soul were extended further, perhaps over the entire body, there would be no need for the sensory organs to be connected to such an extensive nervous system — there would simply be no reason for the optic nerves to extend so far and eventually converge. Obvious logical flaws aside, Descartes has laid out four requirements for the seat of the soul: free movement, indivisibility, being a single structure, and being appropriately connected to the relevant parts of the body.

3. Extreme Simplicity: Pierre-Sylvain Régis

As the Cartesian revolution developed so too did anatomical studies, which in turn quickly lead to the downfall of the Cartesian pineal gland theory. This downfall is traditionally ascribed to Nicolas Steno's devastating critique of the pineal gland theory first presented at Thévenot's salon in 1665 and later published in 1669 as the *Discourse on the Anatomy of the Brain*. Steno's criticism most forcefully attacked Descartes' vulnerable anatomical assumptions; namely, regarding the pineal gland's freedom of movement and connection to the rest of the body, whereas the metaphysical hypotheses were broadly ignored.[34] In short, Steno showed that the pineal gland was neither as well connected as Descartes had thought, nor could it move freely.[35] Outside a very few early defenders, the pineal gland as the specific location of mind-body interaction left Cartesian textbooks with hardly a whimper.[36] But the explanatory lacuna left by the exiting pineal gland theory resulted in early Cartesians struggling to accommodate the ever-expanding anatomical knowledge into a robust theory of mind-body interaction. Given Descartes' strict requirements for the location of a "seat of the soul", the Cartesians were left to radically revise the Cartesian doctrine. As we will see in the case of Régis, the lack of appropriate physical organs that match Descartes original requirements, oddly, lead to an ever-decreasing roll for the mind itself, which left Régis with no other option than to locate all human differences *essentially* in the body.

---

to calculate distance. So, I think it is not far off base to claim that his theory actually *requires* that we be perceiving two images in the same way a man feeling for an object with a stick in each hand receives one impression from each hand (Discours, AT VI, 138).

33 AT III, 19.
34 See Raphaële Andrault, 'Human Brain and Human Mind: The Discourse on the Anatomy of the Brain and Its Philosophical Reception', in *Steno and the Philosophers*, ed. by Mogens Lærke and Raphaële Andrault, Leiden, Brill, 2018, p. 87-112. for an excellent discussion of Steno's criticisms.
35 The *Journal des Sçavans* points out, "What Mr. Descartes said in the treatise he wrote on *Man*, is much more ingenious, but it is not very true, if we believe [Steno]" (*Le Journal Des Sçavans*, 10 February, 1670, p. 8.).
36 Louis de la Forge, who was charged with editing and publishing Descartes posthumous *L'Homme*, was perhaps the most prominent apologist on this front.

As the details of the brain's structure developed, Cartesians were quite keen to incorporate as much of the new findings as possible while retaining the basic principle of simplicity in the mind. Like Descartes, Régis incorporated many of these anatomical findings, including detailed diagrams, to account for variation in mental abilities and mental faculties.[37] For example, with a deeper understanding of the location and composition of brain fibers, Régis was able to forward a hypothesis as to why young people had different learning abilities than the elderly. According to Régis, this comes from young brain fibers being more malleable and thus more apt to take on the traces and marks associated with memory and learning.[38] As we age, these fibers become harder and less suitable to taking on new traces, which leads him to conclude that ages 30-70 are ideal for reasoning.[39]

Variance in one's judgment is also most visible in the very young. Rather than some lack of intellectual maturity or lack of familiarity with the experience of clear and distinct perceptions, as Descartes would have it, Régis's explanation depends on physical causes in the brain. As he describes it, when the nerves in the brain acquire some consistency, the imagination becomes "clearer and more distinct".[40] But because the imagination plays an outsized role in reasoning in Régis's system, these physical changes also result in corresponding changes in one's judgment and reasoning abilities. In fact, according to him, good or bad judgment is completely reducible to the various flows of animal spirits and the traces they leave — the more accurate one's judgement is, the cleaner the traces are in the brain.[41] These fibers, and how they interact with the spirits, also cause some people who have very delicate fibers to be incapable of penetrating deep truths, as even minor distractions can occupy their entire consciousness.[42]

So, part of someone's inability to come to truth might simply be because of their age-related defects in the physical structure of the brain, but the question becomes how far these physical limitations extend into the intellectual realm. Just as we saw in Descartes, one of the basic problems Cartesians faced was fixing the number of faculties/abilities the mind had essentially and those it had merely accidentally. Implicit in Régis's account is the idea that, due to the mind's simplicity, its actions are fundamentally different than actions in a corporeal body. For example, altering the course of a projectile involves the relationship of various parts of the body in motion and the parts of the body it impacts against, as well as the relative relationship of the parts of surrounding bodies that establish its motion; but the soul has no parts and, therefore, cannot be interrupted or fail in the same way as a projectile's motion can. In his final work, *Usage de la raison et de la foy* published

---

37 For more detail on Régis incorporation of other experimental discoveries, see CLARKE.
38 Along the same lines as Malebranche above, Régis argues that the malleability of brain fibers is also shared in women, which makes them particularly bad imagining anything that they are not directly exposed to (*Cours*, III, p. 309).
39 *Cours*, III, p. 309.
40 *Cours*, III, p. 319.
41 *Cours*, III, p. 320.
42 *Cours*, III, p. 321.

in 1704, Régis clearly adopts the thesis that only physical objects were capable of locomotion and change.[43] That being the case, the mind, considered in itself as a spiritual substance, is outside space and time and thus incapable of any temporal change.[44] Because of this, any interference or interruption can only be explained by a bodily process imposing itself on the mind through the unique nature of the mind-body union. While the details are radical when compared to Descartes' own version of simplicity,[45] the conclusion regarding the interruption of mental processes by physical ones is not that far removed. In the *Passions of the Soul* and some of his correspondence, Descartes often relies on the tight connection between the mind and the body to explain mental distractions — where if something is happening in the nerves or brain, it will necessarily have a phenomenal component that can interrupt a willed-thought.[46] However, Régis goes considerably further than Descartes in how much he eliminates from the soul's powers. For example, in book eight of his *Cours Entier*, on physics, Régis considers whether or not free will can be considered as an efficient cause in a body, as he claims the ancient philosophers believed. If the will were an efficient cause over something like memory, one would be able to remember things perfectly on command. Given that we are often unable to recall certain memories when desired, we have to conclude that the will alone is not an efficient cause.[47]

4. Simplicity Extended and Reversing the Cartesian Explanation

As we just saw, Régis argues from causal fallibility in mental abilities to the necessity of a physical cause. This marks the most significant difference between Régis and Descartes yet. Before we look at the philosophical and anatomical context that leads Régis to this position, it will be important to quickly lay out exactly why this type of argument from causal fallibility would be borderline nonsensical under Descartes' system. For Descartes, like Régis, the fallibility of a mental process is nothing out the ordinary. We regularly fail to remember something, get distracted in our reasoning, or let our passions obscure our perception of the good. Further, Descartes is in agreement that part of the causal story of many of those errors or frustrated mental efforts will reside in the body. However, for Descartes, there is simply no problem in claiming that the will is the efficient cause of a failed attempt

---

43 PIERRE-SYLVAIN RÉGIS, *Usage de la raison et de la foy*, Paris, Jean Cousson, 1704, p. 3.
44 *Cours*, III, p. 3-4. This also forms the basis of Régis's empiricism (ROGER ARIEW, 'Cartesian Empiricism', *Revue Roumaine de Philosophie*, 50 (2006), p. 71-84; SCHMALTZ, p. 179-180).
45 There is, for example, no indication in Descartes that he thinks the mind is atemporal or incapable of change due to its simplicity.
46 This type of claim is repeated often in the *Passions* (AT XI 348-351; CSM I 338-339), and to Elisabeth as well (Descartes to Elisabeth, 6 October 1645, AT IV 310; CSMK 270). Descartes even goes so far as to claim the body is the cause of any opposition to reason in us (*Passions* AT XI 364-365; CSM I 346).
47 *Cours*, III, p. 74-75.

to recall something. Descartes' theory of memory is rather simplistic: folds in the brain are used to register various sensations and impressions through the manner in which they are folded and how the passages within those folds restrict the various flows of animal spirits. When anyone wants to remember something, the soul forms a volition, which in turn creates a force on the pineal gland that then inclines itself in one direction or another, impacting animal spirits and sending them on a path to where that memory is stored and returning to the pineal gland. However, there are any number of things that might frustrate those animal spirits: the folds themselves might have been changed or the memory shifted to a different part of the brain, a passion might dramatically change blood flow and lead to a redirection of animal spirits in the brain, or you might simply be bonked on the head at the right moment. But in all these cases, the soul, via the pineal gland, is still the efficient cause of any memory recall. In a same way, one's inability to draw a perfect circle is partly due to deficiencies in the will — the will did not appropriately moderate itself to take into account the imperfections or difficulties in the various bodily mechanisms to complete its desired task. For Descartes then, error can simply be the result of the will lacking the relevant experience. Why then would Régis not resort to some similar type of causal story? My claim is that the answer to this question has to do with the changing anatomical explanations available to Cartesians.

As mentioned earlier, by the 1690's the pineal gland theory had long been out of favor. However, the pineal gland theory served not only in anatomical explanation but also in metaphysical explanation. In other words, even though the pineal gland theory was quite dead, there was still a need for a substitute to explain how bodily sensations were transmitted as phenomena to the mind and how/where the mind was able to act on the body. Yet, there is no easy substitute for the pineal gland. Descartes' requirements of simplicity, indivisibility, freedom of motion, and appropriate connection to the nervous system left little room for anatomical interpretation, which is exactly why Steno's criticism were so successful. So, to fill this lacuna, Régis needed to expand his description of the brain and compromise on the original requirements for an account of the physical seat of mind-body interaction. Much of Régis's account here relies on Raymond Vieussens' new descriptions of the brain, specifically the centrum semiovale. Régis determines this particular part of the brain to be the point where the soul is able to interact with the body, thus replacing Descartes' pineal gland hypothesis.

However, the centrum semiovale cannot be considered a direct replacement for the pineal gland for at least two reasons. First, the centrum semiovale has multiple parts; it contains animal spirits, has portions where the animal spirits are kept in reserve, is itself directly connected with other sections of the brain, and has an indefinite number of different passages through which the animal spirits flow. In this regard, Régis completely abandons Descartes' requirement for indivisibility and unity. Second, the centrum semiovale is properly the seat of the imagination. While Descartes also claimed the pineal gland as the seat of imagination, Régis's account commits him to much more. For Descartes, to be the seat of imagination was to be the point where the animal spirits converged and impressed an image on a single surface that could then be transmitted to the mind. In this theory, we can picture the pineal gland essentially as a projector screen, whereas the actual projector, with all its constitutive parts and processes, were located elsewhere in the brain. However, for Régis, the centrum semiovale is actually carrying out the mechanical image processing itself, so is a combination of projector and screen.[48] Further, the centrum semiovale can also retain impressions and traces left by the various flows of animal spirits produced in the organ itself. In other words, Régis' centrum semiovale's internal make up is in a continual state of change, whereas part of Descartes' justification for using the pineal gland as the seat of the soul was precisely that it could not change.[49] Making lasting impressions on the gland itself would entail it had distinguishable parts, and if it had parts, it could be divided—it would also mean that it was not a homogenous whole and thus would not provide a single unit for the soul to act upon.[50]

Régis's theory obviously comes with its own share of philosophical baggage that Descartes was attempting to avoid. One of the key advantages of Descartes' theory was a simple answer as to why the soul did not extend throughout the body.[51] In other words, why can't the soul interact directly with the eye, or directly cause one's hands to move? Fundamentally, Descartes' response was anatomically and metaphysically based. On the one hand, anatomical studies revealed that there was a complex network of veins, arteries, nerves, glands, etc., that were all interconnected and that many of these connections could be traced to the brain. According to the prevailing sentiment of the day, God's creations could only be produced from the simplest methods, without extraneous detail or undue complication, so in discovering these anatomical networks, we also discover that they are necessary for sending and receiving signals from the soul. On the other hand, the soul was a simple entity, capable of only receiving one impression at time, which would require a unique and singular organ to interact with. But Régis's theory was forced to move beyond these arguments as the pineal gland was no longer a viable option and there was no other suitable organ to substantiate either the physical or metaphysical requirements. This leaves Régis with no principled reason, that I can find, to reject the possibility of the soul extending throughout the entire body, given that he brings no objection to the seat of the soul growing dramatically in size and number of parts as compared to the simplicity of the pineal gland.[52] With so many parts, Régis would suffer a number of potential criticisms if he claimed the soul was able to act as an efficient cause on

---

48 *Cours*, III, 294-297.
49 That is, did not change much (or undergo certain types of change). In Descartes' view, the pineal gland could be impacted by disease and was in a near constant state of motion, but he went to great lengths to minimize these changes; he explicitly rules out the pineal gland having any internal memory, as Régis seems to allow (AT III 20 and AT III 123).
50 Descartes explicitly rejected this (Descartes to Meyssonnier, 29 January 1640, AT III 20).
51 While Descartes sometimes claims the soul occupies the entire body, in a sense, I am speaking here of the causal and sensory powers of the soul extending throughout the body (*Passions*, AT XI 351; CSM I 339-340).
52 Instead, Régis's strategy is to reduce the powers in the separated soul. If, for example, the soul could move bodies, it would stand to reason it could affect the sensory organs at any location. To solve this, Régis simply deprives the soul of any type of efficient causation between the body and the mind, thus side stepping the problem (*Cours*, III, p. 268).

the centrum semiovale. For example, he would have to answer whether or not the soul could act on multiple areas of the centrum at once, whether it could sense the entirety of the centrum at all times, and how much force the soul could apply to counteract the natural flows of animal spirits, etc. Understandably, to address the problems associated with a larger seat of the soul, Régis simply outsources almost the entirety of one's mental faculties to the brain, thus switching the burden from metaphysical limitations to physical limitations.

It's tempting to see Régis as a reluctant materialist, perhaps pulling more theory from Hobbes than just his ethics. However, I think this would be a misunderstanding of Régis' general strategy. When we look at how Descartes conceptualized the basic faculties of the mind, his underlying argument was that whatever the mind cannot do of its own nature must be done in the body. So, because corporeal images shared nothing in common with an incorporeal mind, there must be some type of physical correlate to justify our ability. On the other hand, Régis' argument seems to move in just the opposite direction. Instead of seeking the limits of the mind, Régis focused on finding the limits of body; whatever was incompatible with the body's nature must be in the mind. As it turns out, Régis believes that almost all mental faculties can be explained through the physical just as well as memory and imagination could be for Descartes. Indeed, it appears the only thing that the body cannot truly account for is the phenomenological experience associated with those bodily motions (and perhaps the will), which forces Régis to associate any principle of difference among souls essentially in the body.

5. Conclusion

By the time Régis was able to publish his textbook, the pineal gland theory of mind-body interaction had already been regulated to the trash bin of history. That being said, there was no easy replacement that fit Descartes' original requirements. The change in the accepted anatomy meant that not only does the location of the suitably connected organ need to change, enlarge, and complexify, as there was no longer any other suitable organ to meet each of Descartes' requirements, but moreover, some of the metaphysical arguments need to drop away as well. The "doubling argument" based on the mind's perceived inability to receive multiple signals as a unified experience, or the demand for a simple indivisible organ, could no longer mesh with significantly more complicated centrum semiovale as Régis found described by Vieussens. With this requirement gone, the ground was cleared for the brain to take on significantly more complicated tasks, like reasoning and judgement. Indeed, given the complexity of the centrum semiovale, Régis would have found it difficult to explain exactly why so many different parts were needed to account for the limited processes of just imagination, sensation, and memory as Descartes had it.

When we come to see what the principle of difference is in Régis's philosophy, we can now appreciate that there was a genuine disparity between the two thinkers here. On the surface level, it looks as though both Régis and Descartes can account for difference in the standard Cartesian manner: through variations in the composition of individual human bodies. However, that is not the full picture. While both Descartes and Régis give an embodied theory of human experience, Régis's theory is, in a way, *more* embodied. Descartes can account for error, false judgement, and cloudy reasoning through the opposition between the mind and body and he is only able to do this because the soul acts at a single point.[53] If, on the contrary, the soul could act over the entire brain, Descartes would no longer be able to account for how we could fail to remember something in the same way that the soul is always aware of the position of the pineal gland (though indirectly). When Régis expanded the seat of the soul, mental fallibility needed a new explanation that could only avoid these types of problems by reducing the mental to the physical. But this comes with significant moral implications. Whereas Descartes can still appeal to a defective will, when accounting for poor judgment, Régis cannot. A brain that is formed differently will consequently result in a different way of thinking that cannot be circumvented in ways that Descartes advocates for in his theory of the passions.[54] In short, the rallying cry that "the mind has no sex" is simply not applicable to Régis's brand of Cartesianism.

---

53 CSM I, 346; AT XI, 364-365.
54 For more on Régis' take on the passions of the soul, see ANTONELLA DEL PRETE, 'La Théroie Des Passions de Régis', in *Les Passions de l'âme et Leur Réception Philosophique*, ed. by Vincent Carraud and Giulia Belgioioso, Turnhout, Belgium, Brepols, 2020, p. 531-546.

LAURYNAS ADOMAITIS

Beyond Mechanical Life

Biological Processes in the Seventeenth Century

▼ ABSTRACT Some early modern natural philosophers accepted that life sciences are fundamentally based on processes rather than things. Most clearly it comes out in Hooke who named processes "the steps or foundations of our Enquiry". Bacon too had relied on the notion of *meta-schematismus* or an underlying process to conceptualize structural change of living organisms. The notion of *meta-schematismus* carried through to early modern pathology where diseases were considered to have their own developmental processes. However, processes were not conceptualized by the early modern thinkers to bypass the prior concept of organism. Despite the fact that they embraced process-based ontology, they still used a static methodology that relied on the notions of organism and states of organism. A qualitatively different methodology that embraced temporal dynamics of processes came to light with technological advancements, like the *in vivo* labelling of cell lineage.

▼ KEYWORDS Early modern Biology, Processual Philosophy Of Biology, Robert Hooke, Francis Bacon

1. Introduction

Recent scholarship has argued that the most natural framework for contemporary life sciences considers biological processes (as opposed to things, like organisms or individuals) as the most basic entity of study.[1] This paper seeks to show the historical roots of process-based biology.

---

1 JOHN DUPRÉ and DANIEL J. NICHOLSON, "A Manifesto for a Processual Philosophy of Biology", in *Everything Flows: Towards a Processual Philosophy of Biology*, ed. by J. Dupre and D. Nicholson, Oxford, Oxford University Press, p. 3-48.

Laurynas Adomaitis • CEA-Saclay/Larsim, Gif-sur-Yvette, France. Contact: <laurynas. adomaitis@cea.fr>

The consensus is that early modern natural philosophers considered things (atoms and extended substances) and not processes to be the most basic entities in biology.[2] Descartes's philosophy of organism consisted of the general contention that all organic phenomena undergo formation, just like the rest of the cosmos, according to the mechanical laws of matter in motion. The outcome of Descartes' first claim was the polemical beast-machine hypothesis, which claims that all the behavior of animals could be explained mechanically, without supposing the existence of a "soul" distinct from matter. Descartes' philosophy of organic life was related to his rebuilding of the world, in its general as well as particular patterns, from exclusively mechanical principles.

This paper is a cross-period study of the alternative view to Descartes' mechanical explanation of life that relied on biological processes. Some major early modern biologists accepted the process-based biology. Their definition of a fundamental process consisted in a passing from one degree of complexity to another. This biological notion of a process later informed medical debates on the pathological formation of diseases. Yet a proper definition of a process was lacking. It was partly due to the inability to actually observe processes in action, as predicted by Bacon. A major break in identifying processes was achieved by contemporary techniques like the in vivo labelling in cell lineage studies. The historical definition of processes relied on states and organisms while the contemporary definition replaced them by labelling marks and fate maps. This allowed to formulate a cumulative definition of processes that account for actual (not merely inferred) change over time. The main take-away from this is that process-based biology is not without its history, yet the early modern understanding of what a process is was conceptually lacking in comparison to contemporary views.

2. Process-based Biology and Development

A recent influential approach to the life sciences holds that "the living world is a hierarchy of processes, stabilized and actively maintained at different timescales".[3] *Process-based biology* considers processes (as opposed to things, like organisms or individuals) to be the most basic entity of study in the life sciences. One important caveat for the *Process-based biology* is that it does not seek to eliminate the substantive notions, like an organism. It maintains that processes are more basic.

---

2 The literature on Descartes' philosophy of organism is vast and devoid of complete consensus, but here I rely on a broad understanding. For a detailed description see THEO VERBEEK, ed., *Descartes et Regius, Autour de l'explication de l'esprit humain*, Amsterdam, Rodopi, 1993; FRANÇOIS DUCHESNEAU, *Le modèle du vivant de Descartes à Leibniz*, Paris, Vrin, 1998; DENNIS DES CHENE, *Spirits&Clocks: Machine and Organism in Descartes*, Ithaca, Cornell University Press, 2001; RAPHAËLE ANDRAULT, *La raison des corps. Mécanisme et sciences médicales*, Paris, Vrin, 2016; FABRIZIO BALDASSARRI, *Il metodo al tavolo anatomico. Descartes e la medicina*, Rome, Aracne, 2021.
3 DUPRÉ and NICHOLSON, *Manifesto*, p. 3.

Dupré and Nicholson present liver as an example:

> if we take for example a liver, we see that it provides enabling conditions for the persistence of the organism of which it is a part, but also for the hepatocytes that compose it. Outside a very specialized laboratory, a hepatocyte can persist only in a liver. And reciprocally, in order to persist, a liver requires both an organism in which it resides, and hepatocytes of which it is composed. A key point is that these reciprocal dependencies are not merely structural, but are also grounded in activity. A hepatocyte sustains a liver, and a liver sustains an organism, by doing things. This ultimately underlies our insistence on seeing such seemingly substantial entities as cells, organs, and organisms as processes.[4]

This does not mean that liver is not a thing. However, its reality as a thing is based in more fundamental processes, like that of sustaining the life of its host organism. The live interaction between the organ and the organism is more basic than a structural description of the body which is, according to this view, an abstraction: "Mechanical models, assuming fixed machine-like ontologies, are at best an abstraction from the constantly dynamic nature of biological processes".[5] Thus *Process-based biology* does not reject the substantive notions but claims that they are based in more fundamental processual notions.

There seems to be no universally accepted definition of a process. However, in most general terms, it is said to rely on two other notions — time and change: "Processes are extended in time: they have temporal parts [...] Equally central to the concept of process is the idea of change. A process depends on change for its occurrence".[6] The implications for the philosophy of biology are that the process-based methodology should aim towards dynamical change rather than observation of stable states.

For example, in developmental biology, the life cycle is taken to be the most fundamental biological process: "In this framework [*viz.* developmental systems theory], development (ontogeny) is the reconstruction of a life cycle using resources passed on by previous life cycle".[7] Life cycle as a whole is a process composed of lower dynamical processes (like embryonic development) and it gives rise to a higher evolutionary development which is a process that involves multiple life cycles of individuals and their environment.

Most importantly, process-based developmental biology implies that developmental interactions are dynamical and temporal. Griffith and Stotz, following Lerner and Ford,[8] explain that "In this 'static interaction' the values of two variables measured

---

4 *Ibid.*, p. 3.
5 JOHN DUPRÉ, *Processes of Life: Essays in the Philosophy of Biology*, Oxford, Oxford University Press, p. 71.
6 DUPRÉ and NICHOLSON, *Manifesto*, p. 11-12. Dupré and Nicholson also suggest a more technical term of "dynamicity" instead of "change", see *Manifesto*, p. 13.
7 PAUL GRIFFITHS and KAROLA STOTZ, "Developmental systems theory as a process theory" in *Everything Flows: Towards a Processual Philosophy of Biology*, ed. by J. Dupre and D. Nicholson, Oxford, Oxford University Press, p. 225.
8 DONALD H. FORD and RICHARD M. LERNER, *Developmental Systems Theory: An Integrative Approach*, Sage, Newbury Park, 1992.

before development, such as shared genes and shared environment, are shown to interact with each other. In contrast, dynamic interaction must be studied as a temporally extended process".[9] So, under the static understanding of development, measurements are made on the fixed states before and after the developmental event and then a process or dependency is inferred from the variance. On the other hand, dynamical system analysis relies on the temporal understanding of development which is continuous rather than divided into fixed states.

On a broader scale, mechanical and static models are considered to be just abstract snapshots by the *Process-based biology*. Instead, on all hierarchical levels biology is based in temporal processes and any substantive or fixed description is an idealization:

> The processes of life are of course massively heterogeneous. This heterogeneity is expressed, for example, when we inventory the thousands of chemical species to be found at any instant in a cell. Although such an inventory is a static snapshot of a dynamic entity — at best an idealized description of the cell, therefore — the molecules we distinguish are more or less transient foci of causal power, real nodes in the astonishingly complex causal nexus that drives the cellular processes.[10]

The advocates of the *Process-based biology* consider it as a fundamentally recent approach with some roots in the organicism of the mid-twentieth century. They argue that earlier thinkers were discouraged to analyze processes by the revival of atomism in the early modern period: "Although the scientific revolution is often thought of as a revolt from Aristotelianism, it was certainly not a rejection of substantialism. A central reason for this was the revival of atomism by Boyle, Newton, and others".[11]

In this paper I argue that the thesis that processes are the fundamental entity of study in biology extends to much earlier times, at least to 1620. However, early modern life scientists did not draw the same methodological conclusions that are suggested in Dupré and Nicholson, Griffith and Stotz, or Lerner and Ford. Some major early modern life scientists and physicians believed in the process ontology but still relied on a methodology that presupposed organisms and states of organisms. Lastly, a case will be made that a qualitatively different methodology for developmental biology can be conceived with the help of modern techniques, like the *in vivo* labelling.

3. Early Modern Views on Fundamental Processes

Seventeenth century presented natural philosophy with the reinvigoration of debates about the generation of animals. In sexual generation, some important questions were raised as to how an embryo is formed and what is the process of its development. Galenist theory — one of the dominating factions alongside Aristotelism — is well described by Preus: "female seed is expelled from the ovaries at the time of coition

---

9 Griffiths and Stotz, *Developmental systems theory*, p. 234.
10 Dupré, *Processes of Life*, p. 72.
11 Dupré and Nicholson, *Manifesto*, p. 6.

in such manner that both seeds meet in the womb, mix, and form a membrane; the female seed serves as food for the semen in its development, then the development follows, with *pneuma* bringing about the development of Galen's three major organs, liver, heart, and brain".[12] Aristotelians advocated a more independent development of the fetus which began with the formation of the heart which was the primary and necessary organ for the fetus to become an individual. Having developed a heart, it would begin its own independent formation.

William Harvey followed the Aristotelian idea of independent formation but wanted to pin down the moment in which the fetus becomes an individual more precisely. Finally, a series of dissections of fertilized chicken eggs made him reject both Galenist and Aristotelian views of embryonic development:

> I am therefore of opinion that we are to reject the views of certain physicians, indifferent philosophers, who will have it that three principal and primogenate parts arise together, viz.: the brain, the heart, and the liver; neither can I agree with Aristotle himself, who maintains that the heart is the first engendered and animated part; for I think that the privilege of priority belongs to the blood alone.[13]

As the discoverer of the proper function of the heart,[14] Harvey knew that a fully functional heart required the circulatory system to properly serve its purpose and thus it could not be the very first thing that is formed in an animal. Thus, he drew his attention to much earlier stages of the development. The first autonomous motion that he was able to observe in fertilized chicken eggs was the "pulsating" motion of what seemed a simple droplet of blood. That was the point in which he determined that the autonomous action of the individual would begin and end: "so that as pulsation commences in it and from it, so, in the last struggle of mortal agony, does motion also end there".[15]

An embryo for Harvey was an individual — a *punctum saliens* — from its very first movements. However, it had no inherent features or structure. It was difficult to understand how a simple point (*punctum*) of liquid blood can develop into a fully formed organism. There seemed to be disparity between the complex nature of an adult and the simplicity of the *punctum saliens*. Harvey admitted his ignorance on this question, as he writes to Giovanni Nardi towards the end of his life:

> All of these accidents must inhere in the geniture and semen, and accompany that specific thing, by whatever name you call it, from which an animal is not only produced, but by which it is afterwards governed, and to the end of its life preserved. As all this, I say, is not readily accounted for.[16]

---

12 ANTHONY PREUS, "Galen's criticism of Aristotle's conception theory", *Journal of the History of Biology* 10/1 (1977): 83-84.
13 WILLIAM HARVEY, *The Works of William Harvey*, London, Sydenham Society, 1847, p. 373.
14 WILLIAM HARVEY, *Exercitatio Anatomica de Motu Cordis et Sanguinis in Animalibus*. William Fitzer, Frankfurt, 1628. For a confrontation between Harvey's and Descartes' epistemology, see Benjamin Goldberg's contribution to this volume.
15 HARVEY, *Works*, p. 374.
16 HARVEY, *Works*, p. 610-611. A related and likewise unsolved problem through natural explanation for Harvey was heredity, see STAFFAN MÜLLER-WILLE, "Figures of Inheritance, 1650-1850", in *Heredity*

The major question for Harvey and many other life scientists at the time was the passing of an organism from one degree of complexity to another. The early modern observational biologists, sometimes called the microscopists, eagerly engaged with the question of development. They recognized the need to explain the passing between the degrees of complexity without postulating artificial jumps.[17]

Ultimately, a notion emerged to describe the passage between the stages of complexity that unified biological development. That notion was a biological process. A process was understood as the passage from a simpler state of an organism to a more complex state.[18] To use a *Preliminary definition*:

> P is a developmental biological process iff P is required for an organism O to pass from the state S_1 to the state S_2 where S_2 is more complex than S_1.

One exemplary work on fundamental biological processes is Robert Hooke's *Micrographia* (1665). Smith calls it "the founding document of early modern microscopy as a domain of scientific inquiry."[19] At the very onset of the investigation, Hooke sets out an agenda to begin his analysis with the simple bodies and proceed to increasing complexity:

> we must endevour to follow Nature in the more plain and easie ways she treads in the most simple and uncompounded bodies, to trace her steps, and be acquainted with her manner of walking there, before we venture our selves into the multitude of meanders she has in bodies of a more complicated nature [...] We will begin these our Inquiries therefore with the Observations of Bodies of the most simple nature first, and so gradually proceed to those of a more compounded one.[20]

Hooke chooses the point of the needle as the first and, supposedly, the simplest body in the common imagination, representing the "physical point"[21]. However, he soon emphasizes that observed through the microscope the apex of the needle looks blunt and more like conical frustrum than a sharp cone. He reaches a similar conclusion in relation to lines: "The sharpest Edge hath the same kind of affinity to

---

Produced: At the Crossroads of Biology, Politics, and Culture, 1500-1870, ed. by Staffan Müller-Wille and Hans-Jörg Rheinberger, Cambridge, MA, MIT Press, 2007, p. 177-204.

17 The so-called principle of continuity was an important maxim for early modern philosophers and scientists, see FRANÇOIS DUCHESNEAU, *Organisme et corps organique de Leibniz à Kant*, Paris, Vrin, 2018 for an overview.
18 The developmental process differs from just a process in that development necessarily has increasing complexity, whereas other processes might have decreasing or equivalent complexity. It is interesting to observe that according to our discussion below Hooke mostly dealt with development, whereas Bacon's agenda applies equally to all processes, or *meta-schematismi*.
19 JUSTIN E. H. SMITH, "Introduction", in *The Problem of Animal Generation in Early Modern Philosophy*, ed. by Justin E. H. Smith, Cambridge, Cambridge University Press, 2006, p. 10.
20 ROBERT HOOKE, *Micrographia: or Some Physiological Descriptions of Minute Bodies Made by Magnifying Glasses*, London, Royal Society, 1665, p. 1.
21 *Ibid.*, p. 1.

the sharpest Point in Physicks, as a line hath to a point in Mathematicks"[22] Hooke observes the edge of a razor and concludes that in fact it "appeared a rough surface of a very considerable bredth from side to side"[23], so nothing like a sharp line.

Proceeding in the order of complexity, Hooke microscopically observed woven wool and silk cloths, subtle glass threads and drops, flint and steel sparks, then sand, kidney stones, ice and snow, a porous stone (probably Ketton stone, although Hooke calls it "Kettering-stone"),[24] charcoal, petrified bodies, small plants, mold, moss, polyporaceae, nettle leaves, various seeds, skin, hair, fish scales, bee sting, bird feathers, insect body parts, and, finally, individual insects. Supposedly, from Hooke's initial agenda, they are increasingly complex states of organisms. They are surely not the states of the same organism — it is not the case that a particular speck of sand developed into a particular instance of mold, etc. However, given a concrete complex state of an organism (S_3) it is reasonable to say that its formation must presuppose some simpler state (S_2) and a process (P_2) through which it passed to this more complex state, while the simpler state (S_2) presupposes another simpler state (S_1) with another process (P_1), etc. Otherwise the formation of the higher states would be unintelligible.

Hooke's methodological discussion about process comes out best in Observation XX: "Of blue Mould, and of the first Principles of Vegetation arising from Putrefaction".[25] His stepping stone is the observation of the "Blue and White and several kinds of hairy mouldy spots"[26] on various plants and meats which upon closer look appeared to be "nothing else but several kinds of small and variously figur'd Mushroms [...] excited to a certain kind of vegetation".[27] The vegetation, according to Hooke, is perpetuated by the putrefaction of the substance on which the mushrooms grow. These mushrooms had a considerable complexity, even so that full description of the shapes would be too long and "would not have suited so well with my design in this Treatise".[28] Thus the white mushrooms were an organism in a relatively complex state (S_4).

Hooke goes on to say that he should enquire into the formation of these mushrooms because: "the figure and method of Generation in this concrete seeming to me, next after the Enquiry into the formation, figuration, or chrystalization of Salts, to be the most simple, plain, and easie; and it seems to be a medium through which he must necessarily pass, that would with any likelihood investigate the *forma informans* of Vegetables".[29] So it seems that the understanding of the formation of mold, according

---

22 Ibid., p. 4.
23 Ibid., p. 4.
24 HOOKE, *Micrographia*, p. 24. An analysis of the original specimens of Hooke is in DEREK HULL, "Robert Hooke: A fractographic study of Kettering — stone", *Notes and Records of the Royal Society* 51 (1997), p. 45-55. Hull also replicates some of Hooke's initial observations using reproductions of period instruments.
25 HOOKE, *Micrographia*, p. 125.
26 Ibid., p. 125.
27 Ibid., p. 125.
28 Ibid., p. 125.
29 Ibid., p. 126.

to Hooke, is essential in understanding the formation of vegetables because mold — a simpler organism at state S_4 — "seems to be a medium through which [a vegetable] must necessarily pass"[30] to become a more complex organism at S_5. So according to the *Preliminary definition*, at least from the complexity of the vegetable we can deduce that there was a simpler state of that organism — mold or white mushroom — and they were united by a process.

Furthermore, Hooke observes that mold is also not a completely simple organism, so its formation presupposes something even more basic, namely, salts, while salts presuppose the formation of a globular shape, while the latter requires geometrical construction:

> I think that he shall find it a very difficult task, who undertakes to discover the form of Saline crystallizations, without the consideration and prescience of the nature and reason of a Globular form, and as difficult to explicate this configuration of Mushroms, without the previous consideration of the form of Salts; so will the enquiry into the forms of Vegetables be no less, if not much more difficult, without the fore-knowledge of the forms of Mushroms, these several Enquiries having no less dependance one upon another then any select number of Propositions in Mathematical Elements may be made to have.[31]

So, in summary, starting with an organism at the stage of mold (S_4) we see that it both informs the formation of vegetables (S_5) and is informed by the formation of salts (S_3), while the formation of salts is informed by the globular formation (S_2), and the latter is informed by geometrical construction (S_1). Importantly, these states are in succession as regards their complexity, so that from S_1 to S_5 an organism is becoming continuously more complex. This means that the processes from P_1 to P_5 are developmental processes.

So far Hooke has been referring only to various states of organisms but not the processes that unify their development. However, immediately after the discussion of states $(S_1\text{-}S_4)$ he adds:

> Nor do I imagine that the skips from the one [sc. state] to another will be found very great, if beginning from fluidity, or body without any form, we descend gradually, till we arrive at the highest form of a bruite Animal's Soul, making the steps or foundations of our Enquiry, Fluidity, Orbiculation, Fixation, Angulization, or Crystallization Germination or Ebullition, Vegetation, Plantanimation, Animation, Sensation, Imagination.[32]

There are several things to take from this quote. First, Hooke suggests that the development between states is without great skips or jumps, implying that it was a rather continuous process with multiple stages. Second, the simplest state of body

---

30 *Ibid.*, p. 126.
31 *Ibid.*, p. 127.
32 HOOKE, *Micrographia*, p. 127.

is fluidity, i.e. "a body without any form".³³ Fluidity is the bedrock of development which does not presuppose a simpler state, so it is the S_0. Hooke began his description with what the common opinion might hold to be physical points and lines, i.e. the simplest bodies. But since he has observed that they were not as simple as it might seem, something else must be the beginning of development. That something is here described as fluidity. This also coincides with Harvey's description of the *punctum saliens*, according to which "the privilege of priority belongs to the blood alone".³⁴ Blood, of course, is a form of liquid. So Hooke is at least indirectly tackling Harvey's problem of how structure can arise from liquid in the formation of an embryo. Third, in Hooke's developmental system, the highest natural state that is subject to biological enquiry is "the highest form of a bruite Animal's Soul".³⁵ This presupposes that the explanation of the rational soul that is characteristic of human beings requires something beyond biology. In general, the early modern life scientists did not always draw the analogy from the generation of animals to the generation of humans.³⁶

Lastly, and most importantly, all developmental states are linked through fundamental biological processes which Hooke exhaustively lists above. Processes are the steps that are required for an organism to ascend in the developmental complexity. We can reconstruct Hooke's scheme of biological development as follows:

S_0 [Fluidity] + P_0 [Orbiculation] -> S_1 [Sphere] + P_1 [Fixation] -> S_2 [Residue] + P_2 [Crystallization] -> S_3 [Salt] + P_3 [Germination] -> S_4 [Mold] + P_4 [Vegetation] -> S_5 [Vegetable] + P_5 [Plantanimation] -> S_6 [Zoophyte] + P_6 [Animation] -> S_7 [Animal] + P_7 [Sensation] -> S_8 [Sensitive animal] + P_8 [Imagination] -> S_9 [brute Animal's Soul].

In the end, biological development is comprised of ten states of complexity and nine processes that describe the passage of an organism through all of them. Hooke's description is perfectly in line with our *Preliminary definition*:

P is a developmental biological process iff P is required for an organism O to pass from the state S_1 to the state S_2 where S_2 is more complex than S_1.

---

33 *Ibid.*, p. 127. Hooke seems to be using the notion of "form" not in its technical Aristotelian use but more similarly to the common meaning of "figure" or "shape". In other words, unbound liquid has no geometrical form.
34 HARVEY, *Works*, p. 373.
35 HOOKE, *Micrographia*, p. 127.
36 Bitbol-Hespériès describes the relation between human and animal development in the period: "the development of the fetus remained strongly linked with the activity of a soul, generally divided into its 'vegetative' component, found in plants as well as animals, and its 'sensitive' component, found exclusively in animals. Finally, human beings alone were held to have a rational or intellective soul", ANNIE BITBOL-HESPÉRIÈS, "Monsters, Nature, and Generation from the Renaissance to the Early Modern Period: The Emergence of Medical Thought", in *The Problem of Animal Generation in Early Modern Philosophy*, ed. by Justin E. H. Smith, Cambridge, Cambridge University Press, 2006, p. 51. Hooke remains within the bounds of this conception.

What is more, Hooke describes these processes as "the steps or foundations of our Enquiry"[37] implying that the description of biological development (the passing from simpler states of organisms to more complex ones) essentially relies on processes as its basic notion or foundation. This general thesis echoes the contemporary approach of treating processes as the foundations of developmental biology discussed in the first section.

Although Hooke practiced or at least endorsed the process-based approach to developmental biology, the general idea was already conveyed by Bacon. In the second book of the *Novum Organum* (1620) Bacon discusses the formation of bodies. Formation is a broader notion than development since it comprises the processes that have decreasing complexity as well as an increasing one. So, formation includes development alongside transformation and deterioration of organisms. Talking of formation, Bacon distinguishes between two kinds of approaches to its study. The first kind is the analysis of the simple qualities of bodies and a subsequent recreation of the body from these qualities. From this perspective, the formation is artificial and follows the primary analysis of the basic qualities of a body. Bacon gives the example of gold:

> For example, the following things are all found together in gold; it is tawny coloured; it is heavy with a certain weight; it is malleable or ductile to a certain degree; [...] and so on for the rest of the natures which are found together in gold. Thus this kind of axiom derives the object from the forms of simple natures. For he who knows the forms and methods of superinducing tawny colour, weight, ductility, stability, melting, solution and so on, and their degrees and manners, will take pains to try to unite them in some body, and from this follows the transformation into gold.[38]

This approach implies that certain bodies or materials can be artificially reproduced and, thus, it "affords vast opportunities to human power".[39] Yet it has its drawbacks. The way that, say, a chemist might try to recreate gold with its qualities might not be the same process in which nature generates gold. This is especially true for living organisms which are not recreated by artifice. So Bacon recognizes the need for another approach, which is more fitting for the study of living organisms:

> But the second kind of axiom (which depends on the discovery of the latent process) does not proceed by simple natures, but by compound bodies as they are found in nature in the ordinary course of things. This is so, for example, [...] in the process by which plants are generated, from the first solidifying of the sap in the soil, or from seeds, up to the formed plant, with constant succession of motion, and with diverse yet continuous efforts of nature; likewise, of the orderly progress of the generation of animals from conception to birth.[40]

---

37 HOOKE, *Micrographia*, p. 127.
38 FRANCIS BACON, *The New Organon*. Translated by Lisa Jardine and Michael Silverthorne, Cambridge, Cambridge University Press, 2006, p. 105.
39 Ibid., p. 105.
40 Ibid., p. 105.

Bacon's second kind of approach (or axiom) is a study of organisms that also takes into account its natural environment: "For this investigation looks not only at the generation of bodies, but also at other movements and workings of nature".[41] However, apart from environment, there is another thing that is required by the second approach — "the latent process".[42] He goes on to describe the latent process as follows: "we do not mean actual measures, signs or stages of a process which are visible in bodies, but a wholly continuous process which for the most part escapes the senses".[43] So the latent process is not something that is evident in the apparent states of bodies or animals. It is rather the continuous process that underlies the development of the organism up to a particular state. Bacon also provides this description of the latent process:

> Example: in every case of generation and transformation of a body we have to ask what is lost and disappears; what remains and what accrues; what expands and what contracts; what is combined, what is separated; what is continuous, what interrupted; what impels, what obstructs; what prevails, what submits; and several other questions.[44]

These seem to be the conditions of identifying the underlying process. It appears that, according to Bacon, we can infer the nature of the latent process without the *in vivo* observation of it. What is needed is to take two states of a body or organism before and after the generation or transformation and identify the changes, therefore inferring what must have being going on between these two states. This was essentially the methodology of Hooke who observed the different states of organisms and tried to infer the underlying processes that would be required to pass from one state to another in increasing complexity. As we shall see, the same approach carried through to later pathology and medicine.

What we have been calling "states" and "processes" had a peculiar terminology in Bacon. He had called them *schematismus* and *meta-schematismus*, accordingly. He describes them already in book one, as one of the idols of the tribe: "The human understanding is carried away to abstractions by its own nature, and pretends that things which are in flux are unchanging. But it is better to dissect nature than to abstract; [...] We should study matter, and its structure (schematismus), and structural change (meta-schematismus), and pure act, and the law of act or motion".[45] According to Bacon, what is commonly assumed to be fixed and substantive, might actually be changing and transforming in the latent structures and processes. Therefore, what might appear to be a fixed under an abstract form, might actually be in flux and in the process of transformation. The investigation of the real processes must refer to the "structure (schematismus), and structural change (meta-schematismus)"[46] of matter, not the apparent state of organisms.

---

41 Ibid., p. 105.
42 Ibid., p. 105.
43 Ibid., p. 106.
44 Ibid., p. 106.
45 Ibid., p. 45.
46 Ibid., p. 46.

Bacon opposes the study of the (meta-)schematismus to the "Observation of nature and of bodies in their simple parts", which "fractures and diminishes the understanding".[47] Bacon criticizes the latter because it "is so concerned with the particles of things that it almost forgets their structures".[48] At the same time, the understanding of the (meta-)schematismus must go beyond what is seen with the naked eye:

> But much the greatest obstacle and distortion of human understanding comes from the dullness, limitations and deceptions of the senses; [...] thought virtually stops at sight; so that there is little or no notice taken of things that cannot be seen. [...] And all the more subtle structural change [*meta-schematismus*] in the parts of dense objects (which is commonly called alteration, although in truth it is movement of particles) is similarly hidden.[49]

In sum, Bacon recognized that the study of living organisms must not rely on stable forms or substances. It must look at the underlying structure (*schemtismus*) and underlying processes (*meta-schematismi*) which is hidden from ordinary view. What on the surface appears to be stable and substantive in fact relies on a more fundamental process. The latent process is a passing between structural states. Also, the underlying process manifests itself in relation to its environment. However, its discovery relies on inference from the results of the process, i.e. the structures that it produces.

Bacon's variation of the *Preliminary definition* of the fundamental biological processes could be summarized as follows:[50]

> P is a fundamental biological process (*meta-schematismus*) iff P is required for an organism O to pass from the state S_1 to the state S_2, where S_1 and S_2 are structural (*schematismi*) and observed in their natural environment.

In general, Bacon was convinced that the latent biological processes or *meta-schematismi* were undiscovered by his time: "All these things are unknown and unbroached by the sciences (which are currently practised by the dullest and most unsuitable persons)".[51] The reason for that was the inability of the human eye to see the underlying structure of things: "For since every natural action is transacted by means of the smallest particles, or at least by things too small to make an impression on the senses, no one should expect to master or modify nature without taking the appropriate means to grasp and take note of them".[52] The appropriate means that

---

47 *Ibid.*, p. 47.
48 *Ibid.*, p. 47.
49 *Ibid.*, p. 45.
50 Notice that Bacon does not speak solely of developmental processes that follow increasing complexity. In fact, Bacon's main contribution to development was a study of aging rather than development: "Bacon gave more thought to the question of increasing longevity than any other natural philosopher of the early-modern era, working out, from the mid-1610s onwards, a detailed account of the causes of aging and various suggestions as to how the process might be retarded and perhaps even stopped", STEPHEN GAUKROGER, *Francis Bacon and the Transformation of Early-Modern Philosophy*. Cambridge, Cambridge University Press, 2004, p. 96.
51 Bacon, *New Organon*, p. 105.
52 *Ibid.*, p. 107.

Bacon is referring to is exactly what Hooke had — the microscope: "microscopes, lately invented, which (by remarkably increasing the size of the specimens) reveal the hidden, invisible small parts of bodies, and their latent structure [*schematismus*] and motions".[53]

Bacon was calling for an investigation into the microscopic processes (*meta-schematismi*) that constitute the change of a body or organism from what state (*schematismus*) to another. J. S. Brewer has called the meta-schematismi "the great object of all scientific physics" (page) for Bacon. However, a proper investigation of them required the observation of the underlying structures of organisms. There seems to be continuity between Bacon's methodological agenda and Hooke's observations which both treated processes as a fundamental object of study in biology. In fact, Hooke's *Micrographia* has been called the "best commentary on Bacon" (Ellis 1879: 25).[54] A similar approach carried through to later pathology and medicine.

4. Pathological Processes in Early Modern Medicine

The notion of "*meta-schematismus*" in early modern medicine, and especially pathology, was defined as the transformation of a disease. In other words, like living organisms are subject to development and fundamental biological process (in Hooke and Bacon), so diseases have their own development and formation. This developmental process can lead a disease take up another form in the same organism.

The usage of the term mostly spread in Germany and was presented with the following definition in the *Pathologie* (1798) of Wilhelm Gottfried Ploucquet: "The transition to another disease either is just a change in the form of the disease, which basically remains the same (*meta-schematismus*), or it becomes a *sequela* of another nature"[55]. Usually, a *meta-schematismus* was distinguished form a *metastasis* which was the transfer of the same disease into another place in a body. Philipp Karl Hartmann in the *Theoria morbi* (1828) explains this distinction:

> The transition of one disease into another is *meta-schematismus*, and that which follows from the primary is the secondary disease. There are primary diseases which already hold the seed of the secondary disease in their folds and when the primary ones spread to the certain degree, they will necessarily give rise to the secondary. For example, an abscess from a strong inflammation, an adynamic fever[56] from inflammatory fever. The matter generated by the primary disease and

---

53 Ibid., p. 171.
54 Robert Leslie Ellis, "General Preface", in *The Collected Works of Francis Bacon*, ed. by R. L. Ellis and J. Spedding, London, Longmans, 1879, p. 25.
55 Wilhelm Gottfried Ploucquet, *Pathologie mit allgemeiner Heilkinde in Verbindung gesezt*, Tübingen, Heerbrand, 1798, p. 50.
56 *Febris adynamica* was conceived as a fever, characterized by diminution of the cerebral functions and muscular activity.

retained in the body can bring about the same disease and given the occasion cause new bouts. This is what is *metastasis* which leads to the disease in another part.[57]

There is a disagreement of terminology between the two definitions. Ploucquet suggests that *meta-schematismus* is "just a change in the form of the disease"[58] whereas Hartmann suggests it is a "transition of one disease into another".[59] So the disagreement lies in the understanding of the states of a disease — are they different forms of one disease, or a mutated disease is actually something else? This question, however, is not critical in view of the process of pathological transformation since both Ploucquet and Hartmann agree that the primary state (be it disease or a form of disease) is a requisite for the secondary, so that the primary diseases "already hold the seed of the secondary disease in their folds".[60]

In this sense, pathological processes could be defined in a similar way to the *Preliminary definition* above:

> PP is a fundamental pathological process (*meta-schematismus*) iff PP is required for a disease D to pass from the state S_1 to the state S_2 where S_1 is a primary disease, and S_2 is a secondary disease.

The study of such processes could obviously have important implications for medicine. It could be useful to prevent the formation of secondary diseases, as well as provide treatment. For example, when Johann Christian Reil inquired into polycholia, i.e. the excessive secretion of bile, he had split his results into two volumes. One, which was his thesis, was dedicated to the description of the disease (*Tractatus de Polycholia*, 1782) and another to its various *meta-schematismi* (*Fragmenta meta-schematismi polycholiae*, 1783). Reil proposes an extensive list of diseases which might develop from the excessive bile. Reil seems to share the view of Hartmann that *meta-schematismi* are propagated by the material created by the primary disease. In Reil's case, that material was obviously bile. He claimed that: "In the other part I proposed what is the origin an nature of the mater of bile, yet it will be in our interest to know its qualities and investigate the various diseases that arise due to these diverse qualities to establish more certain prognosis as well as the whole treatment".[61] So in Reil's view, knowing the development of the disease is certainly helpful for both prognosis and treatment.

One example of a disease caused by the elevated production of bile, according to Reil, is skin cancer.[62] First, "when the blackest and thick bile matter, obstructed by the finest fabric of the glands, is spread out and hardens, we say that a black bile scirrhous has arisen".[63] According to this description, the excess of thickened

---

57 PHILIPP KARL HARTMANN, *Theoria Morbi, seu pathologia generalis*, Vienna, Wimmer, 1828, p. 322.
58 PLOUCQUET, *Pathologie*, p. 50.
59 HARTMANN, *Theoria Morbi*, p. 322.
60 *Ibid.*, p. 322.
61 JOHANN CHRISTIAN REIL, *Fragmenta meta-schematismi polycholiae*, Halle, Grunert, 1783, p. 10.
62 The relationship between black bile and cancer was commonplace in the eighteenth century, see ALANNA SKUSE, *Constructions of Cancer in Early Modern England: Ravenous Natures*, Houndmills, Palgrave, 2015, p. 31-37.
63 REIL, *Fragmenta*, p. 92.

black bile develops into a scirrhous which, according to the definition above, is a secondary disease to polycholia.⁶⁴ So we can say that the scirrhous (S_2) has arisen by a *meta-schematismus*, or a fundamental pathological process from polycholia (S_1). The process itself is characterized by Reil as the hardening and thickening of the black bile material. Furthermore, "when the stagnant black bile matter upon impact becomes loosened, moving, and irritated, the scirrhous develops into cancer".⁶⁵ So we see that the scirrhous (S_2) further develops into cancer (S_3) by a commotion of the thickened black bile matter. Reil describes the process in significant detail:

> the liquified matter, gains the disgusting, most acidic, and metal eroding pungency that spills out when absorbed and has a putrid smell, corrodes its surroundings, causes their inflammation and scarring. With the liver being obstructed, and with the perpetual polycholia, the continuous irritation of the affected place invites the black bile to attach on the wound from the blood that is circulating around. That is why people who die from cancer always have porous liver obstructed with rocks and a colon filled with a bilious nature.⁶⁶

It is clear from this description that Reil is drawing conclusions about the process of the development of cancer from its previous formation, i.e. from the *meta-schematismus* of polycholia (S_1) into scirrhous (S_2); and from the subsequent states of the already formed cancerous sub product ("the liquified matter")⁶⁷ and the state of the dead organism. The information about the process is deduced from the states of the disease that precede and succeed it.

Lastly, the treatment prescribed by Reil for this condition relies directly on the reconstructed process. His suggestion is to get ahead of the condition and treat the earlier states of the cancerous development, i.e. the polycholia (S_1): "In the treatment we must take care of the obstacles of the secretion of liver, clogging, stagnations and obstructions" (94), so that the bile matter would not form into scirrhous (S_2), and, ultimately, into cancer (S_3).

In sum, we see that in both methodological works of Ploucquet and Hartmann, and in the applications by Reil, pathological development or *meta-schematismi* were an important ingredient of the prognosis of the development and the treatment of a disease. These medical applications certainly followed the earlier biological investigations into the biological developmental processes. They share a similar methodology geared towards the identification of the biological and pathological processes. Therefore, it seems that the focus on processes has precedents in the early modern life sciences.

---

64 Hajdu explains the relationship between scirrhous and cancer: "In the second half of the eighteenth century, the prevailing view was that scirrhus (tumor firm to touch) was different from cancer, [...] Symptomatic scirrhus was regarded as hard and ill-defined tumor deep under the skin and in fatty tissues that often degenerated to cancer" STEVEN I HAJDU, "A note from history: Landmarks in history of cancer, part 3", *Cancer*, 118 (2012), p. 1155.
65 REIL, *Fragmenta*, p. 93.
66 REIL, *Fragmenta*, p. 93.
67 REIL, *Fragmenta*, p. 93.

However, there is something in the contemporary methodology that was completely unavailable to the early modern biologists and physicians. That is the possibility to observe the developmental processes *in vivo*, without inferring them from the states that precede or result from a certain developmental stage. In all the cases discussed above, and all the definitions employed, biological processes are dependent on the states from which they are inferred:

> P is a developmental biological process iff P is required for an organism O to pass from the state S1 to the state S2 where S2 is more complex than S1.

> P is a fundamental biological process (*meta-schematismus*) iff P is required for an organism O to pass from the state S1 to the state S2 where S1 and S2 are structural (*schematismi*) and observed in their natural environment.

> P is a fundamental pathological process (*meta-schematismus*) iff P is required for a disease D to pass from the state S1 to the state S2 where S1 is a primary disease, and S2 is a secondary disease.

In all these cases the definition of P depends on the definition of organism, disease and their states. In other words, they are static definitions and do not consider interactions to be temporal and dynamical processes: "In this 'static interaction' the values of two variables measured before development [...]. In contrast, dynamic interaction must be studied as a temporally extended process".[68]

Every description of a process presented above — be it Hooke's formation of mold, Bacon's vegetation from seeds, or Reil's cancerous formation — was inferred from the surrounding states (S_n and S_{n+1} for every P_n or PP_n). Early modern biologists and physicians inferred the continuous process behind the states but they did not have a way to record the observations continuously. So they had to rely on the observations of static states and infer processes from them.

In contemporary developmental biology there is an emerging technology that allows to directly capture the processes by the so-called *in vivo* labelling. A combination of techniques allows to mark cell lineage from the initial stages of development to the much later ones without interrupting the natural process. As Woodworth, Girskis, and Walsh explain:

> No longer limited to observing the development of transparent organisms or tracking a small number of cells with serially diluted dyes, biologists can now access a variety of methods for tracing lineage forwards from the application of a genetic label. In addition, recent advances in sequencing, particularly genome sequencing of single cells, allow lineage tracing to be carried out retrospectively, reconstructing lineage decisions that occurred months or years before sequencing.[69]

---

68 GRIFFITHS and STOTZ, *Developmental systems theory*, p. 234.
69 MOLLIE B. WOODWORTH, KELLY M. GIRSKIS, and CHRISTOPHER A. WALSH, "Building a lineage from single cells: genetic techniques for cell lineage tracking" *Nature Reviews Genetics* 18/4 (2017), p. 230-244.

Such techniques provide a qualitatively different methodology of dealing with processes in biology and medicine. The early modern authors had no way to record actual processes and had to rely on their reconstruction from the surrounding states. Yet different techniques of *in vivo* labeling and time-lapse imaging[70] offer the opportunity to mark a particular cell lineage and capture the development *in vivo*.

In 1929 Walter Vogt applied a process in which a vital dye and agar chips were used to mark a region of an amphibian embryo. The marked cells could be traced through the developmental processes of the embryo. Vogt was able to create the first fate map which shows which regions of the developing organism came from the marked regions of the embryo.

Vogt observed the development of an amphibian embryo by first producing markers in the regions of the embryo and then observing the same markers throughout gastrulation and organogenesis. Vogt's technique was supplemented by many contemporary approaches to mark cells and uncover the cell lineage in developing embryos. Most importantly, some contemporary techniques allow to trace cell lineage not only prospectively (by placing markers in advance and observing change) but also retrospectively: "retrospective lineage tracing follows cells backwards to read endogenous marks [...] that have accumulated over the lifetime of an organism".[71]

Contemporary marking techniques can provide a substantially different definition of a developmental process in biology:

> P is a developmental biological process iff P comprises markers $M_0 \ldots M_n$ according to their lineage (i.e. change) in the fate map from t_0 to t_n.

First of all, this definition is very much in line with the *Process based-biology* which, as discussed above, considered the two essential elements of a process to be time ("Processes are extended in time: they have temporal parts"[72]) and change ("A process depends on change for its occurrence"[73]).

Also notice that this definition gets rid of the notions of states and organisms which pervaded the early modern definitions. The latter were inefficient because what they described to be states of an organism were in fact unrelated organisms (like salt and insects) or unrelated states and materials (like bile and skin cancer). This is exchanged for markers which do not allow for such confusion because if a particular marker M_1 is observed at t_0 and then at t_1, the process defined by this change must relate to the same organism and the same region of development. Markers are used to record the actual developmental process, so there is much less need for speculative inference.

---

70 *In vivo* labeling is often supplemented by time-lapse imaging that helps to capture the dynamical development: "time-lapse imaging has brought with it a radical dynamization, not only of the descriptive models of development, but also of the theories of development themselves", cf. LAURA NUÑO DE LA ROSA, "Capturing Processes: the Interplay of Modelling Strategies and Conceptual Understanding in Developmental Biology", in *Everything Flows*, p. 266.
71 WOODWORTH, GIRSKIS, and WALSH, *Building a lineage*.
72 DUPRÉ and NICHOLSON, *Manifesto*, p. 11.
73 Ibid., *Manifesto*, p. 12.

Fate maps also help to predict and retrace developmental processes. It could seem that fate maps themselves depend on the discovery of the processes implying circularity. Yet the circular definition is not vicious because the markers in the processes under investigation and the known fate maps need not be identical. For example, let us take two processes P_1 and P_2. P_1 comprises markers M_0 to M_1 which are already contained in the fate map, so we already know what will happen to these markers from t_0 to t_1. However, it might happen — and in fact it does happen, since the vital dyes tend to fade, and other techniques have their own limitations — that we succeed to observe P_1 from t_0 to t_2 for the first time. In this case, the observation is not trivial since the information was not contained in the fate map and *eo ipso* the fate map is improved by the consideration of P_1 because it extends the fate map from t_0 to t_1 to t_0 to t_2. Similarly, assuming that P_1 from t_0 to t_2 is now contained in the fate map, P_2 from t_0 to t_2 might still be informative by comprising more markers. It might consider not only M_0 to M_1 but also M_2 which also reveals what happens to the region marked by M_2 which was not contained in the fate map in the same time. Therefore, instead of being a *petitio principii*, this definition offers a way to conceptualize the increasing knowledge of biological process through *in vivo* labeling.